Organizations: Structure and Behavior

The Wiley Series in
MANAGEMENT AND ADMINISTRATION

ELWOOD S. BUFFA, *Advisory Editor*
University of California, Los Angeles

MANAGEMENT SYSTEMS
Peter P. Schoderbek

OPERATIONS MANAGEMENT: PROBLEMS AND MODELS, SECOND EDITION
Elwood S. Buffa

PROBABILITY FOR MANAGEMENT DECISIONS
William R. King

PRINCIPLES OF MANAGEMENT: A MODERN APPROACH, THIRD EDITION
Henry H. Albers

MODERN PRODUCTION MANAGEMENT, THIRD EDITION
Elwood S. Buffa

CASES IN OPERATIONS MANAGEMENT: A SYSTEMS APPROACH
James L. McKenney and Richard S. Rosenbloom

ORGANIZATIONS: STRUCTURE AND BEHAVIOR, VOLUME I, SECOND EDITION
Joseph A. Litterer

ORGANIZATIONS: SYSTEMS, CONTROL AND ADAPTATION, VOLUME II
Joseph A. Litterer

MANAGEMENT AND ORGANIZATIONAL BEHAVIOR: A MULTIDIMENSIONAL
APPROACH
Billy J. Hodge and Herbert J. Johnson

MATHEMATICAL PROGRAMMING: AN INTRODUCTION TO THE DESIGN
AND APPLICATION OF OPTIMAL DECISION MACHINES
Claude McMillan

DECISION MAKING THROUGH OPERATIONS RESEARCH
Robert J. Thierauf and Richard A. Grosse

QUALITY CONTROL FOR MANAGERS & ENGINEERS
Elwood G. Kirkpatrick

PRODUCTION SYSTEMS: PLANNING, ANALYSIS AND CONTROL
James L. Riggs

ORGANIZATIONS:

Structure and Behavior

VOLUME I

Second Edition

JOSEPH A. LITTERER

University of Massachusetts

JOHN WILEY & SONS, INC.

NEW YORK · LONDON · SYDNEY · TORONTO

10 9 8 7 6 5 4
Library of Congress Catalogue Card Number: 77-88314

SBN 471 54109 5 (cloth)   SBN 471 54110 9 (paper)

Printed in the United States of America

Preface

THERE ARE A NUMBER OF PURPOSES FOR WHICH AN ANTHOLOGY OF WRITINGS on organizations might be prepared. One would be to present the latest work in the field. Another would be to bring together the important work in a particular approach to organizations, such as theories of decision making in organizations. A third would be to assemble those writings that treat the basic issues, developments, and topics in the field. These different purposes would have distinctly different implications for a new edition of the anthology. With the first approach, each new edition would likely be a new collection. With the last approach, new editions would include only very important new work, with many of the selections likely to remain in one edition after another. The impetus for new editions then would only come, in part, from new developments in the field.

The purpose of this book can be stated quite simply: to bring together the most important writings on organizations. Doing this is a bit more difficult. There is the problem of scope—what are we defining as the area of organizations? There is a problem of depth—how intensively are various aspects to be covered? Then, of course, the nastiest of all problems, what are the most important writings within those boundaries?

Several ideas have led us to believe that the answers to these problems used in the first edition should be modified. The scope of the subject should be expanded to include (as separate topics) control and systems, which had been lumped with other topics in the first edition. A number of topics should be examined more intensively: work flows, conditional aspects for combinations of various organization elements, and impact of environment on organizational matters, to name the more important. Finally, this dynamic field has produced a number of important developments in theory and empirical research in recent years, providing us with more of a selection. All of these factors combine to make a new edition necessary.

This expansion in boundaries and the newer work that has come out have greatly magnified the difficulty noted in the first edition, namely, the amount of material that ought to be included is so large that it far exceeds the capacity of a single (or several) volumes. To permit the selection to do any reasonable justice to the field, it was decided to bring out the second edition in two volumes. This decision raised the problem of how to divide the selections between the two volumes so that the volumes would be as self-contained as possible, yet would permit the items in each to be relatively easy to integrate.

The scheme adopted is provided by Boulding, who has observed that we can differentiate among systems on the basis of levels of abstraction.[1] At the most elementary level are structures or frameworks. They identify parts and the relationship among them in a static fashion. Here we study anatomy, classification schemes for plants, rocks, or insects; or positions, departments, and hierarchical levels into which they are placed. At the second level, the parts move and do something in a fixed and predetermined way. This is identified as the level of clockworks. Here we are concerned with completeness and fit and, in the most elementary fashion, with functions and purposes. For our purposes, we call this the level of the simple steady state. It is here that we study mechanics or kinematics, friction, work flow, or conflict. We apply this study to automatic washing machines or production control systems.

At the next level, things become more complex. Now we are interested not only in the intended purpose but whether it is actually being achieved. For example, an automatic washer, once started, will go through all cycles, whether the clothes in the machine are dirty or not or, for that matter, even if there are no clothes in the washer. At this new level, performance is compared with a standard or goal and, when deviating, is adjusted. Here our concern is not that tools be used as desired, but with organisms that have the capacity to control their own operations to achieve an end. Control is studied not as compliance but as cybernetics. This control involves not only the performance of the total organism but also the adjustment the parts make to one another. We are therefore concerned with the interdependency of the parts in a way only hinted at on the previous levels.

At the fourth level, we are concerned with the interrelationship between the organism and others in its environment. The third level is that of closed systems, the fourth of open systems. Added to the question of how to adjust performance to meet objectives is the far more complex issue of how to change objectives to meet new requirements of the environment. Boulding identifies several additional levels, but they are less well understood and have not yet been reached by organizations in their developments.

Volume I deals with the first two levels as they pertain to organizations: Structure and the Simple Steady State. Volume II will deal with the third and fourth levels of abstraction and will deal with Systems, Cybernetics, and Open and Closed Systems.

Most of the selections retained from the first edition (twelve have been deleted) appear in Volume I. Some, notably those dealing with organizational adaptation, have been moved to the second volume. Both volumes have been organized to reflect the levels-of-abstraction concept, but both the subject and the readings make it impossible to follow it exactly.

I am grateful for the kind cooperation of the authors and publishers of the material reproduced.

Joseph A. Litterer

Friendship Long Island, Maine, 1969

[1] Kenneth E. Boulding, "General System Theory—The Skeleton of a Science," *Management Science*, April 1956, pp. 197–208.

Preface to the First Edition

THIS BOOK IS ABOUT ORGANIZATIONS, PRIMARILY LARGE ORGANIZATIONS; for example, business corporations, government agencies, or service institutions such as hospitals. This is a large topic which can be approached in many ways. We can, for example, study the subject from a detached, outside point of view where organizations are examined by type, shape, products, inputs; in short, study what is known *about* the topic. Or, the subject can be approached from the point of view of a person planning or operating an organization, who is concerned with what an organization can do, what problems or issues develop relevant to an organization, what alternatives are open in coping with these issues, and what the consequences of these alternatives are. This approach is concerned with *what happens in* an organization; how organization activities are allocated, what makes coordination difficult, and how integration is obtained. We are concerned in this book with the organizational processes about which the manager, actual or potential, will have to make decisions in developing or operating an organization.

The above is a statement of intent but, alas, not of what this book accomplishes. The book falls short of realizing this ideal for several reasons. First, although our knowledge of organizations is growing rapidly, we admittedly have a great deal more to learn. Second, even to present all we do know of the topic would require several volumes. Hence a decision was made about the content of the book. It is intended as an introduction to the basic, well-established material of the field for the reader who has little or no background in this subject.

The book was prepared to be used in advanced undergraduate or graduate level courses, or by the interested business or government executive. The book can be used in a separate, single-semester course with no prerequisite work, or can be used following a course in Human Relations or Administrative Behavior where individual and group behavior have been covered.

One of the things which have made the study of organizations trying is that there is not one but several approaches to, or schools of thought on, the subject. Often the differences have been noted by the adherents of one school, with the implication, and sometimes the direct assertion, that the other school (s) are in error and that the one to which the writer belongs is the only way to salvation. Unfortunately, much energy has been expended in establishing and maintaining these positions, often obscuring the fact that the opposing schools of thought contain elements that could fit together into a concept larger and more inclusive than any of them. Observing these actions, we are reminded of the fable of how the disputes between the blind men examining an elephant kept them from developing a real understanding of what an elephant looked like.

Selections for this book were chosen from the major schools of thought to be representative of the different approaches and are arranged to suggest ways in which they might be integrated. Although differences between these schools of thought are discussed, particular attention is given to areas where they can support or supplement each other. Some elements that enable different schools of thought to be bridged, or linked, are identified. Again, these are intentions and guides to action, illustrated by a few applications of bridging elements, rather than complete accomplishments.

Joseph A. Litterer

Urbana, Illinois
January, 1963

Contents

PART ONE: INTRODUCTION   1

Introductory Comment   2

Organization Theory: An Overview and an Appraisal,
     William G. Scott   15

Bureaucracy, *Max Weber*   29

Formal Organization, *Chester I. Barnard*   40

On Organizational Goals, *Fritz J. Roethlisberger and*
     William J. Dickson   51

A Structure-Function Approach to Organization, *Robert S. Weiss*   58

**PART TWO: THE FORMAL STRUCTURE OF
ORGANIZATION**   63

Introduction to Part Two   64

Division of Work   73

The Division of Labor, *Charles Babbage*   73

The Division of Basic Company Activities, *Ernest Dale*   76

Top Management Organization, *Paul Holden, Lounsbury S. Fish*
     and *Hubert L. Smith*   87

Selections from "Scientific Management," *Fredrick Taylor*   95

Toward the New Organization Theories: Some Notes on "Staff,"
     Robert T. Golembiewski   99

Coordination and Integration   105

The Coordinative Principle, *James Mooney*   105

Structure and Coordination, *Luther Gulick*   107

Doctrine, *James Mooney*   111

Authority   115

Perceptions of Organizational Authority: A Comparative
    Analysis, *Robert L. Peabody*   115
Compliance as a Comparative Base, *Amitai Etzioni*   121

Organization Style   133

Decentralization, *Peter Drucker*   133
Overcoming Obstacles to Effective Delegation,
    William H. Newman   146
Program Management, Organizing for Stability and Flexibility,
    Joseph A. Litterer   150

**PART THREE: THE EMERGENT INFORMAL
ORGANIZATION STRUCTURE**   157

Introduction to Part Three   158

Some Basic Concepts   167

Social Systems, *George Homans*   167
Status and Status Hierarchies, *Burleigh Gardner and
    David G. Moore*   189

The Informal Organization   197

The Informal Organization, *Philip Selznick*   197
Selections From Quota Restriction and Goldbricking in a
    Machine Shop, *Donald Roy*   200
Efficiency and "the Fix": Informal Intergroup Relations in a
    Piecework Machine Shop, *Donald Roy*   204
Work Group Behavior and the Larger Organization,
    Leonard R. Sayles   215

Integration of the Individual into the Organization   223

Cosmopolitans and Locals, *Alvin W. Gouldner*   223
Social Control in the Newsroom: A Functional Analysis,
    Warren Breed   229
Bureaucratic Structure and Personality, *Robert K. Merton*   240

Effects of Formal Structural Elements on Behavior   249

The Man on the Assembly Line, *Charles R. Walker and
    Robert H. Guest*   249
Selections From Social and Psychological Consequences of
    the Longwall Method of Coal-Getting, *E. L. Trist
    and K. W. Bamforth*   263

Co-operation and Competition in a Bureaucracy, *Peter M. Blau*   276
Selections From The Impact of Budgets on People, *Chris Argyris*   282

PART FOUR: ORGANIZATIONS AS CLOCKWORKS: THE SIMPLE STEADY STATE   297

Introduction to Part Four   298

Work Flow   303

Work Flow as the Basis for Organization Design,
Eliot O. Chapple and Leonard R. Sayles   303
Vertical and Horizontal Communication in Formal Organizations,
Richard L. Simpson   319

The Organization as a System   325

Product Innovation and Organization, *Jay W. Lorsch*   325
Rationality in Organizations, *James D. Thompson*   336
Administrative Rationality, Social Setting, and Organizational
Development, *Stanley H. Udy, Jr.*   343
Cognitive Limits on Rationality, *James G. March and
Herbert A. Simon*   352

Adjustments in the System: Filling Positions in the Managerial Hierarchy   373

Strategy Leniency and Authority, *Peter M. Blau*   373
About the Functions of Bureaucratic Rules, *Alvin W. Gouldner*   378
Engineer the Job to Fit the Manager, *Fred Fiedler*   388

Conflict   397

Conflicts between Staff and Line Managerial Officers,
Melville Dalton   397
Interdepartmental Conflict and Cooperation: Two Contrasting
Studies, *John M. Dutton and Richard E. Walton*   407

PART FIVE: DETERMINANTS OF AND CONSTRAINTS ON STRUCTURE   423

Introduction to Part Five   424

The Effects of Scale   427

Organizational Size and Functional Complexity: A Study
Of Administration in Hospitals, *Theodore R. Anderson
and Seymour Warkov*   427

Organizational Size, Rules, and Surveillance, *William A. Rushing* 432

Development of Organization Roles   441

The Influence of Technological Components of Work upon
  Management Control, *Gerald D. Bell*   441
Predictability of Work Demands and Professionalization
  as Determinants of Workers' Discretion, *Gerald D. Bell*   446
Administrative Role Definition and Social Change,
  Andrew Gunder Frank   453
Differentiation of Roles in Task-Oriented Groups,
  Harold Guetzkow   459
The Experimental Change of a Major Organizational Variable,
  Nancy C. Morse and Everett Reimer   475

Author Index

Subject Index

PART ONE

Introduction

P A R T   O N E

ONE OF THE DOMINANT CHARACTERISTICS of our era is the existence of large-scale organizations. This prevalence of organizations and their influence on modern life is not always viewed as an unmixed blessing. There are those who are concerned with the power large organizations have in our social, political, and economic life. Still another group is concerned with the tremendous, often subtle influence that organizations can have on the individual. They see organizations subverting the individualistic nature of man and molding him into a cog in a large impersonal entity. On the other hand, there are those who view large-scale organizations as one of the primary factors in developing our modern society to its high level of physical well-being. Obviously, these different points of view deal with very fundamental issues relevant to organizations. We begin with them primarily to dispose of them, for although they are of vital importance, they are outside the scope of this book. The point of view taken here is that organizations do exist, are numerous, and have a very profound impact on our individual and collective lives. It is accepted that the prevalence of organizations will not only continue but in all probability increase in the future. The purpose

of this book is to bring about a better understanding of organizations in order to help make them more fruitful for all concerned. Before leaving this issue completely, we wish to examine both the prevalence and the importance of organizations a bit further, thereby establishing a background against which the rest of the book can be placed.

General Considerations about Organizations

Perhaps the prevalence of organizations can be appreciated by examining the number to which each of us belong and to contrast this situation with that which existed only a few generations earlier. Not too many decades ago, large portions of our population lived in rural settings in which the most significant social structures were the family and the immediate community. Only occasionally did the majority of our population come in contact with a large, complex organization, such as the government or the military. Today this has been sharply changed. The bulk of our population lives in the city, where larger organizations have always been more prevalent. Even those portions of the population living in rural areas are influenced by and are members of many more large organizations than were their forefathers. From the time we enter school, most of us are in at least one and perhaps several organizations. Anything that looms so large in the lives of so many people in today's world is a matter of great importance.

Organizational Effectiveness

It is not the prevalence of organizations alone that makes them important for us to study. We live today in a world of vast abundance. Our material bounty is usually mentioned, and it might also be noted that many artistic things are available in larger quantities and to more people than ever before in history.

Many things have made this bounty possible. One frequently cited factor has been the development of our technical knowledge. But it has also been pointed out that this knowledge would be relatively useless unless we were able to develop organizations to use it. A knowledge of how to make automobiles requires large numbers of people to make parts and to assemble them. Behind them there must be other large numbers of people to make the varieties of steel, paint, and fabric that are used. All of these require still others who can make the tools they use, and so on. It is further argued that our technical knowledge could not have become so extensive without large organizations to provide the time, resources, and tools needed for research.[1] A key question running through this book is how do organizations produce these results. We have two ways of looking at organization results. The first is the question of whether we are able to achieve any result at all. Is the organization effective? The second is a question of whether the organization produces the result at the lowest cost, for example, is it efficient? Assuming that we want to build a Grand Coulee Dam, we need an organization if it is going to be done at all. On the other hand, organizations with different forms can build the dam at different cost in money, time, lives, etc.

[1] Tom Burns and G. M. Stalker, *The Management of Innovation*, Quadrangle Books, Chicago, 1962 (see Chapter 2).

Some Advantages and Requirements of Organization

One idea that implicitly or, many times, explicitly underlies formal organization thinking is the assumption of a central source of authority within the organization that has some legitimate basis for existence. In government we recognize as a legitimate base the will of the people which, in democratic processes, can elect a President who then becomes the central source of executive authority in a federal government. In a business firm we recognize a legitimate base or source of authority to be the owners or stockholders who appoint, through the Board of Directors, a president who is the central authority of the firm. This central authority, be it a person or a board, has the prerogative, in fact the necessity, of delegating portions of this authority to subordinates who will carry out their subdivided tasks within the organization. This, then, extends from the very top of the organization, through various levels, down to the first-line supervisor and, in fact, even to the worker. Each level has a smaller and more narrowly defined sector of authority. We can, therefore, rank positions in an organization on the basis of the authority they possess. A legitimate base of authority within an organization, centralized in the hands of a position at the top of the organization, is an essential component for the classical school of organization. It is also a matter that has not gone unchallenged from the behavioral point of view.

A formal organization, however, has another advantage, which has not yet been noted. In institutionalizing organizational tasks in positions with specified duties and responsibilities, the organization becomes less dependent on any one individual. This is true whether the institutionalization be at the worker or the managerial level.

Let us state it this way. If someone in a group performs a special job that is very important, a job that he has developed himself through his own interest and that involves skill known only to himself, then the group or organization is highly dependent upon him. When this individual dies or leaves, the service he has been rendering is permanently removed.

If what a person contributes to an organization or group is not completely prescribed by his personal skill, but is prescribed in a job description, rules, or procedures, the group or organization becomes less dependent on him as an individual. When the occupant of the position leaves, another can be placed in it and trained to do a known set of activities.

Let us return to the material bounty many of us in this country enjoy. This increase in abundance has freed us, in the United States at least, to a considerable degree, from the fear of want. In addition to freedom from the specter of starvation which haunts much of the world, we have, even at the lowest levels of our society, a relatively large amount of free time. We can use this leisure for hobbies, the pursuit of pleasure, self-improvement, or other desirable activities. We might describe the life of an individual in today's world of large complex organizations as one of performing his own unique task within the organization while expending a relatively small proportion of time. From this he is able to acquire an extraordinarily wide array of goods, services, and also free time. This is indeed a comfortable and attractive picture, but in it there is an element that, although frequently ignored, is of fundamental importance.

Perhaps the simplest way to develop this point is to examine certain aspects of the life of a member of a large contemporary organization. Let us look at an individual who works as a quality control engineer. His education and experience have all been directed toward increasing his competence in the area of quality control. Such specialization, incorporating high degrees of expertness, is recognized as one of the fundamental characteristics of modern organizations. Let us imagine for a moment that we had at our disposal a time machine and could move our quality control expert back to the time of the frontier in our country. Many things would be different for him. One of the most significant differences would be that he would change from a person who was quite important in his local organization because of his special knowledge and unique contribution to one of the most useless people in his environment. In all likelihood he would not know how to milk a cow, ride a horse, plant a crop, skin a bear, make soap, store food through the winter, or any of the other simple but vitally important things nec-

essary in a frontier community. There would be nothing on which he could use his special knowledge and skill. He would only have his brawn, and he would have to put it at the disposal of anyone who had the knowledge to direct it.

It is necessary to recognize that as a consequence of our large-scale organizations, we have been able to develop high degrees of individual specialization. This has made us efficient but has also made us highly dependent on our organizations, our society, and each other. The same point holds for subunits within an organization. The work of the production department is highly interrelated with other departments, such as sales, engineering, and purchasing. Its success in producing goods is only partially dependent on itself and, to no small degree, dependent on the success with which these other units do their work. To carry this thinking one step further, an organization such as a business firm is highly dependent on other business firms in the economy, as is so dramatically illustrated when there is a steel or railroad stike.

In summary, organizations, as they have increased in size and number, have tended to bring about much greater specialization which, in turn, has produced a much higher order of interdependency among all organizational elements.

Organization Solidarity

One view holds that this dependency of individuals on each other and on organizations will generate strong positive feelings toward them. From this will grow a strong solidarity among interdependent people [2] and support for the organization of which they are members. We certainly see strong *esprit de corps* among team members, or crews of ships or bombers, and people often have deep and lasting loyalties to organizations of all types. Yet the fact remains that the opposite often develops. People also resent their dependency on others and find the very characteristics of organizations that make them so productive of goods and leisure very unsatisfying to some of

[2] Emile Durkheim, *The Division of Labor in Society*, The Free Press, New York, 1960.

their most human characteristics.[3] They react with anger, withdraw and end up dissatisfied with, and often alienated from, the organizations they are in.

Philosophers and social scientists have been and are very concerned with this frustration in and alienation from organizations. It constitutes one of the underlying themes throughout both this and the next volume. We shall see that each approach to the study of organizations has a prescription for solving this central issue. In some ways, the most distinctive difference among approaches is on the proposals and assumptions underlying them for solving this problem. While it may be easy to recognize the importance and prevalence of organizations in our modern life, even to recognize how highly dependent we are on organizations and therefore on each other as linked by these organizations, it is still surprising how frequently we fail to take into account the impact of organizations on our lives and on events in the world about us. We tend to think in individualistic terms. Hence, when two people are continually having arguments or fighting with each other, their clash is commonly described as a personality conflict. Perhaps it is, but in many instances the root of the difficulty can be more accurately described as an organizational problem. A not uncommon situation occurs when one of two men who are supposed to be on the same level of the organization is dependent on the other for assistance in successfully completing his responsibilities. The likelihood of difficulty increases greatly if the second party receives no credit or has to detract from his own performance to help the first person.

As an illustration of this situation, let us envision a production manager who is plagued by high production costs resulting from high labor costs largely incurred when machines break down and workers sit around idle while repairs are made. He knows that many of these delays are hours long because the maintenance department, which does not report to him, does not have the necessary repair parts in stock, but has to send out to a supplier when they are needed. The production manager feels quite strongly that his high production costs could be sharply reduced if the maintenance department could give him quicker service. On the other hand, the maintenance supervisor believes that to stock the vast number of parts needed for repair of the company equipment would require an enormous inventory, which would be very expensive for his department. Since he is probably under continuous pressure to keep costs down, as is the production manager, he is reluctant to keep an inventory on any parts which are not used regularly. In such a situation the production manager is likely to be continually badgering the maintenance supervisor for quicker repairs, which the latter will not be able to provide because of his understandable reluctance to provide the inventories that are necessary. Once such a condition is recognized, it is readily understood that the situation is the source of friction. It is not understanding the effects of the condition that makes the study of organizations difficult but, rather, seeing the situation at all.

The Complexity and Diversity of Views about Organizations

The study of organizations is both new and old. Writings about organizations can be traced back for thousands of years. Some sound organizational advice is found, for example, in the Bible. The study of organizations has begun in different places at different times and has been approached from different points of view. As a result, we have a number of different schools of thought and a number of literatures on organizations. One of the difficulties in dealing with the subject today is this multiplicity of literatures. In a book such as this, which attempts to draw together the most pertinent items from several literatures, these different points of view, using different vocabularies on different levels of abstraction, can be confusing to the reader. As we go from one literature to another, it sometimes seems that the authors are talking about quite different and unrelated topics. We can even find instances where, thoroughly convinced of the rightness of their own point of view, authors from one school of thought heatedly deny the validity or usefulness of the ideas of another,

[3] For an interesting discussion of this see George Homans, *Social Behavior: Its Elementary Forms*, Harcourt, New York, 1961.

opposing school of thought. The particular selections have been chosen and edited so as to reduce this source of confusion as much as possible without distorting the real variety and vitality of the literature.

The Classical School of Thought on Organizations

One approach to organizations, and the oldest as far as a continuing systematic literature is concerned, is the so-called classical school. Its modern roots go back at least to the days of Frederick Taylor, Harrington Emerson, and Henry Fayol. The classical point of view holds that work or tasks can be so organized as to accomplish efficiently the objectives of the organization. An organization is viewed as a product of rational thought concerned largely with coordinating tasks through the use of legitimate authority. It is based on the fundamental and usually implicit assumption that the behavior of people is logical, rational, and within the same system of rationality as that used to formulate the organization. It is an analytical approach developing normative models. That is, on the basis of deduction from some assumptions, it attempts to specify what an organization should be.

In the classical point of view, the manager or executive responsible for the organization plans a set of tasks or jobs that presumably include all of the activities necessary to accomplish the objective or objectives of the organization. People are thought of as the means through which the objectives are accomplished. They are looked on primarily as individuals, with the only connections between them being provided by the organization. It is presumed that the people who are assigned to these jobs will perform them exactly as specified. As will be noted later, the classical theorists do not necessarily presume that people will do this naturally. They work on the assumption, however, that through selection, training or indoctrination, just treatment and pay, or a combination of all three, people can be brought to the point of filling the jobs exactly as specified. At this fundamental point, we find the weakest part of the classical approach to organizations and the one to which the behavioral or naturalistic school of thought has made its most significant contributions.

In summary, the classical school of organizations has as its main elements objectives, tasks, rational behavior, coordination of effort, efficiency, just treatment and rewards, and authority.

The Naturalistic School of Organizations

Contrasted to the classical point of view is what might be called the behavioral or empirical school, which holds that organizations spring naturally or spontaneously from the association of people who have common or mutually supportive needs, interests, or objectives.[4] Hence, from this point of view, there need not be anything consciously planned about an organization. Organizations rest instead on the basic needs, both physical and emotional, of people. This approach has received great attention in the last several decades and has developed into a large and rapidly expanding series of studies about the collective behavior of people. They have shown, for example, that people tend to have a much broader and varied set of behavior than is called for, or for that matter anticipated, in the classical point of view. This approach has done much to increase our understanding of the very important fact that many things are done in organizations which are not directly related to the formal goals that the classical approach considers.

The naturalistic point of view has taken as its main topic of interest the behavior of people in groups or collectivities. It recognized early that many things influence the behavior of individuals in groups other than the formal specifications laid down by an organizational plan or orders from superiors who have formal authority. Sometimes behavior of individuals in groups is exactly what superiors or job descriptions call for. At other times it may be almost a direct opposite. In many cases, perhaps most, it is to some degree different from what is formally called for. For example, at times we find employees working very hard

[4] For a discussion of this point of view see Alvin W. Gouldner, "Organization Analysis," in Robert K. Merton, Leonard Broom, and Leonard S. Cottrell, *Sociology Today*, Basic Books, New York, 1959, pp. 400–428.

and exceeding the levels of production standards established by the company executives. In other cases we find them quite consistently flaunting these standards to hold the level of production down. One of the interesting contributions of the behavioral point of view has been the identification of fundamental factors that can explain both the compliance with production standards set by higher management and the consistent violation of the same standards.

The roots of this approach go back for many years. The bulk of our material, however, has been largely developed since the time of the now famous Hawthorne studies in the 1920's and 1930's. It has been produced by students of management, industrial sociologists, and industrial psychologists and now draws heavily on the work of many social psychologists and, more recently, cultural anthropologists.

The development of this approach to the study of organizations, with its rapidly expanding mass of data, has posed a major dilemma for the student of organizations. It would at first glance appear that there are two opposing, contradictory schools of thought which we must choose between. Actually the situation is both more, and less, complicated.

The Systems Concept of Organization

To make things more complicated there has slowly, but gradually, emerged yet a third view of organizations. This approach looks upon organizations as systems of parts each of which makes a contribution to the operation of the organization and each of which is dependent on other aspects of the system for its own needs. These systems of parts are self-adjusting to disturbances which keep purposes from being met as desired. Furthermore, organizations are seen as parts of still larger systems, such as societies, economic systems, etc., and also containing subsystems such as groups and individuals.

These different approaches to organizations are explored in some detail by the first reading in this book (Scott)[5] and appear in total or in part in many later sections.

One concept that will make this subject less complicated is the realization that there are not just governmental organizations or business organizations, formal organizations or informal organizations, but that there is a general topic of organizations of which these are but variants. Each variation being made of the same parts formed to different dimensions and perhaps assembled differently. One of the purposes of this book is to draw together, from many areas and diverse points of view, material that will contribute to an overall understanding of organizations. The sum total of the contributions from these many sources does not at the moment yield a complete and fully integrated concept. Many areas, topics, or issues still have to be studied and explored, and the relationships among them must be analyzed much more adequately. This book, then, is only a step in a direction in which work must still be done.

Fortunately, we now have knowledge that enables us to form some bridges between major concepts and research in the field of organizations which, until not too long ago, had to be treated as separate and somewhat unrelated topics. Some of the items included, therefore, deal with theories and research that link the major schools of thought on organizations, and all of them have been arranged to give a perspective that will heighten the interrelation of the different points of view.

What Are Organizations?

In this book an organization is considered to be a purposeful social unit. That is, it consists of a number of people who perform differentiated tasks while filling differentiated roles, offices, or positions and whose actions are coordinated so that their individual outputs are integrated. This brief and general statement leads to a number of points that should be made more explicit.

Let us begin with considering what is involved in creating an organization. Organizations come into being when two conditions prevail. First, someone is motivated to create an organization. The motive comes from a realization that an end can be better achieved

[5] Papers included in the readings portion of this book will be identified by the author's name in parentheses, for example, (Scott), at related places in the introductory material.

through an organization and, hence, is the desirable solution (Weber). A government may set up a bureau to fight fires, rather than leave citizens do it for themselves. A group of investors may establish a firm because they can get a better return on their funds than by handling them individually. A community may establish a hospital for similar reasons. However, certain preconditions must be met. Namely, there must be people willing to serve in the organization, who are capable of communicating with each other to accomplish a common purpose (Barnard).

The observation that people must be willing to serve in an organization raises the question of why they should do so. The answer is that they too expect to have some of their goals or needs satisfied through the organization. Hence an organization must deliver two kinds of outputs, or fill two types of purposes or goals. The first is the technical or economic product which the society, community, or larger organization (such as a government) will find useful, and the second is to satisfy the needs of the members of the organization. (Roethlisberger and Dickson). Hence, organizations not only satisfy multiple goals but these goals are of different types. Some of the most difficult problems in organization arise because these goals are viewed as being mutually exclusive. Employees may want higher wages, but to award them would force an increase in the price of the goods or services provided the community at large. At the same time, the goals are interdependent, for if users are given very low prices through reducing wages, employees will leave the company, and no goods will be produced. A central problem in any organization then, is to bring about conditions where various parties interested in an organization feel that their goals are being satisfied to a degree that will permit them to give it their support.

At issue here is cooperation among organization members. In turn, necessary cooperation rests on members of an organization perceiving their actions as contributing to an organizational goal (Barnard). Hence, although people in an organization may have different private objectives, there must be a synthesis or a selection of an encompassing objective to produce an organizational goal to which organization members can see their actions contributing.

A very simple illustration is a situation where three men all want to cross a bay for quite different personal reasons. One may want to see his girl friend, another to get medical treatment, the third to pay his taxes. To cross the bay, they have to row a boat. Unfortunately, both the distance and weather make it impossible for a person to row himself across. At least two men will be needed at the oars and a third to bail. They decide to join forces and go together, thereby forming an organization. The organizational objective is to get the boat across the bay. This is different from, although closely related to, their individual objectives. What makes this organization work is that they see their individual actions contributing to the organizational goal of getting across the bay so that they may accomplish their private objectives. Conversely, the more difficult it is for organizational members to perceive this relation the more difficult coordination becomes.

Once an organization is in existence, still further problems arise. As organization members become immersed in doing their work, it becomes difficult, because of this preoccupation and because of geographical distances, for them to communicate. This makes it difficult, perhaps impossible, for them to coordinate their efforts even if they want to. To cope with this condition, to aid in communication and coordination, a separate group of organization members are necessary who are the executive or managers of the organization (Barnard).

Organization as a Set of Intervening Factors

Let us examine more closely this last observation that managers are provided to make sure that the necessary communication and coordination takes place. When doing this work, those who occupy managerial positions are not directly involved in doing the work of the organization, such as physically assembling washing machines. While quite essential, their influence is indirect and their general function facilitative. Organizations provide a host of things that facilitate goal achievement and that create the conditions that permit people to work in a coordinated, efficient fashion. An organization, then, can be viewed as a set of intervening factors that link peoples' desire for goal attainment and that link resources and finished goods and services to these goals.

Perhaps this concept of intervening factors or variables can be clarified by a simple illustration. At the beginning of World War II, the aircraft industry expanded enormously in order to satisfy the wartime needs for aircraft. Many new people were drawn into these plants from all over the country for both monetary and patriotic reasons. To put it another way, the people working in these firms were interested in the same end result, namely, to make airplanes, as were the owners of the firm and the government. We might assume that having this objective would be all that was necessary for them to work hard and remain on the job. Actually, there was a great deal of turnover. Investigation showed that one of the key factors related to this turnover was the highly unstable social relations within certain departments. People were being moved in or moved out of the departments very rapidly, transferred from one job to another within the department or, in some other way, prevented from getting acquainted with each other and building up friendship associations. In other departments, however, where conditions were much more stable, the turnover and absenteeism rate was much lower. In terms we have been using, in order to accomplish its objective of making airplanes, the firm needed people who not only worked hard but stayed on the job. To achieve this condition, the company had to provide some degree of social stability, which would permit people to get acquainted and develop friendship groups. Hence, in order to accomplish the objective of making large quantities of airplanes, it was necessary to provide another factor, namely, stable interpersonal relations. Therefore, a man building an organization needs to give effort and attention to building such intervening factors as cohesive, stable work groups in order to accomplish the ends in which he was interested.

Let us explore this matter a little more fully. By intervening factors or variables, we mean things which, although they do not directly produce the end objective, are in some way related to producing it. In any business firm, for example, we expect to find a wage payment plan. A wage payment plan does not directly get washing machines made, but it does re-

ward the people within the organization for making the parts or components that go into the end products which are the objectives of the firm. Some of the effort of management, then, has been diverted in setting up this intervening factor, and another portion, although probably smaller, will be continually diverted to keep it functioning.

The Scope of Organizations as Covered in This Book

One of the difficulties in discussing the field of organizations is the scope of the subject matter. To some, organization is properly the study of whole cultures or societies. To others, it is the study of small groups. Needless to say, between these extremes, there are a number of intermediate concepts of how inclusive the study of organizations should be.

To delimit the area we shall cover here, it may be useful to draw an analogy to viewing a drop of water under a microscope. If at first the drop is examined under very low power of magnification, we can see the largest bodies or particles contained in the drop of water quite easily. Several things should be noted, however. First, even under low magnification it is probably impossible to see the boundaries of the drop of water itself. This has become too large for our point of view. At the same time, attached to or around the large particles in the drop are small specks or blurs which, as yet, are too small for us to see clearly. When we change to a higher power of magnification, however, some of these smaller specks become quite sharp and clear and fill a large portion of our viewing area. If we look closely, we note, for example, that some of the little blurs or specks turn out to be legs or feelers on the larger bodies we noticed earlier and that these larger bodies have now become so large that they blur into the background and extend far beyond our range of vision. Similarly, if we look closely, there are now additional new blurs or specks, invisible at the lower power of magnification, which have now become visible, although hardly large or clear. This illustration is used for two purposes: first, to bring out the fact that something like an organization consists of several "levels" of parts or units; and second, that although the units at

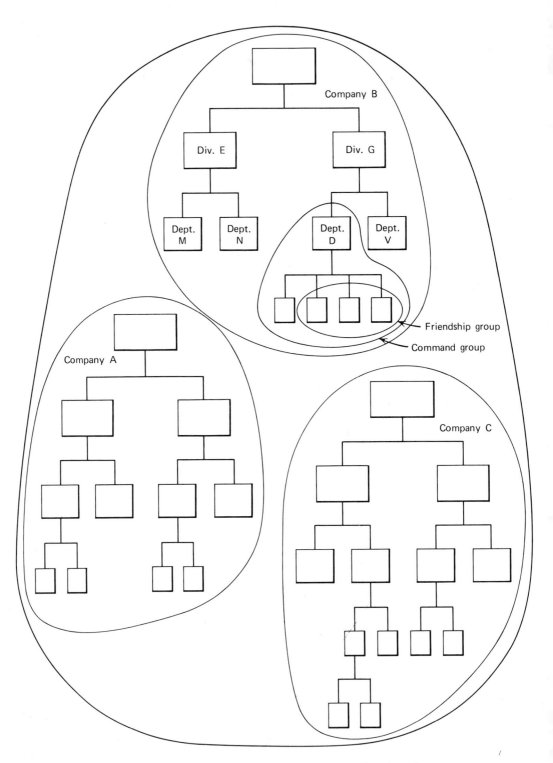

Fig. 1. *Levels at which organizations can be viewed.*

one "level" can be examined separately, the different levels are closely related.

Looking along one dimension of human affairs we might consider whole economies as organizations. Hence, we would have a French economy or an English economy or an economy in the metals industry and an economy in the clothing industry. Looking more closely we would find that any one of these economies is made up of a collection of companies. At the same time, looking still more closely within each of these companies, we notice that there are divisions and departments (Fig. 1) which, in turn, contain command groups (that is, a superior and his immediate subordinates) some members of which have formed into a still different form of unit, a friendship group or clique. If we wanted to carry this even further, of course, we could make the individual our point of examination and look at the things that bear on him. Although it may be desirable to include all these levels in our study of organizations, it is unrealistic to attempt to include them all in one beginning volume. Here we consider a few levels, beginning with the organization at the level of the company or, if you will, the army or the hospital, and the subunits within it down to and including the small face-to-face group. We shall be quite concerned with studying each of these elements and the interrelations among them. Factors or influences coming from outside the organization, such as those from the industry or the economy at one end, or from the personalities or cultures of the individual at the other, will be recognized and their influence taken into account. They will, however, be considered as "givens" to the system. In short, culture, economy, and personality are exogenous factors, whereas departments, tasks, interpersonal relations, communication systems, and similar matters are endogenous variables.

An Approach to Examining Organizations

A number of classes of phenomena can be noted about organizations. Among the more prominent are structure, process, and product. By structure, we mean the identification of the elements in an organization and relations between them. Process has two meanings: one,

the sequence of events or phases by which organization and its elements, such as structure, develop or change; the other, the sequence of events or interactions between elements and structure, once they are established. By product is meant the outputs of an organization. This could include both the technical accomplishments, such as making a commodity or rendering a service, and the satisfaction of the wants and needs of the organizational members both as individuals and collectivities.

All of these—structure, process, and product —are linked together. A change in one results in a change in the others. Furthermore, the process of devising tasks and assigning individuals to them results in a structure; yet this very structure may generate problems with which additional processes will have to cope, thereby creating additional or changed structures. Hence the processes are continuous and the alterations in the other elements continuous also (Weiss).

The Structure of This Book

When beginning a discussion of organizations, we are faced with a very difficult problem that comes, in part, from the scope and the complexity of the subject. It is analogous to starting from scratch to describe the living human body. We might be most interested in how the body speaks, thinks, learns, grows, ages, moves, but we would hardly start with these. Most likely, we would begin by identifying the parts. But even this elementary starting point requires some decisions before we can begin. For example, would we begin by taking the parts in alphabetic order going from adrenal gland to the zygot cell? Lacking any knowledge, we might, but, since we know something about the body, we would probably follow the useful practice of grouping parts into simple systems and describing first the bones and their relationship to one another as they form the skeleton, then go to the circulatory system, then to the nervous system, and so on. Before going further, let us pause and note that we have made several additional decisions. First, we have decided to describe not only the part but its position relevant to other parts like it. Second, in our discussion we would probably explain the functions of some of the bones (parts) and combinations of parts. For example, we would note that the bones in the skull fit together to make an enclosed space that functions to protect the contents.

Once these elementary systems of parts had been described, we could then go on to identify which muscles were connected with particular bones to bring about motion and then to discuss the role of nerves in starting and controlling motion. That is, we would explain the relationships between simple systems as they combine into larger, more complex systems. Our descriptions at this point become more complex not only because of this aggregation of simpler elements but because the things these larger systems do is so much more complex. Explaining how a motion comes about, such as the simple reflex motion of drawing our hand away from a hot object, is more involved than explaining that the bones of the cranial cavity can protect the contents. When we get to sophisticated motions such as threading a needle, the scope and operation of the system involved is very complex. It is much more difficult to explain than reflex motion and can only be approached after several other things have been developed.

This book will follow a similar approach in discussing organizations. We shall begin with identifying parts in elementary systems and the relation of and function of the parts in those systems. Then we shall examine how these subsystems fit together to produce a result, but at the level of kinematics and mechanics. Starting and controlling these motions or the controlling of parts and outputs come next, as a much more complex topic.

The book is divided into two volumes. The first covers organizations to the point of how the parts fit together to produce a particular result. The parts are in motion, but their performance and the overall output is determined by their design and, once put in motion, they operate until their source of energy is removed or they wear out. This is the level of simple clockworks. A clock has no way of telling whether it is going too fast or too slow or, for that matter, if it is telling the correct time. It just goes. The second volume takes up control: how actions are started, how the performance of parts is integrated into the whole, how feedback is obtained and used, and how the organization adapts to the environment. Volume I is organized as follows.

Part One. The Formal Organization Structure

In Part One we have been introducing both the topic of organizations and the field of organization study. The readings have been selected to permit us, in a general way, to differentiate organizations from other things, to identify some of the most prominent characteristics, and to introduce the approach which will most frequently be taken to analyze organizations.

Part Two. The Formal Structure Organization

We go next to the study of the formal structure of organization for several reasons. First, it presents an opportunity to become somewhat acquainted with the overall picture of a large, complex organization. Obviously, the whole body is not there but, at least, a general form and skeleton can be presented. Second, it is the logical starting point if we want to examine an organization from the point of view of the actual or potential manager. The formal organization contains many of the elements that the manager can control most directly.

By formal is meant those aspects of organizations which have been, or possibly might be, consciously planned. Hence, much of the classical school of organizations is included in the formal organization area. This category, however, includes more than classical concepts because we intend to build toward a concept of formal organization, which includes any organizational elements that can be planned and specified. Hence, as we learn more about elements needed to satisfy the social needs of people, and these elements reach a state of development where they can be consciously taken into account in planning the organization, they then fall within the province of the formal organization. The formal organization is viewed as a plan by which the efforts of people fit together to accomplish some purpose.

In this volume, our study of organizations begins with the purposes or objectives having been chosen. To put it another way, for the organizational designer, objectives are given. To accomplish them, the work to be done must be broken up or divided into a series of jobs that individuals can perform. One of the early issues centers on just how the work will be divided, for there are many different ways of dividing work, each with certain advantages and certain disadvantages or, equivalently, each with certain returns and certain costs. The task of the planner of an organization is not completed when he has decided on a division of labor because, as noted earlier, the tasks within an organization must also include means of integrating the efforts of organizational members. It is at this point that some of the most serious difficulties arise.

Even when people have fairly well-defined jobs, it is necessary, for example, to inform them when to start work, what to work on, how many units to make, and what to do with the units when completed. Furthermore, we need some way of making sure that people will fill these jobs in the way needed by the organization. This raises questions of authority, its forms and foundations. The various elements of systems of authority, coordination, and division of work can be combined in a number of ways with different effect. The design chosen is determined in part by the objective sought but also by the characteristics or requirements of people who make up the organization. This leads us to the main theme of the next part.

Part Three. The Emergent Informal Organization Structure

The third part of the book also examines structures, but of a different type and from a totally different source. One of the things noted by numerous early writers and investigators of organizational matters was that people within an organization frequently behaved in a way different from that called for by the formal organization plan. To some this appeared to be erratic, unpredictable behavior, but on closer investigation it was found that much of this behavior followed consistent patterns and was based on recognizable factors. It was soon apparent that if we looked at the individual within an organization, we could see that his behavior was not only influenced by the formal structure but that it was also influenced by another structure that grew spontaneously among people. Planned, deliberate structures are called formal, these spontaneous, natural structures are called informal. In some ways and in some areas, this emergent structure could be described as developing from the needs of people and suggesting that this structure should be looked upon as separate and parallel to the formal structure. A more adequate view is that the informal structure grows from the needs of people in a particular situation and, for our study, that situation is the formal organization. The form and function of the informal structure is intimately linked with the formal. To understand the informal organization then, we need not only to know its basic elements and the relations among those elements but also the effects of the formal organization on people that, in turn, generate needs for the informal structure to service. We need also to know the effects of these structures on the performance of the formal structure.

It is now time to make quite explicit a point as yet left unclarified. We are interested in real organizations. Thus, we are interested in the coordinated efforts of real people achieving some purpose. The plan of what they should be doing is hardly an accurate portrayal of what is actually going on. Yet the plan will have a large influence on what they are doing. The informal structure which may detract from, handicap, add to, or extend the intent of the formal organization is also limited as a tool for understanding real organizations. For us, organizations are a more inclusive concept that contains both of these and more. The distinction between them is a convention made for our convenience and to compensate for our limitations. It is easy to lose sight of this point.

Part Four. Organizations as Clockworks: The Simple Steady State

Thus far we have been discussing organizations in static terms. It is time to put these parts into motion.

In accomplishing their purpose, organizations take in some form of input, do something to it, and send a finished result to a user. To do this, decisions are made and transmitted as instructions to others in the organization for execution. Funds received for the product or service supplied to the user are received, recorded, and ultimately used to buy more supplies, pay wages, or for capital expansion. In short, there are flows of money, materials, ideas, instructions, authority, and many other things. These flows occur as people in positions carry out their tasks. Over and above the influence of the division of work, these flows will have a great influence on how a person behaves in filling the requirements of his position. Flows link positions in a very special way. They therefore influence not only what a person will do but with whom he will interact.

In any position, a person will be in a matrix of flows, of different types and importance. From both the organization and individual point of view, the flow concerned with accomplishing the primary purpose of the organization is the most important. It tells us which interdependencies will be considered the most important and where the greatest strains and most frustrating difficulties are likely to occur.

To say that positions or departments are linked by flows, as well as systems of authority and overall organization obligations, does not automatically guarantee that this will be consummated smoothly and effortlessly. Some of the elements covered in the earlier parts of the book are now seen to generate obstacles to a smooth and relatively effortless work flow. However, analysis has revealed some of the mechanics of these difficulties and helped in developing solutions or at least accommodations to them. Two classes of problems are probed. Those involved in getting people to fit into organization positions and those arising between positions as people fill them.

Part Five. Fitting Elements into the Organization

The first four parts lay out some of the basic elements of organizations. With these it is now possible to return to the original topic, structure, and examine it more closely. Initially, we were concerned with identifying structures and their effects. We said little about what gave rise to particular structures or influenced their use and effect. In this last part, we turn our attention to such questions. We examine the effects of organization size and policy and the effects one major structure has on the form and functioning of others. We can hardly do more than suggest what are the determinants of structure, for here the analysis becomes very complex because of the number of variables that have to be handled simultaneously. Yet to ignore these aspects of organizations is to proceed in foolish innocence to make decisions about or evaluations of organizations.

These five parts take us through the organization both in its static form and in its simple steady state. We are now ready for the important and vastly more complex topics of control and adaptation in Volume II.

Organization Theory: An Overview and an Appraisal

WILLIAM G. SCOTT

Man is intent on drawing himself into a web of collectivized patterns. "Modern man has learned to accommodate himself to a world increasingly organized. The trend toward ever more explicit and consciously drawn relationships is profound and sweeping; it is marked by depth no less than by extension." [1] This comment by Seidenberg nicely summarizes the pervasive influence of organization in many forms of human activity.

Some of the reasons for intense organizational activity are found in the fundamental transitions which revolutionized our society, changing it from a rural culture, to a culture based on technology, industry, and the city. From these changes, a way of life emerged characterized by the *proximity* and *dependency* of people on each other. Proximity and dependency, as conditions of social life, harbor the threats of human conflict, capricious antisocial behavior, instability of human relationships, and uncertainty about the nature of the social structure with its concomitant roles.

Of course, these threats to social integrity are present to some degree in all societies, ranging from the primitive to the modern. But, these threats become dangerous when the harmonious functioning of a society rests on the maintenance of a highly intricate, delicately balanced form of human collaboration. The civilization we have created depends on the preservation of a precarious balance. Hence, disrupting forces impinging on this shaky form of collaboration must be eliminated or minimized.

Traditionally, organization is viewed as a vehicle for accomplishing goals and objectives. While this approach is useful, it tends to obscure the inner workings and internal purposes of organization itself. Another fruitful way of treating organization is as a mechanism having the ultimate purpose of offsetting those forces which undermine human collaboration. In this sense, organization tends to minimize conflict, and to lessen the significance of individual behavior which deviates from values that the organization has established as worthwhile. Further, organization increases stability in human relationships by reducing uncertainty regarding the nature of the system's structure and the human roles which are inherent to it. Corollary to this point, organization enhances the predictability of human action, because it limits the number of behavioral alternatives available to an individual. As Presthus points out:

> Organization is defined as a system of structural interpersonal relations . . . individuals are differentiated in terms of authority, status, and role with the result that personal interaction is prescribed. . . . Anticipated reactions tend to occur, while ambiguity and spontaneity are decreased. [2]

In addition to all of this, organization has built-in safeguards. Besides prescribing acceptable forms of behavior for those who elect to submit to it, organization is also able to counterbalance the influence of human action which transcends its established patterns. [3]

From *Journal of the Academy of Management*, Vol. 4, No. 1, April 1961, pp. 7–26. Reprinted with permission of The Academy of Management.
[1] Roderick Seidenburg, *Post-Historic Man* (Boston: Beacon Press, 1951), p. 1.

[2] Robert V. Presthus, "Toward a Theory of Organizational Behavior," *Administrative Science Quarterly*, June, 1958, p. 50.
[3] Regulation and predictability of human behavior are matters of degree varying with different or-

Few segments of society have engaged in organizing more intensively than business.[4] The reason is clear. Business depends on what organization offers. Business needs a system of relationships among functions; it needs stability, continuity, and predictability in its internal activities and external contacts. Business also appears to need harmonious relationships among the people and processes which make it up. Put another way, a business organization has to be free, relatively, from destructive tendencies which may be caused by divergent interests.

As a foundation for meeting these needs rests administrative science. A major element of this science is organization theory, which provides the grounds for management activities in a number of significant areas of business endeavor. Organization theory, however, is not a homogeneous science based on generally accepted principles. Various theories of organization have been, and are being, evolved. For example, something called "modern organization theory" has recently emerged, raising the wrath of some traditionalists, but also capturing the imagination of a rather elite *avant-garde*.

The thesis of this paper is that modern organization theory, when stripped of its irrelevancies, redundancies, and "speech defects," is a logical and vital evolution in management thought. In order for this thesis to be supported, the reader must endure a review and appraisal of more traditional forms of organization theory which may seem elementary to him.

In any event, three theories of organization are having considerable influence on management thought and practice. They are arbitrarily labeled in this paper as the classical,

the neo-classical, and the modern. Each of these is fairly distinct; but they are not unrelated. Also, these theories are on-going, being actively supported by several schools of management thought.

The Classical Doctrine

For lack of a better method of identification, it will be said that the classical doctrine deals almost exclusively with the *anatomy of formal organization*. This doctrine can be traced back to Frederick W. Taylor's interest in functional foremanship and planning staffs. But most students of management thought would agree that in the United States, the first systematic approach to organization, and the first comprehensive attempt to find organizational universals, is dated 1931 when Mooney and Reiley published *Onward Industry*.[5] Subsequently, numerous books, following the classical vein, have appeared. Two of the more recent are Brech's, *Organization*[6] and Allen's, *Management and Organization*.[7]

Classical organization theory is built around four key pillars. They are the division of labor, the scalar and functional processes, structure, and span of control. Given these major elements just about all of classical organization theory can be derived.

1. *The division of labor* is without doubt the cornerstone among the four elements.[8] From it the other elements flow as corollaries. For example, *scalar* and *functional* growth requires specialization and departmentalization of functions. Organization *structure* is naturally dependent upon the direction which specialization of activities travels in company development. Finally, *span of control* problems result

---

ganizations on something of a continuum. At one extreme are bureaucratic type organizations with tight bonds of regulation. At the other extreme are voluntary associations, and informal organizations with relatively loose bonds of regulation.

This point has an interesting sidelight. A bureaucracy with tight controls and a high degree of predictability of human action appears to be unable to distinguish between destructive and creative deviations from established values. Thus the only thing which is safeguarded is the *status quo*.
[4] The monolithic institutions of the military and government are other cases of organizational preoccupation.

[5] James D. Mooney and Alan C. Reiley, *Onward Industry* (New York: Harper and Brothers, 1931). Later published by James D. Mooney under the title *Principles of Organization*.
[6] E. F. L. Brech, *Organization* (London: Longmans, Green and Company, 1957).
[7] Louis A. Allen, *Management and Organization* (New York: McGraw-Hill Book Company, 1958).
[8] Usually the division of labor is treated under a topical heading of departmentation, see for example: Harold Koontz and Cyril O'Donnell, *Principles of Management* (New York: McGraw-Hill Book Company, 1959), Chapter 7.

from the number of specialized functions under the jurisdiction of a manager.

2. *The scalar and functional processes* deal with the vertical and horizontal growth of the organization, respectively.[9] The scalar process refers to the growth of the chain of command, the delegation of authority and responsibility, unity of command, and the obligation to report.

The division of the organization into specialized parts and the regrouping of the parts into compatible units are matters pertaining to the functional process. This process focuses on the horizontal evolution of the line and staff in a formal organization.

3. *Structure* is the logical relationships of functions in an organization, arranged to accomplish the objectives of the company efficiently. Structure implies system and pattern. Classical organization theory usually works with two basic structures, the line and the staff. However, such activities as committee and liaison functions fall quite readily into the purview of structural considerations. Again, structure is the vehicle for introducing logical and consistent relationships among the diverse functions which comprise the organization.[10]

4. *The span of control* concept relates to the number of subordinates a manager can effectively supervise. Graicunas has been credited with first elaborating the point that there are numerical limitations to the subordinates one man can control.[11] In a recent statement on the subject, Brech points out, "span" refers to ". . . the number of persons, themselves carrying managerial and supervisory responsibilities, for whom the senior manager retains his over-embracing responsibility of direction and planning, co-ordination, motivation, and control." [12] Regardless of interpretation, span of control has significance, in part, for the shape of the organization which evolves

through growth. Wide span yields a flat structure; short span results in a tall structure. Further, the span concept directs attention to the complexity of human and functional interrelationships in an organization.

It would not be fair to say that the classical school is unaware of the day-to-day administrative problems of the organization. Paramount among these problems are those stemming from human interactions. But the interplay of individual personality, informal groups, intraorganizational conflict, and the decision-making processes in the formal structure appears largely to be neglected by classical organization theory. Additionally, the classical theory overlooks the contributions of the behavioral sciences by failing to incorporate them in its doctrine in any systematic way. In summary, classical organization theory has relevant insights into the nature of organization, but the value of this theory is limited by its narrow concentration on the formal anatomy of organization.

Neoclassical Theory of Organization

The neoclassical theory of organization embarked on the task of compensating for some of the deficiencies in classical doctrine. The neoclassical school is commonly identified with the human relations movement. Generally, the neoclassical approach takes the postulates of the classical school, regarding the pillars of organization as givens. But these postulates are regarded as modified by people, acting independently or within the context of the informal organization.

One of the main contributions of the neoclassical school is the introduction of behavioral sciences in an integrated fashion into the theory of organization. Through the use of these sciences, the human relationists demonstrate how the pillars of the classical doctrine are affected by the impact of human actions. Further, the neoclassical approach includes a systematic treatment of the informal organization, showing its influence on the formal structure.

Thus, the neoclassical approach to organization theory gives evidence of accepting classical doctrine, but superimposing on it modifications resulting from individual behavior,

---

[9] These processes are discussed at length in Ralph Currier Davis, *The Fundamentals of Top Management* (New York: Harper and Brothers, 1951), Chapter 7.

[10] For a discussion of structure see: William H. Newman, *Administrative Action* (Englewood Cliffs: Prentice-Hall, Incorporated, 1951), Chapter 16.

[11] V. A. Graicunas, "Relationships in Organization," *Papers on the Science of Administration* (New York: Columbia University, 1937).

[12] Brech, *op. cit.*, p. 78.

and the influence of the informal group. The inspiration of the neoclassical school was the Hawthorne studies.[13] Current examples of the neoclassical approach are found in human relations books like Gardner and Moore, *Human Relations in Industry*,[14] and Davis, *Human Relations in Business*.[15] To a more limited extent, work in industrial sociology also reflects a neoclassical point of view.[16]

It would be useful to look briefly at some of the contributions made to organization theory by the neoclassicists. First to be considered are modifications of the pillars of classical doctrine; second is the informal organization.

Examples of the Neoclassical Approach to the Pillars of Formal Organization Theory. 1. The *division of labor* has been a long standing subject of comment in the field of human relations. Very early in the history of industrial psychology study was made of industrial fatigue and monotony caused by the specialization of the work.[17] Later, attention shifted to the isolation of the worker, and his feeling of anonymity resulting from insignificant jobs which contributed negligibly to the final product.[18]

Also, specialization influences the work of management. As an organization expands, the need concomitantly arises for managerial motivation and coordination of the activities of others. Both motivation and coordination in turn relate to executive leadership. Thus, in part, stemming from the growth of industrial specialization, the neoclassical school has developed a large body of theory relating to motivation, coordination, and leadership. Much

of this theory is derived from the social sciences.

2. Two aspects of the *scalar and functional* processes which have been treated with some degree of intensity by the neoclassical school are the delegation of authority and responsibility, and gaps in or overlapping of functional jurisdictions. The classical thory assumes something of perfection in the delegation and functionalization processes. The neoclassical school points out that human problems are caused by imperfections in the way these processes are handled.

For example, too much or insufficient delegation may render an executive incapable of action. The failure to delegate authority and responsibility equally may result in frustration for the delegatee. Overlapping of authorities often causes clashes in personality. Gaps in authority cause failures in getting jobs done, with one party blaming the other for shortcomings in performance.[19]

The neoclassical school says that the scalar and functional processes are theoretically valid, but tend to deteriorate in practice. The ways in which they break down are described, and some of the human causes are pointed out. In addition the neoclassicists make recommendations, suggesting various "human tools" which will facilitate the operation of these processes.

3. *Structure* provides endless avenues of analysis for the neoclassical theory of organization. The theme is that human behavior disrupts the best laid organizational plans, and thwarts the cleanness of the logical relationships founded in the structure. The neoclassical critique of structure centers on frictions which appear internally among people performing different functions.

Line and staff relations is a problem area, much discussed, in this respect. Many companies seem to have difficulty keeping the line and staff working together harmoniously. Both Dalton[20] and Juran[21] have engaged in re-

---

[13] See: F. J. Roethlisberger and William J. Dickson, *Management and the Worker* (Cambridge: Harvard University Press, 1939).

[14] Burleigh B. Gardner and David G. Moore, *Human Relations in Industry* (Homewood: Richard D. Irwin, 1955).

[15] Keith Davis, *Human Relations in Business* (New York: McGraw-Hill Book Company, 1957).

[16] For example see: Delbert C. Miller and William H. Form, *Industrial Sociology* (New York: Harper and Brothers, 1951).

[17] See: Hugo Munsterberg, *Psychology and Industrial Efficiency* (Boston: Houghton Mifflin Company, 1913).

[18] Probably the classic work is: Elton Mayo, *The Human Problems of an Industrial Civilization* (Cambridge: Harvard University, 1946, first printed 1933).

[19] For further discussion of the human relations implications of the scalar and functional processes see: Keith Davis, *op. cit.*, pp. 60–66.

[20] Melville Dalton, "Conflicts between Staff and Line Managerial Officers," *American Sociological Review*, June, 1950, pp. 342–351.

[21] J. M. Juran, "Improving the Relationship between Staff and Line," *Personnel*, May, 1956, pp. 515–524.

search to discover the causes of friction, and to suggest remedies.

Of course, line-staff relations represent only one of the many problems of structural frictions described by the neoclassicists. As often as not, the neoclassicists will offer prescriptions for the elimination of conflict in structure. Among the more important harmony-rendering formulae are participation, junior boards, bottom-up management, joint committees, recognition of human dignity, and "better" communication.

4. An executive's *span of control* is a function of human determinants, and the reduction of span to a precise, universally applicable ratio is silly, according to the neoclassicists. Some of the determinants of span are individual differences in managerial abilities, the type of people and functions supervised, and the extent of communication effectiveness.

Coupled with the span of control question are the human implications of the type of structure which emerges. That is, is a tall structure with a short span or a flat structure with a wide span more conducive to good human relations and high morale? The answer is situational. Short span results in tight supervision; wide span requires a good deal of delegation with looser controls. Because of individual and organizational differences, sometimes one is better than the other. There is a tendency to favor the looser form of organization, however, for the reason that tall structures breed autocratic leadership, which is often pointed out as a cause of low morale.[22]

The Neoclassical View of the Informal Organization. Nothing more than the barest mention of the informal organization is given even in the most recent classical treatises on organization theory.[23] Systematic discussion of this form of organization has been left to the neoclassicists. The informal organization refers to people in group associations at work, but these associations are not specified in the "blueprint" of the formal organization. The informal organization means natural groupings of people in the work situation.

In a general way, the informal organization appears in response to the social need—the need of people to associate with others. How-

ever, for analytical purposes, this explanation is not particularly satisfying. Research has produced the following, more specific determinants underlying the appearance of informal organizations.

1. The *location* determinant simply states that in order to form into groups of any lasting nature, people have to have frequent face-to-face contact. Thus, the geography of physical location in a plant or office is an important factor in predicting who will be in what group.[24]

2. *Occupation* is a key factor determining the rise and composition of informal groups. There is a tendency for people performing similar jobs to group together.[25]

3. *Interests* are another determinant for informal group formation. Even though people might be in the same location, performing similar jobs, differences of interest among them explain why several small, instead of one large, informal organizations emerge.

4. *Special issues* often result in the formation of informal groups, but this determinant is set apart from the three previously mentioned. In this case, people who do not necessarily have similar interests, occupations, or locations may join together for a common cause. Once the issue is resolved, then the tendency is to revert to the more "natural" group forms.[26] Thus, special issues give rise to a rather impermanent informal association; groups based on the other three determinants tend to be more lasting.

When informal organizations come into being they assume certain characteristics. Since understanding these characteristics is important for management practice, they are noted below:

1. Informal organizations act as agencies of *social control*. They generate a culture based on certain norms of conduct which, in turn, demands conformity from group members. These standards may be at odds with the values

[22] Gardner and Moore, *op. cit.*, pp. 237–243.
[23] For example: Brech, *op. cit.*, pp. 27–29; and Allen, *op. cit.*, pp. 61–62.
[24] See: Leon Festinger, Stanley Schachter, and Kurt Back, *Social Pressures in Informal Groups* (New York: Harper and Brothers, 1950), pp. 153–163.
[25] For example see: W. Fred Cottrell, *The Railroader* (Palo Alto: The Stanford University Press, 1940), Chapter 3.
[26] Except in cases where the existence of an organization is necessary for the continued maintenance of employee interest. Under these conditions the previously informal association may emerge as a formal group, such as a union.

set by the formal organization. So an individual may very well find himself in a situation of conflicting demands.

2. The form of human interrelationships in the informal organization requires *techniques of analysis* different from those used to plot the relationships of people in a formal organization. The method used for determining the structure of the informal group is called sociometric analysis. Sociometry reveals the complex structure of interpersonal relations which is based on premises fundamentally unlike the logic of the formal organization.

3. Informal organizations have *status and communication* systems peculiar to themselves, not necessarily derived from the formal systems. For example, the grapevine is the subject of much neoclassical study.

4. Survival of the informal organization requires stable continuing relationships among the people in them. Thus, it has been observed that the informal organization *resists change*.[27] Considerable attention is given by the neoclassicists to overcoming informal resistance to change.

5. The last aspect of analysis which appears to be central to the neoclassical view of the informal organization is the study of the *informal leader*. Discussion revolves around who the informal leader is, how he assumes this role, what characteristics are peculiar to him, and how he can help the manager accomplish his objectives in the formal organization.[28]

This brief sketch of some of the major facets of informal organization theory has neglected, so far, one important topic treated by the neoclassical school. It is the way in which the formal and informal organizations interact.

A conventional way of looking at the interaction of the two is the "live and let live" point of view. Management should recognize that the informal organization exists, nothing can destroy it, and so the executive might just as well work with it. Working with the informal organization involves not threatening its existence unnecessarily, listening to opinions expressed for the group by the leader, allowing group participation in decision-making situations, and controlling the grapevine by prompt release of accurate information.[29]

While this approach is management centered, it is not unreasonable to expect that informal group standards and norms could make themselves felt on formal organizational policy. An honestly conceived effort by managers to establish a working relationship with the informal organization could result in an association where both formal and informal views would be reciprocally modified. The danger which at all costs should be avoided is that "working with the informal organization" does not degenerate into a shallow disguise for human manipulation.

Some neoclassical writing in organization theory, especially that coming from the management-oriented segment of this school, gives the impression that the formal and informal organizations are quite irreconcilable factors in a comnpay. The formal organizations are distinct, and at times, interaction which takes place between the two is something akin to the interaction between the company and a labor union, or a government agency, or another company.

The concept of the social system is another approach to the interactional climate. While this concept can be properly classified as neoclassical, it borders on the modern theories of organization. The phrase "social system" means that an organization is a complex of mutually interdependent, but variable, factors.

These factors include individuals and their attitudes and motives, jobs, the physical work setting, the formal organization, and the informal organizations. These factors, and many others, are woven into an overall pattern of interdependency. From this point of view, the formal and informal organizations lose their distinctiveness, but find real meaning, in terms of human behavior, in the operation of the system as a whole. Thus, the study of organization turns away from descriptions of its component parts, and is refocused on the system of interrelationships among the parts.

One of the major contributions of the Hawthorne studies was the integration of Pareto's

[27] Probably the classic study of resistance to change is: Lester Coch and John R. P. French, Jr., "Overcoming Resistance to Change," in Schuyler Dean Hoslett (editor) *Human Factors in Management* (New York: Harper and Brothers, 1951) pp. 242–268.

[28] For example see: Robert Saltonstall, *Human Relations in Administration* (New York: McGraw-Hill Book Company, 1959), pp. 330–331; and Keith Davis, *op. cit.*, pp. 99–101.

[29] For an example of this approach see: John T. Doutt, "Management Must Manage the Informal Group, Too," *Advanced Management*, May, 1959, pp. 26–28.

idea of the social system into a meaningful method of analysis for the study of behavior in human organizations.[30] This concept is still vitally important. But unfortunately some work in the field of human relations undertaken by the neoclassicists has overlooked, or perhaps discounted, the significance of this consideration.[31]

The fundamental insight regarding the social system, developed and applied to the industrial scene by the Hawthorne researchers, did not find much extension in subsequent work in the neoclassical vein. Indeed, the neoclassical school after the Hawthorne studies generally seemed content to engage in descriptive generalizations, or particularized empirical research studies which did not have much meaning outside their own context.

The neoclassical school of organization theory has been called bankrupt. Criticisms range from "human relations is a tool for cynical puppeteering of people," to "human relations is nothing more than a trifling body of empirical and descriptive information." There is a good deal of truth in both criticisms, but another appraisal of the neoclassical school of organization theory is offered here. The neoclassical approach has provided valuable contributions to the lore of organization. But, like the classical theory, the neoclassical doctrine suffers from incompleteness, a shortsighted perspective, and lack of integration among the many facets of human behavior studied by it. Modern organization theory has made a move to cover the shortcomings of the current body of theoretical knowledge.

Modern Organization Theory

The distinctive qualities of modern organization theory are its conceptual-analytical base, its reliance on empirical research data and, above all, its integrating nature. These qualities are framed in a philosophy which accepts the premise that the only meaningful way to study organization is to study it as a system.

As Henderson put it, the study of a system must rely on a method of analysis, ". . . involving the simultaneous variations of mutually dependent variables." [32] Human systems, of course, contain a huge number of dependent variables which defy the most complex simultaneous equations to solve.

Nevertheless, system analysis has its own peculiar point of view which aims to study organization in the way Henderson suggests. It treats organization as a system of mutually dependent variables. As a result, modern organization theory, which accepts system analysis, shifts the conceptual level of organization study above the classical and neoclassical theories. Modern organization theory asks a range of interrelated questions which are not seriously considered by the two other theories.

Key among these questions are: (1) What are the strategic parts of the system? (2) What is the nature of their mutual dependency? (3) What are the main processes in the system which link the parts together, and facilitate their adjustment to each other? (4) What are the goals sought by systems? [33]

Modern organization theory is in no way a unified body of thought. Each writer and researcher has his special emphasis when he considers the system. Perhaps the most evident unifying thread in the study of systems is the effort to look at the organization in its totality. Representative books in this field are March and Simon, *Organizations*,[34] and Haire's anthology, *Modern Organization Theory*.[35]

Instead of attempting a review of different writers' contributions to modern organization theory, it will be more useful to discuss the various ingredients involved in system analysis. They are the parts, the interactions, the processes, and the goals of systems.

The Parts of the System and Their Interdependency. The first basic part of the system is the *individual*, and the personality structure he brings to the organization. Elementary

[30] See: Roethlisberger and Dickson, *op. cit.*, Chapter 24.

[31] A check of management human relations texts, the organization and human relations chapters of principles of management texts, and texts on conventional organization theory for management courses reveals little or no treatment of the concept of the social system.

[32] Lawrence J. Henderson, *Pareto's General Sociology* (Cambridge: Harvard University Press, 1935), p. 13.

[33] There is another question which cannot be treated in the scope of this paper. It asks, what research tools should be used for the study of the system?

[34] James G. March and Herbert A. Simon, *Organizations* (New York: John Wiley and Sons, 1958).

[35] Mason Haire (editor) *Modern Organization Theory* (New York: John Wiley and Sons, 1959).

to an individual's personality are motives and attitudes which condition the range of expectancies he hopes to satisfy by participating in the system.

The second part of the system is the formal arrangement of functions, usually called the *formal organization*. The formal organization is the interrelated pattern of jobs which make up the structure of a system. Certain writers, like Argyris, see a fundamental conflict resulting from the demands made by the system, and the structure of the mature, normal personality. In any event, the individual has expectancies regarding the job he is to perform; and, conversely, the job makes demands on, or has expectancies relating to, the performance of the individual. Considerable attention has been given by writers in modern organization theory to incongruencies resulting from the interaction of organizational and individual demands.[36]

The third part in the organization system is the *informal organization*. Enough has been said already about the nature of this organization. But it must be noted that an interactional pattern exists between the individual and the informal group. This interactional arrangement can be conveniently discussed as the mutual modification of expectancies. The informal organization has demands which it makes on members in terms of anticipated forms of behavior, and the individual has expectancies of satisfaction he hopes to derive from association with people on the job. Both these sets of expectancies interact, resulting in the individual modifying his behavior to accord with the demands of the group, and the group, perhaps, modifying what it expects from an individual because of the impact of his personality on group norms.[37]

Much of what has been said about the various expectancy systems in an organization can also be treated using status and role concepts. Part of modern organization theory rests on research findings in social-psychology relative to reciprocal patterns of behavior stemming from role demands generated by both the formal and informal organizations, and role perceptions peculiar to the individual. Bakke's *fusion process* is largely concerned with the modification of role expectancies. The fusion process is a force, according to Bakke, which acts to weld divergent elements together for the preservation of organizational integrity.[38]

The fifth part of system analysis is the *physical setting* in which the job is performed. Although this element of the system may be implicit in what has been said already about the formal organization and its functions, it is well to separate it. In the physical surroundings of work, interactions are present in complex man-machine systems. The human "engineer" cannot approach the problems posed by such interrelationships in a purely technical, engineering fashion. As Haire says, these problems lie in the domain of the social theorists.[39] Attention must be centered on responses demanded from a logically ordered production function, often with the view of minimizing the error in the system. From this standpoint, work cannot be effectively organized unless the psychological, social, and physiological characteristics of people participating in the work environment are considered. Machines and processes should be designed to fit certain generally observed psychological and physiological properties of men, rather than hiring men to fit machines.

In summary, the parts of the system which appear to be of strategic importance are the individual, the formal structure, the informal organization, status and role patterns, and the physical environment of work. Again, these parts are woven into a configuration called the organizational system. The processes which link the parts are taken up next.

The Linking Processes. One can say, with a good deal of glibness, that all the parts mentioned above are interrelated. Although this observation is quite correct, it does not mean too much in terms of system theory unless

---

[36] See Chris Argyris, *Personality and Organization* (New York: Harper and Brothers, 1957), esp. Chapters 2, 3, 7.

[37] For a larger treatment of this subject see: George C. Homans, *The Human Group* (New York: Harcourt, Brace and Company, 1950), Chapter 5.

[38] E. Wight Bakke, "Concept of the Social Organization," in *Modern Organization Theory*, Mason Haire (editor) (New York: John Wiley and Sons, 1959) pp. 60–61.

[39] Mason Haire, "Psychology and the Study of Business: Joint Behavioral Sciences," in *Social Science Research on Business: Product and Potential* (New York: Columbia University Press, 1959), pp. 53–59.

some attempt is made to analyze the processes by which the interaction is achieved. Role theory is devoted to certain types of interactional processes. In addition, modern organization theorists point to three other linking activities which appear to be universal to human systems of organized behavior. These processes are communication, balance, and decision making.

1. Communication is mentioned often in neoclassical theory, but the emphasis is on description of forms of communication activity, i.e., formal-informal, vertical-horizontal, line-staff. Communication, as a mechanism which links the segments of the system together, is overlooked by way of much considered analysis.

One aspect of modern organization theory is study of the communication network in the system. Communication is viewed as the method by which action is evoked from the parts of the system. Communication acts not only as stimuli resulting in action, but also as a control and coordination mechanism linking the decision centers in the system into a synchronized pattern. Deutsch points out that organizations are composed of parts which communicate with each other, receive messages from the outside world, and store information. Taken together, these communication functions of the parts comprise a configuration representing the total system.[40] More is to be said about communication later in the discussion of the cybernetic model.

2. The concept of *balance* as a linking process involves a series of some rather complex ideas. Balance refers to an equilibrating mechanism whereby the various parts of the system are maintained in a harmoniously structured relationship to each other.

The necessity for the balance concept logically flows from the nature of systems themselves. It is impossible to conceive of an ordered relationship among the parts of a system without also introducing the idea of a stabilizing or an adapting mechanism.

Balance appears in two varieties—quasi-automatic and innovative. Both forms of balance act to insure system integrity in face of changing conditions, either internal or external

to the system. The first form of balance, quasi-automatic, refers to what some think are "homeostatic" properties of systems. That is, systems seem to exhibit built-in propensities to maintain steady states.

If human organizations are open, self-maintaining systems, then control and regulatory processes are necessary. The issue hinges on the degree to which stabilizing processes in systems, when adapting to change, are automatic. March and Simon have an interesting answer to this problem, which in part is based on the type of change and the adjustment necessary to adapt to the change. Systems have programs of action which are put into effect when a change is perceived. If the change is relatively minor, and if the change comes within the purview of established programs of action, then it might be fairly confidently predicted that the adaptation made by the system will be quasi-automatic.[41]

The role of innovative, creative balancing efforts now needs to be examined. The need for innovation arises when adaptation to a change is outside the scope of existing programs designed for the purpose of keeping the system in balance. New programs have to be evolved in order for the system to maintain internal harmony.

New programs are created by trial and error search for feasible action alternatives to cope with a given change. But innovation is subject to the limitations and possibilities inherent in the quantity and variety of information present in a system at a particular time. New combinations of alternatives for innovative purposes depend on:

(*a*) the possible range of output of the system, or the capacity of the system to supply information.

(*b*) the range of available information in the memory of the system.

(*c*) the operating rules (program) governing the analysis and flow of information within the system.

(*d*) the ability of the system to "forget" previously learned solutions to changed problems.[42] A system with too good a memory

[40] Karl W. Deutsch, "On Communication Models in the Social Sciences," *Public Opinion Quarterly*, 16 (1952), pp. 356–380.

[41] March and Simon, *op. cit.*, pp. 139–140.
[42] Mervyn L. Cadwallader, "The Cybernetic Analysis of Change in Complex Social Organization," *The American Journal of Sociology*, September, 1959, p. 156.

might narrow its behavioral choices to such an extent as to stifle innovation. In simpler language, old learned programs might be used to adapt to change, when newly innovated programs are necessary.[43]

Much of what has been said about communication and balance brings to mind a cybernetic model in which both these processes have vital roles. Cybernetics has to do with feedback and control in all kinds of systems. Its purpose is to maintain system stability in the face of change. Cybernetics cannot be studied without considering communication networks, information flow, and some kind of balancing process aimed at preserving the integrity of the system.

Cybernetics directs attention to key questions regarding the system. These questions are: How are communication centers connected, and how are they maintained? Corollary to this question: what is the structure of the feedback system? Next, what information is stored in the organization, and at what points? And as a corollary: how accessible is this information to decision-making centers? Third, how conscious is the organization of the operation of its own parts? That is, to what extent do the policy centers receive control information with sufficient frequency and relevancy to create a real awareness of the operation of the segments of the system? Finally, what are the learning (innovating) capabilities of the system? [44]

Answers to the questions posed by cybernetics are crucial to understanding both the balancing and communication processes in systems.[45] Although cybernetics has been applied largely to technical-engineering problems of automation, the model of feedback, control, and regulation in all systems has a good deal of generality. Cybernetics is a fruitful area which can be used to synthesize the processes of communication and balance.

3. A wide spectrum of topics dealing with types of decisions in human systems makes up the core of analysis of another important process in organizations. Decision analysis is one of the major contributions of March and Simon in their book *Organizations*. The two major classes of decisions they discuss are decisions to produce and decisions to participate in the system.[46]

Decisions to produce are largely a result of an interaction between individual attitudes and the demands of organization. Motivation analysis becomes central to studying the nature and results of the interaction. Individual decisions to participate in the organization reflect on such issues as the relationship between organizational rewards versus the demands made by the organization. Participation decisions also focus attention on the reasons why individuals remain in or leave organizations.

March and Simon treat decisions as internal variables in an organization which depend on jobs, individual expectations and motivations, and organizational structure. Marschak [47] looks on the decision process as an independent variable upon which the survival of the organization is based. In this case, the organization is viewed as having, inherent to its structure, the ability to maximize survival requisites through its established decision processes.

The Goals of Organization. Organization has three goals which may be either intermeshed or independent ends in themselves. They are growth, stability, and interaction. The last goal refers to organizations which exist primarily to provide a medium for association of its members with others. Interestingly enough these goals seem to apply to different forms of organization at varying levels of complexity, ranging from simple clockwork mechanisms to social systems.

These similarities in organizational purposes have been observed by a number of people, and a field of thought and research called general system theory has developed, dedicated to the task of discovering organizationed universals. The dream of general system theory is to create a science of organizational universals, or if you will, a universal science using com-

---

[43] It is conceivable for innovative behavior to be programmed into the system.

[44] These are questions adapted from Deutsch, *op. cit.*, 368–370.

[45] Answers to these questions would require a comprehensive volume. One of the best approaches currently available is Stafford Beer, *Cybernetics and Management* (New York: John Wiley and Sons, 1959).

[46] March and Simon, *op. cit.*, Chapters 3 and 4.

[47] Jacob Marschak, "Efficient and Viable Organizational Forms" in *Modern Organization Theory*, Mason Haire (editor) (New York: John Wiley and Sons, 1959), pp. 307–320.

mon organizational elements found in all systems as a starting point.

Modern organization theory is on the periphery of general system theory. Both general system theory and modern organization theory study:

1. the parts (individuals) in aggregates, and the movement of individuals into and out of the system.

2. the interaction of individuals with the environment found in the system.

3. the interactions among individuals in the system.

4. general growth and stability problems of systems.[48]

Modern organization theory and general system theory are similar in that they look at organization as an integrated whole. They differ, however, in terms of their generality. General system theory is concerned with every level of system, whereas modern organizational theory focuses primarily on human organization.

The question might be asked, what can the science of administration gain by the study of system levels other than human? Before attempting an answer, note should be made of what these other levels are. Boulding presents a convenient method of classification:

1. The static structure—a level of framework, the anatomy of a system; for example, the structure of the universe.

2. The simple dynamic system—the level of clockworks, predetermined necessary motions.

3. The cybernetic system—the level of the thermostat, the system moves to maintain a given equilibrium through a process of self-regulation.

4. The open system—level of self-maintaining systems, moves toward and includes living organisms.

5. The genetic-societal system—level of cell society, characterized by a division of labor among cells.

6. Animal systems—level of mobility, evidence of goal-directed behavior.

7. Human systems—level of symbol interpretation and idea communication.

8. Social system—level of human organization.

9. Transcendental systems—level of ultimates

and absolutes which exhibit systematic structure but are unknowable in essence.[49]

This approach to the study of systems by finding universals common at all levels of organization offers intriguing possibilities for administrative organization theory. A good deal of light could be thrown on social systems if structurally analogous elements could be found in the simpler types of systems. For example, cybernetic systems have characteristics which seem to be similar to feedback, regulation, and control phenomena in human organizations. Thus, certain facets of cybernetic models could be generalized to human organization. Considerable danger, however, lies in poorly founded analogies. Superficial similarities between simpler system forms and social systems are apparent everywhere. Instinctually based ant societies, for example, do not yield particularly instructive lessons for understanding rationally conceived human organizations. Thus, care should be taken that analogies used to bridge system levels are not mere devices for literary enrichment. For analogies to have usefulness and validity, they must exhibit inherent structural similarities or implicitly identical operational principles.[50]

Modern organization theory leads, as it has been shown, almost inevitably into a discussion of general system theory. A science of organization universals has some strong advocates, particularly among biologists.[51] Organization theorists in administrative science cannot afford to overlook the contributions of general system theory. Indeed, modern organization concepts could offer a great deal to those working with general system theory. But the ideas dealt

[48] Kenneth E. Boulding, "General System Theory—The Skeleton of a Science," *Management Science*, April, 1956, pp. 200–202.

[49] *Ibid.*, pp. 202–205.

[50] Seidenberg, *op. cit.*, p. 136. The fruitful use of the type of analogies spoken of by Seidenberg is evident in the application of thermodynamic principles, particularly the entropy concept, to communication theory. See: Claude E. Shannon and Warren Weaver, *The Mathematical Theory of Communication* (Urbana: The University of Illinois Press, 1959). Further, the existence of a complete analogy between the operational behavior of thermodynamic systems, electrical communication systems, and biological systems has been noted by: Y. S. Touloukian, *The Concept of Entropy in Communication, Living Organisms, and Thermodynamics*, Research Bulletin 130, Purdue Engineering Experiment Station.

[51] For example see: Ludwig von Bertalanffy, *Problem of Life* (London: Watts and Company, 1952).

with in the general theory are exceedingly elusive.

Speaking of the concept of equilibrium as a unifying element in all systems, Easton says, "It (equilibrium) leaves the impression that we have a useful general theory when in fact, lacking measurability, it is a mere pretence for knowledge." [52] The inability to quantify and measure universal organization elements undermines the success of pragmatic tests to which general system theory might be put.

Organization Theory: Quo Vadis? Most sciences have a vision of the universe to which they are applied, and administrative science is not an exception. This universe is composed of parts. One purpose of science is to synthesize the parts into an organized conception of its field of study. As a science matures, its theorems about the configuration of its universe change. The direction of change in three sciences, physics, economics, and sociology, are noted briefly for comparison with the development of an administrative view of human organization.

The first comprehensive and empirically verifiable outlook of the physical universe was presented by Newton in his *Principia*. Classical physics, founded on Newton's work, constitutes a grand scheme in which a wide range of physical phenomena could be organized and predicted. Newtonian physics may rightfully be regarded as "macro" in nature, because its system of organization was concerned largely with gross events of which the movement of celestial bodies, waves, energy forms, and strain are examples. For years classical physics was supreme, being applied continuously to smaller and smaller classes of phenomena in the physical universe. Physicists at one time adopted the view that everything in their realm could be discovered by simply subdividing problems. Physics thus moved into the "micro" order.

But in the nineteenth century a revolution took place motivated largely because events were being noted which could not be explained adequately by the conceptual framework supplied by the classical school. The consequences

of this revolution are brilliantly described by Eddington:

From the point of view of philosophy of science the conception associated with entropy must I think be ranked as the great contribution of the nineteenth century to scientific thought. It marked a reaction from the view that everything to which science need pay attention is discovered by microscopic dissection of objects. It provided an alternative standpoint in which the centre of interest is shifted from the entities reached by the customary analysis (atoms, electric potentials, etc.) to qualities possessed by the system as a whole, which cannot be split up and located—a little bit here, and a little bit there. . . .

We often think that when we have completed our study of *one* we know all about *two*, because "two" is "one and one." We forget that we have still to make a study of "and." Secondary physics is the study of "and"—that is to say, of organization.[53]

Although modern physics often deals in minute quantities and oscillations, the conception of the physicist is on the "macro" scale. He is concerned with the "and," or the organization of the world in which the events occur. These developments did not invalidate classical physics as to its usefulness for explaining a certain range of phenomena. But classical physics is no longer the undisputed law of the universe. It is a special case.

Early economic theory, and Adam Smith's *Wealth of Nations* comes to mind, examined economic problems in the macro order. The *Wealth of Nations* is mainly concerned with matters of national income and welfare. Later, the economics of the firm, micro-economics, dominated the theoretical scene in this science. And, finally, with Keynes' *The General Theory of Employment Interest and Money*, a systematic approach to the economic universe was re-introduced in the macro level.

The first era of the developing science of sociology was occupied by the great social "system builders." Comte, the so-called father of sociology, had a macro view of society in that his chief works are devoted to social reorganization. Comte was concerned with the inter-

[52] David Easton, "Limits of the Equilibrium Model in Social Research," in *Profits and Problems of Homeostatic Models in the Behavioral Sciences*, Publication 1, Chicago Behavioral Sciences, 1953, p. 39.

[53] Sir Arthur Eddington, *The Nature of the Physical World* (Ann Arbor: The University of Michigan Press, 1958), pp. 103–104.

relationships among social, political, religious, and educational institutions. As sociology progressed, the science of society compressed. Emphasis shifted from the macro approach of the pioneers to detailed, empirical study of small social units. The compression of sociological analysis was accompanied by study of social pathology or disorganization.

In general, physics, economics, and sociology appear to have two things in common. First, they offered a macro point of view as their initial systematic comprehension of their area of study. Second, as the science developed, attention fragmented into analysis of the parts of the organization, rather than attending to the system as a whole. This is the micro phase.

In physics and economics, discontent was evidenced by some scientists at the continual atomization of the universe. The reaction to the micro approach was a new theory or theories dealing with the total system, on the macro level again. This third phase of scientific development seems to be more evident in physics and economics than in sociology.

The reason for the "macro-micro-macro" order of scientific progress lies, perhaps, in the hypothesis that usually the things which strike man first are of great magnitude. The scientist attempts to discover order in the vastness. But after macro laws or models of systems are postulated, variations appear which demand analysis, not so much in terms of the entire system, but more in terms of the specific parts which make it up. Then, intense study of mircocosm may result in new general laws, replacing the old models of organization. Or, the old and the new models may stand together, each explaining a different class of phenomenon. Or, the old and the new concepts of organization may be welded to produce a single creative synthesis.

Now, what does all this have to do with the problem of organization in administrative science? Organization concepts seem to have gone through the same order of development in this field as in the three just mentioned. It is evident that the classical theory of organization, particularly as in the work of Mooney and Reiley, is concerned with principles common to all organizations. It is a macro-organizational view. The classical approach to organization, however, dealt with the gross anatomical parts and processes of the formal organization. Like classical physics, the classical theory of organization is a special case. Neither are especially well equipped to account for variation from their established framework.

Many variations in the classical administrative model result from human behavior. The only way these variations could be understood was by a microscopic examination of particularized, situational aspects of human behavior. The mission of the neoclassical school thus is "micro-analysis."

It was observed earlier, that somewhere along the line the concept of the social system, which is the key to understanding the Hawthorne studies, faded into the background. Maybe the idea is so obvious that it was lost to the view of researchers and writers in human relations. In any event, the press of research in the microcosmic universes of the informal organization, morale and productivity, leadership, participation, and the like forced the notion of the social system into limbo. Now, with the advent of modern organization theory, the social system has been resurrected.

Modern organization theory appears to be concerned with Eddington's "and." This school claims that its operational hypothesis is based on a macro point of view; that is, the study of organization as a whole. This nobility of purpose should not obscure, however, certain difficulties faced by this field as it is presently constituted. Modern organization theory raises two questions which should be explored further. First, would it not be more accurate to speak of modern organization theories? Second, just how much of modern organization theory is modern?

The first question can be answered with a quick affirmative. Aside from the notion of the system, there are few, if any, other ideas of a unifying nature. Except for several important exceptions,[54] modern organization theorists tend to pursue their pet points of view,[55] suggesting they are part of system theory, but not troubling to show by what mystical means they arrive at this conclusion.

The irony of it all is that a field dealing with systems has, indeed, little system. Modern organization theory needs a framework, and it needs an integration of issues into a common conception of organization. Admittedly, this

[54] For example: E. Wight Bakke, *op. cit.*, pp. 18–75.
[55] There is a large selection including decision theory, individual-organization interaction, motivation, vitality, stability, growth, and graph theory, to mention a few.

is a large order. But it is curious not to find serious analytical treatment of subjects like cybernetics or general system theory in Haire's *Modern Organizational Theory* which claims to be a representative example of work in this field. Beer has ample evidence in his book *Cybernetics and Management* that cybernetics, if imaginatively approached, provides a valuable conceptual base for the study of systems.

The second question suggests an ambiguous answer. Modern organization theory is in part a product of the past; system analysis is not a new idea. Further, modern organization theory relies for supporting data on microcosmic research studies, generally drawn from the journals of the last ten years. The newness of modern organization theory, perhaps, is its effort to synthesize recent research contributions of many fields into a system theory characterized by a reoriented conception of organization.

One might ask, but what is the modern theorist reorienting? A clue is found in the almost snobbish disdain assumed by some authors of the neo-classical human relations school, and particularly, the classical school. Re-evaluation of the classical school of organization is overdue. However, this does not mean that its contributions to organization theory are irrelevant and should be overlooked in the rush to get on the "behavioral science bandwagon."

Haire announces that the papers appearing in *Modern Organization Theory* constitute, "the ragged leading edge of a wave of theoretical development."[56] Ragged, yes; but leading no! The papers appearing in this book do not represent a theoretical breakthrough in the concept of organization. Haire's collection is an interesting potpourri with several contributions of considerable significance. But readers should beware that they will not find vastly new insights into organizational behavior in this book, if they have kept up with the literature of the social sciences, and have dabbled to some extent in the esoterica of biological theories of growth, information theory, and mathematical model building. For those who have not maintained the pace, *Modern*

Organization Theory serves the admirable purpose of bringing them up-to-date on a rather diversified number of subjects.

Some work in modern organization theory is pioneering, making its appraisal difficult and future uncertain. While the direction of this endeavor is unclear, one thing is patently true. Human behavior in organizations, and indeed, organization itself, cannot be adequately understood within the ground rules of classical and neo-classical doctrines. Appreciation of human organization requires a *creative* synthesis of massive amounts of empirical data, a high order of deductive reasoning, imaginative research studies, and a taste for individual and social values. Accomplishment of all these objectives, and the inclusion of them into a framework of the concept of the system, appears to be the goal of modern organization theory. The vitality of administrative science rests on the advances modern theorists make along this line.

Modern organization theory, 1960 style, is an amorphous aggregation of synthesizers and restaters, with a few extending leadership on the frontier. For the sake of these few, it is well to admonish that pouring old wine into new bottles may make the spirits cloudy. Unfortunately, modern organization theory has almost succeeded in achieving the status of a fad. Popularization and exploitation contributed to the disrepute into which human relations has fallen. It would be a great waste if modern organization theory yields to the same fate, particularly since both modern organization theory and human relations draw from the same promising source of inspiration—system analysis.

Modern organization theory needs tools of analysis and a conceptual framework uniquely its own, but it must also allow for the incorporation of relevant contributions of many fields. It may be that the framework will come from general system theory. New areas of research such as decision theory, information theory, and cybernetics also offer reasonable expectations of analytical and conceptual tools. Modern organization theory represents a frontier of research which has great significance for management. The potential is great, because it offers the opportunity for uniting what is valuable in classical theory with the social and natural sciences into a systematic and integrated conception of human organization.

---

[56] Mason Haire, "General Issues," in Mason Haire (editor), *Modern Organization Theory* (New York: John Wiley and Sons, 1959), p. 2.

Bureaucracy

MAX WEBER

CHARACTERISTICS OF BUREAUCRACY. Modern officialdom functions in the following specific manner:

I. There is the principle of fixed and official

From *From Max Weber: Essays in Sociology,* edited and translated by H. H. Gerth and C. Wright Mills. Copyright 1946 by Oxford University Press. Reprinted with permission of the publisher.

jurisdictional areas, which are generally ordered by rules, that is, by laws or administrative regulations.

1. The regular activities required for the purposes of the bureaucratically governed structure are distributed in a fixed way as official duties.

2. The authority to give the commands required for the discharge of these duties is distributed in a stable way and is strictly delimited

by rules concerning the coercive means, physical, sacerdotal, or otherwise, which may be placed at the disposal of officials.

3. Methodical provision is made for the regular and continuous fulfilment of these duties and for the execution of the corresponding rights; only persons who have the generally regulated qualifications to serve are employed.

In public and lawful government these three elements constitute "bureaucratic authority." In private economic domination, they constitute bureaucratic "management." Bureaucracy, thus understood, is fully developed in political and ecclesiastical communities only in the modern state, and, in the private economy, only in the most advanced institutions of capitalism. Permanent and public office authority, with fixed jurisdiction, is not the historical rule but rather the exception. This is so even in large political structures such as those of the ancient Orient, the Germanic and Mongolian empires of conquest, or of many feudal structures of state. In all these cases, the ruler executes the most important measures through personal trustees, table-companions, or court-servants. Their commissions and authority are not precisely delimited and are temporarily called into being for each case.

II. The principles of office hierarchy and of levels of graded authority mean a firmly ordered system of super- and subordination in which there is a supervision of the lower offices by the higher ones. Such a system offers the governed the possibility of appealing the decision of a lower office to its higher authority, in a definitely regulated manner. With the full development of the bureaucratic type, the office hierarchy is monocratically organized. The principle of hierachical office authority is found in all bureaucratic structures: in state and ecclesiastical structures as well as in large party organizations and private enterprises. It does not matter for the character of bureaucracy whether its authority is called "private" or "public."

When the principle of jurisdictional "competency" is fully carried through, hierarchical subordination—at least in public office—does not mean that the "higher" authority is simply authorized to take over the business of the "lower." Indeed, the opposite is the rule. Once established and having fulfilled its task, an office tends to continue in existence and be held by another incumbent.

III. The management of the modern office is based on written documents ("the files"), which are preserved in their original or draught form. There is, therefore, a staff of subaltern officials and scribes of all sorts. The body of officials actively engaged in a "public" office, along with the respective apparatus of material implements and the files, make up a "bureau." In private enterprise, "the bureau" is often called "the office."

In principle, the modern organization of the civil service separates the bureau from the private domicile of the official, and, in general, bureaucracy segregates official activity as something distinct from the sphere of private life. Public monies and equipment are divorced from the private property of the official. This condition is everywhere the product of a long development. Nowadays, it is found in public as well as in private enterprises; in the latter, the principle extends even to the leading entrepreneur. In principle, the executive office is separated from the household, business from private correspondence, and business assets from private fortunes. The more consistently the modern type of business management has been carried through the more are these separations the case. The beginnings of this process are to be found as early as the Middle Ages.

It is the peculiarity of the modern entrepreneur that he conducts himself as the "first official" of his enterprise, in the very same way in which the ruler of a specifically modern bureaucratic state spoke of himself as "the first servant" of the state.[1] The idea that the bureau activities of the state are intrinsically different in character from the management of private economic offices is a continental European notion and, by way of contrast, is totally foreign to the American way.

IV. Office management, at least all specialized office management—and such management is distinctly modern—usually presupposes thorough and expert training. This increasingly holds for the modern executive and employee of private enterprises, in the same manner as it holds for the state official.

V. When the office is fully developed, official activity demands the full working capacity of the official, irrespective of the fact that his obligatory time in the bureau may be

[1] Frederick II of Prussia.

firmly delimited. In the normal case, this is only the product of a long development, in the public as well as in the private office. Formerly, in all cases, the normal state of affairs was reversed: official business was discharged as a secondary activity.

VI. The management of the office follows general rules, which are more or less stable, more or less exhaustive, and which can be learned. Knowledge of these rules represents a special technical learning which the officials possess. It involves jurisprudence, or administrative or business management.

The reduction of modern office management to rules is deeply embedded in its very nature. The theory of modern public administration, for instance, assumes that the authority to order certain matters by decree—which has been legally granted to public authorities—does not entitle the bureau to regulate the matter by commands given for each case, but only to regulate the matter abstractly. This stands in extreme contrast to the regulation of all relationships through individual privileges and bestowals of favor, which is absolutely dominant in patrimonialism, at least in so far as such relationships are not fixed by sacred tradition.

THE POSITION OF THE OFFICIAL. All this results in the following for the internal and external position of the official:

I. Office holding is a "vocation." This is shown, first, in the requirement of a firmly prescribed course of training, which demands the entire capacity for work for a long period of time, and in the generally prescribed and special examinations which are prerequisites of employment. Furthermore, the position of the official is in the nature of a duty. This determines the internal structure of his relations, in the following manner: Legally and actually, office holding is not considered a source to be exploited for rents or emoluments, as was normally the case during the Middle Ages and frequently up to the threshold of recent times. Nor is office holding considered a usual exchange of services for equivalents, as is the case with free labor contracts. Entrance into an office, including one in the private economy, is considered an acceptance of a specific obligation of faithful management in return for a secure existence. It is decisive for the specific nature of modern loyalty to an office that, in the pure type, it does not establish a relationship to a *person*, like the vassal's or disciple's faith in feudal or in patrimonial relations of authority. Modern loyalty is devoted to impersonal and functional purposes. Behind the functional purposes, of course, "ideas of culture-values" usually stand. These are *ersatz* for the earthly or supra-mundane personal master: ideas such as "state," "church," "community," "party," or "enterprise" are thought of as being realized in a community; they provide an ideological halo for the master.

The political official—at least in the fully developed modern state—is not considered the personal servant of a ruler. Today, the bishop, the priest, and the preacher are in fact no longer, as in early Christian times, holders of purely personal charisma. The supra-mundane and sacred values which they offer are given to everybody who seems to be worthy of them and who asks for them. In former times, such leaders acted upon the personal command of their master; in principle, they were responsible only to him. Nowadays, in spite of the partial survival of the old theory, such religious leaders are officials in the service of a functional purpose, which in the present-day "church" has become routinized and, in turn, ideologically hallowed.

II. The personal position of the official is patterned in the following way:

1. Whether he is in a private office or a public bureau, the modern official always strives and usually enjoys a distinct *social esteem* as compared with the governed. His social position is guaranteed by the prescriptive rules of rank order and, for the political official, by special definitions of the criminal code against "insults of officials" and "contempt" of state and church authorities.

The actual social position of the official is normally highest where, as in old civilized countries, the following conditions prevail: a strong demand for administration by trained experts; a strong and stable social differentiation, where the official predominantly derives from socially and economically privileged strata because of the social distribution of power; or where the costliness of the required training and status conventions are binding upon him. The possession of educational certificates—to be discussed elsewhere [2]

[2] Cf. *Wirtschaft und Gesellschaft*, pp. 73 ff. and part II [German editor's note].

—are usually linked with qualification for office. Naturally, such certificates or patents enhance the "status element" in the social position of the official. For the rest this status factor in individual cases is explicitly and impassively acknowledged; for example, in the prescription that the acceptance or rejection of an aspirant to an official career depends upon the consent ("election") of the members of the official body. This is the case in the German army with the officer corps. Similar phenomena, which promote this guild-like closure of officialdom, are typically found in patrimonial and, particularly, in prebendal officialdoms of the past. The desire to resurrect such phenomena in changed forms is by no means infrequent among modern bureaucrats. For instance, they have played a role among the demands of the quite proletarian and expert officials (the *tretyj* element) during the Russian revolution.

Usually the social esteem of the officials as such is especially low where the demand for expert administration and the dominance of status conventions are weak. This is especially the case in the United States; it is often the case in new settlements by virtue of their wide fields for profit-making and the great instability of their social stratification.

2. The pure type of bureaucratic official is *appointed* by a superior authority. An official elected by the governed is not a purely bureaucratic figure. Of course, the formal existence of an election does not by itself mean that no appointment hides behind the election —in the state, especially, appointment by party chiefs. Whether or not this is the case does not depend upon legal statutes but upon the way in which the party mechanism functions. Once firmly organized, the parties can turn a formally free election into the mere acclamation of a candidate designated by the party chief. As a rule, however, a formally free election is turned into a fight, conducted according to definite rules, for votes in favor of one of two designated candidates.

In all circumstances, the designation of officials by means of an election among the governed modifies the strictness of hierarchical subordination. In principle, an official who is so elected has an autonomous position opposite the superordinate official. The elected official does not derive his position "from above" but "from below," or at least not from a superior authority of the official hierarchy but from powerful party men ("bosses"), who also determine his further career. The career of the elected official is not, or at least not primarily, dependent upon his chief in the administration. The official who is not elected but appointed by a chief normally functions more exactly, from a technical point of view, because, all other circumstances being equal, it is more likely that purely functional points of consideration and qualities will determine his selection and career. As laymen, the governed can become acquainted with the extent to which a candidate is expertly qualified for office only in terms of experience, and hence only after his service. Moreover, in every sort of selection of officials by election, parties quite naturally give decisive weight not to expert considerations but to the services a follower renders to the party boss. This holds for all kinds of procurement of officials by elections, for the designation of formally free, elected officials by party bosses when they determine the slate of candidates, or the free appointment by a chief who has himself been elected. The contrast, however, is relative: substantially similar conditions hold where legitimate monarchs and their subordinates appoint officials, except that the influence of the followings are then less controllable.

Where the demand for administration by trained experts is considerable, and the party followings have to recognize an intellectually developed, educated, and freely moving "public opinion," the use of unqualified officials falls back upon the party in power at the next election. Naturally, this is more likely to happen when the officials are appointed by the chief. The demand for a trained administration now exists in the United States, but in the large cities, where immigrant votes are "corralled," there is, of course, no educated public opinion. Therefore, popular elections of the administrative chief and also of his subordinate officials usually endanger the expert qualification of the official as well as the precise functioning of the bureaucratic mechanism. It also weakens the dependence of the officials upon the hierarchy. This holds at least for the large administrative bodies that are difficult to supervise. The superior qualification and integrity of federal judges, appointed by the President, as over against elected judges in the United States is well known, although both types of officials have been selected primarily in terms of party considerations. The great changes in American metropolitan administrations demanded by reformers have proceeded essentially from elected mayors working with an apparatus of officials who were appointed by them. These reforms have thus come about in a "Caesarist" fashion. Viewed technically, as an organized form of authority, the efficiency of "Caesarism," which often grows out of democracy, rests in general upon the position of the "Caesar" as a free trustee of the masses (of the army or of the citizenry), who is unfettered by tradition. The "Caesar" is thus the unrestrained master of a body of highly qualified military officers and officials whom he selects freely and personally without regard to tradition or to any other considerations. This "rule of the personal genius," however, stands in contradiction to the formally "democratic" principle of a universally elected officialdom.

3. Normally, the position of the official is held for life, at least in public bureaucracies; and this is increasingly the case for all similar structures. As a factual rule, *tenure for life* is presupposed, even where the giving of notice or periodic reappointment occurs. In contrast to the worker in a private enterprise, the official normally holds tenure. Legal or actual life-tenure, however, is not recognized as the official's right to the possession of office, as was the case with many structures of authority in the past. Where legal guarantees against arbitrary dismissal or transfer are developed, they merely serve to guarantee a strictly objective discharge of specific office duties free from all personal considerations. In Germany, this is the case for all juridical and, increasingly, for all administrative officials.

Within the bureaucracy, therefore, the measure of "independence," legally guaranteed by tenure, is not always a source of increased status for the official whose position is thus secured. Indeed, often the reverse holds, especially in old cultures and communities that are highly differentiated. In such communities, the stricter the subordination under the arbitrary rule of the master, the more it guarantees the maintenance of the conventional seigneurial style of living for the official. Because of the very absence of these legal guarantees of tenure, the conventional esteem for the official may rise in the same way as, during the Middle Ages, the esteem of the

nobility of office[3] rose at the expense of esteem for the freemen, and as the king's judge surpassed that of the people's judge. In Germany, the military officer or the administrative official can be removed from office at any time, or at least far more readily than the "independent judge," who never pays with loss of his office for even the grossest offense against the "code of honor" or against social conventions of the salon. For this very reason, if other things are equal, in the eyes of the master stratum the judge is considered less qualified for social intercourse than are officers and administrative officials, whose greater dependence on the master is a greater guarantee of their conformity with status conventions. Of course, the average official strives for a civil-service law, which would materially secure his old age and provide increased guarantees against his arbitrary removal from office. This striving, however, has its limits. A very strong development of the "right to the office" naturally makes it more difficult to staff them with regard to technical efficiency, for such a development decreases the career-opportunities of ambitious candidates for office. This makes for the fact that officials, on the whole, do not feel their dependency upon those at the top. This lack of a feeling of dependency, however, rests primarily upon the inclination to depend upon one's equals rather than upon the socially inferior and governed strata. The present conservative movement among the Badenia clergy, occasioned by the anxiety of a presumably threatening separation of church and state, has been expressly determined by the desire not to be turned "from a master into a servant of the parish."[4]

4. The official receives the regular *pecuniary* compensation of a normally fixed *salary* and the old age security provided by a pension. The salary is not measured like a wage in terms of work done, but according to "status," that is, according to the kind of function (the "rank") and, in addition, possibly, according to the length of service. The relatively great security of the official's income, as well as the rewards of social esteem, make the office a sought-after position, especially in countries which no longer provide oppor-

[3] *Ministerialen.*
[4] Written before 1914 [German editor's note].

tunities for colonial profits. In such countries, this situation permits relatively low salaries for officials.

5. The official is set for a *"career"* within the hierarchical order of the public service. He moves from the lower, less important, and lower paid to the higher positions. The average official naturally desires a mechanical fixing of the conditions of promotion: if not of the offices, at least of the salary levels. He wants these conditions fixed in terms of "seniority," or possibly according to grades achieved in a developed system of expert examinations. Here and there, such examinations actually form a character *indelebilis* of the official and have lifelong effects on his career. To this is joined the desire to qualify the right to office and the increasing tendency toward status group closure and economic security. All of this makes for a tendency to consider the offices as "prebends" of those who are qualified by educational certificates. The necessity of taking general personal and intellectual qualifications into consideration, irrespective of the often subaltern character of the educational certificate, has led to a condition in which the highest political offices, especially the positions of "ministers," are principally filled without reference to such certificates. . . .

TECHNICAL ADVANTAGES OF BUREAUCRATIC ORGANIZATION. The decisive reason for the advance of bureaucratic organization has always been its purely technical superiority over any other form of organization. The fully developed bureaucratic mechanism compares with other organizations exactly as does the machine with the non-mechanical modes of production.

Precision, speed, unambiguity, knowledge of the files, continuity, discretion, unity, strict subordination, reduction of friction and of material and personal costs—these are raised to the optimum point in the strictly bureaucratic administration, and especially in its monocratic form. As compared with all collegiate, honorific, and avocational forms of administration, trained bureaucracy is superior on all these points. And as far as complicated tasks are concerned, paid bureaucratic work is not only more precise but, in the last analysis, it is often cheaper than even formally unremunerated honorific service.

Honorific arrangements make administrative work an avocation and, for this reason alone, honorific service normally functions more slowly; being less bound to schemata and being more formless. Hence it is less precise and less unified than bureaucratic work because it is less dependent upon superiors and because the establishment and exploitation of the apparatus of subordinate officials and filing services are almost unavoidably less economical. Honorific service is less continuous than bureaucratic and frequently quite expensive. This is especially the case if one thinks not only of the money costs to the public treasury—costs which bureaucratic administration, in comparison with administration by notables, usually substantially increases —but also of the frequent economic losses of the governed caused by delays and lack of precision. The possibility of administration by notables normally and permanently exists only where official management can be satisfactorily discharged as an avocation. With the qualitative increase of tasks the administration has to face, administration by notables reaches its limits—today, even in England. Work organized by collegiate bodies causes friction and delay and requires compromises between colliding interests and views. The administration, therefore, runs less precisely and is more independent of superiors; hence, it is less unified and slower. All advances of the Prussian administrative organization have been and will in the future be advances of the bureaucratic, and especially of the monocratic, principle.

Today, it is primarily the capitalist market economy which demands that the official business of the administration be discharged precisely, unambiguously, continuously, and with as much speed as possible. Normally, the very large, modern capitalist enterprises are themselves unequalled models of strict bureaucratic organization. Business management throughout rests on increasing precision, steadiness, and, above all, the speed of operations. This, in turn, is determined by the peculiar nature of the modern means of communication, including, among other things, the news service of the press. The extraordinary increase in the speed by which public announcements, as well as economic and political facts, are transmitted exerts a steady and sharp pressure in the direction of speeding up the tempo of administrative reaction towards various situations. The optimum of such reaction time is normally attained only by a strictly bureaucratic organization.[5]

Bureaucratization offers above all the optimum possibility for carrying through the principle of specializing administrative functions according to purely objective considerations. Individual performances are allocated to functionaries who have specialized training and who by constant practice learn more and more. The "objective" discharge of business primarily means a discharge of business according to *calculable rules* and "without regard for persons."

"Without regard for persons" is also the watchword of the "market" and, in general, of all pursuits of naked economic interests. A consistent execution of bureaucratic domination means the leveling of status "honor." Hence, if the principle of the free-market is not at the same time restricted, it means the universal domination of the "class situation." That this consequence of bureaucratic domination has not set in everywhere, parallel to the extent of bureaucratization, is due to the differences among possible principles by which polities may meet their demands.

The second element mentioned, "calculable rules," also is of paramount importance for modern bureaucracy. The peculiarity of modern culture, and specifically of its technical and economic basis, demands this very "calculability" of results. When fully developed, bureaucracy also stands, in a specific sense, under the principle of *sine ira ac studio*. Its specific nature, which is welcomed by capitalism, develops the more perfectly the more the bureaucracy is "dehumanized," the more completely it succeeds in eliminating from official business love, hatred, and all purely personal, irrational, and emotional elements which escape calculation. This is the specific nature of bureaucracy and it is appraised as its special virtue.

The more complicated and specialized modern culture becomes, the more its external supporting apparatus demands the personally detached and strictly "objective" *expert*, in lieu of the master of older social structures, who was moved by personal sympathy and favor, by grace and gratitude. Bureaucracy offers the attitudes demanded by the external apparatus of modern culture in the most favorable combination. As a rule, only bureaucracy has established the foundation for the administration of a rational law conceptually systematized on the basis of such enactments as the latter Roman imperial period first created with a high degree of technical perfection. During the Middle Ages, this law was received along with the bureaucratization of legal administration, that is to say, with the displacement of the old trial procedure which was bound to tradition or to irrational presuppositions, by the rationally trained and specialized expert. . . .

THE CONCENTRATION OF THE MEANS OF ADMINISTRATION. The bureaucratic structure goes hand in hand with the concentration of the material means of management in the hands of the master. This concentration occurs, for instance, in a well-known and typical fashion, in the development of big capitalist enterprises, which find their essential characteristics in this process. A corresponding process occurs in public organizations.

The bureaucratically led army of the Pharaohs, the army during the later period of the Roman republic and the principate, and, above all, the army of the modern military state are characterized by the fact that their equipment and provisions are supplied from the magazines of the war lord. This is in contrast to the folk armies of argicultural tribes, the armed citizenry of ancient cities, the militias of early medieval cities, and all feudal armies; for these, the self-equipment and the self-provisioning of those obliged to fight was normal.

War in our time is a war of machines. And this makes magazines technically necessary, just as the dominance of the machine in industry promotes the concentration of the means of production and management. In the main, however, the bureaucratic armies of the past, equipped and provisioned by the lord, have risen when social and economic development has absolutely or relatively diminished the stratum of citizens who were economically able to equip themselves, so that their number was no longer sufficient for putting the re-

---

[5] Here we cannot discuss in detail how the bureaucratic apparatus may, and actually does, produce definite obstacles to the discharge of business in a manner suitable for the single case.

quired armies in the field. They were reduced at least relatively, that is, in relation to the range of power claimed for the polity. Only the bureaucratic army structure allowed for the development of the professional standing armies which are necessary for the constant pacification of large states of the plains, as well as for warfare against far-distant enemies, especially enemies overseas. Specifically, military discipline and technical training can be normally and fully developed, at least to its modern high level, only in the bureaucratic army.

Historically, the bureaucratization of the army has everywhere been realized along with the transfer of army service from the proper-tied to the propertyless. Until this transfer occurs, military service is an honorific privilege of propertied men. Such a transfer was made to the native-born unpropertied, for instance, in the armies of the generals of the late Roman republic and the empire, as well as in modern armies up to the nineteenth century. The burden of service has also been transferred to strangers, as in the mercenary armies of all ages. This process typically goes hand in hand with the general increase in material and intellectual culture. The following reason has also played its part everywhere: the increasing density of population, and therewith the intensity and strain of economic work, makes for an increasing "indispensability" of the acquisitive strata [6] for purposes of war. Leaving aside periods of strong ideological fervor, the propertied strata of sophisticated and especially of urban culture as a rule are little fitted and also little inclined to do the coarse war work of the common soldier. Other circumstances being equal, the propertied strata of the open country are at least usually better qualified and more strongly inclined to become professional officers. This difference between the urban and the rural propertied is balanced only where the increasing possibility of mechanized warfare requires the leaders to qualify as "technicians."

The bureaucratization of organized warfare may be carried through in the form of private capitalist enterprise, just like any other business. Indeed, the procurement of armies and their administration by private capitalists has been the rule in mercenary armies, especially

those of the Occident up to the turn of the eighteenth century. During the Thirty Years' War, in Brandenburg the soldier was still the predominant owner of the material implements of his business. He owned his weapons, horses, and dress, although the state, in the role, as it were, of the merchant of the "putting-out system," did supply him to some extent. Later on, in the standing army of Prussia, the chief of the company owned the material means of warfare, and only since the peace of Tilsit has the concentration of the means of warfare in the hands of the state definitely come about. Only with this concentration was the introduction of uniforms generally carried through. Before then, the introduction of uniforms had been left to a great extent to the arbitrary discretion of the regimental officer, with the exception of individual categories of troops to whom the king had "bestowed" certain uniforms, first, in 1620, to the royal bodyguard, then, under Frederick II, repeatedly.

Such terms as "regiment" and "battalion" usually had quite different meanings in the eighteenth century from the meanings they have today. Only the battalion was a tactical unit (today both are); the "regiment" was then a managerial unit of an economic organization established by the colonel's position as an "entrepreneur." "Official" maritime ventures (like the Genoese *maonae*) and army procurement belong to private capitalism's first giant enterprises of far-going bureaucratic character. In this respect, the "nationalization" of these enterprises by the state has its modern parallel in the nationalization of the railroads, which have been controlled by the state from their beginnings.

In the same way as with army organizations, the bureaucratization of administration goes hand in hand with the concentration of the means of organization in other spheres. The old administration by satraps and regents, as well as administration by farmers of office, purchasers of office, and, most of all, administration by feudal vassals, decentralize the material means of administration. The local demand of the province and the cost of the army and of subaltern officials are regularly paid for in advance from local income, and only the surplus reaches the central treasure. The enfeoffed official administers entirely by payment out of his own pocket. The bureaucratic

[6] *Erwerbende Schichten.*

state, however, puts its whole administrative expense on the budget and equips the lower authorities with the current means of expenditure, the use of which the state regulates and controls. This has the same meaning for the "economics" of the administration as for the large centralized capitalist enterprise.

In the field of scientific research and instruction, the bureaucratization of the always existing research institutes of the universities is a function of the increasing demand for material means of management. Liebig's laboratory at Giessen University was the first example of big enterprise in this field. Through the concentration of such means in the hands of the privileged head of the institute, the mass of researchers and docents are separated from their "means of production," in the same way as capitalist enterprise has separated the workers from theirs.

In spite of its indubitable technical superiority, bureaucracy has everywhere been a relatively late development. A number of obstacles have contributed to this, and only under certain social and political conditions have they definitely receded into the background. . . .

THE PERMANENT CHARACTER OF THE BUREAUCRATIC MACHINE. Once it is fully established, bureaucracy is among those social structures which are the hardest to destroy. Bureaucracy is *the* means of carrying "community action" over into rationally ordered "societal action." Therefore, as an instrument for "societalizing" relations of power, bureaucracy has been and is a power instrument of the first order—for the one who controls the bureaucratic apparatus.

Under otherwise equal conditions, a "societal action," which is methodically ordered and led, is superior to every resistance of "mass" or even of "communal action." And where the bureaucratization of administration has been completely carried through, a form of power relation is established that is practically unshatterable.

The individual bureaucrat cannot squirm out of the apparatus in which he is harnessed. In contrast to the honorific or avocational "notable," the professional bureaucrat is chained to his activity by his entire material and ideal existence. In the great majority of

cases, he is only a single cog in an ever-moving mechanism which prescribes to him an essentially fixed route of march. The official is entrusted with specialized tasks and normally the mechanism cannot be put into motion or arrested by him, but only from the very top. The individual bureaucrat is thus forged to the community of all the functionaries who are integrated into the mechanism. They have a common interest in seeing that the mechanism continues its functions and that the societally exercised authority carries on.

The ruled, for their part, cannot dispense with or replace the bureaucratic apparatus of authority once it exists. For this bureaucracy rests upon expert training, a functional specialization of work, and an attitude set for habitual and virtuoso-like mastery of single yet methodically integrated functions. If the official stops working, or if his work is forcefully interrupted, chaos results, and it is difficult to improvise replacements from among the governed who are fit to master such chaos. This holds for public administration as well as for private economic management. More and more the material fate of the masses depends upon the steady and correct functioning of the increasingly bureaucratic organizations of private capitalism. The idea of eliminating these organizations becomes more and more utopian.

The discipline of officialdom refers to the attitude-set of the official for precise obedience within his *habitual* activity, in public as well as in private organizations. This discipline increasingly becomes the basis of all order, however great the practical importance of administration on the basis of the filed documents may be. The naive idea of Bakuninism of destroying the basis of "acquired rights" and "domination" by destroying public documents overlooks the settled orientation of *man* for keeping to the habitual rules and regulations that continue to exist independently of the documents. Every reorganization of beaten or dissolved troops, as well as the restoration of administrative orders destroyed by revolt, panic, or other catastrophes, is realized by appealing to the trained orientation of obedient compliance to such orders. Such compliance has been conditioned into the officials, on the one hand, and, on the other hand, into the governed. If such an appeal is successful it brings, as it were, the disturbed mechanism into gear again.

The objective indispensability of the once-existing apparatus, with its peculiar, "impersonal" character, means that the mechanism —in contrast to feudal orders based upon personal piety—is easily made to work for anybody who knows how to gain control over it. A rationally ordered system of officials continues to function smoothly after the enemy has occupied the area; he merely needs to change the top officials. This body of officials continues to operate because it is to the vital interest of everyone concerned, including above all the enemy.

During the course of his long years in power, Bismarck brought his ministerial colleagues into unconditional bureaucratic dependence by eliminating all independent statesmen. Upon his retirement, he saw to his surprise that they continued to manage their offices unconcerned and undismayed, as if he had not been the master mind and creator of these creatures, but rather as if some single figure had been exchanged for some other figure in the bureaucratic machine. With all the changes of masters in France since the time of the First Empire, the power machine has remained essentially the same. Such a machine makes "revolution," in the sense of the forceful creation of entirely new formations of authority, technically more and more impossible, especially when the apparatus controls the modern means of communication (telegraph, et cetera) and also by virtue of its internal rationalized structure. In classic fashion, France has demonstrated how this process has substituted *coups d'état* for "revolutions": all successful transformations in France have amounted to *coups d'état*. . . .

THE POWER POSITION OF BUREAUCRACY. Everywhere the modern state is undergoing bureaucratization. But whether the *power* of bureaucracy within the polity is universally increasing must here remain an open question.

The fact that bureaucratic organization is technically the most highly developed means of power in the hands of the man who controls it does not determine the weight that bureaucracy as such is capable of having in a particular social structure. The ever-increasing "indispensability" of the officialdom, swollen to millions, is no more decisive for this question than is the view of some representatives of the proletarian movement that the economic indispensability of the proletarians is decisive for the measure of their social and political power position. If "indispensability" were decisive, then where slave labor prevailed and where freemen usually abhor work as a dishonor, the "indispensable" slaves ought to have held the positions of power, for they were at least as indispensable as officials and proletarians are today. Whether the power of bureaucracy as such increases cannot be decided *a priori* from such reasons. The drawing in of economic interest groups or other non-official experts, or the drawing in of non-expert lay representatives, the establishment of local, inter-local, or central parliamentary or other representative bodies, or of occupational associations—these *seem* to run directly against the bureaucratic tendency. How far this appearance is the truth must be discussed in another chapter rather than in this purely formal and typological discussion. In general, only the following can be said here:

Under normal conditions, the power position of a fully developed bureaucracy is always overtowering. The "political master" finds himself in the position of the "dilettante" who stands opposite the "expert," facing the trained official who stands within the management of administration. This holds whether the "master" whom the bureaucracy serves is a "people," equipped with the weapons of "legislative initiative," the "referendum," and the right to remove officials, or a parliament, elected on a more aristocratic or more "democratic" basis and equipped with the right to vote a lack of confidence, or with the actual authority to vote it. It holds whether the master is an aristocratic, collegiate body, legally or actually based on self-recruitment, or whether he is a popularly elected president, a hereditary and "absolute" or a "constitutional" monarch.

Every bureaucracy seeks to increase the superiority of the professionally informed by keeping their knowledge and intentions secret. Bureaucratic administration always tends to be an administration of "secret sessions": in so far as it can, it hides its knowledge and action from criticism. Prussian church authorities now threaten to use disciplinary measures against pastors who make reprimands or other admonitory measures in any way accessible to third parties. They do this because the pastor, in making such criticism available, is "guilty" of facilitating a possible criticism of the church authorities. The treasury officials of the Persian shah have made a secret doctrine of their budgetary art and even use secret script. The official statistics of Prussia, in general, make public only what cannot do any harm to the intentions of the power-wielding bureaucracy. The tendency toward secrecy in certain administrative fields follows their material nature: everywhere that the power interests of the domination structure toward *the outside* are at stake, whether it is an economic competitor of a private enterprise, or a foreign, potentially hostile polity, we find secrecy. If it is to be successful, the management of diplomacy can only be publicly controlled to a very limited extent. The military administration must insist on the concealment of its most important measures; with the increasing significance of purely technical aspects, this is all the more the case. Political parties do not proceed differently, in spite of all the ostensible publicity of Catholic con-

gresses and party conventions. With the increasing bureaucratization of party organizations, this secrecy will prevail even more. Commerical policy, in Germany for instance, brings about a concealment of production statistics. Every fighting posture of a social structure toward the outside tends to buttress the position of the group in power.

The pure interest of the bureaucracy in power, however, is efficacious far beyond those areas where purely functional interests make for secrecy. The concept of the "official secret" is the specific invention of bureaucracy, and nothing is so fanatically defended by the bureaucracy as this attitude, which cannot be substantially justified beyond these specifically qualified areas. In facing a parliament, the bureaucracy, out of a sure power instinct, fights every attempt of the parliament to gain knowledge by means of its own experts or from interest groups. The so-called right of parliamentary investigation is one of the means by which parliament seeks such knowledge. Bureaucracy naturally welcomes a poorly informed and hence a powerless parliament—at least in so far as ignorance somehow agrees with the bureaucracy's interests. . . .

Formal Organizations

CHESTER I. BARNARD

An organization comes into being when (1) there are persons able to communicate with each other (2) who are willing to contribute action (3) to accomplish a common purpose. The elements of an organization are therefore

From Chester I. Barnard, *The Functions of the Executive*. Cambridge, Mass.: Harvard University Press, copyright, 1938, by the President and Fellows of Harvard College. Pp. 82–95, 104–113. Reprinted with permission of the publisher.

(1) communication; (2) willingness to serve; and (3) common purpose. These elements are necessary and sufficient conditions initially, and they are found in all such organizations. The third element, purpose, is implicit in the definition. Willingness to serve, and communication, and the interdependence of the three elements in general, and their mutual dependence in specific coöperative systems, are matters of experience and observation.

For the continued existence of an organ-

40

ization either *effectiveness* or *efficiency* is necessary;[1] and the longer the life, the more necessary both are. The vitality of organizations lies in the willingness of individuals to contribute forces to the coöperative system. This willingness requires the belief that the purpose can be carried out, a faith that diminishes to the vanishing point as it appears that it is not in fact in process of being attained. Hence, when effectiveness ceases, willingness to contribute disappears. The continuance of willingness also depends upon the satisfactions that are secured by individual contributors in the process of carrying out the purpose. If the satisfactions do not exceed the sacrifices required, willingness disappears, and the condition is one of organization inefficiency. If the satisfactions exceed the sacrifices, willingness persists, and the condition is one of efficiency of organization.

In summary, then, the initial existence of an organization depends upon a combination of these elements appropriate to the external conditions at the moment. Its survival depends upon the maintenance of an equilibrium of the system. This equilibrium is primarily internal, a matter of proportions between the elements, but it is ultimately and basically an equilibrium between the system and the total situation external to it. This external equilibrium has two terms in it: first, the effectiveness of the organization, which comprises the relevance of its purpose to the environmental situation; and, second, its efficiency, which comprises the interchange between the organization and individuals. Thus the elements stated will each vary with external factors, and they are at the same time interdependent; when one is varied compensating variations must occur in the other if the system of which they are components is to remain in equilibrium, that is, is to persist or survive.

We may now appropriately consider these elements and their interrelations in some detail, having in mind the system as a whole. In later chapters we shall consider each element in greater detail with reference to its variability in dependence upon external factors, and the interrelations of the elements as deter-

mining the character of the executive functions.

Willingness to Coöperate. By definition there can be no organization without persons. However, as we have urged that it is not persons, but the services or acts or action or influences of persons, which should be treated as constituting organizations,[2] it is clear that *willingness* of persons to contribute efforts to the coöperative system is indispensable.

There are a number of words and phrases in common use with reference to organization that reach back to the factor of individual willingness. "Loyalty," "solidarity," "*esprit de corps*," "strength" of organization, are the chief. Although they are indefinite, they relate to intensity of attachment to the "cause," and are commonly understood to refer to something different from effectiveness, ability, or value of personal contributions. Thus "loyalty" is regarded as not necessarily related either to position, rank, fame, remuneration, or ability. It is vaguely recognized as an essential condition of organization.

Willingness, in the present connection, means self-abnegation, the surrender of control of personal conduct, the depersonalization of personal action. Its effect is cohesion of effort, a sticking together. Its immediate cause is the disposition necessary to "sticking together." Without this there can be no sustained personal effort as a contribution to coöperation. Activities cannot be coördinated unless there is first the disposition to make a personal act a contribution to an impersonal system of acts, one in which the individual gives up personal control of what he does.

The outstanding fact regarding willingness to contribute to a given specific formal organization is the indefinitely large range of variation in its intensity among individuals. If all those who may be considered potential contributors to an organization are arranged in order of willingness to serve it, the scale gradually descends from possibly intense willingness through neutral or zero willingness to intense unwillingness or opposition or hatred. The *preponderance of persons in a modern society always lies on the negative side* with reference to any particular existing or poten-

[1] See definitions in *The Functions of the Executive*, Chapters II and V, pp. 19 and 55 ff., also Chapter XVI.

[2] Page 72 [of *The Functions of the Executive*].

tial organization. Thus of the possible contributors only a small minority actually have a positive willingness. This is true of the largest and most comprehensive formal organizations, such as the large nations, the Catholic Church, etc. Most of the persons in existing society are either indifferent to or positively opposed to any single one of them; and if the smaller organizations subordinate to these major organizations are under consideration the minority becomes of course a much smaller proportion, and usually a nearly negligible proportion, of the conceivable total.

A second fact of almost equal importance is that the willingness of any individual cannot be constant in degree. It is necessarily intermittent and fluctuating. It can scarcely be said to exist during sleep, and is obviously diminished or exhausted by weariness, discomfort, etc., a conception that was well expressed by the saying "The spirit is willing, but the flesh is weak."

A corollary of the two propositions just stated is that for any given formal organization the number of persons of positive willingness to serve, but near the neutral or zero point, is always fluctuating. It follows that the aggregate willingness of potential contributors to any formal coöperative system is unstable—a fact that is evident from the history of all formal organizations.

Willingness to coöperate, positive or negative, is the expression of the net satisfactions or dissatisfactions experienced or anticipated by each individual in comparison with those experienced or anticipated through alternative opportunities. These alternative opportunities may be either personal and individualistic or those afforded by other organizations. That is, willingness to coöperate is the net effect, first, of the inducements to do so in conjunction with the sacrifices involved, and then in comparison with the practically available net satisfactions afforded by alternatives. The questions to be determined, if they were matters of logical reasoning, would be, first, whether the opportunity to coöperate grants any advantage to the individual as compared with independent action; and then, if so, whether that advantage is more or less than the advantage obtainable from some other coöperative opportunity. Thus, from the viewpoint of the individual, willingness is the joint effect of personal desires and reluctances; from the viewpoint of organization it is the joint effect of objective inducements offered and burdens imposed. The measure of this net result, however, is entirely individual, personal, and subjective. Hence, organizations depend upon the motives of individuals and the inducements that satisfy them.

Purpose. Willingness to coöperate, except as a vague feeling or desire for association with others, cannot develop without an objective of coöperation. Unless there is such an objective it cannot be known or anticipated what specific efforts will be required of individuals, nor in many cases what satisfactions to them can be in prospect. Such an objective we denominate the "purpose" of an organization. The necessity of having a purpose is axiomatic, implicit in the words "system," "coördination," "coöperation." It is something that is clearly evident in many observed systems of coöperation, although it is often not formulated in words, and sometimes cannot be so formulated. In such cases what is observed is the direction or effect of the activities, from which purpose may be inferred.

A purpose does not incite coöperative activity unless it is accepted by those whose efforts will constitute the organization. Hence there is initially something like simultaneity in the acceptance of a purpose and willingness to coöperate.

It is important at this point to make clear that every coöperative purpose has in the view of each coöperating person two aspects which we call (1) the coöperative and (2) the subjective aspect, respectively.

1. When the viewing of the purpose is an *act of coöperation*, it approximates that of detached observers from a special position of observation; this position is that of the interests of the organization; it is largely determined by organization knowledge, but is personally interpreted. For example, if five men are coöperating to move a stone from A to B, the moving of the stone is a different thing in the organization view of each of the five men involved. Note, however, that what moving the stone means to each man personally is not here in question, but what he thinks it means to the organization *as a whole*. This includes the significance of his own effort as

an element in coöperation, and that of all others, in his view; but it is not at all a matter of satisfying a personal motive.

When the purpose is a physical result of simple character, the difference between the purpose as objectively viewed by a detached observer and the purpose as viewed by each person coöperating *as an act of coöperation* is ordinarily not large or important, and the different coöperative views of the persons coöperating are correspondingly similar. Even in such cases the attentive observer will detect differences that result in disputes, errors of action, etc., even though no *personal* interest is implicated. But when the purpose is less tangible—for example, in religious coöperation —the difference between objective purpose and purpose as cooperatively viewed by each person is often seen ultimately to result in disruption.

We may say, then, that a purpose can serve as an element of a coöperative system only so long as the participants do not recognize that there are serious divergences of their understanding of that purpose as the object of coöperation. If in fact there is important difference between the aspects of the purpose as objectively and as coöperatively viewed, the divergencies become quickly evident when the purpose is concrete, tangible, physical; but when the purpose is general, intangible, and of sentimental character, the divergencies can be very wide yet not be recognized. Hence, an objective purpose that can serve as the basis for a coöperative system is one that is *believed* by the contributors (or potential contributors) to it to be the determined purpose of the organization. The inculcation of belief in the real existence of a common purpose is an essential executive function. It explains much educational and so-called morale work in political, industrial, and religious organizations that is so often otherwise inexplicable.[3]

2. Going back to the illustration of five men moving a stone, we have noted "that what moving the stone means to each man personally is not here in question, but what he thinks it means to the *organization as a whole.*" The distinction emphasized is of first importance. It suggests the fact that every participant in an organization may be regarded as having a dual personality—an organization personality and an individual personality. Strictly speaking, an organization purpose has directly no meaning for the individual. What has meaning for him is the organization's relation to him—what burdens it imposes, what benefits it confers. In referring to the aspects of purpose as coöperatively viewed, we are alluding to the *organization* personality of individuals. In many cases the two personalities are so clearly developed that they are quite apparent. In military action individual conduct may be so dominated by organization personality that it is utterly contradictory of what personal motivation would require. It has been observed of many men that their private conduct is entirely inconsistent with official conduct, although they seem completely unaware of the fact. Often it will be observed that participants in political, patriotic, or religious organizations will accept derogatory treatment of their personal conduct, including the assertion that it is inconsistent with their organization obligations, while they will become incensed at the slightest derogation of the tenets or doctrines of their organization, even though they profess not to understand them. There are innumerable other cases, however, in which almost no organization personality may be said to exist. These are cases in which personal relationship with the coöperative system is momentary or at the margin of willingness to participate.

In other words we have clearly to distinguish between organization purpose and individual motive. It is frequently assumed in reasoning about organizations that common purpose and individual motive are or should be identical. With the exception noted below, this is never the case; and under modern conditions it rarely even appears to be the case. Individual motive is necessarily an internal, personal, subjective thing; common purpose is necessarily an external, impersonal, objective thing even though the individual interpretation of it is subjective. The one exception to this general rule, an important one, is that the accomplishment of an organization purpose becomes itself a source of personal satisfaction and a motive for many individuals in many organizations. It is rare, however, if ever, and

[3] This will be expanded in Chapter XVII [of *The Functions of the Executive*].

then I think only in connection with family, patriotic, and religious organizations under special conditions, that organization purpose becomes or can become the *only* or even the major individual motive.

Finally it should be noted that, once established, organizations change their unifying purposes. They tend to perpetuate themselves; and in the effort to survive may change the reasons for existence. I shall later make clearer that in this lies an important aspect of executive functions.[4]

Communication. The possibility of accomplishing a common purpose and the existence of persons whose desires might constitute motives for contributing toward such a common purpose are the opposite poles of the system of coöperative effort. The process by which these potentialities become dynamic is that of communication. Obviously a common purpose must be commonly known, and to be known must be in some way communicated. With some exceptions, verbal communication between men is the method by which this is accomplished. Similarly, though under crude and obvious conditions not to the same extent, inducements to persons depend upon communication to them.

The method of communication centers in language, oral and written. On its crudest side, motions or actions that are of obvious meaning when observed are sufficient for communication without deliberate attempt to communicate; and signaling by various methods is an important method in much coöperative activity. On the other side, both in primitive and in highly complex civilization "observational feeling" is likewise an important aspect of communication.[5] I do not think it is generally so

recognized. It is necessary because of the limitations of language and the differences in the linguistic capacities of those who use language. A very large element in special experience and training and in continuity of individual association is the ability to understand without words, not merely the situation or conditions, but the *intention.*

The techniques of communication are an important part of any organization and are the preëminent problems of many. The absence of a suitable technique of communication would eliminate the possibility of adopting some purposes as a basis for organization. Communication technique shapes the form and the internal economy of organization. This will be evident at once if one visualizes the attempt to do many things now accomplished by small organizations if each "member" spoke a different language. Similarly, many technical functions could hardly be carried on without special codes; for example, engineering or chemical work. In an exhaustive theory of organization, communication would occupy a central place, because the structure, extensiveness, and scope of organization are almost entirely determined by communication techniques. To this aspect of communication much of the material in subsequent chapters will be devoted.[6] Moreover, much specialization in organization originates and is maintained essentially because of communication requirements.

Effectiveness of Coöperation. The continuance of an organization depends upon its ability to carry out its purpose. This clearly depends jointly upon the appropriateness of its action and upon the conditions of its environment. In other words, effectiveness is prima-

---

[4] See also Chapters II and III [of *The Functions of the Executive*].
[5] The phrase "observational feeling" is of my coining. The point is not sufficiently developed, and probably has not been adequately studied by anyone. I take it to be at least in part involved in group action not incited by any "overt" or verbal communication. The cases known to me from the primitive field are those reported by W. H. R. Rivers on pages 94–97 of his *Instinct and the Unconscious* (2nd edition Cambridge University Press, 1924), with reference to Polynesia and Melanesia. One case is summarized by F. C. Bartlett, in *Remembering* (Cambridge University Press, 1932), at p. 297. Rivers states in substance

that in some of the relatively small groups decisions are often arrived at and acted upon without having ever been formulated by anybody.

I have observed on innumerable occasions apparent unanimity of decision of equals in conferences to quit discussion without a word to that effect being spoken. Often the action is initiated apparently by someone's rising; but as this frequently occurs in such groups *without* the termination of the meeting, more than mere rising is involved. "Observational feeling," I think, avoids the notion of anything "occult."
[6] Especially in Chapter XII, latter half [of *The Functions of the Executive*].

rily a matter of technological [7] processes. This is quite obvious in ordinary cases of purpose to accomplish a physical objective, such as building a bridge. When the objective is non-physical, as is the case with religious and social organizations, it is not so obvious.

It should be noted that a paradox is involved in this matter. An organization must disintegrate if it cannot accomplish its purpose. It also destroys itself by accomplishing its purpose. A very large number of successful organizations come into being and then disappear for this reason. Hence most continuous organizations require repeated adoption of new purposes. This is concealed from everyday recognition by the practice of generalizing a complex series of specific purposes under one term, stated to be *"the* purpose" of this organization. This is strikingly true in the case of governmental and public utility organizations when the purpose is stated to be a particular kind of service through a period of years. It is apparent that their real purposes are not abstractions called "service" but specific acts of service. A manufacturing organization is said to exist to make, say, shoes; this is its "purpose." But it is evident that not making shoes in general but making specific shoes from day to day is its series of purposes. This process of generalization, however, provides in advance for the approximate definition of new purposes automatically—so automatically that the generalization is normally substituted in our minds for the concrete performances that are the real purposes. Failure to be effective is, then, a real cause of disintegration; but failure to provide for the decisions resulting in the adoption of new purposes would have the same result. Hence the generalization of purpose which can only be defined concretely by day-to-day events is a vital aspect of permanent organization.

Organization Efficiency. It has already been stated that "efficiency" as conceived in this treatise is not used in the specialized and limited sense of ordinary industrial practice or in the restricted sense applicable to technological processes. So-called "practical" efficiency has little meaning, for example, as applied to many organizations such as religious organizations.

Efficiency of effort in the fundamental sense with which we are here concerned is efficiency relative to the securing of necessary personal contributions to the coöperative system. The life of an organization depends upon its ability to secure and maintain the personal contributions of energy (including the transfer of control of materials or money equivalent) necessary to effect its purposes. This ability is a composite of perhaps many efficiencies and inefficiencies in the narrow senses of these words, and it is often the case that inefficiency in some respect can be treated as the cause of total failure, in the sense that if corrected success would then be possible. But certainly in most organization—social, political, national, religious—nothing but the absolute test of survival is significant objectively; there is no basis for comparison of the efficiencies of separate aspects. . . . The emphasis now is on the view that efficiency of organization is its capacity to offer effective inducements in sufficient quantity to maintain the equilibrium of the system. It is efficiency in this sense and not the efficiency of material productiveness which maintains the vitality of organizations. There are many organizations of great power and permanency in which the idea of productive efficiency is utterly meaningless because there is no material production. Churches, patriotic societies, scientific societies, theatrical and musical organizations, are cases where the original flow of *material* inducements is toward the organization, not from it—a flow necessary to provide resources with which to supply material inducements to the small minority who require them in such organizations.

In those cases where the primary purpose of organization is the production of material things, insufficiency with respect to the non-material inducements leads to the attempt to substitute material inducements for the non-material. Under favorable circumstances, to a limited degree, and for a limited time, this substitution may be effective. But to me, at least, it appears utterly contrary to the nature of men to be sufficiently induced by material or monetary considerations to contribute enough effort to a coöperative system to enable it to be productively efficient to the degree necessary for persistence over an extended period.

If these things are true, then even in purely economic enterprises efficiency in the offering

[7] Using "technological" in the broad sense emphasized in Chapter III [of *The Functions of the Executive*].

of non-economic inducements may be as vital as productive efficiency. Perhaps the word efficiency as applied to such non-economic inducements as I have given for illustration will seem strange and forced. This, I think, can only be because we are accustomed to use the word in a specialized sense.

The non-economic inducements are as difficult to offer as others under many circumstances. To establish conditions under which individual pride of craft and of accomplishment can be secured without destroying the material economy of standardized production in coöperative operation is a problem in real efficiency. To maintain a character of personnel that is an attractive condition of employment involves a delicate art and much insight in the selection (and rejection) of personal services offered, whether the standard of quality be high or low. To have an organization that lends prestige and secures the loyalty of desirable persons is a complex and difficult task in efficiency—in all-round efficiency, not one-sided efficiency. It is for these reasons that good organizations—commercial, governmental, military, academic, and others—will be observed to devote great attention and sometimes great expense of money to the non-economic inducements, because they are indispensable to fundamental efficiency, as well as to effectiveness in many cases.[8]

The theory of organization set forth in this chapter is derived from the study of organizations which are exceedingly complex, although it is stated in terms of ideal simple organizations. The temptation is to assume that, in the more complex organizations which we meet in our actual social life, the effect of complexity is to modify or qualify the theory. This appears not to be the case. Organization, simple or complex, is always *an impersonal system of coördinated human efforts;* always there is purpose as the coördinating and unifying principle; always there is the indispensable ability to communicate, always the necessity for personal willingness, and for effectiveness and efficiency in maintaining the integrity of purpose and the continuity of contributions. Complexity appears to modify the quality and form

of these elements and of the balance between them; but fundamentally the same principles that govern simple organizations may be conceived as governing the structure of complex organizations, which are composite systems.   . . .

The Growth of Organizations

[I]t will be noted that when the origin of organization is spontaneous, or is the result of the initiative of one man, or is the deliberate creation of a parent organization, the beginning is small. The organization comes into being when two or more persons begin to coöperate to a common end. Where there is division by schism, rebellion, this is likewise true, but is usually not so recognized because attention is given to the final breakup of a large complex organization. What takes place beforehand is the growth of a new counter organization or independent organization supported by the efforts of individuals who may in part still continue to support the older organization. So far as I have learned, this beginning is always small; that is, it results from the spontaneous acceptation of a new purpose, independent of and perhaps definitely conflicting with the older purpose, by a small group; or it is prompted by one individual who associates others with himself. Hence, all organizations of complex character grow out of small, simple organizations.[9] It is impossible for formal organizations to grow except by the process of combining unit organizataions already existing, or the creation of new units of organization to be added to those in an existing complex.

It may, therefore, be said that all large for-

---

[8] The economics of coöperative systems and their relation to organizations is presented in Chapter XVI [of *The Functions of the Executive*].

[9] Perhaps this will be clearer if the process is visualized of trying to organize a group of one hundred or five hundred men. Under the most favorable circumstances, i.e., when they are willing to be organized because there has come about some consensus of opinion as to purpose or objective, the mass must be broken up into small groups with group leaders. Only when by this process unit organizations have been created is it possible to combine these units into a complex organization that can manage itself.

In this connection, I should regard a mob not as a formal organization, simple or complex, but a special type of informal organization, until it has formal leaders.

mal organizations are constituted of numbers of small organizations.[10] It is impossible to create a large organization except by combining small organizations.[11]

The basic organization, if measured by the number of persons simultaneously contributing to it, is usually quite small—from two to fifteen or twenty persons, and probably not having an average of more than ten. Certain special types of simple organization, however, are very large, just as in biology some cells, such as birds' eggs, are very large. The largest of such organizations which I have observed are a full orchestra or orchestra and chorus; and a public speaker and his audience, which under radio technique reaches enormous size.[12]

[10] I exclude the very extreme and special case of large audiences as being of limited pertinence to a discussion of the functions of the executive.

[11] The origins of the major organizations being historically so remote, and the processes of reorganization being apparently often directed from central points or by central authority, we are much under the delusion that large mass organizations are subdivided as a secondary process, the mass having first been created. This is the order in which intellectually we approach the understanding of most large complex organizations; it is the method of analysis, of breaking down a whole into parts. Thus, if we wish to study a government organization or a large telephone system, we may often effectively begin with the constitution, the major departments, the parent company, etc. But this procedure is as if we subdivided a trunk of a tree or a piece of flesh into fibres and membranes and finally into cells, being misled into thinking that these subdivisions developed after the existence of an undifferentiated protoplasm of the same mass.

Many theoretical and practical errors arise from employing this analytical approach except for immediate limited purposes. For it is, I think, as true of organization as it is of all living things that they grow by the multiplication of cells and begin with single cells. It is true that quite often a fusion of two existing simple or complex organizations into one complex organization takes place; but fundamentally the growth is from single-cell organizations.

[12] A descriptive catalogue and classification of organizations from the standpoint of unit size would be of interest in a more exhaustive treatment. For example, clubs furnish an illustration of rather units which are partly structured by "working" units (staff, officers, committees and official meetings of members), and temporary "playing" or "social" units.

The clue to the structural requirements of large complex organizations lies in the reason for the limitations of the size of simple organizations. The limitations are inherent in the necessities of intercommunication.[13] In Chapter VII we discussed communication between persons as an essential element of coöperative systems; it is also the limiting factor in the size of simple organizations and, therefore, a dominant factor in the structure of complex organizations. We must now consider why this is true.

Under most ordinary conditions, even with simple purposes, not many men can see what each is doing or the whole situation; nor can many communicate essential information regarding or governing specific action without a central channel or leader. But a leader likewise is limited in time (and capacity) in communicating with many persons contemporaneously, especially if they are widely separated so that he must move about. In practice a limit of usually less than fifteen persons obtains, and for many types of coöperation five or six persons is the practicable limit.

These limits are widely exceeded in certain special cases, chiefly those where the action involved is that of extreme habitual practice within narrow limits, as in military drill and orchestral performance, where there are both individual and collective habituation and a precise special system of language or some other special means of communication; and those where the action is limited substantially to one person, the others being relatively passive, as in an audience. In this case the organization is practically limited (at least for the time being) to communication in one direction only.[14] Moreover, in the case of audiences and speakers, this communication is an end in itself.

Fundamentally, communication is necessary to translate purpose into terms of the concrete action required to effect it—what to do and when and where to do it. This necessitates knowledge of the conditions of the environment, and of the action under way. Under very

[13] These limitations, therefore, arise out of the joint effect of physical, biological, and social factors. See Chapter V [of *The Functions of the Executive*].

[14] Where not limited to one direction, a leader—moderator, chairman, i.e., an executive—is required.

simple and usually temporary conditions and with small numbers of persons the communication problem often appears simple, but under many conditions, even with small numbers, a special channel of communication is required. For if all talk at once there is confusion; and there is indecision particularly as to timing of actions. This creates the necessity for a leader. The size of the unit, therefore, usually is determined by the limitations of effective leadership. These limitations depend upon (1) the complexity of purpose and technological conditions; (2) the difficulty of the communication process; (3) the extent to which communication is necessary; (4) the complexity of the personal relationships involved, that is, of the social conditions.

1. It is clear that when the purpose is not simple—that is, when its requirements are complex and not obvious, or the conditions require precision of coördinated movements, or the nature of the individual action necessary is difficult to grasp by the actor (or by the leader)—much more communication is necessary than under the contrary conditions.

2. It is also evident that the difficulty of the communication process has an important bearing on the size of the organization unit. There are many things that are difficult to communicate by words—in some matters it is impossible. When the difficulty is great it is evident that the time required may limit the number between whom communication may be effectively had; for example, communication perhaps must be accomplished by demonstration.

3. It is apparent that if each actor can see what the other is doing and can see the situation as a whole, the amount of positive communication is reduced. Thus, if five men are working together on a simple task (say pulling a boat into the water) little communication is required; but if five men are coördinating efforts under conditions such that they cannot see each other and the whole situation, constant communication is often necessary. Moreover, if men know what to do from previous experience and can work on the basis of habit and acquired skill, a minimum of communication is required; or if they are accustomed to working together, a special language which they evolve cuts down the time of communication.

4. The complexity of the relationships in any group increases with great rapidity as the number of persons in the group increases. If the simplest possible relationship between two persons is that of "knowing" each other as accomplished by a mutual introduction, then the relational complexity at the very least increases as follows:

NUMBER IN GROUP	NUMBER OF RELATIONSHIPS	INCREASE IN RELATIONSHIPS WITH EACH ADDITION TO GROUP
2	1	—
3	3	2
4	6	3
5	10	4
6	15	5
7	21	6
8	28	7
9	36	8
10	45	9
15	105	—
20	190	—
50	1225	—

The relationships between persons in a group will be "active" in a great variety of subgroupings which may constantly change. If A, B, C, D, and E constitute a group of five, then subgroups may be made as follows: ten pairs, ten triplets, five groups of four, one of five. If only one person be added to the group of five, the possible subgroups become: fifteen pairs, twenty triplets, fifteen groups of four, six groups of five, and one of six.

A person has relationships not only with others individually and with groups, but groups are related to groups. As the number of possible groups increases, the complexity of group relationship increases in greater ratio.[15]

The complexity of relationships within groups is important in two aspects: technologically and socially. Technologically, the burden of coördination, that is, the communication function of a leader, will increase in the proportion that the relationships increase; and the ability of individuals and groups without leadership to coördinate is also quickly outrun with increase in the size of groups. The same

[15] A suggestive exposition of this subject in quantitative terms is given by V. A. Graicunas' "Relationship in Organization," reprinted in *Papers on the Science of Administration*, edited by Gulick and Urwick (New York: Institute of Public Administration, 1937).

is true of the social or informal organization relationships. The capacity of persons to maintain social relationships is obviously limited. If the technological group is larger than is adapted to social limitations, the social organization groupings cannot correspond to the technological requirements. Since a large part of the communication of organizations is informal, the burden on formal channels is thereby increased.[16]

These factors, and probably others also, limit the size of the fundamental organization cell. I shall call the simple basic organization form a "unit" organization. It differs from the ideal organization of Chapter VII in that it is never found isolated from other organizations and is always subordinate to some other formal organization directly or indirectly, being ultimately subordinate to and dependent upon either a church or a state or both.

The size of a unit organization being usually restricted very narrowly by the necessities of communication, it follows that growth of organization beyond the limits so imposed can only be accomplished by the creation of new unit organizations, or by grouping together two or more unit organizations already existing. When an organization grows by the addition of the services of more persons it is compelled, if it reaches the limit of size, to establish a second unit; and henceforward it is a complex of two unit organizations. All organizations except unit organizations are a group of two or more unit organizations. Hence, a large organization of complex character consists not of the services of individuals directly but of those of subsidiary unit organizations. Nowhere in the world, I think, can there be found a large organization that is not composed of small units. We think of them as having descended from the mass, whereas the mass can only be created from the units.[17]

[16] See also discussion on p. 225 [of *The Functions of the Executive*]. I have strongly the opinion that there may be substantial variations in social satisfactions related to disparities between the size of organizations as determined technologically by organization purpose and the size of "natural" social groups. "Natural" would be affected by the personalities involved.
[17] A group of two or more unit organizations may coöperate as a whole without a formal superior organization or leader. Under many conditions

Usually when two and always when several unit organizations are combined in one complex organization, the necessities of communication impose a super-leader, who becomes, usually with assistants, an "overhead" unit of organization. Similarly, groups of groups are combined into larger wholes. The most obvious case of complex structure of this type is an army. The fact that these large organizations are built up of small unit organizations is neglected in the spectacular size that ensues, and we often pass from the whole or major divisions to "men." The resulting dismissal from the mind of the inescapable practice of unit organization often leads to utterly unrealistic attitudes regarding organization problems.

The Executive Organization

In a unit organization there are executive functions to be performed, but not necessarily by a single individual continuously. They may be performed alternately by the several persons who contributed to the organization. In complex organizations, on the other hand, the necessities of communication result almost invariably in the localization of the executive functions of the subordinate unit organizations normally in one person. This is necessary for reasons of formal communication; but it is also necessary to establish executive organizations, that is, those units specializing in the executive functions. The execu-

this is observed, especially where two small organizations (or a large and a small) work together under contract for specified purposes. The method of communication is primarily that of conference. Because of our habit of considering an organization as a group of persons rather than as systems of coöperative services of persons, the usually temporary combinations that are made as a result of contracts or agreements are not recognized as organizations, since they have no name or common officials. Most large building operations are so organized, however; and it will be readily seen that a very large part of the organized activities of today are carried on by temporary limited combinations under contracts without a general coordinating "authority." The state, through the law of contracts and the provisions of courts, is a general formal executive in these cases in limited degree; but the real general executive is custom, etc.

tives of several unit organizations as a group, usually with at least one other person as a superior, form an executive organization. Accordingly, persons specializing in the executive functions in most cases are "members" of, or contributors to, two units of organization in one complex organization—first, the so-called "working" unit, and second, the executive unit. This is clearly seen in practice, it being customary to recognize a foreman, or a superintendent of a shop section, or a captain, at one time or from one point of view as a "member" of his gang, shop crew, or company, at another time or from another point of view as a member of a "district management group," or the "shop executives' group," or the "regimental organization." Under such conditions a single concrete action or decision is an activity of two different unit organizations. This simultaneous contribution to two organizations by a single act appears to be the critical fact in all complex organization; that is, the complex is made an organic whole by it. Here again, it will be noted that the definition of formal organization as an impersonal system of efforts and influences is supported by the facts more closely in accord with concrete phenomena than the "group membership" idea. One person often functions in or contributes services to several different units of the same complex organization, as well as to different external organizations. For payroll, and many other formal purposes, it is convenient to regard every person as being "in" only one unit organization; but this is merely a matter of convenience for certain purposes, and is misleading as to the actual operation of organizations even for many other practical purposes.

The size of executive units of organizations is limited generally by the same conditions that govern the size of unit organizations of other kinds. When there are many basic working units, therefore, there must be several primary executive unit organizations, from the heads of which will be secured the personnel of superior executive units. And so on, in extensive pyramids of executive units in very large complex organizations.[18]

In summary, we may say that historically and functionally all complex organizations are built up from units of organization, and consist of many units of "working" or "basic" organizations, overlaid with units of executive organizations; and that the essential structural characteristics of complex organizations are determined by the effect of the necessity for communication upon the size of a unit organization.

[18] Professor Philip Cabot, in a published address, once quoted my opinion that organizations are best regarded as circular or spherical, with the chief executive positions in the center. This was based on discussions with him and an unpublished manuscript which he was kind enough to examine. I have, however, followed the conventional figures here, because they are well established, and because there appears to be no practicable way to diagram the system of authoritative communication that does not result in a "pyramid" (usually in two-dimensional perspectives, however) which put the chief executive positions at the top They also are frequently located on top floors. Probably all spatial figures for organization are seriously misleading; but if they are used to cover the functioning of organizations as distinguished from its structural aspects, either the center of a circle or of a sphere better suggests the relationships. The nearest approach to this, I think, is the practice of regarding the location of G.H.Q. in field armies as *behind* the lines centrally.

On Organizational Goals

FRITZ J. ROETHLISBERGER AND
WILLIAM J. DICKSON

The Two Major Functions of an Industrial Organization

An industrial organization may be regarded as performing two major functions, that of producing a product and that of creating and distributing satisfactions among the individual members of the organization. The first function is ordinarily called economic. From this point of view the functioning of the concern is assessed in such terms as cost, profit, and technical efficiency. The second function, while it is readily understood, is not ordinarily designated by any generally accepted word. It is variously described as maintaining employee relations, employee good will, co-operation, etc. From this standpoint the functioning of the concern is frequently assessed in such terms as labor turnover, tenure of employment, sickness and accident rate, wages, employee attitudes, etc. The industrial concern is continually confronted, therefore, with two sets of major problems: (1) problems of external balance, and (2) problems of internal equilibrium. The problems of external balance are generally assumed to be economic; that is, problems of competition, adjusting the organization to meet changing price levels, etc. The problems of internal equilibrium are chiefly concerned with the maintenance of a kind of social organization in which individuals and groups through working together can satisfy their own desires.

Ordinarily an industrial concern is thought of primarily in terms of its success in meeting problems of external balance, or if the problems of internal equilibrium are explicitly recognized they are frequently assumed to be

From Fritz J. Roethlisberger and William J. Dickson, *Management and the Worker*, Harvard University Press, Cambridge, Mass., 1939, pp. 552–562. Reprinted with permission of the publisher.

separate from and unrelated to the economic purpose of the enterprise. Producing an article at a profit and maintaining good employee relations are frequently regarded as antithetical propositions. The results of the studies which have been reported indicated, however, that these two sets of problems are interrelated and interdependent. The kind of social organization which obtains within a concern is intimately related to the effectiveness of the total organization. Likewise, the success with which the concern maintains external balance is directly related to its internal organization.

A great deal of attention has been given to the economic function of industrial organization. Scientific controls have been introduced to further the economic purposes of the concern and of the individuals within it. Much of this advance has gone on in the name of efficiency or rationalization. Nothing comparable to this advance has gone on in the development of skills and techniques for securing co-operation, that is, for getting individuals and groups of individuals working together effectively and with satisfaction to themselves. The slight advances which have been made in this area have been overshadowed by the new and powerful technological developments of modern industry.

The Technical Organization of the Plant

In looking at an industrial organization as a social system it will first be necessary to examine the physical environment, for this is an inseparable part of any organization. The physical environment includes not only climate and weather, but also that part of the environment which is owned and used by the organization itself, namely, the physical plant, tools, machines, raw products, and so on. This latter part of the factory's physical environment is ordered and organized in a certain

51

specified way to accomplish the task of technical production. For our purposes, therefore, it will be convenient to distinguish from the human organization this aspect of the physical environment of an industrial plant and to label it the "technical organization of the plant." This term will refer only to the logical and technical organization of material, tools, machines, and finished product, including all those physical items related to the task of technical production.

The two aspects into which an industrial plant can be roughly divided—the technical organization and the human organization—are interrelated and interdependent. The human organization is constantly molding and re-creating the technical organization either to achieve more effectively the common economic purpose or to secure more satisfaction for its members. Likewise, changes in the technical organization require an adaptation on the part of the human organization.

The Human Organization of the Plant

In the human organization we find a number of individuals working together toward a common end: the collective purpose of the total organization. Each of these individuals, however, is bringing to the work situation a different background of personal and social experiences. No two individuals are making exactly the same demands of their job. The demands a particular employee makes depend not only upon his physical needs but upon his social needs as well. These social needs and the sentiments associated with them vary with his early personal history and social conditioning as well as with the needs and sentiments of people closely associated with him both inside and outside of work.

The Individual

It may be well to look more closely at the sentiments the individual is bringing to his work situation. Starting with a certain native organic endowment the child is precipitated into group life by the act of birth. The group into which the child is born is not the group in general. The child is born into a specific family. Moreover, this specific family is not a family in isolation. It is related in certain ways to other families in the community. It has a certain cultural background—a way of life, codes and routines of behavior, associated with certain beliefs and expectations. In the beginning the child brings only his organic needs to this social milieu into which he is born. Very rapidly he begins to accumulate experience. This process of accumulating experience is the process of assigning meanings to the socio-reality about him; it is the process of becoming socialized. Much of the early learning period is devoted to preparing the child to become capable of social life in its particular group. In preparing the child for social participation the immediate family group plays an important role. By the particular type of family into which the child is born he is "conditioned" to certain routines of behavior and ways of living. The early meanings he assigns to his experience are largely in terms of these codes of behavior and associated beliefs. As the child grows up and participates in groups other than the immediate family his leanings lose, although never quite entirely, their specific family form. This process of social interaction and social conditioning is never-ending and continues from birth to death. The adult's evaluation of his surroundings is determined in a good part by the system of human interrelations in which he has participated.

The Social Organization of the Plant

However, the human organization of an industrial plant is more than a plurality of individuals, each motivated by sentiments arising from his own personal and private history and background. It is also a social organization, for the members of an industrial plant—executives, technical specialists, supervisors, factory workers, and office workers—are interacting daily with one another and from their associations certain patterns of relations are formed among them. These patterns of relations, together with the objects which symbolize them, constitute the social organization of the industrial enterprise. Most of the individuals who live among these patterns come to accept them as obvious and necessary truths and to react as they dictate. Both the kind of behavior that is expected of a person and the kind of behavior he can expect from others are prescribed by these patterns.

If one looks at a factory situation, for example, one finds individuals and groups of individuals who are associated at work acting in certain accepted and prescribed ways toward one another. There is not complete homogeneity of behavior between individuals or between one group of individuals and another, but rather there are differences of behavior expressing differences in social relationship. Some relationships fall into routine patterns, such as the relationship between superior and subordinate or between office worker and shop worker. Individuals conscious of their membership in certain groups are reacting in certain accepted ways to other individuals representing other groups. Behavior varies according to the stereotyped conceptions of relationship. The worker, for example, behaves toward his foreman in one way, toward his first-line supervisor in another way, and toward his fellow worker in still another. People holding the rank of inspector expect a certain kind of behavior from the operators—the operators from the inspectors. Now these relationships, as is well known from everyday experiences, are finely shaded and sometimes become complicated. When a person is in the presence of his supervisor alone he usually acts differently from the way he acts when his supervisor's supervisor is also present. Likewise, his supervisor acts toward him alone quite differently from the way he behaves when his own supervisor is also there. The subtle nuances of relationship are so much a part of everyday life that they are commonplace. They are taken for granted. The vast amount of social conditioning that has taken place by means of which a person maneuvers himself gracefully through the intricacies of these finely shaded social distinctions is seldom explicitly realized. Attention is paid only when a new social situation arises where the past social training of the person prevents him from making the necessary delicate interpretations of a given social signal and hence brings forth the "socially wrong" response.

In the factory, as in any social milieu, a process of social evaluation is constantly at work. From this process distinctions of "good" and "bad," "inferior" and "superior," arise. This process of evaluation is carried on with simple and ready generalizations by means of which values become attached to individuals and to groups performing certain tasks and operations. It assigns to a group of individuals performing such and such a task a particular rank in the established prestige scale. Each work group becomes a carrier of social values. In industry with its extreme diversity of occupations there are a number of such groupings. Any noticeable similarity or difference, not only in occupation but also in age, sex, and nationality, can serve as a basis of social classification, as, for example, "married women," the "old-timer," the "white-collared" or clerical worker, the "foreign element." Each of these groups, too, has its own value system.

All the patterns of interaction that arise between individuals or between different groups can be graded according to the degree of intimacy involved in the relationship. Grades of intimacy or understanding can be arranged on a scale and expressed in terms of "social distance." Social distance measures differences of sentiment and interest which separate individuals or groups from one another. Between the president of a company and the elevator operator there is considerable social distance, more for example than between the foreman and the benchworker. Social distance is to social organization what physical distance is to physical space. However, physical and social distance do not necessarily coincide. Two people may be physically near but socially distant.

Just as each employee has a particular physical location, so he has a particular social place in the total social organization. But this place is not so rigidly fixed as in a caste system. In any factory there is considerable mobility or movement. Movement can occur in two ways: the individual may pass from one occupation to another occupation higher up in the prestige scale; or the prestige scale itself may change.

It is obvious that these scales of value are never completely accepted by all the groups in the social environment. The shop worker does not quite see why the office worker, for example, should have shorter hours of work than he has. Or the newcomer, whose efficiency on a particular job is about the same, but whose hourly rate is less than that of some old-timer, wonders why service should count so much. The management group, in turn, from the security of its social elevation, does not often understand what "all the fuss is about."

As was indicated by many of the studies, any person who has achieved a certain rank in the prestige scale regards anything real or imaginary which tends to alter his status adversely as something unfair or unjust. It is apparent that any move on the part of the management may alter the existing social equilibrium to which the employee has grown accustomed and by means of which his status is defined. Immediately this disruption will be expressed in sentiments of resistance to the real or imagined alterations in the social equilibrium.

From this point of view it can be seen how every item and event in the industrial environment becomes an object of a system of sentiments. According to this way of looking at things, material goods, physical events, wages, hours of work, etc., cannot be treated as things in themselves. Instead they have to be interpreted as carriers of social value. The meanings which any person in an industrial organization assigns to the events and objects in his environment are often determined by the social situation in which the events and objects occur. The significance to an employee of a double-pedestal desk, of a particular kind of pencil, or of a handset telephone is determined by the social setting in which these objects appear. If people with double-pedestal desks supervise people with single-pedestal desks, then double-pedestal desks become symbols of status or prestige in the organization. As patterns of behavior become crystallized, every object in the environment tends to take on a particular social significance. It becomes easy to tell a person's social place in the organization by the objects which he wears and carries and which surround him. In these terms it can be seen how the introduction of a technical change may also involve for an individual or a group of individuals the loss of certain prestige symbols and, as a result, have a demoralizing effect.

From this point of view the behavior of no one person in an industrial organization, from the very top to the very bottom, can be regarded as motivated by strictly economic or logical considerations. Routine patterns of interaction involve strong sentiments. Each group in the organization manifests its own powerful sentiments. It is likely that sometimes the behavior of many staff specialists which goes under the name of "efficiency" is as much a manifestation of a very strong sentiment— the sentiment or desire to originate new combinations—as it is of anything strictly logical.

This point of view is far from the one which is frequently expressed, namely, that man is essentially an economic being carrying around with him a few noneconomic appendages. Rather, the point of view which has been expressed here is that noneconomic motives, interests, and processes, as well as economic, are fundamental in behavior in business, from the board of directors to the very last man in the organization. Man is not merely—in fact is very seldom—motivated by factors pertaining strictly to facts or logic. Sentiments are not merely things which man carries around with him as appendages. He cannot cast them off like a suit of clothes. He carries them with him wherever he goes. In business or elsewhere, he can hardly behave without expressing them. Moreover, sentiments do not exist in a social vacuum. They are the product of social behavior, of social interaction, of the fact that man lives his life as a member of different groups. Not only does man bring sentiments to the business situation because of his past experiences and conditioning outside of business, but also as a member of a specific local business organization with a particular social place in it he has certain sentiments expressing his particular relations to it.

According to this point of view, every social act in adulthood is an integrated response to both inner and outer stimuli. To each new concrete situation the adult brings his past "social conditioning." To the extent that this past social conditioning has prepared him to assimilate the new experience in the culturally accepted manner, he is said to be "adjusted." To the extent that his private or personal view of the situation is at variance with the cultural situation, the person is called "maladjusted."

The Formal Organization of the Plant

The social organization of the industrial plant is in part formally organized. It is composed of a number of strata or levels which differentiate the benchworker from the skilled mechanic, the group chief from the department chief, and so on. These levels are well defined and all the formal orders, instructions, and compensations are addressed to them. All such factors taken together make up the formal organization of the plant. It includes the systems, policies, rules, and regulations of the plant which express what the relations of one person to another are supposed to be in order to achieve effectively the task of technical production. It prescribes the relations that are supposed to obtain within the human organization and between the human organization and the technical organization. In short, the patterns of human interrelation as defined by the systems, rules, policies, and regulations of the company, constitute the formal organization.

The formal organization of an industrial plant has two purposes: it addresses itself to the economic purposes of the total enterprise; it concerns itself also with the securing of cooperative effort. The formal organization includes all the explicitly stated systems of control introduced by the company in order to achieve the economic purposes of the total enterprise and the effective contribution of the members of the organization to those economic ends.

The Informal Organization
of the Plant

All the experimental studies pointed to the fact that there is something more to the social organization than what has been formally recognized. Many of the actually existing patterns of human interaction have no representation in the formal organization at all, and others are inadequately represented by the formal organization. This fact is frequently forgotten when talking or thinking about industrial situations in general. Too often it is assumed that the organization of a company corresponds to a blueprint plan or organization chart. Actually, it never does. In the formal organization of most companies little explicit recognition is given to many social distinctions residing in the social organization. The blueprint plans of a company show the functional relations between working units, but they do not express the distinctions of social distance, movement, or equilibrium previously described. The hierarchy of prestige values which tends to make the work of men more important than the work of women, the work of clerks more important than the work at the bench, has little representation in the formal organization; nor does a blueprint plan ordinarily show the primary groups, that is, those groups enjoying daily face-to-face relations. Logical lines of horizontal and vertical co-ordination of functions replace the actually existing patterns of interaction between people in different social places. The formal organization cannot take account of the sentiments and values residing in the social organization by means of which individuals or groups of individuals are informally differentiated, ordered, and integrated. Individuals in their associations with one another in a factory build up personal relationships. They form into informal groups, in terms of which each person achieves a certain position or status. The nature of these informal groups is very important, as has been shown in the Relay Assembly Test Room and in the Bank Wiring Observation Room.

It is well to recognize that informal organizations are not "bad," as they are sometimes assumed to be. Informal social organization exists in every plant, and can be said to be a necessary prerequisite for effective collaboration. Much collaboration exists at an informal level, and it sometimes facilitates the functioning of the formal organization. On the other hand, sometimes the informal organization develops in opposition to the formal organization. The important consideration is, therefore, the relation that exists between formal and informal organizations.

To illustrate, let us consider the Relay Assembly Test Room and the Bank Wiring Observation Room. These two studies offered an interesting contrast between two informal working groups; one situation could be characterized in almost completely opposite terms from the other. In the Relay Assembly Test Room, on the one hand, the five operators changed continuously in their rate of output up and down over the duration of the test, and yet in a curious fashion their variations in output were insensitive to many significant changes introduced during the experiment. On the other hand, in the Bank Wiring Observation Room output was being held relatively constant and there existed a hypersensitivity to change on the part of the worker—in fact, what could almost be described as an organized opposition to it.

It is interesting to note that management could draw from these studies two opposite conclusions. From the Relay Assembly Test Room experiment they could argue that the company can do almost anything it wants in the nature of technical changes without any perceptible effect on the output of the workers. From the Bank Wiring Observation Room they could argue equally convincingly that the company can introduce hardly any changes without meeting a pronounced opposition to them from the workers. To make this dilemma even more striking, it is only necessary to recall that the sensitivity to change in the one case occurred in the room where no experimental changes had been introduced whereas the insensitivity to change in the other case occurred in the room where the operators had been submitted to considerable experimentation. To settle this question by saying that in one case the situation was typical and in the other case atypical of ordinary shop conditions would be to beg the question, for the essential difference between the two situations would again be missed. It would ignore the social setting in which the changes occurred and the meaning which the workers themselves assigned to the changes.

Although in both cases there were certain informal arrangements not identical with the formal setup, the informal organization in one room was quite different from that in the other room, especially in its relation to the formal organization. In the case of the Relay Assembly Test Room there was a group, or informal organization, which could be characterized as a network of personal relations which had been developed in and through a particular way of working together; it was an organization which not only satisfied the wishes of its members but also worked in harmony with the aims of management. In the case of the Bank Wiring Observation Room there was an informal organization which could be characterized better as a set of practices and beliefs which its members had in common—practices and beliefs which at many points worked against the economic purposes of the company. In one case the relation between the formal and informal organization was one of compatibility; in the other case it was one of opposition. Or to put it another way, collaboration in the Relay Assembly Test Room was at a much higher level than in the Bank Wiring Observation Room.

The difference between these two groups can be understood only by comparing the functions which their informal organizations performed for their members. The chief function of the informal group in the Bank Wiring Observation Room was to resist changes in their established routines of work or personal interrelations. This resistance to change, however, was not the chief function of the informal group in the Relay Assembly Test Room. It is true that at first the introduction of the planned changes in the test room, whether or not these changes were logically in the direction of improvement, was met with apprehension and feelings of uneasiness on the part of the operators. The girls in the beginning were never quite sure that they might not be victims of the changes.

In setting up the Relay Assembly Test Room with the object of studying the factors determining the efficiency of the worker, many of the methods and rules by means of which management tends to promote and maintain efficiency—the "bogey," not talking too much at work, etc.—were, in effect, abrogated. With the removal of this source of constraint and in a setting of heightened social significance (because many of the changes had differentiated the test room girls from the regular department and as a result had elevated the social status within the plant of each of the five girls) a new type of spontaneous social organization developed. Social conditions had been established which allowed the operators to develop their own values and objectives. The experimental conditions allowed the operators to develop openly social codes at work and these codes, unhampered by interference, gave a sustained meaning to their work. It was as if the experimenters had acted as a buffer for the operators and held their work situation steady while they developed a new type of social organization. With this change in the type of social organization there also developed a new attitude toward changes in their working environment. Toward many changes which constitute an unspecified threat in the regular work situation the operators became immune. What the Relay Assembly Test Room experiment showed was that when innovations are introduced carefully and with regard to the actual sentiments of the workers, the workers are likely to develop a spontaneous type of informal organization which will not only express more adequately their own values and significances but also is more likely to be in harmony with the aims of management.

Although all the studies of informal organization at the Hawthorne Plant were made at the employee level, it would be incorrect to assume that this phenomenon occurs only at that level. Informal organization appears at all levels, from the very bottom to the very top of the organization.[1] Informal organization at the executive level, just as at the work level, may either facilitate or impede purposive co-operation and communication. In either case, at all levels of the organization informal organizations exist as a necessary condition for collaboration. Without them formal organization could not survive for long. Formal and informal organizations are interdependent aspects of social interaction.

[1] Barnard, C. I., *The Functions of the Executive*, Harvard University Press, 1938, pp. 223–4.

A Structure-Function Approach to Organization [1]

ROBERT S. WEISS

As our graduate seminars teach us, there are many points of view from which human behavior may be studied: as motivations or as the outcome of social forces; as an expression of neuromuscular set or of the history of a society; genetically or contemporaneously. The problems of organization are similarly susceptible to more than one approach. Two orientations are discernible in our work to date: an emphasis on organization as a setting within which human beings spend a part of their life, and alternatively, an emphasis on organization as a social form. In the one case the individual is figure and the organization ground. In the other it is the other way around.

Which of these emphases is the more appropriate in a given situation depends on the problem to be dealt with. The effect of the organization on the well-being of its members is best studied by concentrating on the members. The functioning of the organization is best understood by concentrating on the organization itself.

The social scientist who is interested in human beings in organizations, rather than in the organization itself, tends to conceptualize problems in terms of the motivations of the individuals who become members of the organization; the rewards, punishments, or other influences the organization brings to bear on them; and the consequent satisfaction or dissatisfaction of the members. He tends to see the history of the organization, the techniques it uses

From *Journal of Social Issues*, **12** (**2**), 61–67. Reprinted by permission of *The Journal of Social Issues*.
[1] Much of this material will appear in Robert S. Weiss, *Processes of Organization*, to be published by the Survey Research Center. The theory is based on the points of view expressed by Theodore Newcomb, Talcott Parsons, Amos Hawley, and Marion Levy. The sections having to do specifically with organization draw on the work of Max Weber, Chester Barnard, Herbert Simon, E. Wight Bakke, and Philip Selznick.

to maintain itself as a functioning unit, its power blocs, cliques, and divisions, its lines of authority, its structure and function, all as background material. He may be interested in these things and quite sensitive to them, but they are useful in his analysis only as they bear on what happens to the member of the organization.

Where the individual emphasis involves the organization only as it bears on its members, the organizational approach deals with individuals only as they contribute to the organization. The organization is conceptualized from the very beginning completely apart from its members. One way in which this can be done is by thinking of the organization as a structure of offices and relations between offices, like the models chemists make of molecular structures, with different colored balls to represent atoms, and rods which connect the balls to represent chemical bonds. The atoms are offices; jobs to be filled, with titles, authorities, and responsibilities. The bonds are working relationships among offices. It is true that individuals must fill the offices before the organization can function, but their motivations and goals are secondary questions. The more primary questions have to do with the operation of the organization; how tasks are assigned to offices; what the range is within which individuals are adaptable to demands made on them by the organization; how coordination comes about among the staff of the organization.

Unfortunately the molecular figure emphasizes the structure of the organization at the expense of its functions. A fuller statement would be that the organization is a social form which has the following characteristics:

(a) a set of individuals in *offices*,

(b) individual responsibility for definite tasks—*functional activities*—which are parts of a division of labor,

(c) an *organizational goal* to which the activities of the staff contribute, and

58

(d) a stable system of coordinative relationships, i.e., a *structure*.

An *office* is a position in the organizational structure in regard to which role prescriptions exist: i.e., there are shared expectations among the members of the organization regarding the duties to be performed by the individual who occupied the office. In addition the office has associated with it a title, a salary scale, formal specifications of duties, and a place on an organizational chart. These latter elements are formal representations of expectations regarding the duties, privileges, and proper coordinative relationships of the individual who fills the office.

Individuals in organizations habitually function as occupants of offices, as is apparent at those exceptional times when they do not; at office parties, for example. Then the staff members are faced with the serious problem of finding new ways to relate to one another.

The organization allocates to offices tasks which then become the responsibilities of whoever fills the office. These tasks contribute to the organization's efforts to reach a goal. In this sense, they are *functional activities*.

The method of allocation of functional activities adopted by the organization contrasts severely with the method of more informal groups. In the group anyone who recognizes something which has to be done, and is capable of doing it, is likely to set about it. In the family an executive will answer the phone, the door, and the mail, and will type his own letters. The same executive doing the same things in his office would be drawing attention to something unusual in his situation, perhaps that his secretary was overworked or incompetent. The jobs still require doing, but they're someone else's responsibility. In the organization, one has a definite job, and one does it, and that is that.

The *organizational goal* is the basis for the existence of the jobs, and of the organization. Individuals, by doing their jobs, help the organization reach its goal. The organizational goal may not be a personal goal of all, or even of any, of its members. All the organization asks is that its members be committed to doing a good job. It assumes that if they do their job well, they will thereby contribute to the goals of the organization adequately enough. The leaders of the organization may be required to show deeper commitment, since their roles require an ability to identify actively with the collectivity they are heading. Yet they do not *set* the organization's goals any more than do other members. Leaders may come and leaders may go, and the organization will maintain its direction.

We will find no organizations without goals, but it is of interest to speculate on what such a social form might be like. Franz Kafka's inventions probably capture the essential elements: an organization which strives for nothing, where there is no reason for one activity to be preferred to another, except perhaps tradition. The total effect is of unbearable pointlessness.

The goal of the organization is embedded in the organization's very definition. The organization is defined from its beginning as a collectivity for the achievement of something. From then on, as individuals become members of the organization, they "understand" the organization, identify with it, as a collectivity with definite aims. The aims may not be their personal aims, but they can pitch in and help with them nevertheless. And, by reference to them, they can estimate what actions will serve the collectivity, and what actions will impede its progress.

The high ranking executives of an organization do have a special role in relation to the organization's goals. They are responsible for the development of a *program*, a plan of action for the organization, by which the goal may be achieved. This program should not be thought of as setting the goal, in any way. Instead it interprets it—operationalizes it—and sets the means.

Turning now to the *organizational structure*, it should be noted that the co-workers of an individual tend to remain the same over time and, if the individual leaves the organization, his replacement will pick up most of the relationships he maintained. The overall system of coordinative relationships changes only slowly in the ordinary course of events, and it is in part this stability which is emphasized by the phrase "organizational structure." It should also be noted that the structure of the organization reflects the organization's division of labor; the distribution of the total task among the staff. It is possible to think of the structure as the characteristic of the organization which reflects its method of operation in the same way that anatomy reflects physiology. The routes of coordination, and thus the way in which the segmented functional activities are integrated with each other, are embodied in the organizational structure.

The organization, as a social form which achieves its goals through the coordinated effort of individuals in offices, faces three basic problems:

(1) the problem of the *allocation* of responsibility for particular functional activities to particular members of the organization;

(2) the problem of acceptance of responsibility by the member of the organization (referred to as the problem of *adaptation*);

(3) the problem of the *coordination* of the functional activities of the members of the organization.

If the assumption is made that these problems are continuous in their demands, and that any breakdown in the way they are met would be disastrous to the organization, then their solutions must also be continuously in evidence. To convey this the solutions to these problems may be thought of as continuous *processes*, each necessary to the maintenance of the organization.

To quite an extent the processes are built into the organization, although they require a properly trained staff member to make them work. One process of coordination, for example, may be based on the allocation to an important executive of the responsibility for allocating tasks to others and checking on their completed work. He will be expected to do his own job in such a way that his subordinates' efforts are coordinated. But even here coordination is dependent on the executive being someone who knows how to supervise, and the lower level personnel being individuals who know how to work under supervision.

The question regarding individuals which is relevant to an organizational approach is not so much "How is the individual affected by the organization?" as it is "What does the organization require of the individual?" What seems to be the case is that the organization requires, once it has conveyed to the member what his job is, that he *accept* the assignment fully enough to perform it adequately. Different levels of acceptance are required of the individual, depending on the job. The elevator operator, the switchboard girl, and the filing clerk perform adequately so long as they know the formal requirements of their role and contrive to meet them. The executive who must choose from many courses of action the course which is best for the organization, represent and interpret the organization to subordinates and others, and serve as a flexible yet reliable link among separate units, must identify with his job much more fully.

While individual acceptance of the job is a process crucial for the organization, it is one over which it has only partial control. The organization may try to make its jobs as desirable as possible, and may hire individuals who have done well elsewhere, but beyond this it can only rely on the individual to be motivated to do his job. It cannot itself supply the motivation. On the other hand, the organization can count on the individual's basic desire to do a good job, and willingness to identify with the organization as a collectivity.

These two psychological tendencies in the organization member—desire to do a good job, and willingness to identify with the organization—allow the organization a certain amount of leeway in its construction of jobs, and allow it to de-emphasize authority relations and sanctions for poor performance. The source of these tendencies may, perhaps, be traced to a socialization theme in America. The baseball team of nine-year-olds may settle the assignment of positions on the basis of ownership of ball, bat, and gloves, assuming that the owner of the equipment is entitled to determine its use. But a group only a few years older will have the best pitcher pitching, and the boy who is best at getting on base as the first batter. The socialization theme is partly learning to take a role, but more than that, it is learning to contribute to a collectivity through taking a role.

From this cultural emphasis would develop good organization members: individuals who can understand the necessity for accepting a role as a way of contributing to a collectivity. Some positions would require the good organization member more than others. The lower level executive, and particularly the nonspecialist, who cannot make of his job what he wants, and cannot expect a job tailored to a person with his training, might do best if he were a good organization member. The organization, so long as it can hire this kind of person, designs its jobs accordingly.

Yet the range of activities to which an individual may be expected to adapt is not unlimited. The organization will first be required to combine responsibilities in a way acceptable to most potential staff members. In addition it must associate with these responsibilities rewards sufficient to keep the staff member preoccupied with mastering the activities allocated to him, even when other jobs in other organizations become available.

The organization which has constructed jobs that are difficult to staff is in a serious way once it begins to lose the staff it has. A vicious circle may develop of problem, inadequate solution, further problem. Since the organization is understaffed, the remaining members are forced to take on activities which would not ordinarily be parts of their job. If the activities are beneath them, they threaten their sense of occupational status. If the activities are of high status, the employees resent the allocation of tasks for which they are not qualified and not paid. If the organization seeks a solution by curtailing its goals, so that it no longer requires some functional activities, the goal which is dropped is likely to be its most idealistic, just because it is this goal which is least related to the problem of organizational survival. Some staff members are likely to have identified strongly with it, the more so since the organization began to have trouble, and its loss will result in *their* demoralization. So, while the organization may count on a range of adaptability among its members, it is imperative that it not construct its jobs so that they overstep this range. The good organization member takes up some of the slack; the organization must take up the rest.

This particular relationship between individual and organization is a reflection of the larger American scene. A different culture would require a different kind of organization, or, possibly, might support none at all. For example, the German emphasis on role-taking as an element in superior-subordinate relationships, in contrast to the American emphasis on role-taking as a way of pitching in, is reflected in organizations where there is much more emphasis on lines of authority, and much less emphasis on informal communication. One would guess the result to be a more efficient, less flexible organization, capable of fixing a higher basic level of contribution from its members, but incapable of sponsoring creativity. It would be traditional, rather than innovating, except as innovation is introduced

by leaders; more responsive to the demands of chief executives, but less responsive to the needs, demands, and wishes of the rank and file; in general, dependent on leadership rather than on cooperation.[2]

The question of the kind of organization which would be supported by a different culture from our own is a different kind of question from one asking how organizations meet the needs and goals of their members. It has to do with the organization as a social form, with its own problems and properties, responsive to the culture of which it is a part. For the right problem—one example of which arises when we think about exporting along with our surplus goods the organizational forms which produced them—it is the right approach. Then it is as practical to think about the organization as the unit of analysis as, in other situations, it is to concentrate on the individual.

Suppose that the inferences regarding German adaptation to role demands are correct; that here adaptation is founded on early experiences with a strongly hierarchic family struc-

[2] A German student of industrial psychology and I discussed the way group decision might work out in the American factory and in the German factory. We took the problem of deciding on a vacation time. In the American factory there would be give and take, probably ending with a vote, and the agreement that the majority should rule. In the German factory the first suggestion would be that the foreman decide. If the foreman said, "No, you men decide," the men would individually state the period best for them: "May," "early August," and so on. If the foreman then said, "We can't shut down the plant all that time; you have to decide on *one* time," they would say, "All right. You decide on one time. We have told you our preferences." Further insistence by the foreman on group decision would be met by increased opposition among the men. The difference is that Americans are able to see themselves as forming a group, aside from their working relationships. The Germans are a group only as they are led by their foreman. The informal group is a potentiality in America in a way it probably is not in Germany. For a description of the problems met in attempting to work with Germans as one would with Americans, see Jeanne Watson and Ronald Lippitt, *Learning Across Cultures.* Ann Arbor: University of Michigan, 1955, pp. 75–96. The experiences of the authors with group decision involving visiting German students are uniformly discouraging.

ture and a strongly hierarchic school system. What must we recognize as necessary modifications of our understanding of organization as we move from the American to the German? Perhaps most strongly affected will be coordination processes, which, even in the most formal American organizations, leave to the individual some responsibility for coordination with others. In the German organization we must expect the peer relationship this involves to be not so trustworthy. Instead we should expect a more elaborate formal system for the achievement of coordination, with heavier responsibility on centrally placed executives. We should be willing to grant sharper status differentials between levels, commensurate with the sharply increasing responsibility. We should be wary regarding group decision, not because the tradition is different, but because the prerequisites of group decision are not met. By thinking about the organization and its requirements it is possible to identify the differences in the character of the staff which must be taken into account, and to suggest the differences in organization which must follow.

This is pure speculation, and submitted only as an example of an application of organization-level conceptualization. Its leading idea is that we must understand what organization really is, and how it works, if we are to plan organizations. If we have this understanding, we can work toward social forms which are effective in their settings, and which in achieving their goals utilize and express, rather than clash with, the personalities of their staffs. Without this understanding we can only design our organizations from tradition, projection, and the unrealistic extrapolation of experience from one situation to another.

The Formal Structure

of Organization

P A R T   T W O

IF YOU WERE to drive past a factory owned by a large automobile manufacturer and notice that the plant made electrical components which were used in the firm's automobiles, you would be observing a tangible manifestation of an organization plan. One part of this plan had determined that part of the work of manufacturing automobiles was to be handled by dividing up the overall task in such a way that people worked on items of a similar nature, in this case electrical components. Another vital part of the plan was concerned with coordinating the work in the various plants and of the people in the plants to make sure that the final result, in this case the automobile, was produced as efficiently as possible. The magnitude of this task can perhaps be appreciated by noting that a number of automobile manufacturers have several hundred thousand employees, and by noting further that any one of the cars made by these companies probably had several thousand employees directly involved in its manufacture. To make the task still more difficult, these employees were in a number of plants located over a fairly large geographical area. The fact that the efforts of these numerous people resulted in an automobile rather than in utter chaos and frustration is indeed very remarkable.

A premise on which a formal organization rests is that the sum total of the efforts of people when organized will be greater than the sum of their individual efforts when unorganized. To put it more simply, if each of the several hundred thousand employees working for one of the typical automobile manufacturers was to be put to work on a separate automobile, the likelihood is that very few automobiles would ever be completed and that these few would take a very long time to produce. The same people properly organized can produce hundreds of thousands of automobiles each year. In this section on formal organization, we are concerned with the plans used to organize the efforts of people.

Organization Goals

A fundamental characteristic of organizations noted earlier is that they are purposeful entities. Therefore, the goals or objectives toward which organizations are directed are of great interest in a very particular way. As mentioned earlier, we are not concerned in

64

this volume with the examination of the particular goals or objectives that an organization *should* have. Hence, we are not concerned with whether or not a company should have an objective of obtaining a certain percentage return on its investment, or that it should have objectives that are concerned with both the private advantage of the owners and service to the community. These are policy decisions made before planning the organization or, if you will, before the formal organization is created.

The relation between goals and an organization is analogous to that between the purpose of a building and its design; for example, the architect is told to design a structure that will serve as a warehouse. His client tells him what purpose the building is to serve to support his objectives. The purpose of the building will be of great importance in determining its size, appearance, cost, etc. The adequacy of the building will largely be determined by how well it serves the purpose for which it was intended. Similarly, with an organization, its goals or purpose determine many of its characteristics and also serve as a measure of how adequate the organization is. The initial question before the person establishing a formal organization is: what type of organization will satisfy or accomplish the goals or objectives?

An organization, just as a building, is not created in a vacuum. Along with a set of goals, the planner of an organization draws on (1) a set of resources, such as capital and the technical knowledge he can use, and (2) conditions, that is, a type of competition, an economy, which the organization must face. All influence the organization. A second question must therefore be asked: what type of organization can accomplish the goals we have with the resources available and under the conditions facing us?

An analysis of these factors in connection with his knowledge of organizations may well lead the planner to conclude that a satisfactory organization is not possible or at least not possible without accepting additional and, perhaps, previously unanticipated "costs," which may well result in the goals being redefined. This is one way that organizations have an influence on goals and objectives—by delimiting the possible goals and conditions under which they are obtainable.

An organization has more than a delimiting influence on its goals, however, in that goal formation or, perhaps more accurately, reformation can be considered a continuing process of an organization. In this volume, however, goals will be considered as "givens." In the next volume, attention will be given both to the effects of changes in goals on the organization and some ways in which organizational goals are changed.

Division of Labor

We have in part answered the question of what a formal organization does, but we have not really considered what it is. That is, what is this conscious plan or system that coordinates the efforts of people?

Probably the single most important aspect of organization is that it provides for a division of labor. By this we mean that in order to accomplish an operating objective, a certain amount of work has to be accomplished and, rather than have one person do it all himself, we divide up the work and allocate it to different individuals or, perhaps, groups. Carried to its logical conclusion, this gives everyone his own unique job in which he can specialize. As each person does his unique task, the products of his efforts fit together with those of others in the organization to complete the overall objective or goal of the organization. A division of labor that gives each person a small portion of the overall task has many advantages for the organization (Babbage).

The central concept and advantages of division of labor are rather readily recognized. What may not be so obvious are the many different ways in which work can be divided. One of the real difficulties in applying division of labor is not deciding the question of whether it should be used but deciding what form this division should take. There are two major forms of division of labor, each of which has a number of subforms.

The first of the major forms might be classified as a horizontal division of labor, which involves breaking up the task to be handled. To illustrate this, let us look at the job of getting a leaky boat to shore. Some people in the boat may be given the job of bailing, others may be given the task of rowing, and still others may be given the job of lookout to search for land or any rescue ship that may appear on the horizon. The objective is clear—to use the boat to reach safety—a number of tasks are involved in accomplishing this, and they have been divided among the occupants of the boat.

The other main form of the division of labor may be called a vertical division. We recognize that in almost any group where work is divided there is a central figure who may be called the foreman, the squad leader, the supervisor, or any one of a number of titles, who is responsible for seeing that a group of people receive task assignments and perform them in the proper fashion. This person has a unique or special job also, but it is of a different order from those of bailing the boat or pulling at the oars. His task, as Barnard has pointed out in Part-One, is one of supervision, coordination, direction, and motivation.

The Anatomy of Formal Organization

As we consider some of the basic characteristics of formal organizations, it may be well to see what meaning they have for the shape, form or, as we call it here, anatomy of formal organizations. Perhaps the simplest way to begin is to use a symbolic representation of an organization. Probably the most typical portrayal of a formal organization is a chart like that shown in Fig. 2.

Before examining this particular chart in detail, it may be well to say a few words about organization charts in general. Such a chart represents an attempt to depict *some* elements of the formal organization and not the total organization. It is a schematic presentation that identifies positions, their groupings, and their reporting relations. Although it may show which position has authority over another, such as position *a* having authority over position *b* (Fig. 2), it does not tell us very much else about the authority relations that impinge on *b*. For example, it gives us no indication at all of the extent of the authority that position *a* has over *b*. Is *a*, for example, able to fire the occupant of position *b*, or does his authority only extend to making recommendations for wage increases? Furthermore, does it not show us any of the authority that another position, such as that of a quality control inspector, has over position *b*? In short, although these schematic representations of the formal organiza-

tion can be exceedingly useful, we should at the same time always be cognizant of the fact that they contain only limited amounts of information.

Looking at Fig. 2, then, we note a series of rectangles, each representing a position in which the occupant is expected to perform certain tasks or activities. If the organization represented a company making and selling washing machines, we would expect those people at level 1 to be directly involved with the product, making or selling it. The positions above them we recognize as supervisory or managerial positions that are in some way involved in executing the managerial function, which makes it possible for those at level 1 to carry out their assignments effectively. As we go from level 1 to level 4, the authority in each position increases, and the position at the top of the organization is the seat of central authority that ties all the company activities together.

From what has been said up to now, we could obtain the impression that in going from a position on, say, level 2 to one on level 3, we would meet essentially the same type of situation, only with more authority and responsibility attached. This is not entirely the case. As we go from one level to another, not only does the responsibility and authority increase but the nature of the job changes in a very significant way. Those at level 2 are primarily concerned with supervising the day-to-day activities of people in a rather tangible, concrete world. As we go higher in the organization, the time horizon within which a person works extends further into the future, and the issues dealt with become less concrete.

This has been described in a number of ways. One useful distinction is to say that at the top of the organization, the occupants of positions are primarily concerned with establishing organizational policy that will guide the overall organization, whereas those at the lower levels are involved with carrying out these top-level decisions. This makes a very distinctive difference in the nature of the work performed at various levels (Holden, Fish, and Smith). One profound difference results from the separation of planning from execution. The advantages of this are considered here (Taylor). The disadvantages will be examined in later parts of this volume.

One thing Fig. 2 suggests is that at the top of

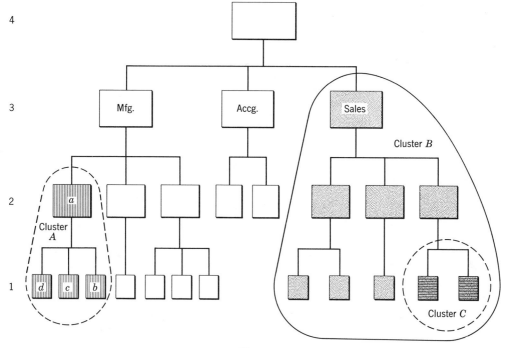

Fig. 2

the organization there is one position that serves as the central or chief executive responsible for the overall affairs of the organization. Although the affairs of the organization do fall into the province of a central authority, there is no reason why this must be invested in one person and, in fact, in many cases it consists of a number of people and positions arranged in different ways (Holden, Fish, and Smith).

Another thing we notice about Fig. 2 is that positions in the organization have been grouped as, for example, happened with cluster A. Let us presume that in cluster A positions b, c, and d all work on the washing machines that the company makes. It could well be that they are all involved with performing similar operations involved in making parts to be later assembled into washers. If so, we recognize these positions as being grouped because they work on a common process. On the other hand, we might find that position b is involved with assembling several parts of the washer into a jig, position c is involved with spot-welding them, and position d is involved with spray painting the items just welded. If this is the case, we find them grouped according to the product on which they work.

Within an organization, positions can be grouped in a number of ways (Dale).

Within any organization, there are very likely to be several different types of groupings used. At one level, as in cluster B, it might be by business function, such as selling, and at another level, such as cluster C, it might be by geographical area. The question is, what combinations of different types of departments should an organization have? A considerable number of alternatives are open. The real answer lies in determining what purpose the groupings must serve in the organization.

We have covered most of the items shown in Fig. 2. One last grouping remains—the accounting department shown reporting to the top executive. One thing we note about this department is that it is not as directly involved with the purpose of the organization as are the other two principal clusters we have discussed —manufacturing and sales. It represents a division of managerial work on the basis of managerial function, rather than by business function, area, or some other criteria. Because of the more indirect nature of its activities, we recognize this as what is typically called a staff department (Golembiewski). Few areas of organization are under as much constant scrutiny and questioning as is the area of staff. In actual organizations, we frequently hear of conflicts between line and staff positions, some of which are examined in later portions of this book. The theory about staff is frequently found at variance with practice, creating demands that it be both reexamined and reconstituted. This is being done and, in the future, we shall doubtless have more extended and more adequate theories of staff. For the moment, the selection chosen presents a statement of current, classical organization theory about staff.

Coordination and Integration

Division of work, with its subsequent specialization, permits the efficient completion of jobs or the efficient production of subparts or services. However, organizations do not exist to make parts or supply parts of services. The parts must be assembled into finished products, the individual performances coordinated to achieve the desired end result. The very essence of organizations is coordinated effort (Mooney). In examining the necessity for a vertical division of labor, we run into some of the basic limitations or difficulties connected with the horizontal or task division of labor. What this division of labor does is to specify the activities that must be performed and also who will do them. At first glance it might seem enough to know that one man will bail the boat and a second will pull on the right oar and a third on the left oar, but is it? Even the simplest boating experience will dramatize the fact that the oars must be pulled in unison. In short, there is a need for coordination. In a boat with reasonably skilled rowers who see where their individual efforts contribute to the organization objective, people may be able, through their willingness to cooperate, to provide the necessary coordination themselves. As noted earlier, however, if these conditions are not met, the coordination may have to come from another source. As organizations grow larger or as jobs become more specialized, it becomes more difficult for people to see where their efforts contribute the overall objectives, and additional means for coordination must be provided.

Division of labor, then, has many great advantages, but it has its cost. It requires the provision of some means of coordinating the different jobs that result from the division of labor. It is important to recognize early that the greater the degree to which this division of labor is carried and, therefore, the more unique each job becomes, the greater becomes this need of providing some means for coordination. A foreman supervising a group of men digging a ditch, where each of them does the same job with a shovel, has a relatively simple job of coordination and can therefore supervise a fairly large number of men. On the other hand, a foreman supervising people who each have a quite different job that is interrelated with the others in the department has a much more difficult task of coordination and can supervise only a smaller number of people. The executive who has reporting to him a number of work units all of which are doing the same task and are not very highly interrelated will be able to handle a considerable number of work units each with their own local supervisor. Such is the case, for example, for the regional manager of a shoe store chain in that each of the stores reporting to him handles the same line of products and does the same thing, namely, sell shoes. On the other hand, a manager who has a number of work units that are quite different and are also highly interrelated reporting to him can have far fewer reporting to him. In building an organization, then, one must consider how to divide and group tasks in order to be able not only to achieve the efficiency of work in individual positions and departments but to provide coordination between them (Gulick). Thus far, we have said that the principle means by which the formal organizations provide the necessary coordination is through its managerial group or hierarchy. Employees know when or how to do things because the superior (a) gives them direct orders or (b) some administrative apparatus, such as production schedules, instruction sheets, or rules, indirectly conveys this information to them. The assumption underlying much of the writings of the classical school of organization writers was that when workers received orders, they would follow them, and thus the effort would be coordinated with others. Hence the first step is for subordinates to accept orders. If they did not, it was assumed that there was something wrong with the subordinates or with the organization, or both. It has been obvious to many writers of the classical school that people not only did not accept orders but often deliberately disobeyed them; that rather than be loyal and supportive of their organizations, they were disgusted with them and stayed in them only out of dire economic necessity. Present (more in body than in spirit), many workers were at the least apathetic and often antagonistic toward the organization.

In examining and prescribing for this antagonism toward and alienation from organizations, the classical writers took a position that organizations were instruments through which people achieved their ends. Workers then should be treated with justice and paid fairly for what they did and not be expected or forced to do work beyond their physical or mental skills and capacities (Taylor). Managements of organizations were often seen as failing to do this. They did not pay fairly for work done. They did encourage people to exceed their physical capacities. It was thought that these conditions came about, in part, because managements allowed the workers to plan their own work methods which, it was held, they were incapable of doing. The solution to the problem was better management which could be achieved (1) by having superiors take on the planning of work, (2) through the use of proper techniques as time and motion study to design jobs that people could handle efficiently and easily, and (3) by employing a fair wage scheme to pay employees adequately (Taylor). These logical extensions to formal organizations substituted new problems for those they solved and often intensified others greatly for reasons we shall examine in the next part.

But there is another way in which coordination can be achieved. This is the voluntary coordination that occurs when people know the goal of the organization, want to attain it, and know what has to be done. We witness this coordination frequently, most conspicuously in those organizations in which people have high *esprit de corps*, such as sports teams, armies, etc. (Mooney). The desirability of *esprit de corps* from which this spontaneous coordination springs has been frequently cited. The ways to attain it are as frequently conspicuous by their absence. Mooney, however, has suggested that a key step is to inculcate the organization members with the organization purpose and values and, in this way, make the goals of all organization members the same.

Authority

When we witness one person doing what another has told him we see the manifestation of authority—the right to command the actions of others. From what we have been discussing, the importance of authority is obvious. Unfortunately, the source of authority is not. Many early writers assumed that authority came from some ultimate source such as the gods, the people, or the law. The position at the top of the organization would receive this authority and then would delegate authority to lower members of the organization, members on each level receiving smaller amounts than those above them. This was a neat explanation which, however, did not always seem to fit what actually was going on. The search for better explanations has lead to the identification of several types and sources of authority (Peabody). However, if we take one of these types of authority, we still find that the response to people is very varied and, to explain this variance, we have to take into account the way in which the person relates to the organization (Etzioni). A person who is alienated from an organization responds differently than a person who is deeply committed to it.

This brings us to a point where we will digress briefly from the discussion of organizations to the types of models used to analyze them. Briefly speaking, our models until now have been of the simple cause-effect type. We say, "when we increase variable A then variable B will decrease." In our discussion above, we observed that it had been found that, for adequate explanation of authority, we had not only to note the type of authority exerted to achieve a desired behavior but also that a certain type of relationship between the person and the organization prevailed at the time the authority was exerted. We call these conditional models and say, "if condition Z prevails then when we use A, B will occur." We shall find conditional models occurring with increasing frequency as we continue.

Organizational Style

Up to now we have been considering both the elements and the anatomy of organizations. We are in the position of an architectural student who has learned, on the one hand, that he has to put up with forces of gravity, tension, and stress in beams, the wracking of walls, and the pressure of wind as a set of building elements and, on the other, has learned that buildings consist of foundations, walls, roofs, floors, windows, and doors. Once he is aware of these things, he is ready to start using these components to design buildings. The components can go together in a wide variety of ways. When designing a house, we can make it a Georgian style or a modern contemporary style and still have a house, and so it is with the elements in an organization. They can be combined in a variety of ways that might be called styles.

In the field of organization perhaps the most important differences in style are those that range along a continuum between centralized and decentralized organization. Although these style differences have many characteristics, probably the most important are those relevant to decision making. In brief, when positions at the lower levels of the organization have a fairly broad array of decision-making authorities, we have a decentralized organization, and when positions at the lower level of the organization are primarily concerned with executing decisions which, for the most part, are made toward the top of the organization, we have a centralized organization.

Although centering attention on decision making narrows our scope of discussion considerably, it still leaves us with a rather enormous area because decision making is an exceedingly complex topic. Let us consider some of the differences that can occur in the nature of decision making. We have, for example, the issue of the scope of the decision. Does a person make a decision as to what will be done, how it will be done, and when it will be done? Or is he told what will be done, when it will be done, and left with the decision of how? Quite obviously, the latter situation has far fewer decision-making prerogatives than the

former. Another issue in describing the nature of decision making is the degree of autonomy given the executive. If an executive is given a broad area within which to work and is authorized to make many types of decision, being held accountable for profit and loss results at the end of the year, he has far more autonomy in decision making than another executive who makes decisions about what, when, and how but must obtain clearance for each decision from higher authorities and be accountable for each along the way.

The choice of which style to adopt is not an easy one. In truth, no organization is ever completely centralized or completely decentralized. Furthermore, most organizations are continually shifting between the two organizational styles. In this book, we have chosen two rather detailed examinations of organization style. Drucker discusses in detail how the General Motors Corporation scheme of decentralization operates.

The classical concept of formal organization views an organization as having a central source of authority and responsibility. At the creation of an organization, then, authority and responsibility may be conceived of as being totally contained in the hands of one person. As he acquires subordinates who will occupy the positions beneath him to carry out their portion of the organization work, he is faced with the task of distributing part of the central authority and responsibility to subordinates. This process is called delegation.

It is usually recognized that although responsibilities can be delegated, they can by no means be transferred. When the superior gives some authority and responsibility to a subordinate, he does not relieve himself of the responsibility for the subordinate's performance. Therefore, to the extent that a subordinate fails to live up to his responsibility, the superior proportionately fails. With this realization in mind, superiors are at times reluctant, quite naturally, to delegate to a subordinate, preferring to retain authority and responsibility for themselves using subordinates to execute their instructions. To achieve workable delegation requires more than a statement of its logical necessity; it also calls for an understanding of conditions on which it must rest and the consequences that can result from its ineffective execution (Newman).

Decentralization was the organizational answer to a number of problems, among them how to reduce the complexity and magnitude of the top-level management work, how to make organizations more flexible, and how to increase the motivation and limited perspective of middle-level managers. Developments in industry and other areas have made it progressively more difficult for even decentralized organizations to effectively support the desired strategies. Both the frequency and magnitude of the changes necessary to cope with the environment have increased. Frequently, to adjust properly, it is necessary to change the basic structuring of the organization, creating new product divisions, rather than merely adjusting operations of established structures. However, changes of this magnitude made it difficult for people to be adequately integrated into the organization and to cooperate even if they wanted to. This, in turn, made it difficult to achieve adequate motivation, coordination, and accountability. In recent years, there has emerged the project or matrix form of organization, which has permitted organizations to better achieve their ends when faced with these conditions (Litterer).

Summary

The formal organization is that part of the organization consciously planned to achieve a purpose or a goal. It specifies tasks to be performed in positions or offices. Rules and procedures establish both requirements for admission and departure from positions and the or-

ganization and, also, the general behavioral requirements while in the organization. It also provides the means of linking individual performances to objectives through a system of control or coordination. As a division of work is established, the type and the magnitude of the coordination to be provided is influenced. For the organization planner then, the decisions he makes to solve one set of problems creates and determines, in part, another set with which he will have to contend.

The basic elements we have been dealing with and refer to in later sections are summarized in Fig. 3. We begin by recognizing that an organization is set up to accomplish some purpose and that this purpose is not only its reason for existence but also has a profound influence on the internal arrangement of the organization. In order to accomplish the objective, it is necessary to promote a division of labor. This division of labor, however, and the rest of the organization are influenced not only by the objectives but also by the technology and resources available to the organization and by the social, economic, and political conditions that the organization faces.

Once a division of labor begins, the immediate necessity arises of promoting coordination between the parts that are now developing. This necessity is satisfied, in part, by (1) a hierarchy exercising an executive function, (2) systems and procedures, and (3) arrangements of organizational units. The result is, first, a set of positions that are defined by a set of tasks or duties; and, second, an arrangement or set of relations between these positions, such as

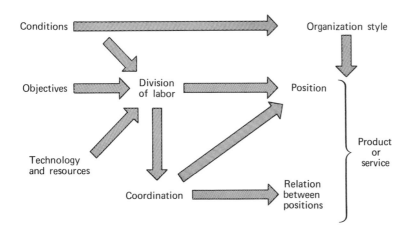

Fig. 3. Relationship of factors influencing and comprising the formal organization.

departments and a hierarchy of superior-subordinate relationships.

The content of the job and, for that matter, the relation between them is influenced not only by the tasks thought necessary to complete the objective but also by other matters, such as organizational style, which may give or deduct duties or authorities from a position on the basis of other factors.

Other factors that influence organization style are the conditions that face the organization. A threatening condition may encourage one style whereas a benign environment may permit a totally different style.

Organizations do not always perform as intended. The most visible area of difficulty has been with people who were supposed to be members of the organization. They fail to cooperate in an optimal fashion and often seem to be either apathetic about the organization or actually hostile to it. Early writers in organization have held this to be a manifestation of poor management or poor organization. The solutions they proposed to improve one or both of these were only partially successful with existing problems and often created new problems. Their view seemed to rest on a number of assumptions:

Organizations were instruments through which people achieved their ends. When people joined organizations they either accepted the organization goal as their own or saw that they could achieve their own through advancing the organization's. People would therefore accept the organization and those filling official capacities in it as sources of legitimate direction and control. They would continue to accept these as legitimate as long as (a) the organization paid them fairly for what they contributed and (b) matched their physical and mental skills and capacities with the assignments and orders given. The organization then consisted of two components. The managerial, which planned and administered an equitable system of tasks and rewards, and those who executed the tasks in return for the rewards.

Much of the rest of this book is concerned with aspects of organizations arising because these assumptions are either inadequate or incomplete. Let it be understood that in making this statement there is no intention to condemn the formal organization concepts. We are, however, trying to clearly point out their limitations in order that: (1) the ideas can more reliably and profitably be used within their area of legitimacy and (2) knowledge from the behavioral approach to organization can be properly and adequately brought to bear on these formal organization concepts.

The Division of Labor

CHARLES BABBAGE

Perhaps the most important principle on which the economy of a manufacture depends, is the *division of labour* amongst the persons who perform the work. The first application of this principle must have been made in a very early stage of society; for it must soon have been apparent, that a larger number of comforts and conveniences could be acquired by each individual, if one man restricted his occupation to the art of making bows, another to that of building houses, a third boats, and so on. This division of labour into trades was not, however, the result of an opinion that the general riches of the community would be increased by such an arrangement; but it must have arisen from the circumstance of each individual so employed discovering that he himself could thus make a greater profit of his labour than by pursuing more varied occupations. Society must have made considerable advances before this principle could have been carried into the workshop; for it is only in countries which have attained a high degree of civilization, and in articles in which there is a great competition amongst the producers, that the most perfect system of the division of labour is to be observed. The various principles on which the advantages of this system depend, have been much the subject of discussion amongst writers on Political Economy; but the relative importance of their influence does not appear, in all cases, to have been estimated with sufficient precision. It is my intention, in the first instance, to state shortly those principles, and then to point out what appears to me to have been omitted by those who have previously treated the subject.

1. *Of the Time Required for Learning.* It will readily be admitted, that the portion of time occupied in the acquisition of any art will depend on the difficulty of its execution; and that the greater the number of distinct processes, the longer will be the time which the apprentice must employ in acquiring it. Five or seven years have been adopted, in a great many trades, as the time considered requisite for a lad to acquire a sufficient knowledge of his art, and to enable him to repay by his labour, during the latter portion of his time, the expense incurred by his master at its commencement. If, however, instead of learning *all* the different processes for making a needle, for instance, his attention be confined to one operation, the portion of time consumed unprofitably at the commencement of his apprenticeship will be small, and all the rest of it will be beneficial to his master: and, consequently, if there be any competition amongst the masters, the apprentice will be able to make better terms, and diminish the period of his servitude. Again, the facility of acquiring skill in a single process, and the early period of life at which it can be made a source of profit, will induce a greater number of parents to bring up their children to it; and from this circumstance also, the number of workmen being increased, the wages will soon fall.

2. *Of Waste of Materials in Learning.* A certain quantity of material will, in all cases, be consumed unprofitably, or spoiled by every person who learns an art; and as he applies himself to each new process, he will waste some of the raw material, or of the partly manufactured commodity. But if each man commit this waste in acquiring successively every process, the quantity of waste will be much greater than if each person confine his attention to one process; in this view of the subject, therefore, the division of labour will diminish the price of production.

From *On the Economy of Machinery and Manufactures.* London: Charles Knight, 1832, pp. 169–176.

3. Another advantage resulting from the division of labour is, *the saving of that portion of time which is always lost in changing from one occupation to another*. When the human hand, or the human head, has been for some time occupied in any kind of work, it cannot instantly change its employment with full effect. The muscles of the limbs employed have acquired a flexibility during their exertion, and those not in action a stiffness during rest, which renders every change slow and unequal in the commencement. Long habit also produces in the muscles exercised a capacity for enduring fatigue to a much greater degree than they could support under other circumstances. A similar result seems to take place in any change of mental exertion; the attention bestowed on the new subject not being so perfect at first as it becomes after some exercise.

4. *Change of Tools.* The employment of different tools in the successive processes is another cause of the loss of time in changing from one operation to another. If these tools are simple, and the change is not frequent, the loss of time is not considerable; but in many processes of the arts the tools are of great delicacy, requiring accurate adjustment every time they are used; and in many cases the time employed in adjusting bears a large proportion to that employed in using the tool. The sliding-rest, the dividing and the drilling-engine, are of this kind; and hence, in manufactories of sufficient extent, it is found to be good economy to keep one machine constantly employed in one kind of work: one lathe, for example, having a screw motion to its sliding-rest along the whole length of its bed, is kept constantly making cylinders; another, having a motion for equalizing the velocity of the work at the point at which it passes the tool, is kept for facing surfaces; whilst a third is constantly employed in cutting wheels.

5. *Skill Acquired by Frequent Repetition of the Same Processes.* The constant repetition of the same process necessarily produces in the workman a degree of excellence and rapidity in his particular department, which is never possessed by a person who is obliged to execute many different processes. This rapidity is still further increased, from the circumstance that most of the operations in factories, where the division of labour is carried to a considerable extent, are paid for as piece-work. It is difficult to estimate in numbers the effect of this cause upon production. In nail-making, Adam Smith has stated, that it is almost three to one; for, he observes, that a smith accustomed to make nails, but whose whole business has not been that of a nailer, can make only from eight hundred to a thousand per day; whilst a lad who had never exercised any other trade, can make upwards of two thousand three hundred a day.

In different trades, the economy of production arising from the last-mentioned cause will necessarily be different. The case of nail-making is, perhaps, rather an extreme one. It must, however, be observed, that, in one sense, this is not a permanent source of advantage; for, though it acts at the commencement of an establishment, yet every month adds to the skill of the workmen; and at the end of three or four years they will not be very far behind those who have never practised any other branch of their art. Upon an occasion when a large issue of bank-notes was required, a clerk at the Bank of England signed his name, consisting of seven letters, including the initial of his Christian name, five thousand three hundred times during eleven working hours, besides arranging the notes he had signed in parcels of fifty each.

6. *The Division of Labour Suggests the Contrivance of Tools and Machinery to Execute its Processes.* When each process, by which any article is produced, is the sole occupation of one individual, his whole attention being devoted to a very limited and simple operation, improvements in the form of his tools, or in the mode of using them, are much more likely to occur to his mind, than if it were distracted by a greater variety of circumstances. Such an improvement in the tool is generally the first step towards a machine. If a piece of metal is to be cut in a lathe, for example, there is one particular angle at which the cutting-tool must be held to insure the cleanest cut; and it is quite natural that the idea of fixing the tool at that angle should present itself to an intelligent workman. The necessity of moving the tool slowly, and in a direction parallel to itself, would suggest the use of a screw, and thus arises the sliding-rest. It was probably the idea of mounting a chisel in a frame, to

prevent its cutting too deeply, which gave rise to the common carpenter's plane. In cases where a blow from a hammer is employed, experience teaches the proper force required. The transition from the hammer held in the hand to one mounted upon an axis, and lifted regularly to a certain height by some mechanical contrivance, requires perhaps a greater degree of invention than those just instanced; yet it is not difficult to perceive, that, if the hammer always falls from the same height, its effect must be always the same.

When each process has been reduced to the use of some simple tool, the union of all these tools, actuated by one moving power, constitutes a machine. In contriving tools and simplifying processes, the operative workmen are, perhaps, most successful; but it requires far other habits to combine into one machine these scattered arts. A previous education as a workman in the peculiar trade, is undoubtedly a valuable preliminary; but in order to make such combinations with any reasonable expectation of success, an extensive knowledge of machinery, and the power of making mechanical drawings, are essentially requisite. These accomplishments are now much more common than they were formerly; and their absence was, perhaps, one of the causes of the multitude of failures in the early history of many of our manufactures.

Such are the principles usually assigned as the causes of the advantage resulting from the division of labour. As in the view I have taken of the question, the most important and influential cause has been altogether unnoticed, I shall re-state those principles in the words of Adam Smith:

The great increase in the quantity of work, which, in consequence of the division of labour, the same number of people are capable of performing, is owing to three different circumstances: first, to the increase of dexterity in every particular workman; secondly, to the saving of time, which is commonly lost in passing from one species of work to another; and, lastly, to the invention of a great number of machines which facilitate and abridge labour, and enable one man to do the work of many.

Now, although all these are important causes, and each has its influence on the result; yet it appears to me, that any explanation of the cheapness of manufactured articles, as consequent upon the division of labour, would be incomplete if the following principle were omitted to be stated.

That the master manufacturer, by dividing the work to be executed into different processes, each requiring different degrees of skill or of force, can purchase exactly that precise quantity of both which is necessary for each process; whereas, if the whole work were executed by one workman, that person must possess sufficient skill to perform the most difficult, and sufficient strength to execute the most laborious, of the operations into which the art is divided. *

---

* I have already stated that this principle presented itself to me after a personal examination of a number of manufactories and workshops devoted to different purposes; but I have since found that it had been distinctly pointed out, in the work of Gioja, *Nuovo Prospetto delle Scienze Economiche,* 6 tom. 4to. Milano, 1815, tom. i. capo iv.

The Division of Basic Company Activities

General Analysis

The Division of Basic Company Activities.
The alternative methods for dividing the work of a company toward the accomplishment of its objectives are numerous. They traditionally include function, product, location, customers, process, equipment, and time. It should be noted that in many companies these various bases of division are combined, and coordinated by checks and balances. But there is usually one predominant type of subdivision of the major company activities, made by the chief executive officer himself, called "basic subdivision," "basic delegation," or "departmentation."

The first step in the division of work is the determination of the primary responsibilities of the enterprise—that is, the purpose of the enterprise, and the major functions necessary to accomplish it. Thus, in a manufacturing enterprise, production is one basic responsibility; in merchandising, it may be advertising; in public utilities, the maintenance of equipment; in the liquor business, the determination of credit risk; in flour milling, the purchase of flour.

The principal or primary subdivision of the activities of an enterprise may then be divided on the following bases:

From *Planning and Developing the Company Organization Structure*. New York: American Management Association, 1952, pp. 25–38. Reprinted with permission of the publisher.

1. FUNCTION. Major subdivision by function, subject-matter or principal activities is found in many enterprises where actual control throughout all hierarchies and over all locations is exercised by the heads of managerial functions—such as finance; production (including plant design, construction and maintenance, purchasing); manufacture; engineering (product design or research, possibly quality control); law (claims, tax laws, corporate affairs); human relations (relations to stockholders, employees, community, government); sales (marketing, advertising). Many companies are so subdivided at the top. This arrangement has the advantages of specialization. More importantly, it should make possible adequate time for basic long-run planning and major decision-making and consultation for those in charge of the major management functions. But it may result in interdepartmental jealousies and conflicts over the limits of authority. It is also subject to considerable conflict among the local plant managers in multi-plant organizations. An example of a functional type of organization setup is shown in the organization chart of the Dictaphone Corporation (Fig. 1).

There appears to be a certain degree of uniformity in basic managerial functions of the top organization structure, at least in very large companies, as is shown in the accompanying illustrations of abbreviated organization charts (Figs. 2–4). Of particular interest is the abbreviated organization chart of Stan-

76

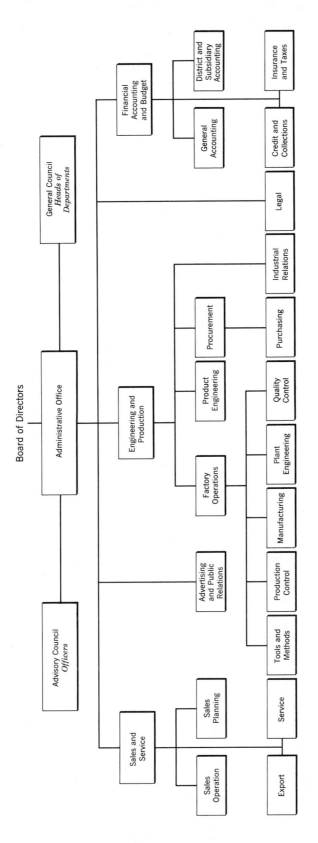

Fig. 1. A functional organization (the Dictaphone Corporation).

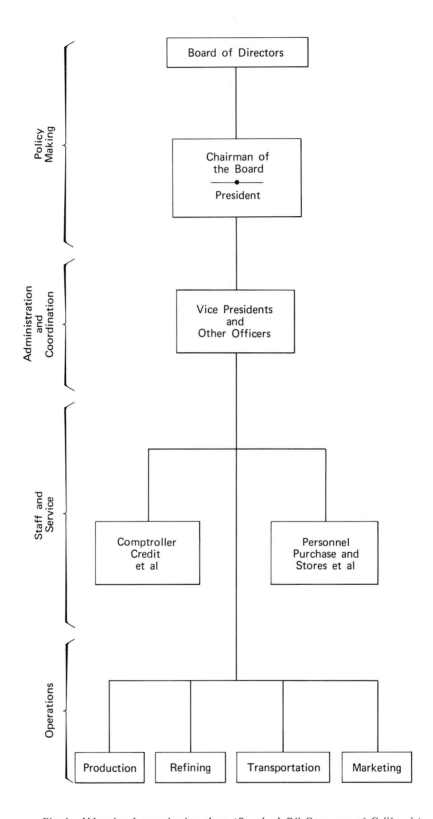

Fig. 2. Abbreviated organization chart (Standard Oil Company of California).

dard Oil Company of California (Fig. 2), which employs the use of the conventional line and staff organization plan and, in addition, identifies in vertical arrangement the following basic functional groups: Policy Making, Administration and Coordination, Staff and Service, and Operations.

2. PRODUCT. Management activities may be grouped on the basis of the major types of products or services marketed, and sold separately. This kind of grouping is used by some large companies manufacturing a diverse product line.

At General Foods Corporation and International Harvester Company, the major subdivisions of work are on a product basis. Other examples are found in merchandising, automobiles, chemicals and meat packing. Grouping by product has the advantage of bringing together and coordinating in one place major activities required to make a particular product (purchasing, engineering, production, distribution, etc.). Such an arrangement provides a particularly sound basis for decentralization. It may also make possible close control and accounting comparability through central staff agencies.

Even in the "mono-product plants" (as General R. Johnson, President of Johnson & Johnson, describes them) it may be wise to make "little ones out of big ones." For example, at the General Electric Company the refrigerator cabinet is made separately from refrigerator compressor units. Or in the production of locomotives, the cabs and running gear are made in separate sections, erected and assembled in another section; the rotating units are made in another shop; and control gadgets in still another. In making control gadgets of infinite variety, the necessity for a multi-product plant really arises.

Figure 5 shows the product organization at The Kendall Company, a medium-sized company which is famous for its work in scientific management. It shows a basic organization built about three major products. It also shows in an interesting way the provision of staff services to these line divisions, the operation of which is decentralized, while coordination and control are centralized.

3. LOCATION (also called territorial or geographical division or departmentation). Under this type of arrangement, all activities performed in a particular area are brought together. It is found in companies serving customers on a national or international scale—e.g., the liquor business, railroads, chain stores, life insurance companies, the overseas branches of motor car and oil companies. The product and locational principles may be combined, with different factories in different locations devoted to the production of different types of products (e.g., General Motors).

The major subdivisions of oil companies are often on a regional basis, since the natural unit of work centers around the major oil producing fields. Production and selling or the selling function alone may often be subdivided on a regional basis. The advantage of such a division is that the power of decision-making is concentrated near the source of origin and is all-inclusive, with functional central control. It prevents the losses of efficiency that arise when a company spreads out too thinly. It ensures that careful account is taken of local conditions—an important factor, since the problems of selling may be different in different parts of the country. It makes it possible to take advantage immediately of favorable opportunities arising on the spot. It permits coordination on a manageable scale. It facilitates operation in times of emergency or war. Finally, it provides opportunity for training of lower executives in a wide range of activities so that qualified men will be available to fill vacancies in higher jobs.

Figure 6 illustrates territorial or geographical division of company activities.

4. CUSTOMERS. Major subdivision on a customer basis occurs in certain fields—radio and television, for example. Here emphasis is principally on selling programs to individual clients, such as a cigarette company, a soap manufacturer, etc. Lower level subdivisions on a customer basis are found, for example, on railroads (Pullman and Coach travellers), and insurance companies (type of policy-holders, sometimes divided by groups of serial numbers).

In a broader sense, not only customers, but other parties connected with the enterprise may be represented on the organization chart. Figure 7 shows such a division of functions in terms of management communications to its

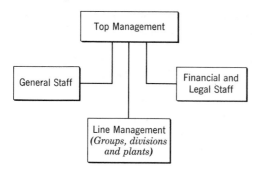

Fig. 3. *Abbreviated organization chart (General Motors Corporation).*

own people at all levels—stockholders, suppliers, financiers, the consumer audience and the general audience. While the usual organization chart shows the structure of the management hierarchy, this chart shows the inter-relationships (and their absence) between the various "publics" connected with the enterprise. It shows the functions which fall into natural groupings and the combinations of functions which are possible in various managerial activities. For instance, in preparing the company annual report, its uses and the varying interests of the different groups may be indicated by such a chart. (This chart was prepared by A. F. Arnold, designer and management consultant to industry.)

5. PROCESS. In integrated textile concerns, major divisions may be made on the basis of operational sequence—e.g., spinning, weaving, bleaching, dyeing, inspection, boxing, shipping. In steel and men's and women's clothing subdividing is often based on the process.

6. EQUIPMENT. In certain fields, equipment determines major subdivisions. In a secretarial school, for example, the subdivisions may be determined by the chief instruments whose operation is taught, such as the typewriter, the stenotyping machine, the comptometer, etc. (often identical with process).

7. TIME. Division of work may be based on time sequences, with the work broken down under the categories of planning, execution and control. Thus the first major business division would be devoted to the formulation of objectives, methods of accomplishing them, forecasts and budgets. The second major division would be devoted to the execution of the plans, and would correspond roughly to

the major operating group in a business. The third major division is devoted to the control of the results of execution in the light of the objectives and plans of the business.

To present an illustration, at one prominent company the general manager has three principal assistants, each of whom is responsible to him for one of the three main aspects of management, i.e., planning, execution, and control. There are three aspects of planning. In order to do a job one must analyze it carefully and study the available resources. Next, one must balance resources against the job, and design the job to fit the resources. The program must be scheduled on a time basis, and must meet certain set standards of quality and quantity. All these activities are found under the First Vice President. In another corporation this might be a continuing function of the secretariat of a general policy or planning committee. Although the committee may be made up of certain heads of subordinate departments, the permanent secretariat is in fact the Office of the Vice President. Second, general management is supplied with a Vice President for Operations, charged with the execution of the company's program. He is responsible for the day-to-day coordination, direction and supervision of the company's affairs. To his desk come the thousand and one issues which demand prompt decisions to expedite the efficient execution of any large and complex program. And, finally, in the jurisdiction of the Third Vice President is the function of controllership. His is the job of keeping the progress of the company under scrutiny, comparing it constantly with its program. One might say that this Third Vice President serves the other two. He serves the

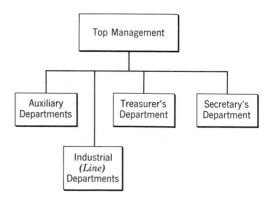

Fig. 4. *Abbreviated organization chart (Du Pont).*

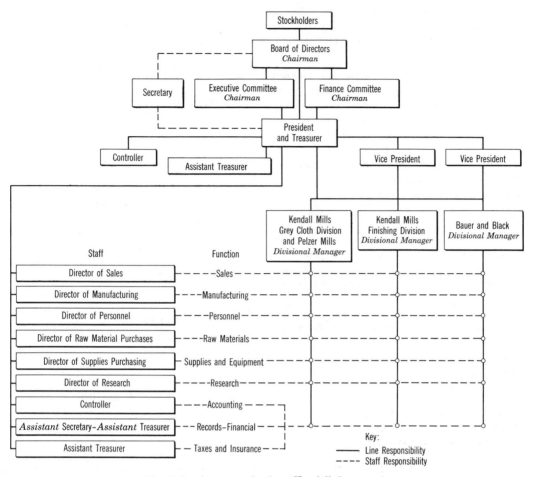

Fig. 5. Product organization (Kendall Company).

planner by making prognosticative analyses, and by analysis of past performance which can serve as the basis for future program activities. Obviously, he is a most valuable aid to the General Manager, because he is able to make decisions on the basis of *all* the facts—not merely those which happen to come to him in connection with specific problems.

8. THE "HARMONIOUS OVERLAP." Another method of work division may be useful, particularly in research work which must be speedily completed to meet competition or fulfill an urgent customer requirement. It can sometimes be applied to a variety of rush jobs.

This method of work division may be best explained by recounting Dr. Alexander Sachs' conference with the late President F. D. Roosevelt in 1939 on dividing the work on the atomic bomb construction:

F.D.R. was worried whether an atomic weapon could be ready in time to decide the outcome of the war. Dr. Sachs had estimated the project might cost two billions, and honestly told the President that, ordinarily, it would take 25 years to do the job. He explained to F.D.R. that he had searched the history of human thought for an example of how time could be telescoped.

He found the example in music, he says. The composer of music has ways of making time three-layered. Remember the old round you used to sing: "Are you sleeping, etc?" Three tunes going at once, harmoniously overlapping each other. This, he advised, was what must be done with the atomic project.

"When you start one part of the project, assume you have finished it successfully, and start the next as if you had." That is exactly what was done, probably for the first time with such a huge undertaking. It worked.[1]

9. COORDINATION AND BALANCE. An attempt has been made to bring together the various factors of organizational planning in such a way that each acts as a check or balance on the others. In his *Design for Industrial Co-ordination*,[2] Robert W. Porter set out a technique for coordinating the basic functions in the field of industrial organization. He set up seven major categories for classifying industrial activities, with three subsidiary classifications for each:

1. The problems of policy, performance and compensation, identified as technical problems.

2. The problems of planning, production and inspection, identified as functional problems.

3. The problems of administration, management and operation, identified as jurisdictional problems.

4. The problems of communication, cooperation and control, identified as organizational problems.

[1] From "How F. D. R. Planned to Use the A-Bomb," by Nat S. Finney, *Look Magazine*, March 14, 1950, page 25, copyright 1950 by Cowles Magazines, Inc.
[2] Harper & Brothers, New York, 1941.

5. The problems of executive capacity dealing with intellect, volition and ethics, identified as leadership problems.

6. The problems of employee stimulation, application and discipline, identified as institutional problems.

7. The problems of expectancy, efficiency and economy, identified as measurement problems.

The author attempts, on the basis of wide practical experience, to bring out the interoperation and relationships of the 21 elements of performance, so that staff needs can be reduced, while the coordination process is improved. It is claimed that this plan of division has the advantages of economizing staff services, improving communication, cutting down jurisdictional problems, and providing better balance in general.

The foregoing are some general guides for determining how the work of the organization may be subdivided, and what consequences may follow. Their specific application will depend upon the special needs of the enterprise. There is no indication from this list that any one way of grouping activities is better than another. If one basis is adopted, then other bases will have to be intermixed. Even when a proper primary basis of dividing work has been decided on, its specific limits must be determined. For example, suppose it has been decided that it will be best to divide

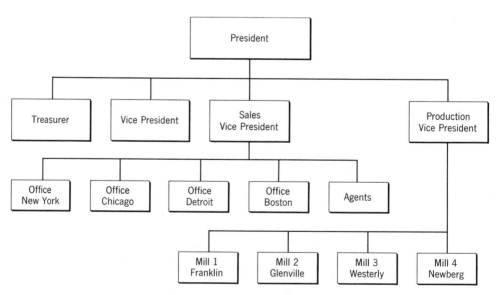

Fig. 6. Territorial division of activities (American Felt Company).

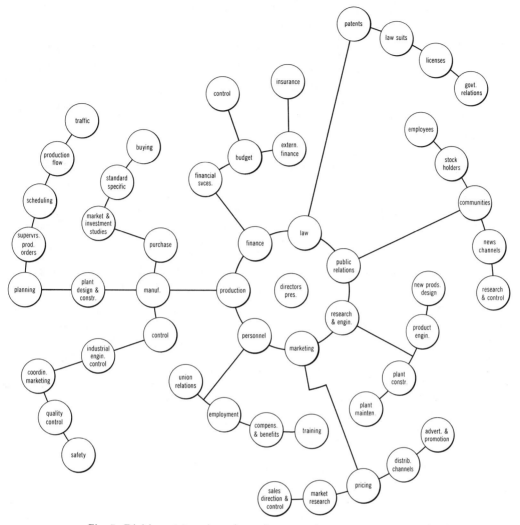

Fig. 7. Division of functions shown in terms of management communication.

sales activities on a territorial basis. This still leaves open the question as to how the territories are to be split up. It is not always practical to determine sales territories by geographical boundaries. The problem must be solved in terms of selling a particular article in a particular situation.

For these reasons it is necessary to develop criteria which are helpful in deciding which method of grouping to use. That method should then be chosen which satisfies best the criteria under consideration, and is best adapted to individual needs.

Criteria for Determining the Division of Basic Activities

In general, the various functions which must be performed to accomplish the objectives of the enterprise should be so assigned as to obtain the greatest possible advantage from the division of labor:

1. Work should be so divided that the incumbent of a position should be able to become a specialist and increase his knowledge on the particular job assigned to him.

2. Special abilities should be used to the full.

3. Groups of people (divisions, departments) should comprise a workable, homo-

geneous and separate field of activity. The nature of their work should be similar or complementary (the former is probably more important in the lower executive ranks, the latter more important in the upper ranks).

Three major criteria may be distinguished for dividing work—economic and non-economic criteria and the size of the company.

Economic Efficiency. Economic criteria relate to business efficiency. These in turn may be evaluated in terms of saving money, contributing more to the company's revenue, in the speed or accuracy of transacting business.

That particular grouping of activities should be chosen which will make the greatest contribution to the profitability of the enterprise. This may take many different forms, some of which are discussed below.

1. MAJOR CONTRIBUTIONS TO SURVIVAL AND PROFITABILITY. In the early stages of a company's growth the fundamental problem is that of economic survival. This may require improvement of the production process so that goods will be turned out on time and within the proper cost limits. It may require successful acquisition of sources of raw materials, as in the timber industry and mining. Or, most commonly, it may require acquisition of cash through sales to meet current expenses and to build up a reserve of working capital. These basic objectives tend to become the major function in the business, with the executive in charge becoming in fact the most important official in the business.

Once production or sales have reached satisfactory levels and have become more or less stabilized, they may well lapse into secondary activities, while research and control become dominant. The primary aim at this point may be technical superiority. If this is under pressure by competitors, or the company itself is forging ahead, this very instability will greatly increase the importance of the technical function—especially if the firm's competitive superiority rests on it. The development by the research or style department of innovations which will accelerate the growth of the company are likely to be primary functions. Or the primary activity, from the standpoint of profits, may be that of integration, consolidation and establishment of central control. Once the firm has reached its final stage of growth and is at the point of defending its share of

the market, sales may again become predominant.

2. The company may wish to take full advantage of *specialization* and therefore may group together similar functions or specialties. Thus the selling function is often divided into groups of closely related products—in a food company, confectionery products, for example, may be grouped together so that salesmen can devote themselves to selling one product group well rather than dissipate their efforts over many products. Similarly, activities which serve the same purpose may be most efficiently grouped together—e.g., recruitment, interviewing, testing, hiring and induction may be handled by the employment department, while the employee benefit activities are handled separately by a welfare department.

3. LINES OF COMMUNICATION may be shortened by a particular type of grouping. Thus specific functions in subsidiary plants may communicate directly with the corresponding headquarters function without going through the local plant manager—e.g., control and auditing.

4. DUPLICATION may be reduced or abolished by consolidating a particular function which was previously widely scattered, e.g., the consolidation of the personnel function into a headquarters department.

5. BALANCE may be improved and better operating results attained by combining different parts of a job under several men into one complete job under one man. Joseph B. Hall, President of The Kroger Company, describes such a change in operations as follows:

Until the past few years, we operated on a functional basis with one man responsible for buying and another man responsible for selling. Sometimes there was friction between these men. If, for instance, merchandise failed to sell, the sales promotion man claimed that the merchandise was inferior; whereupon the buyer would intimate that the sales promotion man had missed his true vocation and should be farming or cleaning the streets. The situation was somewhat like that between the meat managers and the grocery managers; in both cases it was difficult to hold men responsible when each man handled only a part of the complete job.

Railroads have experienced similar cleavages between different parts of the system.

6. The extent of delegated authority may be widened so that lower executives have a greater *power of decision-making*. This has the advantage that people on the spot who are most familiar with the problems can make better and speedier decisions.

7. UNIFORMITY AND CONSISTENCY of policy may be brought about. For example, if a personnel department is set up, there is likely to result greater uniformity in pay for similar jobs, more consistent policies with regard to merit rating and promotion, hiring and training.

8. CONTROL may be improved. Work may be so divided that similar units are created so that there is better comparability of selling and production efforts. On the other hand, control may be improved by separating inspection activities from the group—e.g., separation of the financial or auditing function from a subsidiary plant, separating credit from sales for fear salesmen will be too easy on the creditors.

9. Activities may be grouped in the department which makes the *most effective use* of them. For example, a company might consider having the production department take over the training function from the personnel department if this is the best way to gain acceptance from foremen and hourly-rated employees.

10. COMPETITION may be the criterion for dividing activities. Accordingly, the work may be split up into different departments or factories so that the results are fairly comparable. For example, in cement companies the work is distributed to different plants which are usually highly comparable. Sometimes it may be necessary to proceed on the opposite line of reasoning and join two types of work in order to suppress competition which hurts the total effort of the company.

11. JOB INTEREST may be severely impaired by over-specialization of individual jobs as well as of whole departments. Where work is divided too finely, with little variation or change, the monotony may obscure the meaning of the job and its relation to the end product, and give rise to job dissatisfaction and quits. Over-specialization is likely to require extra supervision (to deal with the resulting discontent) and an elaborate system of formal controls.

Non-economic Factors. There may be important *non-economic* factors to consider in the division of work. These frequently make for *autonomy* in a particular activity. Thus a special division may be set up to look after special interests connected with the enterprise, e.g., a division on stockholder relations or local community relations. Or the division is created to arouse *attention* to the particular activity—defense work, governmental relationships, safety (Central Maine Power Company), executive health, or salary evaluation. At the National Biscuit Company, for example, the head of the Sanitation Department reports directly to the president because the company attaches primary importance to the maintenance of sanitary conditions. Or a special division may be created for a *particular man*—to feather his ego, to "kick him upstairs," to take account of reduced abilities, or to retain some of his services on retirement (e.g., the position of Honorary Chairman of the Board). Division of work may have to be fitted to traditional arrangements within the company. For example, both the production and sales manager may have equal standing in a subsidiary and be given equal powers, but there may be no plant manager. Or the office manager may take over personnel work because there may not be enough of it to justify a full-time division. Or a particular division may continue to occupy an important position within the company simply because it has existed for a long time—e.g., in one company the engineer in charge of bridge-building (the oldest activity in the company) headed up a major division and reported to the president long after bridge-building had become a minor activity. *Preconceived ideas* and principles, and excessive reliance on formality may also be powerful factors in structuring a business enterprise.

Finally, the *personal interests* or hobbies of the chief executive may play a role. For example, Mac Fisheries were originally added to the Lever soap business in order to facilitate sale of the catch of fishermen of some islands on the West Coast of Scotland in whose development the first Lord Leverhulme took a private interest.

Obviously, not all the factors mentioned above are either rational or desirable determinants of the division of work within an enterprise. However, their existence should be taken into account and the reasons for their existence understood before any attempt is made to change the status quo.

Size of Company. The final major criterion for dividing the work of the organization is the size of the company. The importance of the chief problems faced by the top management varies as the company grows. Hence the major functions exercised and supervised

3. The most important ability on the part of heads of large companies in managerial ability or skills, and the more important the company the greater the place occupied by this ability.

4. Commercial and financial ability play a relatively more important part in the case of heads of small and middle-sized companies than they do in the case of larger companies.

5. As one goes up the scale of industrial concerns the managerial coefficient increases at the expense of the rest, which tend to even out, approximating up to one-tenth of the total evaluation.

It is clear that the larger the size of the business the greater the emphasis on broad managerial functions, such as planning, forecasting, organizing, commanding, coordinating and controlling.

Relative Importance of Requisite Abilities of Personnel in Industrial Concerns

	REQUISITE ABILITIES						
	MAN-AGERIAL %	TECH-NICAL %	COM-MERCIAL %	FINAN-CIAL %	SE-CURITY * %	ACCOUNT-ING %	TOTAL EVALUA-TION %
One-man business	15	40	20	10	5	10	100
Small firm	25	30	15	10	10	10	100
Medium-sized firm	30	25	15	10	10	10	100
Large firm	40	15	15	10	10	10	100
Very large firm	50	10	10	10	10	10	100
State enterprise	60	8	8	8	8	8	100

* Safeguarding property, avoiding social disturbances in the broad sense and any influence endangering the life of the business.

by the chief executive are likely to change also. This may be illustrated by the Work Table which the great French industrialist, Henri Fayol, drew up.[3]

From this table the following conclusions may be drawn:

1. The most important ability of the head of the small industrial company is technical ability.

2. As one goes up the chain of command, the relative importance of managerial ability increases and that of technical ability declines. Equilibrium between these two obtains in medium-sized companies.

[3] From Henri Fayol, *General and Industrial Management*, Sir Isaac Pitman & Sons, Ltd., London, 1949, pp. 10–11. Translator Constance Storres.

Conclusion

The most important criterion for the division of work is that of economic efficiency. This should lead to specialization, full utilization of abilities and homogeneity between groups.

Where this criterion is paramount, the basic functions (i.e., those supervised by the chief executive) are those which make the greatest contribution toward profitability. However, the economic criterion, it should be remembered, must usually be modified in the light of non-economic needs. Both need to be fitted to the particular stage of the growth and the special requirements of the company.

Top-Management Organization

PAUL HOLDEN, LOUNSBURY S. FISH, AND HUBERT L. SMITH

The importance of a sound and clean-cut plan of top-management organization in facilitating and contributing to the effectiveness of corporate administration cannot be overemphasized. In a few of the companies studied this field has obviously been given the attention and study it deserves. In many others it is evident that further clarification and development are needed.

The Three Basic Zones or Levels of Top Management

In order to clarify this stratum of organization, it should be recognized that there are three distinct and separable zones or levels of top management. They differ as to function, and as to the viewpoint, requisite background, and experience of the responsible personnel. These three zones may be characterized as follows:

ZONE 1. THE TRUSTEESHIP FUNCTION is to represent, safeguard, and further the stockholders' interests, determine the basic policies and the general course of the business, appraise the adequacy of over-all results, and in general protect and make the most effective use of the company's assets. This field is the exclusive province of the board of directors.

ZONE 2. THE GENERAL-MANAGEMENT OR ADMINISTRATIVE FUNCTION includes the active

From *Top-Management Organization and Control.* New York: McGraw-Hill Book Co., 1951, pp. 15–18, 20–29. Copyright 1951 by McGraw-Hill Book Co. Reprinted with permission of the publisher.

planning, direction, co-ordination, and control of the business as a whole, within the scope of basic policies established and authority delegated by the board. In other words, this function involves the determination of objectives, of operating policies, and of results. This broad co-ordinative function is variously handled (*a*) by the chief executive, (*b*) by the chief executive and a part-time council of divisional executives, (*c*) by a full-time group of general executives, or (*d*) by a managing board of directors.

ZONE 3. THE DIVISIONAL- OR DEPARTMENTAL-MANAGEMENT FUNCTION includes the management of the major divisions or departments of the company by executives fully responsible and accountable to general management for the successful conduct of their respective operations. This zone embraces the topmost level of executives concerned primarily with a particular division of the company rather than with the enterprise as a whole.

In many companies these three fundamental and separable levels of top management appear to be indistinct and confused. In some instances two or even three of these fields are administered by the same identical group of executives, as in the case of some managing boards. This frequently results in the assumption by a single agency of an excessive burden in trying to cover these three distinct functions. It is also difficult for executives steeped in the pressing problems and demands of divisional management to divorce themselves from their divisional interests and assume the broader viewpoint needed in the determination of policies, objectives, and long-range plans for the best interests of the company as a whole.

It is believed that a clear conception of the proper functions, responsibilities, and relationships of these three levels of management affords an effective basis (*a*) for testing the adequacy of any company's plan of top organization, (*b*) for making sure that each field is entrusted to a "team" whose composition and qualifications are best adapted to do that particular job, and (*c*) for passing the burden of management detail down to those in the best position to assume it.

Zone 1. Trusteeship Function (Board of Directors)

In this country the stockholders seldom bother, even once a year, to attend personally to the affairs of the corporations they own. As owners these stockholders have definite interests to be considered and protected. The business of a corporation must be conducted in such a way as to preserve its assets. Good judgment must be exercised in setting long-range policies, in selecting the officers, in checking results of operations, and in guiding generally the affairs of the business.

Obviously several thousand stockholders cannot personally manage the business. Therefore, they select a small group upon whom they rely to look after their interests in the enterprise. This group is the board of directors.

The point of view of the board of directors must by the nature of this relationship be identical with that of the stockholders. At all meetings of the board this viewpoint should outweigh any other consideration. In fact, the fundamental concept of the first zone or level of management is management for the benefit of those who own the business.

This point of view is not always easily maintained. Many directors are also full-time executives whose interests as members of management may momentarily be at variance with those of the stockholders.

Functions of the Board of Directors. It may be argued that all transactions of the business are or should be for the interest of the stockholders. At what point, therefore, should the trusteeship of the stockholders' interests, as such, cease and other more direct forms of management begin? In other words, how far should the board of directors enter into the management of the business in order properly to discharge the trusteeship function?

In substantially all the companies reviewed, the board of directors establishes broad basic policies, handles major financial matters, selects the officers and sets their salaries, and takes care of other matters of a similar character. In addition, it receives reports from the management on the company's operation since the last meeting, and passes judgment as to whether, in view of circumstances, the results are satisfactory.

These duties are of such a nature that they can be handled satisfactorily at periodic meetings. Broad policies are not subject to current fluctuation, but stand for relatively long periods. Results of operations are usually shown by monthly statistical and financial reports. Consequently, boards of directors meet at infrequent intervals. Of the thirty-one companies studied, twenty-one have monthly meetings, six meet quarterly, and only four meet oftener than monthly. Some twenty-six of the companies rely upon an executive committee of the board to handle matters requiring board action which cannot await a regular meeting.

In most companies there seems to be an unwritten but well-understood allocation of certain management decisions between the board and general management. But in addition there is a large middle ground within which the chief executive uses his discretion as to whether or not a program shall be decided by general management or presented to the board. In many such instances the action taken by general management is subsequently submitted to the board for ratification.

Any sound plan of management might well begin with the determination and definition of the functions, responsibilities, and limits of authority to be reserved for the board, and those to be delegated to general management. It is only by a clear delineation of functions that each group will know exactly what part it is to play in the management of the company as a whole. In some concerns this separation of functions has been made, and the field and duties of the board have been included as the first section of the organization manual. . . . In such companies top management has been made easier, simply because specific duties have been established, and each level can concern itself with its own particular assignment. . . .

Zone 2. General-Management or Administrative Function

The general-management function may be characterized as the active planning, direction, co-ordination, and control of the business as a whole, within the scope of basic policies established and authority delegated by the board. While both the board of directors and general management are concerned with the interests of the company as a whole, the former performs a judicial and intermittent function, that is, the appraisal and approval of major proposals and results, whereas the latter exercises an active and continuous function, involving the initiation, formulation, co-ordination, and development of those proposals and results.

Among the functions which appear to fall logically within this conception of general management are the following:

1. Maintenance of a sound and effective plan of company organization, with functions, responsibilities, and limits of authority clearly defined and properly allocated.

2. Maintenance of fully qualified personnel in all management positions.

3. Farsighted planning and clarification of general objectives.

4. Maintenance of effective systems of control over such general activities as capital expenditures, operating expenditures and results, manpower, wages, salaries, product line, and prices.

5. Review and approval of major appropriations, budgets, appointments, and salary changes as provided under these systems of control, within the limits delegated to it by the board and above the limits delegated by it to divisional executives.

6. Determination of general operating policies.

7. Recommendation to the board on matters requiring its action.

8. General co-ordination of major operating plans.

9. Appraisal of divisional or departmental performance and results.

Among the thirty-one companies studied, four plans for organizing the general-management function are found: (1) In some companies the chief executive handles this field, calling informally upon his fellow officers and divisional executives for advice and counsel as he may feel the need. (2) In other cases, the chief executive and a council of divisional or departmental executives perform the same function. (3) Other companies have set up a group of general executives to concentrate full time upon the problems of general management. (4) And, finally, in a few companies, a managing board of directors handles this field, as well as performing its natural trusteeship function. These four plans for organizing general management, as they were observed in the different companies, may be characterized and appraised as follows:

General Management through Chief Executive. One-third of the companies rely upon the chief executive, usually the president, to carry the major burden of general management, consulting informally with divisional executives as he deems necessary. Occasionally this amounts to a "one-man show." More frequently there is such close consultation between the chief executive and his fellow officers in regard to all major moves as to approximate council action. Unless the latter condition prevails this arrangement is subject to the following analysis:

ADVANTAGE. Tendency to expedite executive action.

DISADVANTAGES. Possibility that action may be taken without adequate consideration of all important aspects.

Lack of well-rounded experience, viewpoint, and knowledge of all major operations, which are available only through group consideration, and which are valuable aids to and checks upon the chief executive's judgment.

Tendency to overload the chief executive with matters that could be handled satisfactorily by others.

Inability of the chief executive, through lack of time and energy, to accomplish satisfactorily all the important functions and objectives of general management.

Failure to develop fellow officers to major stature through sharing the responsibility of general management with them.

Consequent maximum disruption of the enterprise when the chief executive finally retires or leaves the business.

General Management through Chief Executive and Council of Divisional Executives. Another third of the participating companies look to the chief executive and a part-time but formally constituted and representative council of divisional executives, called together from their divisional duties as necessary, to handle the broad administrative functions of general management. Characteristics of this plan may be summarized as follows:

1. The president (sometimes together with a chairman, vice-chairman, or executive vice-president) is the only executive devoting full time to general management.

2. In a few companies, he makes some of the decisions and exercises some of the functions of general management himself, taking up other matters with the council. In other companies, nearly all the decisions appear to be reached through the council, in order to assure that all aspects of each matter are given adequate consideration.

3. In all cases, the council, variously termed executive council, president's cabinet, officers' board, operating committee or management advisory committee, is a formally constituted agency, with members appointed by the chief executive, holding regular meetings weekly or oftener as required to transact business. Authority of the group is that delegated by the chief executive, who may ordinarily overrule any decision of the cabinet.

4. Council membership ranges from five to seventeen with an average of eight. Besides the chief executive, it usually includes the principal divisional executives whose interests or advice are most often of general concern.

Divisional members of these part-time councils devote their major time and attention to divisional interests, getting together as necessary to advise with the president in regard to general problems. The relative merits of this plan of general management appear to be as follows:

ADVANTAGE. Regular participation of representative divisional executives in council deliberations should assure adequate consideration of divisional interests and points of view. In addition, such participation should result in better understanding of and compliance with council action.

DISADVANTAGES. In the largest companies the problem of general management becomes so complex that it is questionable whether or not the part-time attention of a representative group of divisional executives is sufficient to find and chart the most profitable course for the business to follow, involving as it does the forecasting of general conditions, formulation of operating policies and objectives, co-ordination of plans, review and approval of major proposals, and appraisal of results.

It is difficult for divisional executives, absorbed in their day-to-day divisional problems and responsibilities, to cast this all aside and take a sufficiently broad company-wide viewpoint to be fully effective in the field of general management during the few hours a week in which they may serve on the council.

Insufficient attention is often devoted to broad planning for and direction of the business as a whole, because these can, without immediately apparent results, be deferred in favor of seemingly more pressing divisional matters.

There is a natural tendency for divisional executives to bring into the council divisional problems which properly need never concern it.

General Management through a Council of General Executives. In one-fourth of the companies studied, particularly those which have devoted the most attention to organization planning, the boards of directors have delegated the field of general management to a full-time group or council of general executives. This group determines operating policies and objectives and concentrates upon the broad direction, co-ordination, and control of the business as a whole. In order that they may devote their full time and energies to this important purpose, council members are usually relieved of direct responsibility for individual divisions or departments through effective delegation to divisional executives.

This arrangement for handling the general-management function, which appears to be particularly effective and toward which there is a discernible trend among the larger concerns, has the following typical characteristics:

1. In all those companies having such a plan, the board confines its sphere to proper trusteeship functions, the intermittent character of which necessitates meeting not oftener than once a month.

2. The executive council usually consists of the three to nine (average six) top active officers of the company, ordinarily the president and ranking vice-presidents, so chosen as to embrace a wide range of experience, back-

ground, and knowledge of the company's principal operations, such as manufacturing, marketing, and finance. As a rule, it is largely the same group that represents management on the board.

3. This group meets daily to weekly as required to transact its business, but the members devote their full time to the broad interests of the company as a whole.

4. While the members are not, as a rule, in charge of any specific phase of the company's operations, this responsibility being effectively delegated to divisional executives, they are usually looked to by the other members of the council and by divisional executives for consultation, co-ordination, and advice within the field of their special experience and background. Thus, particularly in companies which are set up on a product-division basis, council members with a broad manufacturing, marketing, or financial background are able to provide the necessary functional co-ordination between divisions.

5. This is ordinarily done on an advisory basis, however, divisional executives being accountable to the council, not to its individual members. In almost no case would a divisional executive expect to receive a "yes" or "no" decision from an individual council member; such decisions emanate only from the council as a whole. In this connection, it is noteworthy that in companies working under this plan even the president usually takes action through the council rather than as an individual.

6. In the words of one company, the council consists of a president and several "assistant presidents," each of whom has the same company-wide interest and viewpoint as the chief executive, thus multiplying the seasoned consideration of corporate problems.

7. Divisional executives consult members of the council to secure the benefit of their advice on major problems, to enlist their support on specific proposals in advance of council action, and to keep them informed as to what is going on. These contacts are voluntary, not mandatory, and though usually made with a designated council member, divisional executives are free to consult with any of the members at will.

8. Every effort is made to hold divisional executives fully responsible and accountable for successful conduct of their respective operations. They are expected to make their own decisions in regard to strictly divisional matters and to burden council members only with matters whose character or magnitude, as delimited by the council, make them of general concern. Even these matters are presented as well-considered and substantiated proposals for the council's final action.

9. Divisional executives appear frequently before the council, either at their own instigation to present some matter for decision, or upon request to explain or defend proposals or results.

This plan of general management appears to have the following advantages and disadvantages over other plans observed:

ADVANTAGES. Each of the three zones of top management is occupied by a separate agency, designed and constituted to do the most effective job in that particular field. This is broadly true even though usually all members of the general-management group and some members of the divisional-management group may also function as directors at periodic board meetings.

With a small group of top executives concentrating full time on the problems of general management and divorced from the problems and administrative routine of divisional management, the broad planning, direction, and co-ordination so vital to the success of the business as a whole are facilitated and assured.

The small executive group is able to take action easily, effectively, and informally, calling in divisional executives for specialized counsel and advice as necessary.

The time and energy of the top and, presumably, highest-paid officers and executives are devoted to the broad problems of the company as a whole, instead of being dissipated in handling responsibilities which divisional executives with their specialized experience may appropriately assume.

Throwing the full responsibility of divisional management and administration upon divisional executives serves to develop these men to their full potentialities.

DISADVANTAGES. Smaller companies may not feel able to afford a separate group of major executives concentrating on the broad, general aspects of the business as a whole, preferring to call in divisional executives to consult with the chief executive on general problems as necessary.

In such smaller organizations, too, the problems of general direction and co-ordination are less complex and may not require the full time of a general executive group to do them justice.

General Management through the Board of Directors. Two of the thirty-one companies studied rely upon a managing board of full-time executives to handle the entire burden of general management as well as their natural trusteeship function. In comparison with other plans observed, this arrangement is subject to the following appraisal:

ADVANTAGES. Most of the principal functions and activities are directly represented in management deliberations through membership of the responsible executives on the board of directors.

General management is kept thoroughly familiar with all major aspects of the business.

Co-ordination of interdivisional interests and development of a company-wide viewpoint are facilitated.

DISADVANTAGES. Such a large group (the full board of directors) is unwieldy in taking management action.

It is necessary to involve the whole board for frequent and extended periods in deliberation over problems that affect and are of prime interest to only a few members.

With the divisional management so heavily represented there is a natural tendency to burden the general group with the consideration of purely divisional problems which properly need never concern it.

Zone 3. Divisional- or Departmental-Management Function

Divisional management provides the active direction and management of the respective parts or divisions of the company within the scope of operating policies and authority delegated by general management. These parts may be operating departments, such as manufacturing and marketing, or staff departments, product divisions, regional divisions, or subsidiary companies.

Divisional executives are therefore defined as the topmost executives directly in charge of one or more of these divisions or departments, whether they be called vice-presidents, directors, general managers, managers, or presidents (as in the case of some subsidiaries). They are all directly accountable to the chief executive or to general management for the successful conduct of their respective parts of the business.

Divisional executives are distinguished from general executives in that they are immediately concerned with divisional or departmental rather than company-wide interests. A thorough knowledge of divisional operations and problems is therefore of greater moment than a wide knowledge, experience, and viewpoint of the company as a whole which are so important in the zone of general management.

The following considerations are of primary importance in the successful functioning of divisional management:

LOGICAL DIVISIONS. Whatever the nature of the division assigned to each divisional executive, whether a functional division, like manufacturing or marketing, a staff department, a product division, or a subsidiary company, sound organization requires that it be a logical, separable, clean-cut part of the whole. This facilitates the clear conception and definition of functions, objectives, and relationships, and, through the fact that records of performance naturally follow the same channels, makes it possible to measure divisional results effectively.

In some companies, certain divisional executives appear to have an unrelated hodgepodge of activities under their direction. In other companies, the primary divisions are confined to single major functions, product divisions, departments, or logical groups of closely related activities. This appears to facilitate their effective management by permitting concentration and specialization of executive attention.

NUMBER OF DIVISIONS. The number of divisions reporting directly to general management varies widely. In one well-organized company practically all activities head up to four divisional vice-presidents in charge of manufacturing, marketing, financial, and purchasing activities, respectively. The other extreme is reached in the case of a company set up on a product-division basis, where there are ten product-division managers and fourteen staff and service department heads, all report-

Table 1. Four Basic Types of Top-Management Organization

This chart illustrates the four general methods found among the participating companies for organizing the three levels of top management. It will be observed that the principal point of difference relates to the arrangement for handling the general-management function.

THE THREE ZONES OF TOP MANAGEMENT	TYPE A	TYPE B	TYPE C	TYPE D
ZONE 1 TRUSTEESHIP MANAGEMENT Representing, safeguarding, and furthering stockholders' interests; determining basic policies and broad course of the business; reviewing and appraising over-all results	*Board of Directors* Meeting usually monthly or quarterly	*Board of Directors* Meetings usually monthly or quarterly	*Board of Directors* Meeting usually monthly or quarterly	*Board of Directors* Meeting weekly or oftener as necessary
ZONE 2 GENERAL MANAGEMENT Planning, directing, co-ordinating, and controlling the business as a whole—determining objectives, establishing operating policies, and securing results—within the scope of basic policies established and authority delegated by the board	*Chief Executive* Consulting informally with individual departmental executives as necessary	*Chief Executive* Working in conjunction with a formally constituted *Council of Divisional Executives* Who are called together as necessary from their departmental duties Meeting weekly or oftener as occasion demands	*Council of General Executives* Consisting of the chief executive and a few other top officers who devote full time to the interests of the business as a whole, delegating to departmental or divisional executives wide responsibility for management of specific operations Meeting several times a week	*Board of Directors* Meeting several time a week
ZONE 3 DIVISIONAL MANAGEMENT Standing fully accountable to general management for the successful conduct of the respective departments, divisions, or subsidiaries of the company	*Divisional Executives* Including all executives, regardless of rank or title, who are directly responsible to general management for their respective departments, divisions, or subsidiaries	*Divisional Executives* Including all executives, regardless of rank or title, who are directly responsible to general management for their respective departments, divisions, or subsidiaries	*Divisional Executives* Including all executives, regardless of rank or title, who are directly responsible to general management for their respective departments, divisions, or subsidiaries	*Individual Directors* Devoting major attention to the management of their respective departments, divisions, and subsidiaries.

93

ing to the president. It appears that under this latter arrangement, unless some special provision is made to the contrary, the demands upon the president's time for maintaining necessary contacts with such a large number of divisional executives might prove burdensome. There is a prevalent conviction that the number of subordinates reporting to a single executive should be definitely limited in order that each may get the attention he needs without overburdening his principal.

RESPONSIBILITY, AUTHORITY, AND ACCOUNTABILITY. General management, whether it consists of the president or a full-time group of general executives, should keep itself free of divisional detail, concentrating its full time and energy upon the larger problems of overall direction and control. Divisional executives should be expected to handle their strictly divisional problems without burdening their principals, assuming as nearly full proprietary responsibility and accountability for the successful conduct of divisional operations as is consistent with the need for over-all coordination and control. The most effective steps found among the participating companies for insuring and furthering this objective are:

Clear-cut delineation of the functions, responsibilities, and relationships of each divisional executive through job specifications in the organization manual.

Delegation to divisional executives of adequate authority, commensurate with these responsibilities, within limits specifically defined.

The establishment of definite objectives and suitable measures of what constitutes the divisional job well done. This may take the form of budgetary planning, standards of performance, or other devices of control.

Effective current comparison and appraisal of actual results against the preplanned objectives, and the taking of necessary action to stimulate improvement where it is needed.

A conscious effort on the part of general executives to render advice and counsel as requested, but to give no decisions, as individuals, within the field delegated to divisional executives. The latter are expected to make up their own minds, take appropriate action, and stand accountable for results.

Insistence that matters presented for the action of general management be submitted in the form of well-substantiated proposals or recommendations.

Effective use of staff agencies to analyze and digest proposals as a preliminary to general management's consideration.

Selections from "Scientific Management"

Bricklaying is one of the oldest of our trades. For hundreds of years there has been little or no improvement made in the implements and materials used in this trade, nor in fact in the method of laying bricks. In spite of the millions of men who have practised this trade, no great improvement has been evolved for many generations. Here, then, at least, one would expect to find but little gain possible through scientific analysis and study. Mr. Frank B. Gilbreth, who had himself studied bricklaying in his youth, became interested in the principles of scientific management, and decided to apply them to the art of bricklaying. He made an intensely interesting analysis and study of each movement of the bricklayer, and one after another eliminated all unnecessary movements and substituted fast for slow motions. He experimented with every minute element which in any way affects the speed and the tiring of the bricklayer.

He developed the exact position which each of the feet of the bricklayer should occupy with relation to the wall, the mortar box, and the pile of bricks, and so made it unnecessary for him to take a step or two toward the pile of bricks and back again each time a brick is laid.

He studied the best height for the mortar box and brick pile, and then designed a scaffold, with a table on it, upon which all the materials are placed, so as to keep the bricks, the mortar, the man, and the wall in their proper relative positions. These scaffolds are adjusted, as the wall grows in height, for all of the bricklayers by a laborer especially detailed for this purpose, and by this means the bricklayer is saved the exertion of stooping down to the level of his feet for each brick and each trowelful of mortar and then straightening up again. Think of the waste of effort that has

gone on through all these years, with each bricklayer lowering his body, weighing, say, 150 pounds, down two feet and raising it up again every time a brick (weighing about 5 pounds) is laid in the wall! And this each bricklayer did about one thousand times a day.

As a result of further study, after the bricks are unloaded from the cars, and before bringing them to the bricklayer, they are carefully sorted by a laborer, and placed with their best edge up on a simple wooden frame, constructed so as to enable him to take hold of each brick in the quickest time and in the most advantageous position. In this way the bricklayer avoids either having to turn the brick over or end for end to examine it before laying it, and he saves, also, the time taken in deciding which is the best edge and end to place on the outside of the wall. In most cases, also, he saves the time taken in disentangling the brick from a disorderly pile on the scaffold. This "pack" of bricks (as Mr. Gilbreth calls his loaded wooden frames) is placed by the helper in its proper position on the adjustable scaffold close to the mortar box.

We have all been used to seeing bricklayers tap each brick after it is placed on its bed of mortar several times with the end of the handle of the trowel so as to secure the right thickness for the joint. Mr. Gilbreth found that by tempering the mortar just right, the bricks could be readily bedded to the proper depth by a downward pressure of the hand with which they are laid. He insisted that his mortar mixers should give special attention to tempering the mortar, and so save the time consumed in tapping the brick.

Through all of this minute study of the motions to be made by the bricklayer in laying bricks under standard conditions, Mr. Gilbreth has reduced his movements from eighteen motions per brick to five, and even in one case to as low as two motions per brick. He has given all of the details of this analysis to the profession in the chapter headed "Motion Study," of his book entitled "Bricklaying Sys-

From Fredrick Taylor, "Scientific Management" in *Scientific Management*, Harper, New York, 1947, pp. 77–85, 122–123. Reprinted with permission of the publisher.

tem," published by Myron C. Clerk Publishing Company, New York and Chicago; E. F. N. Spon, of London.

An analysis of the expedients used by Mr. Gilbreth in reducing the motions of his bricklayers from eighteen to five shows that this improvement has been made in three different ways:

First. He has entirely dispensed with certain movements which the bricklayers in the past believed were necessary, but which a careful study and trial on his part have shown to be useless.

Second. He has introduced simple apparatus, such as his adjustable scaffold and his packets for holding the bricks, by means of which, with a very small amount of cooperation from a cheap laborer, he entirely eliminates a lot of tiresome and time-consuming motions which are necessary for the bricklayer who lacks the scaffold and the packet.

Third. He teaches his bricklayers to make simple motions with both hands at the same time, where before they completed a motion with the right hand and followed it later with one from the left hand.

For example, Mr. Gilbreth teaches his bricklayer to pick up a brick in the left hand at the same instant that he takes a trowelful of mortar with the right hand. This work with two hands at the same time is, of course, made possible by substituting a deep mortar box for the old mortar board (on which the mortar spread out so thin that a step or two had to be taken to reach it) and then placing the mortar box and the brick pile close together, and at the proper height on his new scaffold.

These three kinds of improvements are typical of the ways in which needless motions can be entirely eliminated and quicker types of movements substituted for slow movements when scientific motion study, as Mr. Gilbreth calls his analysis, time study, as the writer has called similar work, are applied in any trade.

Most practical men would (knowing the opposition of almost all tradesmen to making any change in their methods and habits), however, be skeptical as to the possibility of actually achieving any large results from a study of this sort. Mr. Gilbreth reports that a few months ago, in a large brick building which he erected, he demonstrated on a commercial scale the great gain which is possible from

practically applying his scientific study. With union bricklayers, in laying a factory wall, twelve inches thick, with two kinds of brick, faced and ruled joints on both sides of the wall, he averaged, after his selected workmen had become skilful in his new methods, 350 bricks per man *per hour;* whereas the average speed of doing this work with the old methods was, in that section of the country, 120 bricks per man per hour. His bricklayers were taught his new method of bricklaying by their foreman. Those who failed to profit by their teaching were dropped, and each man, as he became proficient under the new method, received a substantial (not a small) increase in his wages. With a view to individualizing his workmen and stimulating each man to do his best, Mr. Gilbreth also developed an ingenious method for measuring and recording the number of bricks laid by each man, and for telling each workman at frequent intervals how many bricks he had succeeded in laying.

It is only when this work is compared with the conditions which prevail under the tyranny of some of our misguided bricklayers' unions that the great waste of human effort which is going on will be realized. In one foreign city the bricklayers' union have restricted their men to 275 *bricks per day* on work of this character when working for the city, and 375 per day when working for private owners. The members of this union are probably sincere in their belief that this restriction of output is a benefit to their trade. It should be plain to all men, however, that this deliberate loafing is almost criminal, in that it inevitably results in making every workman's family pay higher rent for their housing, and also in the end drives work and trade away from their city, instead of bringing it to it.

Why is it, in a trade which has been continually practised since before the Christian era, and with implements practically the same as they now are, that this simplification of the bricklayer's movements, this great gain, has not been made before?

It is highly likely that many times during all of these years individual bricklayers have recognized the possibility of eliminating each of these unnecessary motions. But even if, in the past, he did invent each one of Mr. Gilbreth's improvements, no bricklayer could alone increase his speed through their adoption because it will be remembered that in all cases several bricklayers work together in a row and that the walls all around a building must grow at the same rate of speed. No one bricklayer, then, can work much faster than the one next to him. Nor has any one workman the authority to make other men cooperate with him to do faster work. It is only through *enforced* standardization of methods, *enforced* adoption of the best implements and working conditions, and *enforced* cooperation that this faster work can be assured. And the duty of enforcing the adoption of standards and of enforcing this cooperation rests with the *management* alone. The *management* must supply continually one or more teachers to show each new man the new and simpler motions, and the slower men must be constantly watched and helped until they have risen to their proper speed. All of those who, after proper teaching, either will not or cannot work in accordance with the new methods and at the higher speed must be discharged by the *management*. The *management* must also recognize the broad fact that workmen will not submit to this more rigid standardization and will not work extra hard, unless they receive extra pay for doing it.

All of this involves an individual study of and treatment for each man, while in the past they have been handled in large groups.

The *management* must also see that those who prepare the bricks and the mortar and adjust the scaffold, etc., for the bricklayers, cooperate with them by doing their work just right and always on time; and they must also inform each bricklayer at frequent intervals as to the progress he is making, so that he may not unintentionally fall off in his pace. Thus it will be seen that it is the assumption by the management of new duties and new kinds of work never done by employers in the past that makes this great improvement possible, and that, without this new help from the management, the workman even with full knowledge of the new methods and with the best of intentions could not attain these startling results.

Mr. Gilbreth's method of bricklaying furnishes a simple illustration of true and effective cooperation. Not the type of cooperation in which a mass of workmen on one side together cooperate with the management; but that in which several men in the management (each one in his own particular way) help each workman individually, on the one hand,

by studying his needs and his shortcomings and teaching him better and quicker methods, and, on the other hand, by seeing that all other workmen with whom he comes in contact help and cooperate with him by doing their part of the work right and fast.

The writer has gone thus fully into Mr. Gilbreth's method in order that it may be perfectly clear that this increase in output and that this harmony could not have been attained under the management of "initiative and incentive" (that is, by putting the problem up to the workman and leaving him to solve it alone) which has been the philosophy of the past. And that his success has been due to the use of the four elements which constitute the essence of scientific management.

First. The development (by the management, not the workman) of the science of bricklaying, with rigid rules for each motion of every man, and the perfection and standardization of all implements and working conditions.

Second. The careful selection and subsequent training of the bricklayers into first-class men, and the elimination of all men who refuse to or are unable to adopt the best methods.

Third. Bringing the first-class bricklayer and the science of bricklaying together, through the constant help and watchfulness of the management, and through paying each man a large daily bonus for working fast and doing what he is told to do.

Fourth. An almost equal division of the work and responsibility between the workman and the management. All day long the management work almost side by side with the men, helping, encouraging, and smoothing the way for them, while in the past they stood one side, gave the men but little help, and threw on to them almost the entire responsibility as to methods, implements, speed, and harmonious cooperation.

The necessity for systematically teaching workmen how to work to the best advantage has been several times referred to. It seems desirable, therefore, to explain in rather more detail how this teaching is done. In the case of a machine-shop which is managed under the modern system, detailed written instructions as to the best way of doing each piece of work are prepared in advance, by men in the planning department. These instructions represent the combined work of several men in the planning room, each of whom has his own specialty, or function. One of them, for instance, is a specialist on the proper speeds and cutting tools to be used. He uses the slide-rules which have been above described as an aid, to guide him in obtaining proper speeds, etc. Another man analyzes the best and quickest motions to be made by the workman in setting the work up in the machine and removing it, etc. Still a third, through the time-study records which have been accumulated, makes out a timetable giving the proper speed for doing each element of the work. The directions of all of these men, however, are written on a single instruction card, or sheet.

Toward the New Organization Theories: Some Notes on "Staff" *

ROBERT T. GOLEMBIEWSKI

ORGANIZATION THEORY is fast approaching a major reshaping.[1] The burgeoning of the behavioral sciences, most prominently in small-group analysis, erodes the bases of traditional organization theory at a microscopic level: [2] knowledge of group and personality properties sharply reveals the theory's inadequacies.

Reprinted from *Midwest Journal of Political Science*, Vol. V, No. 3 (August, 1961), 237–246.
* This title requires explanation. There eventually will be a general *empirical theory* of organization, that is, a statement of what is related to what under various conditions. Such an empirical theory will permit the development of any number of *goal-based, empirical theories*. These theories will prescribe the conditions under which various sets of objectives may be attained.

This article points toward the development of new organization theories, both empirical and goal-based empirical. Hence the title above.

In contrast, the literature suffers from the unfortunate emphasis upon *an* organization theory. Indeed, the traditional theory of organization (to be analyzed presently) is often offered as universally valid in both descriptive and prescriptive senses. That is, the traditional organization theory is presented as the general empirical theory. Moreover, the theory is presumed to be the only goal-based empirical theory worth developing. The distinctions between theory-types will be reflected in the analysis. Thus both the descriptive and the prescriptive adequacy of traditional organization theory will be scrutinized here. By way of preview, this theory does not describe reality. Moreover, when the conditions prescribed by the theory do exist, the expected consequences often do not result. The theory-types, and their methodological implications, are considered in more detail in this author's " 'The Group Basis of Politics': Notes on Analysis and Development," *American Political Science Review*, 54 (December, 1960), 962–971.

[1] Mason Haire (ed.), *Modern Organization Theory* (New York: Wiley, 1959).
[2] Robert T. Golembiewski, "The Small Group and Public Administration," *Public Administration Review*, 19 (Summer, 1959), 149–156.

Moreover, a critical literature of long standing complements this challenge to students of organization at a macroscopic level. For example, Stahl has argued that the traditional concept of "staff" as advisor of, and subordinate to, "line" units at all levels "not only *should not be* the case but *is not* and *never has been* the case." [3]

This paper contributes to this reshaping of organization theory through an examination of the intimate relations between traditional organization theory and the concept of "staff" it supports. The focus is upon the relation of Stahl's position and the revamping of traditional organization theory, which Stahl did not consider. The purpose is to complement what Stahl did, not to indict him for what he did not intend to do.

The burden of this analysis may be abstracted. Three main themes—although they are not considered seriatim—dominate the treatment. The traditional "staff" concept, it will be shown, is a derivative from a general theory of organization whose purportedly empirical propositions inadequately reflect reality. Moreover, the "staff" concept is inadequate for describing relations within and among organizations. Finally, the traditional "staff" concept often does not lead to effective administration even when individuals act in the ways it prescribes. The analysis builds toward these three themes by considering, in order: the skeleton of Stahl's argument; some ideal concepts of "staff"; the traditional "staff" concept as a derivative from a general theory of organization; the method of the general theory of organization and, environmental changes which have undercut the general the-

[3] O. Glenn Stahl, "More on the Network of Authority," *Public Administration Review*, 20 (Winter, 1960), 35 (my emphases). See also his "Straight Talk About Label Thinking," *Public Administration Review*, 6 (Autumn, 1946), 362–367; and "The Network of Authority," *Public Administration Review*, 18 (Winter, 1958), ii–iv.

ory of organization and, thus, the traditional "staff" concept.

The Network of Authority

Stahl recently has argued his thesis that "line" and "staff" are hardly "distinguishable as indicators of power status" in two brief pieces.[4] The following propositions (in Stahl's wording) summarize his thesis: [5]

1. that so-called staff units usually do and must necessarily carry out functions of command.
2. that there are some activities for which there is an inescapable need for organization adherence [which activities the so-called staff units are in the best position to police];
3. that a staff activity is no more a restricted, specialized function than . . . line segments . . . ;
4. that staff functions, having to do with *how* things are done more than *what* is done, assume a special importance in the public service;
5. that it is convenient to think of line and staff as "program" functions and "sustaining" functions, respectively, which interlace with each other in a *network;* that the chief executive controls the organization by means of both vertical "program" channels and the horizontal "sustaining" channels; and
6. . . . that conflicts are reconciled and communication facilitated at lower levels in the organization when there is no presumption of unvarying command superiority of line over staff.

Some "Staff" Concepts

Two themes outline this section: (1) that the literature about "staff" is not monolithic, and practice is ever more variegated; but (2) that nevertheless, in terms of central tendencies, a concept has been emphasized which stands in sharp contrast to Stahl's position.

Both themes can be developed by outlining several *ideal styles* of the relations of agencies or individuals performing "sustaining" functions with those performing "program" functions. "Staff" will not be differentiated in terms of the designations commonly assigned to agencies ("general staff," for example) or to individuals ("chief of staff" or "assistant-to," for example). The three styles analyzed, however, will cover the full range of ideal relations of any "sustaining" activity with any "program" activity.[6]

The "colleague" style of "staff," first, implies formal authority independent of—and sometimes superior to—the "line." Consider the German practice of sending direct representatives of headquarters into critical battle areas, not as "line" commanders but as chiefs of staff. These chiefs of staff participated in, and sometimes assumed, command. Their relations with "line" commanders thus were fluid. As one commentator described these relations: [7]

Always the commander commands through the chief and the chief's orders even older subordinate commanders have to follow without murmur . . . How far the chief can go in issuing orders without the knowledge of his commander is a question that can be decided only between the two and cannot be judged by any outsider.

The concluding sentence is a crucial one. The relations of the "staff" man and the field commander cannot be described simply. They will be determined "only between the two." Moreover, the "colleague" concept of "staff" does not hide the relation of a superior "line" official who is a direct representative of headquarters with a subordinate "line" official in the field. Indeed, the traditional notions of "line" (see the third "staff" concept below) do not apply. For a bargaining situation is implicit in the "colleague" concept. And the traditional "line-staff" distinction permits no such indeterminacy.

---

[4] "The Network of Authority"; and "More on the Network of Authority."

[5] "More on the Network of Authority," *loc. cit.,* p. 35.

[6] The designations above, for example, are employed in Ernest Dale and Lyndall F. Urwick, *Staff in Organization* (New York: McGraw-Hill, 1960), pp. 80–109. The concern here is with idealized relations. This is an analytical convenience rather than an assumption about behavior.

[7] Hans von Seeckt, *Gedanken eines Soldaten* (Berlin: Verlag für Kulturpolitik, 1929), p. 163.

The fluidity of the "colleague" concept has this intention: to encourage the active participation in the command function of individuals whose formal positions encourage differing orientations to problem situations. The factors of jurisdiction and pressure of time, for example, would encourage such differing orientations. Jurisdiction-wise, the field commander would tend to emphasize those conditions dominant in his problem area, the "staff" man to be more oriented toward overall policy and strategy. Temporally, the here-and-now would tend to be of most concern to the field commander. A longer-run view would tend to influence the "colleague."

This first concept, then, attempts to provide for the integration of the "part" and the "whole," which is one of the base problems of administration. (In the case of a personnel "staff" service, or similar organization-wide function, the "whole" would be the functional area, the "part" the personnel matters of any administrative unit.) But, significantly, this first concept of "staff" does not attempt to handcuff organizationally either the commander or the "colleague." For, by implication, to do so would result in the inadequate expression of either particularistic or overall considerations.

A second concept of "staff" implies less indeterminacy. This second concept may be called the "alter ego" type. To illustrate the type, the U. S. Army's *Staff Officers' Field Manual* noted that the "staff of a unit consists of the officers *who assist the commander in his exercise of command*." Such assistance is of a quite intimate nature. For the staff officer is enjoined to "live inside the mind of the commanding general, and know what his policies are, even though they have not been announced." [8] This "living inside of" may be reflected, for example, in orders signed by the staff officer "in the name of the commander." Field Marshal Montgomery's *Memoirs* give a precise picture of the relations involved. He articulated his notion of "line-staff" relations in this way: [9]

> I appointed de Guingand Chief of Staff . . . ; every order given by him would be regarded as coming from me and would be obeyed instantly.
> [The night of the major battle of the African war, I] went to bed early. At 9:40 p.m. the barrage of over 1,000 guns opened, and the Eighth Army went into attack. At that moment I was asleep in my caravan. . . .
> [The battle went poorly.] De Guingand rightly issued orders for a conference at my Tactical HQ . . . and then woke me and told me what he had done. I agreed.

The "alter ego" concept of "staff," then, restricts behavior far more than the "colleague" concept. The "alter ego's" orders are to be obeyed, but these orders merely articulate for the commander. There is no provision for the bargaining implied in the "colleague" concept. The "staff" man assumes the personality of the commander, ideally, rather than asserts his own.

Despite the wide usage of these two "staff" concepts and their reputation for getting results,[10] American students of organization—especially in Public Administration—generally have chosen a third concept. It can be characterized as the "neutral and inferior instrument" concept. It is, of course, very familiar. White described it in these terms in his very influential text: [11]

> line authorities . . . are the central elements of any administrative system; staff and auxiliary agencies are necessary in a large and complex organization, *but they are secondary*. They serve the line; the line serves the people.

Thus "staff" in this concept is: "outside the lines of command"; "deliberate organization for

[8] War Department, *Staff Officers' Field Manual: The Staff and Combat Orders* (Washington: 1940), p. 1, is the source of the description. The nature of the assistance is described by Richard M. Leighton, *History of Control Division, ASF, 1942–45* (Historical Section, Control Division, Army Service Forces, April 1946, mimeo'd), p. 205.

[9] Bernard Law Montgomery, *The Memoirs of . . . the Viscount Montgomery of Alamein* (Cleveland: World Publishing Co., 1958), pp. 93–94 and 118.
[10] See Alvin Brown, *The Armor of Organization* (New York: Hibbert Printing Co., 1953), pp. 92–97.
[11] Leonard D. White, *An Introduction to the Study of Public Administration* (New York: Macmillan, 1955), p. 195.

thought rather than execution"; and "purely advisory." Illustratively, no orders can be issued by the "staff" official who respects the "neutral and inferior instrument" concept of "staff." Nor need such orders be obeyed, *in theory*, were they to be issued. In contrast, the two previous concepts (and especially the "colleague" concept) include ample room for "staff" work inside the lines of command, for execution as well as thought, and for action as well as advice.

The three concepts of "staff," then, cover a broad range of ideal relations. This range of relations may be represented by a funnel. The "colleague" concept is represented by the funnel's wide mouth. It provides broad scope for "staff" behavior. The "alter ego" concept is represented by some cross-sectional area further down the cone of the funnel. And the "neutral and inferior" concept is represented by the narrow tube of the funnel, signifying a very restricted range of sanctioned behaviors. More succinctly, the "colleague" concept is most akin to the position for "staff" recommended by Stahl. The "neutral and inferior instrument" concept, in contrast, is the target of Stahl's criticism.

The three concepts illustrate the variations in "staff" usage. Two cautions, however, must be observed. First, no distinctions are made between "private staffs" and, for example, "staffs" which are themselves complex organizations. For many purposes, such distinctions are crucial. Moreover, second, the aim is simply the outline of possible styles of idealized relations of "program" and "sustaining" functions. Thus the important question of the organizational set-up which would encourage, for example, "colleague"-type relations is not considered.

The "Principles" of Traditional Organization Theory

The explanation of the general choice of the "neutral and inferior instrument" concept by students of organization is a complex problem. The emphasis here is upon a single, but major, explanatory factor: the "staff" concept is merely the protruding tip of the larger body of organization theory which, in general, is reflected in the literature of both business and public administration. This derivative nature of "staff" implies an important point of analyt-

ical strategy. It does not suffice to analyze the derivations of a theory. For, even if one of the off-shoots of such an underlying theory is expertly nipped, the theory still remains.[12] And no doubt it will induce a similar derivation in time. Consequently, this analysis will resist the temptation to concentrate upon the interesting difficulties implied by the "neutral and inferior instrument" concept, such as the maintenance of the separation of "service" and "control" which is required by the concept.[13]

There is wide agreement about the properties of the "principles" common to public and business administration.[14] Hundreds of volumes on traditional organization theory emphasize such "principles" as specialization, one-line authority and responsibility, and unity of command. These "principles"—although they do not exhaust the usual lists—are the more central ones of traditional organization theory. And they are also most useful in demonstrating the derivative nature of the "neutral and inferior instrument" concept of "staff." These "principles," in the order listed above, are framed in propositions such as these:

1. Administrative efficiency is increased by specialization of the work process.
2. Administrative efficiency is increased when organization members are arranged in a definite hierarchy of authority from top to bottom and of responsibility from bottom to top, with a single head at the apex and a broad base at the bottom.
3. Administrative efficiency is increased if the unity of command is preserved, that is, if each organization member reports to but one superior.

[12] Perhaps the most expert nipping of "staff" was contributed by Herbert A. Simon, Donald V. Smithburg, and Victor Thompson, *Public Administration* (New York: Knopf, 1956), esp. pp. 280–291.

[13] For a discussion of some of these problems, see Frank M. Stewart, "Purchasing of Highway Equipment in Texas," *American Political Science Review*, 29 (May, 1930), 409–15; Willard W. Hogan, "A Dangerous Tendency in Government," *Public Administration Review*, 6 (Summer, 1946), 235–239; and Stahl, "Straight Talk About Label Thinking," *loc. cit.*

[14] See, for example, John M. Pfiffner and Frank P. Sherwood, *Administrative Organization* (Englewood Cliffs: Prentice-Hall, 1960), esp. pp. 52–95.

The "neutral and inferior instrument" concept of "staff" is most consistent with the "principles." Of course, all three ideal concepts of "staff" seem to respect the "principle" of specialization, and little wonder, given its unhappy vagueness. The "principles" of one-line authority and unity of command, however, could be logically at home only with the "neutral and inferior instrument" concept of "staff." Thus "staff" became "purely advisory" and "outside the lines of command." No other concept of "staff" could have avoided so completely any challenge to traditional organization theory.

The molding of the "staff" concept to one-line authority and unity of command received several assists. The apparently greater importance of the "line" functions under the then-existing technology, for example, had this effect. Similarly, an empirically naïve but widely professed notion of "popular control" in a democracy provided such an assist in Public Administration. The implicit rationale underlying the central "principles" of one-line authority and unity of command, to develop the point, takes this form: this is a democracy; in a democracy, the people must control the government; but the people elect (quasi-) directly only the chief executive; therefore, the president must control administrative officers.[15] Given the assumption that the "line" should be and/or is fundamentally different from "staff," the convenient alternative was to make "staff" subordinate to the "line." This avoided some embarrassing questions, but posed others.

There also were practical, as well as theoretical, reasons for fitting the "staff" concept to the "principles" of one-line authority and

unity of command. These practical reasons encouraged the adoption of the "neutral and inferior instrument" concept in business as well as public administration. Thus one of the embarrassing problems which the traditional "staff" formulation seemed to solve was the acute one of making some peace with patterns of organization which existed before the advent of "staff" aid. These patterns, in sum, were based upon the one-line authority and unity of command of traditional organization theory. The "principles," then, were reinforced by resistance to change. For "staff" units posed a real challenge to the "principles" and to organization practice as well: the purpose of "staff" units was to perform functions "line" officials had performed. The "neutral and inferior instrument" concept at once left the dogma undisturbed and reduced resistance by "line" officials.

Near the turn of this century, to explain, the position of the "line" supervisor was an uncomplicated one. The first-line supervisor, for example, had control, period. He normally hired and fired, scheduled production, set and administered wages, and so on. By 1930, however, many of the foreman's previous functions had passed to "staff" agencies. Thus Personnel, Production Scheduling, Accounting, and the like developed as separate organizational functions. The supervisor no longer controlled, period.

The "neutral and inferior instrument" concept eased the transition. For it seemed to avoid the difficulty implicit in an overt threat to the power of the "line," while meeting the need of rapid and increased specialization attendant on techological advances and growth in the scale of enterprises. This balance is a delicate one. For, after all, the work of the new "staff" had been done by "line" officials, somehow. And the "line" naturally valued their contributions and experience above what often seemed the pretensions of the new specialists. As Dale and Urwick frame this problem and the way in which the traditional "staff" concept seemed to resolve it: [16]

. . . the introduction of many of the forms of specialization in personnel, industrial engineering, research, and so on, to which business is now well accustomed, appeared [absurd and unnatural] to line departmental

[15] This is, of course, a bald statement. Consequently, it is easy to fault. Thus the people elect legislators, and sometimes judges, in addition to a chief executive; and in some states, administrative officers other than governors also are elected; and so on. But such a bald statement—in more or less diluted form—underlies even sophisticated commentary, e. g., much of the literature on government reorganization. The argument above, for example, pervades the *Report* of the President's Committee on Administrative Management (Washington, D.C.: Government Printing Office, 1937). Relevantly, legislative control of administration is understressed (to put it mildly); the independent regulatory commissions draw particularly heavy criticism; and so on.

[16] Dale and Urwick, *op. cit.*, pp. 163–165.

managers and foremen early in this century. They opposed their introduction lustily, and progressive business leaders who realized the necessity for these innovations if their undertakings were to survive were hard put.
. . .

So the fur flew, and harassed chief executives in business after business were driven into a hysteria of assurances that staff specialists were not meant to do what they had manifestly been hired to do. The line managers were solemnly told that the staff men were "purely advisory" and that no one need take their advice if they did not want to. . . .

This explanation provided by the "neutral and inferior instrument" was, to Dale and Urwick, "a glaring example of the irrational."

The alliance—irrational or not—of the "principles" and the "neutral and inferior instrument" concept has proved a stable and lasting one. This lasting alliance constitutes the next explanatory burden. Thus the tendentiousness of both the "principles" and the traditional "staff" concept in the face of massive contradictory evidence will be illustrated. In addition, an attempt will be made to explain this persisting bias in terms of the method of the organization theory which supports the "neutral and inferior instrument" concept of "staff."

The inadequacies of traditional organization theory often have been stressed.[17] This critical literature expresses logical, empirical, and value reservations about the traditional theory. This literature need not and cannot be reviewed here in any detail. We may content ourselves with an overview which focuses upon a limited portion of a single aspect of the case against the "principles," their lack of specificity. Traditional organization theory, to begin, has important logical defects. The "principles" of specialization and the pair of unity of command and one-line authority, for example, reflect two unreconciled strains of traditional organization theory. As Simon concluded in his classic paper: [18]

What is needed to decide the issue is a principle of administration that would enable one to weigh the relative advantages of the two courses of action. But neither the principle of unity of command nor the principle of specialization·is helpful in adjudicating the controversy. They merely contradict each other without indicating any procedure for resolving the contradiction.

Moreover, the "principles" are not well grounded empirically. Value questions are also begged by this empirical footlooseness. To illustrate, the "principles" do not specify the behavioral conditions under which they will apply to man *qua* man, as opposed to man as a mechanical system. This is empirically inelegant. Such empirical specification, existing research demonstrates, will require major revamping of traditional organization theory.[19] This empirical shortcoming also implies a moral insensitivity. For it runs the great risk of obscuring the fact that these behavioral conditions are value-loaded, and must be evaluated in terms other than whether these conditions exist or not.

Similarly, the "principles" are offered as size- and level-universal. That is, they are allegedly applicable to administrative units of all sizes and at all levels.[20] But actually they reflect a low-level preoccupation. The kinship between the "principles" and the organization theory derived by Taylor from his time-and-motion analysis, to explain, often has been emphasized. And it is the case (as one student noted) "that Taylor never went beyond the foreman." [21] The "principles" conveniently, if illegitimately, extrapolated Taylor's low-level working propositions to all organization levels. This extrapolation assumes that which requires study. Consequently, the more levels in an organization to which the "principles" are applied, the less satisfactory the fit with empirical conditions is likely to be.

[17] See the spate of early studies emphasizing the non-empirical nature of the "principles," for example. One of the earlier efforts of this kind is F. W. Coker's, "Dogmas of Administrative Reform," *American Political Science Review*, 16 (August, 1922), 399–411.

[18] Herbert A. Simon, "The Proverbs of Administration," *Public Administration Review*, 6 (Winter, 1946), 53–67. The quotation from this article in this paragraph is from p. 55.

[19] Much relevant data is summarized by Chris Argyris, *Personality and Organization* (New York: Harper, 1957).

[20] The point is raised and criticized by Norman M. Pearson, "The Budget Bureau: From Routine Business to General Staff," *Public Administration Review* 3 (Spring, 1943), 127.

[21] Norman M. Pearson, "Fayolism as the Necessary Complement of Taylorism," *American Political Science Review*, 39 (February, 1945), 69.

The Coordinative Principle

JAMES MOONEY

Organization begins when people combine their efforts for a given purpose. We have shown this by the simple illustration of two people uniting their efforts to lift and move some weighty object. This combination, however, is not the first principle of organization. It is only an illustration of organization itself.

To find the first principle, let us carry the illustration a step further. The efforts of these two lifters must be coordinated, which means that they must act together. If first one lifted, and then the other, there would be no unity of action, and hence no true organization of effort. Coordination first appeared in organization when one of those hairy, slow-witted ancestors of ours assumed authority and gave the guttural equivalent of "Heave ho!" *Here, then, we find the first principle of organization.*

Coordination therefore, is the orderly arrangement of group effort, to provide unity of action in the pursuit of a common purpose.

When we call *coordination* the first principle, we mean that this term expresses the principles of organization *in toto*; nothing less. This does not mean that there are no subordinated principles; it simply means that all the others are contained in this one of coordination. The others are simply the principles through which coordination operates and thus becomes effective.

As coordination contains all the principles of organization, it likewise expresses all the purposes of organization, in so far as these purposes relate to its internal structure. To avoid confusion we must keep in mind that there are always two objectives of organization, the *internal* and the *external*. The latter may be anything, according to the purpose or interest that calls the group together, but the internal objective is coordinative always.

AUTHORITY. In some spheres of organization the external objective is not continuous. This is true of army organizations in peace-time, when all external objectives are in abeyance, and the army merely waits for mobilization day, for the day of action. In every form of organization, however, the internal objective must be constant. This internal objective is organized efficiency, and everything that is essential to such efficiency is expressed in the single word "coordination." There can be no waiting for "M-day" in coordination. It is a constant necessity in organization, essential to the existence of the organization itself.

As coordination is the all-inclusive principle of organization, it must have its own principle and foundation in *authority*, or the supreme coordinating power. Always, in every form of organization, this supreme authority must rest somewhere, else there would be no directive for any coordinated effort.

The term "authority," as here used, need not imply autocracy. Where true democracy prevails, this authority rests with the group as a whole, as it rests in our government with the people of the United States. In the simplest and most compact forms of democratic organization it is represented in the entire group, assembled at one time, in one place. Examples in secular government are separated as widely in

From *Principles of Organization*, New York: Harper and Brothers, 1947, pp. 5–8. Reprinted with permission of the publisher.

time as the ecclesia of ancient Athens and the present New England town meeting.

In whatever form it may appear, this supreme coordinating authority must be conceived simply as the source of all coordination, and not necessarily as the coordinating directive that runs through the entire organization. In a democracy like our own this authority rests with the people, who exercise it through the leaders of their choice.

The distinction between authority and leadership is such a vital one that it will in due course be considered at greater length. It is sufficient here to observe that the supreme coordinating authority must be prior to leadership in logical order, for it is this coordinating force that makes the organization. Leadership, on the other hand, always presupposes the organization. There can be no leader without something to lead. Leadership, of course, must exercise a derived authority. In absolutist forms of government the supreme coordinating authority usually exercises its own leadership, but this fact does not alter their essential difference.

Just as vital as the distinction between authority and leadership is that between authority and power, two terms so often confused. Power in the psychic sense—that is, ability to do things—is distinctly an individual possession. When we speak of the power of an organization we mean that this power has become collective through coordinated effort.

Authority, on the other hand, is a right. Hence we use the expression "moral authority," and may say of some great teacher, as was said of Jesus, the greatest of all teachers, that he speaks "as one having authority," which means that he has a moral right to speak as he does. In organization, authority is likewise a right, because it inheres legitimately in the structure of the organization. The distinction in the political sphere between de jure and de facto governments is based on the difference between the right of authority, acquired through some procedure recognized as legitimate, and the mere possession of power, however obtained.

The same observations apply to the exercise of authority, a truth that is not altered by the fact that authority rests on *moral right*. Rights cannot be divorced from duties, and if authority does not use its rights with due solicitude relative to these duties, it is sooner or later bound to fall. No organization has any prospect of stability if moral factors are not its basis.

Structure and Co-ordination

LUTHER GULICK

Interrelation of Systems of Departmentaliza-tion. Students of administration have long sought a single principle of effective depart-mentalization just as alchemists sought the phi-losophers' stone.[1] But they have sought in vain. There is apparently no one most effective system of departmentalism.

Each of the four basic systems of organiza-tion [2] is intimately related with the other three, because in any enterprise all four elements are present in the doing of the work and are embodied in every individual workman. Each member of the enterprise is working for some major purpose, uses some process, deals with some persons, and serves or works at some place.

If an organization is erected about any one of these four characteristics of work, it be-comes immediately necessary to recognize the other characteristics in constructing the sec-ondary and tertiary divisions of the work. For example, a government which is first divided on the basis of place will, in each geographical department, find it necessary to divide by purpose, by process, by clientele, or even again by place; and one divided in the first instance by purpose may well be divided next by process and then by place. While the first or primary division of any enterprise is of very great significance, it must none the less be said that there is no one most effective pattern for determining the priority and order for the introduction of these inter-dependent principles. It will depend in any case upon the results which are desired at a given time and place. . . .

The major purpose of organization is co-ordination, as has been pointed out above. It should therefore be noted that each of the four principles of departmentalization plays a

---

From "Notes on the Theory of Organization" in *Papers on the Science of Administration* by L. Gulick and L. Urwick, pp. 31–37. Reprinted with permission of the publisher, The Institute of Public Administration, copyright 1937 by The Institute of Public Administration.
[1] Charles A. Beard, "The Administration and Pol-itics of Tokyo." Macmillan, New York, 1923, Ch. 3; A. E. Buck, "Administrative Consolidation in State Governments," 5th ed. National Municipal League, New York, 1930; Great Britain, Ministry of Reconstruction, Report of the Machinery of Government Committee. H. M. Stationery Office, London, 1918; Luther Gulick, "Principles of Ad-ministration," *National Municipal Review*, vol. 14, July, 1925, pp. 400–403; W. F. Willoughby, "Prin-ciples of Public Administration." John Hopkins Press, Baltimore, 1927, Part I, Ch. 5.
[2] Purpose, Process, Clientele or Material, Place [ed.].

different rôle in co-ordination. In each case the highest degree of co-ordination takes place within the departments set up, and the greatest lack of co-ordination and danger of friction occurs between the departments, or at the points where they overlap.

If all of the departments are set up on the basis of purpose, then the task of the chief executive in the field of co-ordination will be to see that the major purposes are not in conflict and that the various processes which are used are consistent, and that the government as it touches classes of citizens or reaches areas of the community is appropriate, rational, and effective. He will not have to concern himself with co-ordination within the departments, as each department head will look after this.

If all of the departments are set up on the basis of process, the work methods will be well standardized on professional lines, and the chief executive will have to see that these are co-ordinated and timed to produce the results and render the services for which the government exists, and that the service rendered actually fits the needs of the persons or areas served.

If place be the basis of departmentalization, that is, if the services be decentralized, then the task of the chief executive is not to see that the activities are co-ordinated locally and fit the locality, but to see that each of these services makes use of the standard techniques and that the work in each area is part of a general program and policy.

If the work of the government be departmentalized in part on the basis of purpose, in part on the basis of process, in part on the basis of clientele, and in part on the basis of place, it will be seen that the problems of co-ordination and smooth operation are multiplied and that the task of the executive is increased. Moreover, the nature of his work is altered. In an organization in which all of the major divisions follow one philosophy, the executive himself must furnish the inter-departmental co-ordination and see that things do not fall between two stools. In an organization built on two or more bases of departmentalization, the executive may use, for example, the process departments as a routine means of co-ordinating the purpose departments. None the less the task of the executive is extraordinarily complicated. There is also great danger in such an organization that one department may fail to aid or actually proceed to obstruct another department. When departments cross each other at right angles, the danger of collision is far greater and far more serious than when their contacts are along parallel lines at their respective outer limits.

THE HOLDING COMPANY IDEA. A large enterprise engaged in many complicated activities which do not require extensive or intimate co-ordination may need only the loosest type of central co-ordinating authority. Under such conditions, each activity may be set up, on a purpose basis, as virtually independent, and the central structure of authority may be nothing more than a holding company. In practice various industrial holding companies, particularly in the power field, require little or no co-ordination whatsoever. They have no operating services in common, and seem to have few interrelations except in finance. It has been suggested that the larger governmental units are in comparable position, and that they may well be looked upon not as single enterprises like the Ford Motor Company, but rather as if they were each holding companies like the American Telephone and Telegraph Company, or General Motors. From this point of view, the government of the United States would be the parent company, and each department would be an independent subsidiary. While the parent company would give certain central services and require conformity to certain central plans and policies, each subsidiary, that is each department, would be given extensive freedom to carry on as it saw fit, and the President at the center of the parent company would not pretend to do more than prevent conflict and competition.

This point of view is helpful to the student of administration in that it brings out two important factors:

1. It makes clear the important difference between the operating functions and departments, such as agriculture, war, and labor, and the co-ordinating and central services, such as the budget, planning, and personnel. In the holding company analogy, the former would be subsidiaries, while the latter would be functions of the parent company; and

2. It directs attention to the kind of service to which the central agencies, including the President and the Cabinet, should limit themselves in any case. If the co-ordinating agencies

of the government would look upon themselves as holding company officials and staff, they would devote their energies to the larger problems of co-ordination, and would leave to the departments and their staffs the internal problems of operation.

While this attitude toward the respective functions of the operating and the co-ordinating services of the government may be valuable for certain purposes, it cannot be accepted as the sound theoretical foundation for the consideration of the federal government, or of any of the governments of the states or larger cities. It is not a satisfactory analogy for four important reasons:

1. There is but one board of directors in the governmental set-up, and a single avenue of democratic responsibility;

2. The interrelations between the various departments are many and intimate, requiring extensive and continuous co-ordination;

3. In government there must be highly developed uniform standards and methods, particularly in finance and personnel; and

4. There is in government no simple, final measure of successful operation of subsidiaries like the profit and loss statement in business. Supervisory relations must be intimate and complete, not distant and limited.

In the actual operation of the larger American governmental units we are, as a matter of fact, confronted at the same time by too much activity by the co-ordinating authorities, and by too little co-ordination. This anomalous situation seems to come about because of the lack of understanding both by experts and by laymen of the true function of the chief executive; because of the lack of proper managerial staffs attached to the chief executive; and because of the tendency of legislative bodies to step over the line into administration and to meddle with appointments. It must be recognized that the chief executive of any enterprise has but a limited amount of time and energy at his command. These he can use either in participating in detail in the administration of a few activities, or in dealing broadly with the policies and problems of many activities. If the task of the executive is first of all co-ordination, it would seem that the latter is his true function. But in any large enterprise, the executive cannot perform this function intelligently or skillfully unless he has adequate assistance. Where he is denied

such assistance, he must act either tardily or ruthlessly, and an executive who recoils from either course is immediately drawn down into the minutiae of administration and fails to perform his main job.

In public administration the holding company concept is helpful if it is used to emphasize the need of broad co-ordination and the methods of achieving it. It must be recognized, however, that government is actually not a holding company at all.

OTHER MEANS OF INTERDEPARTMENTAL CO-ORDINATION. In the discussion thus far it has been assumed that the normal method of interdepartmental co-ordination is hierarchical in its operation. That is, if trouble develops between a field representative (X) of one department and the field representative (A) of another department, that the solution will be found by carrying the matter up the line from inferior to superior until the complaint of Mr. X and the complaint of Mr. A finally reach their common superior, be he mayor, governor or President. In actual practice, there are also other means of interdepartmental co-ordination which must be regarded as part of the organization as such. Among these must be included planning boards and committees, interdepartmental committees, co-ordinators, and officially arranged regional meetings, etc. These are all organizational devices for bringing about the co-ordination of the work of government. Co-ordination of this type is essential. It greatly lessens the military stiffness and red tape of the strictly hierarchical structure. It greatly increases the consultative process in administration. It must be recognized, however, that it is to be used only to deal with abnormal situations and where matters of policy are involved, as in planning. The organization itself should be set up so that it can dispose of the routine work without such devices, because these devices are too dilatory, irresponsible and time-consuming for normal administration. Wherever an organization needs continual resort to special co-ordinating devices in the discharge of its regular work, this is proof that the organization is bad. These special agencies of co-ordination draw their sanction from the hierarchical structure and should receive the particular attention of the executive authority. They should not be set up and forgotten,

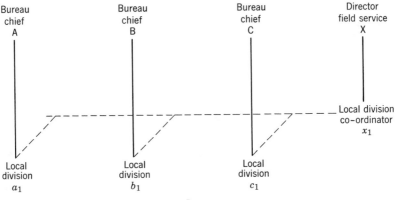

Fig. 1

ignored, or permitted to assume an independent status.

The establishment of special regional co-ordinators to bring about co-operation in a given region between the local representatives of several central agencies presents special difficulties. There are three chief plans which have been tried. One is the device of propinquity, the juxtaposition of offices in the same building or city, and reliance on ordinary daily contact. Another is the establishment of a loose committee, or "conference," meeting locally from time to time to discuss local problems of co-ordination, under a local chairman who is actually nothing but a presiding officer and formulator of agenda. A third plan is the establishment of such groups under the chairmanship of a regional co-ordinator designated by and responsible to a central office of co-ordination of field service. When this is attempted, to whom should the head of the field service be subordinate? For example, in the accompanying diagram [Fig. 1] to whom should X report? Certainly not to A, or to B, or to C. The central director of a co-ordination field service must be on a par with the central directors of the services which are being co-ordinated in the field, or possibly even on a higher plane.

In the devices of co-ordination, one must recognize also joint service contracts and co-incident personnel appointments. Independent agencies may be pulled together in operation through such use of the same staff or service. There are many illustrations of the former, especially in engineering services. The county agent who is at the same time a county, a state, and a federal official is an example of the latter.

A great obstacle in the way of all of these plans of co-ordination is found in the danger of introducing confusion in direction through the violation of the principle of unity of command, and also in the difference in the level of authority of those who are brought together in any interdepartmental or intergovernmental co-ordinating arrangement. The representatives of the Department of Agriculture, for example, may have a large measure of responsibility and power, and may therefore be in a position to work out an adjustment of program through conference and to agree to a new line of conduct, but the representatives of the Army, coming from an entirely different kind of an organization, are sure to be in a position where they cannot make any adjustments without passing the decision back to headquarters.

Doctrine

JAMES MOONEY

Mutual Service. Community of interest is the legitimate basis of every organization. In searching for its psychic fundaments we find that it can mean only *mutuality of interest*. This in turn implies mutual duties, which means the obligation to *mutual service*. This obligation is universal, transcending, therefore, the sphere of organization. As expressed in the ancient Roman juridical maximum *do ut des* (I give that thou mayest give), it is the manifest basis of all human relations.

In a special sense, however, it has an application within the sphere of organization. Here it is the moral phase of the principle of coordination. It is for this reason that organizations of all kinds, whether governmental, religious, military, or industrial, furnish our best human examples of the spirit of mutual service.

Although the formal technique of organization has, until recent years, received but scant attention, the humanistic phases of organization have an extensive literature. In this literature the obligation to mutual service is called by various names, among them cooperation, integration, functional relating, and integrated functioning. All these terms suggest the formal as well as the human side of coordination, which shows how impossible it is to separate them. We must keep in mind that organizations are the creations of people, and hence that everything that is formal in organized forms must rest on psychic fundaments.

A true coordination must be based on a real community of interest in the attainment of the desired object. It is equally true that a community of interest that is real, not only in the objective sense but likewise in everybody's consciousness, can come only through a real

community of understanding. This means not merely that administration and members must understand each other, but that each and all must understand what the real purpose is and, furthermore, that every group represented in the organization must understand how and why the attainment of this purpose is essential to the welfare of all.

The reason, we think, is obvious. Mutuality of interest or, let us say, a common interest, does not, so far as human consciousness is concerned, constitute an *identity* of interest. The only conceivable means of attaining a true integration of all group interests in organization is through administrative policies that will make this community of interest a more tangible reality to every member of the group.

It is evident that every element of psychic coordination is a necessity in the establishment of harmony in all internal relations. Even this statement, however, does not include everything necessary in a truly coordinated efficiency. Before we leave this subject of coordination, therefore, let us consider one more element, especially conspicuous in church and military organization, which has its lessons for organizers in every sphere.

Doctrine. Coordination implies an aim or objective. But it does not follow, even where there is a true mutual interest, a mutual understanding, and a degree of mutual participation, that each and every member of the organization does in fact carry in his mind a deep understanding of the objective and how it may be attained. Among the higher officials, those who are responsible for results, this understanding should be ever present. They should know, furthermore, that the more this understanding seeps down through all ranks and grades, until all are permeated with it, the greater will be the coordinated effort and the greater the strength of the organization

From *The Principles of Organization*. New York: Harper and Brothers, 1947, pp. 8–13. Reprinted with permission of the publisher.

for the accomplishment of its purpose. It is the necessary means to this end that brings us in contact with the significant word "doctrine."

To most people this word has a religious favor, and well it may, for, of all forms of organization, religious associations are the ones that are most deeply imbued with its spirit. But the word itself has a broader meaning. We see this illustrated in the various applications of the title "doctor," which means simply the teacher, representative, or practitioner of a doctrine. There is, indeed, a doctrine for every conceivable form of collective human effort.

Doctrine in the primary sense means the *definition of the objective*. In religious associations this doctrine is based on faith, as formally stated in the *creed*. In industrial organizations it is the attainment of a *surplus through service*. In governmental organization we find different and constantly changing doctrines, but always a doctrine of some sort, however varied its interpretations by the leaders and statesmen of history. In this primary sense doctrine is synonymous with the objective.

When we consider, however, the *procedure necessary to attain the objective* we encounter the secondary meaning of the word, which it seems a misnomer to call secondary, for it often transcends the primary meaning in practical importance. This fact the following examples will show.

With a physician or surgeon the doctrine of the objective is obvious. It is to make the patient well. But the doctrine of procedure and its application call for a thorough training and wide experience. Likewise, the doctrine of the military objective is simple. According to the school of Foch and Napoleon, it is the forcing of a decision through the overthrow of the adversary. The necessary procedure, however, constitutes a highly technical art, in which all the principles of military strategy and tactics are involved.

This point is vital in all forms of coordinated effort. Always there is sure to be a doctrine of procedure of some kind, but it is not enough to have such a doctrine, nor is it sufficient for the doctrine to be a sound one. Above all, it is essential that this doctrine shall, in the popular phrase, be "sold" to everyone concerned. Every member of an organization should not only know its doctrine, but he should feel it and absorb it until he lives in its atmosphere and makes it the guide of all his acts.

A doctrine of procedure does not mean a body of set rules that must be accepted as though they were articles of faith. We shall presently discuss more broadly the distinction between rules and principles in organization. "Indoctrination" in the military sense means simply the inculcation of those principles which serve as the guide of the military man, whatever the situation he is compelled to face.

To find a simpler illustration of unity of doctrine, and its necessity in the attainment of any group objective, we may turn to the field of sports, such as our national games of baseball and football, where groups are competing and where success in the attainment of the purpose depends on coordinated effort. In these sports there is a real functional differentiation of duties. In the formal sense, however, the problems of organization are all predetermined by the rules of the game. The primary objective also is so simple that the shortest word will state it. It is to *win*.

When we come, however, to procedure, in other words, to the means necessary to win, we find emerging in each case a real doctrine which accounts for the high importance of the baseball manager and the football coach. Tracing each doctrine through all the intricacies of baseball and football strategy we find that it rests, as it must, on the first principle of organization, namely, coordination of effort. This coordination, so essential to victory in any sport where a number of players combine their efforts for a common purpose, has given us the splendid word "teamwork."

Another illustration in a different sphere is the coordination of a symphony orchestra. Here the purpose is the production of a collective harmony, not as a means to an end but as an end in itself. To attain this end each individual musician merges himself in the common purpose. Functionalism in an orchestra is as varied as the nature of the different instruments. In the orchestra these individual functions derive their importance solely from their contribution to the common purpose, and the relation of each musician's function to this purpose is ever present in the instant result. This fact of the objective resulting instantly from the initial coordination makes the orchestra the supreme symbol and the simplest illustration of a coordinated effort.

Discipline. One other factor essential to organized efficiency must not be overlooked. Organized efficiency in the pursuit of any objective demands a doctrine, but the efficient application, even of the soundest doctrine, demands in turn an organized *discipline*. By this we mean something more vital than the discipline imposed by command. That is essential, but even more vital is the discipline which command must impose on itself, for such discipline is the first necessity to ensure a truly organized efficiency. Without such self-discipline at the top it would be useless to expect it anywhere else down the line. The commander of a battleship is subjected to a greater degree of discipline than a bluejacket. Even the pope must every year wash the feet of a beggar and must go to confession twice a week. Discipline by example we may call it, but such examples are essential to the discipline of any organization.

The sum of these observations is that the strength of an organization is determined by its spirit, that the spirit must be determined by the purpose and the means necessary to its attainment, and that these means imply a doctrine out of which the spirit of an organization grows and on which it lives. On the other hand, no organization can live on its spirit alone. Coordination must have its formalism, which means its technique or method by which its power is directed to the attainment of the purpose.

Perceptions of Organizational Authority:
A Comparative Analysis

ROBERT L. PEABODY

Authority relations are an integral component of organizational behavior. Clarification of the concept of authority would seem to be essential to the development of systematic organization theory.[1] Despite numerous attempts at conceptual clarification and a growing body of empirical inquiries focusing on organization behavior, Herbert A. Simon could conclude in 1957 that "there is no consensus today in the management literature as to how the term 'authority' should be used."[2] For Simon, the source of the difficulty lay in the failure of many writers to distinguish between "(1) a specification of the set of behaviors to which

they wish to apply the term 'authority'; and (2) a specification of the circumstances under which such behaviors will be exhibited."[3] The first problem, one of definition, or the way in which the term "authority" will be used, continues to plague students of administration.[4] There seems to be considerable agreement, however, on an important facet of the second problem, namely, identification of the bases of authority that facilitate its acceptance.

The Bases of Authority

This study is focused upon organizational authority in its several forms. Although authority is initially based on formal position, legitimacy, and the sanctions inherent in office, its acceptance is conditioned by several additional factors. In analyzing such related phenomena

From Robert L. Peabody, "Perceptions of Organizational Authority: A Comparative Analysis," *Administrative Science Quarterly*, Vol. 6, March 1962, pp. 463–472. Reprinted with permission of The Administrative Science Quarterly.

[1] This article is based on the author's doctoral dissertation at Stanford University entitled "Authority in Organizations: A Comparative Study" (1960). The research was financed in part by a grant from the Stanford University Committee on Research in Public Affairs. Further revision was made possible by a Brookings Institution Research Fellowship for 1960–1961. For helpful comments on earlier versions of this paper I am indebted to Heinz Eulau and Robert A. Walker of Stanford University, James D. Thompson of the University of Pittsburgh, and F. P. Kilpatrick, Milton Cummings, and M. Kent Jennings of the Brookings Institution.

[2] *Administrative Behavior* (2d ed.; New York, 1957), pp. xxxiv–xxxv. For criticism of Simon's "operational definition" of authority and Simon's rejoinder see Edward C. Banfield, The Decision-making Schema, *Public Administration Review*, 17 (1957), 278–285, and Simon, "The Decision-making Schema": A Reply, *ibid.*, 18 (1958), 60–63.

[3] *Administrative Behavior*, p. xxxv.

[4] For a more recent unsuccessful attempt at an operational definition, see Daniel J. Duffy, Authority Considered from an Operational Point of View, *Journal of the Academy of Management*, 2 (Dec. 1959), 167–175. For a more traditional viewpoint of authority see Merten J. Mandeville, The Nature of Authority, *Journal of the Academy of Management*, 3 (Aug. 1960), 107–118. While numerous definitions of authority occur in the literature of administration and organization theory, a review of these writings reveals considerable variation, vagueness, and ambiguity. For extended comment, see the author's review of the literature of organizational authority (cited in note 1) and a closely parallel review of leadership theories by Warren G. Bennis, Leadership Theory and Administrative Behavior: The Problem of Authority, *Administrative Science Quarterly*, 4 (1959), 259–301.

as professional competence, experience, and leadership, which modify and condition the exercise of formal authority, several different approaches could be taken. Some sociologists, for example Robert K. Bierstedt, would clearly distinguish between authority, competence, and leadership, reserving the label "authority" for hierarchical status relationships between incumbents of formal positions in organizations.[5] Other students of administration, notably Herbert A. Simon and Robert V. Presthus, would broaden the meaning of authority to include additional bases beyond formal position and the sanctions inherent in office.[6] Everyday usage of the word and much of the interview data of this inquiry seem to support the more inclusive interpretations of Simon and Presthus. However, the development of a science of administration may necessitate either a restriction of the term "authority" to a more precise technical meaning or an abandonment of the term for purposes of rigorous theory building.[7] Which of these two usages of the term is finally adopted is not as important as making clear the implications of each. The bases of *formal* authority—legitimacy, position, and the sanctions inherent in office—need to be distinguished from the sources of *functional* authority, most notably, professional

competence, experience, and human relations skills, which support or compete with formal authority.[8]

Rather than attempt an exhaustive review of the literature, five contributors to the study of authority relations in organizations—Max Weber, Lyndall F. Urwick, Herbert A. Simon, Warren G. Bennis, and Robert V. Presthus—will be singled out as illustrative of a growing consensus as to the importance of several bases of authority which condition its acceptance. While not all these social scientists have placed emphasis on the same sources of authority and while they have frequently used different words to convey similar meanings, the essential points of agreement can be classified under four broad categories: (1) authority of legitimacy; (2) authority of position, including the sanctions inherent in position; (3) authority of competence, including both technical skills and experience, and (4) authority of person, including leadership and human relations skills (see Table 1).

Authority of Legitimacy. Unlike the related concepts of power and influence, the concept of authority has implicit in it the notion of legitimacy or ethical sanctification. Philosophers

---

[5] "The Problem of Authority," Morroe Berger, Theodore Abel, and C. H. Page, eds., *Freedom and Control in Modern Society* (New York, 1954), pp. 67–81. In an earlier paper, Bierstedt defined authority as "institutional power," which appears to be a concept of authority somewhat broader than formal status relationships (An Analysis of Social Power, *American Sociological Review*, 15 [1950], 736).
[6] Simon, "Authority," in C. M. Arensberg *et al.*, *Research in Industrial Human Relations* (New York, 1957), pp. 104–106; Herbert A. Simon, D. W. Smithburg, and V. A. Thompson, *Public Administration* (New York, 1950), pp. 189–201; Presthus, Authority in Organizations, *Public Administration Review*, 20 (1960), 86–91.
[7] "In the initial stages of scientific inquiry, descriptions as well as generalizations are stated in the vocabulary of everyday language. The growth of a scientific discipline, however, always brings with it the development of a system of specialized, more or less abstract, concepts and of a corresponding technical terminology." See Carl G. Hempel, Fundamentals of Concept Formation in Empirical Science, *International Encyclopedia of Unified Science* (Chicago, 1952), II, No. 7, p. 1.

[8] In general, functional authority supports formal authority. In a given superior-subordinate relationship, it is the superior's lack of functional authority or the subordinate's possession of greater competence, experience, or personal skills which tends to undermine formal authority. Competition may also occur between incumbents of equal formal rank, but different task or specialist orientations, as for example between the controller and the merchandise manager of a department store. Finally, competition between functional and formal authority may occur where hierarchical channels are ambiguous, a condition frequently characteristic of staff-line relationships. Cf. Victor A. Thompson's distinction between hierarchical and nonhierarchical authority, Hierarchy, Specialization, and Organizational Conflict, *Administrative Science Quarterly*, 5 (1961), 499. See also, Melville Dalton, "Conflicts between Staff and Line Managerial Officers," *American Sociological Review*, 15 (1950), 342–351; O. Glenn Stahl, "The Network of Authority," *Public Administration Review*, 18 (1958), ii–iv; O. Glenn Stahl, "More on the Network of Authority," *Public Administration Review*, 20 (1960), 35–37; Robert T. Golembiewski, "Toward the New Organization Theories: Some Notes on 'Staff,'" *Midwest Journal of Political Science*, 5 (1961), 237–259.

Table 1. The Bases of Authority

| | FORMAL AUTHORITY | | FUNCTIONAL AUTHORITY | |
	LEGITIMACY	POSITION	COMPETENCE	PERSON
Weber *	Legal	....	Rational authority	Traditional authority
	Legal order	Hierarchical office	Technical knowledge, experience	Charismatic authority
Urwick †		Formal, conferred by the organization	Technical, implicit in special knowledge or skill	Personal, conferred by seniority or popularity
Simon ‡	Authority of legitimacy, social approval	Authority of sanctions	Authority of confidence (technical competence)	Techniques of *persuasion* (as distinct from authority)
Bennis §		Role incumbency	Knowledge of performance criteria	Knowledge of the human aspect of administration
Presthus ‖	Generalized deference toward authority	Formal role or position	Technical expertise	Rapport with subordinates, ability to mediate individual needs

* Max Weber, *The Theory of Social and Economic Organization*, A. M. Henderson and Talcott Parsons, trans., Talcott Parsons, ed. (New York, 1947), pp. 328, 339.

† L. Urwick, *The Elements of Administration* (London, 1944), p. 42.

‡ Herbert A. Simon, "Authority," in Conrad M. Arensberg, *et al.*, eds., *Research in Industrial Human Relations* (New York, 1957), pp. 104–106; H. A. Simon, D. W. Smithburg, V. A. Thompson, *Public Administration* (New York, 1950), pp. 189–201.

§ Warren G. Bennis, "Leadership Theory and Administrative Behavior: The Problem of Authority," *Administrative Science Quarterly*, 4 (1959), 288–289.

‖ Robert V. Presthus, "Authority in Organizations," *Public Administration Review*, 20 (1960), 88–91.

have long struggled with the complex and continuing problems of political authority, couched in the language of social contract theories and doctrines of political obligation.[9] The employment relationship, evolving out of the relationship between master and servant, has frequently been phrased in the same language.[10] Those in authority have the *right* to demand obedience; those subject to authority have the *duty* to obey.[11] Max Weber, whose influence permeates almost all studies of bureaucracy, classifies the types of authority "according to the kind of claim to legitimacy typically made by each." [12] While both traditional authority and charismatic authority are owed to a *person*, the chief or charismatic

[9] See, for example, Carl J. Friedrich, ed., *Authority* (Cambridge, Mass., 1958), or Bertram de Jouvenel, *Sovereignty* (Chicago, 1957).

[10] Reinhard Bendix, *Work and Authority in Industry* (New York, 1956).

[11] Simon, Smithburg, and Thompson, *op. cit.*, p. 180.

[12] *The Theory of Social and Economic Organization*, A. M. Henderson and Talcott Parsons, trans., Talcott Parsons, ed. (New York, 1947), p. 325.

leader, "in the case of legal authority, obedience is owed to the legally established impersonal order." [13] As Parsons and Gouldner have pointed out, Weber sets forth but does not elaborate on several additional bases of legal-rational authority, for example, hierarchical office and technical knowledge and experience.[14] Other writers, most notably Simon and Presthus, have further developed these concepts of the underlying bases of authority. While Simon uses "authority of legitimacy" in the narrower sense utilized here, Presthus extends the concept of "legitimation" to include all processes by which authority is accepted, reserving the concept of a "generalized deference to authority" (which in turn reflects the process of individual socialization), for this narrower sense of ethical sanctification.[15] For Simon, it is through the indirect mechanism of social approval from the particular reference group that the motive of legitimacy obtains its greatest force.[16] But whether used in the broad or narrow sense, authority of legitimacy is inextricably fused in reality with a second source or base frequently discussed in the literature, that is, authority of position.

Authority of Position. As Robert K. Merton restates Weber's classic treatment of authority based on hierarchical office: "Authority, the power of control which derives from an acknowledged status, inheres in the office and not in the particular person who performs the official role." [17] That is to say, when a person becomes a member of an organization he is already predisposed to accept orders given to him by persons acknowledged to be his superiors by their position in the formal organizational chart. As March and Simon make this point:

In joining the organization [the employee] accepts an authority relation; i.e., he agrees that within some limits (defined both explicitly and implicitly by the terms of his employment contract) he will accept as the premises of his behavior orders and instructions supplied to him by the organization.[18]

Although their language has been different, writers such as Urwick, Bennis, and Presthus all have had reference to much the same thing when they discussed formal authority, role incumbency, and formal position.

Simon, among others, has given the authority of position an extended interpretation in his discussion of the authority of rewards and sanctions inherent in office. His assertions that "the most important sanctions of managers over workers in industrial organizations are (*a*) power to hire and fire, (*b*) power to promote and demote, and (*c*) incentive rewards," are equally true of public organizations.[19] Both participants in a superior-subordinate relationship are aware of the disparities in sanctions which support the relationship. However, while the subordinate is subject to the commands of the superior, the superior is dependent on the subordinate to get the job done. The supervisor engages in periodic ratings of his workers, ratings which affect promotion, pay raises, and even the chances of keeping the job. But if subordinates take no initiative, solve no problems for themselves, do everything the superior asks them, but *no more*, the superior will soon be faced with the impossible task of trying to do every job in the organization by himself.[20] On the other hand, as long as subordinates know that a superior controls ultimate sanctions to compel obedience if his orders are resisted, authority cannot be defined solely in terms of acceptance or consent.[21] But even this advantage possessed by the superior is not without its costs. As Peter M. Blau points out, the continued use of sanctions, or threat of their use, will in the long run undermine authority. "This is the dilemma of bureaucratic authority: it rests on the power of sanction but is weakened by frequent resort to sanctions in operations." [22]

[13] *Ibid.,* p. 328.
[14] Parsons, in *ibid.,* n. 4, pp. 58–60; Gouldner, "Organizational Analysis," in Robert K. Merton, Leonard Broom, and Leonard S. Cottrell, Jr., eds. *Sociology Today* (New York, 1959), pp. 400–423.
[15] Presthus, *op. cit.,* n. 8, p. 88.
[16] "Authority," *op. cit.,* p. 106.
[17] *Social Theory and Social Structure* (rev. ed.; Glencoe, 1957), p. 195.

[18] *Organizations* (New York, 1958), p. 90.
[19] "Authority," *op. cit.,* p. 104.
[20] Harold J. Leavitt, *Managerial Psychology* (Chicago, 1958), pp. 150–151.
[21] Robert V. Presthus, Toward a Theory of Organizational Behavior, *Administrative Science Quarterly,* 3 (1958), 57.
[22] *Bureaucracy in Modern Society* (New York, 1956), pp. 76–77.

One consequence of this relationship of mutual dependency with disparate sanctions is that the superior must broaden the base of his authority if he is to secure the active cooperation of his subordinates in order to achieve organizational goals. Formal authority flowing from legitimacy and organizational status almost invariably must be supported by authority based on professional competence and human relations skills.

Authority of Competence. While the authority of competence is not limited to formal hierarchical relationships, and indeed frequently cuts across the formal channels of communication, possession of experience and appropriate technical skills by the superior obviously greatly enhances the acceptance of his formal authority by his subordinates. In general, authority based on technical knowledge and authority based on experience are closely related, although distinctions can be made between these two subtypes of the authority of competence. Familiarity with certain operations can only be gained from day-to-day confrontation of problems. What may be a crisis for the beginner is routine to the old hand. Technical knowledge, in contrast with experience, is more apt to come from professional training, for example, specialized graduate education. Indeed, when promotional opportunities arise, seniority may frequently compete with technical proficiency; therefore the prerequisites for most supervisory positions stress both professional training and experience.

There remains, however, a more fundamental ambivalence regarding bases of authority in organizations. As Gouldner asserts, "one of the deepest tensions in modern organization, often expressed as a conflict between the line and staff groups, derives from the divergence of . . . two bases of authority"—authority legitimized by incumbency in office and authority based on professional competence.[23] Not only do subunits of organizations differ as to the importance attached to these two bases of authority, but different kinds of organizations,[24]

over different time periods,[25] and within different cultures [26] also seem to emphasize one or the other of these bases of authority. While a number of writers have commented upon an increasing tendency toward reliance on professional competence with an attending decline in the perceived legitimacy of hierarchical authority, evidence suggests that the strategic location and influence of those in hierarchical roles often enables them to resist specialist claims. As Victor A. Thompson shows, control of the organization's distribution system remains in hierarchical hands:

> Above what might be considered a market minimum, the satisfactions which the organization has to offer are distributed according to hierarchical rank. They include, in addition to money, deference, power, interesting activities and associations, conveniences, etc. Because these goods are distributed according to status rank, and access to any rank is controlled by . . . hierarchical position, these positions acquire great power. . . .[27]

The tension between positional and specialist authority, which appears to be endemic in hierarchical organizations, may sometimes be mediated by a fourth basis of authority, authority of person.

Authority of Person. Authority based on legitimacy, position, and competence can be analytically distinguished from the authority of person. Such a distinction takes a number of forms in the literature. As already suggested, Weber makes use of the distinction between authority based on office and authority based

[23] *Op. cit.*, p. 414. See Thompson, *op. cit.*, for an extended analysis of conflict arising from growing inconsistencies between specialist and hierarchical roles.
[24] James D. Thompson and Frederick L. Bates, Technology, Organization, and Administration, *Administrative Science Quarterly*, 2, (1957), 332–

334; Amitai Etzioni, Authority Structure and Organizational Effectiveness, *Administrative Science Quarterly*, 4 (1959), 43–67.
[25] Morris Janowitz, Changing Patterns of Organizational Authority: The Military Establishment, *Administrative Science Quarterly*, 3 (1959), 473–493; Bendix, *op. cit.*
[26] Walter B. Miller, Two Concepts of Authority, *American Anthropologist*, 57 (1955), 271–289; Stephen A. Richardson, Organizational Contrasts on British and American Ships, *Administrative Science Quarterly*, 1 (1956), 189–207; Elliot Jaques *The Changing Culture of a Factory* (London, 1951), p. 254; Heinz Hartmann, *Authority and Organization in German Management* (Princeton, 1959), pp. 5–7.
[27] *Modern Organization* (New York, 1961), p. 65.

on personal attributes to differentiate the first of his three pure types of authority,—legal-rational authority (itself containing seeds of other bases of authority) from his second and third types—traditional and charismatic authority.[28] Both Henri Fayol and Chester Barnard make similar distinctions between what Fayol referred to as "official authority" and "personal authority" and what Barnard described as "authority of position" and "authority of leadership."[29] A number of social scientists, including Bierstedt, Blau, Gibbs, Selznick, and Urwick, have made analytical distinctions between authority and leadership.[30] The focus

in this study is not so much on personal or informal leader-follower relations, but rather on the *fusion* of leadership skills—be it charisma or routinized human relations skills—in a person who *also* occupies a position of authority; not on leadership as personal quality, but on leadership as an organizational function.[31] Thus, as Bennis, Presthus, and others have suggested, "the knowledge of the human aspect of administration," "the ability to mediate individual needs," and the possession of certain leadership traits by a superior enhance the frequency and extent of acceptance of formal authority on the part of his subordinates.[32]

Before reporting some results from an empirical inquiry of authority relations which seem to support a fourfold typology of authority, several assumptions underlying the selection of field setting, working hypothesis, and methodology of this study should be made explicit.

[28] Weber, *op. cit.*, p. 328.
[29] Fayol, *General and Industrial Management*, Constance Storrs, trans. (London, 1949), pp. 19–21; Barnard, *The Functions of the Executive* (Cambridge, Mass., 1937), p. 173.
[30] Bierstedt, *op. cit.*, pp. 70–71; Peter M. Blau, *The Dynamics of Bureaucracy* (Chicago, 1955), p. 178; Cecil A. Gibbs, "Leadership," in Gardiner Lindzey, ed., *Handbook of Social Psychology* (Reading, Mass., 1954), II, 882; Philip Selznick, *Leadership in Administration* (Evanston, Ill., 1957), p. 24; L. F. Urwick, *Leadership in the Twentieth Century* (New York, 1957), p. 37.

[31] Alex Bavelas, Leadership: Man and Function, *Administrative Science Quarterly*, 4 (1960), 491.
[32] Bennis, *op. cit.*, pp. 283–287; Presthus, Authority in Organizations, p. 91.

Compliance as a Comparative Base

AMITAI ETZIONI

A Definition of Compliance

Compliance is universal, existing in all social units. It is a major element of the relationship between those who have power and those over whom they exercise it (Simmel, 1896). Despite its universality, it has been chosen as a base for this comparative study because it is a central element of organizational structure. The emphasis on compliance within the organization differentiates the latter from other types of social units. Characteristics of organizations such as their specificity, size, complexity and effectiveness each enhances the need for compliance. And in turn, compliance is systematically related to many central organizational variables.

Compliance refers both to a relation in which an actor behaves in accordance with a directive supported by another actor's power, and to the orientation of the subordinated actor to the power applied.[1]

By *supported* we mean that those who have power manipulate means which they command in such a manner that certain other actors find following the directive rewarding, while not following it incurs deprivations. In this sense, compliance relations are asymmetric (or "vertical"). But it is not assumed that the subordinates have no power, only that they have less.[2]

The power-*means*, manipulated to support the directives, include physical, material, and symbolic rewards and deprivations. Organizations tend to allocate these means systematically and strive to ensure that they will be used in conformity with the organizational norms.

The *orientation of the subordinated actor* can be characterized as positive (commitment) or negative (alienation). It is determined in part by the degree to which the power applied is considered legitimate by the subordinated actor, and in part by its congruence with the line of action he would desire. We refer to this orientation, whether positive or negative, as *involvement* in the organization. In sum, there are two parties to a compliance relationship: an actor who exercises power, and an actor, subject to this power, who responds to this subjection with either more or less alienation or more or less commitment.

The next task is to use compliance as here defined to develop an analytical base for the classification of organizations. This is done in three steps. First, three kinds of *power* are differentiated; then, three kinds of *involvement* are specified; and finally, the associations of kinds of power with kinds of involvement are indicated. These associations—which constitute *compliance relationships*—then serve as the basis of our classification of organizations.

Three Kinds of Power: A Comparative Dimension

A Classification of Power. Power is an actor's ability to induce or influence another actor to carry out his directives or any other norms he supports.[3] Goldhamer and Shils state that "a person may be said to have power to the extent that he influences the behavior of others in accordance with his own intentions." (p. 171). Of course, "his own intentions" might be to influence a person to follow others' "intentions" or those of a collectivity.

From Amitai Etzioni, *Complex Organizations*, Free Press, New York, 1961, pp. 3–22. Reprinted with permission of the publisher.

[1] For other usages of the term see Bendix (1947, pp. 502–507) and Zetterberg (1957).
[2] See Parsons (1957, p. 139); cf. Dahrendorf (1954, p. 169).

[3] See Parsons (1951, p. 121). See also Lasswell and Kaplan (1950, pp. 74–102); Easton (1952, p. 116); Dahl (1957); and Cartwright (1959).

In organizations, enforcing the collectivity norms is likely to be a condition determining the power-holder's access to the means of power.

Power positions are positions whose incumbents regularly have access to means of power. Statements about power positions imply a particular group (or groups) who are subject to this power. For instance, to state that prison guards have a power position implies the subordination of inmates. In the following analysis we focus on power relations in organizations between those higher and those lower in rank. We refer to those in power positions, who are higher in rank, as *elites* or as organizational *representatives*. We refer to those in subject positions, who are lower in rank, as *lower participants*.

Power differs according to the *means* employed to make the subjects comply. These means may be physical, material, or symbolic.[4]

Coercive power rests on the application, or the threat of application, of physical sanctions such as infliction of pain, deformity, or death; generation of frustration through restriction of movement; or controlling through force the satisfaction of needs such as those for food, sex, comfort, and the like.

Remunerative power is based on control over material resources and rewards through allocation of salaries and wages, commissions and contributions, "fringe benefits," services and commodities.

Normative power rests on the allocation and manipulation of symbolic rewards and deprivations through employment of leaders, manipulation of mass media, allocation of esteem and prestige symbols, administration of ritual, and influence over the distribution of "acceptance" and "positive response." (A more eloquent name for this power would be persuasive, or manipulative, or suggestive power. But all these terms have negative value connotations which we wish to avoid.)

There are two kinds of normative power. One is based on the manipulation of esteem, prestige, and ritualistic symbols (such as a flag or a benediction); the other, on allocation and manipulation of acceptance and positive response (Parsons, 1951, p. 108). Although both powers are found both in vertical and in horizontal relationships, the first is more frequent in vertical relations, between actors who have different ranks, while the second is more common in horizontal relations, among actors equal in rank—in particular, in the power of an "informal" or primary group over its members. Lacking better terms, we refer to the first kind as *pure normative power*, and to the second as *social power*.[5] Social power could be treated as a distinct kind of power. But since powers are here classed according to the means of control employed, and since both social and pure normative power rest on the same set of means—manipulation of symbolic rewards—we treat these two powers as belonging to the same category.

From the viewpoint of the organization, pure normative power is more useful, since it can be exercised directly down the hierarchy. Social power becomes organizational power only when the organization can influence the group's powers, as when a teacher uses the class climate to control a deviant child, or a union steward agitates the members to use

---

[4] We suggest that this typology is exhaustive, although the only way we can demonstrate this is by pointing out that every type of power we have encountered so far can be classified as belonging to one of the categories or a combination of them.

Boulding, Neuman, and Commons have suggested similar typologies. Boulding has developed a typology of "willingness" of persons to serve organizational ends which includes identification, economic means, and coercion. He suggests, however, that identification should be seen as an "economic" way of inducing willingness, a position which we believe is unacceptable to most sociologists (see Boulding, 1953, p. xxxi; and Niebuhr, "Coercion, Self-Interest, and Love," *ibid.*, pp. 228–44). Neuman has suggested that "three basic methods are at the disposal of the power group: persuasion, material benefits, violence" (1950, p. 168). Commons distinguishes among physical, economic, and moral power (1957, pp. 47–64). Janowitz analyzes international relations using the concepts of "economic resources, violence, and persuasion" (1960, p. 258). See also Deutsch (1953, pp. 218 ff.).

[5] This distinction draws on the difference between social and normative integration, referred to by Parsons, Bales, and Shils (1953, p. 182) as the distinction between the "integrative" and the "latent pattern maintenance" phases. In a volume in progress, Shils distinguishes between social and ideological primary groups (private communication). Coleman (1957, p. 255) has pointed to the difference between group-oriented and idea-oriented attachments.

their informal power to bring a deviant into line.

Organizations can be ordered according to their power structure, taking into account which power is predominant, how strongly it is stressed compared with other organizations in which the same power is predominant, and which power constitutes the secondary source of control. Two methodological problems raised by such an ordering are discussed in Chapter XII, pages 297–8.

Neutralization of Power. Most organizations employ all three kinds of power, but the degree to which they rely on each differs from organization to organization. Most organizations tend to emphasize only one means of power, relying less on the other two.[6] Evidence to this effect is presented below in the analysis of the compliance structures of various organizations. The major reason for power specialization seems to be that when two kinds of power are emphasized at the same time, over the same subject group, they tend to neutralize each other.

Applying force, for instance, usually creates such a high degree of alienation that it becomes impossible to apply normative power successfully. This is one of the reasons why rehabilitation is rarely achieved in traditional prisons, why custodial measures are considered as blocking therapy in mental hospitals, and why teachers in progressive schools tend to oppose corporal punishment.

Similarly, the application of remunerative powers makes appeal to "idealistic" (pure normative) motives less fruitful. In a study of the motives which lead to purchase of war bonds, Merton pointed out that in one particularly effective drive (the campaign of Kate Smith), all "secular" topics were omitted and the appeal was centered on patriotic, "sacred" themes. Merton asked a sample of 978 people:

[6] In more technical language, one can say that the three continua of power constitute a three-dimensional property space. If we collapse each dimension into high, medium, and low segments, there are 27 possible combinations or cells. Our hypothesis reads that most organizations fall into cells which are high on one dimension and low or medium on the others; this excludes 18 cells (not counting three types of dual structures discussed below). On multi-dimensional property space, see Barton (1955, pp. 40–52).

"Do you think that it is a good idea to give things to people who buy bonds?"

Fifty per cent were definitely opposed in principle to premiums, bonuses and other such inducements, and many of the remainder thought it a good idea only for "other people" who might not buy otherwise. (1946, p. 47)

By omitting this [secular] argument, the authors of her scripts were able to avoid the strain and incompatibility between the two main lines of motivation: unselfish, sacrificing love of country and economic motives of sound investment. (*Ibid.*, p. 45)

It is possible to make an argument for the opposite position. It might be claimed that the larger the number of personal needs whose satisfaction the organization controls, the more power it has over the participants. For example, labor unions that cater to and have control over the social as well as the economic needs of their members have more power over those members than do unions that focus only on economic needs. There may be some tension between the two modes of control, some ambivalence and uneasy feeling among members about the combination, but undoubtedly the total control is larger. Similarly, it is obvious that the church has more power over the priest than over the average parishioner. The parishioner is exposed to normative power, whereas the priest is controlled by both normative and remunerative powers.

The issue is complicated by the fact that the *amount* of each kind of power applied must be taken into account. If a labor union with social powers has economic power which is much greater than that of another union, this fact may explain why the first union has greater power in sum, despite some "waste" due to neutralization. A further complication follows from the fact that neutralization may also occur through application of the "wrong" power in terms of the cultural definition of what is appropriate to the particular organization and activity. For example, application of economic power in religious organizations may be less effective than in industries, not because two kinds of power are mixed, but because it is considered illegitimate to use economic pressures to attain religious goals. Finally, some organizations manage to apply two kinds of power abundantly and without much waste through neutralization, because they segregate the application of one power from that of the other. The examination below of combat armies and labor unions supplies an illustration of this point.

We have discussed some of the factors related to the tendency of organizations to specialize their power application. In conclusion, it seems that although there can be little doubt that such a tendency exists, its scope and a satisfactory explanation for it have yet to be established.

Three Kinds of Involvement: A Comparative Dimension

Involvement, Commitment, and Alienation. Organizations must continually recruit means if they are to realize their goals. One of the most important of these means is the positive orientation of the participants to the organizational power. *Involvement* [7] refers to the cathectic-evaluative orientation of an actor to an object, characterized in terms of intensity and direction.

The intensity of involvement ranges from high to low. The direction is either positive or negative. We refer to positive involvement as *commitment* [8] and to negative involvement as *alienation*.[9] (The advantage of having a third

term, *involvement*, is that it enables us to refer to the continuum in a neutral way.[10]) Actors can accordingly be placed on an involvement continuum which ranges from a highly intense negative zone through mild negative and mild positive zones to a highly positive zone.[11]

Three Kinds of Involvement. We have found it helpful to name three zones of the involvement continuum, as follows: *alienative,* for the high alienation zone; *moral,* for the high commitment zone; and *calculative,* for the two mild zones. This classification of involvement can be applied to the orientations of actors in all social units and to all kinds of objects. Hence the definitions and illustrations presented below are not limited to organizations, but are applicable to orientations in general.

ALIENATIVE INVOLVEMENT. Alienative involvement designates an intense negative orientation; it is predominant in relations among hostile foreigners. Similar orientations exist among merchants in "adventure" capitalism, where trade is built on isolated acts of exchange, each

[7] *Involvement* has been used in a similar manner by Morse (1953, pp. 76–96). The term is used in a somewhat different way by students of voting, who refer by it to the psychological investment in the outcome of an election rather than in the party, which would be parallel to Morse's usage and ours. See, for example, Campbell, Gurin, and Miller (1954, pp. 33–40).

[8] Mishler defined *commitment* in a similar though more psychological way: "An individual is committed to an organization to the extent that central tensions are integrated through organizationally relevant instrumental acts." Cited by Argyris (1957, p. 202). See also Mishler (1953); Abramson, Cutler, Kautz, and Mendelson (1958), p. 16; H. P. Gouldner (1960, p. 469); and Becker (1960, pp. 35ff.).

[9] We draw deliberately on the associations this term has acquired from its usage by Marx and others. For a good analysis of the idea of alienation in Marxism, and of its more recent development, see Bell (1959 and 1960, pp. 335–68). See also D. G. Dean (1960, pp. 185–89).

[10] An example of empirical indicators which can be used to translate the involvement continuum into directly observable terms is offered by Shils and Janowitz (1948, pp. 282–83). They classify "modes of social disintegration" in the armed forces as follows: desertion; active surrender; passive surrender; routine resistance; "last-ditch" resistance. In the terms used here, these measures indicate varying degrees of involvement, from highest alienation (desertion) to highest commitment (last-ditch resistance).

Nettler (1958) has developed a 17-item unidimensional scale which measures alienation from society. It seems that a similar scale could be constructed for measuring alienation from or commitment to organizational power without undue difficulties. Kornhauser, Sheppard, and Mayer (1956, pp. 147–48) have developed a 6-item scale, measuring the orientation of union members to their organization, which supplies another illustration of the wide use and measurability of these concepts, which are central to our analysis (for some further specifications, see Chapter XII).

[11] Several sociologists have pointed out that the relationship between intensity and direction of involvement is a curvilinear one: the more positive or negative the orientation, the more intensely it is held (Guttman, 1947, 1950, 1954, pp. 229–30; Suchman, 1950; McDill, 1959).

side trying to maximize immediate profit (Gerth and Mills, 1946, p. 67). Such an orientation seems to dominate the approach of prostitutes to transient clients (K. Davis, 1937, pp. 748–49). Some slaves seem to have held similar attitudes to their masters and to their work. Inmates in prisons, prisoners of war, people in concentration camps, enlisted men in basic training, all tend to be alienated from their respective organizations.[12]

CALCULATIVE INVOLVEMENT. Calculative involvement designates either a negative or a positive orientation of low intensity. Calculative orientations are predominant in relationships of merchants who have continuous business contacts. Attitudes of (and toward) permanent customers are often predominantly calculative, as are relationships among entrepreneurs in modern (rational) capitalism. Inmates in prisons who have established contact with prison authorities, such as "rats" and "peddlers," often have predominantly calculative attitudes toward those in power (Sykes, 1958, pp. 87–95).

MORAL [13] INVOLVEMENT. Moral involvement designates a positive orientation of high intensity. The involvement of the parishioner in his church, the devoted member in his party, and the loyal follower in his leader are all "moral."

There are two kinds of moral involvement, pure and social. They differ in the same way pure normative power differs from social power. Both are intensive modes of commitment, but they differ in their foci of orientation and in the structural conditions under which they develop. Pure moral commitments are based on internalization of norms and identification with authority (like Riesman's inner-

directed "mode of conformity"); social commitment rests on sensitivity to pressures of primary groups and their members (Riesman's "other-directed"). Pure moral involvement tends to develop in vertical relationships, such as those between teachers and students, priests and parishioners, leaders and followers. Social involvement tends to develop in horizontal relationships like those in various types of primary groups. Both pure moral and social orientations might be found in the same relationships, but, as a rule, one orientation predominates.

Actors are means to each other in alienative and in calculative relations; but they are ends to each other in "social" relationships. In pure moral relationships the means-orientation tends to predominate. Hence, for example, the willingness of devoted members of totalitarian parties or religious orders to use each other. But unlike the means-orientation of calculative relationships, the means-orientation here is expected to be geared to needs of the collectivity in serving its goals, and not to those of an individual.

As has been stated, the preceding classification of involvement can be applied to the orientations of actors in all social units and to all kinds of objects. The analysis in this book applies the scheme to orientations of lower participants in organizations to various organizational objects, in particular to the organizational power system. The latter includes (1) the directives the organization issues, (2) the sanctions by which it supports its directives, and (3) the persons who are in power positions. The choice of organizational power as the prime object of involvement to be examined here follows from a widely held conception of organization as an administrative system or control structure. To save breath, the orientation of lower participants to the organization as a power (or control) system is referred to subsequently as *involvement in the organization*. When other involvements are discussed, the object of orientation—for example, organizational goals—is specified.

Organizations are placed on the involvement continuum according to the modal involvement pattern of their lower participants. The placing of organizations in which the participants exhibit more than one mode of involvement is discussed in a later chapter.

---

[12] For a description of this orientation in prisons see Clemmer (1958, pp. 152ff.). Attitudes toward the police, particularly on the part of members of the lower classes, are often strictly alienative. See, for example, Banfield (1958). Illustrations of alienative orientations to armies are found in Norman Mailer, *The Naked and the Dead*, and Erich Maria Remarque, *All Quiet on the Western Front*.

[13] The term moral is used here and in the rest of the volume to refer to an orientation of the actor; it does not involve a value-position of the observer (see Parsons and Shils, 1952, pp. 170ff.).

Compliance as a Comparative Base

A Typology of Compliance. Taken together, the two elements—that is, the power applied by the organization *to* lower participants, and the involvement in the organization developed *by* lower participants—constitute the compliance relationship. Combining three kinds of power with three kinds of involvement produces nine types of compliance, as shown in the accompanying table.[14]

A Typology of Compliance Relations

KINDS OF POWER	KINDS OF INVOLVEMENT		
	Alienative	Calculative	Moral
Coercive	1	2	3
Remunerative	4	5	6
Normative	7	8	9

The nine types are not equally likely to occur empirically. *Three*—the diagonal cases, 1, 5, and 9—*are found more frequently than the other six types.* This seems to be true because these three types constitute *congruent* relationships, whereas the other six do not.

THE CONGRUENT TYPES. The involvement of lower participants is determined by many factors, such as their personality structure, secondary socialization, memberships in other collectivities, and so on. At the same time, organizational powers differ in the kind of involvement they tend to generate. When the kind of involvement that lower participants have because of other factors [15] and the kind of involvement that tends to be generated by the predominant form of organizational power are the same, we refer to the relationship as *congruent.* For instance, inmates are highly alienated from prisons; coercive power tends to alienate; hence this is a case of a congruent compliance relationship.

Congruent cases are more frequent than noncongruent ones primarily because congru-

ence is more effective, and organizations are social units under external and internal pressure to be effective. The effective application of normative powers, for example, requires that lower participants be highly committed. If lower participants are only mildly committed to the organization, and particularly if they are alienated from it, the application of normative power is likely to be ineffective. Hence the association of normative power with moral commitment.

Remuneration is at least partially wasted when actors are highly alienated, and therefore inclined to disobey despite material sanctions; it is also wasted when actors are highly committed, so that they would maintain an effective level of performance for symbolic, normative rewards only. Hence the association of remuneration with calculative involvement.

Coercive power is probably the only effective power when the organization is confronted with highly alienated lower participants. If, on the other hand, it is applied to committed or only mildly alienated lower participants, it is likely to affect adversely such matters as morale, recruitment, socialization, and communication, and thus to reduce effectiveness. (It is likely, though, to create high alienation, and in this way to create a congruent state.)

THE INCONGRUENT TYPES. Since organizations are under pressure to be effective, the suggestion that the six less effective incongruent types are not just theoretical possibilities but are found empirically calls for an explanation. The major reason for this occurrence is that organizations have only limited control over the powers they apply and the involvement of lower participants. The exercise of power depends on the resources the organization can recruit and the license it is allowed in utilizing them. Involvement depends in part on external factors, such as membership of the participants in other collectivities (e.g., membership in labor unions [16]); basic value commitments (e.g., Catholic versus Protestant religious commitments [17]); and the personality

---

[14] A formalization of the relationship between rewards-allocation (which comes close to the concept of power as used here) and participation (which, as defined, is similar to the concept of involvement) has been suggested by Breton (1960).

[15] "Other factors" might include previous applications of the power.

[16] On the effect of membership in labor unions on involvement in the corporation, see Willerman (1949, p. 4); L. R. Dean (1954); Jacobson (1951); and Purcell (1953, pp. 79, 146).

[17] See W. F. Whyte et al. (1955, pp. 45–46). Protestants are reported to be more committed to

structure of the participants (e.g., authoritarian [18]). All these factors may reduce the expected congruence of power and involvement.

A DYNAMIC HYPOTHESIS. Congruent types are more effective than incongruent types. Organizations are under pressure to be effective. Hence, to the degree that the environment of the organization allows, *organizations tend to shift their compliance structure from incongruent to congruent types* and *organizations which have congruent compliance structures tend to resist factors pushing them toward incongruent compliance structures.*

Congruence is attained by a change in either the power applied by the organization or the involvement of lower participants. Change of power takes place when, for instance, a school shifts from the use of corporal punishment to stress on the "leadership" of the teachers. The involvement of lower participants may be changed through socialization, changes in recruitment criteria, and the like.[19]

Because the large majority of cases falls into the three categories representing congruent compliance, these three types form the basis for subsequent analysis. We refer to the coercive-alienative type as *coercive compliance;* to the remunerative-calculative type as *utilitarian compliance;* and to the normative-moral type as *normative compliance.* Students of organizational change, conflict, strain, and similar topics may find the six incongruent types more relevant to their work.

Compliance and Authority. The typology of compliance relationships presented above highlights some differences between the present approach to the study of organizational control and that of studies conducted in the tradition of Weber. These studies tend to focus on authority, or legitimate power, as this concept is defined.[20] The significance of authority has been emphasized in modern sociology in the past, in order to overcome earlier biases that overemphasized force and economic power as the sources of social order. This emphasis, in turn, has led to an overemphasis on legitimate power. True, some authority can be found in the control structure of lower participants in most organizations. True, authority plays a role in maintaining the long-run operations of the organization. But so does nonlegitimated power. Since the significance of legitimate power has been fully recognized, it is time to lay the ghost of Marx and the old controversy, and to give full status to both legitimate and nonlegitimate sources of control.

Moreover, the concept of authority does not take into account differences among powers other than their legitimacy, in particular the nature of the sanctions (physical, material, or symbolic) on which power is based. All three types of power may be regarded as legitimate by lower participants: thus there is normative,[21] remunerative, and coercive authority

the values of saving and productivity, whereas Catholics are more concerned with their social standing in the work group. This makes for differences in compliance: Protestants are reported to be more committed to the corporation's norms than Catholics.

[18] For instance, authoritarian personality structure is associated with a "custodial" orientation to mental patients (Gilbert and Levinson, 1957, pp. 26–27).

[19] We return to this dynamic perspective in Chapter IV, after introducing the concepts of goal and effectiveness. See pages 87–88.

[20] For various definitions and usages of the concept see Friedrich (1958). For a formalization of the concept in relation to power and to leadership, see Barton (1958). For a psychological discussion of legitimate power see French and Raven (1959, pp. 158–61).

[21] The concept of "normative authority" raises the question of the difference between this kind of authority and normative power. There is clearly a high *tendency* for normative power to be considered legitimate and thus to form an authority relationship. The reason for this tendency is that the motivational significance of rewards and deprivations depends not only on the objective nature of the power applied, but also on the meaning attached to it by the subject. Coercive and remunerative means of control are considerably less dependent on such interpretations than normative ones. Most actors in most situations will see a fine as a deprivation and confinement as a punishment. On the other hand, if the subject does not accept as legitimate the power of a teacher, a priest, or a party official, he is not likely to feel their condemnation or censure as depriving. Since normative power depends on manipulation of symbols, it is much more dependent on "meanings," and, in this sense, on the subordinate, than other powers. But it is by no means necessary that the application of normative power always be regarded as legitimate.

A person may, for example, be aware that an-

(differentiated by the kind of power employed, for instance, by a leader, a contractor, and a policeman).[22] But these powers differ in the likelihood that they will be considered legitimate by those subjected to them. Normative power is most likely to be considered legitimate; coercive, least likely; and remunerative is intermediate.

Finally, it is important to emphasize that involvement in the organization is affected both by the legitimacy of a directive and by the degree to which it frustrates the subordinate's need-dispositions. Alienation is produced not only by illegitimate exercise of power, but also by power which frustrates needs, wishes, desires. Commitment is generated not merely by directives which are considered legitimate but also by those which are in line with internalized needs of the subordinate. Involvement is positive if the line of action directed is conceived by the subordinate as both legitimate and gratifying. It is negative when the power is not granted legitimacy and when it frustrates the subordinate. Involvement is intermediate when either legitimation or gratification is lacking. Thus the study of involvement, and hence that of compliance, differs from the study of authority by taking into account the effects of the cathectic as well as the evaluative impact of directives on the orientation of lower participants.

Lower Participants and Organizational Boundaries

Before we can begin our comparisons, the following questions still remain to be answered. Why do we make compliance of lower participants the focus of the comparison? Who exactly are "lower participants"? What are the lower boundaries of an organization? In answering these questions, we employ part of the analytical scheme suggested above, and thus supply the first test of its fruitfulness.

Why Lower Participants? Compliance of lower participants is made the focus of this analysis for several reasons. First, the control of lower participants is more problematic than that of higher participants because, as a rule, the lower an actor is in the organizational hierarchy, the fewer rewards he obtains. His position is more deprived; organizational activities are less meaningful to him because he is less "in the know," and because often, from his position, only segments of the organization and its activities are visible.[23] Second, since we are concerned with systematic differences among organizations (the similarities having been more often explored), we focus on the ranks in which the largest differences in compliance can be found. An inter-organizational comparison of middle and higher ranks would show that their compliance structures differ much less than those of the lower ranks (see Chapter IX, pp. 201–3).

Who Are Lower Participants? Organizational studies have used a large number of concrete terms to refer to lower participants: employees, rank-and-file, members, clients, customers, inmates.[24] These terms are rarely defined. They are customarily used to designate lower participants in more than one organization, but none can be used for all.

Actually, these terms can be seen as reflecting different positions on at least three analytical dimensions.[25] One is the *nature* (direction and intensity) of the actors' *involvement* in the organization. Unless some qualifying adjectives such as "cooperative" or "good" are

---

other person has influenced his behavior by manipulation of symbolic rewards, but feel that he had no right to do so, that he ought not to have such power, or that a social structure in which normative powers are concentrated (e.g., partisan control over mass media; extensive advertising) is unjustified. A Catholic worker who feels that his priest has no right to condemn him because of his vote for the "wrong" candidate may still fear the priest's condemnation and be affected by it.

[22] For another classification of authority, which includes authority of confidence, of identification, of sanctions, and of legitimacy, see Simon, Smithburg, and Thompson (1959, p. 189).

[23] The term *visible* is used here and throughout this book as defined by Merton: "the extent to which the norms and the role-performances within a group are readily open to observation by others." (1957, pp. 319 ff.)

[24] For one of the best discussions of the concept of participation, its definition and dimensions, see Fichter (1954, Part I, *passim*).

[25] The difference between concrete and analytic membership in corporations has been pointed out by Feldman (1959).

introduced, *inmates* implies alienative involvement. *Clients* designates people with alienative or calculative involvement. *Customers* refers to people who have a relatively more alienative orientation than clients; one speaks of the clients of professionals but not ordinarily of their customers. *Member* is reserved for those who have at least some, usually quite strong, moral commitment to their organization. *Employee* is used for people with various degrees of calculative involvement.

A second dimension underlying these concrete terms is the degree to which lower participants are *subordinated* to organizational powers. Inmates, it seems, are more subordinated than employees, employees more than members, and members more than clients. A study in which subordination is a central variable would take into account that it includes at least two subvariables: the extent of control in each area (e.g., "tight" versus remote control); and the scope of control, measured by the number of areas in which the subject is subordinated. Such refinement is not required for our limited use of this dimension.

A third dimension is the amount of *performance* required from the participants by the organization: it is high for employees, low for inmates, and lowest for clients and customers.[26]

Using concrete terms to designate groups of participants without specifying the underlying dimensions creates several difficulties. First of all, the terms cannot be systematically applied. Although "members" are in general positively involved, sometimes the term is used to designate lower participants with an alienative orientation. Archibald, for instance, uses this term to refer to members of labor unions who are members only *pro forma* and who see in the union simply another environmental constraint, to which they adjust by paying dues.

[26] Participants of a social unit might also be defined as all those who share an institutionalized set of role-expectations. We shall not employ this criterion since it blurs a major distinction, that between the organization as such and its social environment. Members of most groups share such role-expectations with outsiders.

A criterion of participation which is significant for other purposes than ours is whether lower participants have formal or actual powers, such as those reflected in the right to vote, submit grievances, or strike.

Most workers entered the yards not merely ignorant of unions, but distrustful of them. . . . They nonetheless joined the unions, as they were compelled to do, with little protest. They paid the initiation fees, averaging not more than twenty dollars, much as they would have bought a ticket to the county fair: it costs money, but maybe the show would be worth the outlay. As for dues, they paid them with resignation to the principle that all joys of life are balanced by a measure of pain. (1947, pp. 131–32)

The term *customers* suggests that the actors have no moral commitments to their sources of products and services. But sometimes it is used to refer to people who buy from cooperatives, frequent only unionized barbers, and remain loyal to one newspaper—that is, to people who are willing to suffer some economic loss because they see in these sources of service something which is "good in itself"—people who, in short, have some moral commitments.

Any moral commitment on the part of mental patients, designated as *inmates*, is viewed either with surprise or as a special achievement of the particular mental hospital; on the other hand, members of labor unions are "expected" to show moral commitment and are labeled "apathetic" if they do not. The fact that some mental patients view their hospital as their home, and thus are positively involved, whereas labor union members may see their organization as a secondary group only, is hidden by the terminology employed. The same point could be made for differences in performance and in subordination.

Although the use of such concrete terms leads to overgeneralization, by implying that all lower participants of an organization have the characteristics usually associated with the label, they can also impede generalization. An illustration is supplied by studies of parishioners. Many of these studies focus on problems of participation, such as "apathy," high turnover, and declining commitment. But rarely are comparisons drawn, or insights transferred, from the study of members of voluntary associations and political organizations. Actually, all these organizations are concerned with the moral commitment of lower participants who have few performance obligations and little subordination to the organization.

Another advantage of specifying the analytical dimensions underlying these concepts is that the number of dimensions is limited, whereas the number of concrete terms grows continuously with the number of organizations studied. Thus the study of hospitals introduces patients; the analysis of churches brings up parishioners; and the examination of armies adds soldiers. Following the present procedure, we can proceed to characterize the lower participants of additional organizations by the use of the same three dimensions.

lytical terms such as alienative, calculative, and moral can be applied equally well to participants at all levels of the organizational hierarchy.

Ideally, in a book such as this, we should refer to lower participants in analytical terms, those of various degrees of involvement, subordination, and performance obligations. Since this would make the discussion awkward, the concrete terms are used, but only to refer to *typical* analytical constellations. *Inmates* are lower participants with high alienation, low

Table 1. Analytical Specifications of Some Concepts Referring to Lower Participants *

LOWER PARTICIPANTS	NATURE OF INVOLVEMENT (INTENSITY AND DIRECTION)	SUBORDINATION	PERFORMANCE OBLIGATIONS
Inmates	High, negative	High	Low
Employees	Low, negative or positive	Medium	High
Customers	Low, negative or positive	None	Low
Parishioners	High, positive	Low	Low
Members	High, positive	Medium to Low	Low
Devoted Adherents	High, positive	High	High

* This table contains a set of definitions to be used. It is not exhaustive, either in concepts referring to lower participants or in possible combinations of "scores" on the various dimensions.

Specifying the underlying dimensions enables us not only to formulate analytical profiles of a large variety of lower participants, but also to compare them systematically with each other on these three dimensions. For instance, "soldiers" (in combat) are high on all three dimensions, whereas inmates are high on subordination and alienation but low on performance; employees are medium in involvement and subordination, but high on performance obligations. The import of such comparisons will become evident later.

Finally, whereas concrete terms tend to limit analysis to participants at particular levels, ana-

performance obligations, and high subordination. The term will not be used to refer to other combinations which are sometimes found among lower participants in prisons. *Members* is used to refer only to lower participants who are highly committed, medium on subordination, and low on performance obligations; it is not used to refer to alienated lower participants in voluntary associations. Similarly, other terms are used as specified in Table 1.

Lower versus Higher Participants. Higher participants have a "permanent" power advantage over lower participants because of their organizational position. Thus, by definition, higher participants as a group are less *subordinated* than lower participants. Often, though not in all organizational types, they are also more *committed*, and have more *performance obligations* (if we see decision making and other mental activities as performances). Thus the three dimensions which serve to distinguish among various types of lower participants also mark the dividing line between lower and higher participants. These very dimensions also enable us to suggest a way to delineate the organizational boundaries—that is, to distinguish between participants and non-participants.

Organizational Boundaries. Students of organizations must often make decisions about the boundaries of the unit they are studying: who is a participant, who an outsider. March and Simon, for example, take a broad view of organizational boundaries: "When we describe the chief participants of most business organizations, we generally limit our attention to the following five major classes: employees, investors, suppliers, distributors, and consumers" (1958, p. 89).

We follow a narrower definition and see as participants all actors who are high on at least one of the three dimensions of participation: involvement, subordination, and performance. Thus, students, inmates, soldiers, workers, and many others are included. Customers and clients, on the other hand, who score low on all three criteria, are considered "outsiders."

We should like to underscore the importance of this way of delineating the organizational boundaries. It draws the line much "lower" than most studies of bureaucracies, which tend to include only persons who are part of a formal hierarchy: priests, but not parishioners; stewards, but not union members; guards, but not inmates; nurses, but not patients. We treat organizations as collectivities of which the lower participants are an important segment. To exclude them from the analysis would be like studying colonial structures without the natives, stratification without the lower classes, or a political regime without the citizens or voters.

It seems to us especially misleading to include the lower participants in organizational charts when they have a formal role, as privates in armies or workers in factories, and to exclude them when they have no such status, as is true for parishioners or members. This practice leads to such misleading comparisons as seeing the priests as the privates of the church and teachers as the lowest-ranking participants of schools, in both cases ignoring the psychological import of having "subordinates." One should not let legal or administrative characteristics stand in the way of a sociological analysis. However, the main test of the decision to delineate the organization as we have chosen follows: it lies in the scope, interest, and validity of the propositions this approach yields.

Summary

Compliance patterns were chosen as the basis for our comparative study of organizations because compliance relations are a central element of organizational structure. It distinguishes organizations from other collectivities because organizations require more compliance than other collectivities do, and it is systematically related to many other organizational variables.

Compliance refers both to a relation in which an actor behaves in accordance with a directive supported by another person's power and to the orientation of the subject to the power applied. There are three kinds of power: coercive, remunerative, and normative; and three kinds of involvement: alienative, calculative, and moral. There are, therefore, nine possible types of compliance. Three of these types (congruent types) are more effective than the other six; they are also empirically much more frequent. These three types form the basis of our comparative study.

Each organizational rank has its own compliance structure. We focus on the compliance structure of lower participants, first because their compliance is more problematic than that of higher participants, and second because organizations can be most fruitfully distinguished from each other at this level.

Lower participants are actors who are high on at least one of the three dimensions of participation: involvement, performance obligations, and subordination. An examination of concrete terms often used to refer to different groups of lower participants shows that they can be seen as positions on these three analytical dimensions, which also enable us also to delineate systematically the boundaries of organizations. We are now ready to engage in the first major substantive step: classification of organizations according to their compliance structures.

REFERENCES

Davis, K. The sociology of prostitution. *A. socio. Rev.*, 1937, **2**, 744–755.

Gerth, H. H., & Mills, C. W. *From Max Weber: Essays in Sociology*. New York: Oxford University Press.

Goldhamer, H., & Shils, E. A. Types of power and status. *Am. J. Soc.*, 1939, **45**, 171–182.

March, J. G. & Simon, H. *Organizations*. New York: Wiley, 1958.

Merton, R. K. *Mass Persuasion: The Social Psychology of a War Bond Drive*. New York: Harper, 1946.

Parsons, T. *The Social System*. Glencoe, Ill.: The Free Press, 1951.

Simmel, G. Superiority and subordination as subject-matter of sociology. *Am J. Soc.*, 1896, **2**, 167–189, 392–415.

Sykes, G. M. *The Society of Captives*. Princeton, N.J.: Princeton University Press, 1958.

Weber, M. *The Theory of Social and Economic Organization*. London: Wm. Hodge, 1947.

Decentralization

PETER DRUCKER

In this study General Motors is considered only as an example of the social structure and of the institutional problems of the big-business corporation. No attempt will be made to give a description of General Motors as such, or of its history—let alone of its products and results. However, an elementary knowledge of the main outlines of the organization and of its policies will be useful.

The domestic manufacturing properties of General Motors can be classed in three groups according to their main peace-time products. First in employment and volume of business comes the automobile and truck group: Chevrolet, Buick, Oldsmobile, Pontiac, Cadillac and General Motors Truck. To this group belongs also the Fisher Body Division, which produces the bodies for all automobile divisions and which works in closest contact with them. Most of the Fisher plants, though managed separately by the Body Division, are physically combined with the assembly plants of the automobile producers.

The second group consists of the manufacturers of automobile accessories who produce most of the accessory needs of the automobile plants. A good many of the accessory producers sell also outside of General Motors. In addition to the spare parts and replacement business which is very important for practically all accessory divisions, some of them, notably the producers of spark plugs, roller bearings, ball bearings and electrical motors, sell directly to other industrial producers who

in some cases account for more than fifty per cent of total sales. To this group also belongs Frigidaire—both historically and according to its manufacturing and engineering problems—which sells exclusively to the public.

The third group of manufacturing properties consists of three Diesel engine producers in Cleveland, Detroit and La Grange, Illinois, whose products comprise small Diesel engines for trucks, marine Diesel engines, and the huge Diesel-electric locomotives which pull America's stream-lined trains. The Allison engine division producing aircraft engines also belongs in this group of non-automotive engine producers.

During the war General Motors added to these three main foci of activities a number of aircraft producing plants located on the Eastern seaboard; these plants which were under one management and organized in the Eastern Aircraft Division presented a special reconversion problem.

These three groups of manufacturing properties are organized in about thirty divisions ranging in size from Chevrolet and Fisher Body, which would be among the largest American businesses by themselves, to small one-plant appliance divisions, employing in peacetime less than a thousand men. Each of these divisions has its own divisional manager who is served by almost as complete a staff as if he were heading an independent business: production manager, chief engineer, sales manager, comptroller, personnel manager, etc.; in other words, each division is organized as an autonomous unit. The three largest of these divisions: Chevrolet, Fisher Body and Buick, are represented in the top management by their own divisional managers. The other divisions are organized in groups according to their products, each under a group executive who, as a vice-president of General Motors, acts as representative of his group in the central management of the corporation and as adviser and representative of central management for the divisional managers of his group.

Side by side with this organization according to products there is, as a part of central management, a set of functional service staffs: manufacturing, engineering, sales, research, personnel, finance, public relations, law, etc., each under its own vice-president. These staff organizations advise both central management and the divisional managers, act as liaison between the divisions and formulate corporation policies.

The "line organization"—the manufacturing divisions—is headed by the President and his two Executive Vice-Presidents; the "staff work" is headed by the Chairman of the Board who is the Chief Executive Officer of General Motors, and by the Vice-Chairman of the Board. These five officials form a team. They work through and with two closely co-ordinated committees, one on policy, one on administration. In addition to top management these committees contain the senior administrative and staff officers of the company, former officers now on the Board of Directors, and representatives of the major stockholders.

These two committees are the central organ of co-ordination, decision and control, and may well be called the government of General Motors. They pass on all major decisions in the fields of policy and administration. They hear periodic reports on conditions, problems and achievements in all branches of the business. And they are the court of last appeal should there be serious disagreements on policy within the organization. Hence all members of these committees—whether departmental executives in charge of service staffs or divisions, or members of top management—are almost automatically informed at all times about the work of all divisions, about all important problems and decisions in all fields, and also about the great line and, the over-all policies of the company. These functions, integration of "staff" and "line," combination of a variety of experiences and special backgrounds into one policy, presentation of the over-all picture to all the senior men, may well be more impor-

tant in the normal course of affairs than the decision-making power of the committees.

Each of these two top committees meets regularly to discuss and to decide. The actual executive work is, however, done by a number of specialized sub-committees, each in charge of a field such as engineering, labor, finance, public relations, distribution, etc. These sub-committees are very much smaller. They are built around a number of men from the field in question. The vice-president in charge of the appropriate service staff usually acts as the chairman. The membership includes experts in the field both from central management and from the divisions. But on each sub-committee there sit also several members of the top-management team and senior executives from other fields to balance the sectional viewpoint of the experts, to bring in a broader background of experience, and to relate the work of the sub-committee to the corporation as a whole. These sub-committees, in monthly meetings, actually work out the recommendations and presentations on which the two top committees act.*

Neither this sketch nor an organization chart can, of course, show the outsider how the organization actually functions. But it should give some impression of the administrative and organizational problems that have to be solved in order to make it run efficiently. There is the sheer size of the business—250,000 workers in peacetime, twice that number during the war. There is a problem of diversity: not only do the finished products—over two hundred in

---

* I have not come across much evidence that theories of governmental organization or historical examples had any considerable influence on the development of General Motors' managerial organization. The impetus seems to have been supplied mainly by experience and needs. Yet, there is a remarkably close parallel between General Motors' scheme of organization, and that of the two institutions most renowned for administrative efficiency: that of the Catholic Church and that of the modern army as first developed by the Prussian General Staff between 1800 and 1870 and later adopted everywhere. I tend to think that this scheme represents one of the basic solutions to the problem of institutional organization for survival and efficiency—the other one being the system of checks and balances between organs constructed upon contrasting principles of rule, for instance the one-man executive, committee-judiciary and many-men legislature of the American Constitution.

peacetime—range from a Diesel-electric locomotive costing $500,000 to a bolt costing a fraction of a cent; the production units required range from gigantic plants with 40,000 employees to machine shops. There is a problem in autonomy: the five hundred men of ability, experience and ambition who are needed in major executive jobs in order to turn out all these different finished products of General Motors could not possibly be organized and managed from the top. There is also a problem of unity: with the bulk of the company's products focused on one final utility, the automobile, and therefore directed towards the same market, the divisions could not be left to their own devices but must be one in spirit and in policy. Divisional management must be both autonomous and directed; central management must at the same time give effective, unifying leadership and be confined to regulation and advice.

General Motors could not function as a holding company with the divisions organized like independent companies under loose financial control. Central management not only has to know even minor details of divisional management but the top officials have to exercise the power, the prestige and the influence of real bosses. On the other hand General Motors could not function as a centralized organization in which all decisions are made on the top, and in which the divisional managers are but little more than plant superintendents. Divisional managers too must have the authority and standing of real bosses.

Hence General Motors has become *an essay in federalism*—on the whole, an exceedingly successful one. It attempts to combine the greatest corporate unity with the greatest divisional autonomy and responsibility; and like every true federation, it aims at realizing unity through local self-government and vice versa. This is the aim of General Motors' policy of decentralization.

Decentralization, as the term is usually understood, means division of labor and is nothing new. In fact, it is one of the prerequisites of any management whether that of a business or of any army. But in General Motors usage, decentralization is much more than that. In over twenty years of work, first from 1923 to 1937 as President, since then as Chairman of the Corporation, Mr. Alfred P. Sloan, Jr., has developed the concept of decentralization into

a philosophy of industrial management and into a system of local self-government. It is not a mere technique of management but an outline of a social order. Decentralization in General Motors is not confined to the relations between divisional managers and central management but is to extend in theory to all managerial positions including that of foreman; it is not confined in its operation within the company but extends to the relations to its partners in business, particularly the automobile dealers; and for Mr. Sloan and his associates the application and further extension of decentralization are the answer to most of the problems of modern industrial society.

THE AIMS OF DECENTRALIZATION. Because General Motors considers decentralization a basic and universally valid concept of order, I asked several General Motors executives—particularly men well below the top—what in their opinion decentralization seeks to achieve. The following is a summary of the views of a good many different people. One man gave an unusually full statement of what he believed to be the aims and achievements of the policy of decentralization that was of particular interest because he himself had joined General Motors only two years earlier after a distinguished career in another big business organized on radically different lines; his statement —completely unrehearsed as my question was sprung at him in the course of an informal chat—has therefore been regarded as particularly valuable.

We shall have occasion later to discuss the question how much of its program decentralization actually realizes; here are the advantages claimed for it:

1. The speed with which a decision can be made, the lack of any confusion as to who makes it and the knowledge of the policies on which the decision is based by everybody concerned.

2. The absence of any conflict between the interests of the divisions and those of General Motors.

3. The sense of fairness in dealing among executives, the certainty that a good job will be appreciated, the confidence and feeling of security that comes when personality-issues, intrigues and factionalism are kept under control.

4. The democracy of management and its

informality. Nobody throws his weight around, yet there is never any doubt where the real authority lies. Everybody is free to criticize, to talk and to suggest; yet once the decision is taken, nobody tries to sabotage it.

5. The absence of a gap in the executive group between the "privileged few" and the "great many." "Mr. Wilson (the President) could not arrogate to himself any right he does not accord to his associates."

6. There is a very large management group. Thus there is always a supply of good and experienced leaders, able to take top responsibility.

7. Decentralization means that weak divisions and weak managers cannot ride for any length of time on the coat tails of successful divisions, or trade on their own past reputation.

> At the company I came from [this from the informant mentioned above] nobody ever knew whether the foundry was run efficiently or not, whether our foundry manager was a good or a bad manager; the foundry costs were centrally merged in the general costs. In General Motors, this foundry would be a division, so that the costs and the results of foundry operations would at once be visible to everybody.

8. Decentralization means the absence of "edict management" in which nobody quite knows why he does what he is ordered to do. Its place is taken by discussion and by policies which are public and which are arrived at as a result of the experiences of all the people concerned.

> Perhaps my greatest surprise when I joined General Motors [so again the above-mentioned informant] came when I attended my first 'Sloan meeting' [see below] and saw the extent to which even minor executives are informed of the reasons for company policies, and are encouraged to speak their mind freely and to express their opinions, however much they disagree with central management. In. . . . [the company where my informant had spent twenty years and where he had risen from apprentice to chief engineer] even senior executives were never told the reason for any central management decision.

It is obvious from this summary—as indeed it was obvious in my talks—that the executives of General Motors do not only consider decentralization to be the correct concept for the organization of a big business but that they feel that, at least on the level of top management, the concept has been realized and its aims achieved.

CENTRAL AND DIVISIONAL MANAGEMENT. Decentralization, as said above, is not considered as confined to top management but a principle for the organization of all managerial relationships. It was developed, however, out of the problems of co-ordinating central and divisional management into one whole. It has been tested most thoroughly on the top level of General Motors; and it has been most generally accepted and most successful on this level. Hence we shall study the meaning and the effects of the policy of decentralization by analyzing the relationships between central and divisional managements.

Central management has twofold functions under a system of decentralization. It is at the same time the servant of the divisional managers, helping them to be more efficient and more successful in their autonomy, and the boss of the corporation. And in this role it has to weld several hundred aggressive, highly individual and very independent divisional top executives into one team. These two jobs are apparently contradictory but actually interdependent. Their solution is attempted in various ways: (1) through the power of central management to set the goals for each division and for the whole corporation; (2) through its power to define the limits of authority of the divisional manager and through the power to appoint and remove divisional managers; (3) through its constant check on divisional problems and progress; (4) through relieving the divisional manager of all concern with problems that are not strictly part of the process of production and selling; (5) and finally through offering him the best obtainable advice and help through the service staffs of central management.

1. The manufacturing program of the various divisions has to be approved by central management, particularly as far as the car divisions are concerned; central management sets the price range within which Chevrolet, Buick, etc. operate. Beyond this range they cannot go without specific authorization. But no attempt is made to prevent Oldsmobile, for instance,

from trying to displace the low-priced Buick car. No attempt is made to tell Chevrolet what prices to pay the Fisher Body Division for its bodies. No attempt is made to force any of the car divisions to buy its accessories, such as lamps, from one of the General Motors divisions if the manager of a car division can show that he can get better value elsewhere.

Similarly in respect to the Diesel divisions, it is central management that will have to decide whether the overlapping production programs of two of these divisions—the result of historical developments antedating their acquisition by General Motors—are to be maintained or whether each division is to specialize on one type of engine.

Central management not only delimits the divisions against each other, it fits them into a general pattern as part of the unified corporation. It establishes the general over-all aim and allots to each division its role on the team. It establishes a total production goal on the basis of an analysis of the economic situation and assigns to each division its minimum quota. It determines how much capital to allot to each division.

Above all, central management thinks ahead for the whole Corporation. It is thus differentiated from divisional management not only in power and function but in time. A good divisional manager is fully as much concerned with the future as with the present; indeed one way to distinguish a divisional manager from divisional employees—some of whom, such as the managers of a few large plants owned by the big divisions, have many more people working for them than the manager of a small division—is by the divisional manager's responsibility for the long-term future of the business he runs. But it is not his responsibility to decide in what direction his division should develop; that is the responsibility of central management however much it may rely on the advice of divisional management. It is also the responsibility of central management to foresee problems and to work out solutions in advance. Central management furthermore works out major policy decisions applicable to problems common to all divisions. Finally, it decides on expansion into new lines—for instance on the expansion into the Diesel field, on the acquisition of new properties and the establishment of new divisions. *Of all the functions of central management, this responsibility to think ahead is perhaps the most important as it more than anything else makes General Motors a unified institution with but one purpose.*

2. Central management determines the limits within which the divisional manager operates. Within General Motors this is usually expressed by saying that central management makes policy decisions, while the divisional manager is in charge of administration. This is, of course, a misunderstanding. Every executive down to the lowliest assistant foreman makes policy decisions; and every executive, up to the Chairman of the Board, has administrative duties. But central management determines both the areas of decision for the divisional manager, and the general rules to which his decisions have to adhere. To phrase it in terms of constitutional law, policy decisions of a divisional manager must rest on an explicit or implicit delegation of policy-making power and must conform to implicit or explicit commands or be *ultra vires*.

And behind this, as an ultimate recourse, there is the absolute power of central management to remove a divisional manager and to appoint a new man in his stead. Obviously it is a rare and grave decision to dismiss the manager of a division, and it is regarded as most important by central management that it should be taken not on the basis of a personal impression regarding the man's ability and achievement, but on the basis of objective records. But this is voluntary self-restraint on the part of central management which does not affect its unquestioned final power of removal.

3. More in evidence in every day business conduct is the control through contact which central management exercises over divisional managers. Largely this is informal and a question of advice, discussion or mutual respect built up over years of collaboration. The vice-president in charge of a group of divisions, for instance, has a very real power; but it is rarely, if ever, exercised in the form of orders. Rather it makes itself felt through suggestions made in discussing problems or achievements of the division, in discussing central-management decisions, or as a result of the respect the divisional manager has for a man who, as is usually the case, has successfully been a divisional manager himself. The same kind of informal but very real control is exercised by the subcommittees of the Policy and Administration Committees with whom managers discuss their

problems, plans and policies, and, as will be discussed later, by the service staffs.

However there is a formal safeguard of central-management control, a formal veto power on all capital investments beyond a certain limit and on the hiring of executive personnel beyond a certain salary. This veto power is rarely exercised as a divisional manager is unlikely to make such a proposal without the support of his group-executive and of the appropriate service-staff. But it has the important result that practically every major policy decision of the divisions has to be discussed extensively with central management.

Equally important is central management's role in helping the divisional manager to be as effective as possible.

4. To this end the divisional manager is relieved of all worry over financial matters. As president of an independent company, he would have to spend a great deal of his time in obtaining the capital necessary for expansion. This worry is taken off his shoulders completely. It is the job of central management to obtain the capital for him for any program that has been decided upon as desirable. The same holds for legal matters. Also, General Motors has a uniform accounting system supervised and managed centrally. Finally, most union contracts and all negotiations in labor matters are handled centrally by a staff of the Corporation under a vice-president; this is, however, not the result of a decision to relieve the divisional manager of a worry only incidental to the business such as underlies the centralized handling of financial, legal and accounting matters, but is the result of the demand of the United Automobile Workers Union for a uniform contract for the company; and the wisdom of such a centralized labor policy is hotly debated within the Corporation.

5. Finally, the divisional managers are served through the service staffs of central management. Their first function is to advise the divisional manager whenever he feels in need of such advice. It is, for instance, quite customary for a newly appointed divisional manager to come to the Detroit office to obtain advice on the distribution of the bonus (see below) within his division. During the war the manufacturing staff at Central Office worked out the basic manufacturing processes for many war products upon the request of the divisions; it is typical however of the way these staff agencies work that the final details of production and improvements in working methods were left entirely to the division.

Another important function of the staff agencies is to act as liaison between the various divisions, and particularly as centers of information on new or improved methods. If, for instance, one division has worked out a new way of treating cast aluminum which cuts down costs by five per cent, the other divisions interested in this or similar problems will at once be informed by the service staff. In this way, the service staffs attempt to make sure that all over General Motors the most advanced methods are used. In the same way, information about new problems that have arisen in one division and about difficulties to be encountered with a new product, a new method or a new labor policy is collected and transmitted to all the other divisions to save time and avoid costly errors. Similarly, the staff experts make available to the divisions the most up-to-date methods developed outside of General Motors, whether in research, in merchandising, in the handling of public relations, etc. This service function of central management alone probably is worth considerably more to the divisions than the one-half of one per cent of turnover that is charged by General Motors for the upkeep of the entire central management.

It should be emphasized that the staff agencies in their relations with the divisions rely on suggestions and advice, and that they have no direct authority whatsoever over the divisional manager and his policies. Of course they might appeal to top management in a last attempt to force an obstructionist divisional manager into line; this, however, is a theoretical rather than a practical recourse. In the normal course of events the service staffs have to "sell themselves" to the divisional manager, and have to rely on their ability to convince the divisional management and on their reputation and achievements. No divisional manager is under compulsion to consult the service staff or to take their advice. Yet the relationship between service staffs and divisional managers is on the whole quite frictionless.

Just as the service staffs apprise the divisional management of all important developments outside of his own division, they inform central management of all important developments within the divisions. To the service staffs—though not exclusively to them—central management owes its knowledge of the details of production, engineering, distribution and personnel management throughout the business, which is one of the most important factors in the teamwork between the policy-makers at the top and the administrators in the division.

Finally, it is the job of the service staff to formulate future policies in closest collaboration with both divisional managers and central management. The staff agencies themselves cannot lay down policies; they can only recommend. They must convince both the central management dealing with broad problems of corporation policy and the divisional managers with their concrete tasks, before any of their recommendations will be accepted as general Corporation policy.

Like any formal analysis of a functioning organization this description fails to convey what is really the most important thing: the way in which the organs of central management work. It gives only an outline of the frame within which central management operates, and not the picture itself. When we turn to the *divisional manager*, we cannot give even the frame. The nearest description of his status and operations might be to say that within the limits of policy and decision set for him by central management, he operates on his own as the boss of his outfit. He is in complete charge of production and sales. He hires, fires and promotes; and it is up to him to decide how many men he needs, with what qualifications and in what salary range—except for top executives whose employment is subject to a central-management veto. The divisional manager decides the factory layout, the technical methods and equipment used. He works out the capital requirements of his division and plans for expansion and for new plants—though central management must approve of major investments. The divisional manager is in charge of advertising and public relations for his division. He buys his supplies independently from suppliers of his own choice. He determines the distribution of production within the several plants under his jurisdiction, decides which lines to push and decides on the methods of sale and distribution. He makes contracts with dealers and gives or cancels their franchises. In everything pertaining to operations he is as much the real head as if his division were indeed an independent business. According to the estimate of several divisional managers—corroborated by members of the central management—ninety-five per cent of all decisions fall within his jurisdiction.

But this description, while correct, fails to convey one intangible though very significant fact: the atmosphere of a team of which the divisional manager is a member. There is no "General Motors atmosphere" and very definitely no "General Motors type." In fact I am greatly struck by the difference of atmosphere between divisions, and by the variety of personality and background between individual divisional managers. This variety is not only permitted, it is definitely encouraged by central management; for it is held that every man will do his best job when he does it his own way, and that each division will do its best job when it feels a pride in its tradition, manners and social climate. Hence central management refrains as much as possible from telling a division how to do its job; it only lays down what to do. Yet the divisional manager, though left alone as long as he does a good job, is conscious of his place on a team.

This is largely the result of two broad policies which will be discussed later in some detail: the system of impersonal yardsticks by which the performance of divisional managers is measured objectively in terms of their contribution to the team, and the interchange of factual and personal knowledge by which the divisional managers are kept informed of their place in the team, and of the work of the team. But the dual position of the divisional manager as being at one and the same time the autonomous boss of his division and a member of a unified team shows best in the administration of the General Motors Bonus Plan—which in itself is an important reason why this dualism works without too much tension.

General Motors sets aside each year a considerable part of its net profit for bonuses to executive employees, to be paid in General Motors shares (during the last years a cash alternative has been offered for part of the bonus to enable the recipients to pay wartime income taxes on the bonus without having to sell General Motors stock; this is, however, considered a temporary expedient). Top management decides how much bonus each divisional manager is to receive as his own personal compensation. It also decides the total to be allotted to each division for distribution among the employees below the rank of divisional manager. While guided by a formula expressing both the total results of the corporation and an appraisal of the results of the division, central management is independent in these decisions. Who is eligible for participation in the bonus is also decided centrally for all divisions; participation is usually confined to men above the income level of a general foreman. Finally there is a definite and strongly recommended pattern of bonus distribution. The more important a man's position the greater should be his stake in the profit; while bonuses in the lower ranks of management should be a relatively unimportant "extra," bonuses of higher executives should be a major source of income though very elastic.

But within these general rules and recommendations the divisional manager decides how the bonus is to be distributed among his subordinates. He may single out one department for a special award or penalize another. He may reward or penalize individuals. To safeguard against arbitrary or partisan decisions he has to obtain the approval of central management before he can make radical departures from precedent, and has to explain his reasons. Once approved, however, his decision is final.

For General Motors executives, particularly for the senior men, the bonus is in normal years a very important part of their income. Hence the power of the divisional manager to decide on its distribution makes him the boss in a very real sense though the general rules and the veto power of central management over the plans of the divisional manager make it difficult for him to be arbitrary or spiteful or to play favorites. At the same time the stake the divisional manager himself has in a bonus which represents both the results of his own division and the results of the whole business, tends to give him a strong incentive to do his best in running his division and to play a cooperative part on the team that is General Motors.

The bonus enables the divisional manager to be both independent and a member of the group. Under normal business and tax conditions the divisional manager even of a small division should become in a few years a moderately wealthy man, if he keeps his bonus stock as he is strongly urged to do. Thus he will soon be financially independent. He need not hesitate to express his own opinion, to object to corporation policy, or to run his own division his own way; for he does not have to keep his job at all costs, nor does he regard himself as in any way inferior to the men in central management; they may be much wealthier than he is but the difference is one of degree rather than one of kind. At the same time his prosperity is directly bound up with the prosperity of General Motors, the shares of which are usually his major asset. It is not a decisive factor in the working of the system of decentralized management that the executives of the company are the largest individual (that is non-corporate) shareholders as a result of the bonus plan, and that General Motors shares are the major assets of most of its executives; but it is important.

A TWO-WAY FLOW. Division of powers and of functions, unity in action—this definition of a federal union would be a fairly accurate description of the aim of General Motors' policy of decentralization. Such a union cannot rest on blind obedience to orders. It must be based on an understanding of each other's problems, policies, approaches, mutually between central management and divisional managers. Every one must not only know what is expected of him but also how his neighbor will act and why. It is a problem which all large organizations have to solve. Concretely, General Motors could not function if every decision had to be approved by a few overworked men in New York or Detroit. At the same time, it could not function if these men at the helm did not know of every major move within the business. Similarly, it could not function if the divisional managers had to determine basic policy at every step; and it could not function if they did not know and understand policy decisions and the reasons behind them. The first requirement of General Motors' management is, therefore, that as many of its executive employees as possible understand the policies, the problems and the program of the company and of its divisions. Both information and decision must flow continually in two directions: from central management to the divisions, from the divisions to central management.

We have already mentioned some of the devices used. The vice-president in charge of a group of divisions acts as a constant liaison on policy and performance between head office and division. The service staffs provide liaison in the technical fields not only between central management and divisions but between the divisions themselves. The sub-committees through which top management works have members from the divisions and call in divisional executives all the time to advise and be advised. In addition, there are special meetings to create common understanding, which are being held twice a year in Detroit under the chairmanship of Mr. Sloan, and at which important or acute problems are discussed. At these meetings the results of the various divisions are also shown and reasons for success and failure are discussed. Suggestions from the divisions or from central management are brought up for debate and unplanned but effective personal contacts are established between central management and divisional personnel. About two to three hundred people attend these meetings regularly; an equal number is invited in rotation. Thus practically every senior employee—beginning perhaps at the level of plant superintendent—has an opportunity to see the business as a whole, to see his place in it and to familiarize himself with the basic policies and the program of the company.

These meetings have been held for more than ten years and have been singularly successful. However, the group was felt to be too large to establish the personal contact between central office and divisional personnel that is necessary for the general understanding of policies and problems on which General Motors depends. Therefore the "Sloan meetings" in Detroit are now being supplemented by smaller meetings in the various centers of production in which members of the central management meet for several days with local executives of the divisions. The attendants at these meetings include all the people who are invited to the "Sloan meetings" and a number of lesser employees from the local plants and offices. Similar meetings are being held with dealers.

By these means managerial employees of the corporation are kept informed on policies and problems: they are also constantly brought into the determination of policies. No important policy decision is made without consulting the divisional executives affected by it. It is the right as well as the duty of every managerial employee to criticize a central management decision which he considers mistaken or ill-advised. In fact, the one definition I could obtain of who is considered an executive in General Motors was: "A man who would be expected to protest officially against a policy decision to which he objects." Such criticism is not only not penalized; it is encouraged as a sign of initiative and of an active interest in the business. It is always taken seriously and given real consideration.

Central management does not of course base its decisions on the votes of the divisional personnel. It may completely disregard the opinions of divisional management. But in turning down a divisional executive it will attempt to explain to him its reasons. It is a standing rule that central management is to rely on persuasion and on rational proof rather than on an order. In debatable matters central management often prefers to wait until the divisional managers have themselves come and requested a policy decision rather than dictate from the top.

An example may illustrate the nature of this relationship. Several years ago, it was laid down as a general policy that all foremen should be on a salary basis rather than on hourly pay, and should enjoy seniority in layoffs over all hourly workers. During the war the number of foremen doubled. The new foremen were given the same status as the old foremen, lest they feel deprived of the relative security of seniority and thus in a worse position than the hourly workers in the event of a postwar depression. This decision was seriously attacked by several divisional managers who felt that it demoralized the old foremen who should be distinguished in some way as the permanent supervisory force of the company. The divisional managers brought their argument before the central management which at once agreed to reconsider the whole matter.

On the other hand central management does not hesitate to interfere directly and even ruthlessly whenever the interests or policies of the business are at stake. There is perhaps no greater contrast than that between the consideration shown to a divisional manager in all matters pertaining to the management of his division, and the co-operation expected of him in all matters where his conduct and policies directly affect the company as a whole. It is precisely here that the General Motors concept of central management functions pays its highest dividends. Because policy matters are usually discussed well in advance of the time when they become pressing, they can be handled leisurely and discussed freely and carefully. This, it is claimed, makes it possible to give all concerned a chance to think things through and to speak their minds without causing dangerous delay. Above all it makes it possible for central management to acquaint itself with the views of divisional management and vice versa. As a result when the time comes to put the policy into action everybody should know what he is supposed to do and why; every divisional manager should not only know where general policy begins and his autonomy stops but he should also accept the general policy as something he has helped formulate. Thus the question whose responsibility a certain decision is, will arise rarely, if ever.

FREEDOM AND ORDER. The impression that emerges from an analysis of the aims of General Motors' policy of organization is one of great individual liberty in which every man— at least among the three to five hundred first- and second-line executives—is to be allowed as much responsibility as he is willing to assume. There is little emphasis on title, rank or formal procedure. Indeed, the one thing that is most stressed by all executives is the "informality" that exists in the relationships among the members of this group and in the division of their work. This raises the question how General Motors avoids the dangers which according to age-old experience threaten every federal and especially every committee form of government: the danger of a deadlock between co-ordinated organs, the danger of a break-up of the organization in factionalism, intrigues and fights for power. It has always been a basic axiom of political theory that freedom such as General Motors accords to the members of its top management group is only possible within a clearly defined order with a strict division of authority and responsibility. General Motors, however, seems to lack largely what might be called a clear division of powers. Yet decisions must obviously be arrived at without too much delay or uncertainty as to who is entitled to make them, so as to enable the corporation to function in a highly competitive market. The question thus arises what it is that makes this "informality" possible. Can it be based solely on good will

and on good intentions? Or does it require a strict frame of objective policy as a condition of individual freedom? This, needless to say, is not a new but a very old question of politics —known in this country perhaps best as it appears in the conflict between Jeffersonian and Hamiltonian ideas of politics.

There is a tendency within General Motors to explain its functioning as owing to human individual good will rather than to institutional structure. There is a good deal to back up such an explanation. There can be no doubt that the informality, the reliance on information and persuasion, and the absence of "edict management" reflect accurately the personality of the man who developed General Motors to its present position—Alfred P. Sloan, Jr., for more than twenty years its active head. It is also certain that without Mr. Sloan's personality the system could never have grown up and established itself. Yet the tendency which underlies this "personality" explanation, to seek the basis of a political order in the personality of the ruler or in the good will of the citizens, is actually a very dangerous one. That it is current within General Motors is a potential weakness as it implies a lack of understanding by the organization of the factors from which it derives its strength. If it were true that the General Motors' system rested on individual good will, it could hardly survive the life span of one man. It would also have validity only for an organization headed by one particular type of personality and could not be regarded as a general model of industrial organization, which is precisely what General Motors aspires to be. Finally—and this is probably the most dangerous point for General Motors itself— such a belief might lead to a false sentimentalism, which evaluates executives according to the lip-service they pay to humanitarian principles, rather than according to their achievements.

Actually, General Motors' decentralization does not rest on the good will of the men in top management positions. It could, if necessary, function without the personal qualities which Mr. Sloan has shown in his long administration. Indeed it has been functioning with senior executives whose personalities were the very opposite of his, and who had nothing of the informality and of the respect for their fellow workers which would seem to be required. There must thus be an objective, impersonal frame of reference to make possible if not mandatory the freedom of decentralized management. This objective frame is given in the use of modern methods of cost accounting and market analysis as an impersonal yardstick to measure achievement of both policy-makers and production men.

This objective yardstick is comprised of two sets of measurements which apply equally to divisional management and its subordinates and to central management and its policy decisions: (1) Base pricing which gives an objective measure of the efficiency of the Corporation and of its subdivisions as a producer; (2) Competitive market standing which shows automatically and immediately the efficiency of the Corporation as a seller. Together these two gauges are supposed to show over-all efficiency and supply an immediate and objective check on decisions and policies.

The function of the system of base pricing is to measure the productive efficiency of all units of the business and also to eliminate from the measurement of productive costs all extraneous and transient factors, particularly those introduced by the fluctuations of the business cycle. Its core is that careful analysis of all the cost factors that enter into production at various rates of capacity which is the basis of modern accounting. This makes it possible to determine at one glance whether a certain division —or a department within a division—is producing with greater or lesser efficiency than the norm, and why. It also shows whether a good result is attributable to an increase in efficiency or to an improvement in methods, or whether it is the result of purely accidental factors for which management cannot claim credit. Above all, it makes it impossible to be deceived by a high profit in boom years if such profit is actually purchased at the expense of productive efficiency, that is at the risk of a permanent impairment of the company's strength. Conversely, it prevents a divisional manager from being blamed for the disappointing returns of a depression year when actually the result was caused by factors over which he had no control. Thus, a divisional manager will be held accountable for a deterioration of productive efficiency even when it is concealed by an increase in total profits; and he will get the credit for any strengthening of managerial efficiency, even when as the result of bad business conditions, his division operates at a

loss. The cost analysis of base pricing thus gives an objective standard of manufacturing efficiency.

The instrument of base pricing also furnishes a yardstick for policy decisions—both before they are taken and afterwards. It shows the factors of productive efficiency that are likely to be affected by a policy decision, thus substituting facts for personal differences of opinion in policy arguments. It shows how costs will be affected by policy decisions deemed necessary or advisable not for reasons of productive efficiency but for such reasons as labor policy, merchandising, public relations, etc.

Base pricing also shows the use made of General Motors' capital. It measures the rate of return on capital invested and the factors: rate of capacity at which the plants operate, lifetime of the productive equipment, etc., on which this rate depends. The assumptions under which any given investment is made can thus be isolated and checked against actual economic developments all the time. It thus furnishes a basis for policy decisions on expansion and measures the advisability of proposed new capital investments.

It is indicative of the concept of management that is embodied in General Motors organization that the cost analysis underlying base pricing is made by the divisions—just as it is customary in a good many divisions to have the department heads such as superintendents and foremen make the cost analysis for their jobs. The necessary check is supplied by a comparison of the cost analysis of each division with those of other divisions within the company making comparable products or using comparable methods—one reason for the company's insistence on uniform accounting practices throughout all divisions.

Efficient production is only one element in the success of a business in a free-enterprise economy, and has to be complemented by ability to sell one's products in the market. Hence, in General Motors an objective analysis of the market and of the competitive standing of the products is used as the second measurement. The consumer's decisions and preferences are combined with the facts of the engineer to give an impersonal basis for decisions and for the evaluation of performance. Again the problem is how to eliminate purely extraneous fluctuations in measuring performance. This is done for the car-producing divisions by measuring their achievement and competitive standing not in terms of total sales but according to the ratio of their sales to total automobile sales in their price range. A car division which would show a loss in percentage of its potential market would be considered as losing ground even though—as a result of prosperous business conditions—it might roll up high absolute sales figures. On the other hand, it is generally understood that the management of Cadillac has been doing an outstanding job over the last fifteen years, even though the dollar volume of sales has gone down sharply. The share of the division in the total sales of high-priced cars has risen; the fall in absolute sales volume is thus not chargeable to Cadillac but to a shrinkage of the market for higher priced cars over which the Cadillac management has had no control and for which it can not be blamed.

Since the accessory divisions produce largely for use within General Motors their efficiency could not be measured in terms of their competitive standing on the consumer's market. Hence they are measured by a different—and perhaps even a more severe—standard, their ability to supply the car divisions at lower cost than any outsider. As mentioned above, no car division is under compulsion to buy from the accessory divisions, or under compulsion to pay the prices demanded by them. To obtain the custom of the car divisions, each accessory division must be able to meet the lowest prices of outside accessory manufacturers and to satisfy the quality and styling requirements of the car divisions. Most of them are therefore subjected to the test of competition as much as the car divisions. And while individual car buyers will often decide on the basis of habit or advertising appeal, that is on economically non-rational grounds, the accessory producers have to satisfy a buyer who is interested only in tangible and provable economic factors.

The yardstick of market performance is based on the assumption that consumers' buying preferences and even their prejudices are as much objective facts for the producer as are the facts and figures of engineering and accounting which underlie base pricing. It is as necessary to analyze the consumer's preferences as it is to analyze cost factors. Without knowledge of the elements which make up the consumer's decision, it would be impossible to find the causes of faulty selling performance or

to plan rationally for improvements in the competitive position of a division, or of the business as a whole. Hence, General Motors has built up a comprehensive consumer research organization.

The combination of these two elements of objective analysis, base pricing and competitive market standing, has made possible a considerable degree of production planning. Annually each division submits estimated schedules for the next year in which it gives tentative figures for sales, costs and expected capital requirements on the assumption of a good, an average, and a bad year for the industry as a whole. It also indicates which of these three estimates it considers most likely on the basis of its knowledge of business conditions, trends in the used-car market, etc. By correlating the estimates of the various divisions, central management obtains a fairly representative picture of conditions in the industry as a whole. By closely checking this composite judgment of the producing and selling personnel against the analysis of the consumer research staff and of the company's economists, a result is obtained which should not only be fairly reliable but which also is comprehensible to the executives, thus setting an objective frame for the work of the members both of central and of divisional management.

Through measuring the efficiency and achievement of both policy decision and administration against the objective criteria of cost and efficiency, of return on the invested capital, and of competitive standing in the market, General Motors aims at the elimination of personal and subjective elements in the relationship between boss and subordinate, central management and divisional management. The questions, how efficient is a man, how successful is he, and how important is he to the company, do not have to be decided on the basis of subjective preference. In fact, they should not have to be decided at all; they should be answered clearly by the objective yardstick that records efficiency and achievement immediately and automatically. The President of the company does not have to tell a divisional manager that he is not satisfied with him; the divisional manager knows it anyhow by looking at the figures based on his own cost and market analysis. Similarly, the President does not have to justify a promotion to the colleagues of the promoted man;

he has the man's record which is known within the company. Also the objective yardstick should limit the personal element in policy decisions. If a man's opinion or suggestion are overruled it should be not because of the higher rank of the boss, but because the facts are against him. That would make it possible for superiors freely to admit mistakes to their subordinates—perhaps the most important thing in human relations. In fine, this objective yardstick should not only make possible informal and friendly personal relations, a spirit of teamwork and a free and frank discussion. It should also—at least, that is what the people in General Motors claim—make the organization of management as a team on a federal basis natural and almost inevitable by erecting strong barriers of fact against action based on nothing but seniority and rank.

Overcoming Obstacles to Effective Delegation

WILLIAM H. NEWMAN

"Go West, young man!" was Horace Greeley's counsel for success a century ago. Today, in management circles, the common advice is: "Delegate. Decentralize."

Why is this advice so often disregarded? Many management practices are open to uncertainty and debate, but there is substantial agreement in this country on the desirability of delegation. Experience, especially during the last war, has shown a remarkable capacity in people down the line to shoulder responsibility and get results. We also know that wise delegation is an important training device and helps build morale. Yet, in company after company, executives frankly admit that they do not delegate as much as they can and should.

The malady is not universal, of course. The production achievements of American business would not have been possible without assignment of tasks—and accompanying freedom of action—to literally millions of individuals. Still, in large companies and small ones, we hear:

He's overworked but he won't let go.

There's a good man if only his boss would turn him loose.

Everybody agrees it's a one-man show but we can't seem to break the pattern.

If we could overcome the obstacles to delegation in such cases as these, the resulting resiliency and flexibility would add further strength to the company and our business

From *Management Review*, January 1956, pp. 36–41. Reprinted with permission of American Management Association.

structure. What, then, is the nature of the difficulty?

To sharpen the problem, let us set aside the cases where the boss, at any level—president, district manager, superintendent, or first-line supervisor—does not want to delegate. Some bosses are little Napoleons who can satisfy their egos only by keeping all the authority to make decisions within their own hands. Also, the boss's boss may hold such a tight rein that the junior man does not dare delegate further. Then, there are some men in executive positions who haven't given enough thought to management *per se* to recognize the advantages of decentralization. A lack of desire to delegate for such reasons as these is a problem in itself.

But what of the cases where effective delegation is lacking even though it is recognized as desirable? All too often the boss may give lip-service to delegation and sincerely agree that it is desirable, but for some reason the right to decide—with corresponding responsibility and initiative—does not pass down the line.

Effective delegation centers around a personal relationship between two individuals: The boss and his immediate subordinate. The boss, who is accountable for achieving certain results, looks to the subordinate for the performance of parts of the job, and toward this end gives him permission to take certain action. The greater the freedom of action, the higher the degree of delegation. The subordinate, on the other hand, accepts an obligation to use his talents to accomplish the mission.

In practice, this is typically a growing and shifting relationship between the two men. The freedom and initiative which the subordinate is expected to exercise can rarely be spelled out in detail; the substance of the delegation takes on real meaning in the working habits which are developed from day to day. These habits and attitudes, in turn, are shaped by the subtle interplay of the two personalities involved.

The personal adjustments involved in effective delegation cannot be created by an order from the president or a page in the organization manual. Formal statements regarding organization have an influence, of course, as does company tradition. An organization plan, however, does not become reality until it is incorporated into the behavior pattern of the specific individuals involved. This is the point where delegation so often breaks down.

A closer look at some of the tugs and pulls on the two people involved in delegation may reveal blocks to desired behavior. The following list suggests some of the common pitfalls. An executive who is plagued with a failure of real delegation to occur at a specific point in his organization may well find the root of the trouble among these stumbling blocks. At the least the analysis gives an approach which can profitably be applied to such weak spots.

Let us look first at some of the reasons why executives are loath to delegate and then turn our attention to common reasons why subordinates hesitate to take responsibility.

REASONS FOR RELUCTANCE TO DELEGATE. 1. Some executives get trapped in the "*I can do it better myself*" *fallacy*. A man who is both conscientious and has high standards of performance is naturally tempted to perform himself any activity that he can do better than his subordinates. This may be anything from writing advertising copy to directing repair work when a machine breaks down. Assuming that the executive really can do the job better (which is not true quite so often as he thinks it is), the executive must nevertheless reconcile himself to turning the job over to someone whose performance will be "good enough." The choice the executive has to make is not between the quality of work he or his assistant will do on the specific task; instead, he should compare the improvement in performance resulting from doing the work himself against the benefits to the total operation which will arise from devoting his attention to planning and supervision, which only he is in a position to per-

form. Only after an executive accepts emotionally and intellectually the idea that his job requires getting the most things done through other people will full use be made of delegation.

2. *Lack of ability to direct* is another barrier to successful delegation. The executive must be able to communicate to his subordinate, often far in advance, what is to be done. This means that the executive must (*a*) think ahead and visualize the work situation, (*b*) formulate objectives and general plans of action, and then (*c*) communicate these to his subordinate. After the two men have worked together for a period of time, this process may be extremely informal, but it is still important that the three key elements be present.

All too often executives have not cultivated this ability to direct. The author remembers well one of his first bosses, a very friendly individual with shrewd business judgment, who simply could not tell a man working for him what he wanted done more than a few hours ahead of time. Life for subordinates was a bit precarious because success depended upon guessing how the boss's mind would work before the boss himself had formulated his ideas. Here was a man who wanted desperately to delegate, but could do so only for repetitive situations because he was unable to identify and communicate the essential features of his long-range plans.

3. A third possible block to effective delegation is *lack of confidence in subordinates*. Here, the executive hesitates to turn things over to his subordinate because:

> He'll take care of the details all right but miss the main point.
>
> I'm not sure of his judgment in a pinch.
>
> He has ideas but doesn't follow through.
>
> He's too young to command the respect of the other men.

—or some other doubt about the ability to get the job done.

When this kind of a situation is open and recognized, the remedy is clear. Either training should be started immediately or, if this is impractical, a new subordinate found. Often the situation is by no means so clear-cut, however. The lack of confidence may be subjective and almost unconscious. Where this is so, the executive is likely to give lip-service to delegation but in the actual working relationship won't let go.

4. A related obstacle to delegation is *absence of selective controls which give warning of impending difficulties.* Problems beyond those covered by the delegation may arise, and the executive naturally wants to avoid being caught with no warning. Consequently, the executive needs some "feedback" on what is going on. Such information is also useful for counseling and for appraising final results. While care must be taken that the control system does not undermine the very essence of delegation, it is also true that the executive cannot completely abdicate his responsibilities. Unless the executive has confidence in the adequacy of the controls set up he probably will be very cautious about delegating.

5. Finally, the executive may be handicapped by *a temperamental aversion to taking a chance.* Even with clear instructions, proper subordinates and selective controls, there still remains the possibility that something will go wrong. The greater the number of subordinates and the higher the degree of delegation, the more likely it is that sooner or later there will be trouble. The executive who delegates takes a calculated risk. Over a period of time, he expects that the gains from delegation will far offset the troubles that arise. Until the executive sees this characteristic of his job, and adjusts to it emotionally as well as intellectually, he is likely to be reluctant to delegate.

These five obstacles to effective delegation are all related to the attitudes of the boss—the man who is doing the delegating. Fortunately, the attitudes of most men can be modified, at least in intensity. So, when you are faced with a specific situation where authority is in fact not being delegated as it should be, look first for reasons why the executive may be reluctant to turn over authority to someone else.

WHY SUBORDINATES AVOID RESPONSIBILITY. Delegation, as noted above, is a two-sided relationship. Even when the boss is ready and able to turn over authority, there may be reasons why the subordinate shrinks from accepting it. Something within the subordinate himself or in the relationship with his boss may become a block. Let us look at some likely difficulties on the part of the subordinate.

1. Often the subordinate finds it *easier to ask the boss* than decide for himself how to deal with a problem. Making a wise decision is usually hard mental work, and men are perpetually seeking formulas or short cuts to avoid this labor. If a man finds that he can take a half-baked idea or a problem to his boss and get an answer, it is natural for him to do so. In addition, making one's own decisions carries with it responsibility for the outcome. Asking the boss is a way of sharing, if not shifting, this burden. Over a period of time, asking the boss becomes a habit and the man develops a dependence upon his boss rather than on himself.

A habit of taking all the non-routine and tough decisions to the boss can best be broken by an agreement between the two men concerned to mend their ways. If the practice is of long standing, perhaps the executive will have to resort to stubborn refusal even to give advice. Then, after a period of "throw him in the water and let him swim," a more healthy coaching relationship can be established. The distinction between advice, decision and orders will, however, remain slippery and the boss must constantly be on his guard that his advice does not undercut the attitudes of initiative and responsibility he is striving to build.

2. A second factor which deters a man from embracing greater responsibility is the *fear of criticism* for mistakes. Much depends upon the nature of the criticism. Negative criticism is often resented where constructive review might be accepted. "The old man sure raised the roof, but I swear I don't know what I'd do differently if it happened again."

"Unreasonable" criticism is likely to evoke even sharper reactions. Unreasonableness, in this situation, must be defined in terms of the feeling of the subordinate. If he feels that unfavorable results were beyond his control, that his duties and authority were not clear, that his actions were wise in terms of the situation as he knew it at the time, or that he has not been given an opportunity to explain his side of the story, the criticism will have a cowing effect.

Negative or unreasonable criticism given publicly in a way which embarrasses a man before fellow workers adds salt to the wound. The impact of such criticism on a man's willingness to take on new responsibility is direct. He naturally will be inclined to be cautious and play it safe, if he has learned from experience that taking on more risk may result in an embarrassing and unwarranted bawling out. The subordinate's feeling is, "Why should I stick my neck out for that guy?"

3. Most men hesitate to accept responsibility when they believe they *lack the necessary information and resources* to do a good job. The enthusiasm of a newly appointed training director in an industrial company, for example, was dampened when he found he had virtually no equipment and very poor secretarial help. Then, when top management officials not only were too busy to see him, but also failed to keep him advised of changes in company planning which affected training needs, he lost most of his remaining initiative. Here again, much depends upon attitudes and expectations. It is possible for a person reared in a restraining web of budgetary and personnel limitations to accept responsibility knowing full well he will have to battle for each step he takes. Generally, however, the frustrations that go along with inadequate information and resources create in the man an attitude which rejects further assignments. Such a barrier makes effective delegation difficult indeed.

4. A fourth obstacle to accepting responsibility is simply that the subordinate may already have *more work than he can do*. True, such an overload may be the man's own fault; for example, he may make poor use of his own time or fail to hire trained, competent assistants even though he has the authority to do so. But, from the point of view of his willingness to accept responsibility, the cause of the overwork is not the critical point. If he already feels overburdened, he will probably shy away from new assignments which call for thinking and initiative.

5. *Lack of self-confidence* stands in the way of some men's accepting responsibility. The boss believes the man can do the job and is willing to take the risk of the outcome, but the man is unsure of himself and doesn't like to take the plunge. Ordering the man to have self-confidence will have little effect. In many cases, however, self-confidence may be developed by carefully providing experience with increasingly difficult problems to help the man sense his own potentialities. To be sure, some men may not have the psychological make-up to carry heavy responsibilities—but here, again, World War II provided us with many examples of far greater latent ability than appeared on the surface.

6. Finally, *positive incentives may be inadequate*. As already noted, accepting additional responsibility usually involves more mental work and emotional pressure. In the lower ranks of some companies, there is some social stigma on the "eager beaver" who is pushing to get ahead. Also, there is more or less risk of failure; failure is unpleasant and may result in embarrassing removal from the job. For these reasons, there should be positive inducements for accepting delegated responsibility. These inducements may take all sorts of forms, such as pay increases, better opportunity for promotion, fancier title, recognized status in the organization, more pleasant working conditions, additional power, personal recognition and approval by respected members of the enterprise, and other rewards both tangible and intangible. The important point is that the specific subordinate affected by delegation should be provided with a positive incentive which is important to him.

CONCLUSIONS. We see, then, a variety of possible reasons why a subordinate may hesitate to accept new responsibilities. These and other points which might be added to the list emphasize the need to think about the specific individuals involved and the factors which will affect their reactions to a change in delegation of authority.

Fortunately, many delegations encounter none of these obstacles, and in other situations there may be only one or two points which interfere with effective delegation. In any case, the list of common reasons for reluctance on the part of the boss and of the subordinate suggests potential difficulties to look for, and provides a frame of analysis that should be useful even when the specific points don't happen to fit a given situation.

The main thing that all of us who are enthusiastic about delegation and decentralization ought to remember is that the carrying out of such plans requires the adjustment of atttiudes and behavior patterns of specific individuals and a workable adjustment in their relationships. Such adjustments are a normal occurrence in a dynamic society, but we must recognize that they take time and that some individuals are more adaptable than others. Our best plans will come to naught until these personal adjustments have been made.

Program Management: Organizing for Stability and Flexibility

JOSEPH A. LITTERER

"Change is not made without inconvenience, even from worse to better." So wrote Dr. Johnson in the preface to his famous dictionary—and though I would hesitate to nominate that monumental tome for inclusion in any manager's "five-foot shelf," here, surely, is an observation that the modern businessman would do well to keep firmly in mind. It's a rare manager indeed who hasn't run into a host of the "inconveniences" involved in keeping up with the times and making necessary improvements in the organization.

Getting a new plant, production process, or field sales force to the point where it operates smoothly can be a difficult and frustrating job. And when at last things have shaken down and the new setup is running smoothly, the executives who have lived through the experience are inclined to draw a deep breath and devoutly hope that they won't have to go through it again for a long time to come. Almost invariably, though, the hope is a vain one: Hardly has the dust settled than another massive upheaval already looms on the horizon.

For some organizations, in fact, major changes are almost the order of the day. Many companies, for instance, now derive a considerable, if not the greater part of their income from products that didn't even exist ten years ago. Others are changing in other directions, such as expanding into overseas markets. In these growth situations existing facilities and personnel are continuously being reshuffled, new plants have to be built and staffed, and new sales units developed. And the signs all point to more, not fewer, of these adaptations to change, with all the confusion, frustration, and waste that seem inevitably to accompany them, sometimes for a considerable length of time.

Inevitable though they may be, these upsetting characteristics of change can be brought under some measure of control. By way of example, I propose to discuss here one type of change—organizational—and one technique that can make it simpler—program management.

At the outset, it might be a good idea to define the term "organization," because it is used in so many ways today. My definition is a rather broad one, since it includes both technical and social structures. By this I mean not only tasks, jobs, or positions and the relations between them—the traditional formal organization—but also the informal relations among the members, and the relations of individuals to their work.

In some ways, of course, it would be highly desirable if no organizational changes ever had to be made. This would insure the continuance of established relationships and increase their stability. As it is, directly or indirectly, most organizational changes alter interpersonal relations. Old work groups are broken up, and new ones formed; people may be assigned to work where it is difficult for them to adjust to new colleagues. Such changes in social relations can have a serious effect on both individual and organizational performance.

Thus, in their study of aircraft plants, Mayo and Lombard found that an absence of relatively stable work groups resulted in a high rate of turnover and apathy.[1] And Chester Barnard, in a hypothetical discussion of what might happen to the New Jersey Bell Telephone Company if all the executives except the president were replaced by experienced and competent executives from other companies in the Bell System, predicted that the company

---

From *Personnel*, Vol. 40, 1963, pp. 25–34. Reprinted by permission of the American Management Association.

[1] E. Mayo and G. F. Lombard, *Teamwork and Labor Turnover in the Aircraft Industry of Southern California.* (Business Research Studies No. 32.) Harvard Business School, Division of Research, 1944.

would not operate normally more than 12 hours because "no one would know the local conditions and how to interpret the changes in the environment to which the organization has constantly to adjust." [2]

Here we see the root of the organization planner's dilemma. On the one hand, he is faced with the fact that events outside his company, as well as developments within it, make frequent change more and more imperative. On the other, he has to weigh the costs in lowered morale, turnover, extra effort and errors, and the confusion caused by the disruption of established organizational relationships. How is he to reconcile these conflicting pressures?

Program Pioneers

Some practical guidance on this problem is forthcoming from one segment of the American economy that has had to adjust to more drastic and accelerated change than most—the defense industry. Because the problems it has encountered in this respect have been more crucial than in other industries, the solutions the defense companies have developed should offer a guide for handling organizational change in other situations. Here is an illustration drawn largely from the experience of one company, but representative of many others in the industry.

For many years this company had been an important source of parts for the aircraft industry. Its success had been in no little degree due to its excellent equipment and highly skilled employees, assets that enabled it to keep up with increasingly difficult production problems as the industry advanced. Major divisions were on a product basis, but since many products were dependent upon a principal manufacturing process, they tended also to be in many ways process divisions. Thus, foundry work was a key process in the division making hydraulic fittings, and machining in the section making superchargers. The executives in these various manufacturing divisions were excellent technical men who had established sound relationships within their units.

A few years after World War II it became apparent to the company's top management

[2] C. F. Barnard, "Education for Executives," *The Journal of Business*, October, 1945, pp. 175–182.

that missiles would be the important defense weapon in the future, while the airplane would gradually lose its importance. Such being the case, the company executives faced the need to make a major shift to handle many new products, and to service new customers. Though they recognized the importance of the stable relationships in their production departments, they were willing to disrupt them for the sake of the new business; the question was, which missile business would they service, the liquid fuel or the solid fuel? There was considerable debate about their relative merits at the time, and it wasn't an easy question to decide, but management recognized that it would be disastrous if it reorganized to service one type of missile and then found a few years later that the other type had come out on top. As it turned out, however, the company was able to avoid this ticklish decision entirely. Instead, it made some minor regroupings to strengthen its existing process type of organization and installed an extensive system of program management.

Program management is an organizational device, found today mostly in the defense industry but having advantages that make it useful in many other areas where the same fundamental problems exist. Most companies engaged in defense work have several contracts in addition to their regular nonmilitary business, and each individual project requires only part of the activity in each major division of the company. The basic idea in program management is for the company to appoint a program manager for each contract to coordinate all phases of work on it in the various divisions.

Programs Change, People Don't

By adopting this approach, the company I described coordinated the efforts of specialized areas on its projects, and at the same time kept the personnel and facilities in their established locations. When one contract was finished, the specialized groups working on it were simply reassigned to new, and often quite different programs.

Of course, as far as the program manager and his staff are concerned in this setup, there are bound to be fairly frequent and sometimes abrupt changes, as contracts are completed and new ones are taken on. These employees, however, are usually only a small group of accountants, control clerks, and perhaps a few engineers, and with the exception of them, the organization goes along unchanged: The individual employee continues to report to the same superior, and work with the same people with the same equipment in the same location, even though the specific assignment may change with a new contract. The end result of their efforts may be different, but the important relationships remain stable.

This stability is all the more valuable because the amount of work that a given department does on a project is not uniform from start to finish. For instance, in the early stages there probably is particular attention to research or engineering and relatively little work on tooling or manufacturing, whereas several months later this emphasis is reversed. Thus, with program management the company avoids organizational disruption not only when it shifts from one project to another, but also when it makes the more frequent changes within each project's life cycle.

Companies in the defense field have also adopted program management to coordinate multiple programs. For example, some companies, after taking on a number of defense contracts and assigning them to major components of the organization, have found that the newest or largest project gets the most attention from higher management, and this emphasis is mirrored at lower levels of management. Naturally, a department head with several contracts to work on will give priority to the ones his superiors are most interested in, and as a result other contracts are neglected and frequently fall so far behind schedule that finally higher management has to step in. What this means is an on-again, off-again pattern of priorities, with individual contracts getting a great deal of attention at one time and relatively little at another—a frustrating and wasteful irregularity in scheduling. Program management has proved to be an effective method of insuring that work on all contracts proceeds smoothly; through the various program managers higher management has continuing reports on the progress of all projects and can keep them in balance.[3]

There is a third problem area in which program management can come up with the answers. This is the pressure to reduce lead time, which again, though not peculiar to the defense industry, is more acute there than in many others.

To reduce lead time, work on defense contracts is often conducted in a parallel or concurrent fashion, rather than serially. To illustrate, if work were to be performed serially on a new airplane, the sequence might be (1) developing and building a new engine; (2) designing and building a new airframe to utilize the new power plant; and (3) developing a new radar system for the new aircraft. Such a progression permits each new part to be made with a clear relationship to the equipment with which it will be integrated; it is a safe but slow way of developing a major new weapon. But the over-all lead time can be greatly shortened if the development and manufacture of major components are carried out simultaneously, that is, in this case, with the design and manufacture of power plant, airframe, and radar system going on all at the same time.[4]

Coordination a Must

The advantages here are obvious, but so are the risks. One risk is that a key component design may turn out to have technical bugs. Another possibility is that if the development of a component lags seriously while the others proceed on schedule, that one roadblock may hold up the whole procession. Careful coordination is vital, and here again the concept of program management shows its worth. Let's see just how it functions.

The sequence I mentioned above is, of course, oversimplified. Actually, there is a great deal more to the development of so

[3] A. Vleck, Jr., "Minimizing Line-Staff Friction at Martin Baltimore: Functional-Operational Organizational Structure," in *Line-Staff Relationships in Production* (Special Report No. 18), American Management Association, 1957, pp. 39–52.

[4] For an interesting discussion of this problem, upon which parts of these comments are based, see: Hearings before the Subcommittee for Special Investigations of the Committee on Armed Services, House of Representatives, 86th Congress, April–August, 1959, *Weapon System Management and Team System Concept in Government Contracting*.

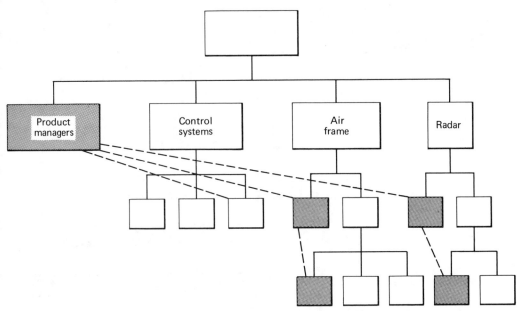

Fig. 1. Hierarchy of program managers for components of final weapon.

complex a mechanism as an airplane. The program manager finds himself chiefly concerned with coordination of work on a number of components made either in subsidiary departments of his own company or by subcontractors, and to help with this coordination, each of the subordinate departments or subcontractors will in turn have a program manager. Thus, there is usually a hierarchy of program-manager positions, all coordinating different phases of work on the components. (See Figure 1.) At any one of these levels, and at the same time, work may be begun *functionally*—designing, tooling, manufacturing, and so on—on both the over-all product and components. To explain this point in detail, we'll take another concrete example, the manufacture of an electronic component.

In making advanced electronic equipment there are a number of highly complicated problems, but basically they divide into two categories—design of the equipment, and manufacturing and testing it. Ideally, the design of the unit should be completed and models prepared before anyone has to think about designing the test facilities and procedures. If this sequence were followed, however, lead time would be stretched out uneconomically, since designing test facilities and procedures and building and installing them involve consider-

able engineering in themselves. To avoid this lengthy serial process, the design of the testing facilities and procedures is started while the design of the electronic equipment itself is still going on. (See Figure 2.)

Certain characteristics of the equipment are known almost from the beginning—conditions of use, performance requirements, and the like —and once some of these over-all characteristics have been established it is possible to go ahead with designing the test facilities with some assurance. This seems a simple way to shorten the lead time and it is, but by the same token the problems of coordination between the equipment design and the test design become much more critical. There must be a rapid and accurate transmission of information about progress and problems in the concurrent work.

To provide this there is usually a program manager in each of the major functional departments involved in making a component—design engineering, tool engineering, and so on.[5] The program manager at one level would

[5] For a discussion of the work, problems, and pressures of the project manager at the engineering level, see: P. O. Gaddis, "The Project Manager," *Harvard Business Review*, May–June, 1959, pp. 89–97.

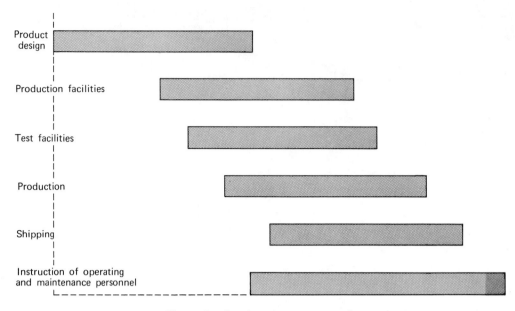

Fig. 2. Overlapping of concurrent tasks.

thus work with two kinds of subordinate program managers, some responsible for coordinating work on the *functions* of making the component and others responsible for coordinating work on the *parts* that go into the component.

This brings up another advantage of program management: As the work of the program manager shifts from specifying performance characteristics to engineering characteristics, he has increasing control over component selection and like details. For instance, when various components are turned over to subcontractors they often select different parts for the component than might have been chosen by the prime contractor. With more detailed specifications, the program manager can standardize component selection and thereby simplify the number of parts to be stocked for repairs.[6]

Now that we have a general picture of program management and some of the principal reasons why companies have turned to this organizational device, a more detailed examination of how it actually operates is in order.

[6] For further discussion, see: F. Hamlin, "More Logical Spending for Navy's Weapons," *Armed Forces Management,* January, 1960, pp. 19–21.

Program management may be handled in a variety of ways, depending on the size of the company, its organization, and the nature of the program it undertakes, among other factors. For purposes of illustration, though, I'll take a fairly large company, with a well-developed program-management system.

Structure of the Program

When this company gets a contract from the government, the over-all administration of the contract is assigned to the company division best able to handle it. The vice president in charge of that division then appoints a program manager, who is responsible to him for administering the contract.

The program manager may have only a few people reporting to him—a secretary, an accountant or two, and perhaps a few other assistants—so it is evident that he does not control and coordinate work by controlling people. Rather, he must rely on persuasion, personal leadership, and control of important managerial procedures and processes. It should be remembered, too, that he is frequently responsible for preparing information on the planned and actual position of all technical, manufacturing, and financial aspects of his program.

On a complex job it is impossible for one man or one small central staff to do all this, so this structure is repeated in the other parts of the company working on this particular contract. In other words, when another division or department is designated to do part of the work on the program, the head of that unit appoints his own program manager. (The title may be changed slightly, i.e., to project manager or program representative, in order to differentiate the level or scope of responsibility.) These second-level program managers do the same thing for their units and subordinate units, and so on down the line. Program managers in organizational units carrying out a portion of an over-all program are responsible to the top program manager for all phases of scheduling, planning, budgets, and reports of progress on the project within their area. This group of program managers spotted in different organizational units comprise the team or committee responsible for seeing that the contract obligations of the company are completely fulfilled.

Two Kinds of Direction

Thus, the team of program managers have a great deal to say about company activities on their program. What, then, one might ask, is left for the rest of the management group to do? Essentially, the regular management group are responsible for delivering whatever item or service is necessary to the program according to the time, technical, and cost specifications the program-management team have set, and all have agreed to.

One company I know of makes a formal distinction between the *program direction* exercised by the program managers and the *operational direction* exercised by the department and division executives. It distinguishes between the two in this way:

Operational direction defines how program direction will be carried out. Provision of such direction basically involves: planning the facilities and work methods; organizing the people; assigning the work tasks; and providing the leadership and con-

trols necessary for successful work completion. . . .

Control is provided through such vehicles as authority to: obtain needed facilities, equipment, and material; determine work hours; hire, train, motivate, and discipline people; and approve work results.

Program direction defines program requirement which must be met. . . . Provision for such direction includes: serving as a focal point of customer contact; developing and approving Statements of Work . . . and Plans of Action for proposals; approving contracts and contract changes; interpreting contractual requirements; and approving issuance of General Orders and other standard work-authorizing documents. . . . Inasmuch as program management is accountable for successful accomplishment of assigned program, they must have authority to exercise control when necessary. Program control basically involves continuous checking. . . .

Vehicles for checking compliance with requirements include: approval of all major action documents affecting work scope, schedules, or costs of the program; developing and approving master program and planning documents; approving engineering specifications; reviewing and approving program budgets; and approving budget requirements. . . .[7]

It is easy to see that the program manager in this company is in an extremely strong position to direct over-all planning on his program and to control subsidiary and subordinate planning. The division and department managers are given a set of objectives and target dates and are required to meet them. They operate as they see fit, but must present over-all plans to the program manager for approval.

What Programs Have in Common

As I have already noted, the details of program management will differ from company to company; some have fewer levels with far less authority than the one I described above, while in others the reverse is true.

[7] Autonetics Division of North American Aviation, Inc., "Executive Policy EP-2," December, 1961, pp. 3–4.

Program Management
Not Without Its Dangers

Though an enthusiastic advocate of program management, L. B. Young, general manager of Bendix Corporation's systems division, warns that it has its pitfalls, too.

In a recent interview with *Armed Forces Management*, Mr. Young said, "The major danger appears to be that if this is pursued too far we . . . may tend to prove Parkinson's law, and create a burden in administrative load which is both uneconomical and inefficient. I am particularly concerned that too great an emphasis may be placed on statistics and the filling out of various forms. I cannot emphasize too strongly the need for personal understanding and leadership. Data and procedures should be tailored to assist the capable manager. More data and less managerial competence won't get the same results."

Mr. Young went on to say, "I think it is essential that any major system effort have the full-time attention of a group assigned to its specific management problems. However, we must be careful that the project management effort does not exceed the program implementation effort."

In every case, however, there are some constants: All are designed to guide and control changing numbers of complex projects, providing coordination for these projects but at the same time permitting the company to maintain a stable organization for the great majority of its employees. The success of all program-management systems rests with the skills of the program manager and the relationships he is able to establish with the division and departmental executives. His role is a trying one in spite of (and at times because of) the considerable authority he wields.[8]

To summarize, business organizations must choose among a number of possible organization designs, which, even though they don't always conflict, are frequently not mutually supportive. There are definite advantages to large-scale operations, specialization, and organizational stability; yet all of these tend to make an organization unwieldly and slow to adjust to changing conditions. Increased pressure for greater flexibility and more adequate control of complex operations has forced some companies into newer organizational arrangements, one of which is a product division type of structure and/or increased decentralization of decision making. This is a satisfactory solution for a wide range of conditions. It is often found wanting, however, when a company takes on tasks requiring support from many areas of the firm, support that in turn needs close coordination to insure meeting stringent technical, cost, and time specifications.

Perhaps even more important is the stepped-up tempo of these companywide changes. Previous practices might suggest setting up a separate division or department to handle a new company obligation, but such an organizational structure simply does not adapt to the rapid changes in the nature of these new tasks and the varying volume of different kinds of work involved in them.

As I have shown, these conditions are most sharply drawn in the defense industry, but they are more and more evident in other segments of the economy. And it is at this point that program management has distinct advantages to offer, even though no organizational arrangement or device is a permanent or perfect solution.

[8] Gaddis, *op. cit.* For an interesting analysis of the work of the research project manager brought to the author's attention while this paper was being completed, see also: K. Davis, "A Preliminary Study of Management Patterns of Research Project Managers in Manufacturing in the Phoenix Area," Arizona State University, 1961.

The Emergent Informal

Organization Structure

PART THREE

WE HAVE SEEN that some theorists have viewed organizations as instruments through which people achieve their ends. While correct, this statement can and has been given an excessively narrow interpretation. As a result, attention was given to establishing equitable or just ways of distributing the accomplishments of organized effort for satisfying goals or needs outside the organization. Missed was the important point that, for many members, the organization was the environment in which they lived while these objectives were achieved. Furthermore, some of the properties that made organizations effective and efficient instruments for goal attainment were also the very properties that made them uncomfortable or unsatisfactory as environments within which to live. The immediate environment that people experience is certainly one of the principal determinants of their behavior. Consequently, earlier theorists found people behaving in ways not called for in their formal organization plans. It was behavior neither explained nor anticipated through these theories.

This unanticipated behavior has received a great deal of attention in the last four decades, and we have learned a great deal about its origins. While unanticipated, it is nonetheless, to a large degree, caused by the formal organization. Some of the effects of the formal organization plan are fairly direct, as when we find decisions on the type and extent of division of work-determining to content of jobs and the opportunities for socializing at work which, in turn, influences the satisfactions that individuals can derive from their work (Walker and Guest, Trist and Bamforth), or the effects of control procedures like budgets or behavior (Argyris).

In this section, we are interested in the actual behavior that emerges in a formal organization. We shall examine some of the important research that has helped us better to understand this behavior and its relationship to the designed aspects of the organization. Perhaps the most famous of the studies that have contributed to this understanding were the Hawthorne studies conducted by Elton Mayo, Fritz Roethlisberger, and other associates at Harvard University, but these studies have received major additions from the fields of social psychology, industrial sociology and, more recently, anthropology.

One thing soon apparent from these studies was that within large organizations a great deal of effort is expended by organizational members on activities that do not directly support organizational goals. Investigators found, for example, that people spent a lot of time in social activities that had nothing directly to do with the task they were supposed to be accomplishing. Investigators also spent a good deal of time examining the activities of people who resisted or thwarted organization objectives. The well-known practice of work restrictions, by which employees establish the maximum amount that they will produce (probably below the standards established by management), is only one of these phenomena.

Investigations went considerably beyond a mere classification of different types of non-goal behavior. It was rapidly established that the behavior was not something capricious, necessarily disloyal, random, or unpredictable but that, instead, it fell into regular and consistent patterns that might persist over long periods of time and serve very definite functions. What should be noted is that the functions were important not necessarily for the formal organization but for the people within the organization as individuals and, particularly, as members of groups or informal organizations.

Up until this point, the tendency had been to think primarily of people either as individuals or as occupants of positions in large, impersonal structures. Much behavior in an organization, however, is only understandable when we examine it as a manifestation of group life. Hence, these researches added a neglected but exceedingly important factor to our thinking about organizations.

When probing deeper into the patterns and functions of group behavior, the investigators found that much of it actually was conforming with rules or standards, that other portions of it were under the direction of people who occupied informal superior or leadership positions, and that the people in groups knew full well that deviations from these rules or standards, or violation of the directions from the informal superiors, would result in some disciplinary action. In short, much of the behavior on investigation turned out to be controlled behavior.

Here was what organization theorists had been concerned with all along—people behaving according to rules and standards or following orders within a system of control. The point that is exceedingly important, however, is that investigators showed that the rules and standards, the orders and control that influence a very large portion of the behavior of the organization members were not established by the formal organization or the members of the managerial hierarchy. Instead, these organizational elements were components of what has now come to be called the informal organization. They are not formally prescribed by a central, "legitimate" authority but, rather, spring up out of the situation and have their roots in the needs and requirements of people. The nature of informal organizations is explained more thoroughly in a moment, but first a digression is necessary.

Some Problems With Terms

One of the difficulties with this area is the problem of deciding which words to use to cover the ideas considered. Already we have been using "small groups" and "informal organizations" in an interchangeable fashion. Many of the investigations in this area have focused on the small group in an attempt to understand what it is, how it operates, and why it operates as it does. The term "informal organizations," as used here, includes something larger and more inclusive than one group. It has among other implications the idea that a person can be and, in fact, is a member of more than one small group. Hence, if we are to study the totality of influences on him other than those coming from the formal organization, we have to include the influences of several small groups, not all equal, perhaps, but all in some way significant.

There are other influences that properly belong to the topic of informal organizations but extend beyond any one small group or, for that matter, a collection of small groups, which may be included within one organizational unit. For example, status can be discussed relevant to one group, or it can be discussed relevant to a collection of groups within a formal organization, or it can be discussed relevant to a whole social system or culture. This multiplicity and looseness in the use of such terms makes it difficult to talk with precision about what should be included in a discussion of the informal organization. For our purposes, we consider the informal organization to be those aspects of the total organization not included in the formal organization area. Such a view of informal organization will include certain structural properties, processes, and products, and it will quite properly consist of a number of related, perhaps overlapping, small groups. For purposes of exposition, however, we follow the convention adopted by many writers in the field and discuss these matters as if there were just one group. This short cut is taken in order to reduce the cumbersomeness of always talking about a multiplicity of small groups. It would be erroneous to suggest that this approach or convention does not inject some distortion into our thinking about organizations. It certainly limits the things we include, since it tends to exclude conceptually the very difficult problem, faced by an organizational member, of reconciling the multiplicity of pressures placed on him by the formal organization and the different small groups of which he is a member (Blau, Breed, Sayles).

An Overall Framework for the Analysis of Social Behavior

The study of informal organization has grown rapidly in the last thirty years or so and is continuing to grow. As a result, we have been able to do little more than touch on a few of the more important aspects of behavior and group properties. Important and invaluable as these properties are, they do have some limitations from the point of view taken in this book. We need more fundamental or underlying concepts, both fewer in number and more inclusive in scope. They must be able to take into account that (as has been partially noted), at times, the informal organization is a product of the formal. Furthermore, these new concepts must account for the fact that the formal organization is continually modified by the informal (Selznick). This new approach will have to account for these reciprocal influences. One model of social phenomena that meets these requirements is proposed by George Homans in his book *The Human Group*.[1]

Homans begins by suggesting that we look at the total social system which constitutes the small group. Within this total social system, he claims most things can be classified into one of

three categories: (1) the activities of the group members, by which he means the individual's physical motions; (2) the interactions of the group members, by which he means any transaction between two or more members of the group; and (3) sentiments. This is a broad and exceedingly slippery dimension, but essentially it includes all the feelings, the beliefs, the hopes that the people within the group have.

In Homans' view these three factors are intimately linked together and, therefore, a change in one will be expected to produce a change in at least one other. For example, he makes the supposition that if two people interact frequently, they will develop positive sentiments (feelings of friendship) toward each other. The model would also hold that two people who share a common activity or who perform similar activities will likely seek each other out because they presume that people who do the same thing must be somewhat similar to themselves. Hence, common activities will lead to interaction which, in turn, will result in an increase in the strength of sentiments, presumably positive. Finally, of course, to complete this system, it follows that people who like each other will interact frequently and will select activities that permit them to interact. Obviously, this is an exceedingly general system. It does, however, help us relate three things in a useful fashion: (1) the things people do; (2) the interactions between people; and (3) the things they feel, believe, or hold important.

Homans goes one step further and makes another distinction. He says that the total social system in which people find themselves can be divided into two parts: the internal system and the external. The external system is set up by the forces or environment outside the individual or the group. In many instances, this is the company or the organization which, as part of its job assignments, requires that people perform certain activities and, in performing these activities, interact with certain other people.

The external system, then, brings people together with certain relations, although hardly all, established and assigns them activities in the form of jobs or duties. At first they may be strangers but soon they become acquainted and may become friends forming strong social ties. Their life together now has a meaning

---

[1] Harcourt Brace, New York, 1950.

which includes a social base, an internal system, in addition to the technical base. The nature of, in fact the very existence of, their social life springs from the technical arrangements of the external system. Once their social life is established, the internal system will, or at least can, have a significant influence on the external system. Homans' model of a social system gives us a very useful tool for analyzing what effect the formal organization will have on the social life of people. In turn, it enables us to explore the effects that the informal organization will have on the behavior the formal organization specifies but may not be receiving. Needless to say, this gives us a most useful tool for bridging the formal and the informal organizations. It also permits us to talk about organizational elements, such as jobs, in a more inclusive, precise manner, without being restricted to dealing with these elements in just formal or informal organization terms.

In the discussion on Homans' model, one element was left undeveloped, namely, the sentiments coming from the external system. Homans identifies these sentiments as those which a person brings into a particular situation from his previous environment or background. Needless to say, this element could have great influence on the small group. It explains, in part, why taking a collection of people and putting them into the same work situation in which they are interacting does not guarantee that they will all grow to like each other. Bringing people together who have different, perhaps opposing, values may result in bitter hostility rather than friendship. We see in a later section the importance of this possibility.

Homans' concepts have been discussed at considerable length. First, they provide us with an exceedingly useful tool for relating a number of informal and formal organization concepts. The Homans model, however, is also difficult to understand in that its variables are exceedingly broad, frequently contain slippery elements, and the interrelations are very complex. It does require us to recognize that a social system can only be understood when all the elements are considered at the same time in relation to all the other elements. The elements of Homans' concept will be repeatedly referred to in later sections, and even when not specifically noted, they will provide a useful framework for incorporating material from later papers into an overall concept of what is actually happening within an organization.

Properties of the Informal Organization

In general, informal organizations emerge to buffer individuals from the harshness or impersonality of formal organizations, to provide some things that formal organizations do not provide and, not infrequently, to create additional means with which organization members can better perform their formal assignments (Selznick, Roy, Sayles). In short, they produce things consumed within the organization by its members. As a productive instrument, it too has its structural properties.

Norms

One of the conspicuous items in the literature is the organization members' practice of establishing quota restrictions. Here are definite standards of how much a person should produce. Typically we think of a quota restriction as a ceiling on the amount of work a person will be permitted to produce. Such a ceiling may be considerably below the level of output that management or the time-study engineers have specified. It is not as frequently noted that some minimum levels of production are established informally. The circumstances under which these minimums exist can be quite revealing.

Quota restrictions on production are one of the many different types of standards that are established by the informal organization for the behavior of organizational members. They are usually called norms. The processes by which these are established and the purposes they fill are far from simple; in fact, on investigation, they turn out to be exceedingly complex. The wide variety of norms, or informal standards, not only guide the behavior of the individual in his relation with management or the formal organization but also guide his relations with other members of the informal organization.

A point perhaps not stressed frequently enough is that many of these norms pertain to the relations people have in getting their work done. We have earlier noted that few formal organizations take into account everything necessary to complete the technical aspects of a task or position assignment. Consequently, in order to do the work assigned to him, a person frequently has to add many things that are not called for in the formal organization plan, additions which may require him to obtain the support and assistance of other people (Roy, 1954).

The norms of the informal group, like the rules of the formal organization, have connected with them means for enforcement that both reward behavior which conforms to the standard and discipline or penalize behavior which deviates. There are a great many different ways in which member behavior is controlled by the informal organization. A variety of illustrations are contained in the selections in this book (Roy, Sayles, Selznick).

Leader-Follower Relations

At one time, there was a tendency to consider workers on the job as a more or less homogeneous group in which everyone was on the same level. Few ideas could be more misleading, for a number of different structural arrangements have been uncovered. Within a small group, investigators have found those who fill the leadership functions of pointing to new directions, coordinating the work of others, and holding the group together. Others can be classified as being in follower positions. Such leaders are not formally appointed but are accepted by the members of the group. Several things should be noted about leadership in a small group or informal organization. First, the leadership function may actually be carried out by a number of individuals. Within a group, there may be a multiplicity of leaders, each functioning in a different aspect of group activity. One person may serve as leader, when it comes to setting new directions or making plans or specifying the steps to be followed in accomplishing group objectives. These are the informal task leaders. Another leader may be concerned with the social activities within the group, making it a pleasant place to be by his wit or personality and thereby helping to hold it together. He is the informal social leader.

Communications

One fact, which has been repeatedly observed in investigations and which we all are likely to see in our daily experiences, is that people who are in groups, cliques, or gangs tend to reach an understanding on things very quickly. To put it briefly, they communicate easily and well among themselves. Once a piece of information enters a group, it usually is not too long before everyone within the group knows it. This perhaps comes about because of a common fund of interest, common experiences, and a shared vocabulary that enables members of a group to communicate easily and precisely with each other.

Communications, or the need for information about the world, is perhaps one of the basic reasons for the existence of small groups. People want to belong to groups in order, among other things, to obtain information about the world around them. By going to our friends, our cliques, our lodges, or our fraternities, we pick up information, which we otherwise might not obtain. We also obtain interpretations of facts that have come to us, but whose meanings we perhaps find difficult to ascertain.

This is exceedingly important to have in mind, because we would have an extremely restricted view of the small group if we merely looked on it as an instrument for controlling member behavior. Since an informal organization is so important in getting information to people and interpreting information, it serves a very important role in forming people's opinions and impressions of the world.

The suspicions that workers may have about management when a system of work standards is established may be based on the fact that management does engage in rate-cutting practices. On the other hand, management may not have had any such intentions at all. It may only have engaged in activities that people have interpreted as possibly leading to rate-cutting practices. Often, these interpretations are formed and perpetuated by groups. As far as the final behavior of the individuals is concerned, it does not matter whether management had the intention or not, as long as people think it did. If anything is to be done about their behavior, we must be aware of its real basis. For management merely to protest its innocence will do little more than clear its conscience about a frustrating situation. Such statements of innocence will not be likely to eliminate the suspicions of the workers. Management must, instead, take into account the view of the work standard that their employees have developed in their group and work with it.

Values

This leads us to one of the phenomena very frequently noted both by scientific investigators and lay observers, namely, that members of groups, cliques, or gangs frequently share or hold in common certain values, opinions, or beliefs. In fact, some people define groups in this way. Regardless of what they are, we can always be sure that an informal group will have shared values. Understanding the group values will be very important for understanding how the group operates and the influence it has on the behavior of its individual members. People have probably had some of these values for a long time. We find people who hold similar values coming together to form a group composed on the basis of their shared values. At other times, we can find that values are developed among people who are already in a group and that the values are then a product rather than an antecedent of group life.

Status

One use of values is in ranking things such as positions and the people who occupy them into what are called status hierarchies. Status appears in one way or another in many of the items included in this book (Roy, Homans), but only one deals directly with the topic (Gardner and Moore). For this reason, it is necessary to consider the topic at some length here.

In a general way, we consider status as the social ranking of people. We recognize and frequently use ranking terms of people in our community or on the job or in our church; some people are "upper-class," others are perhaps "middle-class," and there are also those who are "low-class." We all have some idea of what the overall social order is and a pretty

good idea of where people fit in this ranking. We understand without too much difficulty that physicians rank very high in social status and that street cleaners rank low in status. Status structures, however, are important not only in understanding where people fit within a community but also where they fit within a work group. For example, in a restaurant, we find that the people who work on fish are thought to be in a lower status position than those who work on beef.

Status structures define not only where categories of occupations fit, such as cooks and physicians, but also may define an individual's position within any category. Hence, a person will have a position first because he is in the category of a cook, which he knows is somewhere beneath a physician but above a street cleaner. Within the cook's category, however, this position may be more specifically defined by the type of material on which he works. This opens up several important issues. First, there are a number of status structures. Some are general, applying to large categories or groupings of people, and others are quite special and specific. As a result, it is frequently possible to define not only the class of a person but also his position within the class.

A second issue is that, whereas some of us may understand well the overall and common types of status structure, we are frequently unacquainted with the rather special ones that may exist within different categories. Consequently, the management of a restaurant may fully understand that the cooks rank somewhere between physicians and street cleaners, but may not understand that within the category of cooks there are sharp status distinctions. Hence a careless or innocent grouping of jobs by the management on the presumption that all cooks are the same could run into serious problems by disturbing some of the status hierarchies that people in this class of work consider quite important. Therefore, the organization planner who will group tasks and assign people to the tasks so that they will do an adequate job must take into account not only the way the jobs and skills will fit together to accomplish the task, but what the arrangements will mean to the occupants of the positions.

A third consideration is of considerable importance. We have noted that there are a great many status structures. Some, as we have seen, dovetail nicely, enabling each person to be placed in a rather definite niche. This, however, is usually on an occupational basis. There are many status hierarchies that do not fit in this neat fashion and, in fact, may not fit at all. For example, in many situations, seniority in the company or in the department or age are matters of status ranking. At the same time, the community in which a person lives gives him a certain status. Furthermore, education, parentage, wealth, and many other factors also define a person's status. In short, each of us have positions in a number of status hierarchies. It is possible, therefore, for a person to find himself rather high on one status hierarchy, in a middle position on another, and in a rather low position on still a third hierarchy. As we might suspect, this can and frequently does cause problems. No one will ever occupy the same relative position on all the status hierarchies, and most of us seem to have accepted and adjusted to some incongruities. On the other hand, when a person occupies highly different positions on status hierarchies that are important to him, we may find serious morale problems and behavior that evidences either considerable frustration or an attempt to bring about some reconciliation of his highly different positions.

From the position of the organization planner, it is necessary first to understand the different types of status that exist and, second, to recognize that these status relations will, in the minds of people within an organization, define certain types of relations as proper. When the formal organization sets up jobs or job relations that seem incompatible with these informally proper relations, some behavioral consequences can be expected.

The Individual in the Organization

An underlying question we have been exploring is how we can account for the behavior, both intended and not, of people in organizations. In part, we have said that it is determined by the structure (both planned and emergent) and directed by orders, instructions, rules, norms, etc. This pushes the inquiry to how one learns of the rules and norms, how one knows which orders must be followed and which can be ignored. The answer is that there are a number of learning experiences, some formal, some informal, through which a new person in the organization learns "how things are done around here" (Breed, Merton). Lessons well learned are rewarded, again both formally and informally (Merton, Roy). As a result, people become attached to the system that rewarded them.

This sounds simple enough and would seem basically supportive of the organization. But there are several problems. Sometimes, these processes can teach unintended (in fact, undesired) things, leading to dysfunctional consequences (Merton). At other times organizations may not be able to give or even control directly the means to satisfy the aspirations of individuals and as a result they may have interests, sources of influence, and loyalties outside the occupation, as when people give their loyalty to their occupation group and adapt their behavior to gain the approval of other members of this occupation rather than to get it from other organizational members. Hence, it is possible to have some people highly motivated to do their work well and relating primarily to the organizations they are in—locals —and others equally motivated who are interested in the approval of others in the occupation, most of whom may be outside the organization—cosmopolitans (Gouldner).

Summary and Conclusions

In Part One of this book, we considered some of the direct and positive effects of organizational decisions. It is necessary to consider the less obvious, and perhaps negative, consequences of these decisions. To do this, we need a knowledge of the informal organization and the ways it can be influenced by the formal. On examination, the informal organization was found to have a leadership structure, rules, standards, or norms, and ways of rewarding compliance with, or punishing deviations from, norms, thereby controlling people. In short, the informal organization meets with our general definition of an organization quite well, for it presents a set of relations among people that produces something; in this instance, however, the product is used by members. These relations, however, are products of social life and not the results of a central, rational plan based on some legitimate source of authority.

Many things were noted about informal organizations; many more could be noted. To simplify our examination of this part of the organization and also to provide a base for relating it to the formal organization, attention was given to a scheme for classifying elements of the social situation we were examining and also for relating the various classes of phenomena. The major variables were identified as sentiments, interactions, and activities, all mutually related. It was further recognized that some activities, interactions, and sentiments could be considered as coming from without a particular social situation. These would include the beliefs and values people bring with them into a situation, the activities assigned as part of a formal job, and the interactions required in the execution of these duties. On the other hand, another set could be considered as springing from the social situation where people interact with those whose company they enjoy and perhaps share activities with them. The former grouping we called the external system, the latter the internal system. These elements are shown in Fig. 1.

Parts Two and Three deal with the formal and the informal organization and cover what has been our traditional ways of viewing an organization. For purposes of investigation or explanation, it is frequently necessary to break a large topic into pieces and deal with one piece at a time. As long as the parts are recognized as a division based to a degree on expediency, this is not a particularly dangerous step.

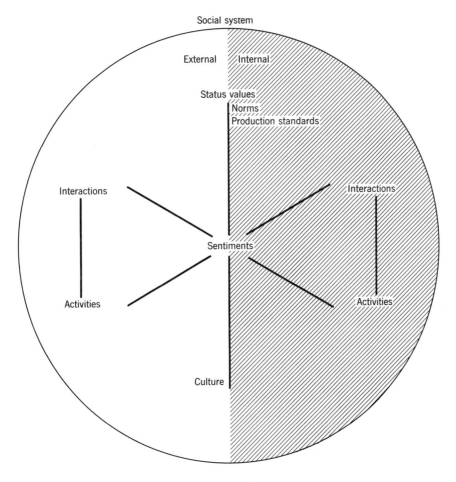

Fig. 1

Nevertheless, when we lose sight of the fact that we are dealing with pieces of a larger whole and begin to consider the parts as wholes in themselves, serious difficulties arise. This seems to have happened to some who have been studying organizations. Therefore, as these two parts have been developed, partic-ular attention has been given to identifying certain elements that will be particularly useful in developing links or bridges between the two approaches to organizations in order to join them eventually into a larger picture of an organization.

Social Systems

GEORGE HOMANS

This chapter is a tough one, perhaps the toughest in the book, but we had better know the worst at once. It tries to do two things at the same time. First, it tries to show how the kinds of generalization we shall be interested in are reached: how we go from simple descriptions

From *The Human Group*. New York: Harcourt, Brace and Co., 1950, pp. 25–40, 90–107, 108–113, 118–119. Copyright 1950 by Harcourt, Brace and World and reprinted with their permission.

of social events to uniformities in the behavior of a limited number of persons and groups and finally to generalizations that may apply to all groups. Second, it tries to define the words, or concepts, that will come into these highest generalizations. As we shall see, the two jobs mesh with one another and must be carried on together.

One of the big problems of sociology, as of all social science, is semantic: the problem of the relation between the words used and the observations made. The meanings of words are usually given by definitions, but the trouble with definitions, as one of the first great semanticists, Lord Bacon, pointed out, is that "the definitions themselves consist of words, and those words beget others: so that it is necessary to recur to individual instances, and those in due series and order."[1] Bacon meant that the end of the chain of words must be anchored in an act something like the one by which a mother teaches her child the meaning of the word *cow:* she points at the beast and says the word. Acts of this kind are not available to us. We are not in the open air watching a group in action, and we cannot learn the meaning of sociological concepts by having someone point to various items in the behavior of the group and, as he does so, name the concepts. But we can do the next best thing. We can take the descriptions of group behavior made by good observers, persons who, unlike ourselves, have been watching groups in the open air; we can point to certain things they saw and give these things names. The names are the concepts.

Our work presupposes the direct observation of human behavior. It does not for the most part deal with what men write in answer to a questionnaire or what they say when a research assistant has his foot in the door. It deals with what men say and do on the ordinary occasions of ordinary life. This kind of fact is surprisingly hard to collect; it demands an observer who is not himself so much a part of the situation that he cannot view it with a fresh eye, and one who does not, by the mere fact of his presence, change what would otherwise be said and done. Anthropologists who live with the tribes they study and who back up their lengthy questionings of native informants with firsthand observations of daily life collect this kind of material, and so do a few sociologists who study groups and communities in our own society. Our work relies on theirs. Some social scientists find this kind of material hard and unsatisfying to work with: it can seldom be converted into statistics and always leaves unanswered many interesting questions—and they shy away from it. Nevertheless·it is the stuff of everyday existence, and we start with it here.

EVENTS IN THE SINGLE GROUP. We are going to begin with a description of everyday social events in a society not our own. The world is a stage, and one of its many scenes opens:

> The room is low and rectangular. The left wall is filled by a door, closed, and a big stone fireplace, fitted for cooking. Chairs and benches are set around the fireplace. Against the back wall a table stands, and to the right of the table a colored picture hangs over a cabinet containing a small figure. The right wall is taken up by a dresser, full of kitchen gear and crockery, on one side of which is a door and on the other a staircase leading upstairs. Through a window over the table a yard, with a cart in it, is seen in dim light.
>
> A woman opens the door, right, and comes into the room. She goes to the fireplace, rakes together the ashes on the hearth, some of them still alive, puts on new fuel, and rekindles the blaze. Then she fills a kettle with water and hangs it on a hook over the fire. When it boils, she makes tea; meanwhile she lays out dishes, cutlery, bread, and milk on the table, and gets ready to cook eggs.
>
> A middle-aged man and two younger ones enter, exchange a few words with the woman, pull up chairs, sit down at the table, and begin to eat. The woman herself does not sit, but stands by, ready to bring up more food and drink if the men ask for them. When the men have eaten, the older one says to the younger ones, "Well, we'd better be off." They go out.
>
> By this time a girl has joined the woman in the room, but not until the men have left do the two sit down for their meal. Before they have finished, crying is heard outside, right. The woman leaves and later returns carrying a young child in her arms. She fondles and comforts it, then feeds it in its turn.
>
> She turns to the girl, who is already washing the dishes, with a remark about making butter. . . .[2]

We need not go on. This scene, or something much like it, has been enacted millions of times in the history of mankind, and it

[1] F. Bacon, *Novum Organum*, Bk. I, aphorism lix.

[2] Adapted from C. M. Arensberg and S. T. Kimball, *Family and Community in Ireland*, 35.

shows, of course, a farm family beginning a working day. It is not an American farm family, though families of this sort were common not so long ago in America and survive in some places still. It is a countryman's family in the southwest of Ireland. Farm families, differing from this one in some outward appearances, but perhaps not very different in essentials, have for centuries formed the foundations of society in Europe, the Near East, India, China, and much of the Americas. This social unit is characteristic of many of the countries that have the largest populations. Only in recent years and in a few places have we begun to see the appearance of a new kind of family. The old-fashioned farm family —if we may call it that—is still the commonest of human groups.

The scene is familiar. We begin and end with the familiar and are lucky to be able to do so, but the important point at the moment is not the familiarity of the scene. It is rather that a scene like this is part of the raw material of sociology: a description of a series of *events*, in each of which at one particular place and time a person did certain things, in certain physical surroundings, perhaps with certain implements and together with certain other persons. All science begins with process, the flux of things, the passing scene. Generalization must be true to events. We forget their vividness at our peril. And how refreshing they are! "Here," we can say, "is one kind of certainty. No matter how we interpret them, and no matter how far they fall short of telling the whole story, these things, at least these things, *happened*."

There can be little interpretation of, generalization from, single events. We can learn much—and it is good discipline, too—from trying merely to report, that is, from trying to describe human behavior in words altogether flat, simply descriptive, devoid of interpretation. In any strict sense, it cannot be done. Any noun implies some context; even a word like *table* implies something about the use of a physical object. But in the effort to leave out at least the higher levels of meaning, we can discover how much meaning we regularly put into our descriptions. Perhaps we shall see how easy it is to commit ourselves to an interpretation before we know what we are doing.

Our description of the farm family beginning the day is just such a flat description as a playwright might write in setting the opening scene of his play. The meaning unfolds only as the action of the play develops. Thus the older woman is not called the mother of the family, nor the man the father. "Mother" and "father" assume a certain scheme of social relationships, and from the single scene we cannot be sure that we are dealing with that kind of scheme. It is better to begin with distinctions like those between man and woman, youth and age. In the same way, the cabinet is not called a shrine. If we had called it that, we should have been assuming something that the single scene cannot tell us. Nevertheless, there are items in the description that might be remembered, should he run across them again, by anyone anxious to build up a picture of the relationships between the members of the family. For instance, the older man gives orders to the two younger ones or at least gives the signal to go out and begin the day's work. The woman likewise points out to the girl the job—making butter—that the two of them will do in the course of the day. Both women wait for the men to finish eating before they sit down themselves. The older woman comforts and plays with the baby. And so on. An observer builds up his picture of social relationships from repeated events like these.

CUSTOM. The next stage in the analysis of human behavior—and it always implies the first—is reached when we recognize simple recurrences in events, recurrences at different intervals. To go back to our farm family, we note that almost every day the men go out to work in the fields; that every year, at about the same season, they dig potatoes; that in this work the father directs the activities of the sons. The women do the chores around the house but do not work in the fields; so long as there is a youngster in the house, the mother feeds it, goes to it when it cries, comforts and protects it. And so on. The behavior of the members of a group is a symphony, a symphony that may have discords. There are different voices—as the wood winds are a voice in a symphony—each with its themes, which come in at different intervals, sometimes quietly, sometimes loudly, sometimes in the foreground, sometimes in the background. Often there is a conductor who is himself a voice, and there are recurrences in the group of voices, in the movement as a whole. Like lazy listeners, we who are at the symphony never hear all the voices and all their harmonies. We hear only the ones we are interested in hearing.

These recurrences in social behavior, when recognized as recurrences, are called customs. For the moment we are simply going to accept custom as a fact, giving notice at the same time that the fact raises an important question, which will be considered in a later chapter. We mention the question now only to show we are aware of it. Some students of society are inclined to take the recurrences in the behavior of a group for granted. They are interested in the details of particular customs, but not in custom itself as an aspect of group life. Other students go further, as Edmund Burke did years ago, and see custom as useful, even necessary. Men cannot plan for the future without relying on the massive regularities of expected behavior. Yet when everything intelligent has been said about the usefulness of custom, one more profound question remains: What makes custom customary? For the brute fact is that customs do change. In view of the constantly varied forces playing on society, it is amazing that anything can be recognized as persistent. The recurrences are miracles, not commonplaces; and miracles, if they happen often, are just the things we should study most closely. As soon as we do, we find that nothing is more defenseless than a custom, alone. Not single customs, but systems of custom, survive. Anthropologists used to talk about the "tyranny of custom" as if custom were a mold pressing social organization into a shape. This view is misleading. Custom is not something outside of, and apart from, social organization but is implicit in organization. These are large generalizations. We state them now, but only in a much later chapter shall we try to back them up. By that time we hope to have the tools to do the job.

The usual descriptions of groups consist of statements of custom, that is, recurrences in human behavior at different places or at different intervals. "The Irish countrymen live on isolated farms." . . . "The men of a Tikopia village commonly put out to sea together when they go fishing." The books and articles that are our sources, that we must work with, are full of such remarks. But we must never forget, having a lively sense of the shifting sands on which we build, that statements of custom, if they are worth anything, are founded on repeated observations of individual events in single scenes. With this in mind, let us return to the Irish farm family, and now study a description of the relationships between its members, particularly father, mother, and son. The description is a statement of custom: a summary of the recurrences in many single scenes like the one with which this chapter opened.

The growing child ordinarily sees his father as owner and principal worker of the farm. When the whole family group of father, mother, children, and whatever other relatives may be living with them, works in concert, as at the potato planting, the turf cutting, and the haymaking, it is the father who directs the group's activities, himself doing the heavy tasks. . . .

In his earliest childhood, of course, the mother looms larger in the child's consciousness than the father. The child's first duties, as soon as he can speak and walk, are to run on petty errands to neighbors and near-by "friends." Soon he is taking his father's meals to him in the fields or going on errands to the nearest shop. Until he is seven and has gone through First Communion, his place is in the house with the women, and his labor is of very little importance. After First Communion, at six or seven, he begins to be thrown more with his elder brothers, and comes to do small chores which bring him more and more into contact with his father and with the other men of the neighborhood . . . But not till he passes Confirmation and leaves school (generally at the same time) does he take on full men's work. Even then, as he becomes adult and takes on more and more of the heavy tasks of the farm work, he never escapes his father's direction, until his father dies or makes over the farm to him at his marriage . . .

It goes without saying that the father exercises his control over the whole activity of the "boy." It is by no means confined to their work together. Indeed, the father is the court of last resort, which dispenses punishment for deviations from the norm of conduct in all spheres. Within the bounds of custom and law he has full power to exercise discipline. Corporal punishment is not a thing of the past in Ireland, and, especially in the intermediate stages of the child's development, from seven to puberty, it gets full play.

It is during those years that the characteristic relationship between father and son is developed in rural communities. The son has suffered a remove from the previous almost exclusive control of its mother, in which an affective content of sympathy and indulgence was predominant, and is brought into contact for the first time with the father and older men. But the transfer is not completed. There is a hiatus in his development through the years of school when his participation in men's work and his relationship with his father has little chance of developing into an effective partnership. A real union of interests does not take place until after Confirmation and school-leaving, when for the first time his exclusive contacts and his entire day-to-day activity, particularly in farm work, will be with his father and the older men.

This fact colors greatly the relationship of father and son, as far as affective content goes. There is none of the close companionship and intimate sympathy which characterizes, at least ideally, the relationship in other groups. Where such exists, it is a matter for surprised comment to the small farmers. In its place there is developed, necessarily perhaps, a marked respect, expressing itself in the tabooing of many actions, such as smoking, drinking, and physical contact of any sort, which can be readily observed in any small farm family. Coupled with this is the lifelong subordination . . . which is never relaxed even in the one sphere in which farmer father and son can develop an intense community of interest—farm work. Nothing prevents the development of great mutual pride, the boy in his experienced and skillful mentor, tutor, and captain in work, and the man in a worthy and skillful successor and fellow workman, but on the other hand everything within the behavior developed in the relationship militates against the growth of close mutual sympathy. As a result, the antagonisms inherent in such a situation often break through very strongly when conflicts arise . . .

On the other hand, the relationship of mother and son has a very different content. Like that between father and son, it is the product of years of development. It is marked, too, by a similar retention of subordinate status on the part of the son. In farm work the boy is subject to the commands of his mother even when, fully adult, he has passed over exclusively to men's work. . . . But within the scope of such a subordination there is a quite different affective history. The relationship is the first and earliest into which a child enters. It is very close, intimate, and all-embracing for the first years of life; only gradually does the experience of the child expand to include brothers, sisters, and last, the older male members of the household.

Until seven, the child of either sex is the constant companion of its mother. If the family is numerous an elder child, usually a sister, may take over much of the mother's role, but the mother is always near-by. As the woman works in the house or fields, the child is kept by her side. In the house it usually sits in a crib by the fire or plays about on the floor, but always within sight and sound. It learns its speech from its mother, amid a flood of constant endearments, admonitions, and encouragements. The woman's work never separates her from the child. Custom imposes no restraints or interruptions in her solicitude. She looks after its comforts, gives it food, dresses it, etc. She constantly exercises restraints and controls over it, teaching it day by day in a thousand situations the elements of prudery, modesty and good conduct.

The controls she exercises are of a different kind from those of the father. She is both guide and companion. Her authority most often makes itself felt through praise, persuasion, and endearment. Only when a grave breach of discipline demands a restraining power greater than hers, or when an appeal to ultimate authority is needed, does the father begin to play his role. Especially in the years before puberty, the farm father enters the child's cognizance as a disciplinary force. The barriers of authority, respect, extra-household interests, and the imperatives of duty rather than of encouragement make it difficult for any intimacy to develop.

Even after Confirmation the child's relationship to his mother is not materially weakened. He becomes confirmed, it is true, in a masculine scorn for feminine interests and pursuits, but he can and must still look for protection to his mother against a too-arbitrary exercise of his father's power. In family disputes the mother takes a diplomatic, conciliatory role. From her intermediary position she can call upon the strongest ties between herself and her sons to restore rifts in parental authority and filial submission.

Throughout the years of the son's full activity in the farm economy under the father's leadership, the mother still remains the source of comfort and the preparer of food and is still infinitely solicitous of his welfare. It is only at marriage that the bond is broken . . . If the child must leave the farm for other walks of life, the closest possible relationship is still maintained. When one goes home, it is to see one's mother. There is always an attempt to carry on a correspondence. In exile, the bond lingers as a profound sentimental nostalgia.[3]

Before we go on to our main purpose, we must get some preliminaries out of the way. This passage describes a relationship between three persons, not the conventional triangle of a love story but the triangle that has father, mother, and son at its corners. The pattern of the relationship is clearly marked—which is a reason why we chose a description of an Irish family and not one of an American family. The latter is more familiar to us but its pattern is not so easily characterized. In the Irish family the relationship between mother and son is one of warm affection, the relationship between father and son is one of admiration mixed with respect. Moreover, these relationships are not peculiar to Ireland: it is interesting how often the pattern repeats itself in farm families, and indeed in other families, all over the world. Nor are these relationships inevitable. It is not simply "natural" that a son should love his mother, though we all like to think it is. He loves his mother be-

cause the repeated, thousand-times-repeated, events in which the two are brought together are of a certain kind. From earliest childhood she cares for him; but change her behavior and the emotion would change too. In like manner, the son's feeling for the father is colored by the father's control over him in the many-times-repeated events of farm work. Nor, to go a step further, are the two series of events —the events determining these mother-son and father-son relationships—isolated from the rest of the world. Instead they are related to the division of labor and assignment of authority in a going farm enterprise, surviving in an environment.

We shall not be misled by the use of the words "the child," "his mother," and "his father" in the singular. These are shorthand for "children," "mothers," and "fathers." An anthropologist would say that the passages quoted above tell us some of the customs of Irish countrymen, a statistician that they may perhaps express some kind of average in the behavior of a certain number of groups—Irish farm families—over a certain span of time. The statistician might find fault with the passages for not letting him know the relation between the "sample" and the "universe," that is, the relation between the number of groups directly observed and the larger number for whose behavior the average is supposed to hold good. He might also find fault with the passages for giving us no idea of the number of groups—there must be a few—whose behavior deviates in some degree from the average. He might say that the statements are by implication quantitative but that they do not let an outsider make any judgment of their quantitative reliability. His criticisms are good, and they can be answered only by raising new questions: How much more effort, in men, time, and money, would be needed to get the kind of data he wants? Given a limited supply of all three, how far would getting his kind of data interfere with getting a wider, though admittedly less reliable, coverage of group behavior? These are questions not of scientific morality but of strategy and, in the broad sense, economics: getting the most for one's money. They themselves beg for quantitative answers. And we might finally ask the different and more searching question: How far does the craving to get the kind of data a statistician considers reliable lead social scientists to take

[3] Reprinted by permission of the publishers from Conrad Maynadier Arensberg and Solon Toothaker Kimball, *Family and Community in Ireland,* Cambridge, Mass.: Harvard University Press, 1940, pp. 51–60.

up questions for which this kind of data can easily be secured instead of questions that are interesting for other reasons? To which the statistician might reply: If we are not getting what I want, are we getting anything on which we can found a science? We should keep these questions in mind, for much of the material we shall be working with is not of the kind the statistician wants.

DEFINITION OF CONCEPTS. Let us go back over our work so far. We began with a flat description of events within a single group; then we went on to a statement of the customs of an unspecified but limited number of groups: the families of Irish countrymen. The next step is a long one; in fact it will take up the rest of this book. We shall set up some hypotheses—and they will remain hypotheses because we shall only set them up, not prove them—that may sum up a few aspects of social behavior in an unlimited number of groups all over the world. There is no use saying now what these hypotheses are; we shall find out soon enough, and one move in particular we must make before we can formulate any hypotheses of high generalization, such as ours will be. We must define a few of the concepts that come into them. Though we cannot do so by pointing at objects and saying the concept, we can take the next best step. We can examine a passage like the one above, point out certain words in it, ask ourselves whether the aspects of social behavior to which the words refer have anything in common, and then, if they do, give a name to this common element. The name is the concept. We might have written a passage of our own for this purpose, but anyone can solve a problem if he sets it up himself. It is much more convincing to use someone else's passage, as we have done.

ACTIVITY. Let us look, then, at certain words and phrases in this passage, and first, perhaps, at words like these: *potato planting, turf cutting, haymaking, corporal punishment, smoking, drinking, gives food, dresses, looks after, plays, sits, walks, speaks, talks, First Communion, Confirmation.* In the passage we can pick out many more such words, and also some of greater generality, like *work* and *activity.* Let us agree that they have something in common, without committing ourselves on the question whether this something is im-

portant. They all refer to things that people do: work on the physical environment, with implements, and with other persons. If we want to be precise, we can say that all these words and phrases refer in the end to movements of the muscles of men, even though the importance of some of the movements, like talk and ceremonies, depends on their symbolic meaning. We shall speak of the characteristic they have in common as an *element* of social behavior, and we shall give it a name, as a mere ticket. It might be called *action,* if *action* had not been given a more general meaning, or *work,* if *work* did not have a special meaning in the physical sciences and may yet have an analogous one in sociology. Instead of either of these, we shall call it *activity,* and use it, in much the same way that it is used in everyday speech, as an analytical concept for the study of social groups.

We call activity an element, not implying that it is some ultimate, indivisible atom of behavior. It is no more than one of the classes into which we choose to divide something that might be divided in other, and less crude, ways. In fact we call it an element just because the vagueness of that word gives us room to move around in. Above all we must realize that activity is not a variable like temperature in physics: it cannot be given a single series of numerical values. Instead, a number of aspects of activity might be measured. We are sometimes able to measure the *output* or rate of production of certain kinds af activity, for instance, factory work, and sometimes the *efficiency* of activity, the relation to input to output. We might even be able to assign an index to the degree of *similarity* of one activity to another. And so on. These are true variables, at least in possibility, though we could not give them numerical values in every piece of research. In later chapters we shall have to make sure, when we speak of activity, which particular variable we have in mind.

INTERACTION. Going back now to the passage we are working with, let us look at expressions like these: the boy is *thrown with* his elder brothers; he comes more and more *into contact with* his father; he never *escapes from* his father's direction; he *participates* in the men's work; he is a *companion* of his mother; he goes to *see* his mother, and so on. The element that these phrases have in common is more or less mixed with other things, for in our language one word seldom states one clear idea. For instance, what does the word *see* mean in the phrase "going to see someone"? Yet there is a common element, and it seems to be some notion of sheer interaction between persons, apart from the particular activities in which they interact. When we refer to the fact that some unit of activity of one man follows, or, if we like the word better, is stimulated by some unit of activity of another, aside from any question of what these units may be, then we are referring to *interaction*. We shall speak of interaction as an element of social behavior and use it as an analytical concept in the chapters that follow.

We may find it hard to think consistently of interaction as separate from the other elements of behavior, but we shall have to do so in this book, and the fact is that in our everyday thinking we often keep it separate without realizing as much. When we say "Tom got in touch with Harry," or "Tom contacted Harry," or "Tom was an associate of Harry's," we are not talking about the particular words they said to one another or the particular activities they both took part in. Instead we are talking about the sheer fact of contact, of association. Perhaps the simplest example of interaction, though we should find it complex enough if we studied it carefully, is two men at opposite ends of a saw, sawing a log. When we say that the two are interacting, we are not referring to the fact that both are sawing: in our language, sawing is an *activity*, but to the fact that the push of one man on the saw is followed by the push of the other. In this example, the interaction does not involve words. More often interaction takes place through verbal or other symbolic communication. But when in the armed forces men talk about the chain of command, or in a business ask what officers report to what other ones, they are still talking about channels of communication—the chains of interaction—rather than the communications themselves or the activities that demand communications.

Just as several variables are included under the concept of activity, so several are included under interaction. We can study the *frequency* of interaction: the number of times a day or a year one man interacts with another or the members of a group interact with one another. We can measure the ratio between the amount of time one man is active, for instance, talking, and the *duration* of his interlocutor's activity. Or we can study the *order* of interaction: Who originates action? Where does a chain of interactions start and where does it go? If Tom makes a suggestion to Dick, does Dick pass it on to Harry? [4] Once again, we shall have to make sure from time to time that we are talking about one variable under interaction and not another. Our observations of this element can often be rather precise and definite, which gives them infinite charm for persons of a certain temperament.

When we called the first of our elements *activity*, we may have been using the obvious and appropriate word. But in calling the second element *interaction*, are we not needlessly using a strange word when a familiar one is on hand? Why not speak of *communication* rather than *interaction*? Our answer is: The word *communication* is neither general enough in one sense nor specific enough in another. When people think of communication, they think of communication in words, but here we are including under interaction both verbal and nonverbal communication. What is more, the word *communication* is used in several different ways in everyday speech. It may mean the content of the message, signal, or "communication" being transmitted, or the process of transmission itself, as when people speak of "methods of communication," or to the sheer fact, aside from content or process of transmission, that one person has communicated with another. Only to the last of these three do we give the name of interaction, and the unfamiliarity of the word may underline the fact that its meaning is specific. Nevertheless we shall, from time to time, when there is no risk of confusion, use the word *communication* in place of *interaction*, so that our language will not sound hopelessly foreign.

SENTIMENT. Now let us go back to our passage again and consider another set of words and phrases: *sentiments of affection, affective*

<hr>

[4] For a systematic discussion of interaction as an element of social behavior, see E. D. Chapple, with the collaboration of C. M. Arensberg, *Measuring Human Relations* (Genetic Psychology Monographs, Vol. 22 (1940)).

content of *sympathy* and *indulgence*, *intimate sympathy*, *respect*, *pride*, *antagonism*, *affective history*, *scorn*, *sentimental nostalgia*. To these we shall arbitrarily add others, such as *hunger* and *thirst*, that might easily have come into the passage. What can we say these words have in common? Perhaps the most we can say, and it may not be very much, is that they all refer to internal states of the human body. Laymen and professional psychologists call these states by various names: drives, emotions, feelings, affective states, sentiments, attitudes. Here we shall call them all *sentiments*, largely because that word has been used in a less specialized sense than some of the others, and we shall speak of *sentiment* as an element of social behavior.

Notice the full range of things we propose to call sentiments. They run all the way from fear, hunger, and thirst, to such probably far more complicated psychological states as liking or disliking for individuals, approval or disapproval of their actions. We are lumping together under this word some psychological states that psychologists would certainly keep separate. Our employment of the concept *sentiment* can only be justified by what we do with it, so that at the moment all we can ask is indulgence for our failure in orthodoxy.

We must now consider a question that may not seem important but that has come up again and again, in one form or another, ever since the behaviorists first raised it. We can *see* activities and interactions. But if sentiments are internal states of the body, can we see them in the same way? It is true that a person may say he feels hungry or likes someone, and that in everyday life, if we are dealing with him, we take account of what he has to say about his own feelings. But scientists may be forgiven for believing that subjective judgments are treacherous things to work with. They are not reliable; we cannot tell whether two persons would reach the same judgment under the same circumstances, and reliability is the rock on which science is built. Some scientists even believe that they can reach important generalizations, in psychology and sociology, without paying any attention whatever to subjective judgments; and they would ask us whether there is anything we can point to as sentiment that has not already been included under activity and interaction. Can it be independently observed? Perhaps in some animals the

more violent sentiments can be so observed. In a dog or cat, pain, hunger, fear, and rage are marked by measurable changes in the body, particularly in the glands of internal secretion.[5] We assume that this is also true of human beings, but few of the necessary measurements can easily be made. For mild sentiments such as friendliness, and these are the ones we shall be working with most often here, we are not sure how far the bodily changes occur at all. The James-Lange theory that a sentiment and a set of visceral changes are one and the same thing cannot be driven too far. On an occasion that might conceivably have called for emotion, the undamaged human being reacts so as to cut down the amount of visceral change taking place. The body mobilizes for action, if that is appropriate, and reduces the merely emotional changes.

Science is perfectly ready to take leave of common sense, but only for a clear and present gain. Lacking more precise methods for observing sentiments, since the biological methods can only be used in special circumstances, have we anything to gain by giving up everyday practice? Have we not rather a good deal to lose? And what is everyday practice? In deciding what sentiments a person is feeling, we take notice of slight, evanescent tones of his voice, expressions of his face, movements of his hands, ways of carrying his body, and we take notice of these things as parts of a whole in which the context of any one sign is furnished by all the others. The signs may be slight in that the physical change from one whole to another is not great, but they are not slight so long as we have learned to discriminate between wholes and assign them different meanings. And that is what we do. From these wholes we infer the existence of internal states of the human body and call them anger, irritation, sympathy, respect, pride, and so forth. Above all, we infer the existence of sentiments from what men say about what they feel and from the echo that their words find in our own feelings. We can recognize in ourselves what they are talking about. All those who have probed the secrets of the human heart have known how misleading and ambiguous these indications can sometimes be, how a man can talk love and mean hate, or

[5] See W. B. Cannon, *Bodily Changes in Pain, Hunger, Fear, and Rage.*

mean both together, without being aware of what he is doing. Yet we act on our inferences, on our diagnoses of the sentiments of other people, and we do not always act ineffectively. In this book we are trying to learn how the elements of our everyday social experience are related to one another. Leaving out a part of that experience—and sentiment is a part—would be reasonable only if we had a better kind of observation to take its place. Some sciences have something better; ours does not yet.

We may end with a practical argument. This book is, in one of its intentions, an effort to bring out the generalizations implicit in modern field studies of human groups. If the men who made the studies felt that they could infer and give names to such things as sentiments of affection, respect, pride, and antagonism, we shall see what we can do with their inferences, remembering always that a more advanced theory than ours may have to wait for more precise and reliable observations. No theory can be more sophisticated than the facts with which it deals.

Under the element of *sentiment*, several different kinds of studies can and have been made. Perhaps the best-known ones are carried on by the public opinion pollsters and attitude scalers using questionnaires they get people to answer. Especially when they try to find out the *number* of persons that approve or disapprove of, like or dislike, a proposal for action or a candidate for public office, they are studying at least one variable under this element. Often they go further and try to discover not only how many persons approve or disapprove but the *conviction* with which they do so: whether they are sure they are right, feel somewhat less sure, or remain undecided. The pollsters may also try to find out the *intensity* of the sentiments concerned: a man may disapprove of something intellectually and yet not feel strongly about it. His emotions may not have been deeply aroused. . . .

The External System

The environment and its influences will be different for each group considered; . . . we note that the group is, at the moment we study it, persisting or surviving in its environment; and we infer, not unnaturally, that the behavior of the group must be such as to allow it to survive in the environment. Then we turn to the elements of group behavior: sentiment, activity, and interaction, and we say that the *external system* is the state of these elements and of their interrelations, so far as it constitutes a solution—not necessarily the only possible solution—of the problem: How shall the group survive in its environment? We call it external because it is conditioned by the environment; we call it a system because in it the elements of behavior are mutually dependent. The external system, plus another set of relations which we shall call the *internal system*, make up the total social system.

At the risk of anticipating some later steps in our argument, let us take everyone into our confidence on what we are trying to do. When we study a group, one of the first observations we can make is that the group is surviving in an environment, and therefore we say of the group, as of other organisms, that it is, for the moment at least, adapted to its environment. But this word *adaptation* is ambiguous. Does it mean that the characteristics of the group are determined by the environment? No, it does not, for the second observation we can make is that the characteristics of the group are determined by two classes of factors and not one only. These characteristics are determined by the environment, in greater or lesser degree according to the nature of the environment and of the group in question, and also by what we shall call for the time being the internal development of the group. But we are not yet at the end of our difficulties, for the third observation we can make is that the two classes of factors are not independent of one another. Full explanation of our meaning will take the rest of this book, but we can outline our argument now. Assuming that there is established between the members of a group any set of relations satisfying the condition that the group survives for a time in its particular environment, physical and social, we can show that on the foundation of these relations the group will develop new ones, that the latter will modify or even create the relations we assumed at the beginning, and that, finally, the behavior of the group, besides being determined by the environment, will itself change the environment.

In short, the relationship between group and environment is essentially a relationship of action and reaction; it is circular. But perhaps it is safer to say that it sounds circular when described in words and sentences. When we describe a phenomenon in ordinary language, we are bound to start with a particular statement, going on from there to a sequence of further statements, and if the phenomenon is complex and organic, the sequence has a way of coming back sooner or later to the statement with which we started. No doubt a series of simultaneous equations could describe the characteristics of the group more elegantly than words and sentences can, but we do not yet have the equations, and it may be that the equations cannot be set up before the verbal description has been made. If, then, we are limited to ordinary language, and if the tendency of ordinary language is to make the analysis of complex organic wholes sound circular, we propose in this book to relax, to fall in with this tendency of language rather than fight against it, and to analyze the relationship between group and environment as if it were a process having a beginning and an end, even though the point at which the process ends may be the point from which it started. Let us be candid and admit the method is clumsy, though it may be the best we have.

Our method has many analogies in the verbal description of physical processes. In describing a group, our problem is, for instance, a little like the problem of analyzing without the help of mathematics what happens to a set of interlinked springs when one of them is compressed. How shall a man describe in words what happens to a set of springs in a cushion or mattress when he sits on them? If he begins by sitting on any one spring and tries to trace from there the changes that take place in the rest of the springs, he will always find that the last spring in the series is linked back to the first and prevents the first from giving way under his weight as much as he thought it would. This, in fact, is the virtue of the set of springs.

Now let us use a more complicated analogy. We are all more or less familiar with the operation of the gasoline, or internal-combustion, engine. Let us ask ourselves how the operation of this engine was originally explained to us, or, better, how we should go about explaining it to someone else. We should, perhaps, begin by considering only one cylinder, instead of all the cylinders a real engine would have, and we should, just to get our exposition going, assume the cylinder and its contents to be in a certain state. We might, for instance, assume that the piston has reached the top of its stroke, and that the mixture of air and gasoline above the piston is hot and compressed. From then on, we should describe the operations of the engine as proceeding in sequence. A spark explodes the hot mixture; the explosion drives the piston downwards, and the moving piston transmits turning energy to the shaft. As the shaft turns, a system of cams opens valves in the cylinder head that admit a fresh mixture and allow the burnt gas to escape. The turning shaft also causes the piston to rise once more in the cylinder, compressing and heating the fresh mixture; and we are back where we started from, except that we have yet to account for the spark that set the whole process going. A generator is turned by the shaft, and this generator produces the electric current that explodes the mixture in the cylinder. And so the process goes on as long as the gasoline holds out.

The point we want to make is that although these operations in fact take place in a continuing cycle, we must nevertheless, language being what it is, describe them as if they took place in a sequence having a beginning and an end. Therefore we must assume a certain state of affairs at the beginning of our exposition, the existence of which we can account for only at the end. Thus we assume at the beginning the hot, compressed gas and the spark that ignites it, but we cannot account for the gas being in the cylinder, and being heated, compressed, and ignited, until we have reached the end of our explanation. At our convenience, we can choose any point in the cycle as the point from which our exposition starts, but, whatever point we choose, the problem of describing a cycle as a sequence of events still remains.

Now a group is obviously not an internal-combustion engine—our analogy is *only* an analogy—but we shall analyze the characteristics of the group as if we were dealing with some kind of ongoing circular process. No doubt this is not the only way in which the group could be analyzed, and no doubt, once we have finished making our analysis in this way, we shall be able to adopt a better way and throw away the old, just as one discards the scaffolding that has surrounded a house during construction. But having adopted this method of exposition, we encounter the same kind of difficulty we encountered with the gasoline engine. In describing the circular process in ordinary language, we are at liberty to begin at whatever point in the process we choose, but no matter what point that is, we must still assume at the beginning of our description the existence of certain conditions that we can account for only at the end. We choose to begin the analysis of the group with the external system, which we have defined as a set of relations among the members of the group that solves the problem: How shall the group survive in its environment? We do not say that the external system is the only possible solution to the problem. We do not say either that the group could do no worse or that it could do no better and still survive. We merely say that the external system is *one* solution of the survival problem. For us it is the equivalent of the assumption we made in describing the gasoline engine that the mixture was originally hot and compressed and that a spark was ready to explode it. Then, having assumed that some set of relations such as the external system must exist, we shall go on, as we did with the gasoline engine, and try to show why they do in fact exist or why the assumed relations are modified. The emphasis had better be on modification, for there is one great difference between describing the gasoline engine and describing the group. With the gasoline engine we show how the later events in the cycle create the very conditions we assumed in the beginning, whereas with the group we shall show that the later events in the cycle may modify the conditions we assumed in the beginning. We shall have to allow scope for emergent evolution.

Thus the external system first gives us a set of initial conditions from which our exposition can take its departure and then takes account of the fact that the adaptation of the group to its environment is partly determined by the nature of the environment, while leaving us free later to show how this adaptation is also in part determined by the internal development of the group.

To return from the general problem to the particular group we are studying at the moment, the first question we ask of the Bank Wiring group * is this: What does this group need to have in order to keep going in its particular environment? It needs motives (sentiments) on the part of its members, jobs (activities) for them to do, and some communication (interaction) between them. In other words, the members of the group must meet in some degree the plans of the Western Electric Company, and they must be adequately motivated to do so. We shall first take up each element of the external system separately and then in its mutual relations with the others. Until we have done this job we had better not try to define the external system any more rigorously. We must show, and not just say, what we mean.

SENTIMENT. The Bank Wiremen came to the Hawthorne Plant in the first instance with certain motives. The motives were generated by the circumstances of their lives outside the plant, but they were also part of their behavior within it. Some of the motives the men would have recognized: they were working for money, money to get food, to support a family, to buy and keep a car, to take a girl to the movies. These motives were the only ones the planners in the company took into account in devising the wage incentive scheme. Perhaps these were the only motives they thought they could successfully appeal to. At any rate, the men must have had many other reasons for working at Hawthorne that they

---

* The Bank Wiring group were employees of the Western Electric Company who were employed in connecting wires to banks of terminals used in telephone equipment. Some of these employees were placed in a seperate Observation Room where their behavior was intensively studied. This and other related investigations at the Hawthorne Plant of the Western Electric Company are reported in Fritz J. Roethlisberger and William J. Dickson, *Management and the Worker*, Cambridge, Mass.: Harvard University Press, 1939. Homans makes extensive use of the data reported about this group [Ed. note].

might not have admitted so easily: a feeling that a man was not a fully self-respecting citizen unless he had a job, a desire for the prestige outside the factory that comes from working up to a good job within it, the wish to belong to a company that was said to be a good place to work, and so on. These are all, by our definition, sentiments, and these were the motives for work that the men brought to the Bank Wiring Observation Room. Whatever other sentiments their association with their fellow workers might release in the men, these would still have had to be satisfied in some degree. Man does not live by bread alone, but he lives by bread at least. These sentiments were assets to the company in that they led to hard work; they were liabilities in that the company had to satisfy them. Sentiment as an element of co-operation always has this double aspect.

The sentiments we have been talking about are part of what is often called individual self-interest. Let us be clear as to what we mean by this famous phrase. In the first place, it may be that all motives are motives of self-interest in the sense that, given the situation in which he is placed, a man always tries to do as well as he can for himself. What he does may look to outsiders as if it were hurting rather than helping him; it may look impossibly altruistic rather than selfish, and yet modern psychology teaches us that, if we knew the full situation, both the social relationships and the psychological dynamics of the person concerned, we should find all his actions to be self-enhancing. But this is an aside; let us take up the question from another point of view. If we examine the motives we usually call individual self-interest, we shall find that they are, for the most part, neither individual nor selfish but that they are the product of group life and serve the ends of a whole group not just an individual. What we really mean by the celebrated phrase is that these motives are generated in a different group from the one we are concerned with at the moment. Thus from the point of view of the Bank Wiring Observation Room, the desire of a man to earn wages was individual self-interest, but from the point of view of his family it was altruism. Motives of self-interest in this sense are the ones that come into the external system. Sentiments, on the other hand, that are generated within the group we are concerned with at the moment include some of the ones

we call disinterested. Friendship between wiremen is an example. While sentiments of self-interest affected or influenced the behavior of the men in the room, they did not solely determine that behavior. If these sentiments had been alone decisive, output would perhaps have been higher. That both self-interest *and* something else are satisfied by group life is the truth that is hardest for the hard-boiled—and half-baked—person to see. As Mayo says, "If a number of individuals work together to achieve a common purpose, a harmony of interests will develop among them to which individual self-interest will be subordinated. This is a very different doctrine from the claim that individual self-interest is the solitary human motive." [6]

ACTIVITY. The activities of the group were in the first instance planned by the Western Electric Company engineers. Some of the men, with tools and fixtures, wired one kind of equipment; some of the men wired another. Some of the men soldered the connected wires into place on the terminals. Two men inspected the completed switches, both visually and with testing sets. A group chief supervised the whole. A trucker brought supplies into the room and took completed equipments out. Here were a number of different kinds of activity, ranging from manual work with tools through visual observation to activity that was largely verbal: supervision and direction. The activities were in theory different for different persons, and they were organized: each had a part in the production of a completed whole. Furthermore, the men were paid for their work in different amounts, according to a complicated system of group piecework. Note that the Western Electric organization tried to control more of the activities of the group than it was actually able to control. Nevertheless, it did to a very large extent settle what the men should do.

INTERACTION. In the same way, observing the behavior of the men, one could have mapped out a scheme of interaction among them, in abstraction from their sentiments and their activities, and one could have recognized that a part of the scheme was set by the company.

[6] E. Mayo, *The Political Problem of Industrial Civilization*, 21.

There were the necessary interactions between a solderman and the three wiremen he worked for, between an inspector and the wiremen and soldermen whose work he passed judgment on, between the group chief and all the men in the room. Then there were the almost inevitable interactions between the men who were thrown together by the physical geography of the room, especially between the wiremen and soldermen who worked together, some at the front, some in the middle, and some at the back of the room. Finally, the mere fact that all the men were together in a single room tended to increase interaction between each member of the group and every other.

PAIR RELATIONSHIPS. So far we have been doing with the description of the Bank Wiring Observation Room no more than we did . . . with the description of the Irish countryman's family. We have, to be sure, limited ourselves to that part of group behavior that is under the direct influence of the environment, but within this field what we have been doing is the same. We have been making a crude analysis, breaking the behavior of the men down into its elements of sentiment, activity, and interaction. We shall now take a new step in the application of our method, the first step in synthesis. What has been separated must be put together again. We shall study the relationships of mutual dependence among sentiment, activity, and interaction in the external system. More particularly, we shall study the relationships between pairs of elements, of which there are, logically, three: sentiment-activity, activity-interaction, and interaction-sentiment.

There is nothing complicated about the idea of mutual dependence. Just the same, we had better say what we mean by it, as it will come into our thinking over and over again. In physics, Boyle's law states that the volume of a gas in an enclosed space varies inversely with the pressure upon it. The greater the pressure, the smaller the volume of the gas. This statement, which is usually put in the form of an equation, expresses a relationship of mutual dependence, mutual because if either pressure or volume changes, the other variable will change too. If pressure is increased, volume will decrease. But if we choose to begin with volume instead of pressure, we say that if volume increases, pressure must decrease. This kind of relationship is most elegantly expressed

in an equation, but in the field of sociology we should not pretend to use equations until we have data that are thoroughly quantitive. Instead we shall have to describe this kind of relationship in ordinary language, and here we are at once in trouble, because this is just the kind of relationship that ordinary language— at least any of the Western languages—is least well equipped to describe. Ordinary language, with its subjects and predicates, is geared to handling only one independent factor and one dependent factor at a time: someone is always doing something to somebody. Cause-and-effect thinking, rather than mutual-dependence thinking, is built into speech. Yet a situation that can accurately be described in cause-and-effect terms is just the kind that is encountered least often in sociology. Here the cause produces an effect, but the effect reacts upon the cause. In these circumstances, the very first effort to use ordinary language shows how crude a tool it is. Yet we shall do what we can with it, as we have nothing else. We may, for instance, say that an increase in the complexity of the scheme of activity in the external system will bring about an increase in the complexity of the scheme of interaction, but that the reverse is also true. The two are mutually dependent.

One other point should be made but not elaborated at this time. According to Boyle's law, the volume of a gas in an enclosed space varies inversely as the pressure put upon it only if the temperature is held constant during the process. If the temperature does vary, the relationship between volume and pressure will not have the simple form stated by the law. When we study the mutual dependence of two variables, we must somehow take account of the effect on these two of the other variables that enter the system. In the same way, when we make a statement about the mutual dependence of, for instance, interaction and activity, we must never forget that sentiment also comes into the system and may effect the relationships described. It is never enough to say that the relationship holds good "other things being equal." We must try to say what these other things are, and where they are "equal." This raises immense problems, which we shall not try to cope with at this time, if indeed we can ever cope with them adequately in social science.

MUTUAL DEPENDENCE OF SENTIMENT AND ACTIVITY. When we are thinking of the relationship of mutual dependence between sentiment and activity, we speak of sentiments as motives or drives. In the simplest form of the relationship, a motive gives rise to activity, and once the activity is successfully completed, the motive disappears. A man feels hungry; he gets something to eat and his hunger disappears. If his activity does not result in his getting something to eat, new sentiments, which we call frustration will be added to his original hunger, and we say that the activity was unrewarding or even positively punishing. He may then try a new one; if it ends in his getting something to eat, his hunger is allayed, and he will tend to repeat the activity the next time he feels hungry. We now say that the activity is rewarding, but do we mean anything more by this word that we saw the man eat the food and repeat the activity leading to it?

This is the relationship at its simplest. It is much more complicated when the motive is not something like hunger but something like a man's fear that he will be hungry in the future. Suppose that a man is afraid he will be hungry in the future if he does not now start plowing his field and doing other tasks in co-operation with other men that will lead in the end to loaves of bread on his table. The man's hunger is allayed when he gets food, but the fear does not necessarily disappear when the appropriate activities are carried out. Future hunger is still a threat. In these circumstances, *both motives and associated activities persist, both continuously recreated, but if either side of the relationship is changed, the other will be affected.* Returning to our example, we can say that, if for any reason the man is less afraid he will be hungry, he may not work so hard. And if, on the other hand, he finds some new set of activities that will yield more food than the old, he may become less fearful. The relationship between motive and activity is mutual.

This relationship seems to hold good whether the activity in question is obviously and directly useful or, like magic, takes the place of a useful activity that is unknown or impossible. In the absence of anything better to do, men must find even magic rewarding. The relationship also seems to hold good both for the sentiments we share with all men, such as fear,

hunger, thirst, cold, and the like, and for the sentiments generated in a particular social situation, such as the need to be paid wages. Note how in the Bank Wiring Observation Room the company's wage incentive plan tried to establish a particularly close link between one sentiment (the desire for money) and one set of activities (production). That the plan did not altogether achieve its intended results does not mean that this link was unimportant. It means that other sentiments besides the need for money affected output. It is clear, for instance, that the sentiments of Green * . . . — "I'd like a job reading"—, sentiments that presumably were generated by his whole past history and experience in groups outside the plant, were among the forces making his output the lowest in the room. If the interviews with the workers had been reported more fully, we should know much more about the outside influences on the motives of the men.

We need not go further into the mutual dependence of sentiment and activity. After all, most of the science of psychology, and particularly that part called "learning theory," is devoted to studying it, and if we tried to compete with psychology our hopeless inadequacy in that field would be revealed even more clearly than it is already. All we can do is show how some of the problems studied by psychology fit into a general scheme for analyzing group behavior. Remember also that we are now considering only the sentiments that come into the external system. The sentiments of the internal system are rather different in kind, though their mutual dependence with activities is the same as that we have just described.

MUTUAL DEPENDENCE OF ACTIVITY AND INTERACTION. In the external system, the relationship of mutual dependence between activity and interaction links the division of labor with the scheme of communication in the group. In the Bank Wiring Observation Room, the total job of turning out completed equipments was divided into a series of separate activities: wiring, soldering, inspection, trucking, and, not least in importance, supervision. Each separate activity was assigned to a different individual or subgroup, and in many of the activities each unit of work—for instance, completing a single

* Green was one of the employees in the Bank Wiring Observation Room [Ed. note].

level of connections—took a certain length of time. But what has been broken up must be put together again. If finished equipments were to be turned out, interaction had to take place in a certain scheme between the men doing the different jobs.

Thus when a wireman had completed a level on one equipment he moved over to a second one, and that act was the signal for the solderman to begin soldering in place the connections of the first terminal. The wireman had interacted with the solderman: remember that by our definition interaction takes place when the action of one man sets off the action of another. And note that, in this instance, the wireman originated interaction with the solderman: he gave the signal to which the other responded. We can without danger call interaction communication provided we remember that communication is not necessarily verbal. There was no need for words to pass between wireman and solderman in order that communication between them should be effective. In the same way, the solderman's completion of his part of the task was the signal for the inspector to go to work, and if he discovered any defect, he would initiate interaction, almost necessarily verbal this time, with the workman responsible. Thus a continuous process of interaction brought together the separate activities that went into the completion of the product. Finally, if one of the company's regulations was too flagrantly violated, or the process of co-ordination failed at any point, the problem would come to the group chief's attention. Someone would bring the matter up to him, or he himself would initiate interaction to restore the established order.

Generalizing from the Bank Wiring Observation Room, we can say, then, that any division, among the members of a group, of the partial activities that go into the completion of some total activity implies a scheme of interaction among the persons concerned, and that *if the scheme of activities is changed, the scheme of interaction will, in general, change also, and vice versa.* The two are mutually dependent. Sometimes, and this is perhaps the more common situation, a man who is organizing a piece of work begins by dividing it up into separate activities, and then makes the scheme of interaction conform to his division. That is, he treats the scheme of activity as the independent or governing factor. Thus the management of a plant may decide how an operation shall be divided among the workers and then devise an appropriate method of co-ordination. But this presupposes that an appropriate method of co-ordination can be put into effect, and the presupposition may be wrong. That is, the scheme of interaction may sometimes be the governing factor. Surely certain forms of the division of labor among the members of an industrial group were prohibitively expensive in the days before the conveyor belt was invented and made new schemes of interaction possible. In most circumstances, *both* factors are important.[7]

The division of labor makes the cost of work less in human effort or money. For this reason all societies have gone some distance in making their members specialists. From Adam Smith to Henry Taylor the uncriticized assumption was apt to be that the further the division was carried, the greater were the savings effected, that the further a job like shoemaking was broken down into its component specialties, and each assigned to a workman who did nothing else, the less would be the cost of making the shoe. Now we have begun to understand that the division of labor, like any other process, has its point of diminishing returns. Peter Drucker has shown how, in World War II and in some kinds of industrial work where conventional assembly lines could not be set up, the assigning of all the component specialties of any one job to one person or a group of persons, rather than to a number of separate individuals, turned out to be a cheaper way of manufacturing than any other.[8] Why the division of labor may reach a point of diminishing returns should be clear from our analysis. The division of labor is not something in itself; it always implies a scheme of interaction by which the different divided activities are co-ordinated. The indirect costs of setting up this scheme, including the costs that arise if supervision is inadequate, may offset the direct savings from specialization.

THE PYRAMID OF INTERACTION. What we said two paragraphs ago we must now take back in part. It is not universally true that as the

In this and the following discussion, much reliance is placed on C. I. Barnard, *The Functions of the Executive,* ch. VIII.
[8] P. F. Drucker, "The Way to Industrial Peace," *Harper's Magazine,* Vol. 193 (Nov., 1946), 390.

scheme of activity changes the scheme of inter-action will change too. It is not true when the activity in question is supervision or leadership: the process by which departures from a given plan of co-operation are avoided or new plans introduced. In groups that differ greatly in the activities they carry on, the schemes of inter-action between leaders of different levels ·and their followers tend nevertheless to be strik-ingly similar. Let us see what this means by taking up the problem of the *span of control*, as organization experts call it: How many men can be supervised by a single leader? When the activities of a group are of such a kind that they can be co-ordinated largely through one-way interaction from the leader to the follow-ers, then the leader can supervise a rather large number of persons. An example is the con-ductor of a symphony orchestra, who may direct as many as a hundred men. But in gen-eral the interaction must be two-way: the leader gives orders, information, and exhorta-tion to his followers, but they must also supply him with information about themselves and the situation they face. In these circumstances the span of control becomes much smaller. It is significant how often a group of between eight and a dozen persons crops up under the super-vision of a single leader in organizations of many different kinds. The old-fashioned squad in the army is an example. And since the same kind of considerations govern the relations be-tween the leaders of the first level and their own leaders, and so on for higher and higher leaders in groups of larger and larger size, it is easy to see how the scheme of interaction, especially in big organizations, piles up into its characteristic pyramidical, or hierarchical, form. The leader-in-chief appears at the apex of the pyramid, working with a small group of lesser leaders; each lesser leader, level by level, works with his own small group of lead-ers of still lower rank, until finally at the broad base the rank and file are reached.

No matter what activities an organization carries on, this characteristic form of the inter-action scheme tends to appear; it appears in the Catholic Church as surely as it does in an industrial firm or an army. Therefore we must modify our earlier rule and say that *whatever changes occur in the scheme of activities of a group, the scheme of interaction between the leaders of various levels and their followers tends to keep the same general pyramidical*

form. Yet the modification is more apparent than real. If the conflict between the two rules distresses us, we can readily reconcile them. The pyramid scheme of interaction seems to make possible the supervision of the activities of a large number of persons, through two-way interaction between them and leaders of different levels. Whenever, therefore, this par-ticular activity, supervision, remains largely the same from organization to organization, then the scheme of interaction—the pyramid—through which supervision is exercised remains largely the same too. Our rule stated that if the scheme of activity changed, the scheme of interaction changed too. But the rule also implies that if the activity does not change—and the job of supervision is much the same from group to group—the interaction does not change either. The first rule holds after all, the second rule being merely one of its special cases.

The relation between the scheme of activities and the scheme of interaction in an organiza-tion is usually represented by the familiar organization chart, which shows the organiza-tion divided into departments and subdepart-ments, the various officers and subofficers oc-cupying boxes, connected by lines to show which persons are subordinate to what other ones. Every such chart is too neat; it tells what the channels of interaction ought to be but not always what they are. The pyramid-type chart is particularly misleading because it shows only the interaction between superiors and subordinates, the kind of interaction that we shall call, following Barnard, *scalar*.[9] It does not show the interaction that goes on between two or more persons at about the same level of the organization, for instance, between two department heads or, in the Bank Wiring Room, between a wireman and an inspector. This kind of interaction we shall call *lateral* interaction, though we must remem-ber there are borderline cases where the dis-tinction between scalar and lateral interaction disappears. The conventional organization chart represents the scalar but not the lateral interaction. If it were not for the unhappy association with predatory spiders, the facts would be much better represented by a web, the top leader at the center, spokes radiating

[9] C. I. Barnard, *Organization and Management*, 150.

from him, and concentric circles linking the spokes. Interaction takes place along the concentric circles as well as along the spokes. But even the web is too neat a picture.

It is a mistake to think of the pyramid—or the web—scheme of interaction as always created by conscious planning. It is so created in only a few instances, for example, the large formal organizations of modern Western society, and these, in their origins, modeled themselves on previously existing patterns. The pyramid occurs not only where it is planned, as in the Western Electric Company, but also where it is not planned, as in a street gang or primitive tribe. Sometimes the pyramid is imposed on a group, as supervision was imposed on the Bank Wiremen; sometimes, as we shall see, a group spontaneously creates its own pyramid. Sometimes a group, if it is to operate successfully on the environment, needs the pyramid; sometimes a group does not need the pyramid but creates it anyhow. In any event, the fact that a pyramid of interaction may be a practical necessity of effective operations on the environment is no guarantee that the pyramid will appear. As we mentioned earlier, the possiblility of coincidence between the practically necessary and the spontaneously produced is one of the fascinating discoveries that comes from the study of groups as of other organisms, but we shall never explain the existence of the pyramid of interaction or any other such item of group behavior by pointing out that it helps the group to survive in an environment. Even if we assume for the moment that it does help the group to survive, we shall sooner or later go on to examine in detail the mechanisms by which the item in question is produced. We shall study what the philosophers call efficient, rather than final, causes. But we are again running ahead of our argument. The immediate point is that the principles of organization are universal; they are not an invention of the Prussian general staff or of American big business.

The relationship between the scheme of activities and the scheme of interaction is the problem of *organization*, in the narrow sense of that word. When the leaders of military, industrial, and other concerns speak of organization, this is what they mean. For us the word has a much broader meaning, but the narrow one will do no harm so long as we know what it is. Since our concern is with the small group,

we had better not try to attain the higher reaches of organization theory, which apply only to large concerns. But one last point should be made. The complexity of organization does not end with the appearance of the hierarchy of leadership. In big concerns, several different hierarchies arise and intersect one another. The pyramid, from being two-dimensional, becomes three- and multi-dimensional, with several different chains of interaction between the followers and the upper leaders. In the jargon of the experts, a line-and-staff form of organization develops, and we shall have something to say about it in a later chapter, where the subject comes in naturally. For the moment we can summarize in the words of Eliot Chapple and Carleton Coon:

> The coordination needed in any complex technique is impossible without interaction. As we have seen, most complex techniques involve the activities of more than one person, and, in fact, where people practice a number of complex techniques, extensive interactions must take place to coordinate the work of manufacturing, to secure raw materials, and to exchange the goods produced. In other words, the growth of complexity in technical processes goes hand in hand with an increase in the amount of interaction and in the complexity of the interaction pattern.[10]

CONCLUSION. Logically, of course, a third relationship of mutual dependence exists: the mutual dependence of interaction and sentiment, but we shall choose to consider this a part of the internal system, to which we turn in the next chapter. The two aspects of group life that we call the external and the internal sysems are continuous with one another. The line between them can be drawn where we choose, arbitrarily, and we choose to draw it here. The only reason for drawing a line at all is to save words: we now can talk about the external system without repeating everything we have said in this chapter.

What goes into the external system is what we have shown goes in: the best definition is a process of pointing. If we must have a definition in words, we can say that the mutual dependence between the work done in a group

[10] E. D. Chapple and C. S. Coon, *Principles of Anthropology*, 250.

and the motives for work, between the division of labor and the scheme of interaction, so far as these relationships meet the condition that the group survives in an environment—this we shall regularly speak of as the external system. But remember that when we talk of a group's survival in an environment we always deceive ourselves to some degree. The group is not passive before the environment; it reacts. It even defines what its environment shall be. Its purposes make different aspects of the environment important. The relationship between group and environment is never a one-way matter. But we are weak creatures, and our tools of language and analysis are soft. We ought to say everything at once, yet in our desperation we find we have to start somewhere. We have chosen to begin with the environment and its influence on the group. We shall then show how the group, on the foundation of the relationships thus established, elaborates further tendencies of its own, which react so as to modify the adaptation to the environment. This again is not the truth, but a manner of speaking. Yet it is forced on us. What we need now is a willing and provisional suspension of disbelief. Until we have said everything, we shall have said nothing. We shall have to keep many balls in the air at the same time. Regard all our statements as partial truths until the last word and the last modification are in.

The Internal System

Long ago Aristotle wrote: "The city comes into existence in order that men may live; it persists that they may live well." [11] For Aristotle the city meant the small Greek city-state, such as Athens, which was much closer to the small group we are studying in this book than to the mass cities of modern times. At least the members of the governing class could have some direct contact with one another. For Aristotle the city was also the most familiar and important of organized human groups, and much that he says about it, including the remark just quoted, applies to all human groups. Elton Mayo used to make Aristotle's point in different language. He said that there is a tendency for any group of men to complicate

the conditions of their life, to make the conditions more interesting, and that any circumstances interfering with the complication were felt emotionally as frustration. Chester Barnard's statement is still more elaborate.

> When the individual has become associated with a cooperative enterprise he has accepted a position of contact with others similarly associated. From this contact there must arise interactions between these persons individually, and these interactions are social. It may be, and often is, true that these interactions are not a purpose or object either of the cooperative systems or of the individuals participating in them. They nevertheless *cannot be avoided.* Hence, though not sought, such interactions are consequences of cooperation, and constitute one set of social factors involved in cooperation. These factors operate on the individuals affected; and, in conjunction with other factors, become incorporated in their mental and emotional characters. This is an effect which makes them significant. Hence, cooperation compels changes in the motives of individuals which otherwise would not take place. So far as these changes are in a direction favorable to the cooperative system they are resources to it. So far as they are in a direction unfavorable to cooperation, they are detriments to it or limitations of it. [12]

THE ELABORATION OF GROUP BEHAVIOR. Each of these men—Aristotle, Mayo, Barnard—is talking about the same phenomenon. When a number of persons have come together to form a group, their behavior never holds to its first pattern. Social life is never wholly utilitarian: it elaborates itself, complicates itself, beyond the demands of the original situation. The elaboration brings changes in the motives of individuals. This is the point that Barnard stressed especially; and the change in the attitudes of persons, brought about by their membership in groups, is perhaps the central topic of social psychology. But the elaboration also means changes in their activities and inter-

[11] *Politics,* I, 1, 1252b12.

[12] Reprinted by permission of the publishers from Chester Irving Barnard, *The Functions of the Executive*, Cambridge, Mass.: Harvard University Press, 1938, p. 40. See also pp. 45, 52, 120, 286.

actions—changes, in fact, in the organization of the group as a whole.

This elaboration is the subject of the present chapter and the one following. In the last chapter we studied the *external system*—the behavior of a group so far as that behavior represents one possible answer to the question: How does the group survive in its particular environment? In the present chapter we shall begin the study of the *internal system*—the elaboration of group behavior that simultaneously arises out of the external system and reacts upon it. We call the system "internal" because it is not directly conditioned by the environment, and we speak of it as an "elaboration" because it includes forms of behavior not included under the heading of the external system. We shall not go far wrong if, for the moment, we think of the external system as group behavior that enables the group to survive in its environment and think of the internal system as group behavior that is an expression of the sentiments towards one another developed by the members of the group in the course of their life together.

In analyzing the internal system, we shall, as before, use the Bank Wiring Observation Room to illustrate our points, and we shall do so according to a definite plan. In the present chapter we shall take up the internal system as exemplified in the behavior of the group as a whole; in the next chapter we shall take it up as exemplified in the division of the group into cliques. In Chapter 3 we saw that the group was in some sense a unit and in some sense also a grouping of sub-units.

We shall again work with the three main elements of group behavior: activity, sentiment, and interaction, but in describing the internal system we shall find that these elements do not take quite the same form they do in the external system. Instead of the motives for getting a job, we shall have to deal with sentiments developed on the job, such as liking or disliking for other persons, approval or disapproval of the things other persons do. Instead of activities demanded by the job, we shall have to deal with activities spontaneously evolved that serve to express the attitudes of persons toward one another. And instead of interactions required for the co-ordination of practical activities, we shall have to deal with interaction elaborated socially—for fun, so to speak. We call the internal system a system,

just as we called the external system one, because in it all three of the elements of social behavior are mutually dependent, and we shall, as before, take account of the mutual dependence by considering three pair relations: interaction-sentiment, sentiment-activity, and activity-interaction.

MUTUAL DEPENDENCE OF INTERACTION AND SENTIMENT. By the very circumstances in which they were placed, working together in the same room, the Bank Wiremen almost inevitably interacted with one another. They were, as we often say, thrown together. In our description of the external system, we did not go beyond statements like this, but the internal system takes up where the other leaves off. Interaction in the external system gives rise to sentiments that we treat as part of the internal system because they are not brought into the group by its members but released in the members by their life in the group. Specifically the Bank Wiremen, interacting with one another frequently, also became friendly. No doubt there were social isolates in the group, like Capek * and Mazmanian,* and no doubt the specially close friends were also members of the same clique, but it is all too easy in emphasizing the cliques and the anti-social individuals to lose sight of the wide-spread friendliness within the group as a whole. The relationship between association and friendliness is one of those commonly observed facts that we use all the time as a guide for action in practical affairs but seldom make an explicit hypothesis of sociology. We assume that if only we can "get people together," they will like one another and work together better. We also assume that the relationship between interaction and sentiment works in the other direction. If it is true that we often come to like the persons with whom we interact, it is also true that we are prepared to interact with persons we already like. That is, interaction and this particular kind of sentiment are mutually dependent.

Now let us try to make the hypothesis a little more explicit. We can begin by saying that *persons who interact frequently with one another tend to like one another*. But this does

* Members of the Bank Wiring group about whom sociometric data were reported by Roethlisberger and Dickson, *op. cit.* [Ed. note.]

not do justice to the quantitative and relative aspects of the relationship. Our words "like" and "dislike," "friendship" and "antagonism," are misleading. They make us think that there are only two values on the scale. We should think instead of a continuous gradation from hatred to love, with our usual words for the sentiments representing many different values on the scale. And even if we think in these terms, we are still in difficulties. When we say that Hasulak * liked Steinhardt * and disliked Mueller,* we may only mean that he liked Steinhardt more than he liked Mueller. If forced to choose between Mueller and some outsider as a companion, he might have found that he liked Mueller well enough. All our words for liking and disliking have relative and not absolute values. We cannot say how much Hasulak liked the men he knew, unless we have determined a zero point on the scale, a point, perhaps, where one man is indifferent, neither friendly nor hostile, to another. Setting up such a point and measuring the strength of sentiment with reference to it is not an easy task, as the social psychologists who study attitudes know, and we shall not undertake it here. Instead we shall allow for the quantitative aspect of sentiment and the other elements of social behavior by stating some of our hypotheses in differential form; for instance, by stating what small change will take place in the strength of sentiment if there is a small change in the frequency of interaction. Thus we can restate our original hypothesis as follows: *If the frequency of interaction between two or more persons increases, the degree of their liking for one another will increase, and vice versa.* This kind of hypothesis takes account of the fact that some sentiments form a scale without raising the question where the zero point on the scale lies. We should probably state all our later hypotheses in differential form, but we shall not in fact be tediously careful to do so.

But our hypothesis still does not take adequate account of the facts of group behavior. It does not take account of group elaboration or development. For instance, it is not hard to think of the original relationships among the Bank Wiremen being those of the

external system. The members of the group began by being thrown together in a certain room and working on certain jobs. But obviously the observed behavior of the Bank Wiremen went far beyond the original plan of work set up by the company. How shall we describe the process of growth and development? We can at least reformulate our hypothesis as follows: *If the interactions between the members of a group are frequent in the external system, sentiments of liking will grow up between them, and these sentiments will lead in turn to further interactions, over and above the interactions of the external system.* The interactions between Bank Wiremen were in fact more frequent than the setup of work required. It is not just that favorable sentiments increase as interaction increases, but that these sentiments then boost interaction still further. Our theory is that through processes like these a social system builds up or elaborates itself. But how far can the elaboration go? Clearly it cannot go on indefinitely; there must be forces bringing it to a halt; for one thing, the limitations of time will prevent the frequency of interaction from going beyond a certain level. But what is the level and what determines it? We raise these questions without being able to answer them.

A further complication can now be brought in. It was observed that the Bank Wiremen, after a time in the Observation Room, found themselves to some degree antagonistic toward the men remaining behind in the department, and that they expressed their antagonism in claims that the men in the department were in various small matters discriminating against them. In this instance, then, as in so many others, the liking of friends within a group carries with it some dislike of outsiders. The greater the inward solidarity, the greater the outward hostility. As before, this hypothesis is familiar. It is almost the principle of organization in some primitive tribes. A dictator may try to use it, believing that if he can cut down his subjects' interaction with, and inflame their distrust of, foreigners, he can maintain his own power and a primitive unity in his nation. Stated more precisely, the hypothesis is that *a decrease in the frequency of interaction between the members of a group and outsiders, accompanied by an increase in the strength of their negative sentiments toward outsiders, will increase the frequency of*

* Members of the Bank Wiring group about whom sociometric data were reported by Roethlisberger and Dickson, *op. cit.* [Ed. note.]

interaction and the strength of positive sentiments among the members of the group, and vice versa. This hypothesis is in turn a special case of a more general one, which we shall consider later and which may be stated as follows: *the nature of the relationships between the individuals A, B, C, . . . is always determined in part by the relationships between each one of them and other individuals M, N, O, . . .* In the present case, A, B, C, etc., are members of a particular group; M, N, O, etc., are outsiders, and we are considering, in the relationships between these persons, only the elements of interaction and sentiment. . . .

MUTUAL DEPENDENCE OF SENTIMENT AND ACTIVITY. In the Bank Wiring Observation Room group as a whole, we can see the mutual dependence of sentiment and activity most easily in the wide web of helping. There were few occasions when helping another man was required by the necessities of the work—indeed it was forbidden by the company; yet it took place just the same, and many of the men testified that helping and being helped made them feel better. Everyone took part in helping; it was not confined, as were some other activities, to soldering units. In fact it was one of the activities that united the whole group instead of dividing it into cliques, though there were some men, like Taylor, who were helped more than others. On the basis of the Bank Wiring Room, we can, therefore, state the hypothesis that *persons who feel sentiments of liking for one another will express those sentiments in activities over and above the activities of the external system, and these activities may further strengthen the sentiments of liking.* In the same way persons who dislike one another will express their disliking in activity, and the activity will increase the disliking. The circle may be vicious as well as beneficent. Stating the relationship quantitatively, we can expect that any change in the sentiments of persons for one another will be followed by a change in the activities in which they express those sentiments. And the reverse will also be true: any change in the expressive activities—for instance, in the amount of help given—will be followed by a change in the sentiments of liking.

All sentiments seeks expression in action, and if the action is rewarding it will be repeated. The mechanism we are describing here is universal; it applies to the external system as much as it does to the internal. But in the external system the sentiments being expressed are those a person brings to the group from his life outside the group, whereas in the internal system the sentiments—favorable or unfavorable attitudes toward other members of the group—are generated or released in a person by his experience within the group. The activities in which the latter sentiments find expression may be of many kinds. In the Bank Wiring Room they took the form of mutual help. In other groups we shall see other ways of exchanging gifts and favors, and we shall see the appearance of new co-operative activities undertaken by the group as a whole.

MUTUAL DEPENDENCE OF ACTIVITY AND INTERACTION. The intimate relation between activity and interaction is obvious, here as in the external system. In fact it takes an uncomfortable effort of mind to separate them only to put them together again. In the Bank Wiring Room an activity like helping clearly implied interaction between the persons who helped one another and, moreover, an increase of interaction beyond what the wiring job demanded. The process is general. A great deal of social activity—dances, parties—is enjoyed less for the sake of the activity itself, which may be trivial, than for the possibilities of social interaction it affords.

Status and Status Hierarchies

BURLEIGH GARDNER AND DAVID G. MOORE

The idea of relative status, of who outranks whom, is a basic ingredient in our society. Furthermore, it is not a concept which can be readily eliminated or ignored, even though it seems counter to our basic tenet that "all men are equal." We see it in the home, where parents are the superiors of the children, and the older child is superior to or "ahead of" the younger. And the child looks forward to being an adult, the youngest wants to catch up with the eldest, etc. We see it in every organization; and in every community there are those who, by virtue of formal position, ability, birth, possessions, or luck, are looked on as being in some way above or superior to others. We hear it expressed in a myriad of phrases, such as "leading citizens," "no-accounts," "upper crust," "ordinary folks." All this tells us that even in America we have, not a system of pure equality, but one in which there are great differences in social status.

Now there are two kinds of status relations. One is that of the subordinate to his boss, or the enlisted man to his commanding officer. This status relationship involves not only a general difference in rank—the officer is always thought of as superior to his subordinates—but also the right to give orders. It is always connected with specific positions in organizations in which superiors give orders to subordinates. This relationship comprises the chain of command.

The other type of status relation does not involve the right to command. It merely expresses a concept of relative positions, of who outranks whom. For example, an upper-class executive is felt by the community to be somehow superior to the "po-white" fisherman; he

From *Human Relations in Industry*. Homewood: Richard D. Irwin, 1964, pp. 245–257. Reprinted with permission of the publisher.

will be deferred to in many ways, while the fisherman will be ignored; yet the executive, merely because of his high status, has no "right" to give the other orders.

Any organization chart is a diagram of positions occupied by individuals, and each person is identified by his position. Thus John Jones, a machinist, becomes a different person in the organization when he becomes John Jones, a foreman. Furthermore, these different positions fit into systems of ranks, or status hierarchies, in which one is seen as superior to another. These systems are most clearly seen in military organizations, where differences in rank are carefully spelled out so everyone can know who outranks whom.

The supervisory structure is, then, a status system in which it is accepted as a matter of course that each level has more status and prestige than the ones below it. In fact, the words used in discussing it show this status factor. We speak of superiors and subordinates, of higher and lower levels, of up and down, of above and below—all of which imply differences in rank in such a structure. The problem of status or prestige does not end with this simple supervisory hierarchy, however, but intrudes itself into all sorts of situations and in innumerable guises. In fact, the matters of relative status, of where each person fits in terms of it, of how each compares with others, present some of the most interesting and, to those involved, some of the most annoying and painful problems of people at work. Certainly, if no one was ever bothered by the status of himself or others, life would be much simpler for everyone.

As we have seen, the chain of command establishes the most clearly defined hierarchy, with the supervisor outranking the supervised. Now differences in rank extend beyond the command, or supervisory relationship, so that all foremen are considered superior to all workers just as all officers outrank all privates. Thus we have rank hierarchies based on ideas of relative position rather than on face-to-face relationships. And these types of status systems, which are very widespread both within industry and in society generally, have great influence on human behavior. In this chapter, we will examine some of the common types of status hierarchies and their significance in the work situation.

SHOP-OFFICE DISTINCTIONS. In the first place, we find the important status distinction between shop and office or "white-collar" jobs. Despite the talk about the "dignity of labor" and the pleasures of working with your hands, there is an almost universal feeling that the office jobs are in some sense "superior" to the shop jobs and that the person who runs a typewriter or adding machine has a higher status than the person who runs a drill press. This feeling was well expressed by a girl working on a shop job, who said:

> I'd really like to work in the office. Isn't it funny the way office people treat factory people? I don't see any difference between them myself, but the office people think they are so much better than the girls who work in the factory. Lots of them have the same education as the office girls, and we are just as refined as they are. They seem to think that factory girls are loud and rough, but there are just as many girls in the office who drink and smoke and are immoral as the girls in the shop. It just seems that having an office job makes them feel that they're better than we are. I've seen the difference in some people I know. One who came from a farm in Missouri went to school and got an office job. Well, she talks about her office job as much as she can and isn't near as friendly as she used to be. We don't have anything to do with each other any more.
>
> I've noticed it with other girls too. I'll meet them at church and they ask me where I work. I tell them. They ask if I work in factory or office. When I say factory, they say, "Oh," and then ask me if I don't get tired of it, and ask me if it's dirty. Then they take every chance to talk about their office jobs.
>
> My mother feels the same way as these

people do. She says that since I've worked in the factory I've gotten more boisterous. I talk in a louder voice, not as refined as I used to be. Well, you don't like to hear those things. You don't like to feel that something's happening to you.

In this interview, an important characteristic of the status system was expressed, that is, the fact that the person who occupies the higher status position tends to identify himself with the status of his position until it becomes a part of him which he carries into all his contacts with those of lesser status. Thus the girl who had obtained an office job began to draw apart from her former factory friends, and the factory girl was looked down upon by the office girls whom she met in church. And so the status of one's position is not something which is shed when he leaves his job; it is carried with him into all kinds of situations.

This interview also shows the general feeling of superiority which the higher-status group has toward the lower. Not only is their work felt to be of a higher order of importance or value, but they are superior beings. The office group tends to look down upon the shopworkers as inferiors in mind, manner, and morals. The shopworkers have grimy hands and poor taste, they say; they are loudmouthed and use coarse language; they are less educated, or at least less intellectual. Although these attitudes of office workers may seem to be extreme expressions of feelings of superiority, similar feelings are expressed by every high-status group toward their "inferiors." Executives have something of the same attitude toward foremen, foremen toward workers, the old-timers toward the newcomers, the skilled workers toward the semiskilled. In fact, we can safely say that everyone in a factory busies himself from time to time with looking down on someone, looking up to someone, or assuring himself that, in spite of what certain others think, he is just as good as they are. As the girl in the interview said, "We are just as good as they are," and in the next breath voiced her doubts.

STATUS AND WAGES. The rate of pay or earnings is, of course, another important source of status differences. This is quite in keeping with a business or factory as an economic enterprise in which everything is supposedly evaluated in terms of money. Thus the higher the pay, the higher the status of the job or the individual.

The ten-thousand-dollar-a-year man is far superior to the five-thousand-dollar man, or the dollar-forty-an-hour shopworker is superior to the eighty-five-cent man. In the same way, the job that pays a dollar-forty an hour is superior to the eighty-five-cent an hour job. ("Superior" in this sense does not always mean more desirable, since individual tastes in jobs vary considerably.) As a result, every work situation in which there is a gradation of wages has a status hierarchy revolving around these wages and one which is readily upset by any changes in the wage structure.

There is also a status system based upon the different kinds of jobs found in any work group. As a rule, the jobs requiring the most skill are at the top and those requiring the least are at the bottom, although other factors may enter in to disurb such a simple arrangement. For example, a job which receives a great deal of attention and recognition from the boss may become the superior job even though other jobs in the group require more skill. Sometimes, too, jobs acquire status because they are always held by long-service people who receive recognition because of their service.

SENIORITY AND STATUS. Seniority forms the basis for other status differences, with the old-timers feeling that they are somehow superior to the young people and newcomers. In most stable companies there is a feeling toward long-service people something like the attitude toward age which we find in our society generally. The youngsters are thought of as lacking in knowledge and understanding and are expected to give recognition and deference to their elders, while the very old have a place with certain rights and privileges because of their age. The special privileges of old-timers were demonstrated by the nurse in one factory. We quote from an observer's notes:

> In a plant which had, before the war, found it necessary to employ only one nurse, the expansion due to the war brought the need for more nurses.
>
> The original nurse had been with the company thirteen years. Then a male nurse was hired for the 4–12 shift. And when a 12–8 shift started, he was transferred to it. Two more nurses were hired, and since none of them wanted to work 4–12 all the time, it was agreed that they should alternate.

> The nurse who had seniority took one turn at the afternoon shift and then refused to work it again. The doctor and the personnel manager agreed that she need not take her turn; and the other nurses, although they resented this evident favoritism, seemed to feel that it was done because she had been with the company so long.

ORGANIZATIONAL DIFFERENCES. There are also status differences among organizations, and in any plant there are usually certain organizations which are generally thought of as superior to others. The shop-office distinction accounts for some of this, as the strictly office organizations are usually superior to the shop organizations. As a result, a typist or file clerk with the shop department is usually thought to have a poorer," that is lower-status, job than the typist or file clerk in an accounting department. Also, organizations such as engineering or sales, where much of the work requires technical skills or special training, are usually of status superior to shop or accounting organizations. In all such cases the feeling of superiority does not remain merely the prerogative of the salesmen or engineers but carries over even to the most routine jobs in the organization. The office boy in the engineering department, for example, is likely to feel superior to the office boy in the accounting organization.

OCCUPATIONAL HIERARCHIES. We have seen how certain types of jobs carry differences of status. However, this extends often to very elaborate rankings in which there may be recognized differences between many jobs. Thus in many of the skilled trades, we find the hierarchy of apprentice, journeyman, master. In these, a man's position is based upon his progress through a clearly defined system of training and experience.

In addition, we see differences in rank between jobs based on the levels of skill required, such as the semiskilled versus skilled worker. Or the simpler machines are lower than the complicated machines. Or the job that requires long training outranks the one that requires little training. In general, all jobs in a plant can be placed on a scale which expresses the general beliefs as to where each fits in relation to the others.

As we have seen, many of the status systems are based on the characteristics inherent in the work organization. Supervisory rank, levels of skill, wage differences, etc., are largely defined within the organization. However, there are other types of status which are general to the society and are carried over into the work situation. In communities where the particular hierarchies do not already exist, they do not appear in the local industries.

MEN VERSUS WOMEN. In our society, women are traditionally defined as the "weaker sex," subordinate to the male. This traditional role of subordination and inferiority is carried over into the work situation. Women's jobs are thought of as simpler, requiring less skill, or in some way unsuitable for men. And attempts to place women in jobs habitually defined as men's work meet with considerable resistance from men. Also, the man who is placed alongside of women, doing the same work, feels that he is degraded.

NEGRO VERSUS WHITE. Here again we find status differences between the Negro and the white existing in our society. This is expressed in the most extreme form in the deep South, where the Negro is thought of as socially separate and inferior. There he is generally restricted to the lowest status and lowest paid jobs and is rarely permitted to occupy a supervisory position over whites. And while the system is less rigorous in the North, many of the same attitudes and restrictions still exist.

COMPLICATING FACTORS. These status systems are not nicely co-ordinated, however, so that the older person always gets more money, has the better job, or is higher in the supervisory structure. We see old-timers in some of the poorest jobs at the lowest pay. We see bright young executives who, with only short service, have climbed high in the supervisory ranks. We see office jobs paying less than shop jobs, or skilled workers earning more than their foremen. We see innumerable complicating factors, so that it seems impossible to present a simple picture of the status relationships between individuals within any plant or even in any one department.

We do find, however, that there is a feeling that these various status systems *should* be co-ordinated. This is most strongly expressed in the idea that superiors should earn more than their subordinates. Generally in the supervisory structure wages rise rapidly as you go up in the structure, and it is usually felt to be wrong for a foreman to get less pay than his subordinates. There is also some tendency for wages to increase with age, and a feeling that this should be so, especially when the rate of pay is not rigidly tied to the kind of job. Also, the more highly skilled jobs are often held by the long-service people who have worked themselves up. Interestingly enough, the status difference between office and shop is usually not recognized in pay, especially at the lower levels. Apparently the office jobs are sufficiently attractive, especially to girls, that they are preferred even if the wages are lower, so that in many organizations we find these "better" jobs being paid considerably less than the others.

"PLACING" PEOPLE. A matter of common interest and concern to everyone in the factory is the problem of "place" in the social organization. Everyone wants to know where other people "fit" in terms of the functional relations of the work and, what is to many even more important, in terms of the status systems. The newcomer is always faced by the questions, "Who are you?" and "Where do you fit?" In fact, one of the important aspects of getting acquainted on a new job is the process by which the newcomer finds out just where he belongs. He learns with whom he will work and what their relationship is to him and to each other; he learns who are is superiors in the line of authority, who can give him orders and who cannot, to whom he should defer and whom he can ignore. All this is the real function of much of the introduction and conversation which often takes place when a new worker comes into a group. For example, the foreman brings a new man over to Joe Blow on the dinkus assembly line, and the conversation goes like this:

FOREMAN: Joe, this is Jim Blank, who is going to work on this assembly. I wish you would show him how to do the job. (Telling Joe that Jim is new and inexperienced on the job.)

JOE: Howdy, Jim. You ever had any experience with dinkus assembly? (Trying to place Jim a little more accurately.)

JIM: No. I been on a drill press in the gadget department for a couple of years. (Letting Joe know that he is not entirely a greenhorn and has had experience on machines, as well as service with the company.)

JOE: You did? Why I worked over there when I first started eight years ago. Is old Jake, the foreman, still as 'sour-puss' as ever? (Telling Jim that he need not feel that two years of service amounts to much and that he knows about the gadget department also.)

JIM: Well, Jake's a pretty decent guy after all, even if he does act sour at times. I kinda hate to leave the department, but work was getting slack on the drill presses. (Showing a little annoyance at Joe's implied criticism of the gadget department, and also telling Joe that he had not left to get out of the place or because they did not want him.)

JOE: Yeah, I used to like Jake and hated to leave there myself. (Sensing Jim's irritation and trying to express a common attitude.)

Scenes such as this occur constantly; and in every one the individuals are consciously or unconsciously telling each other just where they fit and how they feel about it, and at the same time finding out about each other. When making introductions or when talking about newcomers, there is this same emphasis on "placing" people. Once the individual's place has been established, however, interest in him and gossip about him shifts to other topics.

SYMBOLS OF STATUS. Because of the importance of status, the individual himself is greatly concerned that he be placed properly, at least not in a position inferior to what he actually occupies. The private may be amused to be mistaken for a lieutenant, but the lieutenant who is mistaken for a private is really burned up. Undoubtedly, that is one of the important functions of military insignia. In industry people feel much the same way, with the result that almost every large plant has developed its own insignia, its own set of symbols by means of which everyone can be placed properly in the status system. In general, these symbols are not the simple and obvious types evolved by the Armed Forces but are much more subtle and indirect. The sort of clothes you wear, the desk you sit at, the position of your desk or workbench, the machine you operate, and many other things may indicate status. In fact, these things are often so indirect that the out-sider is not aware that such a symbol system exists at all. Many executives, too, deny that there are such systems; but usually these denials are coupled with an assertion that, even if they do exist, they are wrong and should be abolished. Unfortunately for such a point of view, there is no way to stop people from trying to place one another or to keep them from being concerned about their own status.

Because of the importance of the distinction between shop and office, there is a strong tendency to differentiate between them in many ways, each of which becomes a symbol to indicate the position of the individual. While the nature of the work usually leads to a separation between office and shop groups, the separation itself becomes an important symbol of the difference in status. As a result, most office workers are upset and feel that they have lost status if they are moved from an office location to a shop location even though there is no change in the job. In most large plants where there is a separation of the office and shop organizations, there are usually separate washrooms for the office people; and any attempt to have the office people use the shop washrooms, or to bring shop people into the office washrooms, meets with strong resistance from the office people. To be forced to share lockers or washrooms with these "uncouth and inferior" people is a bitter pill to the office people. In such instances, all sorts of complaints are voiced about the crowded washrooms, about how untidy the shop people are, about how they threw paper towels or cigarettes on the floor or leave the washbasins grimy from their dirty hands, or about their bad manners and unrefined language. This whole attitude was well expressed in the behavior of a typist who had been transferred from an office location to the same work in a shop: rather than use the shop washrooms which were adjacent to her new location, she would walk across a building and up a flight of stairs to a washroom used by an office group.

In many companies there is a payroll distinction, too, between shop and office, the shop-workers being paid by the hour and the office by the week. Since both groups are actually paid every week, there is no obvious difference; yet the different payrolls assume the status differences of the two groups. And to move from the hourly to the weekly or salaried payroll is a step up in the world. In some cases this difference may be accentuated by having different time clocks or a different payday for each group, so that there remains no doubt as to where a person fits. Separate time clocks or paydays are, of course, usually thought of as devices to assist the payroll department in preparing the pay checks, or to spread the work load a bit; but it is surprising how often such devices get mixed up in the status system and become status symbols in themselves. And once they become status symbols, any attempt to change them meets with strong resistance from the people.

An almost universal characteristic of all types of status hierarchies is that certain prerogatives accompany high status; and as one ascends in the structure, he acquires certain rights and privileges which are denied to those below him. Some of these rights have to do with the symbols of status themselves. As one is promoted, he acquires the right to display the insignia of his new place. Others are much more tangible rewards, such as increased freedom from restraints, special rights, additional pay, and so on. For example, the following situation was observed in one small plant:

As more machines were added to the departments, the girls who had the best records in attendance and production or showed aptitude for mechanics were made adjusters. This was considered a promotion, although there was no increase in pay. They had a small measure of authority in that they were responsible for seeing that the operators turned out perfect work and for adjusting the machines to make this possible. Since the adjusters operated the machines during the regular lunch period, they ate alone. There were no bells to ring to signify the beginning and end of their lunch period; so they took a few minutes extra. Although everyone knew about this, nothing was said, so the adjusters felt that they were a little above the ordinary workers.

These symbolic distinctions are well shown, too, in the shop-office division, with the office usually having definite privileges denied to the shop. For example, office workers frequently have a longer lunch hour than shop; they may be free to leave their desks to go to the washroom whenever they please, while the shop is limited to fixed rest pauses. Through the device of the weekly pay, the office workers may take time off or come in late without penalty, while the hourly paid shopworkers are usually paid only for the time they are actually on the job.

It is interesting that foremen are generally on the weekly payroll and so are grouped with the office people. It appears, then, that the ordinary factory is split into two groups, one of which is composed of the hourly paid shopworkers, the other of the weekly paid office workers and the entire superivsory staff. The nonsuperisvory office workers, furthermore, tend to think of themselves as akin to the supervisory and executive group rather than to the shopworkers.

Within the office group itself, there is usually a high development of status symbols. Almost anything in the work situation seems to have potentialities for becoming such a symbol, whether it be a desk, chair, telephone, location, arrangement of furniture, or whatnot. For example, a telephone directory usually becomes a sort of *Who's Who* which reflects status more than phone calls. Whether you have a telephone on your desk, or share one with the next desk, or have none at all may be a direct reflection of your status and is usually interpreted that way. In one large organization, desks were an important symbol: the lowest clerical workers worked at tables, the next level had single-pedestal desks with one bank of drawers, the superiors had larger, double-pedestal desks with two banks of drawers, and so on, up to the plant manager, who had a great big desk of fancy woods. In such a system, to give a man a promotion without the proper desk would have given rise to elaborate speculations as to whether he really rated the title or just what was wrong. It would be like promoting a lieutenant but telling him that he would have to still wear his lieutenant's bars, that he was not really a captain yet. The emphasis on these status symbols in one small factory was described by an office worker, as follows:

This same vice-president has three assistant vice-presidents in his department besides his department manager. He gets them increasingly large bonuses each year. He can't give them all private offices, so he gathers them all into one special corner of the office away from their secretaries, gives them each a desk *and* a table and more space for visitors. Their desks have leather desk pads with green blotters instead of the usual rubber mat, and, on the whole, he keeps them happy. But if one of them were to get a bronze wastebasket, they would each have to have one.

In the same way, offices for executives become important symbols of status. In most large organizations there are certain superior offices which, because of size or location, are preferred. Usually these better offices are occupied by the top-ranking men in the organization and reflect their status. Other offices may fit into the status pattern on the basis of their proximity to the "brass hats." Thus the office next to the president is superior to the one down the hall. Where offices occupy several floors of a tall building, the higher offices usually have the most status. The manager or president usually occupies the top floor, and the lesser officials are found somewhere below. In such cases, moving to a higher floor is getting up in the world in more ways than one. The importance of location as a status symbol affects the people who work for executives, too, so that their secretaries, stenographers, and even their office boys, feel very strongly the status significance of working on the top floor or in the office next to the president's suite. This was described by a girl in the personnel department of one organization, thus:

> Then there is the social problem caused by the physical layout which comprises three floors. The executives' offices are on the tenth. (This is special!) Several departments, including accounting and payroll, are on the ninth. (This is O.K.) There is the eighth floor, with dictaphones, typing, filing. (This is Bargain Basement!) The girls on the eighth feel that the girls on the ninth and tenth look down on them. The secretaries on the tenth floor are supposed to be pretty high-hat. Girls on the ninth beg to be transferred "upstairs."

Among shopworkers, on the other hand, there is not quite so much emphasis upon status symbols. In general, a person's position in the shop is pretty clearly shown by the work he is doing. The man operating an automatic screw machine is obviously different from the sweeper or material handler, the machinist is superior to his helper, and anyone familiar with shopwork can place people easily in the general status system. This does not mean that shopworkers are not concerned about status, but merely that the work itself provides fairly obvious status insignia.

With office people, however, as pointed out, the symbols of status are often a major concern, and changes in them are sure to create disturbances. To account for such emphasis is difficult, but we may present two possible hypotheses. In the first place, the office and supervisory groups probably contain more people who want to improve their status. And these people naturally want to display evidence of any gains; they want people to know where they belong. At the same time, the nature of office work is such that all jobs look alike from a distance; people sitting at desks writing and shuffling papers may be either important executives or the most unimportant clerks. For that reason, it becomes important that the superior people acquire symbols to distinguish them from the rest. (And everyone gets upset if the new clerk gets the desk by the boss or one by the window.)

These status symbols are a constant source of conflict and anxiety. Each watches his equals lest they acquire symbols which he lacks; each longs to have the choice office or the large desk and schemes to get it; each judges the importance of his job by symbols which go with it. As a result, every change in arrangement, every movement of people or organizations, may upset the status systems and cause trouble.

AN EXAMPLE OF STATUS PROBLEMS. A situation involving status problems, changes, and disturbances in one small factory was described by a personnel officer, as follows:

> Fred J., aged 45, was one of the most capable all round machinists in a tool industry of about 350 employees. A year and a half ago he was placed in charge of a night shift in the approximate capacity of superintendent. The night shift had just been started, and none of the day foremen who might have been eligible for the job seemed to want it.
>
> The initial night force was small, but it grew rapidly to a total of 125 employees. The top management never made a clear

announcement of Fred's position as super-intendent. He had the duties of a super-intendent except that one department oper-ated at night as an independent unit. No clear directive was given to the effect that Fred was in complete charge, although it was intended that this should be generally understood up to the point of his being responsible for all night activities except in the one independent department.

A great deal of antagonism having the appearance of jealousy immediately de-veloped among the foremen of the day shift. The day superintendent likewise seemed to resent the fact of there being another superintendent in the plant. He would often challenge Fred's right to deal with operational matters that extended through both shifts. In a showdown be-tween these two, Fred answered the chal-lenge by saying, "All right, let's go up to George's (the general manager's) office right now, and I'll apologize to you in his presence." The offer was declined.

Characteristic expressions of the day fore-man in referring to Fred would run some-what along the lines of "that fellow that's on nights. . . . I don't know what you'd call him. . . . He ain't a superintendent,

and I wouldn't even call him a foreman."

The management says that, had they clearly designated Fred as a superintendent, they would have had a blowup. They had to place him where they did because the job had to be done and there was no one else in the place who would take it and would have their confidence to the same extent.

Over a period of sixteen months Fred seems to have been winning his battle slowly. But the whole thing has been marked by a good deal of antagonism, fre-quent ignoring of notes left by Fred for the day supervision, and quite obvious buck-passing, such as the charging of scrap against the night shift when portions of it belonged unmistakably to the day shift.

In one instance Fred had one of his night operators mark each piece he turned out, a piece which was being produced by both shifts. In the inspector's reports on rejects, all the scrap was charged against the night shift. Fred examined the rejected pieces, found that his man's symbol was not on them, and demanded of the inspector, "How come?" The inspector explained: "The day superintendent told me to charge them that way."

The Informal Organization

PHILIP SELZNICK

This analysis will consider bureaucracy as a special case of the general theory of purposive organization. Recent sociological research has made explicit several conceptions which must serve as essential background for any analysis such as that to follow. Based upon that research, three hypotheses may be introduced here:

1. Every organization creates an informal structure.

2. In every organization, the goals of the organization are modified (abandoned, deflected, or elaborated) by processes within it.

3. The process of modification is effected through the informal structure.

Three recent sociological studies have elucidated these hypotheses.

1. In an intensive examination of a shop department, Roethlisberger and Dickson found clear evidences of an informal structure. This structure consisted of a set of procedures (binging, sarcasm, ridicule) by means of which control over members of the group was exercised, the formation of cliques which functioned as instruments of control, and the establishment of informal leadership. "The men had elaborated, spontaneously and quite unconsciously, an intricate social organization around their collective beliefs and sentiments." [1]

The informal structure of the worker group grew up out of the day-to-day practices of the men as they groped for ways of taking care of their own felt needs. There was no series of conscious acts by which these procedures were instituted, but they were no less binding on that account. These needs largely arose from the way in which the men defined their situation within the organization. The informal organization served a triple *function:* (a) it served to control the behavior of the members of the worker group; (b) within the context of the larger organization (the plant), it was an attempt on the part of the particular group to control the conditions of its existence; (c) it acted as a mechanism for the expression of personal relationships for which the formal organization did not provide. Thus the informal structure provided those avenues of aggression, solidarity, and prestige-construction required by individual members.

The *consequence* of the activity of the men through the informal organization was a deleterious effect upon the professed goal of the organization as a whole: it resulted in the restriction of output. In asserting its control over the conditions of the job, the group wanted above all to protect itself from outside interference, exhibiting a strong resistance to change.

Thus the facts in this empirical investigation illustrate the hypotheses noted above: the creation of an informal organization, the modification of the professed goal (maximum output), and the effectuation of this modification through the informal structure. In addition, three important characteristics of the informal structure were observed in the study: (a) it arises spontaneously; (b) the bases of the relationships are personal, involving factors of prestige, acceptance within the group, friendship ties, etc.; and (c) the relationships are *power* relationships, oriented toward techniques of *control.* These characteristics are general, and they are important for conceiving of the theory of bureaucratic behavior as a

From "An Approach to a Theory of Bureaucracy," *American Sociological Review,* Vol. 8, 1943, pp. 47–48. Reprinted with permission of the author and the publisher, American Sociological Association.

[1] F. J. Roethlisberger, and W. J. Dickson, *Management and the Worker,* Cambridge: Harvard University Press, 1941, 524.

special case of the general theory of organization.

2. C. I. Barnard, in his theoretical analysis of organizational structure, concerned mainly with the problems of the executive, discusses explicitly the character and function of informal structures which arise out of the attempts to solve those problems. By informal structures he means "the aggregate of the personal contacts and interactions and the associated groupings of people" which do not have common or joint purposes, and which are, in fact, "indefinite and rather structureless." [2] He says, further, that "though common or joint purposes are excluded by definition, common or joint results of an important character nevertheless come from such organization." [3]

Barnard lists three functions of informal structures as they operate in formal organizations: (*a*) as a means of communication, establishing norms of conduct between superordinates and subordinates; (*b*) "maintenance of cohesiveness in formal organizations through regulating the willingness to serve and the stability of objective authority"; (*c*) "the maintenance of the feeling of personal integrity, of self-respect, of independent choice." [4] The last mentioned function means simply that the individual's "integrity" is protected by the *appearance* of choice, at the same time that subtle group pressures guarantee control of his actions. Barnard's view of the functions of the informal structure is primarily in terms of the needs of the executive (control through friendship ties, personal authority, a "grape-vine" system, etc.), but it is clear that his analysis agrees with the hypothesis that the informal organization is oriented essentially toward the techniques of control. In the Roethlisberger and Dickson study, it was the worker group which was attempting to control the conditions of its existence; in this case, it is the executive who is doing the same thing.

3. A discussion by Waller and Henderson [5] based on the study of institutions of segregative care, gives further evidence for the theses presented here. The general hypotheses about organizational processes are confirmed by the examination of such structures as private schools, transient camps, prisons, flop-houses, reformatories and military organizations. The authors set the problem in this way:

> Each of our institutions has an idea or purpose—most of them have several purposes more or less compatible with one another—and this idea or purpose gives rise to an institutional structure. The institutional structure consists of a system of organized groups. The interaction of these elements is a principal clue to the understanding of institutions of segregative care. Without a structure, the purpose of an institution would be an empty form of words, and yet the process of translating the purpose into an institutional structure always somehow deflects and distorts it.

It is thus the iron necessity of an organizational structure for the achievement of group goals which creates the paradox to which we have referred. The ideals of those who construct the organization are one thing; the "facts of life" operating independently of and often against those ideals are something else again.

PROFESSED AND OPERATIONAL GOALS. Running an organization, as a specialized and essential activity, generates problems which have no necessary (and often an opposed) relationship to the professed or "original" goals of the organization. The day-to-day behavior of the group becomes centered around specific problems and proximate goals which have primarily an internal relevance. Then, since these activities come to consume an increasing proportion of the time and thoughts of the participants, they are—from the point of view of actual behavior—*substituted* for the professed goals.

The day-to-day activity of men is ordered by those specific problems which have a direct relevance to the materials with which they have to deal. "Ultimate" issues and highly abstract ideas which do not specify any concrete behavior have therefore little direct influence on the bulk of human activities. (The general ideas, of course, may influence action by setting its context and, often, defining its limits.) This is true not because men are evil or un-

[2] C. I. Barnard, *The Functions of the Executive*, Cambridge: Harvard University Press, 1940, p. 115.
[3] *Ibid.*
[4] *Loc. cit.*, pp. 122–123.
[5] W. Waller and W. Henderson, "Institutions of Segregative Care and the Organized Group" (unpublished manuscript), 1941.

intelligent, but because the "ultimate" formulations are not *helpful* in the constant effort to achieve that series of equilibria which represent behavioral solutions to the specific problems which day-to-day living poses. Besides those professed which do not specify any concrete behavior, which are analogous to nonprocedural formulations in science, there are other professed goals which require actions which conflict with what must be done in the daily business of running an organization. In that conflict the professed goals will tend to go down in defeat, usually through the process of being extensively ignored. This phenomenon may be introduced as a fourth hypothesis in the general theory of organization.

Selections from Quota Restriction and
Goldbricking in a Machine Shop

DONALD ROY

QUOTA RESTRICTION. It is "quota restriction" which has received the most attention. The Mayo researchers observed that the bank-wiring group at Western Electric limited output to a "quota" or "bogey."[1] Mayo inferred that this chopping-off of production was due to lack of understanding of the economic logics of management, using the following chain of reasoning: Insistence by management on purely economic logics, plus frequent changes in such logics in adaptation to technological change, results in lack of understanding on the part of the workers. Since the latter cannot understand the situation, they are unable to develop a nonlogical social code of a type that brought social cohesion to work groups prior to the Industrial Revolution. This inability to develop a Grade-A social code brings feelings of frustration. And, finally, frustration results in the development of a "lower social code" among the workers in opposition to the economic

logics of management. And one of the symptoms of this "lower social code" is restriction of output.[2]

Mayo thus joins those who consider the economic man a fallacious conception. Now the operators in my shop made noises like economic men. Their talk indicated that they were canny calculators and that the dollar sign fluttered at the masthead of every machine. Their actions were not always consistent with their words; and such inconsistency calls for further probing. But it could be precisely because they were alert to their economic interests—at least to their immediate economic interests—that the operators did not exceed their quotas. It might be inferred from their talk that they did not turn in excess earnings because they felt that to do so would result in piecework price cuts; hence the consequences would be either reduced earnings from the same amount of effort expended or increased effort to maintain the take-home level.

When I was hired, a personnel department clerk assured me that the radial-drill operators were averaging $1.25 an hour on piecework. He was using a liberal definition of the term

From *American Journal of Sociology*, Vol. 57, No. 5, March 1952, pp. 430–432, 436–437. Reprinted with permission of the publisher, The University of Chicago Press; copyright 1952 by the University of Chicago Press.
[1] Fritz Roethlisberger and J. Dickson, *Management and the Worker* (Cambridge: Harvard University Press, 1939).

[2] Elton Mayo, *Human Problems of an Industrial Civilization* (New York: Macmillan Co., 1938), pp. 119–21.

"averaging." Since I had had no previous machine-shop experience and since a machine would not be available for a few days, I was advised to spend some time watching Jack Starkey, a radial-drill man of high rank in seniority and skill.

One of Starkey's first questions was, "What have you been doing?" When I said I had worked in a Pacific Coast shipyard at a rate of pay over $1.00 an hour, Starkey exclaimed, "Then what are you doing in this place?" When I replied that averaging $1.25 an hour wasn't bad, he exploded:

> "Averaging, you say! Averaging?"
>
> "Yeah, on the average. I'm an average guy; so I ought to make my buck and a quarter. That is, after I get onto it."
>
> "Don't you know," cried Starkey angrily, "that $1.25 an hour is the *most* we can make, even when we *can* make more! And most of the time we can't even make that! Have you ever worked on piecework before?"
>
> "No."
>
> "I can see that! Well, what do you suppose would happen if I turned in $1.25 an hour on these pump bodies?"
>
> "Turned in? You mean if you actually did the work?"
>
> "I mean if I actually did the work and turned it in!"
>
> "They'd have to pay you, wouldn't they? Isn't that the agreement?"
>
> "Yes! They'd pay me—once! Don't you know that if I turned in $1.50 an hour on these pump bodies tonight, the whole God-damned Methods Department would be down here tomorrow? And they'd retime this job so quick it would make your head swim! And when they retimed it, they'd cut the price in half! And I'd be working for 85 cents an hour instead of $1.25!"

From this initial exposition of Starkey's to my last day at the plant I was subject to warnings and predictions concerning price cuts. Pressure was the heaviest from Joe Mucha, day man on my machine, who shared my job repertoire and kept a close eye on my production. On November 14, the day after my first attained quota, Mucha advised:

> "Don't let it go over $1.25 an hour, or the time-study man will be right down here! And they don't waste time, either! They

watch the records like a hawk! I got ahead, so I took it easy for a couple of hours."

Joe told me that I had made $10.01 yesterday and warned me not to go over $1.25 an hour. He told me to figure the set-ups and the time on each operation very carefully so that I would not total over $10.25 in any one day.

Jack Starkey defined the quota carefully but forcefully when I turned in $10.50 for one day, or $1.31 an hour.

> Jack Starkey spoke to me after Joe left. "What's the matter? Are you trying to upset the apple cart?"
>
> Jack explained in a friendly manner that $10.50 was too much to turn in, even on an old job.
>
> "The turret-lathe men can turn in $1.35," said Jack, "but their rate is 90 cents, and ours 85 cents."

Jack warned me that the Methods Department could lower their prices on any job, old or new, by changing the fixture slightly, or changing the size of drill. According to Jack, a couple of operators (first and second shift on the same drill) got to competing with each other to see how much they could turn in. They got up to $1.65 an hour, and the price was cut in half. And from then on they had to run that job themselves, as none of the other operators would accept the job.

According to Jack, it would be all right for us to turn in $1.28 or $1.29 an hour, when it figured out that way, but it was not all right to turn in $1.30 an hour.

Well, now I know where the maximum is —$1.29 an hour.

Starkey's beliefs concerning techniques of price-cutting were those of the shop. Leonard Bricker, an old-timer in the shop, and Willie, the stock-chaser, both affirmed that management, once bent on slashing a piecework price, would stop at nothing.

> "Take these $1.25 jobs. One guy will turn in $1.30 an hour one day. Then another fellow will turn in, say, $1.31 or $1.32. Then the first fellow will go up to $1.35. First thing you know they'll be up to $1.50, and bang! They'll tear a machine to pieces to change something to cut a price!"
>
> In the washroom, before I started work,

Willie commented on my gravy job, the pedestals.

"The Methods Department is going to lower the price," he said. "There was some talk today about it."

"I hope they don't cut it too much," I said. "I suppose they'll make some change in the jigs?"

"They'll change the tooling in some way. Don't worry, when they make up their minds to lower a price, they'll find a way to do it!"[3]

The association of quota behavior with such expressions about price-cutting does not prove a causal connection. Such a connection could be determined only by instituting changes in the work situation that would effect a substantial reduction of "price-cut fear" and by observing the results of such changes.

Even if it should be thus indicated that there is a causal relationship, testing of alternative hypotheses would still be necessary. It may be, but it is not yet known, that "economic determinism" may account for quota restriction in the shop investigated. It may also be, but it is not known, that factors such as Mayo's "failure to understand the economic logics of management" are influential. . . .

PIECEWORK GOLDBRICKING. On "gravy jobs" the operators earned a quota, then knocked off. On "stinkers" they put forth only minimal effort; either they did not try to achieve

[3] John Mills, onetime research engineer in telephony and for five years engaged in personnel work for the Bell Telephone Company, has recently indicated the possibility that there were factors in the bank-wiring room situation that the Mayo group failed to detect: "Reward is supposed to be in direct proportion to production. Well, I remember the first time I ever got behind that fiction. I was visting the Western Electric Company, which had a reputation of never cutting a piece rate. It never did; if some manufacturing process was found to pay more than seemed right for the class of labor employed on it—if, in other words, the rate-setters had misjudged—that particular part was referred to the engineers for redesign, and then a new rate was set on the new part. Workers, in other words, were paid as a class, supposed to make about so much a week with their best efforts and, of course, less for less competent efforts" (*The Engineer in Society* [New York: D. Van Nostrand & Co., 1946], p. 93).

a turn-in equal to the base wage rate or they deliberately slowed down. Jobs were defined as "good" and "bad" jobs, not in terms of the effort or skill necessary to making out at a bare base-rate level, but of the felt attainability of a substantial premium, i.e., 15 cents an hour or more. Earnings of $1.00 an hour in relation to a $1.25 quota and an 85-cent base rate were considered worth the effort, while earnings of 95 cents an hour were not.

The attitude basic to the goldbricking type of restriction was expressed succinctly thus: "They're not going to get much work out of me for this pay!"

Complaints about low piecework prices were chronic and universal in the shop.

> The turret lathe men discussed the matter of making out, one man stating that only half the time could a man make 84 cents day rate on a machine. It was agreed: "What's the use of pushing when it's hard even to make day rate?"

His 50-50 estimate was almost equal to my own experience of 49.6-50.4. Pessimistic though it was, it was less so than usual statements on the subject:

> I asked Jackson if he was making out, and he gave me the usual answer, "No!"
>
> "They ask me how I'm making out, and I always say, 'O.K.' As far as I'm concerned, I'm making out O.K. If they start asking me further, I'll tell them that this place stinks.
>
> "The day man isn't making out either. We get a lot of little jobs, small lots. It's impossible to make out when you're getting small jobs all the time."
>
> Joe was working on a new job, time study on some small pieces tonight. I asked him, "Something good?" and he replied, "Nothing is good any more!"

There seemed to be no relation between a man's ability to earn and his behavior on a "stinker." That the men who most frequently earned the quota goldbricked like the rest on poor jobs appears in the following extracts:

> Al McCann (the man who made quota most often) said that he gives a job a trial, and if it is no good he takes his time. He didn't try to make out on the chucks tonight.
>
> Joe Mucha, my day man, said of a certain

job: "I did just one more than you did. If they don't like it they can do them themselves. To hell with them. I'm not going to bust my ass on stuff like this."

Old Peter, the multiple drill man, said "I ran some pieces for 25 minutes to see how many I could turn out. I turned out 20 at $1\frac{1}{2}$ cents apiece (72 cents an hour). So I smoke and take it easy. I can't make out; so ———— it."

I notice that when Ed Sokolsky, one of the better operators on the line, is working on an operation he cannot make out on, he does not go at his task with vigor. He either pokes around or leaves his machine for long periods of time; and Paul (set-up man) seems always to be looking for him. Steve (supt.) is always bellowing, "Where in hell is Ed?" or "Come on, Ed, let's have some production around here!" Tonight I heard him admonishing Ed again, "Now I want you to work at that machine 'til three o'clock, do you understand?"

Mike Koszyk, regarded as a crack operator: The price was a poor one (a few cents a hundred) and the job tough. Mike had turned out only 9 pieces in 3 hours. When Mike takes his time, he really takes his time!

According to Al, Jack Starkey turned in 40 cents an hour today on his chuck parts. Al laughed, saying, "I guess Jack didn't like this job."

Gus Schmidt, regarded as the best speed-drill operator on the second shift, was timed early in the evening on a job, and given a price of $1.00 per 100 for reaming one hole, chamfering both sides of three holes, and filing burrs on one end of one hole. All that for one cent!

"To hell with them," said Gus.

He did not try to make out.

The possibility of covering "day rate" was ordinarily no spur to the machine operator to bestir himself on a job. A remark of Mucha's was characteristic: "I could have made out," he said, "but why kill yourself for day rate?"

Average hourly earnings of less or even a little more than $1.00 an hour were usually thrown into the "day-rate" category.

Joe Mucha drilled 36 of the bases (at $8.80 per 100) today. "The most I'll ever do until they retime this job is 40," he said. "Do you know, they expect us to do 100? Why, I wouldn't bust my ass to do 50, for $8.00, when day rate is almost that!"

McCann was put to drilling some pieces at $6.50 per 100. I noticed him working furiously and walked over to see what he was doing. He asked me to figure out how many pieces at $6\frac{1}{2}$ cents he had to turn out per hour to make $1.20. When I told him 18 or 19 he said, "I give up," and immediately slowed down.

A few minutes later I met him in the washroom, and he said, "I wouldn't work that hard for eight or ten hours even if I could make out. I thought I'd try it for an hour or so and see what I could do."

He figures that he was making 95 cents an hour. At lunch time he said that he had averaged $1.00 an hour for the two hours and thought maybe he would try to make out.

Efficiency and "the Fix": Informal Intergroup Relations in a Piecework Machine Shop [1]

DONALD ROY

As part of a broader examination and appraisal of the application of piecework incentive to the production line of an American factory this paper essays the simple but largely neglected task of exploring the network of intergroup relations in which the work activity of machine operatives is imbedded. Exploration will be restricted to a limited sector of the total web of interaction in one shop; description will center upon those relationships that provide support to the operator group in its resistance to and subversion of formally instituted managerial controls on production. It is hoped that observations reported here not only will bear upon the practical problem of industrial efficiency but will also contribute to the more general study of institutional dynamics.

This could be considered the third in a series of attempts to make more careful discriminations in an area of research that has been characteristically productive of sweeping generalizations, blanket conceptualizations, or algebraic gymnastics that tend to halt inquiry at the same time that they lay a fog over otherwise easily discerned reality. Data for all three papers were acquired in an investigation of a single work situation by a single technique of social inquiry, participant observation. The writer

was employed for nearly a year as radial-drill operator in one of the machine shops of a steel-processing plant, and he kept a daily record of his observations and experiences relating to work activity and social interaction in the shop. His major interest lay in the phenomenon of restriction of output, or "systematic soldiering," the practice of which various sociological soundings have revealed in the lower depths of our industrial organization. To complete the analogy: the writer donned a diving suit and went down to see what it looked like on the bottom.

One conclusion has already been set forth,[2] namely, that the usual view of output restriction is grossly undifferentiating. Different kinds of "institutionalized underworking" were practiced, each with its characteristic pattern of antecedents and consequences. The blanket term "restriction" was found to cloak all-important contrarieties of work behavior. Machine operatives not only held back effort; sometimes they worked hard. The very common failure to note such contrarieties has tended, of course, to impede the progress of research by checking consideration of the specific conditions under which differences in behavior occur.

A second finding was the discovery of complexity where simple lines of relationship had generally been assumed to exist.[3] When inconsistencies in the operator's behavior seemed

From *American Journal of Sociology*, Vol. 60, No. 3, 1954, pp. 255–266. Reprinted with permission of the publisher, The University of Chicago Press; Copyright 1954 by the University of Chicago Press.

[1] This report is drawn from materials presented in the writer's doctoral dissertation, "Restriction of Output in a Piecework Machine Shop" (University of Chicago, 1952), under the direction of Everett C. Hughes.

[2] Donald Roy, "Quota Restriction and Goldbricking in a Machine Shop," *American Journal of Sociology*, LVII (March, 1952), 427–42.

[3] Donald F. Roy, "Work Satisfaction and Social Reward in Quota Achievement: An Analysis of Piecework Incentive," *American Sociological Review*, XVIII (October, 1953), 507–14.

to contradict the hypothesis that variations in application of economic incentive could account for the variations in work effort, a more intensive examination of response to piecework was undertaken. This disclosed that piecework incentive was not equivalent to economic incentive and that attainment of piecework "quotas" afforded machine operators a complex of rewards in which the strictly economic might or might not play a part.

The third set of observations, to be here discussed, again exhibits complication in a picture that has come to be accepted as simple in design. Here the focus of interest is the structure of "informal" intergroup connections that bear directly upon work behavior at the machine level. The material will not deny the hypothesis that the willingness of operatives to put forth effort is a function of their relationship with management or the widely held affirmation that this relationship is mediated by the organization of operatives into "informal groups." It will indicate, however, that further advances in the understanding of work behavior in the factory may involve attention to minor as well as major axes of intergroup relations. It will show that the relevant constituents of problematic production situations may include "lateral" lines of interaction between subgroups of the work force as well as "vertical" connections between managerial and worker groups.

It will be seen, in other words, that the interaction of two groups in an industrial organization takes place within and is conditioned by a larger intergroup network of reciprocal influences. Whyte has called attention to the limitations of studying groups in "isolation," without regard for the "perspectives of large institutional structures."[4] A second warning might be: The larger institutional structures form networks of interacting groups.

As a bona fide member of an informal group of machine operatives the writer had an opportunity to observe and experience management-work group conflict in its day-to-day and blow-by-blow particulars. Also, he participated in another kind of social process, intergroup co-operation. Not only did workers on the "drill line" co-operate with each other as fellow-members of a combat team at war with management; they also received considerable aid and abetment from other groups of the shop. This intergroup co-operation was particularly evident when operators were trying to "make out," or attain "quota" production, on piecework jobs.

It has been noted in another connection that machine operators characteristically evinced no reluctance to put forth effort when they felt that their group-defined piecework quotas were attainable.[5] It might seem, at first glance, that the supporting of operators during intensive application to "getting the work out" would represent co-operation *with* and not *against* management. However, the truth is that operators and their "allies" joined forces in certain situations in a manner not only unmistakably at variance with the carefully prepared designs of staff experts but even in flagrant violation of strongly held managerial "moral principles" of shop behavior. In short, machine operators resorted to "cheating" to attain their quotas; and since this often involved the collusion of other shop groups, not as mere "accessories after the fact" but as deeply entangled accomplices, any managerial suspicion that swindling and conniving, as well as loafing, were going on all the time was well founded. If the workers' conviction that the echelons of management were packed with men addicted to the "dirty deal" be additionally considered, it might appear that the shop was fairly overrun with crooks. Since a discussion of "contrast conceptions"[6] cannot find a place within the limited scope of this paper, it must suffice at this point merely to declare that the kind of effort made by operators and their aids to expedite production, when they did try to expedite it, was actually in many respects conflict with management.

One belief, universally accepted in the work group, may be phrased thus: "You can't 'make out' if you do things the way management

[4] William F. Whyte, "Small Groups and Large Organizations," in *Social Psychology at the Crossroads*, ed. John R. Rohrer and Muzafer Sherif (New York: Harper & Bros., 1951), pp. 297–312.

[5] Roy, "Work Satisfaction and Social Reward in Quota Achievement," *op. cit.*

[6] See L. Copeland, "The Negro as a Contrast Conception," in *Race Relations and the Race Problem*, ed. E. T. Thompson (Durham: Duke University Press, 1939), and S. Kirson Weinberg, "Aspects of the Prison's Social Structure," *American Journal of Sociology*, XLVII (March, 1942), 717–26.

wants them done." This gem of shop wisdom thus negatively put is hardly a prescription for action, but its obverse, "You've got to figure the angles," gave all hands plenty to do.

According to Al McCann (all names used are fictitious), the "Fagan" of the drill line, "They time jobs to give you just base rates. It's up to you to figure out how to fool them so you can make out. You can't make any money if you run the job the way it's timed."

We machine operators did "figure the angles"; we developed an impressive repertoire of angles to play and devoted ourselves to crossing the expectations of formal organization with perseverance, artistry, and organizing ability of our own. For instance, job timing was a "battle all the way" between operators and time-study men. The objective of the operators was good piecework prices, and that end justified any old means that would work. One cardinal principle of operator job-timing was that cutting tools be run at lower speeds and "feeds" than the maximums possible on subsequent production, and there were various ways of encouraging the institution of adequate differentials. Also, operators deemed it essential to embellish the timing performance with movements only apparently functional in relation to the production of goods: little reachings, liftings, adjustings, dustings, and other special attentions to conscientious machine operation and good housekeeping that could be dropped instanter with the departure of the time-study man.

However, the sophistication of the time-study men usually matched the strategy employed against them. The canniest operators often gave of their best in timing duels only to get "hopeless prices" for their pains:

> Gus Schmidt was timed early in the evening on a job, and given a price of $1.00 per 100 for reaming one hole, chamfering both sides of three holes, and filing burrs on one end of one hole. All that for one cent!
> "To hell with them," said Gus.

This is not to say that the "hopeless price" was always truly hopeless. Since the maintenance of an effective control over job-timing and hence price-setting was an uncertain, often disheartening matter, operators were forced to develop skills for turning bad into good. Under the shaping hands of the "angle-applicators" surprising metamorphoses sometimes took

place. Like the proverbial ugly duckling that finally feathered out into a beautiful swan, piecework jobs originally classified in operator vernacular as "stinkers" came to give off the delightful aroma of "gravy." Without going into the particulars of the various types of operation, one might say that jobs were "streamlined." This streamlining was, of course, at times "rough on the tools" and adverse in its effects on the quality of output. The jettisoning of quality called, necessarily, for a corresponding attention to ways and means of shielding supervisors and inspectors from discovering the sacrifices and consequently brought into further play the social graces of equivocation, subterfuge, and prestidigitation.

Still, the adroitness of the machine operators, inventing, scheming, and conniving unto themselves to make quotas attainable, was not enough. Many "stinkers" would not yield before the whitest heat of intelligence or the most cavalier disregard for company property. An appreciable incidence of failure should not be surprising when it is kept in mind that the black arts of "making out" were not only responses to challenge from management but also stimulations, in circular interaction, to the development of more effective countermagic in the timing process. It would be hard to overestimate the wizardry of the time-study men with pencil and paper in computing "angle-tight" piecework prices. During the latter months of his employment, months that marked the peak of his machine performance, the writer was able to achieve quota earnings approximately half the time that piecework jobs were offered. If this experience is roughly representative of the fortunes of the drill-line group, the battle with the stopwatch men was nip and tuck.

It is to be expected that a group of resourceful operatives, working with persistent intent to "make out" at quota levels, and relying heavily upon illegal practices, would be alert to possibilities of assistance from groups that were able and willing to give it and would not hesitate at further flouting the rules and regulations in cultivating it. It is also to be expected that the upholders of a managerial rational and moral order would attempt to prevent corruptive connections and would take action to stamp out whatever subversive organization did develop. During the eleven-month study, machine operators, including the drill-line men, were enjoying the co-operation of several other shop groups in an illegal facilitation of the "make-out" process. This intergroup network effectively modified certain formally established shop routines, a too close attachment to which would handicap the operators. The "syndicate" also proved adequate in circumventing each of a series of "new rules" and "new systems" introduced by management to expurgate all modifications and improvisations and force a strict adherence to the rules.

The shop groups that conspired with the operators were, namely, the inspectors, the tool-crib men, the time-checkers, the stockmen, and the setup men. With a single exception, these "service" groups stemmed from lines of authority distinct from the one for which the operators formed the base. The one exception was the setup group; it was subordinate to the same set of officials in the "production" line of authority that controlled the operators. A brief description of the duties of each of these service groups and a rough tracing of the sequences of interaction involved in the prescribed work routine of the drill men will indicate the formal pattern of intergroup relations within which informally instituted variations were woven.

THE SETUP MEN. A chief function of the setup men was to assist machine operators in the "setting-up" of jigs and fixtures preparatory to operation of machines in the processing of materials. It included the giving of preliminary aid and advice at the beginning of the production process, at which time the setup men would customarily "run the first piece" to show operators how to do it and to indicate that the setup was adequate to meet work specifications. The duties of the setup men also included "trouble-shooting" on occasions when operators encountered difficulties that effected a lowering of the quality of output below inspection standards or a reduction of the rate of output unsatisfactory to operators or supervisors.

THE INSPECTORS. The chief function of the inspectors was to pass judgment on the quality of the output of the machine operators, either accepting or rejecting work turned out, according to blueprint specifications. Their appraisals came at the beginning of operations, when especially thorough examinations of the first pieces processed were made, and subse-

quently at varying intervals during the course of a job.

THE TOOL-CRIB MEN. The tool-crib attendants served the operators as dispensers of jigs, fixtures, cutting tools, blueprints, gauges, and miscellaneous items of equipment needed to supplement basic machinery and operator-owned hand tools in the processing of materials. They worked inside a special inclosure conveniently located along one of the main arterials of shop traffic and did most of their dispensing across the wide sill of a "window," an aperture which served, incidentally, as locus of various and sundry transactions and communications not immediately relevant to tool-dispensing. There were two other openings into the crib, a door, two steps from the window, and a wide gate, farther down the corridor.

THE STOCKMEN. The stockmen were responsible for conducting a steady flow of materials to the machines for processing. Their work called for the removal of finished work as well as the moving-up of fresh stock and involved a division of labor into two specializations: "stock-chasing" and "trucking." The chief duties of the stock-chasers were to "locate" unprocessed materials in the various storage areas, when operators called for stock, and to direct the activities of the truckers, who attended to the physical transportation.

THE TIME-CHECKERS. The time-checkers worked in another special inclosure, a small "time cage," from which they distributed to the operators the work orders "lined up" by the schedulemen of the Planning Department and within which they registered the starting and completion times of each job. There were four time-registering operations for every work order. First, upon presenting an operator with a work-order slip, the checker would "punch" him "on setup" by stamping a separate order card with a clocking mechanism that registered the hours in tenths. Later, when the operator would call at the cage window to announce completion of all preparatory arrangements for the actual processing of materials, the checker would punch him "off setup" and "on production." Finally, following another operator announcement, the checker would clock the termination of the machining process with a fourth punch. At the time of his terminal punch the operator would report the number of "pieces" completed on the job just concluded and would receive a new work order to start the cycle over again. And, since the terminal punch on the completed job would be registered at the same time as the initial punch on the new one, hours on shift would be completely accounted for.

OPERATOR INTERACTION WITH SERVICE GROUPS. The machine operator's performance of each individual job or order assigned to him involved formal relationships with service groups in well-defined sequences or routines.

First, the operator would receive his work order from the time-checker. Next, he would present the work order to a tool-crib attendant at the crib window as a requisite to receiving blueprints, jigs, cutting tools, and gauges. At the same time, that is, immediately before or after approaching the crib attendant, sometimes while waiting for crib service, the operator would show his work order to a stock-chaser as a requisite to receiving materials to work on. The stock-chaser, after perusing the order slip, occasionally with additional reference to the blueprint, would hail a trucker to bring the necessary stock to the operator's machine. If there were no delay in contacting a stock-chaser or in locating and moving up the stock, a load of materials would await the operator upon his arrival at his machine with equipment from the tool crib.

Upon returning to his machine, the operator would proceed with the work of "setting up" the job, usually with the assistance of a setup man, who would stay with him until a piece was turned out whose quality of workmanship would satisfy an inspector. In appraising a finished piece, the inspector would consult the blueprint brought from the crib for work specifications and then perform operations of measurement with rules, gauges, micrometers, or more elaborate equipment. The inspector might or might not "accept" the first piece presented for his judgment. At any rate, his approval was requisite to the next step in the operator's formal interactional routine, namely, contacting the time-checker to punch "off setup" and "on production."

The operator would ordinarily have further "business" contact with a setup man during the course of production. Even if the job did not "go sour" and require the services of a

"trouble-shooter," the setup man would drop around of his own accord to see how the work was progressing. Likewise, the operator would have further formal contact during the course of his job with inspectors and tool-crib attendants. Each inspector would make periodic "quality checks" at the machines on his "line"; and the operator might have to make trips to the tool crib to get tools ground or to pick up additional tools or gauges. He might also have to contact a stock-chaser or truckers for additional materials.

Upon completion of the last piece of his order the operator would tear down his setup, return his tools to the tool crib, and make a final report to the time-checker. Should the job be uncompleted at the close of a shift, the operator would merely report the number of pieces finished to a checker, and the latter would register a final punchout. The setup would be left intact for the use of the operator coming in to work the next shift.

MAJOR JOB CATEGORIES. Certain variations in types of jobs assigned to operators are pertinent to a discussion of intergroup collusion to modify formal work routines. These variations could be classified into four categories: (1) piecework; (2) time study; (3) rework; and (4) setup.

Each piecework job carried a price per 100 pieces, determined by the timing operations mentioned earlier. Time-study and rework jobs carried no prices. The time-study category included (a) new jobs that had not yet been timed and (b) jobs that had once carried a piecework price. As the label indicates, rework jobs involved the refinishing of pieces rejected either by inspectors or in the assembly process but considered salvageable by reprocessing.

Since time-study and rework jobs carried no piecework prices, operators engaged in these two types of work were paid "day rate," that is, according to an hourly base rate determined in collective bargaining. The base rates represented minimal wage guaranties that not only applied to "day work" but also covered piecework as well. If an operator on piecework failed to exceed his base rate in average hourly earnings on a particular job on a particular day, he would be paid his base rate. Failure to produce at base rate or above on the first day of a piecework job did not penalize an operator in his efforts to earn premium pay on the second day; nor did failure to attain base rate on one piecework job on a given day reduce premiums earned on a second job performed that day.

Not a fourth type of job, but measured separately in time and payment units, were the setup operations. Piecework jobs always carried piecework setups; failure to equal or exceed base rate on setup did not jeopardize chances to earn premium on "production," and vice versa. Time-study jobs frequently carried piecework setups; rework never.

Obviously, these formal work routines may easily be modified to fit the perceived needs of machine operators. Possibilities for the development of "make-out angles" should be immediately apparent in a work situation characterized by job repertoires that included piecework and day-work operations; minimum-wage guaranties uniform for all work done; and separate payment computations by jobs and days worked. If, for instance, time formally clocked as day work could be used to gain a "head start" on subsequent piecework operations, such a transferral might mean the difference between earning and not earning premiums on doubtful piecework jobs. Similarly, time on "hopeless" piecework jobs might be applied to more promising operations; and the otherwise "free time" gained on "gravy" jobs might be consumed in productive anticipation of the formal receipt of ordinarily unrewarding piecework. Especially lush "gravy" jobs might even contribute extra time enough to convert "stinkers" into temporary "money-makers." Realization of such possibilities in any given case would necessarily involve obtaining, without a work order, the following: (1) identification of future operations as listed in sequence on the schedule board inside the time cage; (2) jigs, blueprints, and cutting tools appropriate to the work contemplated; (3) stock to work on; (4) setup help and adivce; (5) inspection service; and (6) "trouble-shooting" assistance as needed. Obviously, this sequence of accomplishments would call for the support of one or more service groups at each step. That the required assistance was actually provided with such regularity that it came to be taken for granted, the writer discovered by observation and personal experience.

The following diary recording of interaction between the writer and a time-checker may be indicative of the extent to which service-group collaboration with the operators in perverting the formal system of work routine had become systematized:

> When I came to punch off the rework, the time-cage girl said, "You don't want to punch off rework yet, do you?"—suggesting that I should get a start on the next job before punching off rework.

Even line foremen, who, in regard to intergroup collusion preferred the role of silent "accessory after the fact," became upset to the point of actual attempted interference with formal rules and regulations when the naïve neophyte failed to meet the expectations of his own informal system.

> Art [foreman] was at the time cage when I punched off the day work of rereaming and on to the piecework of drilling. He came around to my machine shortly after.
> "Say," he said, "when you punch off day work onto piecework, you ought to have your piecework already started. Run a few; then punch off the day work, and you'll have a good start. You've got to chisel a little around here to make money."

Acceptance of such subversive practices did not extend, however, to groups in management other than local shop supervision. The writer was solemnly and repeatedly warned that time-study men, the true hatchet men of upper management, were disposed to bring chiselers to speedy justice.

> Gus went on to say that a girl hand-mill operator had been fired a year ago when a time-study man caught her running one job while being punched in on another. The time-study man came over to the girl's machine to time a job, to find the job completed and the girl running another.

NEW RULES AND NEW SYSTEMS. During the near-year that he spent in the shop the writer felt the impact of several attempts to stamp out intergroup irregularities and enforce conformity to managerial designs of procedure. He coincidentally participated in an upholding of the maxim: "Plus ça change, plus c'est la même chose."

Attempts to tighten controls came in a series of "new rules" or "new systems" promulgated by bulletin-board edicts. How far the beginning of the series antedated the writer's arrival is not known. Old-timers spoke of a "Golden Age" enjoyed before the installation of the "Booth System" of production control; then operators "kept their own time," turning in their work orders as they saw fit and building "kitties" on good jobs to tide them over rainy days on poor jobs.

The first new rule during this study went into "effect" less than two months after the writer was hired. It was designed to tighten controls in the tool-crib sector, where attendants had not only been passing out setups ahead of time but allowing operators or their setup men to enter the toolroom to make the advance pickups themselves. An aim of the new rule was also to curb the operators' practice of keeping "main setups" at the machines instead of turning them in at the completion of operations.

> A new crib ruling went into effect today. A memorandum by Bricker [superintendent] was posted on the side of the crib window. Those who check out tools and jigs must sign a slip in triplicate, keeping the pink one and turning it in with the tools in exchange for the white original, which would constitute proof that the tools had been returned. No new setups would be issued until the old ones had been turned in.

An optimistic perception of the new procedures was expressed by young Jonesy, a tool-crib attendant and otherwise willing conniver with the operators: "Tools are scattered all over the shop. This way we'll have them all in order in the crib, and the fellows can get them anytime they need them."

But multiple-drill operator Hanks, old-timer on the line, drew upon his lengthy experience with managerial efficiency measures and saw the situation differently:

> Hanks commented unfavorably on the new ruling. He and the day man [his machine partner on the other shift] had been keeping the tools for their main setups at their bench, or, rather, under it. This practice, according to Hanks, was to insure their setting up promptly without inordinate waste of time and to insure their having all the tools needed. Hanks said that on a previous occasion he was told to turn

in one of his main setups, which included over a dozen drills, reamers, taps, etc., of varying sizes. He did so, but, when he needed this setup again, the crib man couldn't locate all the tools. He asked Hanks to come back in the crib and help him find them. Hanks refused. After several hours of futile search, Hanks was finally induced to "come back and find his tools." He did so on condition that it would not be on his own time. The foreman agreed to this.

"The same thing is going to happen again," predicted Hanks. "And I'm not going back there to find my tools they scatter all over, on my own time."

Though the operators went through the formality of an exchange of slips when they exchanged setups, the new procedures did not modify the practice of getting setups from the crib ahead of time. Appreciable effects of the new ruling included making more paper work for crib attendants at the same time that more work at assembling setups was thrust upon them. Jonesy's happy prediction did not materialize: the tools were not "always in order." Subsequent events confirmed Hanks's gloomy forebodings:

> It took Paul [setup man] and me several hours to get set up for the sockets, as the setup given was incomplete.

> Some time was spent in looking for an angle plate that was specially made for the job. Both Paul and Steve [superintendent] were irritated because the crib men could not find the plate.

> We spent an hour setting up because we could not find the jig.

Included in the new ruling was a stipulation that blueprints and gauges be turned in by the operators at the end of each shift, though setup paraphernalia other than prints and gauges were to be left at the machines as long as jobs were in operation. Calling for prints and gauges at the beginning of the shift, waiting at the crib window in the line that naturally formed, even when these items were "located" immediately, consumed operator time.

> Owing to the new crib ruling, he [Joe Mucha, the writer's machine partner on

another shift] turned in the tap gauge. I spent 20 minutes trying to get it back again. The crib man could not find it and claimed that Joe had not turned it in. Joe stayed after three o'clock to help me get it, countering the arguments of the crib with the slip that he retained as evidence. Finally the gauge was located in the crib.

I started out a half-hour late on operation 55 on the pedestals, due to delay at the crib waiting to check out the print and gauge that Joe had just turned in.

Four months later the new crib ruling was modified by another that canceled the stipulation regarding the turning-in of blueprints and gauges and called for changes in the paper work of operator–crib-attendant relations. These changes were featured by a new kind of work order, duplicates of which became involved in tool-crib bookkeeping. The change reduced the waste of operator time at the start of shifts, but to the burden of the crib attendants paper-work irritations were now added.

When I punched in on the rework and asked Walt [crib attendant] for a print, he fumed a bit as he sought a duplicate of my new-type yellow work order in a new file of his.

"I haven't been able to find more than one in five duplicates so far," he said. "And there's supposed to be a duplicate for every one."

Walt said tonight, when I presented him with a work-order card for tools, "That makes the twelfth card I've had and no duplicate!"

The tool crib under the new system is supposed to have duplicate work orders in their file of all jobs given operators. These duplicates are to be put in the toolroom files as soon as they are put on the board; and the operators are to sign these duplicates when checking out setups.

The "new system" did operate to handicap operators in that they were not to receive new setups from the crib until they received the new yellow work orders from the time cage to check with the duplicates in the crib. However, setup men roamed at will in the toolroom, grinding tools and fixing jigs, and were

able to help the operators by picking up setups ahead of time for them. Their detailed knowledge of the various setups made it possible for them to assemble the necessary tools without the use of setup cards.

"This is a good job," I said to McCann [now setup man]. "I wish I could get it set up ahead of time, but I guess it's no use trying. I can't get the setup now from the toolroom until I get the new work order from the time girls."

McCann thought a moment. "Maybe I can get the jig and tools out of the crib for you."

McCann did get the jig and tools, and I got a half-hour's head start on the job.

The writer had found Ted, a stock-chaser, and his truckers, George and Louie, willing connivers in the time-chiseling process. They moved up stock ahead of time, even after the new system made presentation of the new work order to the stock-chaser a prerequisite to getting stock. Contrary to first impressions, for all practical purposes the situation was unchanged under the new system.

I could not go ahead with the next order, also a load of connecting rods, because the new ruling makes presentation of a work order to the stock-chaser necessary before materials can be moved up. So I was stymied and could do nothing the rest of the day.

About an hour before I was to punch off the connecting rods, I advised Ted that I would soon be needing another job. He immediately brought over a load of reservoir casings.

The new system also included complication of operator-inspector relations. Inspectors were now to "sign off" operators from completed jobs before new work orders could be issued at the time booth. The "signing-off" process included notation by the inspector of the time of operation completion, a double check on the time-checker's "punch out." This added, of course, to the paper work of inspectors.

Drill-man Hanks's first response to this feature of the new system was "individualistic":

Hanks commented on the new system tonight. He thinks that its chief purpose is to keep the operators from getting ahead on an operation and starting the next job on saved time. He said that the inspector checked him off a job tonight at 4:40, and he was not due to punch in on the next one until 6:10. He changed the time recorded by the inspector on his work slip to 6:10 and went ahead as usual. If he had not done so, there would have been a "gap" of an hour and a half unaccounted for in the records.

The writer found himself "stymied" at first but soon discovered that the new obstacle could be overcome without engaging in such a hazardous practice as "forging."

It was ten o'clock when we were ready to punch off setup, and Johnny [setup man] asked Sam [inspector] to sign me off setup earlier, so that I could make out on setup.

"Punch me off at nine o'clock," I said, not expecting Sam to check me off earlier, and purposely exaggerating Johnny's request.

Sam refused. "I can't do that! If I do that for you, I'll have to do it for everybody!"

Sam seemed somewhat agitated in making the refusal.

A few minutes later he said to Johnny, "Why did you ask me to do that when Hanks was standing there?"

Hanks had been standing by my machine, watching us set up.

"I can't take you off an hour back. Go find out when you punched in on this job in the first place."

Johnny consulted the time-cage girl as to the time I punched on the job, later talked to Sam at Sam's bench while I was working, and came to me with the announcement that it was "fixed up" so that I made out on setup and was credited with starting production at 9:30. This gave me an hour and a half of "gravy."

By the time the "new system" was a month old, Sam was not only doing this for everybody but actually taking the initiative:

When I punched off setup for the eight pieces, Sam asked me if I wanted him to take me off setup at an earlier time in order that I might make out on the setup. I refused this offer, as it wasn't worth the trouble for me to stop to figure out the time.

Instead of looking at the clock when an operator asks to be taken off setup, Sam usually asks the operator, "When do you want to be taken off?"

No sooner had the shop employees adjusted to this "new system" and settled down to normal informal routine than they were shocked by a new pronunciamento that barred admittance to the toolroom to all save superintendents and toolroom employees:

A new crib ruling struck without warning today. Typewritten bulletins signed by Faulkner [shop manager] were posted on the toolroom door, barring admittance to all save the toolroom employees and the two departmental foremen [superintendents], Bricker and Steve. Other foremen and setup men are not to be admitted without permission from Milton, toolroom supervisor.

Hanks predicts that the new ruling won't last out the week.

Stimulated by Hanks's prediction, the writer kept an eye on the toolroom door. The rule seemed to be enforced.

On one occasion tonight Paul [setup man] asked Jonesy to let him into the crib; he was in a hurry about something. But Jonesy shook his head, and Paul had to wait at the crib window with the rest of us.

Johnny, the setup man, predicted that the new ruling would be "tough on" the toolcrib employees, not on setup men.

Johnny says that the new rule is going to be tough on grinders and crib attendants, because setup men and foremen have been doing much of the grinding and have made it easier for them by coming in to help themselves to tools, jigs, etc.

Johnny says that the new rule suits him fine. Now he can just stand at the window and holler and let the toolroom employees do the work.

The line foremen seemed to take offense at the new "exclusion act" and threatened reprisals to the crib attendants.

At quitting time I noticed Gil [line foreman] talking to Walt at the crib window. Gil seemed very serious; Walt was waving his arms and otherwise gesturing in a manner indicating rejection of responsibility. I didn't catch any words but gathered that Gil was voicing disapproval or warning, and after Gil left I said to Walt, "Looks like you're behind the eight-ball now!"

I noticed that Walt's hair was mussed, and he looked a little wild. He denied that he was in any trouble whatsoever; nor was he worried about anything whatsoever.

"I'm just working here!" he exclaimed. "I just go by the cards, and beyond that I've got no responsibility!"

I was curious as to what Gil had told him and asked Johnny later, on the way home. I had noticed that Johnny was standing nearby when Gil was talking to Walt. Johnny said that Gil was telling Walt that from now on the crib was going to be charged with every minute of tool delay to the operators—that, if there was any waiting for tools, Gil was going to make out allowance cards charging these delays to the crib.

Contrary to Hanks's prediction, the new rule did "last out the week," and crowds milled around the crib window.

The boys seemed very much disgusted with the slow service at the tool crib. They crowd around the window (always a crowd there) and either growl or wisecrack about the service.

It was at this time that Jonesy, erstwhile optimist and regarded by shop employees as the most efficient of the crib attendants, decided that he had "had enough." He transferred to the quiet backroom retreat of tool-grinding. But several days later, just ten days since the new rule was promulgated, the sun began to break through the dark clouds of managerial efficiency. Hanks's prediction was off by four days.

While I was waiting for tools at the crib window tonight, I noticed the jockey [turret-lathe man] dash into the tool crib through a door that was left ajar; he was followed soon after by Gil. Later, when the door was closed, Paul shook it and shouted to the attendant, "Let me in!" He was admitted.

Steve [superintendent] called out, "Hey!" when he saw the jockey go into the crib.

When the jockey came out, he spoke to him, and the jockey joshed him back. Steve did not seem to be particularly put out about it.

Soon the boys were going in and out of the crib again, almost at will, and setup men were getting setups ahead of time for operators, ignored by the crib attendants.

I noticed that Johnny and others seemed to be going in and out of the crib again, almost at will.

I noticed tonight that Johnny got into the tool crib by appearing at the door and saying to the attendant, "Let me in!"

So much for Faulkner's order—until he makes a new one!

When I asked Walt for some jaws to fit the chuck I had found, he said, "We've got lots of jaws back here, but I wouldn't know what to look for. You'd better get the setup man to come back here and find you some."

Walt said to me, "I break the rules here, but not too much—just within reason to keep the boys on production."

Faulkner's order still hangs at eye level on the crib door.

"So much for Faulkner's order!" The "fix" was "on" again, and operators and their service-group allies conducted business as usual for the remaining weeks of the writer's employment.

CONCLUSIONS. This rough sketch of the operation of one shop "syndicate" has been no more than indicative of the existence of intergroup co-operation in the lower reaches of factory social structure. No attempt has been made here to account for the aid extended by service groups, though suggestion that this assistance might be part of a larger system of reciprocal obligations has been implicit. It is apparent, for instance, that tool-crib attendants benefited from their practice of admitting operators and setup men to the toolroom to seek and pick up equipment.

A more complete picture of intergroup relations would include conflict, as well as co-operation, between operators and the various service groups. It could be shown, if space permitted, that changes in relationship accompanied, in cyclical fashion, changes in basic conditions of work.

Furthermore, attention has not been drawn to intragroup role and personality variations in intergroup relations. Such additional discriminations and the questions that they might raise in regard to the study of institutional dynamics must be left for future discussion.

As for their possible bearing on practical industrial administration, materials presented here seem to challenge the view held in some research circles that the "human" problem of industrial efficiency lies in faulty communication between an economically "rational" or "logical" management and "nonrational" or "nonlogical" work groups. While nothing has been offered to deny linkage between communication and efficiency, observations reported here suggest examination of the stereotypes of the two parties.[7] And questioning the fitness of the stereotypes may lead to a more fruitful conceptualization of the process that is reputedly in need of attention: communication.

Do we see, in the situation studied, an economically "rational" management and an economically "nonrational" work group? Would not a reversal of the labels, if such labels be used, find justification? Does it not appear that operatives and their allies resisted managerial "logics of efficiency" because application of those "logics" tended to produce something considerably less than "efficiency"? Did not worker groups connive to circumvent managerial ukase in order to "get the work out"? Did not Walt, for instance, break the rules "to keep the boys on production"? May not the common query of industrial workers, "What in the hell are they trying to do up there?" be not merely reflective of faulty communication but also based on a real managerial inadequacy, quite apart from a failure in "explanation"? May it not be assumed that managerial inefficiency is and has been for some time a serious problem to those who labor?

If managerial directives are not the guides to efficient action that they are claimed to be, then, perhaps, "logics of efficiency" would be better designated as "sentiments of efficiency." When failure to "explain" is additionally considered, perhaps bulletin-board pronunciamentos might properly be classified with the various exorcisms, conjurations, and miscellaneous esoteric monkey-business of our primitive contemporaries.

If we conceive of "logical" behavior not as self-contained ratiocinative exercises but as intellectual operations in continuous reciprocal interplay with concrete experience, machine operators and their service-group allies would appear the real holders of "logics of efficiency." Like big-city machine politicians, they develop plans for action that, under given conditions of situational pressures, "work."

But this rejection of commonly held stereotypes cannot lead to mere reversal of invidious distinctions; the situation is far too complex for that. The group life that the writer shared was by no means devoid of "sentiments." To the contrary, operator interaction was rich in shared feelings, attitudes, and practices not only of doubtful bearing on getting the work out but often undeniably preventing production maximization. Nor can it be maintained that management, in applying its "sentiments of efficiency," was always ineffective. Perhaps solution to the human problem of industrial efficiency would best be expedited by abandoning altogether the use of contrasted caricatures handed down to us from a preindustrial social class structure. Instead of concerning ourselves with such blind-alley issues as who is "rational" and who is not, we might recognize with John Dewey that both intellectual and emotional activity are essentials of goal-directed behavior[8] and that the development of effective communication focusing on production goals is a matter of instituting interactional processes that engender ideas, sentiments, and plans for action held in common.

[7] William F. Whyte, "Semantics and Industrial Relations," *Human Organization*, VIII (Spring, 1949), 1–7.

[8] *Art as Experience* (New York: Minton, Balch & Co., 1934), p. 55.

Work Group Behavior and the Larger Organization

LEONARD R. SAYLES

The individual's most immediate and meaningful experiences of work are obtained in the context of the work group and his work associates. The larger organization is experienced by indirection, but membership in the small group contributes directly to the shaping of attitudes and behavior toward the entire world of work. For this reason of potency, therefore, the contribution of the small group to the total organization has been a subject of substantial research by those interested in human relations in industry.

Conceptions of the Work Group

As Whyte observes, the individual is *not* a member of a single group within a larger structure.[1] Rather, he typically interacts in a variety of settings within the organization. It is the task of the researcher to identify those interaction patterns which are focused and concentrated so that it is reasonable to speak of a "group."

From *Research in Industrial Human Relations.* New York: Harper and Brothers, 1957, pp. 131–145. Reprinted with permission of the publisher.

A substantial portion of the material included is from a study by the author sponsored by the Bureau of Industrial Relations of the University of Michigan on the relationship of work group behavior to technological and organizational factors. Our major emphasis is on industrial work groups, although examples will be drawn from other work settings.

[1] William F. Whyte, "Small Groups in Large Organizations," in *Social Psychology at the Crossroads,* John Rohrer and Muzafer Sherif, eds. (New York: Harper, 1951), pp. 303–304.

If we follow all the members of the organization through their hours on the job, or find some "high" vantage point and observe the total of all interactions, we are likely to be impressed with this proliferation of memberships. Most apparent is membership, except for that unique individual, the president, in some *command group;* that is, the employee shares a common supervisor with a number of colleagues. Distinguishable from this group, but closely related, is a *functional* or *task group*—those employees who must collaborate in some fashion if the work task defined by the organization is to be accomplished. In fact, both of these groups are rather well defined by the larger organization, and the group typically retains those boundaries.

However, there are two other kinds of clusterings that tend to overlap and penetrate the organization in unexpected ways. They are not defined by the formal organization and are often included under the general term, informal organization. One has received much attention from researchers: the *friendship clique.* The other is less well studied, but equally important. That is the *interest group.* This is comprised of those employees who share a common economic interest and seek to gain some objective relating to the larger organization.

Memberships in these groups are not exclusive; often they will overlap considerably. However, the motivations of the members, and, more important, their behavior, are distinctive; and we have no reason to believe that the boundaries will be perfectly coincident.

The Command Group. Perhaps the most obvious kind of small group in the large organization is composed of the supervisor and his immediate subordinates. As Jacques observes, the entire organization is composed of interconnected *command groups*, the subordinates in one group being the superiors in their own command group, with the exception of the first level.[2] While we might expect that research would have emphasized this unit of the organization, if we exclude the manifold studies of leadership styles dealt with elsewhere in this volume, there are relatively few systematic explorations of the relationship between the leader and his subordinates as a group, as individuals, and among the subordinates themselves. Jacques' volume is a notable exception.[3] His examination of the command group has a strong psychiatric flavor. He stresses the leader's ambivalence: his *authority* over his subordinates and *dependence* upon them, his sense of isolation, the problem of integrating pair relationships (leader and individual subordinates) with cohesiveness among subordinates, and the mixed feelings of the subordinates as a group who find the leader both expendable and indispensable (one to be protected or exposed?).

The Friendship Clique. This has been conceived as the elementary building block of human organization. As Mayo writes, "Man's desire to be continuously associated with his fellows is a strong, if not the strongest human characteristic."[4]

At the workplace we find a multitude of friendship groups representing the diverse interests of the workers placed there by the organization. The boundaries of these clusterings appear to reflect the employees' off-the-job interests and associations or previous work experience. Age, ethnic background, outside activities, sex, marital status, and so on, comprise the mortar that binds the clique together.

The friendship group has emerged as the agency which welds the individual to the organization. Loyalty, even attachment, to the total organization with its impersonality, extended hierarchy, and social distance becomes ambiguous. However, attachment to the immediate and easily perceived face-to-face group is the predominant reality of organization experience. For the individual it provides a source of personal security in an impersonal environment.

Where cliques are largely nonexistent, as in the rapidly expanding aircraft plants of California, turnover can be enormous. The presumption is that stable social groups take time to crystallize; during the period of formation many potential members will leave voluntarily because they do not find an established unit with which they can affiliate. This in turn inhibits the formation of permanent groups; the process is self-defeating.

Thus Lombard and Mayo conclude that the naive administrator who seeks to break up these cliques because of the inefficiency and wasted motion of the purely social activities involved is actually doing a disservice to the organization.[5] In fact, they find that it takes skillful leadership to encourage their formation, at least in organizations undergoing rapid expansion. A recent well-received text[6] in the field of public administration comes out strongly on the side of encouraging on-the-job social life, concluding that production increased when social conversation was allowed. However, a study employing methods of precise interaction observation is unique in casting some doubts as to the positive correlation

---

[2] Elliot Jacques, *The Changing Culture of a Factory* (New York: Dryden Press, 1952), pp. 273–297.

[3] There are two other noteworthy recent exceptions. Argyris devotes a small volume to the relationship between a plant manager in a medium-sized factory and his immediate subordinates. (Chris Argyris, *Executive Leadership* [New York: Harper, 1954]). Two researchers at the Harvard Business School provide us with a very revealing study of the day-to-day changes in the relationship between a first-line supervisor and assembly-line girls during a period of technological changes —Harriet Ronken and Paul Lawrence, *Administering Changes* (Boston: Graduate School of Business Administration, Harvard University, 1952).

[4] Elton Mayo, *Social Problems of an Industrial Civilization* (Boston: Graduate School of Business Administration, Harvard University, 1945), p. 111.

[5] Elton Mayo and George F. Lombard, *Teamwork and Labor Turnover in the Aircraft Industry of Southern California* (Boston: Graduate School of Business Administration, Harvard University, 1940).

[6] Herbert Simon, Donald Smithburg, and Victor Thompson, *Public Administration* (New York: Knopf, 1950), pp. 113–114.

between social interaction and productivity.[7]

More serious criticism of the universal efficacy of friendship cliques, however, involves considerations of personality and work structure differences. A study of "rate busters" disclosed a significant majority who were indifferent to, if not hostile to, the social groupings they found on the job.[8]

A recent examination of British longshoremen finds that approximately half of the longshoremen on the docks studied have consciously avoided social entanglements of work group membership. Given an opportunity to join semipermanent gangs, they prefer random work assignments that leave them free to come and go at will, with no group responsibility.[9]

Formation of social groups also appears to be a function of the structure of the work situation itself. Argyris, in his Bank study, finds that incidence of informal social groupings among tellers is less than for bank employees who have less interaction with customers.[10] This conclusion would confirm a basic hypothesis of Chapple, that individuals seek some equilibrium in their rate and range of interaction.[11]

From this theoretical approach, we would expect that the whole range of group activities, not just social life, would be influenced by the interaction pattern fostered by the job. The previously cited study by the University of Liverpool researchers, for example, notes that dockworkers who were members of semi-permanent crews were rarely found among the informal leaders of the longshoremen or among the active participants in the union.[12] Moving in the other direction, Lipset concludes that because some jobs handicap workers in maintaining adequate off-the-job relations with other friends (e.g., unusual working hours as among printers, actors, and policemen), they tend to form more closely knit "fellow worker" groups, as evidenced by their record of high participation in local union activities.[13]

Similarly, George Strauss has observed an unusually high degree of membership participation in certain occupational groups involving relative isolation from fellow workers, like insurance salesmen, utility meter readers and substation operators.[14]

Such studies add to the trend toward considering the *need for social relations* as a variable worth studying in itself. It would be interesting to know, for example, whether industrial occupations in which there is high inter-worker dependence in the work process, such that almost constant interaction is required, show less social life than groups characterized by relatively independent operations.

The Task Group. Perhaps one of the most important aspects of small group behavior in large organizations is their relation to the work process itself. The formally designated task builds a group structure, just as do individual social needs and the organizational authority structure.

More specifically, the work process stimulates group controls of (1) work method, (2) output standards or productivity, and (3) relative compensation and prestige relationships.

1. IMPACT ON WORK METHOD. The experience of working in close proximity on a day-to-day basis induces methods that may depart from the organization's original conception of the job, or at least "fills in" the specific details of the operation not specified in the

---

[7] A. B. Horsfall and Conrad Arensberg, "Teamwork and Productivity in a Shoe Factory," *Human Organization*, VIII (Winter 1949), pp. 21 ff.

[8] These men tended to have a rural background emphasizing individualism. Orvis Collins and Donald Roy, "Restriction of Output and Social Cleavage in Industry," *Applied Anthropology*, V (Summer 1946), pp. 1–14.

[9] University of Liverpool, *The Dock Worker* (Liverpool: University Press of Liverpool, 1954), pp. 61 ff.

[10] Chris Argyris, *Organization of a Bank* (New Haven: Labor and Management Center, Yale University, 1954), p. 129.

[11] Eliot D. Chapple, "Applied Anthropology in Industry," in *Anthropology Today*, A. L. Kroeber, ed. (Chicago: University of Chicago Press, 1953), pp. 819–831. Many of the observations in this section are based on the theoretical work of Chapple.

[12] University of Liverpool, *op. cit.,* p. 72.

[13] Seymour M. Lipset, "The Political Process in Trade Unions: A Theoretical Statement," in *Freedom and Control in Modern Society*, Monroe Berger, Theodore Abel, and Charles Page, eds. (New York: Van Nostrand, 1954), pp. 101–102.

[14] Personal correspondence, Professor Strauss, University of Buffalo.

formal work plan. Thus, employees may exchange repetitive jobs, although such trading is illegal; one worker may do two jobs while a colleague rests; or, as Whyte [15] found, they may change the sequence of the operations to reduce tensions and provide short cuts. Roy observed similar "adjustments" in relations among tool room clerks, job sellers, and machinists where the objective was maximizing piece rate earnings.[16]

Some of these informal, or unplanned for, work methods may decrease worker output. For example, workers' machinations in Roy's machine shop tended to overstate make-ready time during job changes. However, other worker innovations, such as those described by Whyte, undoubtedly increase the total product. Gross found that radar teams, through communication circuits set up during off-the-job social periods, were compensating for deficiencies in the information provided by the formal organization.[17]

Similarly researchers have analyzed the initiative exhibited by a group of department store salesmen in evolving a new work pattern that solved a serious internal morale problem created by a new incentive system.[18]

However, the work structure can be designed so that elaborations of the informal group necessarily work in opposition to the major objectives of the organization. Recent studies of changes in the method of mining coal, conducted by the Tavistock Institute in Great Britain, illustrate such organization.[19] The change from jobs completed by small groups of miners in one shift to successive operations carried out by three shifts resulted in reduction of interaction and communication and a consequent decrease in the miners' recognition of their total responsibility for the operation.[20]

Thus the Tavistock studies suggest that the goal of the engineer in designing the technological organization is to provide the work group with a relatively autonomous task so that responsible *internal* leadership can develop. This kind of organizational structure is, in fact, the very essence of decentralization:

> A primary work organization of this type has the advantage of placing responsibility for the complete . . . task squarely on the shoulders of a single, small, face-to-face group which experiences the entire cycle of operations within the compass of its membership. For each participant the task has total significance and dynamic closure.[21]

The development of mutually convenient methods of conducting the work process can extend to the "job" of collective bargaining. We have ample evidence that union-management relationships at the work group level often depart radically from established practices and attitudes prevailing at higher levels, and may in fact contradict these other, more "formal" relationships.[22]

Aside from evolving methods which seem most convenient to work group members, the pattern of doing the job is fitted to the status system of the group. Those members with most prestige, if at all possible, receive the best jobs. Where possible, working location and equipment are similarly "assigned." And where these are not under group control, helping and trading can be adjusted to the status system. The exchange-of-favors system readily responds to the prestige hierarchy. Of course, the evaluation placed on jobs is itself a product of group interaction.

[15] William F. Whyte, "The Social Structure of the Restaurant," *The American Journal of Sociology*, LIV (January 1949), pp. 306–307.

[16] Donald Roy, "Quota Restriction and Goldbricking in a Machine Shop," *The American Journal of Sociology*, LVII (March 1952), pp. 427–442.

[17] Edward Gross, "Some Functional Consequences of Primary Controls in Formal Work Organizations," *American Sociological Review*, XVIII (August 1953), pp. 370–371.

[18] Nicholas Babchuck and William Goode, "Work Incentives in a Self-Determined Group," *American Sociological Review*, XVI (October 1951), p. 686.

[19] E. Trist and K. Bamforth, "Some Social and Psychological Consequences of the Longwall Method of Coal-Getting," *Human Relations*, IV, No. 1 (1951).

[20] The same problem can arise even though the employees are not separated into different time shifts. A study of a textile mill provides us with an example of the impact of worker-machine allocations. Cf. A. K. Rice, "Productivity and Social Organization in an Indian Weaving Shed," *Human Relations*, VI, No. 4 (1953).

[21] Trist and Bamforth, *op. cit.*, p. 6.

[22] Cf. Melville Dalton, "Unofficial Union-Management Relations," *American Sociological Review*, XV (October 1950), pp. 611–619.

The methods evolved within the group for task completion become firmly established. Where outside forces (e.g., technological change) threaten to induce changes, the ranks close and resistance is applied. In part, of course, this may be the natural reaction of the culprit fearing punishment for rule infractions. A more reasonable explanation of the informal group's resistance to change, however, is the intimate relationship between the task group as an entity and the work methods they have evolved. A threat to one is a real threat to the other.

2. IMPACT ON OUTPUT STANDARDS. Probably more attention has been given to this aspect of task group behavior than to any other. Starting with the work of Mathewson, and extending through the Western Electric studies, a long and distinguished line of studies indicate that work groups often formulate quite specific output standards and obtain close conformity from their members in *maintaining* these standards. Productivity itself is increasingly conceived of as a group phenomenon.

Several reasons have been advanced as to why output control occupies a place of such importance in the life of the group. Work standards are one of the most important aspects of the job, which can in some fashion be influenced by worker action. The energy expenditure required by the job is largely determined by the number of units required, rather than by the nature of the job itself. Presumably without group control management would be able to utilize individual differences, and competition for promotion and greater earnings, to obtain higher and higher standards. This would penalize particularly the slower worker and the older employee. It might, however, penalize all workers by cutting piece rates, where such exist, and/or reducing the number of employees required by the operation. "Run away" output might have internal ramifications. We have observed situations where group controls were weak, and younger, low-prestige employees exceeded the production and earnings records of their "betters." The results were calamitous for the status hierarchy of the department and ultimately for the effectiveness of the formal organization.

Output control is a basic objective of group action as well as an essential element in maintaining group stability. Not only the relationship of the members to one another, but the durability of the worker relationship to his job depends on the efficacy of this process. Again we need to note that the resultant is not always unfavorable to management. We have many instances on record where the group has sanctioned increasingly high productivity,[23] rejected fellow workers who could not maintain high output, and resisted threats to existing high quality standards.

Evidently a great deal of the interest in "informal group relations" is the result of this presumed relationship between output standards evolving within the group and actual worker productivity. Wilensky in an earlier chapter [of *Research in Industrial Human Relations*] reviews some of the efforts to find the magic formula to convert group norms from "low" to "high."

Some of the earliest research on productivity was based on the assumption that internal harmony in the work group would produce higher performance records. Increasingly researchers have become disillusioned with the relationship between social satisfaction and worker effort. Perhaps one of the most telling blows to the impetus to devote substantial energies to building work groups that are "sociometrically sound" is the provocative study by Goode and Fowler in a low morale plant. They found "the informal relationships which developed were such as to maintain pressures toward high production in the face of considerable *animosity* toward the owners and *among the workers themselves*."[24] While their findings are severely limited by the somewhat unique environment they chose, it has become recognized that the relationship between friendship and output is a complex one.

More recently, Seashore finds in a study in a large "heavy equipment manufacturing company" that highly "cohesive" work groups are more likely to have output records that di-

[23] Cf. George Strauss, "Group Dynamics and Intergroup Relations," in William F. Whyte and others, *Money and Motivation* (New York: Harper, 1955), pp. 90–96.

[24] William Goode and Irving Fowler, "Incentive Factors in a Low Morale Plant," *American Sociological Review*, XIV (October 1949), p. 624; italics added by author.

verge *in either direction* from plant averages.[25] By implication, then, tightly knit work groups are almost as likely to have notably *poor* production records as outstandingly *good* ones.

The present author is inclined to believe that these inconsistencies in research results are due to an overemphasis on output as a part of informal group equilibrium. Control over output is also a major weapon in the arsenal of the group engaging in conflict with management, other work groups, and even the local union. We need to know more about the *total situation* facing a given work group, including these external factors, before predicting its work performance.

The evolution of the method of *group decision* for gaining acceptance for changes in production methods and output standards is recognition of the potency of group standards. The theory presumes that leadership methods that involve the entire work group in the change process have two major advantages:

(*a*) They can eliminate the major barrier of existing group standards which militate against any change, per se.

(*b*) More positively, they commit the individual to new efforts in the context of his group membership. In a sense, the individual "promises" his fellows to accomplish some change in his behavior. Valuing the opinions of his associates, he feels bound to maintain his agreement.

Ideally the "decision" itself becomes the new standard or norm of conduct for the task group. Similarly efforts to develop plant-wide incentive systems are premised on the assumption that output and effort are dependent on the relation of the work group to the total social system of the plant.[26]

3. IMPACT ON RELATIVE COMPENSATION AND PRESTIGE RELATIONSHIPS. The fact that jobs take on a significant social meaning can be seen in the importance attached to wage differentials within the group itself. For example, we have many instances on record when management assigned an equal value to each job and the group found significant distinguishing char-

acteristics. Jobs ranked by employees as *more important or desirable* are expected to have higher earnings than jobs ranked below. The established hierarchy is reinforced over time by the gradual perfection of the correlation between esteem accorded particular workers and prestige accorded to their jobs. The "more important" workers have moved to the "more important" jobs. (The importance attached to the job is not only a function of the earning capacity but also the quality of the surroundings, equipment, the tempo of the work required, etc.) Problems occur only when changes are introduced which violate the established hierarchy.

A persistent problem has been that jobs which the group evaluates as relatively undesirable may need to be compensated at a higher rate than the "desirable" jobs, in order to attract adequate personnel. However, this differential may be contrary to the status system of the work group. Similarly, jobs evaluated (by the group) as desirable may lack characteristics which would bring them a high rating under the organization's formal ranking plan. These contradictions between the group and the organization's ranking system become more important during periods of relative labor shortage, when new recruits are difficult to obtain and when the group undergoes aging.

While these several concepts of the "informal group" are not identical, and in some cases not even complementary in their basic dimensions, they do have one common feature. All stress equilibrium, the development of a system of interpersonal relations which stabilizes the work situation (among subordinates and between superior and subordinates), an interconnected series of friendship linkages, work flow relationships, output levels, and status-income relations. The objectives are the maintenance of individual and group stability by insuring a predictability of day-to-day events and effecting a *modus vivendi* as between individual on-the-job needs and the requirements of the formal organization.

As such, the *informal group* in any and all of its meanings is serving well-recognized and accepted human needs. Its existence and continued preservation are hardly matters for surprise. The building up of routines, of established methods of accomplishing tasks, of predictable social relationships, of group roles —these are all elements of structuring which

[25] Stanley Seashore, *Group Cohesiveness in the Industrial Work Group* (Ann Arbor: Institute for Social Research, University of Michigan, 1954), p. 98.

[26] Cf. William F. Whyte and others, *Money and Motivation, op. cit.*, p. 225.

social scientists have found typical of the human group. In fact, the elements define the group.

Particularly through the setting and maintenance of group standards, informal groups have protected their memberships from possible indiscretions that might reflect adversely on them all; also they have provided support for the individual, by acting as a buffer to outside organizations and by sustaining him through the provision of *known and acceptable* routines of behaving within the face-to-face work group.

Thus the informal group, as perceived in such studies, *reacts to* the initiations of other organizations, particularly management. Being defined in equilibrium terms, the reaction is always an attempt to *regain* the previous undisturbed state—to protect work methods, social relationships, and output levels incorporated in the norms of the group.

Concerted Interest as the Focus. Workers also band together into *interest groups.* These are formed not only to protect their members but also to exploit *opportunities* to improve their relative position. Improvements can take the form of "looser standards," a preferred seniority position, more overtime, more sympathetic supervision, correction of "inequities," better equipment, and countless other less tangible goals that make the job a better one and that often serve to substitute for the more traditional kinds of promotions and mobility.

Distribution of these benefits may be much influenced by pressures of united and determined informal groups. What management feels is "equitable," just as what the union determines is in the "members' interest," is determined to a large extent by attitudes expressed by those individuals who can support their demands by group reinforcements. Those work groups which for one reason or another are unable to exercise similar power in the market place of the plant are penalized.

This is not the traditional concept of the informal group seeking conformity with established norms of conduct. These are much more "free enterprise" units, interacting in a struggle for maximization of utility. All are not equally aggressive in the struggle for self-improvement or equally well equipped with the wherewithal to do battle via the grievance procedure and the more direct pres-

sure tactics on union and management. Some lack the spirit of combat, others the means, while only a restricted few are endowed with the characteristics associated with sustained "activity" and progress toward the goals they seek.

Much of what we say implies a degree of dual or even treble *disloyalty.* Other groups, management, the union, and fellow workers, are perceived as either barriers or sources of assistance. From the point of view of the interest group, it is not high identification or loyalty that counts, but rather the right tactics in using or ignoring these other aggregations.

Thus, management is neither "good" nor "bad," liked or disliked as such. In fact, this approach suggests that it may not always be fruitful to think in pro-management and pro-union terms. It may well be that a group which is satisfied with *itself,* with its ability to protect and improve its own interests, is more favorable to *both* union and management.[27]

The results for the larger plant may not be a system tending toward equilibrium at all. We might expect that certain combinations of pressure groups actually involve the organization in increasing instability—a trend toward disequilibrium. We have observed plants where the interaction of these groups involves increasingly greater discontent, turmoil, and nonadaptive behavior. That is, their behavior tends to reinforce the very problems it was designed to solve.

Similarly, the internal structure of these groups is much more responsive to changes in its external environment than is often implied in the concept of the informal work group as a relatively durable, impervious entity. Literally overnight, technical changes introduced by management can convert a cohesive task force into a disunited, apathetic "rabble," squabbling over internal differences. Similarly, we have observed a group of weakly-united employees become a force of some magnitude in the social system of the plant within a brief period, with no changes in personnel.

The existence of these *interest group* types suggests that greater attention should be given

[27] These areas . . . [are] further elaborated in the author's . . . study, *Technology and Work Group Behavior* (Ann Arbor: Bureau of Industrial Relations, University of Michigan, 1956).

to matching supervisory "types" with group "types." We have tended to think of effective supervision as being the product of a relationship between a good leader and his group, on the assumption that the group of subordinates was a constant. In fact, variations in the effectiveness of supervision may be as much due to inherent differences in the group itself as to the leadership practices exhibited by the supervisor.

The Internal Dynamics of the Work Group

We have concentrated primarily on the relationship of the small group to the larger organization, the functions served, the "compatibilities" and "incompatibilities." Therefore, we have failed to explore much of the research that stresses the intriguing inner processes of these groups, as semiautonomous organizations. This means neglecting the processes of self-selection and exclusion developed in the work of Moreno and his colleagues in the field of sociometry. We have also omitted the prolific findings of the "group dynamics school" with its emphasis on leadership patterns and role differentiation, factors contributing to cohesiveness, and the impact of the group itself on membership perceptions and attitudes. Bales and his associates at Harvard have probed deeply into the "ebb and flow" of the problem-solving process within the group. The sequential member roles have been analyzed effectively.

For our purposes it would seem appropriate at least to make specific reference to the work of George Homans. His work places substantial emphasis on the relationship of the internal life of the group to the outside environment (primarily the attitudes, organizational structure, and work method induced by management).[28]

[28] George Homans, *The Human Group* (New York: Harcourt Brace, 1950).

"Elaborations" of behavior and sentiment induced in the small group in turn modify the larger organization. While we believe an overemphasis on the concept of *equilibrium* may be misleading, Homans' theorizing does provide a framework within which to relate the small group to the larger organization of which it is a part.

Conclusion

Clusterings of workers-on-the-job all have these characteristics: They stem from the uniqueness of individual personality, which refuses to combine into larger "wholes" without changing those entities. The sum of a group of individuals is something more than the total of the constituents; it is a new organization, because most of the members (there are significant exceptions as we have noted) obtain satisfaction in gaining acceptance as a part of the group, and the group itself wields an influence over its members. Put in another way, there are pressures toward *conformity* within the group. These pressures result in the establishment of accepted ways of living together. The way of life of the group includes a complex system of customs and rules, vested interests, and interaction patterns which govern the relationship of members of the group to one another and to the larger environment of which it is a part.

This observance of group-sanctioned behavior and attitudes "fills out" the rationally conceived organization. What is on paper an organization becomes a "living, breathing" social organism, with all the intricacies, emotions, and contradictions we associate with human relations. While no organization would long persist which did not provide its members with this opportunity for spontaneous "human relations," a major problem of the larger organization becomes one of successfully incorporating the small group.

Cosmopolitans and Locals

ALVIN W. GOULDNER

Sociologists have long since documented the empirical utility of role theory. It may be, however, that concepts stagnate when small theoretical investments yield large imperical dividends. The very currency of role concepts may invite complacency concerning their theoretical clarity.

Although the larger theory of social roles could doubtless profit from serious recasting and systematic reappraisal,[1] this is not the place for so ambitious an undertaking. All that

From *Administrative Science Quarterly*, Vol. 2, No. 3, Dec. 1957, pp. 282–292. Reprinted with permission of the publisher, Graduate School of Business and Public Administration, Cornell University.

The author wishes to thank the Social Science Research Council and the Research Board of the University of Illinois for funds which made possible completion of the analysis of the data. During the course of the research Helen P. Gouldner, Esther R. Newcomb, Henry Bobotek, and Ruth Landman assisted in various parts of the work. Carol Tucker guided the factor analysis through the Illiac. Raymond Cattell, Percy Tannenbaum, and George Suci were generous in allowing consultation with them in connection with the factor analyses. Particular thanks are due Robert K. Merton and Paul F. Lazarsfeld for a painstaking reading of a first draft and for numerous cogent suggestions. Needless to say, responsibility for all errors is entirely the author's.

[1] Such an overhauling seems well begun in the recent volume by S. F. Nadel, *Theory of Social Structure* (Glencoe, Ill., 1957). Efforts moving in a similar direction may also be found in Marion J. Levy, Jr., *The Structure of Society* (Princeton, 1952), pp. 157–166, and in Robert K. Merton, *Social Theory and Social Structure* (Glencoe, 1957), pp. 368–380, 415–420.

will be essayed here are some limited questions relating to role analysis. In particular, an attempt will be made to develop certain distinctions between what will be termed "manifest" and "latent" identities and roles.

Since role theory already encompasses a welter of concepts,[2] the introduction of new concepts requires firm justification. Concepts commend themselves to social scientists only as tools with which to resolve problematic situations. Unless this criterion is insisted upon, there inevitably eventuates a sterile formalism and a needless proliferation of neologisms. We must therefore justify the proposed distinction between manifest and latent roles by indicating the theoretic context from which it emerged and by showing its use in various studies.

Theoretical Considerations. A social role is commonly defined as a set of expectations oriented toward people who occupy a certain "position" in a social system or group. It is a rare discussion of social role that does not at some point make reference to the "position" occupied by a group member. Despite its frequent use, however, the notion of a social "position" is obscure and not likely to provide cleancut directives for social research. Often, it is used as little more than a geometrical metaphor with little value for guiding the empirical studies of behavioral scientists.

It seems that what is meant by a "position"

[2] The variety of these role concepts is well displayed in Erving Goffman, *The Presentation of Self in Everyday Life* (Edinburgh, 1956), and is discussed with great cogency in Joseph R. Gusfield, General Education as a Career, *Journal of General Education*, 10 (Jan. 1957), 37–48.

is the social identity which has been assigned to a person by members of his group. That is, group members may be regarded as acting in the following manner: (1) They observe or impute to a person certain characteristics; they observe certain aspects of his behavior or appearance which they employ as clues to enable themselves to answer the question "Who is he?" (2) These observed or imputed characteristics are then related to and interpreted in terms of a set of culturally prescribed *categories* which have been learned during the course of socialization. Conversely, the culturally learned categories focus attention upon certain aspects of the individual's behavior and appearance. (3) In this manner the individual is "pigeonholed"; that is, he is held to be a certain "type" of person, a teacher, Negro, boy, man, or woman. The process by which the individual is classified by others in his group, in terms of the culturally prescribed categories, can be called the assignment of a "social identity." The types or categories to which he has been assigned *are* his social identities. (4) When this assignment of identity is consensually or otherwise validated in the group, people then "ask themselves" what they know about such a type; they mobilize their beliefs concerning it. Corresponding to different social identities are differing sets of expectations, differing configurations of rights and obligations. In these terms, then, a social role is a shared set of expectations directed toward people who are assigned a given social identity.

Obviously the people in any one group have a variety of social identities. In a classroom, for example, there are those identified as "students," but these same people are also identified as men, women, young, mature, and so on. In the classroom situation, it is primarily their identity as students that others in the group regard as central and properly salient. It is also the expectations congruent with this salient identity that are most appropriately activated and have the fullest claim to application. But while the expectations congruent with the student identity are most institutionally relevant and legitimately mobilizable, it is clear that in various ways certain of the other identities do "intrude" and affect the group's behavior in sociologically interesting ways. For example, there is usually something happening between the students that is influenced by their sexual identities.

It is necessary to distinguish, then, between those social identities of group members which are consensually regarded as relevant to them in a given setting and those which group members define as being irrelevant, inappropriate to consider, or illegitimate to take into account. The former can be called the *manifest* social identities, the latter, the *latent* social identities. Let us be clear that "social identities," manifest or latent, are not synonymous with the concept of social status. Social identities have to do with the way in which an individual is in fact *perceived* and classified by others in terms of a system of culturally standardized categories. Social statuses, however, refer to the complex of culturally standardized categories to which individuals in a group may be assigned; they are sometimes also defined as the hierarchical "position" of the individual in relation to others, as well as the culturally prescribed expectations directed toward those in this position.[3]

[3] The terminological disparities with respect to the definition of "status" barely fall short of being appalling. Among the varying definitions which may be found are the following: (1) "a position in the social aggregate identified with a pattern of prestige symbols . . ." D. Martindale and E. D. Monachesi, *Elements of Sociology* (New York, 1951), p. 540; (2) the "successful realization of claims to prestige . . . the distribution of prestige in a society . . ." H. Gerth and C. W. Mills, *Character and Social Structure* (New York, 1953), p. 307; (3) "a measure of the worth or the importance of the role," R. Freedman, A. H. Hawley, W. S. Landecker, and H. M. Miner, eds., *Principles of Sociology* (New York, 1952), p. 148; (4) "the rank position with respect chiefly to income, prestige, and power—one or all of these," G. Knupfer in R. O'Brien, C. C. Shrag, and W. T. Martin, *Readings in General Sociology* (New York, 1951), p. 274; (5) "a collection of rights and obligations . . ." R. Linton, *The Study of Man* (New York, 1945), p. 113; (6) a "complex of mutual rights, obligations, and functions as defined by the pertinent ideal patterns," T. Parsons, *Essays in Sociological Theory Pure and Applied* (Glencoe, Ill., 1949), p. 42; (7) "a position in the general institutional system, recognized and supported by the entire society . . ." K. Davis, *Human Society* (New York, 1949), p. 87. One could go on. That these varying definitions are not necessarily contradictory is small consolation and certainly no guarantee that they all refer to the same things. Nowhere do these definitions become more opaque than when—as they fre-

Expectations which are associated with the manifest social identities can be termed the manifest social *roles*, while expectations oriented toward the latent identities can be called the latent social roles. Just as others can be oriented toward an individual's latent identities, so, too, can the individual himself be oriented to his own latent identities. This is, of course, to be expected in the light of Mead's role theory, which stresses that an individual's self-conception is a function of the judgments and orientations which significant others have toward him.

At the present time, little systematic attention is given to the functioning of either latent identities or roles. It is too easy to focus on the more evident manifest identities and roles in a group. As a result, even in a world on which Freudian theory has made its impact, many sociologists give little indication of the fact that the people they study in offices, factories, schools, or hospitals are also males and females. The sociologist's assumption often seems to be that the latent identities and roles are as irrelevant as the people whom they are studying conventionally pretend. The fact seems to be, however, that these do affect group behavior.

This is, of course, obvious from the most commonplace of questions. For example: Are the career chances of industrial workers affected by their ethnic identity? Are "old-timers" in a group more or less friendly toward each other than with those of less tenure? Do college professors take note of and behave somewhat differently toward members of the college football team who are taking their courses? Do Unitarian ministers sometimes refer to their "Jewish" parishioners?

While it is obvious that individuals in a group have a variety of social identities, and not merely one, we need conceptual tools that firmly distinguish between different types of social identities and facilitate analysis of the varying ways in which they influence group

behavior. While it is obvious that a group member may have many social identities, it needs to be stressed that not all of them are regarded as equally relevant or legitimately activated in that group. This is precisely the point to which the concepts of latent identities and roles direct attention.

This implies that when group members orient themselves to the latent identities of others in their group, they are involved in a relationship with them which is not culturally *prescribed* by the group norms governing their manifest roles. It implies, also, that they are utilizing reference persons or groups which are not culturally prescribed for those in their roles. Thus the concepts of latent identities and roles focus research on those patterns of social interaction, and lines of orientation, which are not prescribed by the group under study. It would also seem clear that latent identities and roles are important because they exert pressure upon the manifest roles, often impairing conformity with their requirements and endemically threatening the equilibrium of the manifest role system. In contrast, the concept of manifest roles focuses on the manner in which group norms yield *prescribed* similarities in the behavior and beliefs of those performing the same role.

The role of "elders" in a gerontocratic society, with the deference and respect due them by their juniors, is in these terms a manifest role. For, in this case, the rights and obligations of elders are culturally prescribed. Here to be an "elder" is a societally relevant identity. Note, however, that even in the American factory elders may also receive some special consideration and similar if not equal deference from their juniors. Here, however, the role of the elder is a latent one, being based upon an assignment of identity which is not regarded as fully legitimate or as clearly relevant in the factory, even if fully acknowledged in the larger society.

This distinction between manifest and latent roles directs us to search out and specify the latent identities, and the expectations corresponding to them, which crosscut and underlie those which are culturally prescribed in the group under study. The concept of latent roles suggests that people playing *different* manifest roles may be performing *similar* latent roles and, conversely, that those performing the *same* manifest role may be playing *different*

quently do—they refer to a status as a "position" in something. The ready familiarity of the word position seems to induce paralysis of the analytic nerve. Needless to say such terminological confusion begets efforts at neologistic clarification which may then only further becloud the field. We can only hope that this has not happened here.

latent roles. The concept of latent role may then aid in accounting for some of the differences (in behavior or belief) among those in the same manifest role or for some of the similarities among those having different manifest roles. Neither the similarities nor the differences mentioned above need be due to the intrusion of "personality" factors or other individual attributes. They may derive from the nature of the latent roles, that is, from the responses to the latent identities of group members, which yield culturally unprescribed yet structured interactions and orientations with others.

The problem that will be explored in the following analysis is whether there are latent identities and roles of general significance for the study of the modern complex organization. That is, can we discern latent identities and roles which are common to a number of different complex organizations? In this connection, we will explore the possibility that, as distinguished from and in addition to their manifest identities, members of formal organizations may have two latent social identities, here called "cosmopolitan" and "local."[4] Development of these concepts may enable organizational analysis to proceed without focusing solely on the relatively visible, culturally differentiated, manifest organizational identities and roles, but without confining analysis to an undifferentiated blob of "bureaucrats." There are of course other latent identities which are of organizational significance, and, in . . . [a second article] we shall consider a more complex structure of latent identities.

[4] These terms are taken from Robert K. Merton, "Patterns of Influence, Local and Cosmopolitan Influentials," in Merton, *op. cit.* Merton's terms are used with respect to types of roles within communities rather than in connection with formal organizations, as they are here. Moreover, Merton's focus is on the conjunction between influence and cosmopolitans-locals, whereas our analysis applies cosmopolitan and local orientations to role players apart from considerations of their influence. Note, also, the similarity between my own discussion of "latent" identities and roles and that of R. Linton, in T. N. Newcomb and E. L. Hartley, eds., *Readings in Sociology* (New York, 1947), p. 368.

Concerning Cosmopolitans and Locals

A number of prior researches have identified certain role-playing patterns which appear convergent with each other and which, further, seem to be commonly based upon those latent identities which will be called "cosmopolitans."

In a study of a factory,[5] "The General Gypsum Company," I noted a type of company executive which I called the "expert." Experts tend to be staff men who never seem to win the complete confidence of the company's highest authorities and are kept removed from the highest reaches of power. Much like staff men in other companies, these experts can advise but cannot command. They are expected to "sell" management on their plans, but cannot order them put into effect. It is widely recognized that these experts are not given the "real promotions." The expert is under pressure to forego the active pursuit of his specialty if he wishes to ascend in the company hierarchy. Among the reasons for the experts' subordination may be the fact that they are less frequently identified as "company men" than others in the executive group. The "company man," a pervasive category for the informal classification of industrial personnel, is one who is regarded as having totally committed his career aspirations to his employing company and as having indicated that he wishes to remain with it indefinitely. In effect, then, company personnel were using a criterion of "loyalty to the company" in assigning social identities to members of their organization. A company man is one who is identified as "loyal."

Experts are less likely to be identified in this manner in part because their relatively complex, seemingly mysterious skills, derived from long formal training, lead them to make a more basic commitment to their job than to the organization in which they work. Furthermore, because of their intensive technical training, experts have greater opportunities for horizontal job mobility and can fill jobs in

[5] Alvin W. Gouldner, *Patterns of Industrial Bureaucracy* (Glencoe, Ill., 1954). It may be worth mentioning that the research published here represents an effort at deliberate continuity and development of some of the conceptions that emerged in the *Patterns* volume.

many different organizations. As E. C. Hughes would say, they are more likely to be "itinerants." Consequently, experts are less likely to be committed to their employing organization than to their specialty.

The expert's skills are continually being refined and developed by professional peers outside of his employing organization. Moreover, his continued standing as a competent professional often cannot be validated by members of his own organization, since they are not knowledgeable enough about it. For these reasons, the expert is more likely than others to esteem the good opinion of professional peers elsewhere; he is disposed to seek recognition and acceptance from "outsiders." We can say that he is more likely to be oriented to a reference group composed of others not a part of his employing organization, that is, an "outer reference group."

Leonard Reissman's study of the role conceptions of government bureaucrats provides another case in point.[6] Among these is the "functional bureaucrat" who is found to be oriented toward groups outside of his employing bureaucracy and is especially concerned with securing recognition from his professional peers elsewhere. If he is an economist, for example, he wants other economists to think well of him, whether or not they are his organizational associates. The functional bureaucrats are also more likely to associate with their professional peers than with their bureaucratic colleagues. They are less likely than other types of bureaucrats to have sentiments of loyalty to their employing bureaucracy. Finally, more than other bureaucrats their satisfaction with their job depends upon the degree to which their work conforms with professional standards, and they seem to be more deeply committed to their professional skills. In short, Reissman's "functional bureaucrat" is much the same as our "expert," insofar as both tend to manifest lesser organizational loyalty, deeper job commitment, and an outer reference group orientation, as compared with their colleagues.

A third study, by Vernon J. Bentz,[7] of a city college faculty, again indicates the interrelationship of these variables and suggests their relevance in another organizational setting. Bentz divided the college faculty into two groups, those who publish much and those publishing little or nothing. Publication as such is not of course theoretically interesting, but it becomes so if taken as an index of something else. The difficulty is that it is an ambiguous index. Within limits, it seems reasonable to treat it as an index of the degree of commitment to professional skills. However, "high" publication might also indicate a desire to communicate with other, like professionals in different organizations. The high publisher must also take cognizance of the publications which others elsewhere are producing. Thus high publication may also be an index of an outer reference group orientation. High publishers also tend to deemphasize the importance which their own college department had to them and to express the feeling that it had comparatively little control over them. This might be taken to imply a lower degree of commitment or loyalty to that particular group.

Although Bentz's research findings are less direct than the others examined, they do seem to point in the same direction, indicating similarities between the high publisher, the functional bureaucrat, and the expert. They were also particularly useful to my own later study of a college by suggesting indices for some of the significant variables.

These three cases suggested the importance of three variables for analyzing latent identities in organizations: (1) loyalty to the employing organization, (2) commitment to specialized or professional skills, and (3) reference group orientations. Considerations of space do not permit this to be developed here, but each of these studies also found role-playing patterns polar to those discussed. This led us to hypothesize that *two* latent organizational identities could be found. These were:

1. COSMOPOLITANS: those low on loyalty to the employing organization, high on commitment to specialized role skills, and likely to use an outer reference group orientation.

2. LOCALS: those high on loyalty to the employing organization, low on commitment to specialized role skills, and likely to use an inner reference group orientation.

[6] Leonard Reissman, A Study of Role Conceptions in Bureaucracy, *Social Forces*, 27 (1949), 305–310.
[7] Vernon J. Bentz, "A Study of Leadership in a Liberal Arts College" (Columbus, O.: Ohio State University, 1950; mimeo.).

Cosmopolitans and locals are regarded as *latent* identities because they involve criteria which are not fully institutionalized as bases for classifying people in the modern organization, though they are in fact often used as such. For example, "loyalty" usually tends to be taken for granted and is, under normal circumstances, a latent social identity in a rational bureaucracy. For example, it may be preferred, but it is not usually prescribed, that one should be a "company man." While loyalty criteria do become activated at irregular intervals, as, for example, at occasional "testimonial dinners" or during outbursts of organizational conflict and crisis, other criteria for identifying personnel are routinely regarded as more fully legitimate and relevant. For example, skill and competence or training and experience are usually the publicly utilized standards in terms of which performances are judged and performers identified.

While organizations are in fact concerned with the loyalty of their personnel, as indicated by the ritual awarding of gold watches for lengthy years of "faithful service," the dominant organizational orientation toward rationality imposes a ban of pathos on the use of loyalty criteria. Organizational concern with the skill and competence of its personnel exerts pressure against evaluating them in terms of loyalty. Indeed, one of the major dilemmas of the modern organization is the tension between promotions based on skill versus promotions based on seniority, the latter often being an informal index of loyalty. Despite the devotion to rational criteria in the modern organization, however, considerations of loyalty can never be entirely excluded and loyalty criteria frequently serve as a basis for assigning latent identities. In some measure, loyalty to the organization often implies the other two criteria, (1) a willingness to limit or relinquish the commitment to a specialized professional task and (2) a dominant career orientation to the employing organization as a reference group. This linking of organizational criteria is only barely understood by the group members. Thus cosmopolitans and locals are also latent identities because the *conjunction* of criteria involved is not normatively prescribed by the organization.

Each of the other two criteria involved may, however, become an independent basis for assigning organizational identities. For example, in the modern organization people tend to be distinguished in terms of their commitment to their work as well as to their employing organization. A distinction is commonly made between the "cynics" and "clock watchers" or those who are just "doing time," on the one hand, and those who "believe in" or are "fired up" by their task.[8] This distinction is based on the common, if not entirely documented, assumption that the latter are likely to be superior role performers.

It is, however, relatively difficult to know how a person feels about his job; it is easier, and is therefore frequently regarded as more important, to know how he *does* it. Performance rather than belief more commonly becomes the formal criterion for assigning organizational identity. Nonetheless, belief is never totally neglected or discarded but tends, instead, to become a basis on which more latent identities are assigned.

While the significance of reference group orientation varies from one type of organization to another, it remains a commonplace if somewhat subtle criterion for assigning latent identities. In colleges, groups distinguish between "insiders" and "outsiders," sometimes using such informal indices as whether or not individuals orient themselves to certain "schools of thought" or people, share familiarity with a prestigious literature, or utilize certain styles of research. In trade unions, different identities may be assigned to those who orient themselves to political movements or to professional peers in other types of organizations and to those who are primarily oriented to the more limited goals of the union—the "union men." Such identities are not fully institutionalized or legitimated, although they may obliquely impinge on promotions, election to office, and evaluation of performance.

[8] For a broader discussion of this problem, see Howard S. Becker and Blanche Geer, "The Fate of Idealism in Medical School" (unpublished paper, available from authors at Community Studies, Inc., Kansas City, Mo.).

Social Control in the Newsroom:

A Functional Analysis

WARREN BREED

Top leaders in formal organizations are makers of policy, but they must also secure and maintain conformity to that policy at lower levels. The situation of the newspaper publisher is a case in point. As owner or representative of ownership, he has the nominal right to set the paper's policy and see that staff activities are coordinated so that the policy is enforced. In actuality the problem of control is less simple, as the literature of "human relations" and informal group studies and of the professions [1] suggests.

Ideally, there would be no problem of either "control" or "policy" on the newspaper in a full democracy. The only controls would be the nature of the event and the reporter's effective ability to describe it. In practice, we find the publisher does set news policy, and this policy is usually followed by members of his staff. Conformity is *not* automatic, however, for three reasons: (1) the existence of ethical journalistic norms; (2) the fact that staff subordinates (reporters, etc.) tend to have more "liberal" attitudes (and therefore perceptions) than the publisher and could invoke the norms

to justify anti-policy writing; and (3) the ethical taboo preventing the publisher from commanding subordinates to follow policy. How policy comes to be maintained, and where it is bypassed, is the subject of this paper.

Several definitions are required at this point. As to personnel, "newsmen" can be divided into two main categories. "Executives" include the publisher and his editors. "Staffers" are reporters, rewrite men, copy readers, etc. In between there may be occasional city editors or wire editors who occupy an interstitial status. "Policy" may be defined as the more or less consistent orientation shown by a paper, not only in its editorial but in its news columns and headlines as well, concerning selected issues and events. "Slanting" almost never means prevarication. Rather, it involves omission, differential selection and preferential placement, such as "featuring" a pro-policy item, "burying" an anti-policy story in an inside page, etc. "Professional norms" are of two types: technical norms deal with the operations of efficient news gathering, writing, and editing; ethical norms embrace the newsman's obligation to his readers and to his craft and include such ideals as responsibility, impartiality, accuracy, fair play, and objectivity.[2]

Every newspaper has a policy, admitted or

From *Social Forces*, Vol. 33, May 1955, pp. 326–335. Reprinted with permission of the author and the publisher, University of North Carolina Press. Copyright 1955, University of North Carolina Press.

[1] See, for instance, F. J. Roethlisberger and William J. Dickson, *Management and the Worker* (Cambridge: Harvard University Press, 1947); and Logan Wilson, *The Academic Man* (New York: Oxford University Press, 1942).

[2] The best-known formal code is The Canons of Journalism, of the American Society of Newspaper Editors. See Wilbur Schramm (ed.), *Mass Communications* (Urbana: University of Illinois Press, 1949), pp. 236–38.

not.[3] One paper's policy may be pro-Republican, cool to labor, antagonistic to the school board, etc. The principal areas of policy are politics, business, and labor; much of it stems from considerations of class. Policy is manifested in "slanting." Just what determines any publisher's policy is a large question and will not be discussed here. Certainly, however, the publisher has much say (often in veto form) in both long-term and immediate policy decisions (which party to support, whether to feature or bury a story of imminent labor trouble, how much free space to give "news" of advertisers' doings, etc.). Finally, policy is covert, due to the existence of ethical norms of journalism; policy often contravenes these norms. No executive is willing to risk embarrassment by being accused of open commands to slant a news story.

While policy is set by the executives, it is clear that they cannot personally gather and write the news by themselves. They must delegate these tasks to staffers, and at this point the attitudes or interests of staffers may—and often do—conflict with those of the executives.[4] Of 72 staffers interviewed, 42 showed that they held more liberal views than those contained in their publisher's policy; 27 held similar views, and only 3 were more conservative. Similarly, only 17 of 61 staffers said they were Republicans.[5] The discrepancy is more

acute when age (and therefore years of newspaper experience) is held constant. Of the 46 staffers under 35 years of age, 34 showed more liberal orientations; older men had apparently "mellowed." It should be noted that data as to intensity of attitudes are lacking. Some staffers may disagree with policy so mildly that they conform and feel no strain. The present essay is pertinent only insofar as dissident newsmen are forced to make decisions from time to time about their relationship to policy.[6]

We will now examine more closely the workings of the newspaper staff. The central question will be: How is policy maintained, despite the fact that it often contravenes journalistic norms, that staffers often personally disagree with it, and that executives cannot legitimately command that it be followed? The frame of reference will be that of functional analysis, as embodied in Merton's paradigm.[7]

The present data come from the writer's newspaper experience and from intensive interviews with some 120 newsmen, mostly in the northeastern quarter of the country. The sample was not random and no claim is made for representativeness, but on the other hand no paper was selected or omitted purposely and in no case did a newsman refuse the request that he be interviewed. The newspapers where chosen to fit a "middle-sized" group,

---

[3] It is extremely difficult to measure the extent of objectivity or bias. One recent attempt is reported in Nathan B. Blumberg, One-Party Press? (Lincoln: University of Nebraska Press, 1954), which gives a news count for 35 papers' performance in the 1952 election campaign. He concluded that 18 of the papers showed "no evidence of partiality," 11 showed "no conclusive evidence of partiality," and 6 showed partiality. His interpretations, however, are open to argument. A different interpretation could conclude that while about 16 showed little or no partiality, the rest did. It should be noted, too, that there are different areas of policy depending on local conditions. The chief difference occurs in the deep South, where frequently there is no "Republican" problem and no "union" problem over which the staff can be divided. Color becomes the focus of policy.

[4] This condition, pointed out in a lecture by Paul F. Lazarsfeld, formed the starting point for the present study.

[5] Similar findings were made about Washington correspondents in Leo C. Rosten, The Washington Correspondents (New York: Harcourt, Brace,

1937). Less ideological conflict was found in two other studies: Francis V. Prugger, "Social Composition and Training of the Milwaukee Journal News Staff," Journalism Quarterly, 18 (Sept. 1941), pp. 231–44, and Charles E. Swanson, The Mid-City Daily (Ph.D. dissertation, State University of Iowa, 1948). Possible reasons for the gap is that both papers studied were perhaps above average in objectivity; executives were included with staffers in computations; and some staffers were doubtless included who did not handle policy news.

[6] It is not being argued that "liberalism" and objectivity are synonymous. A liberal paper (e.g., PM) can be biased too, but it is clear that few liberal papers exist among the many conservative ones. It should also be stressed that much news is not concerned with policy and is therefore probably unbiased.

[7] Robert K. Merton, Social Theory and Social Structure (Glencoe: Free Press, 1949), esp pp. 49–61. Merton's elements will not be explicitly referred to but his principal requirements are discussed at various points.

defined as those with 10,000 to 100,000 daily circulation. Interviews average well over an hour in duration.[8]

There is an "action" element inherent in the present subject—the practical democratic need for "a free and responsible press" to inform citizens about current issues. Much of the criticism of the press stems from the slanting induced by the bias of the publisher's policy.[9] This criticism is often directed at flagrant cases such as the Hearst press, the *Chicago Tribune* and New York tabloids, but also applies, in lesser degree, to the more conventional press. The description of mechanisms of policy maintenance may suggest why this criticism is often fruitless, at least in the short-run sense.

How the Staffer Learns Policy

The first mechanism promoting conformity is the "socialization" of the staffer with regard to the norms of his job. When the new reporter starts work he is not told what policy is. Nor is he ever told. This may appear strange, but interview after interview confirmed the condition. The standard remark was "Never, in my —— years on this paper, have I ever been told how to slant a story." No paper in the survey had a "training" program for its new men; some issue a "style" book, but this deals with literary style, not policy. Further, newsmen are busy and have little time for recruit training. Yet all but the newest staffers know what policy is.[10] On

[*] The data are taken from Warren Breed, The Newspaperman, News and Society (Ph.D. dissertation, Columbia University, 1952). Indebtedness is expressed to William L. Kolb and Robert C. Stone, who read the present manuscript and provided valuable criticisms and suggestions.

[9] For a summary description of this criticism, see Commission on the Freedom of the Press, *A Free and Responsible Press* (Chicago: University of Chicago Press, 1947), chap. 4.

[10] While the concept of policy is crucial to this analysis, it is not to be assumed that newsmen discuss it fully. Some do not even use the word in discussing how their paper is run. To this extent, policy is a latent phenomenon; either the staffer has no reason to contemplate policy or he chooses to avoid so doing. It may be that one strength of policy is that it has become no more manifest to the staffers who follow it.

being asked, they say they learn it "by osmosis." Sociologically, this means they become socialized and "learn the ropes" like a neophyte in any subculture. Basically, the learning of policy is a process by which the recruit discovers and internalizes the rights and obligations of his status and its norms and values. He learns to anticipate what is expected of him so as to win rewards and avoid punishments. Policy is an important element of the newsroom norms, and he learns it in much the following way.

The staffer reads his own paper every day; some papers *require* this. It is simple to diagnose the paper's characteristics. Unless the staffer is naive or unusually independent, he tends to fashion his own stories after others he sees in the paper. This is particularly true of the newcomer. The news columns and editorials are a guide to the local norms. Thus a southern reporter notes that Republicans are treated in a "different" way in his paper's news columns than Democrats. The news about whites and Negroes is also of a distinct sort. Should he then write about one of these groups, his story will tend to reflect what he has come to define as standard procedure.

Certain editorial actions taken by editors and older staffers also serve as controlling guides. "If things are blue-penciled consistently," one reporter said, "you learn he [the editor] has a prejudice in that regard."[11] Similarly an executive may occasionally reprimand a staffer for policy violation. From our evidence, the reprimand is frequently oblique, due to the covert nature of policy, but learning occurs nevertheless. One staffer learned much through a series of incidents:

> I heard [a union] was going out on strike, so I kept on it; then the boss said something about it, and well—I took the hint and we had less coverage of the strike forming. It was easier that way. We lost the story, but what can you do?

> We used a yarn on a firm that was coming to town, and I got dragged out of bed for that. The boss is interested in this industrial stuff—we have to clear it all through

[11] Note that such executives' actions as blue-penciling play not only the manifest function of preparing the story for publication but also the latent one of steering the future action of the staffer.

him. He's an official in the Chamber. So
. . . after a few times, it's irritating, so I get
fed up. I try to figure out what will work
best. I learn to try and guess what the boss
will want.

In fairness it should be noted that this particular publisher was one of the most dicta-
torial encountered in the study. The pattern
of control through reprimand, however, was
found consistently. Another staffer wrote, on
his own initiative, a series about discrimination against Jews at hotel resorts.

> It was the old "Gentlemen's Agreement"
> stuff, documented locally. The boss called
> me in . . . didn't like the stuff . . . the
> series never appeared. You start to get the
> idea. . . .

Note that the boss does not "command";
the direction is more subtle. Also, it seems that
most policy indications from executives are
negative. They veto by a nod of the head, as
if to say, "Please don't rock the boat." Exceptions occur in the "campaign" story, which
will be discussed later. It is also to be noted
that punishment is implied if policy is not
followed.

Staffers also obtain guidance from their
knowledge of the characteristics, interests, and
affiliations of their executives. This knowledge can be gained in several ways. One is
gossip. A reporter said:

> Do we gossip about the editors? Several
> of us used to meet—somewhere off the
> beaten path—over a beer—and talk for an
> hour. We'd rake 'em over the coals.

Another point of contact with executives is
the news conference (which on middle-sized
papers is seldom *called* a news conference),
wherein the staffer outlines his findings and
executives discuss how to shape the story. The
typical conference consists of two persons,
the reporter and the city editor, and can
amount to no more than a few words. (Reporter: "One hurt in auto accident uptown."
City editor: "Okay, keep it short.") If policy
is at stake, the conference may involve several
executives and require hours of consideration.
From such meetings, the staffer can gain insight through what is said and what is not
said by executives. It is important to say here
that policy is not stated explicitly in the news

conference nor elsewhere, with few exceptions. The news conference actually deals
mostly with journalistic matters, such as reliability of information, newsworthiness, possible "angles," and other news tactics.

Three other channels for learning about executives are house organs (printed for the staff
by syndicates and larger papers), observing
the executive as he meets various leaders and
hearing him voice an opinion. One staffer
could not help but gain an enduring impression of his publisher's attitudes in this incident:

> I can remember [him] saying on election
> night [1948], when it looked like we had a
> Democratic majority in both houses, "My
> God, this means we'll have a labor govern-
> ment." (Q: How did he say it?) He had a
> real note of alarm in his voice; you couldn't
> miss the point that he'd prefer the Republi-
> cans.

It will be noted that in speaking of "how"
the staffer learns policy, there are indications
also as to "why" he follows it.

Reasons for Conforming to Policy

There is no one factor which creates con-
formity-mindedness, unless we resort to a
summary term such as "institutionalized statuses" or "structural roles." Particular factors
must be sought in particular cases. The staffer
must be seen in terms of his status and aspirations, the structure of the newsroom organization and of the larger society. He also must be
viewed with reference to the operations he
performs through his workday, and their consequences for him. The following six reasons
appear to stay the potentially intransigent
staffer from acts of deviance—often, if not
always.[12]

---

[12] Two cautions are in order here. First, it will be
recalled that we are discussing not all news, but
only policy news. Secondly, we are discussing only
staffers who are potential non-conformers. Some
agree with policy; some have no views on policy
matters; others do not write policy stories. Furthermore, there are strong forces in American
society which cause many individuals to choose
harmonious adjustment (conformity) in any situation, regardless of the imperatives. See Erich
Fromm, *Escape From Freedom* (New York:

1. *Institutional Authority and Sanctions.* The publisher ordinarily owns the paper and from a purely business standpoint has the right to expect obedience of his employees. He has the power to fire or demote for transgressions. This power, however, is diminished markedly in actuality by three facts. First, the newspaper is not conceived as a purely business enterprise, due to the protection of the First Amendment and a tradition of professional public service. Secondly, firing is a rare phenomenon on newspapers. For example, one editor said he had fired two men in 12 years; another could recall four firings in his 15 years on that paper. Thirdly, there are severance pay clauses in contracts with the American Newspaper Guild (CIO). The only effective causes for firing are excessive drunkenness, sexual dalliance, etc. Most newspaper unemployment apparently comes from occasional economy drives on large papers and from total suspensions of publication. Likewise, only one case of demotion was found in the survey. It is true, however, that staffers still fear punishment; the myth has the errant star reporter taken off murders and put on obituaries—"the Chinese torture chamber" of the newsroom. Fear of sanctions, rather than their invocation, is a reason for conformity, but not as potent a one as would seem at first glance.

Editors, for their part, can simply ignore stories which might create deviant actions, and when this is impossible, can assign the story to a "safe" staffer. In the infrequent case that an anti-policy story reaches the city desk, the story is changed; extraneous reasons, such as the pressure of time and space, are given for the change.[13] Finally, the editor may contribute to the durability of policy by insulating the publisher from policy discussions. He may reason that the publisher would be embarrassed to hear of conflict over policy and the resulting bias, and spare him the resulting uneasiness; thus the policy remains not only covert but undiscussed and therefore unchanged.[14]

2. *Feelings of Obligation and Esteem for Superiors.* The staffer may feel obliged to the paper for having hired him. Respect, admiration and gratitude may be felt for certain editors who have perhaps schooled him, "stood up for him," or supplied favors of a more paternalistic sort. Older staffers who have served as models for newcomers or who have otherwise given aid and comfort are due return courtesies. Such obligations and warm personal sentiments toward superiors play a strategic role in the pull to conformity.

3. *Mobility Aspirations.* In response to a question about ambition, all the younger staffers showed wishes for status achievement. There was agreement that bucking policy constituted a serious bar to this goal. In practice, several respondents noted that a good tactic toward advancement was to get "big" stories on Page One; this automatically means no tampering with policy. Further, some staffers see newspapering as a "stepping stone" job to more lucrative work: public relations, advertising, free-lancing, etc. The reputation for troublemaking would inhibit such climbing.

A word is in order here about chances for upward mobility. Of 51 newsmen aged 35 or more, 32 were executives. Of 50 younger men, 6 had reached executive posts and others were on their way up with such jobs as wire editors, political reporters, etc. All but five of these young men were college graduates, as against just half of their elders. Thus there is no evidence of a "break in the skill hierarchy" among newsmen.

4. *Absence of Conflicting Group Allegiance.* The largest formal organization of staffers is the American Newspaper Guild. The Guild, much as it might wish to, has not interfered with internal matters such as policy. It has

---

Farrar and Rinehart, 1941), and David Riesman, *The Lonely Crowd* (New Haven: Yale, 1950).
[13] Excellent illustration of this tactic is given in the novel by an experienced newspaperwoman: Margaret Long, *Affair of the Heart* (New York: Random House, 1953), chap. 10. This chapter describes the framing of a Negro for murder in a middle-sized southern city, and the attempt of a reporter to tell the story objectively.

[14] The insulation of one individual or group from another is a good example of social (as distinguished from psychological) mechanisms to reduce the likelihood of conflict. Most of the factors inducing conformity could likewise be viewed as social mechanisms. See Talcott Parsons and Edward A. Shils, "Values, Motives and Systems of Action," in Parsons and Shils (eds.), *Toward a General Theory of Action* (Cambridge: Harvard University Press, 1951), pp. 223–30.

stressed business unionism and political interests external to the newsroom. As for informal groups, there is no evidence available that a group of staffers has ever "ganged up" on policy.

5. *The Pleasant Nature of the Activity.* IN-GROUPNESS IN THE NEWSROOM. The staffer has a low formal status vis-à-vis executives, but he is not treated as a "worker." Rather, he is a co-worker with executives; the entire staff cooperates congenially on a job they all like and respect: getting the news. The newsroom is a friendly, first-namish place. Staffers discuss stories with editors on a give-and-take basis. Top executives with their own offices sometimes come out and sit in on newsroom discussions.[15]

REQUIRED OPERATIONS ARE INTERESTING. Newsmen like their work. Few voiced complaints when given the opportunity to gripe during interviews. The operations required—witnessing, interviewing, briefly mulling the meanings of events, checking facts, writing—are not onerous.

NON-FINANCIAL PERQUISITES. These are numerous: the variety of experience, eye-witnessing significant and interesting events, being the first to know, getting "the inside dope" denied laymen, meeting and sometimes befriending notables and celebrities (who are well-advised to treat newsmen with deference). Newsmen are close to big decisions without having to make them; they touch power without being responsible for its use. From talking with newsmen and reading their books, one gets the impression that they are

proud of being newsmen.[16] There are tendencies to exclusiveness within news ranks, and intimations that such near out-groups as radio newsmen are entertainers, not real newsmen. Finally, there is the satisfaction of being a member of a live-wire organization dealing with important matters. The newspaper is an "institution" in the community. People talk about it and quote it; its big trucks whiz through town; its columns carry the tidings from big and faraway places, with pictures.

Thus, despite his relatively low pay, the staffer feels, for all these reasons, an integral part of a going concern. His job morale is high. Many newsmen could qualify for jobs paying more money in advertising and public relations, but they remain with the newspaper.

6. *News Becomes a Value.* Newsmen define their job as producing a certain quantity of what is called "news" every 24 hours. This is to be produced *even though nothing much has happened.* News is a continuous challenge, and meeting this challenge is the newsman's job. He is rewarded for fulfilling this, his manifest function. A consequence of this focus on news as a central value is the shelving of a strong interest in objectivity at the point of policy conflict. Instead of mobilizing their efforts to establish objectivity over policy as the criterion for performance, their energies are channeled into getting more news. The demands of competition (in cities where there are two or more papers) and speed enhance this focus. Newsmen do talk about ethics, objectivity, and the relative worth of various papers, but not when there is news to get. News comes first, and there is always news to get.[17] They are not rewarded for analyzing

---

[15] Further indication that the staffer-executive relationship is harmonious came from answers to the question, "Why do you think newspapermen are thought to be cynical?" Staffers regularly said that newsmen are cynical because they get close enough to stark reality to see the ills of their society, and the imperfections of its leaders and officials. Only two, of 40 staffers, took the occasion to criticize their executives and the enforcement of policy. This displacement, or lack of strong feelings against executives, can be interpreted to bolster the hypothesis of staff solidarity. (It further suggests that newsmen tend to analyze their society in terms of personalities, rather than institutions comprising a social and cultural system.)

[16] There is a sizeable myth among newsmen about the attractiveness of their calling. For example, the story: "Girl: 'My, you newspapermen must have a fascinating life. You meet such interesting people.' Reporter: 'Yes, and most of them are newspapermen.'" For a further discussion, see Breed, *op. cit.*, chap. 17.

[17] This is a variant of the process of "displacement of goals," newsmen turning to "getting news" rather than to seeking data which will enlighten and inform their readers. The dysfunction is implied in the nation's need not for more news but for better news—quality rather than quantity. See Merton, *op. cit.*, "Bureaucratic Structure and Personality," pp. 154–5.

the social structure, but for getting news. It would seem that this instrumental orientation diminishes their moral potential. A further consequence of this pattern is that the harmony between staffers and executives is cemented by their common interest in news. Any potential conflict between the two groups, such as slowdowns occurring among informal work groups in industry, would be dissipated to the extent that news is a positive value. The newsroom solidarity is thus reinforced.

The six factors promote policy conformity. To state more exactly how policy is maintained would be difficult in view of the many variables contained in the system. The process may be somewhat better understood, however, with the introduction of one further concept—the reference group.[18] The staffer, especially the new staffer, identifies himself through the existence of these six factors with the executives and veteran staffers. Although not yet one of them, he shares their norms, and thus his performance comes to resemble theirs. He conforms to the norms of policy rather than to whatever personal beliefs he brought to the job, or to ethical ideals. All six of these factors function to encourage reference group formation. Where the allegiance is directed toward legitimate authority, that authority has only to maintain the equilibrium within limits by the prudent distribution of rewards and punishments. The reference group itself, which has as its "magnet" element the elite of executives and old staffers, is unable to change policy to a marked degree because first, it is the group charged with carrying out policy, and second, because the policy maker, the publisher, is often insulated on the delicate issue of policy.

In its own way, each of the six factors con-

[18] Whether group members acknowledge it or not, "if a person's attitudes are influenced by a set of norms which he assumes that he shares with other individuals, those individuals constitute for him a reference group." Theodore M. Newcomb, *Social Psychology* (New York: Dryden, 1950), p. 225. Williams states that reference group formation may segment large organizations; in the present case, the reverse is true, the loyalty of subordinates going to their "friendly" superiors and to the discharge of technical norms such as getting news. See Robin M. Williams, *American Society* (New York: Knopf, 1951), p. 476.

tributes to the formation of reference group behavior. There is almost no firing, hence a steady expectation of continued employment. Subordinates tend to esteem their bosses, so a convenient model group is present. Mobility aspirations (when held within limits) are an obvious promoter of inter-status bonds as is the absence of conflicting group loyalties with their potential harvest of cross pressures. The newsroom atmosphere is charged with the related factors of in-groupness and pleasing nature of the work. Finally, the agreement among newsmen that their job is to fasten upon the news, seeing it as a value in itself, forges a bond across status lines.

As to the six factors, five appear to be relatively constant, occurring on all papers studied. The varying factor is the second: obligation and esteem held by staffers for executive and older staffers. On some papers, this obligation-esteem entity was found to be larger than on others. Where it was large, the paper appeared to have two characteristics pertinent to this discussion. First, it did a good conventional job of news-getting and news-publishing, and second, it had little difficulty over policy. With staffers drawn toward both the membership and the reference groups, organization was efficient. Most papers are like this. On the few smaller papers where executives and older staffers are not respected, morale is spotty; staffers withhold enthusiasm from their stories, they cover their beats perfunctorily, they wish for a job on a better paper, and they are apathetic and sometimes hostile to policy. Thus the obligation-esteem factor seems to be the active variable in determining not only policy conformity, but morale and good news performance as well.

Situations Permitting Deviation

Thus far it would seem that the staffer enjoys little "freedom of the press." To show that this is an oversimplification, and more important, to suggest a kind of test for our hypothesis about the strength of policy, let us ask: "What happens when a staffer *does* submit an anti-policy story?" We know that this happens infrequently, but what follows in these cases?

The process of learning policy crystallizes into a process of social control, in which deviations are punished (usually gently) by reprimand, cutting one's story, the withholding of friendly comment by an executive, etc. For example, it is punishment for a staffer when the city editor waves a piece of his copy at him and says, "Joe, don't *do* that when you're writing about the mayor." In an actual case, a staffer acting as wire editor was demoted when he neglected to feature a story about a "sacred cow" politician on his paper. What can be concluded is that when an executive sees a clearly anti-policy item, he blue-pencils it, and this constitutes a lesson for the staffer. Rarely does the staffer persist in violating policy; no such case appeared in all the interviews. Indeed, the best-known cases of firing for policy reasons—Ted O. Thackrey and Leo Huberman—occurred on liberal New York City dailies, and Thackrey was an editor, not a staffer.

Now and then cases arise in which a staffer finds his anti-policy stories printed. There seems to be no consistent explanation for this, except to introduce two more specific subjects dealing first, with the staffer's career line, and second, with particular empirical conditions associated with the career line. We can distinguish three stages through which the staffer progresses. First, there is the cub stage, the first few months or years in which the new man learns techniques and policy. He writes short, non-policy stories, such as minor accidents, meeting activity, the weather, etc. The second, or "wiring-in" stage, sees the staffer continuing to assimilate the newsroom values and to cement informal relationships. Finally there is the "star" or "veteran" stage, in which the staffer typically defines himself as a full, responsible member of the group, sees its goals as his, and can be counted on to handle policy sympathetically.[19]

To further specify the conformity-deviation problem, it must be understood that newspapering is a relatively complex activity. The newsman is responsible for a range of skills and judgments which are matched only in the professional and entrepeneurial fields. Oversimplifications about policy rigidity can be avoided if we ask, "*Under what conditions* can the staffer defy or by-pass policy?" We have already seen that staffers are free to argue news decisions with executives in brief "news conferences," but the arguments generally revolve around points of "newsiness," rather than policy as such.[20] Five factors appear significant in the area of the reporter's power to by-pass policy.

1. The norms of policy are not always entirely clear, just as many norms are vague and unstructured. Policy is covert by nature and has large scope. The paper may be Republican, but standing only lukewarm for Republican Candidate A who may be too "liberal" or no friend of the publisher. Policy, if worked out explicitly, would have to include motivations, reasons, alternatives, historical developments, and other complicating material. Thus a twilight zone permitting a range of deviation appears.[21]

2. Executives may be ignorant of particular facts, and staffers who do the leg (and telephone) work to gather news can use their superior knowledge to subvert policy. On grounds of both personal belief and professional codes, the staffer has the option of selection at many points. He can decide whom to interview and whom to ignore, what questions to ask, which quotations to note, and on writing the story which items to feature (with an eye toward the headline), which to bury, and in general what tone to give the several possible elements of the story.

3. In addition to the "squeeze" tactic exploiting executives' ignorance of minute facts, the "plant" may be employed. Although a paper's policy may proscribe a certain issue from becoming featured, a staffer, on getting a good story about that issue may "plant" it in another paper or wire service through a

---

[19] Does the new staffer, fresh from the ideals of college, really "change his attitudes"? It would seem that attitudes about socio-economic affairs need not be fixed, but are capable of shifting with the situation. There are arguments for and against any opinion; in the atmosphere of the newsroom the arguments "for" policy decisions are made to sound adequate, especially as these are evoked by the significant others in the system.

[20] The fullest treatment of editor-reporter conferences appears in Swanson, *op. cit.*

[21] Related to the fact that policy is vague is the more general postulate that executives seek to avoid formal issues and the possibly damaging disputes arising therefrom. See Chester I. Barnard, *Functions of the Executive* (Cambridge: Harvard University Press, 1947).

friendly staffer and submit it to his own editor, pleading the story is now too big to ignore.

4. It is possible to classify news into four types on the basis of source of origination. These are: the policy or campaign story, the assigned story, the beat story, and the story initiated by the staffer. The staffer's autonomy is larger with the latter than the former types. With the campaign story (build new hospital, throw rascals out, etc.), the staffer is working directly under executives and has little leeway. An assigned story is handed out by the city editor and thus will rarely hit policy head on, although the staffer has some leverage of selection. When we come to the beat story, however, it is clear that the function of the reporter changes. No editor comes between him and his beat (police department, city hall, etc.), thus the reporter gains the "editor" function. It is he who, to a marked degree, can select which stories to pursue, which to ignore. Several cases developed in interviews of beat men who smothered stories they knew would provide fuel for policy—policy they personally disliked or thought injurious to the professional code. The cooperation of would-be competing reporters is essential, of course. The fourth type of story is simply one which the staffer originates, independent of assignment or beat. All respondents, executives and staffers, averred that any employee was free to initiate stories. But equally regularly, they acknowledged that the opportunity was not often assumed. Staffers were already overloaded with beats, assignments, and routine coverage, and besides, rewards for initiated stories were meager or non-existent unless the initiated story confirmed policy. Yet this area promises much, should staffers pursue their advantage. The outstanding case in the present study concerned a well-educated, enthusiastic reporter on a conventional daily just north of the Mason-Dixon line. Entirely on his own, he consistently initiated stories about Negroes and Negro-white relations, "making" policy where only void had existed. He worked overtime to document and polish the stories; his boss said he didn't agree with the idea but insisted on the reporter's right to publish them.

5. Staffers with "star" status can transgress policy more easily than cubs. This differential privilege of status was encountered on several papers. An example would be Walter Winchell

during the Roosevelt administration, who regularly praised the president while the policy of his boss, Mr. Hearst, was strongly critical of the regime. A *New York Times* staffer said he doubted that any copy reader on the paper would dare change a word of the copy of Meyer Berger, the star feature writer.

These five factors indicate that given certain conditions, the controls making for policy conformity can be bypassed. These conditions exist not only within the newsroom and the news situation but within the staffer as well; they will be exploited only if the staffer's attitudes permit. There are some limitations, then, on the strength of the publisher's policy.

Before summarizing, three additional requirements of Merton's functional paradigm must be met. These are statements of the consequences of the pattern, of available alternative modes of behavior, and a validation of the analysis.

Consequences of the Pattern

To the extent that policy is maintained, the paper keeps publishing smoothly as seen both from the newsroom and from the outside, which is no mean feat if we visualize the country with no press at all. This is the most general consequence. There are several special consequences. For the society as a whole, the existing system of power relationships is maintained. Policy usually protects property and class interests, and thus the strata and groups holding these interests are better able to retain them. For the larger community, much news is printed objectively, allowing for opinions to form openly, but policy news may be slanted or buried so that some important information is denied the citizenry. (This is the dysfunction widely scored by critics.) For the individual readers, the same is true. For the executives, their favorable statuses are maintained, with perhaps occasional touches of guilt over policy. For newsmen, the consequences are the same as for executives. For more independent, critical staffers, there can be several modes of adaptation. At the extremes, the pure conformist can deny the conflict, the confirmed deviate can quit the newspaper business. Otherwise, the adaptations seem to run in this way: (1) Keep on the job but blunt the sharp corners of policy where possible ("If I wasn't here the next guy would let *all* that crap go through . . ."); (2) Attempt to repress the conflict amorally and anti-intellectually ("What the hell, it's only a job; take your pay and forget it . . ."); (3) Attempt to compensate, by "taking it out" in other contexts: drinking, writing "the truth" for liberal publications, working with action programs, the Guild and otherwise. All of these adjustments were found in the study. As has been suggested, one of the main compensations for all staffers is simply to find justification in adhering to "good news practice."

Possible Alternatives and Change

A functional analysis, designed to locate sources of persistence of a pattern, can also indicate points of strain at which a structural change may occur. For example, the popular recipe for eliminating bias at one time was to diminish advertisers' power over the news. This theory having proved unfruitful, critics more recently have fastened upon the publisher as the point at which change must be initiated. Our analysis suggests that this is a valid approach, but one requiring that leverage in turn be applied on the publisher from various sources. Perhaps the most significant of these are professional codes. Yet we have seen the weakness of these codes when policy decisions are made. Further leverage is contained in such sources as the professional direction being taken by some journalism schools, in the Guild, and in sincere criticism.

Finally, newspaper readers possess potential power over press performance. Seen as a client of the press, the reader should be entitled to not only an interesting newspaper, but one which furnishes significant news objectively presented. This is the basic problem of democracy: to what extent should the individual be treated as a member of a mass, and to what extent fashioned (through educative measures) as an active participant in public decisions? Readership studies show that readers prefer "interesting" news and "features" over penetrating analyses. It can be concluded that the citizen has not been sufficiently motivated by society (and its press) to demand and apply the information he needs, and to discriminate between worthwhile and spurious information, for the fulfillment of the citizen's role. These other forces—professional codes, journalism schools, the Guild, critics and readers—could result in changing newspaper performance. It still remains, however, for the publisher to be changed first. He can be located at the apex of a T, the crucial point of decision making. Newsroom and professional forces form the base of the T, outside forces from community and society are the arms. It is for the publisher to decide which forces to propitiate.

Suggestions for Validation

The Merton paradigm requires a statement concerning validation of the analysis. Checks could be forthcoming both from social science researchers and from newsmen. If the latter, the newsman should explicitly state the basis for his discussion, especially as regards the types of papers, executives, and staffers he knows. A crucial case for detailed description would be the situation in which staffers actively defied authority on policy matters. Another important test would be a comparative description of two papers contrasted by their situation as regards the six factors promoting conformity, with particular reference to the variable of obligation and esteem held toward superiors, and the factors permitting deviation. In any event, the present exploratory study may serve as a point of departure.

A second type of validation may be suggested. This would focus on the utility of the paradigm itself. Previous studies have been based on functional theory but before the development of the paradigm.[22] Studies of diverse social systems also lend themselves to functional analysis, and such comparative research could function not only to build systematic theory but to test and suggest modifications of the paradigm. Situations characterized by conflict and competion for scarce goals seem particularly well suited to functional analysis. Several points made in the present essay might have been overlooked without the paradigm.[23]

[22] References are cited in Merton, *Social Theory and Social Structure, op. cit.,* and also in the works of Talcott Parsons.
[23] That the paradigm might serve best as a checklist or "insurance," or as a theoretical guide to

Summary

The problem, which was suggested by the age-old charges of bias against the press, focussed around the manner in which the publisher's policy came to be followed, despite three empirical conditions: (1) policy sometimes contravenes journalistic norms; (2) staffers often personally disagree with it; and (3) executives cannot legitimately command that policy be followed. Interview and other data were used to explain policy maintenance. It is important to recall that the discussion is based primarily on study of papers of "middle" circulation range, and does not consider either non-policy stories or the original policy decision made by the publishers.

The mechanisms for learning policy on the part of the new staffer were given, together with suggestions as to the nature of social controls. Six factors, apparently the major variables producing policy maintenance, were described. The most significant of these variables, obligation and esteem for superiors, was deemed not only the most important, but the most fluctuating variable from paper to paper. Its existence and its importance for conformity led to the sub-hypothesis that reference group behavior was playing a part in the pattern. To show, however, that policy is not iron-clad, five conditions were suggested in which staffers may by-pass policy.

Thus we conclude that the publisher's policy, when established in a given subject area, is usually followed, and that a description of the dynamic socio-cultural situation of the newsroom will suggest explanations for this conformity. The newsman's source of rewards is located not among the readers, who are manifestly his clients, but among his colleagues and superiors. Instead of adhering to societal and professional ideals, he re-defines his values to the more pragmatic level of the newsroom group. He thereby gains not only status rewards, but also acceptance in a solidary group engaged in interesting, varied, and sometimes important work. Thus the cultural patterns of the newsroom produce results insufficient for wider democratic needs. Any important change toward a more "free and responsible press" must stem from various possible pressures on the publisher, who epitomizes the policy making and coordinating role.

---

fledgling scholars, is shown by the excellence of an article published before the paradigm—and quite similar to the present article in dealing with problems of policy maintenance in a formal organization: Edward A. Shils and Morris Janowitz, "Cohesion and Disintegration in the Wehrmacht in World War II," *Public Opinion Quarterly*, 12 (Summer 1948), pp. 280–315.

Bureaucratic Structure and Personality

ROBERT K. MERTON

A formal, rationally organized social structure involves clearly defined patterns of activity in which, ideally, every series of actions is func-

From *Social Forces*, Vol. 18, 1940, pp. 560–568. Reprinted with permission of the author and the publisher, University of North Carolina Press. Copyright 1940, University of North Carolina Press.

tionally related to the purposes of the organization.[1] In such an organization there is integrated a series of offices, of hierarchized statuses, in which inhere a number of obliga-

[1] For a development of the concept of "rational organization," see Karl Mannheim, *Mensch und Gesellschaft im Zeitalter des Umbaus* (Leiden: A. W. Sijthoff, 1935), esp. pp. 28 ff.

tions and privileges closely defined by limited and specific rules. Each of these offices contains an area of imputed competence and responsibility. Authority, the power of control which derives from an acknowledged status, inheres in the office and not in the particular person who performs the official role. Official action ordinarily occurs within the framework of preexisting rules of the organization. The system of prescribed relations between the various offices involves a considerable degree of formality and clearly defined social distance between the occupants of these positions. Formality is manifested by means of a more or less complicated social ritual which symbolizes and supports the "pecking order" of the various offices. Such formality, which is integrated with the distribution of authority within the system, serves to minimize friction by largely restricting (official) contact to modes which are previously defined by the rules of the organization. Ready calculability of others' behavior and a stable set of mutual expectations is thus built up. Moreover, formality facilitates the interaction of the occupants of offices despite their (possibly hostile) private attitudes toward one another. In this way, the subordinate is protected from the arbitrary action of his superior, since the actions of both are constrained by a mutually recognized set of rules. Specific procedural devices foster objectivity and restrain the "quick passage of impulse into action." [2]

The ideal type of such formal organization is bureaucracy and, in many respects, the classical analysis of bureaucracy is that by Max Weber.[3] As Weber indicates, bureaucracy involves a clear-cut division of integrated activities which are regarded as duties inherent in the office. A system of differentiated controls and sanctions are stated in the regula-

tions. The assignment of roles occurs on the basis of technical qualifications which are ascertained through formalized, impersonal procedures (e.g. examinations). Within the structure of hierarchically arranged authority, the activities of "trained and salaried experts" are governed by general, abstract, clearly defined rules which preclude the necessity for the issuance of specific instructions for each specific case. The generality of the rules requires the constant use of *categorization*, whereby individual problems and cases are classified on the basis of designated criteria and are treated accordingly. The pure type of bureaucratic official is appointed, either by a superior or through the exercise of impersonal competition; he is not elected. A measure of flexibility in the bureaucracy is attained by electing higher functionaries who presumably express the will of the electorate (e.g. a body of citizens or a board of directors). The election of higher officials is designed to affect the purposes of the organization, but the technical procedures for attaining these ends are performed by a continuous bureaucratic personnel.[4]

The bulk of bureaucratic offices involve the expectation of life-long tenure, in the absence of disturbing factors which may decrease the size of the organization. Bureaucracy maximizes vocational security.[5] The function of security of tenure, pensions, incremental salaries and regularized procedures for promotion is to ensure the devoted performance of official duties, without regard for extraneous pressures.[6] The chief merit of bureaucracy is its technical efficiency, with a premium placed on precision, speed, expert control, continuity, discretion, and optimal returns on input. The structure is one which approaches the com-

[2] H. D. Laswell, *Politics* (New York: McGraw-Hill, 1936), pp. 120–21.

[3] Max Weber, *Wirtschaft und Gesellschaft* (Tübingen: J. C. B. Mohr, 1922), Pt. III, chap. 6, pp. 650–678. For a brief summary of Weber's discussion, see Talcott Parsons, *The Structure of Social Action* (New York: McGraw-Hill, 1937), esp. pp. 506 ff. For a description, which is not a caricature, of the bureaucrat as a personality type, see C. Rabany, "Les types sociaux: le fonctionnaire," *Revue générale d'administration*, LXXXVIII (1907), 5–28.

[4] Karl Mannheim, *Ideology and Utopia* (New York: Harcourt, Brace, 1936), pp. 18n., 105 ff. See also Ramsay Muir, *Peers and Bureaucrats* (London: Constable, 1910), pp. 12–13.

[5] E. G. Cahen-Salvador suggests that the personnel of bureaucracies is largely constituted of those who value security above all else. See his "La situation matérielle et morale des fonctionnaires," *Revue politique et parlementaire* (1926), p. 319.

[6] H. J. Laski, "Bureaucracy," *Encyclopedia of the Social Sciences*. This article is written primarily from the standpoint of the political scientist rather than that of the sociologist.

plete elimination of personalized relationships and of nonrational considerations (hostility, anxiety, affectual involvements, etc.).

Bureaucratization is accompanied by the centralization of means of production, as in modern capitalistic enterprise, or as in the case of the post-feudal army, complete separation from the means of destruction. Even the bureaucratically organized scientific laboratory is characterized by the separation of the scientist from his technical equipment.

Bureaucracy is administration which almost completely avoids public discussion of its techniques, although there may occur public discussion of its policies.[7] This "bureaucratic secrecy" is held to be necessary in order to keep valuable information from economic competitors or from foreign and potentially hostile political groups.

In these bold outlines, the positive attainments and functions of bureaucratic organization are emphasized and the internal stresses and strains of such structures are almost wholly neglected. The community at large, however, evidently emphasizes the imperfections of bureaucracy, as is suggested by the fact that the "horrid hybrid," bureaucrat, has become a *Schimpfwort*. The transition to a study of the negative aspects of bureaucracy is afforded by the application of Veblen's concept of "trained incapacity," Dewey's notion of "occupational psychosis" or Warnotte's view of "professional deformation." Trained incapacity refers to that state of affairs in which one's abilities function as inadequacies or blind spots. Actions based upon training and skills which have been successfully applied in the past may result in inappropriate responses *under changed conditions*. An inadequate flexibility in the application of skills will, in a changing milieu, result in more or less serious maladjustments.[8] Thus, to adopt a barnyard illustration used in this connection by Burke, chickens may be readily conditioned to interpret the sound of a bell as a signal for food. The same bell may

now be used to summon the "trained chickens" to their doom as they are assembled to suffer decapitation. In general, one adopts measures in keeping with his past training and, under new conditions which are not recognized as *significantly* different, the very soundness of this training may lead to the adoption of the wrong procedures. Again, in Burke's almost echolalic phrase, "people may be unfitted by being fit in an unfit fitness"; their training may become an incapacity.

Dewey's concept of occupational psychosis rests upon much the same observations. As a result of their day to day routines, people develop special preferences, antipathies, discriminations and emphases.[9] (The term psychosis is used by Dewey to denote a "pronounced character of the mind.") These psychoses develop through demands put upon the individual by the particular organization of his occupational role.

The concepts of both Veblen and Dewey refer to a fundamental ambivalence. Any action can be considered in terms of what it attains or what it fails to attain. "A way of seeing is also a way of not seeing—a focus upon object A involves a neglect of object B."[10] In his discussion, Weber is almost exclusively concerned with what the bureaucratic structure attains: precision, reliability, efficiency. This same structure may be examined from another perspective provided by the ambivalence. What are the limitations of the organization designed to attain these goals?

For reasons which we have already noted, the bureaucratic structure exerts a constant pressure upon the official to be "methodical, prudent, disciplined." If the bureaucracy is to operate successfully, it must attain a high degree of reliability of behavior, an unusual degree of conformity with prescribed patterns of action. Hence, the fundamental importance of discipline which may be as highly developed in a religious or economic bureaucracy as in the army. Discipline can be effective only if the ideal patterns are buttressed by strong sentiments which entail devotion to one's duties, a keen sense of the limitation of one's authority and competence, and methodical performance of routine activities. The ef-

---

[7] Weber, *op. cit.*, p. 671.
[8] For a stimulating discussion and application of these concepts, see Kenneth Burke, *Permanence and Change* (New York: New Republic, 1935), pp. 50 ff.; Daniel Warnotte, "Bureaucratie et Fonctionnarisme," *Revue de l'Institut de Sociologie*, XVII (1937), 245.

[9] *Ibid.*, pp. 58–59.
[10] *Ibid.*, p. 70.

ficacy of social structure depends ultimately upon infusing group participants with appropriate attitudes and sentiments. As we shall see, there are definite arrangements in the bureaucracy for inculcating and reinforcing these sentiments.

At the moment, it suffices to observe that in order to ensure discipline (the necessary reliability of response), these sentiments are often more intense than is technically necessary. There is a margin of safety, so to speak, in the pressure exerted by these sentiments upon the bureaucrat to conform to his patterned obligations, in much the same sense that added allowances (precautionary over-estimations) are made by the engineer in designing the supports for a bridge. But this very emphasis leads to a transference of the sentiments from the *aims* of the organization onto the particular details of behavior required by the rules. Adherence to the rules, originally conceived as a means, becomes transformed into an end-in-itself; there occurs the familiar process of *displacement of goals* whereby "an instrumental value becomes a terminal value." [11]

Discipline, readily interpreted as conformance with regulations, whatever the situation, is seen not as a measure designed for specific purposes but becomes an immediate value in the life-organization of the bureaucrat. This emphasis, resulting from the displacement of the original goals, develops into rigidities and an inability to adjust readily. Formalism, even ritualism, ensues with an unchallenged insistence upon punctilious adherence to formalized procedures.[12] This may be exaggerated to the point where primary concern with conformity to the rules interferes with the achievement of the purposes of the organization, in which case we have the familiar phenomenon of the technicism or red tape of the official. An extreme product of this process of displacement of goals is the bureaucratic virtuoso, who never forgets a single rule binding his action and hence is unable to assist many of his clients.[13] A case in point, where strict recognition of the limits of authority and literal adherence to rules produced this result, is the pathetic plight of Bernt Balchen, Admiral Byrd's pilot in the flight over the South Pole.

According to a ruling of the department of labor Bernt Balchen . . . cannot receive his citizenship papers. Balchen, a native of Norway, declared his intention in 1927. It is held that he has failed to meet the condition of five years' continuous residence in the United States. The Byrd antarctic voyage took him out of the country, although he was on a ship flying the American flag, was an invaluable member of an American expedition, and in a region to which there is an American claim because of the exploration and occupation of it by Americans, this region being Little America.

The bureau of naturalization explains that it cannot proceed on the assumption that Little America is American soil. That would be *trespass on international questions* where it has no sanction. So far as the bureau is concerned, Balchen was out of the country

---

[11] This process has often been observed in various connections. Wundt's *heterogony of ends* is a case in point; Max Weber's *Paradoxie der Folgen* is another. See also MacIver's observations on the transformation of civilization into culture and Lasswell's remark that "the human animal distinguishes himself by his infinite capacity for making ends of his means." See R. K. Merton, "The Unanticipated Consequences of Purposive Social Action," *American Sociological Review*, I (1936), 894–904. In terms of the psychological mechanisms involved, this process has been analyzed most fully by Gordon W. Allport, in his discussion of what he calls "the functional autonomy of motives." Allport emends the earlier formulations of Woodworth, Tolman, and William Stern, and arrives at a statement of the process from the standpoint of individual motivation. He does not consider those phases of the social structure which conduce toward the "transformation of motives." The formulation adopted in this paper is thus complementary to Allport's analysis; the one stressing the psychological mechanisms involved, the other considering the constraints of the social structure. The convergence of psychology and sociology toward this central concept suggests that it may well constitute one of the conceptual bridges between the two disciplines. See Gordon W. Allport, *Personality* (New York: Henry Holt & Co., 1937), Chap. 7.

[12] See E. C. Hughes, "Institutional Office and the Person," *American Journal of Sociology*, XLIII (1937), 404–413; R. K. Merton, "Social Structure and Anomie," *American Sociological Review*, III (1938), 672–682; E. T. Hiller, "Social Structure in Relation to the Person," *Social Forces*, XVI (1937), 34–44.

[13] Mannheim, *Ideology and Utopia*, p. 106.

and *technically* has not complied with the law of naturalization.[14]

Such inadequacies in orientation which involve trained incapacity clearly derive from structural sources. The process may be briefly recapitulated. (1) An effective bureaucracy demands reliability of response and strict devotion to regulations. (2) Such devotion to the rules leads to their transformation into absolutes; they are no longer conceived as relative to a given set of purposes. (3) This interferes with ready adaptation under special conditions not clearly envisaged by those who drew up the general rules. (4) Thus, the very elements which conduce toward efficiency in general produce inefficiency in specific instances. Full realization of the inadequacy is seldom attained by members of the group who have not divorced themselves from the "meanings" which the rules have for them. These rules in time become symbolic in cast, rather than strictly utilitarian.

Thus far, we have treated the ingrained sentiments making for rigorous discipline simply as data, as given. However, definite features of the bureaucratic structure may be seen to conduce to these sentiments. The bureaucrat's official life is planned for him in terms of a graded career, through the organizational devices of promotion by seniority, pensions, incremental salaries, etc., all of which are designed to provide incentives for disciplined action and conformity to the official regulations.[15] The official is tacitly expected to and largely does adapt his thoughts, feelings, and actions to the prospect of this career. But *these very devices* which increase the probability of conformance also lead to an over-concern with strict adherence to regulations which induces timidity, conservatism, and technicism. Displacement of sentiments from goals onto means is fostered by the tremendous symbolic significance of the means (rules).

Another feature of the bureaucratic structure tends to produce much the same result.

Functionaries have the sense of a common destiny for all those who work together. They share the same interests, especially since there is relatively little competition insofar as promotion is in terms of seniority. In-group aggression is thus minimized and this arrangement is therefore conceived to be positively functional for the bureaucracy. However, the esprit de corps and informal social organization which typically develops in such situations often leads the personnel to defend their entrenched interests rather than to assist their clientele and elected higher officials. As President Lowell reports, if the bureaucrats believe that their status is not adequately recognized by an incoming elected official, detailed information will be withheld from him, leading him to errors for which he is held responsible. Or, if he seeks to dominate fully, and thus violates the sentiment of self-integrity of the bureaucrats, he may have documents brought to him in such numbers that he cannot manage to sign them all, let alone read them.[16] This illustrates the defensive informal organization which tends to arise whenever there is an apparent threat to the integrity of the group.[17]

It would be much too facile and partly erroneous to attribute such resistance by bureaucrats simply to vested interests. Vested interests oppose any new order which either eliminates or at least makes uncertain their differential advantage deriving from the current arrangements. This is undoubtedly involved in part in bureaucratic resistance to change but another process is perhaps more significant. As we have seen, bureaucratic officials affectively identify themselves with their way of life. They have a pride of craft which leads them to resist change in established routines; at least, those changes which are felt to be imposed by persons outside the inner circle of coworkers. This nonlogical pride of craft is a familiar pattern found even, to judge from Sutherland's *Professional Thief*, among pickpockets who, despite the risk, delight in

---

[14] Quoted from the *Chicago Tribune* (June 24, 1931, p. 10) by Thurman Arnold, *The Symbols of Government* (New Haven: Yale University Press, 1935), pp. 201–2. (My italics.)
[15] Mannheim, *Mensch und Gesellschaft*, pp. 32–33. Mannheim stresses the importance of the "Lebensplan" and the "Amtskarriere." See the comments by Hughes, *op. cit.*, 413.

[16] A. L. Lowell, *The Government of England* (New York, 1908), I, 189 ff.
[17] For an instructive description of the development of such a defensive organization in a group of workers, see F. J. Roethlisberger and W. J. Dickson, *Management and the Worker* (Boston: Harvard School of Business Administration, 1934).

mastering the prestige-bearing feat of "beating a left breech" (picking the left front trousers pocket).

In a stimulating paper, Hughes has applied the concepts of "secular" and "sacred" to various types of division of labor; "the sacredness" of caste and *Stände* prerogatives contrasts sharply with the increasing secularism of occupational differentiation in our mobile society.[18] However, as our discussion suggests, there may ensue, in particular vocations and in particular types of organization, the *process of sanctification* (viewed as the counterpart of the process of secularization). This is to say that through sentiment-formation, emotional dependence upon bureaucratic symbols and status, and affective involvement in spheres of competence and authority, there develop prerogatives involving attitudes of moral legitimacy which are established as values in their own right, and are no longer viewed as merely technical means for expediting administration. One may note a tendency for certain bureaucratic norms, originally introduced for technical reasons, to become rigidified and sacred, although, as Durkheim would say, they are *laïque en apparence*.[19] Durkheim has touched on this general process in his description of the attitudes and values which persist in the organic solidarity of a highly differentiated society.

Another feature of the bureaucratic structure, the stress on depersonalization of relationships, also plays its part in the bureaucrat's trained incapacity. The personality pattern of the bureaucrat is nucleated about this norm of impersonality. Both this and the categorizing tendency, which develops from the dominant role of general, abstract rules, tend to produce conflict in the bureaucrat's contacts with the public or clientele. Since functionaries minimize personal relations and resort to categorization, the peculiarities of individual cases are often ignored. But the client who, quite understandably, is convinced of the "special features" of *his* own problem often objects to such categorical treatment. Stereotyped behavior is not adapted to the exigencies of individual problems. The impersonal treatment of affairs which are at times of great personal significance to the client gives rise to the charge of "arrogance" and "haughtiness" of the bureaucrat. Thus, at the Greenwich Employment Exchange, the unemployed worker who is securing his insurance payment resents what he deems to be "the impersonality and, at times, the apparent abruptness and even harshness of his treatment by the clerks. . . . Some men complain of the superior attitude which the clerks have." [20]

Still another source of conflict with the

---

[18] E. C. Hughes, "Personality Types and the Division of Labor," *American Journal of Sociology*, XXXIII (1928), 754–768. Much the same distinction is drawn by Leopold von Wiese and Howard Becker, *Systematic Sociology* (New York: John Wiley & Sons, 1932), pp. 222–25 *et passim*.

[19] Hughes recognizes one phase of this process of sanctification when he writes that professional training "carries with it as a by-product assimilation of the candidate to a set of professional attitudes and controls, *a professional conscience and solidarity. The profession claims and aims to become a moral unit.*" Hughes, *op. cit.*, p. 762 (italics inserted). In this same connection, Sumner's concept of *pathos*, as the halo of sentiment which protects a social value from criticism, is particularly relevant, inasmuch as it affords a clue to the mechanisms involved in the process of sanctification. See his *Folkways* (Boston: Ginn & Co., 1906), pp. 180–181.

[20] " 'They treat you like a lump of dirt they do. I see a navvy reach across the counter and shake one of them by the collar the other day. The rest of us felt like cheering. Of course he lost his benefit over it. . . . But the clerk deserved it for his sassy way.' " (E. W. Bakke, *The Unemployed Man*, New York: Dutton, 1934, pp. 79–80). Note that the domineering attitude was *imputed* by the unemployed client who is in a state of tension due to his loss of status and self-esteem in a society where the ideology is still current that an "able man" can always find a job. That the imputation of arrogance stems largely from the client's state of mind is seen from Bakke's own observation that "the clerks were rushed, and had no time for pleasantries, but there was little sign of harshness or a superiority feeling in their treatment of the men." Insofar as there is an objective basis for the imputation of arrogant behavior to bureaucrats, it may possibly be explained by the following juxtaposed statements. "Auch der moderne, sei es öffentliche, sei es private, Beamte erstrebt immer und geniesst meist den Beherrschten gegenüber eine spezifisch gehobene, 'ständische' soziale Schätzung." (Weber, *op. cit.*, 652.) "In persons in whom the craving for prestige is uppermost, hostility usually takes the form of a desire to humiliate others." (K. Horney, *The Neurotic Personality of Our Time*, New York: Norton, 1937, pp. 178–79.)

public derives from the bureaucratic structure. The bureaucrat, in part irrespective of his position with*in* the hierarchy, acts as a representative of the power and prestige of the entire structure. In his official role he is vested with definite authority. This often leads to an actual or apparent domineering attitude, which may only be exaggerated by a discrepancy between his position within the hierarchy and his position with reference to the public.[21] Protest and recourse to other officials on the part of the client are often ineffective or largely precluded by the previously mentioned esprit de corps which joins the officials into a more or less solidary ingroup. This source of conflict *may* be minimized in private enterprise since the client can register an effective protest by transferring his trade to another organization within the competitive system. But with the monopolistic nature of the public organization, no such alternative is possible. Moreover, in this case, tension is increased because of a discrepancy between ideology and fact: the governmental personnel are held to be "servants of the people," but in fact they are usually superordinate, and release of tension can seldom be afforded by turning to other agencies for the necessary service.[22] This tension is in part attributable to the confusion of status of bureaucrat and client; the client may consider himself socially superior to the official who is at the moment dominant.[23]

Thus, with respect to the relations between officials and clientele, one structural source of conflict is the pressure for formal and impersonal treatment when individual, personalized consideration is desired by the client. The conflict may be viewed, then, as deriving from the introduction of inappropriate attitudes and relationships. Conflict with*in* the bureaucratic structure arises from the converse situation, namely, when personalized relationships are substituted for the structurally required impersonal relationships. This type of conflict may be characterized as follows.

The bureaucracy, as we have seen, is organized as a secondary, formal group. The normal responses involved in this organized network of social expectations are supported by affective attitudes of members of the group. Since the group is oriented toward secondary norms of impersonality, any failure to conform to these norms will arouse antagonism from those who have identified themselves with the legitimacy of these rules. Hence, the substitution of personal for impersonal treatment within the structure is met with widespread disapproval and is characterized by such epithets as graft, favoritism, nepotism, apple-polishing, etc. These epithets are clearly manifestations of injured sentiments.[24] The function of such "automatic resentment" can be clearly seen in terms of the requirements of bureaucratic structure.

---

[21] In this connection, note the relevance of Koffka's comments on certain features of the pecking-order of birds. "If one compares the behavior of the bird at the top of the pecking list, the despot, with that of one very far down, the second or third from the last, then one finds the latter much more cruel to the few others over whom he lords it than the former in his treatment of all members. As soon as one removes from the group all members above the penultimate, his behavior becomes milder and may even become very friendly. . . . It is not difficult to find analogies to this in human societies, and therefore one side of such behavior must be primarily the effects of the social groupings, and not of individual characteristics." K. Koffka, *Principles of Gestalt Psychology* (New York: Harcourt, Brace, 1935), pp. 668-9.

[22] At this point the political machine often becomes functionally significant. As Steffens and others have shown, highly personalized relations and the abrogation of formal rules (red tape) by the machine often satisfy the needs of individual "clients" more fully than the formalized mechanism of governmental bureaucracy.

[23] As one of the unemployed men remarked about the clerks at the Greenwich Employment Exchange: " 'And the bloody blokes wouldn't have their jobs if it wasn't for us men out of a job either. That's what gets me about their holding their noses up.' " Bakke, *op. cit.*, p. 80.

[24] The diagnostic significance of such linguistic indices as epithets has scarcely been explored by the sociologists. Sumner properly observes that epithets produce "summary criticisms" and definitions of social situations. Dollard also notes that "epithets frequently define the central issues in a society," and Sapir has rightly emphasized the importance of context of situations in appraising the significance of epithets. Of equal relevance is Linton's observation that "in case histories the way in which the community felt about a particular episode is, if anything, more important to our study than the actual behavior. . . ." A sociological study of "vocabularies of encomium and opprobrium" should lead to valuable findings.

Bureaucracy is a secondary group mechanism designed to carry on certain activities which cannot be satisfactorily performed on the basis of primary group criteria.[25] Hence behavior which runs counter to these formalized norms becomes the object of emotionalized disapproval. This constitutes a functionally significant defence set up against tendencies which jeopardize the performance of socially necessary activities. To be sure, these reactions are not rationally determined practices explicitly designed for the fulfilment of this function. Rather, viewed in terms of the individual's interpretation of the situation, such resentment is simply an immediate response opposing the "dishonesty" of those who violate the rules of the game. However, this subjective frame of reference notwithstanding, these reactions serve the function of maintaining the essential structural elements of bureaucracy by reaffirming the necessity for formalized, secondary relations and by helping to prevent the disintegration of the bureaucratic structure which would occur should these be supplanted by personalized relations. This type of conflict may be generically described as the intrusion of primary group attitudes when secondary group attitudes are institutionally demanded, just as the bureaucrat-client conflict often derives from interaction on impersonal terms when personal treatment is individually demanded.[26]

The trend toward increasing bureaucratization in Western society, which Weber had long since foreseen, is not the sole reason for sociologists to turn their attention to this field. Empirical studies of the interaction of bureaucracy and personality should especially increase our understanding of social structure. A large number of specific questions invite our attention. To what extent are particular personality types selected and modified by the various bureaucracies (private enterprise, public service, the quasi-legal political machine, religious orders)? Inasmuch as ascendancy and submission are held to be traits of personality, despite their variability in different stimulus-situations, do bureaucracies select personalities of particularly submissive or ascendant tendencies? And since various studies have shown that these traits can be modified, does participation in bureaucratic office tend to increase ascendant tendencies? Do various systems of recruitment (e.g. patronage, open competition involving specialized knowledge or "general mental capacity," practical experience) select different personality types? Does promotion through seniority lessen competitive anxieties and enchance administrative efficiency? A detailed examination of mechanisms for imbuing the bureaucratic codes with affect would be instructive both sociologically and psychologically. Does the general anonymity of civil service decisions tend to restrict the area of prestige-symbols to a narrowly defined inner circle? Is there a tendency for differential association to be especially marked among bureaucrats?

The range of theoretically significant and practically important questions would seem to be limited only by the accessibility of the concrete data. Studies of religious, educational, military, economic, and political bureaucracies dealing with the interdependence of social organization and personality formation should constitute an avenue for fruitful research. On that avenue, the functional analysis of concrete structures may yet build a Solomon's House for sociologists.

[25] Cf. Ellsworth Faris, *The Nature of Human Nature* (New York: McGraw-Hill, 1937), pp. 41 ff.
[26] Community disapproval of many forms of behavior may be analyzed in terms of one or the other of these patterns of substitution of culturally inappropriate types of relationship. Thus, prostitution constitutes a type-case where coitus, a form of intimacy which is institutionally defined as symbolic of the most "sacred" primary group relationship, is placed within a contractual context, symbolized by the exchange of that most impersonal of all symbols, money. See Kingsley Davis, "The Sociology of Prostitution," *American Sociological Review*, II (1937), 744–55.

The Man on the Assembly Line

CHARLES R. WALKER AND ROBERT H. GUEST

There are a lot of good things about my job. The pay is good. I've got seniority. The working conditions are pretty good for my type of work. But that's not the whole story. . . . You can't beat the machine. They have you clocked to a fraction of a second. My job is engineered, and the jigs and fixtures are all set out according to specifications. The foreman is an all right guy, but he gets pushed, so he pushes us. The guy on the line has no one to push. You can't fight that iron horse.

> Worker on an assembly line, interviewed by the authors

Machines alone do not give us mass production. Mass production is achieved by both machines *and* men. And while we have gone a long way toward perfecting our mechanical operations, we have not successfully written into our equation whatever complex factors represent man, the human element.

> Henry Ford II, in a talk before the American Society of Mechanical Engineers, shortly after he was made President of the Ford Motor Company.

The principal social and psychological problems connected with mass production and human nature have been stated many times and in many different forms. Their importance in an age of advancing technology is hardly in dispute. The question has become rather: What shall we do about them?

Here are a few of the common problems. Since individuals react very differently to industrial occupations, what are the personality characteristics of those who adjust quickly to—and appear to thrive on—mechanically paced and repetitive jobs? What, on the other hand, are the personality characteristics of those who suffer mentally and physically on such jobs—and who therefore tend to perform them badly? Can the adjustment problem, in other words, be solved by selection? Or is the modern work environment simply *wrong* for the normal human being?

Or to take an engineering and management approach: In the present state of the mechanical arts, what part of a worker's skill and power can the engineer build into a machine? What must he leave out? Precisely how and to what extent in the most mechanized sectors of our economy does the human equation still affect quantity and quality?

Or again, granted that the principles of mass production such as breakdown of jobs into their simplest constituent parts are sound and vital to efficient manufacture, have we yet found how to combine these principles with equally well authenticated principles of human behavior?

Or taking still another approach, if a man spends a third of his life in direct contact with a mass-production environment, why should we not consider important (to him and to society) the hours of living time he spends inside the factory—as important and valuable, for example, as the product he produces which is consumed outside the factory? We talk of a high standard of living, but frequently we mean a high standard of consumption. Man consumes in his leisure, yet fulfills himself not only in his leisure but in his work. Is our mass-production work environment making such fulfillment more difficult?

A short way to sum up these and a great

From *Harvard Business Review*, Vol. 38, No. 3, May–June 1952, pp. 71–83. Reprinted with permission of the publisher.

many more questions is: To what degree can —or should—men be "adjusted" to the new environment of machines, and to what degree is it possible to adjust or rebuild that environment to fit the needs and personalities of men?

Need for Systematic Study. Despite the tremendous contribution of mass-production methods to the productiveness of the economic system under which we live, and notwithstanding the fact that editors, philosophers, and propagandists have long speculated and written about the beneficent or injurious effects of highly mechanized jobs on human behavior, there has been singularly little systematic effort to discover "whatever complex factors represent man, the human element" in the mass-production method as such. The relatively small number of studies which have been made of assembly-line and other types of repetitive work have been mostly laboratory experiments, not explorations of experience in actual industrial plants.

A notable exception is the series of monographs which for some 25 years have been published from time to time under the auspices of the British Medical Council on the effects of mechanization and the repetitive job on productivity and *mental* fatigue. Even these, however, have only touched occasionally on the subject of assembly lines, and have never at all—to the best of our knowledge—dealt specifically with that advanced sector of a mass-production economy, the final assembly line of a plant making a large, complex product like automobiles.

SURVEY OF AUTOMOBILE ASSEMBLY PLANT. For these reasons the authors undertook two years ago an exploratory survey of a modern automobile assembly plant.[1] This is intended as the first of a series of studies designed to define more clearly the several "human equations" involved in assembly work, to prepare and sharpen tools of research, and to look for proximate and empirical answers to the more acute practical problems posed for men and management.

In this article· we shall emphasize how an

assembly line looks and feels to the men who work on it, rather than its importance to the engineers who designed it, the executives who manage it, or the public who buys its product.

In order to preserve the anonymity of those who freely supplied information—managers, workers, and union leaders—the plant in question has been called Plant X. Over a period of months 180 workers were interviewed in their homes about all phases of their life on "the line." These workers constituted a substantial —and representative—sample of the total number of productive workers in the plant.

Nearly 90% of the men working at Plant X came from jobs where the pace of work was not machine-governed in a strict sense, and from jobs over 72% of which were not repetitive. In short, the area from which they were recruited had few mass-production factories. One might say, then, that these men were like the majority of workers who in the past 30 years have made the transition from occupations characteristic of the first industrial revolution to work environments characteristic of a mass-production era. Their attitudes should be all the more revealing.

Most people, in thinking about an assembly line and the workers on it, focus only on the effect of the line on what a man does hour by hour, even minute by minute, with his mind and his muscles. Any serious study of the human effects of the mass-production method, however, must extend its field of vision. For the method not only impinges directly on a man's immediate or intrinsic job but molds much of the character of the in-plant society of which he is a part, including both his relations with his fellow workers and his relations with management. Accordingly we shall discuss the impact of the mass-production method not only directly but indirectly on human nature.

DEFINITION OF MASS-PRODUCTION METHOD. But what is the "mass-production method?" We must have a definition if our discussion and our findings are to be understandable.

Although the methods of mass production or, more accurately and specifically for our purposes, the methods of *progressive manufacture* have been defined and discussed in different ways by different writers, it is agreed by nearly everyone that these methods derive from at least two fundamental and related

[1] The full details of this survey are being published in book form, *The Man on the Assembly Line*, by the Harvard University Press (June 1952).

ideas: (1) standardization and (2) interchange-ability of parts.

Given these basic ideas, plus the accurate machining methods which make them applicable to manufacture, Ford was able to work out and apply the three following additional "principles" of progressive manufacture: (3) the orderly progression of the product through the shop in a series of planned operations arranged so that the right part always arrives at the right place at the right time; (4) the mechanical delivery of these parts and of the product as it is assembled to and from the operators; and (5) a breakdown of operations into their simple constituent motions.[2]

Let us look now at how these principles translate themselves into job characteristics from the standpoint not of the engineer but of the man on the assembly line. In the first place, most automobile assembly jobs are *mechanically paced* (especially those on the main line). In the second place, since the engineer has broken the jobs down into simple and separate elements and assigned only a few to each man, they are clearly *repetitive*. Among other characteristics of most jobs are these: they have a low skill requirement, permit work on only a fraction of the product, severely limit social interaction, and predetermine for nearly every worker any use he may make of tools and methods.

Taken together, automobile assembly-line jobs exemplify all these characteristics, but not every job exemplifies all of them. Put another way, in spite of many common characteristics, automobile assembly jobs are far from being equal—either as to the quantity or quality of job content or as to the satisfaction or dissatisfaction which workers derive from them. They differ both in the number of the several assembly-line characteristics they exemplify and in the degree of impact of any one characteristic. An understanding of this point must mark the beginning of any serious inquiry into the relation of human behavior to assembly-line work.

Attitude toward Jobs. But that is enough of making distinctions. Now let the men on the

[2] This is a rephrased and slightly more explicit statement of the three principles of mass production as set down in "Mass Production" by Henry Ford in the *Encyclopaedia Britannica*, Fourteenth Edition, Vol. 15, pp. 38–39.

assembly line tell us themselves about their jobs, and tell us also what they like and what they do not like about them. Here are six jobs by way of illustration: two on the main moving line, one off the main line but on a moving conveyer, one off the main line and not on a moving conveyer, one repair job on the line, and one utility job on the line. These six will illustrate at least the principal differences in human impact of mass-production assembly-line jobs. (It should be remembered, however, that these six are not representative of the distribution of jobs in the whole plant, where one-half the jobs are on the *main moving assembly line.* Specifically the distribution of jobs in our sample was as follows: main assembly line, 86; subassembly on moving belt, 28; subassembly not on moving belt, 38; repairmen, 14; utility men, 11; and other, 3.)

ON THE MAIN MOVING LINE. Here is the way the assembler of the baffle windbreaker in the trim department describes his job:

> As the body shell moves along the line, I start putting on a baffle windbreaker (two fenders fit on it) by putting in four screws. Then I put nine clips at the bottom which hold the chrome molding strip to the body. On another type of car there is a piece of rubber which fits on the hood latch on the side and keeps the hood from rattling. I drill the holes in the rubber and metal and fit two screws in. Also I put four clips on the rubber in the rear fender. On another type of body, I put the clips on the bottom molding, and in the trunk space I put two bolts which hold the spare tire clamp. I repeat these things all the time on the same types of car.

How does this man's job measure up in terms of some of the characteristics we have mentioned, particularly pace and repetitiveness?

To begin with, the job is on the main line and the worker rides along on the conveyer, completing his cycle of operations in less than two minutes while the conveyer is moving over a distance of about 30 feet. He then walks to his starting point and begins over again. In short, his pace is directly determined by the moving belt. On the other hand, he is sometimes able to work back up the line and so secure a breather for himself.

The job is clearly repetitive, but there is

some element of variety since between five and ten operations are required to complete the job cycle. There are also different models to be worked on. Comparing the repetitiveness of this job with that of other assembly jobs, it is somewhere in the middle range—far less repetitive than a single-operation job and far more repetitive than the job of a repairman.

Similarly, in the matter of skill it is in the middle as assembly-line jobs go. Because of the number of parts handled, learning time is slightly longer than that for many assembly jobs. The worker reported that it took him a month to do the job properly. As for the expenditure of physical energy, it is a light job.

ALSO ON THE MAIN MOVING LINE. Or consider the job of the worker who installs toe plates and who performs operations typical of short-cycle, on-the-main-line jobs:

> I put in the two different toe plates. They cover the holes where the brake and clutch pedals are. I am inside the car and have to be down on the seat to do my work. On one kind of car I put in the shift lever while another man puts in the toe plates.

While doing his job, this man rides along in the car and must complete the job before he is carried too far. After finishing his work cycle he returns to his station, climbs into another car, and begins another installation. Thus his pace is strictly governed by the moving line. This particular worker told the interviewer that he did not mind the pace.

Such a job which demands but two operations in a two-minute cycle is highly repetitive. Only slight variety is introduced when the man installs a shift lever instead of a toe plate on certain cars.

The job demands very little skill and has a learning period of just two days. Although the worker gets in and out of cars 20 or 30 times an hour, his expenditure of physical energy on the actual assembly operation is slight.

OFF THE MAIN LINE BUT ON A MOVING CONVEYER. The job of a seat-spring builder is typical of those off the main line but on a moving belt:

> I work on a small conveyer which goes around in a circle. We call it a merry-go-round. I make up zig-zag springs for front seats. Every couple of feet on the conveyer

there is a form for the pieces that make up the seat springs. As that form goes by me, I clip several pieces together, using a clip gun. I then put the pieces back on the form, and it goes on around to where the other men clip more pieces together. By the time the form has gone around the whole line, the pieces are ready to be set in a frame, where they are made into a complete seat spring. That's further down the main seat cushion line. The only operation I do is work the clip gun. It takes just a couple of seconds to shoot six or eight clips onto the spring, and I do it as I walk a few steps. Then I start right over again.

This job is clearly paced by a moving conveyer quite as much as if it were on the main line. A comment by the worker regarding his previous job emphasized the point: "I liked the piecework system on my old job. If I wanted to stop for a few minutes, I could. You can't do that here."

As for variety, there is none. The job is highly repetitive, consisting of one set of operations repeated every few seconds on a part which is standard for all models.

The skill requirement is minimum. This worker gave two days at his learning time, with a few days more "in order to do it like I do it now."

As for physical energy, the job would probably be rated as light since the worker guides an automatic hand gun. But there is considerable fatigue because the worker performs the operation standing up.

The worker's over-all estimate of the job is typical. As to what he lived about the job, he mentioned good pay, steady work, and good working hours—in that order of priority. As to what he disliked, he said that he could not set his own pace, that he did not have interesting work, and that his job was physically tiring.

OFF THE MAIN LINE BUT NOT ON A MOVING CONVEYER. We turn to a blower-defroster assembler who works off the main line and not on a moving belt:

> I work at a bench on blower defrosters. The blowers come in two parts. I take one part and attach the blower motor to it. I then connect the fan to the motor shaft. Then I take the other half of the air pipe and put two parts together with fourteen

screws. I test the motor to see if it works, and if it does, I put in a fifteenth screw which grounds it to the pipe. The materials are brought to me and put in a pile by a stock chaser. After I finish, I put each assembled blower on one of six shelves.

Here is an example of a job where pace is only indirectly determined by the main line. The worker must keep his shelves stocked with a supply of blower defrosters, but he has some choice of pace in doing so. He may work fast and "build up a bank," then slow down and take a breather. Or he may choose to work quite steadily. The demands of the stock-chaser who brings him materials and takes away the finished assembly are the determinants of his work pace, rather than the moving conveyer.

There is not much variety since there are only three operations. However, a slight variation is introduced through differences in models. The worker called his job completely repetitive but said he did not mind it.

His job operations require a minimum of skill: "I learned it in a couple of hours, though it took me about a week to get up speed." He does not move around, and the materials he handles are light, so very little physical energy is demanded.

Summing up his job, this worker gave good bosses, good pay, and good working conditions as his first three reasons for liking the job. He mentioned only one thing he disliked: "I cannot do different things."

REPAIRMAN. Here is a job description by a repairman in the car-conditioning section of the chassis department:

I work in a pit underneath the final line. The cars move along over the pit. On the previous assembly operations, the inspectors for the under parts of the car have indicated where parts were missing or damaged or not properly attached. There are any number of things which can be wrong, and they are usually different for each car. Sometimes we have a run of the same thing which we have to work on until they get at the bug earlier in assembly operations. The shock absorbers may be bad, gas line in wrong, brake lines or spring attachments off. I fix whatever I see checked by the inspector. The others in the pit do the same thing. I just work down the line until I get it cleared up. Sometimes

I have to work down a long way on one thing. Other times it's just a simple problem on a number of different things.

This worker is on the main line, but his pace is not strictly governed by the moving conveyer. "We don't feel the pressure of the line since we don't have to do just one thing in a given area and length of time."

The variety the job offers is derived from the nature of the work. "There are any number of things which can be wrong, and they are usually different for each car. . . . There is something different all the time."

As for skill, the job as repairman requires manual skill and mechanical experience. A garage repairman's job would be a good preparation. (The man whose job description is given here had, in fact, worked as a repairman in a garage before coming to Plant X.)

The job varies between light and medium-heavy work, with the expenditure of physical energy called for changing appreciably from job to job and from day to day.

The worker's personal satisfaction with his job was clear. He gave as three reasons for liking the job: "I can set my own pace, I have good working conditions, and I have steady work." He also commented favorably on being able to "use my brains," "do different things," and "choose how the job is to be done."

UTILITY MAN. A utility man in the chassis department describes his job as follows:

I work on the whole length of that part of the chassis line beginning with motor drop up to where the wheels are mounted. My job is to fill in wherever I am needed. A man might be absent or away from the job or may need help on the job.

We start where the motor is lowered onto the frame (motor mount). The clutch assembly is installed and hooked up. Then the exhaust system is attached and the bolts tightened. The clutch assembly bolts and the motor mount bolts are also tightened. In the next area on the line the brake chambers are filled and bled.

Off to the side, the subassembly men put the steering column together. The steering post and the Pittman arm assembly are put in. Further down the line, men put in air cleaners and inject hydraulic fluid for the transmission.

Next, the brakes are tested and the clutch linkage hooked up. The bumper brackets are put on; a serial number is attached next; and then the bumper brackets are tightened up. Finally, the chassis is sprayed, mounted on wheels, and moved on toward body drop. All in all, about 28 men work on these jobs, each man with his own special operation. I go on each of these jobs, depending on where I am needed most. It is different each day. Some of the jobs are hard to learn, so when I take over one on which I haven't had much experience, it's hard to keep up. I have been learning how to do the work ever since I've been in the plant. I can never learn everything because new changes are always being made.

The pace of this utility man's work, since it is on the main line, is as strictly governed as that of any assembly worker. In certain ways he may feel the pressure more acutely than some of those for whom he substitutes, since he has less practice on any single job than its regular holder.

To compensate him, however, there is plenty of variety, for, as he points out, he shifts about among 28 different jobs. Notice how in describing his many tasks this utility man gives a very clear account of the whole segment of assembly operations in the chassis department.

Notice, too, the character of a utility man's skill. It is the sum of many little skills of many repetitive jobs. The learning time is six months to a year. The worker said: "Sometimes I walk up and down checking the line. I ask questions of the different men. I rarely stay on the same job more than a couple of days." That his job is not easy is suggested by an additional comment:

Some days you feel like learning, other days you don't. On jobs that take time to learn, you get disgusted because it's hard to keep up. A utility man, when on a job, has more trouble keeping up than the regular man.

This man mentioned good pay, steady work, and good bosses as the three main reasons for liking his job, in that order. Other items bearing on the immediate job which he liked were "having interesting work, having to use my brains, doing many different things," as in the case of the repairman, and also "talking with others." He had only one complaint about the job: that it was "physically tiring."

SUMMARY OF ATTITUDES TOWARD JOBS. In all of this classification of the automobile assembly workers' jobs, we have clearly been concerned not with an engineering analysis but with factors which have an effect on satisfaction or dissatisfaction with the immediate job. Mechanical pace, repetitiveness, minimum skill requirement, and the other factors were all found reflected in attitudes and feelings.

These examples underline some of the commonest facts and feelings which are part of the daily experience of the productive worker in an assembly plant. To recall a few:

1. Contrary to popular belief, all jobs on an assembly line are not alike, either in skill, variety, learning time, or the degree of satisfaction or dissatisfaction which they offer the average wage earner.

2. There are definite ways on certain jobs to get a break or a breather, such as "working back up the line," or "bank building."

3. There is a general, though not a unanimous, desire to move from highly paced jobs to jobs which are less highly paced, and "off the line."

4. It is evident from the statements of the six workers—which for illustrative purposes we have selected from 180—that other factors such as good pay, a good foreman, and a secure job must be considered in appraising the total index of a worker's satisfaction or dissatisfaction.

Major Reactions of Workers. Looking over the range of factors connected with their immediate jobs by all the men interviewed, we see that the two which were given greatest prominence were (1) mechanical pacing and (2) repetitiveness.

TO MECHANICAL PACING. We asked no direct attitude questions on the first and central characteristic of any automobile assembly plant—the moving conveyer—but nearly every worker expressed his opinions about it when describing his job, when talking about the company, or at some other point in the interview. These free-association comments on pace as governed by the moving conveyer showed that: (1) A large majority of the workers regarded the moving line or belt as an undesirable feature of the job. (2) A small minority expressed themselves as enjoying the excitement of the moving line.

Following are typical comments of workers who were highly critical of the line:

The bad thing about assembly lines is that the line keeps moving. If you have a little trouble with a job, you can't take the time to do it right.

On the line you're geared to the line. You don't dare stop. If you get behind, you have a hard time catching up.

The line speed is too great. More men wouldn't help much. They'd just expect more work out of an individual. There's an awful lot of tension.

I don't like rushing all the time. . . . I don't mind doing a good day's work, but I don't like to run through it.

The work isn't hard; it's the never-ending pace. . . . The guys yell "hurrah" whenever the line breaks down. . . . You can hear it all over the plant.

In contrast, a minority liked the challenge and excitement of keeping up with the line:

I do my job well. I get some satisfaction from keeping up with a rapid-fire job. On days when the cars come off slowly, I sometimes get bored.

I get satisfaction from doing my job right and keeping up with the line.

It makes you feel good . . . when the line is going like hell and you step in and catch up with it.

TO REPETITIVENESS. Turning now to the job characteristic, repetitiveness, our findings are that: (1) A majority of the workers were critical of the repetitive character of their jobs. (2) A minority preferred the repetitive character of their work or were indifferent to it. (3) A large number of workers compared on-the-line jobs unfavorably with off-the-line jobs, because off-the-line jobs offered more variety. We found we were able to correlate the number of operations a man performed (which can serve as a rough measure of repetitiveness) with expressions of interest or lack of interest in his job. The number of operations performed on any given job was determined not

by direct questioning but by analysis of the job descriptions. The workers, however, were asked directly: "Would you say your job was very interesting, fairly interesting, not at all interesting?" The correlation with number of operations was as follows:

OPERATIONS PERFORMED	VERY OR FAIRLY INTERESTING	NOT VERY OR NOT AT ALL INTERESTING
1	19	38
2–5	28	36
5 or more	41	18

In the column of workers giving a positive rating to "interest," the number of workers increases as the number of operations increases. In other words, there is a tendency for interest in work to vary directly with the number of operations performed.

Following are typical comments of those men who were critical of the repetitive nature of their jobs:

I dislike repetition. One of the main things wrong with this job is that there is no figuring for yourself, no chance to use your brain. It's a grind doing the same thing over and over. There is no skill necessary.

I'd rather work for a small company any day. They're interested in doing good work, and they are willing to allot enough time for it. The assembly line is no place to work, I can tell you. There is nothing more discouraging than having a barrel beside you with 10,000 bolts in it and using them all up. Then you get a barrel with another 10,000 bolts, and you know every one of those 10,000 bolts has to be picked up and put in exactly the same place as the last 10,000 bolts.

I'd like to do different things on this job. I get bored. It's the same thing all the time. Cars always coming down the line endlessly every time I look up.

I would like to perform different operations, but I do the same thing all the time. I always know what I'm going to do when I come in. There's nothing to look forward to like there was on my old job.

The monotony is what I don't like. It's pretty noisy, but you get used to that. I'd never get used to the monotony. I dislike the plant for this reason.

It's not a matter of pace. It's the monotony. It's not good for you to get so bored. I do the same thing day after day; just an everlasting grind.

The job gets so sickening—day in and day out plugging in ignition wires. I get through with one motor, turn around, and there's another motor staring me in the face.

A minority of workers who declared that they were indifferent to or preferred doing the same thing over and over again commented as follows:

I keep doing the same thing all the time, but it doesn't make any difference to me.

Repeating the same thing you can catch up and keep ahead of yourself. I like the routine. You can get in the swing of it.

We do the same thing all the time, but I don't mind it really.

I like doing the same thing all the time. I'd rather stay right where I am. When I come in in the morning, I like to know exactly what I'll be doing.

I like to repeat the same thing, and every car is different anyway. So my job is interesting enough.

Explanation of why this minority group either preferred or was indifferent to the factor of repetitiveness in contrast to the majority of workers in our sample would appear to lie in the pattern of their individual personalities. An investigation of the psychological characteristics of men who react this way is clearly suggested. We sought but found no other unique characteristics in the group as regards education, age, or any of the other categories of information we used.

Effect of Human Equation. In the introductory paragraphs of this article we reviewed some of the typical questions on which it was hoped research into the human equation of assembly-line work might throw light, including some of special interest to both the production manager and the engineer: What part

of a worker's skill and power can the engineer build into a machine? What must he leave out? Precisely how and to what extent in the most mechanized sectors of our economy does the human equation still affect quantity and quality?

INFLUENCE OF WORKERS ON QUALITY. So far as assembly lines go, there is still a widespread belief on the part of *outsiders* that the machine has completely taken over and that on mechanized conveyer-line jobs the individual has no influence on quality. There is also a belief widely held by *insiders* (employers and production managers) that, even though the quality of individual performance on a mechanized job may still be important for the final product, the average worker no longer cares or gets satisfaction from doing a good job.

In Plant X, both beliefs were shown to be unfounded.

As many as 79 men in the sample of 180 felt that it was difficult to sustain the kind of quality performance which was expected of them or which they themselves wanted to sustain. To most of the 79, *this was a discouraging and negative feature of the job.*

About half the workers felt it was possible to do the kind of quality job expected of them. Few of these workers, however, had jobs which were strictly line-paced. Rather they included mostly repairmen, utility men, workers on off-line jobs, or men on the line who had longer time cycles or greater freedom to move up and down the line. Typical comments among this group were:

No time limit is set on my job, so I can do it right. I get satisfaction out of really fixing a job. I can usually get this, but sometimes the company doesn't want the cars fixed as well as I'd like to.

I get satisfaction and quality because I have time to complete my job right.

I never let a car go by with my number on it unless it is done right. Maybe some of the men on the line don't get quality.

You can take time to get quality. It's not like on the line when you have to rush so much. And I get satisfaction. It makes me feel good when I put out a good day's work and get no kickbacks.

The effects of poor-quality work on job satisfaction were reflected in many of the comments of men on conveyer-paced jobs:

The cars come too fast for quality. It's quantity instead of quality. I'm doing the best I can, but could do a neater job slower.

On an assembly line you just do it once; if it's wrong, you have no time to fix it. I get no satisfaction from my work. All I do is think about all the things that went through wrong that should have been fixed. My old job was nothing like this.

I try to do quality work, but I'm too rushed. This keeps me from getting pleasure from the work. They say "haste makes waste," and they're getting plenty of both.

I'd rather do less work and do it right. How can you get quality when they don't give you time? The "quality" signs they have mean nothing.

These comments tend to show that the characteristics or components of the assembly man's immediate job do have a significant bearing upon the quality of the product, and that mass production restricts rather than eliminates the "human factor" as a determinant of quality for any given part or for the total product. Most workers were conscious of this fact. For a substantial number, inability to put out quality was a source of irritation while putting out quality was a source of job satisfaction.

Constructive Measures by Management. Are there any measures that management can take to modify on-the-job conditions of work in the interest of greater efficiency and of increased satisfaction for the individual operator?

One answer to this question may be sought in the elements of satisfaction or of compensation which some workers already found in their jobs. To begin with, it should be remembered that there was a minority of workers who preferred or were indifferent to repetitiveness and mechanical pacing. Presumably by improved methods of recruiting and selection this minority could be increased. Then there were a number of men who found their immediate jobs on and off the line satisfying—actually all the repairmen and utility men interviewed with one exception. The only measures needed here are protective—to make sure that the content of these jobs is not diluted.

This still leaves the majority of the production workers. Here the clue to constructive action lies in the fact that many of them reacted favorably to particular features of their jobs:

1. Social interaction breaking the monotony.
2. Enough operations on their particular jobs to give variety.
3. Opportunity to work back up the line and get a breather.
4. Opportunity to build up a bank and get a breather.
5. Opportunity to alternate one set of operations with another set of a substantially different character.
6. Opportunity to alternate jobs with other workers within the same section.
7. A long time cycle encompassing a larger number of operations than usual and of a more interesting character.

A practical directive for management would appear to be exploration of the possibility of extending these and other desirable features, so that more assembly men could share in them. The degree of that extension would necessarily vary with the special circumstances—physical and organizational—of individual plants, and with the ingenuity of management; but there would be few plants where something could not be done in this direction.

Detailed discussion of such measures is beyond the scope of this article, but the tenor of our thinking may be indicated by reference to two of the seven features to which Plant X workers reacted favorably.

JOB ROTATION. Take Number 6—alternation of jobs between workers, a technique often called "rotation." At Plant X we were struck with the unusually high degree of job satisfaction expressed by the members of one work group under a particular foreman. With the permission and encouragement of their foreman, the men were working under a system of job rotation. It was to this system that the members of the group ascribed their relatively high job satisfaction. And to the same system the section foreman owed in part a smoothly running and efficient work unit. Top plant management is now encouraging a more widespread application of this practice.

In connection with any system of job rotation the question immediately comes to mind: Since it requires some effort to learn several jobs instead of one, will not the worker—unless he is exceptional—object? Many managers seem to find it difficult to get workers to change jobs frequently.

The best answer to this question about worker resistance is the pragmatic one. In certain sectors on the line at Plant X rotation *is* working. Moreover, in other industries and on other types of assembly lines the practice of rotation is steadily gaining ground. For most people learning to do something new is hard work, and it is only undertaken when an adequate reward is held out. For a considerable number of assembly-line workers the rewards of variety and of possessing a repertory of skills will be sufficient.

Of course, some resistance to an experiment in rotation is to be expected. The key to the situation lies, we suggest, in the word "experiment." Where rotation has been successfully installed on other types of assembly lines, it has usually been started as an experiment, with management guaranteeing to the work group or to any single individual a return to stationary assignments if desired—and rarely have the workers wished to return.

Another question is: Will the work be done as well or as fast under job rotation? The answer for the Plant X section which practices it is an affirmative. For other work groups in other industries with which the authors are familiar, the answer has also been "yes." Of course there are work situations where job rotation appears either altogether impractical or less efficient. But always the real test is in the over-all and long-term performance of the group. Gains in quality and a drop in turnover or absenteeism may balance some decrease in output, if it occurs.

JOB ENLARGEMENT. Or consider Number 7—a long-time cycle encompassing a larger number of operations than usual and of a more interesting character, sometimes called "job enlargement." Here is a concept and a practice that has proved successful in decreasing monotony without impairing efficiency in certain sectors of other industries. We here suggest that it be introduced experimentally into automobile assembly work.

Job enlargement is simply the recombining of two or more separate jobs into one. Certain plant managers in other industries have been finding that a law of diminishing returns applies to the subdivision of jobs and that a recombination of certain fractured parts has increased efficiency. This points toward a lengthening of time cycles. Job enlargement in the sense in which we suggest it does not mean turning automobile assembly back into the hands of master mechanics with one worker assigned to the assembly of one car. It does mean paying greater attention to psychological and social variables in the determination of time cycles and, by the same token, paying more attention to the *content* of individual jobs.

To one unfamiliar with assembly-line work experience, the difference between a job with five operations and a job with ten, or between a job taking two minutes to perform and a job taking four minutes, might seem a matter far too trivial to concern anyone. Our data have shown that this is not true. Management has a vital interest in such matters; the proper assignment of time cycles throughout an assembly plant will make an important difference in the efficiency of the plant. As for the worker, one of the most striking findings of this study is the psychological importance of even minute changes in his immediate job experience.

At the risk of oversimplification, the point may be summarized this way: Other things being equal, the difference between a satisfied and a dissatisfied worker may rest on whether he has a ten-opration or a five-operation job.

Relationship among Workers. Another place to look for possibilities of improvement is in the area of indirect influences—the impact of mass-production methods on the plant's social structure. Ever since the early studies of Elton Mayo, it has been widely accepted that the character of the "work group" frequently exercises a decisive influence on a worker's efficiency—not to mention on his satisfaction on the job. How did the technology of the automobile assembly line affect the grouping of men at Plant X?

Most workers are located along the "main line" according to the particular manpower requirements of each segment of the assembly process. Each operator works in a limited area completing his own operations independently of others as the car is carried by the conveyer down the line. A particular individual may talk with the men immediately around him, but these men cannot be said to comprise a bona fide work group in the usual sense of the term. Take as an illustration the polishing line. Figure 1 shows in diagrammatic form an actual interaction pattern of a left-front-door polisher, Worker E.

The ten men from A to J comprise a work group of which Worker E is a part, and he has some social contact with all the other nine. His really close contacts, however, are only with C, D, F and G. Note that these four workers comprise a group—*but only from E's point of view*. As to the social relationship pattern of G, his immediate group would consist of E, F, H and I; it would not include C and D, who were clearly members of E's group. Further variations occur, for example, when a line makes a bend or loop and brings men in dif-

ferent sections closer together. Thus each man, because of the nature of conveyer operations, has a slightly different circle of associates from that of the man next to him. So it goes along the entire stretch of a line, a line well over two miles long.

In our interviews these men exhibited little of what the sociologist would call "in-group awareness." Rarely, for example, did they talk about "our team" or "our group" or "the men in our outfit." Instead, the following remark was typical: "I've been here over a year, and I hardly know the first names of the men in the section where I work."

In sharp contrast, however, to the majority of line workers, a minority—principally off-line operators—worked on bona fide teams or crews; that is, they were members of a close working group, were functionally interdepend-

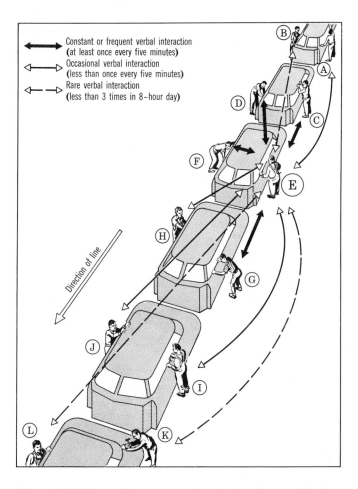

Fig. 1. Social interaction pattern of typical main assembly line worker—polisher in the paint department.

ent, and frequently assisted their fellows or ex-changed operations with them. On charting the interaction pattern of such groups it was found that the frequency of conversational exchange was high and constant for nearly all members of the group. Of greater significance, the group exhibited a marked *esprit-de-corps* not found among the bulk of line operators.

It is clear that the present technology of an automobile assembly line limits social inter-action and does not lend itself to the arrange-ment of men in bona fide teams or crews. It is suggested, however, that in the design of *new* plants, and at periods of retooling or of layout revisions, an effort be made to maximize the opportunities for social interaction and for team relationships.

Relations with Management. Still another area of social relationships—that of worker to supervisor—is crucial to an intelligent under-standing of social organization.

The formal organizational structure of the various production departments in Plant X was similar to that found in many plants. In inter-views with workers we came to know the quality of relationship between workers and supervisors.

FOREMEN. Qualitative comments by the men about their foremen suggested a relatively informal and friendly relationship on the part of the majority. The average foreman had from 15 to 25 men under him, and talking between worker and foreman was generally frequent, friendly, and informal. The sort of remarks one hears about any good foreman were also heard here, as for example: "Our foreman is a real good guy. We're lucky. If he got into trouble, the whole department would back him right up."

There were criticisms of foremen, but usually these were not directed at the in-dividual. Rather they were aimed at the "line" and the role the foreman had to play with reference to the line. As one man said: "After all, the foreman has to be a pusher, and nobody likes to be pushed. He's got to hold his job. If he doesn't push, somebody else will get his job."

Often men exonerated foremen for "push-ing" since they recognized that the compulsion of line production was not the fault of the foremen. One man put it this way: "I guess you'd say the foreman gets along with the men. But they don't need a foreman. *The line is the foreman.* You have to keep up with the line."

HIGHER SUPERVISORS. An interesting finding which came out of the study was the relation-ship, or lack of it, between workers and man-agement above the foreman level. The 180 men in our sample were asked to indicate contacts with supervisors in their department at the general foreman and department-head levels. Only 59 reported that they talked with their general foreman as often as once a week; 15 put it at on to three times a month; and 88 said less than once a month. Contact between workers and upper departmental supervisors was even less, with 70% saying they spoke with their department heads less than once a month. (Departments ranged in size from 200 to 400.)

It is significant in this connection that in a steel fabricating plant which we recently studied the workers talked far more frequently with supervisors above the foreman level. There the nature of the process and the high degree of worker skills made for a closer rela-tionship. It was an everyday experience to find a superintendent in charge of 400 men talking with an individual worker or group of work-ers. He did this because the technical and skilled judgment of the individual worker was important in the production process.

On the automobile assembly line, on the other hand, because of the high degree of mechanization and fractional assembly there appears to be less need for supervisors to dis-cuss production matters with individual work-ers. Management relies on the judgment of the engineer, not the worker. Thus the basic factor which determines the rate and quality of worker-supervisor interaction is the tech-nology of mass production.

Impact on Wage Structure. Not the least important secondary effect of the mass-pro-duction method has been its impact on the wage structure. A leveling of workers' skills has inevitably resulted in a narrowing of dif-ferentials between wage grades, in contrast to industries where the latest mass-production methods have not been applied. For example, in the steel fabricating plant which we investi-gated—a seamless tube mill—the differential between the rates of the lowest and of the highest paid workers was over a dollar an hour.

At Plant X, however, the differential between the lowest paid and the highest paid was around 10 cents for the major categories of production workers, and over half the workers in the production departments received exactly the same hourly wage.

It is obvious that changes in skill levels and in wage categories affect what the wage administrator calls the "system of job progression." Before the application of mass-production methods most industries had many well-defined steps in their ladders of promotion. Mass-production methods, while often raising the general level of wages and bringing other benefits, have knocked out a good many rungs in these promotion ladders. To turn again to the steel mill for contrast: there were as many as seven or eight steps from laborer to roller, each one associated with progressively higher wages, skills, and prestige.

This system of promotion, with its connotations of growth, incentive, and progress, has been weakened or virtually eliminated on the assembly line. Almost any assembly worker can—and some do—say: "There are hundreds of jobs like mine, not much better, not much worse. The differences are so slight—or seem so slight to management—that I am interchangeable." Consequently, to escape a resulting sense of anonymity as much, perhaps, as to escape monotony, the average worker at Plant X does not aspire to climb into another slightly better production job, but rather into a utility man's job or a repairman's job or out of production altogether, where he can be recognized, and where also he can recognize himself, as an individual.

Most of the benefits of the mass-production method are obvious and have often been celebrated. If we are to continue to enjoy them and to expand and refine the method, we should understand more fully its impact on the traditional organization of industry. Surely the problems as well as the promises of mass production are worthy of study.

Conclusion. It is obviously impossible in a single article to do more than sketch some of the problem areas in the broad field of relations between mass production and human nature. Concerning the direct impact of the method on the individual we made a few empirical suggestions and tried to point out at least one direction in which management might seek practical solutions.

But what can be said about the *indirect* impact of mass production on human nature through the character of work groups, the wage structure, and the promotion system? In a negative sense, at least, all these phenomena appear to be related: At Plant X they tended to increase the workers' sense of anonymity within the production enterprise of which they were functional parts. In fact, one way to express the net result of these several influences might be to say that little sense of membership in a common work community existed. (Our evidence showed that to some extent membership in the union gave the worker the feeling of personal identity and "belonging" which neither the shop nor relations with management supplied.)

It seems to us significant that the average worker appeared to be oppressed by this sense of anonymity *in spite of the fact that he declared himself well satisfied with his rate of pay and the security of his job.* The answer to this problem in the most general terms would appear to be a program designed to re-create the sense *and also* the reality of a bona fide work community. And for such a program to be successful we believe that both union and management would have to agree on the measures to be taken.

A comment by a man on the line will suggest the nature of the problem more clearly than many paragraphs of exposition:

> There is a different feeling in this plant. It's much bigger than people around here have ever seen. It's just like the kid who goes up to a grown-up man and starts talking to him. There doesn't seem to be a friendly feeling. At the plant I used to work in there was a different feeling. Everyone spoke to everyone else. . . . Nobody goes to other departments in this plant. The understanding could be better—happier and much easier. Here a man is just so much horsepower.

Perhaps the human needs in Plant X are merely an expression in more explicit terms of the needs of our industrial civilization. The problem of reintegrating the several faculties of man into a significant unity presents itself in many fields—in industry, science, and government, to name but three—in an age of over-specialization.

It is striking that throughout the survey of Plant X both union and management agreed with the authors that the more basic problems to be explored were not those connected with a particular plant, industry, or corporation. Rather they were problems related to technological and organizational trends common to modern industry. Both agreed that modern American civilization as we know it rests upon mass-production principles quite as much as upon the natural resources of the United States. The attitude of both, therefore, was a simple and heartening one: *Since these problems exist, let us get all the facts we can. In time we shall be able to solve them.*

As Saint-Exupéry, the French aviator and author wrote:

The Machine is not an end. . . . It is a tool . . . like the plough.

If we believe that it degrades Man, it is possibly because we lack the perspective for judging the end results of transformations as rapid as those to which we have been subjected. What are two hundred years in the history of the Machine when compared with two hundred thousand years in the history of Man? We have scarcely established ourselves in this country of mines and of central electricity. It is as if we had hardly begun to live in the new house that we have not yet finished building. Everything has changed so rapidly around us: human relations, conditions of work, customs. . . . Every step in our progress has driven us a little further from our acquired habits, and we are in truth pioneers who have not yet established the foundations of our new country.[3]

[3] Antoine de Saint-Exupéry, *Terre des Hommes* (Paris, Gallimard, 1939), p. 58.

Selections from Social and Psychological Consquences
of the Longwall Method of Coal-Getting

E. L. TRIST AND K. W. BAMFORTH

Mechanization and the Problem of Intermediate Organization. With the advent of coal-cutters and mechanical conveyors, the degree of technological complexity of the coal-getting task was raised to a different level. Mechanisation made possible the working of a single long face in place of a series of short faces. In thin seams short faces increase costs, since a large number of "gates" (see Fig. 1) have to be "ripped" up several feet above the height of the seam to create haulage and trav-

elling facilities. In British coal, seams less than 4 ft. in thickness are common, so that there was a tendency to make full use of the possibility of working optimally long rather than optimally short faces. For this reason, and for others also, discussion of which is beyond present scope, the longwall method came into being. Applicable to thick as well as to thin seams, it became the general method of coal-getting in the British industry, enabling the average type of pit, which may contain three or four seams of different thickness, to work its entire coal economically, and to develop its layout and organize its production in terms of a single, self-consistent plan. In America, where

From *Human Relations,* Vol. 4, No. 1, 1951, pp. 6–38. Reprinted with permission of the publisher, Tavistock Publications Ltd., and the authors.

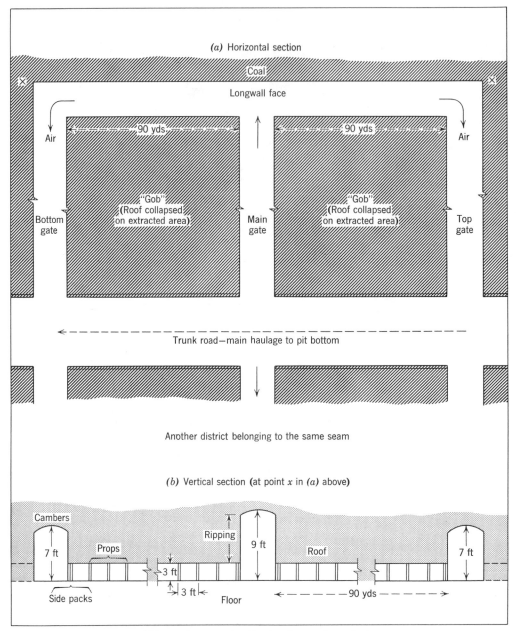

Fig. 1. *Layout of a district, longwall method.*

thick seams are the rule, mechanization has developed in terms of shorter faces and room-and-pillar techniques.

The associated characteristics of mechanized complexity, and of largeness as regards the scale of the primary production unit, created a situation in which it was impossible for the method to develop as a technological system without bringing into existence a work rela-tionship structure radically different from that associated with hand-got procedures. The artisan type of pair, composed of the skilled man and his mate, assisted by one or more labourers, was out of keeping as a model for the type of work group required. Need arose for a unit more of the size and differentiated complexity of a small factory department. A structure of intermediate social magnitude began therefore to emerge. The basic pattern round which the work relationships of the longwall production unit were organized became the cycle group of 40–50 men, their shot-firer and shift "deputies," who were responsible to the pit management for the working as a whole. Only in relation to this total cycle group could various smaller sub-groups secure function and acquire social form.

This centring of the new system on a differentiated structure of intermediate social magnitude disturbed the simple balance that had existed between the very small and very large traditional groups, and impaired the quality of responsible autonomy. The psychological and sociological problems posed by the technological needs of the longwall system were those with respect to which experience in the industry was least, and towards which its traditions were antithetical. The consequences of this conflict between the demands of the new situation and the resources available from past experience will be taken up in the light of the detailed account, which will now be presented, of the longwall system itself.

Features and Difficulties of the Longwall Production Unit as a Whole [1]

The Scale and Spatio-Temporal Structure of the Three-Shift Cycle. In the longwall method, a direct advance is made into the coal on a continuous front; faces of 180–200 yds. being typical, though longer faces are not uncommon. The work is broken down into a standard

series of component operations that follow each other in rigid succession over three shifts of seven and a half hours each, so that a total coal-getting cycle may be completed once in each twenty-four hours of the working week. The shift spread of the 40 workmen needed on an average face is: 10 each to the first ("cutting") and second ("ripping") shifts; 20 to the third ("filling") shift. The amount of coal scheduled for extraction varies under different conditions but is commonly in the neighbourhood of 200 tons per cycle. A medium-size pit with three seams would have 12–15 longwall faces in operation simultaneously.

These faces are laid out in districts as shown in Fig. 1. Since the longwall method is specially applicable to thin seams, Fig. 1 has been set up in terms of a 3-ft. working. The face, extending 90 yds. on either side of the main gate is within average limits for a seam of this thickness. The height of the face area—that of the 3-ft. seam itself—may be contrasted with the 9 ft. and 7 ft, to which the main and side gates have been ripped and built up as permanent structures with cambers and side-packs. By regulation, props must be placed every 3 ft., and the line of props shown in Fig. 1*b* is that placed immediately against a coal-face waiting to be filled off. The area marked "Gob" (to use a term common in mining vernacular) indicates the expanse from which the coal has already been extracted. On this area the roof is left to collapse. Only the tunnels made by the main and side gates, which

---

[1] The procedure followed both in the text and in Figs. 1 and 2 and Table 1 has been to build up a model of the system in terms of the experience of a group of faces similarly run and well known at first hand. What follows is therefore an account of one version of the system, though the version is a common one. Faces exist that are twice as long as that given. In thick seams these may require 40–50 fillers alone (even more), apart altogether from other personnel. In thin seams with high gates more than twice the number of rippers given may be employed, 8 or more on the main gate and some 6–4 on the side gates respectively. On shorter faces there may be only one borer and at least one gummer. Under some conditions packing and drawing-off are separated from belt-

work, and loading-point personnel are included as face workers. There are differences in nomenclature in different areas, e.g. "dinters" for "rippers." Variations arise partly from differences in natural conditions (thickness of seam, hardness of coal, type of roof and floor, etc.), partly from preferences in the matter of lay-out, and partly from the amount and character of the equipment available or judged necessary. Though conveyor serviced, quite a long face may be hand-got if the coal is soft; alternatively, two cutting units may be employed if its is hard and the face exceptionally long. Belts are of several varieties ("floor," "plate," "top," etc.). Where the seam is thick enough to eliminate ripping an approximation may be made to a two-shift system. Productivity varies widely in accordance with these differences, as does smoothness of functioning and the degree of stress experienced. Nevertheless, all are versions of one method. The basic pattern is the same.

are used for ventilation and for haulage and travelling, are kept open. These tunnels may sometimes extend for distances of 2 miles, and even more, before the coal face itself is reached from the trunk road leading from the pit bottom.

In each coal-getting cycle the advance made into the coal is equal to the depth of the undercut. A cut of 6 ft. represents typical practice in a thin seam with a good roof. All equipment has to be moved forward as each cycle contributes to the advance. The detail in the face area is represented in Fig. 2, where the coal is shown cut and waiting for the shot-firer, whose task is the last to be performed before the fillers come on. The combined width of the lanes marked "New Creeping Track" and "New Conveyor Track" equals the depth of 6 ft., from which the coal has been removed by the fillers on the last shift of the previous cycle. As part of the preparation work of the current cycle (before the fillers can come on again), the conveyor has to be moved from its previous position in the "old Conveyor Track" to its present position, shown in Fig. 2, in the "New Conveyor Track," against the face. At the same time the two lines of props on either side of the "Old Creeping Track" are withdrawn (allowing the roof to sag or collapse) and thrown over beside the conveyor for the fillers to use in propping up their roof as they get into the next 6 ft. of coal. The term "creeping track" refers to the single, propped, 3-ft. lane, adjacent to that occupied by the conveyor but on the side away from the coal. It allows free passage up and down the face, and is called a creeping track since in thin seams the low roof makes it necessary for all locomotion to take the form of "creeping," i.e. crawling on the hands and knees.

The mass-production character of the longwall operation necessitates a large-scale, mobile layout of the type described. But the spatiotemporal structure imposed by the long face and the shift sequence makes a difficult habitat when considered as a theatre in which effective communication and good working relationships must be maintained between 40 men, their shot-firer and shift deputies. On the one hand, the group is spread over 200 yds. in a tunnel 2 yds. wide and 1 yd. high, cross-cut only by the main and side gates; on the other, it is spread over 24 hours and divided up in three successive shifts. The production engi-

neer might write a simple equation: 200 tons equals 40 men over 200 yds. over 24 hours. But there are no solutions of equivalent simplicity to the psychological and social difficulties raised. For psychological and social difficulties of a new order appear when the scale of a task transcends the limits of simple spatiotemporal structure. By this is meant conditions under which those concerned can complete a job in one place at one time, i.e., the situation of the face-to-face, or singular group.

Once a job is too big for a singular group, a multiple group comes into existence, composed of a number of sub-groups of the singular type. In these differentiated organizations of intermediate social magnitude, problems of intergroup relationships are superimposed on, and inter-act with, the intra-group tensions of the primary components. In the longwall production unit, the scale of the task introduces the contradiction of spatio-temporal disintegration as a condition of multiple group integration.

The Differentiation and Interdependence of Tasks. Occupational roles express the relationship between a production process and the social organization of the group. In one direction, they are related to tasks, which are related to each other; in the other, to people, who are also related to each other. At workman level, there are seven of these roles in the longwall system—borer, cutter, gummer, beltbreaker, belt-builder, ripper, and filler—which are linked to the component tasks of the production process. In Table 1 the functions of these seven categories in the interrelated technological and social structures are described in detail in a comprehensive table. For analytical purposes, however, it is necessary to treat separately these two different aspects of occupational roles; and, in this section, consideration will be given to the interdependence of component tasks in the production process, and to occupational roles so far as they are related to this. These tasks fall into four groups, concerned with (1) the preparation of the coal-face for shot-firing, (2) shifting the conveyor, (3) ripping and building up the main and side gates, and (4) moving the shot coal on to the conveyor.

The face preparation tasks are all performed on the first shift. They include boring holes for the shot-firer, with pneumatic or electrically operated drills, near the roof of the seam

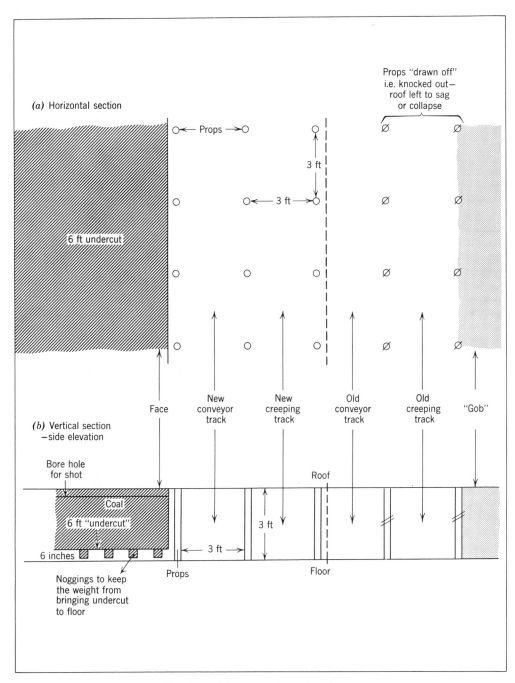

(a) Horizontal section

Props "drawn off"
i.e. knocked out—
roof left to sag
or collapse

O←— Props —→O

3 ft

O   O←— 3 ft —→O

6 ft undercut

O   O   O | ∅   ∅

O   O   O | ∅   ∅

Face   New   New   Old   Old   "Gob"
        conveyor   creeping   conveyor   creeping
        track   track   track   track

(b) Vertical section
  —side elevation

Bore hole
for shot

Roof

Coal

6 ft "undercut"   3 ft

6 inches

3 ft

Props   Floor

Noggings to keep
the weight from
bringing undercut
to floor

Fig. 2. Coal face as set for filling shift.

through to the depth of the undercut, at short distances (within each filler's "length") along the entire expanse of face; driving the coal-cutter so that the blade or "jib" makes an even undercut into the coal some six inches from the floor to whatever depth has been assigned, again along the entire expanse of face; taking out the six inches of coal (called the "gummings") left in the undercut, so that the main weight of coal can drop and break freely when the shots are fired; placing supporting "noggings" underneath it so that this weight does

Table 1. *Occupational Structure in the Longwall System*

SHIFT SEQUENCE	OCCUPATIONAL ROLES	NO. OF MEN	METHODS OF PAYMENT	GROUP ORGANIZATION	TASKS	SKILLS	STATUS DIFFERENCES AND RANKING
First (usually called "cutting" shift). Either night, 8 P.M.–3.30 A.M., or afternoon, 12 noon–7.30 P.M. (borers start an hour earlier). Though alternating between night and afternoon, personnel on the cutting shift are never on days.	Borer	2	Per hole	Interdependent pair on same note.	Boring holes for shot-firer in each stint to depth of undercut.	Management of electric or pneumatic drills, placing of holes, judgment of roof, hardness of coal, etc.	4.5, equal in pair.
	Cutter	2	Per yard	Interdependent pair on same note, front man and back man.	Operating coal-cutter to achieve even cut at assigned depth the entire length of the face; knocking out (front man), re-setting (back man) props as cutter passes. Back man inserts noggings.	Requires rather more "engineering" skill than other coal-face tasks. Mining skills in keeping cut even under changing conditions, watching roof control.	1, front man senior and responsible for cut; back man assists; cutting is the key preparation task.
	Gummer	4	Day wage	Loose group attached to cutters, through front man without supervisory authority.	Cleaning out undercut, so that clear space for coal to drop and level floor for filler. The coal between undercut and floor is called "the gummings."	Unskilled, heavy manual task, which unless conscientiously done creates difficulties for filler, for when gummings left in, the shot simply blows out and coal is left solid.	7, equal in group; some chance of promotion to cutter eventually.

Shift	Role	No.	Payment	Work group	Task	Skill / responsibility	Status
Second (usually called the "ripping" shift). Either night or afternoon alternating with cutting shift. Rippers may start rather later than builders. None of these personnel go on day shift proper.	Belt-breaker	2	Per yard	Interdependent pair on same note.	Shifting belt-engine and tension-end into face clear of rippers; breaking up conveyor in old track, placing plates, etc., ready new track, drawing off props in old creeping track; packing as required.	Belt-breaking is a relatively simple engineering task; engine shifting is awkward and heavy; drawing off and packing involve responsibility for roof control and require solid underground experience.	4.5, equal in pair.
	Belt-builder	2	Per yard	Interdependent pair on same note.	Reassembling conveyor in new track; positioning belt-engine and tension-end in line with this; testing running of reassembled conveyor; placing chocks; packing as required.	As with breaking, the level of engineering skill is relatively simple; inconvenience caused to fillers if belt out of position. The roof control responsibilities demand solid underground experience.	4.5, equal in pair.
	Ripper	8	Cubic measure	Cohesive functionally inter-related group on same note.	To "rip" "dirt" out of main and side gates to assigned heights; place cambers and build up roof into a solid, safe and durable structure; pack up the sides. The ripping team carries out all operations necessary to their task, doing their own boring. The task is . . . seen through by the group [during] . . . one shift.	This work requires the highest degree of building skill among coal face tasks. Some very heavy labour is entailed. Since the work is relatively permanent there is much pride of craft. On the ripper depends the safety of all gates and main ways.	2, the status of the "main ripper" is next to that of the front man on the cutter, but he is not separately paid. The group usually contains all degrees of experience and is egalitarian.

(Continued)

Table 1. Continued

SHIFT SEQUENCE	OCCUPATIONAL ROLES	NO. OF MEN	METHODS OF PAYMENT	GROUP ORGANIZATION	TASKS	SKILLS	STATUS DIFFERENCES AND RANKING
Third (usually called "filling" shift). Either day, 6 A.M.–1.30 P.M., or afternoon, 2 P.M.–9.30 P.M. Never night.	Filler	20	Weight—tonnage on conveyors.	Aggregate of individuals with equal "stints"; all on same note; fractionated relationships and much isolation.	The length of the "stint" is determined by the depth of the cut and the thickness of the seam. Using hand or air pick and shovel, the filler "throws" the "shot" coal on to the conveyor until he has cleared his length, i.e. "filled off." He props up every 2 ft. 6 in. as he works in.	The filler remains in one work place while conditions change. Considerable underground experience is required to cope with bad conditions. Each man is responsible for his own section of roof. Bad work on other shifts makes the task harder. It is heavy in any case and varies in different parts of the wall.	4.5, equal throughout the group; "corner" men are envied, reputation of being good or bad workman is important.
3 shifts	7 roles	40 men	5 methods	4 types	The common background of "underground" skill is more important than the task differences.		Differences in status and weekly earnings are small, apart from the case of the gummers.

not cause it to sag down to the floor while the "cut" is standing during the next shift. These tasks are performed in the order given. Three of the seven work roles are associated with their execution, two men being fully occupied boring the holes, a further two in managing the coal-cutter, and four in clearing out the undercut.

The success of the shots fired at the end of the second shift to make the coal finally ready for the filler depends on the efficiency with which each of these interdependent preparation tasks has been carried out. Bad execution of any one of them diminishes, and may even cancel out, the effect of the shots, with consequent havoc in the lengths of the particular fillers where such breakdowns have occurred. Holes bored too low leave a quantity of coal, difficult to extract, clinging to the roof after the shots have been fired. If the roof is sticky, this gives rise to "sticky tops." Holes not bored through to the full depth of the undercut create the condition of "hard backs," the shots having no effect on this part of the coal. The coal-cutter only too frequently has a tendency to leave the floor and "get up into the coal," producing an uneven cut. This means less working height for the filler, and also less wages, since his tonnage is reduced. When the "gummings" are left in, the shot is wasted; the coal has nowhere to drop and the powder blows out of the hole (usually up the "cutting break" in the roof) so that the mass to be extracted is left solid. Failure to insert noggings, which leads to the cut sagging down, also renders useless the services of the shot-firer.

The group of operations concerned with the conveyor involves—since forward movement is blocked by props which must be left standing—breaking up the sections of belt in the old conveyor track and building them up in the new. Each of these tasks requires two men: the belt-breakers and belt-builders. The dismantling part is done on the first shift in the wake of the cutting operation. The reasons include the necessity of shifting belt-engines and tension-ends out of the gate areas (where they are positioned when the conveyor is working) in order to allow the ripping operation to proceed. The reassembly of the conveyor is the only task performed in the face area during the second shift. Unless the conveyor is properly jointed, set close to the new face, and accurately sighted in a straight

line, a further crop of difficulties arise, and frequent stoppages may interfere with filling. The most modern types of belt, e.g., floor belts, avoid the labour of breaking up and reassembling plates. Belt-engines and tension-ends are cumbersome equipment, but they must nevertheless be shifted every day. Similarly, the last two lines of props have to be taken down and thrown forward.

The third group of tasks comprises those that entail ripping up the roof of the main and side gates to the depth of the undercut, and building them up with a stable roof and firmly packed sides so that haulage- and air-ways can advance with the face. Unless this work is expertly done, the danger of roof falls is acute, with the likelihood both of men and equipment being blocked in the face. This work is carried out by a team of 7–8 rippers.

Only when all these operations have been completed, can the shots be fired and the fillers come on. For the filling operation, the entire face is divided up into equal lengths—except that the corner positions are somewhat shorter in view of difficulties created by the proximity of belt-engines and tension-ends. In a 3-ft. seam, lengths would be 8–10 yds., and some 20 fillers would be required, 10 in each half-face of 90–100 yds. Each filler is required to extract the entire coal from his length, going back to the depth of the 6 ft. undercut. When he has thrown his last load on to the conveyor he has "filled off," i.e., finished his "length" or "stint." As he progresses into his coal, he has the additional task of propping up his roof every 3 ft. As well as a hand-pick and shovel, his tool kit includes an air pick, used for dealing with some of the difficulties created by bad preparation, or in any case when his coal is hard.

At a later point there will be a discussion of the differential distribution of bad conditions among the lengths of a face. Here it may be noted that the face is not "filled off" until each and every length has been cleared, and that until this has been done, the new cycle cannot begin. Disorganization on the filling shift disorganizes the subsequent shifts, and its own disorganization is often produced by the bad preparation left by these teams. Every time the cycle is stopped, some 200 tons of coal are lost.

So close is the task interdependence that the system becomes vulnerable from its need for one hundred per cent performance at each step. The most sensitive interaction is between the face-preparation activities and filling, but it is in relation to this that social organization is weakest. This point will be taken up in later sections.

The Segmented Quality of the Social Organization. With respect to the way in which the work roles have been institutionalized as regards the persons and groups concerned, a basic segregation of the various categories of workers from each other follows from the fact that it has been the traditional practice for a face-worker to be trained in only one of the seven roles, and to spend all or most of his underground life in this one occupation. This basic segregation of roles is intensified by the five different methods of payment described in Table 1, and by the exaggeration of status differences, despite the common background of "underground skill" and the equivalence of earnings (apart from the rather lower rate received by the gummers).

It is still further reinforced by the segregation of shifts. As will be seen from the shift time-tables, the three shifts never meet. Moreover, the two preparation groups alternate on the so-called "back shifts" while the fillers alternate on "days" and "afternoons," so that a far-reaching community, as well as work, split is effected between the fillers and the others. The "back shift" men are either going to or coming from work in the evening, so that they are cut off from normal community activities during the week. Even at week-ends they are down the pit either on Saturday afternoon or Sunday evening.

As regards the primary work groups in which those performing the various roles participate, there are four radically different patterns: the series of interdependent pairs—borers, belt-builders, and belt-breakers; the extended pair organization of the cutters and gummers; the self-sufficient group of eight rippers; and the aggregate of twenty fillers spread out over the 200-yd. face. The uneven social quality of these different types of primary groups will be discussed . . . [later], both with respect to intra- and inter-group relations. This unevenness, taken together with the role and shift segregation, works against the social integration of the cycle group as a whole. Yet, in view of the close interdependence of tasks, the social integration of the total work group is a first essential of the system.

It is submitted that the non-existence of the cycle group as a social whole in face of the interdependence of the component tasks is one of the major contradictions present in the longwall method. The social organization is a simple reflection of the "job breakdown." Because this latter is reintegrated into a technological whole by the task sequence it does not follow that the differentiated role-groups concerned are also and thereby reintegrated into a social whole. Differentiation gives rise to the need for social as well as technological integration. No attempt seems to have been made in the longwall method to achieve any living social integration of the primary and shift groups into which the cycle aggregate has been differentiated. This, of course, is a common omission in mass-production systems. . . .

Four Types of Group Defence

Informal Organization. The functional isolation of the filler within his own group, which leaves him "officially" alone with his "coals," is met by an attempt to develop informal, small-group organization in which private arrangements to help each other out are made among neighbours, in twos, threes, or fours. But these solely interpersonal arrangements are undependable and open to manipulation for anti-social and competitive as well as for mutually protective ends. A number of isolates is left over. The total face group is incapable, except defensively, of acting as a socially responsible whole, since not even private allegiances are owed outside the small informal groups. These in turn are without responsible autonomy; the absence of institutionalized mutual obligation means that there are no statutory group tasks, and each individual can be held ultimately responsible only for clearing his own length. Internal "rows" the more easily break up the informal "coalitions," whose morale tends to be of the clique type.

Examples were, however, given to the writers of stable groups who stuck to each other and worked well over long periods. One informant said of these: "Here things are more like the old times in the pit." Groups of this kind were envied and also criticized for being "too close." They appeared sometimes to be held together by a natural leader, and at others to be made up of individuals of generally good personality. Most informants were agreed that there was a tendency for the extremes to sort themselves out; there were "good" and "bad" faces as well as "good" and "bad" cliques within a particular face aggregate. But all this happened as it might. There was no support from the system.

Isolates, it appears, are either individualists —who "won't even share timber"—or men with bad reputations, with whom others refuse to work. Amongst these are the unconscientious—who "won't help out at the end of a shift" and who are frequently absent—and the helpless—who "cannot learn to look after themselves under bad conditions." Others, whose stamina is deficient (whether through age, illness, or neurosis) and whose lengths are often uncleared in consequence, are dropped from the informal groups.

Only to a very limited extent, therefore, does his informal group organization meet the filler's need for a secure role in a primary group within his own shift. In view of the extent of his dependence on the performance of those in the other two shifts, his need for this foundation is greater than that of any of the other occupational groups, while the resources available to him are fewer.

Reactive Individualism. His small group failing, the filler is thrown on to himself and against others. The second defence against isolation is the development of a reactive individualism, in which a reserve of personal secrecy is apt to be maintained. Among his own shift mates there is competitive intrigue for the better places—middle positions are avoided; from these "it is a long way to creep" —and for jobs in workings where conditions are good there is a scramble.

On some faces described to the writers, fear of victimization was rife, particularly in the form of being sent to work in a "bad place"; the deputy being more easily turned into a persecutor in view of the guilt arising from the intrigue and deception which the men practised both against him and against each other. Against the deputy, advantage is taken of the scope afforded in the underground situation for petty deception over such matters as time of leaving the pit, or the "measure that is sent up" (amount of coal filled on to the con-

veyor). With the deputy, however, men are also prepared to enter into alliance against each other, often for very good reasons—to stop mates from going absent and by so doing throwing more work on to the others.

As regards outside groups, practices of bribing members of the other shifts in the hope of getting a "good deal" in one's own length were mentioned by several informants. Tobacco is taken to the cutter; gummers are stood a pint on Sunday. These practices are to be regarded as symptoms of a state of affairs rather than as widespread in themselves.

The effect of this defensive individualism is to reduce the sense of secure identification in the larger pit collectivity, which was the second principle on which the older equilibrium was based.

Nowhere is the mistrust that shift mates have of each other more in evidence than in controversies over bye-work "slipping off the note." On what is referred to as the "big note" is entered all the contract and bye-work done during the week by the shift aggregate. This note is issued to one man called "the number man" since he is identified by his check-number. In no sense is this individual a representative appointed by his mates. Only rarely is he an informal leader. Customarily he is a "corner man," whose length adjoins the main gate, i.e., the man most conveniently within reach of the deputy. When asked about bye-work he does not always know what has been done at the far ends of the face and he is under no obligation to stop his own work to find out. But though a number of men will grouse about their pay being short, mentioning this or that item as having "slipped off the note," very few ever bother to check up. There are men who have worked on a face for three or four years and never once seen their own big note. Yet these are among the more ready to accuse the corner man or the deputy. The corner man is suspected at least of never forgetting to make the most of his own assignments. To the deputy is ascribed the intention of keeping the costs of his district down. Conspiracy between the two is often alleged. Only when a major rumpus occurs are such suspicions put to the test, but showdowns of this kind are avoided as apt to peter out in squabbles proving nothing.

The competition, intrigue, unwillingness to put allegations to the test and the reserve of personal secrecy, are parts of one pattern. Whatever their personal wishes, men feel under pressure to be out for themselves, since the social structure in which they work denies them membership in any group that can legitimize interdependence. In this respect reactive individualism makes a basic interpretation of the social structure of the filling shift and is the only form of authorized behaviour.

Mutual Scapegoating. Fillers almost never see those who work on the "back shifts," and this absence of contact gives full scope for mutual and irresponsible scapegoating. When there is a crisis, and the filling shift is unable to fill off, the "buck" is passed to the other shifts—or vice versa if disorganization has occurred elsewhere. It is frequently also passed to the deputy, who is blamed for not finding substitutes, and to repair men, brought in, but too old to stand the pace.

For these to pass the buck back to the fillers is fruitless. As they do not exist as a responsible whole, they, as a group, are not there to take the blame, and the individual filler can always exempt himself. Since bad conditions and bad work interact so closely, it is usually difficult to pin blame specifically. Mutual scapegoating is a self-perpetuating system, in which nothing is resolved and no one feels guilty. For all concerned to remain in collusion with such a system is a defence which allows each to make his "anonymous contribution" to the "group mentality," [2] which sabotages both the goal of cycle productivity and the needs of the individual for a membership in a satisfying work-group. So far as this pattern obtains, all strike at each other in a mock war in which no one is hurt yet all suffer.

This defence can also be seen as a "backhanded" attempt to recover the supportive unity lost through reactive individualism in a way that is consistent with it. For all to be "in the bad" together is at least a way of being together. If one's contribution to a group is to help carry the badness of others, the group's contribution to oneself is to allow one to leave some of one's own badness in the group by being granted, for example, the privilege of withdrawal so that one's absence is sanctioned

[2] W. R. Bion, "Experiences in Groups, III," *Human Relations,* Vol. II, No. 1, January, 1949, pp. 13–22.

on a fair share of occasions. This "formula" provides a workable scheme since the tacit agreement is only too plausibly maintained that the badness both of the group and of the individual are exclusively effects of the system which the group is compelled to operate without having power to change, i.e., these effects are regarded as "induced" rather than also as "own" forces. The group and the individual can therefore deny and get rid of their own badness by ascribing it to the system. The good of the group becomes its power to preserve the good of individual members by limiting the degree of their exposure to the bad system. The alternative would be constructive limitation of its real deficiencies so that it might be operated with more productive results and a higher degree of mutual satisfaction.

Not that the system is felt as entirely bad since it is the means by which a living is earned. Moreover, under present conditions this living is a good one, both in terms of wages and of community status. But the benefits which these "goods" bring are not realized in the work activities of the group. They lie outside the work system, which is tolerated as a means to external ends rather than accepted also as an end in itself, worthy of wholehearted pursuit in virtue of the internal satisfactions it affords. When these different aspects of the matter are put together the expectation emerges of a balance being struck which would allow things to tick over, though with a degree of social illness costly alike to productivity and to personal well-being. This expectation accords with reality.

Self-Compensatory Absenteeism. Withdrawal is the fourth form of defence, complementing mutual scapegoating, and absenteeism is to be regarded as a recognized social technique within this pattern. For example, one filler, returning from his week's holiday with pay, complained that the first two shifts had "knocked it all out of him." The gummings had been left in. His coal was solid. He had had the air-pick on all day. "I've tried cursing 'em but it's no use, and pleading with 'em but it's no use. I'll take a day off for this."

When conditions on a face deteriorate, especially in ways that are predictable, absenteeism among fillers sometimes piles up to a point where the remainder have to stay down an extra two or three hours in order to clear the face. Should this situation repeat itself for more than a day or two, those coming on shift often meet at the pit-head baths before presenting themselves for work. If less than a certain number arrive, all go home.

Absenteeism of this self-compensatory type, though carried out as an act of aggrieved defiance against a system, felt in these circumstances as persecutory is an attempt on the part of the individual to prolong his work life at the coal-face. For without the respite of occasional absences, he feels that he would soon become unable to carry on. In view of the accentuated differences both in wages and in status between face workers and repair, haulage, or surface personnel, the goal of remaining at the coal-face for as long as possible would appear to operate as a powerful motivational force in determining the behaviour of the ordinary face-worker. . . .

Conclusions

The fact that the desperate economic incentives of the between-war period no longer operate means a greater intolerance of unsatisfying or difficult working conditions, or systems of organization, among miners, even though they may not always be clear as to the exact nature of the resentment or hostility which they often appear to feel. The persistence of socially ineffective structures at the coal-face is likely to be a major factor in preventing a rise of morale, in discouraging recruitment, and in increasing labour turnover.

The innovations in social organization of face-work groups, which have begun to appear, and the success of some of these developments, suggest that the organizational changes brought about by nationalization provide a not inappropriate opportunity for the experimental working through of problems of the types which have been indicated. It can certainly be said with some confidence that within the industry there exist the necessary resources and creativity to allow widespread constructive developments to take place.

As regards the longwall system, the first need is for systematic study and evaluation of the changes so far tried.[3] It seems to the present writers, however, that a qualitative change will have to be effected in the general character of the method, so that a social as well as a technological whole can come into existence. Only if this is achieved can the relationships of the cycle work-group be successfully integrated and a new social balance be created.

The immediate problems are to develop formal small-group organization on the filling shift and to work out an acceptable solution to the authority questions in the cutting team. But it is difficult to see how these problems can be solved effectively without restoring responsible autonomy to primary groups throughout the system and ensuring that each of these groups has a satisfying sub-whole as its work task, and some scope for flexibility in work-pace. Only if this is done will the stress of the deputy's role be reduced and his task of maintaining the cycle receive spontaneous support from the primary work groups.

It is likely that any attempts in this direction would require to take advantage of the recent trend of training face-workers for more than one role, so that interchangeability of tasks would be possible within work teams. Moreover, the problem of shift segregation will not be overcome until the situation is altered in which one large group is permanently organised round the day shift and the others round the back shifts. Some interchange between roles in preparation and filling tasks would seem worth consideration. Once preparation workers and fillers could experience each other's situations, mutual understanding and tolerance would be likely to increase.

It is to be borne in mind that developments in room-and-pillar methods appear to be stressing the value of the strongly-knit primary work-group and that the most recent advances in mechanization, such as power loaders or strippers, both require work teams of this kind.

[3] One of the most interesting of these is "An Experiment in Continuous Longwall Mining at Bolsover Colliery," W. V. Sheppard, The Institution of Mining Engineers, Annual General Meeting, Jan. 1951.

Co-operation and Competition in a Bureaucracy

This paper discusses performance and variations in competitiveness among twelve interviewers in two small sections of a public employment agency.[1] The duties of the interviewers in both sections were essentially alike. They received requests for workers over the phone. The order forms on which job openings were described were filed in a common pool in each section. Most of the official's time was spent interviewing applicants for jobs. After ascertaining the client's qualifications, the interviewer searched the sectional files for suitable vacancies. If an acceptable job was found, he referred the client to it and later phoned the employer to determine whether the client had been hired.

The statistics which show how many interviews and how many placements each person in the section did are passed around to all interviewers. Of course, you look at them and see how you compare with others. This creates a competitive spirit,

said one of the interviewers, voicing the sentiments of most of his fellows. In a period of job shortages, competition took the form of trying to utilize job openings before anybody else did. Interviewers were so anxious to make

placements that they even resorted to illicit methods. Said one:

> When you take an order, instead of putting it in the box, you leave it on your desk. There was so much hiding of orders under the blotter that we used to ask, "Do you have anything under your rug?" when we looked for an order. You might leave an order you took on the desk, or you might leave it on the desk after you made no referral. . . . Or, you might take an order only partially; you write the firm's name, and a few things; the others you remember. And you leave it on the pad [of order blanks]. You keep on doing this, and all these orders are not in the box.
>
> You can do some wrong filling out. For instance, for a rather low-salary job, you fill out "experience required." Nobody can make a placement on that except you, because you, alone, know that experience isn't required. Or, if there are several openings [on one order], you put the order into "referrals" [file category for *filled* job openings] after you make one placement. You're supposed to put it into "referrals" but stand it up, so that the others can see it. If you don't, you have a better chance of making the next placement than somebody else. And time and again you see four, five openings on one order filled by the same person. [In one case on file eight out of nine openings on one order had been filled by the same interviewer.]

The major opportunity for competitive monopolization of job openings occurred when they were received from employers. Since illicit practices were concealed from the observer, the extent of competition could not be determined through questioning or direct

From *American Journal of Sociology*, Vol. 59, May 1954, pp. 530–535. Reprinted with permission of the publisher, The University of Chicago Press. Copyright 1954, The University of Chicago Press.
[1] These data are part of a study on interpersonal relations in two government agencies conducted under a fellowship of the Social Science Research Council, which is hereby gratefully acknowledged. The entire study is soon to be published under the title "The Dynamics of Bureaucracy."

There were seven interviewers in Section A and five in Section B. Seven of the twelve were women.

observation [2] but was betrayed by the record of official transactions. The extent to which an interviewer filled the vacancies he had re-

ceived over the phone with his own clients in excess of chance expectations furnishes an index of competitiveness. (Col. 4 in Table 1 shows this index; Col. 1–3 present the data on which it is based.)

[2] This is clearly indicated by the comment of one of a group of special interviewers, who were expected to use the job openings of the regular interviewers but usually had great difficulty in doing so: "Oh, they hide everything from us. We got more orders when you [the observer] sat in the middle of that section than ever before. We laughed about it. Interviewers would hand us orders asking whether we could use them—when you were looking. That had never happened before."

STRUCTURAL CONDITIONS AND COMPETITIVENESS. The members of Section A were more competitive than those of Section B. The last two columns in Table 1 also show that the interviewer's competitiveness was related to his productivity in Section A (Pearsonian $r = +.92$), but this was not the case in Section B ($r = -.20$). In other words, hoarding of jobs

Table 1. Competitiveness and Producitvity in Section A and in Section B

	OPENINGS RECEIVED * (1)	REFERRALS MADE BY RECIPIENT (2)	RATIO OF REFERRALS TO OPENINGS (3)	COMPETI- TIVENESS † (4)	PRO- DUCTIVITY ‡ (5)	NUMBER OF PLACEMENTS (6)
Section A:						
Adams	34	19	0.56	3.9	0.70	100
Ahman	62	27	0.44	3.1	0.49	70
Ajax	40	28	0.70	4.9	0.97	139
Akers	71	32	0.45	3.2	0.71	101
Ambros	69	18	0.26	1.8	0.45	65
Atzenberg	106	43	0.41	2.9	0.61	87
Auble	10	3	0.30	2.1	0.39	56 §
Section B						
Babcock	16	7	0.44	2.2	0.53	46
Beers	58	19	0.33	1.6	0.71	62
Bing	51	15	0.29	1.5	0.75	65
Borden	17	7	0.41	2.1	0.55	48 §
Bush	43	19	0.42	2.1	0.97	84
Section A	392	170	0.43	3.0	0.59	590
Section B	185	67	0.36	1.8	0.67	289

* The great differences between interviewers in this column show that some were much more successful than others in inducing employers, or telephone operators, to channel requests for workers to them personally. This form of rivalry does not involve competitive interaction.

† Competitiveness index (col. 4): The proportion of job openings received to which the recipient made a referral (col. 3) times the number of members of the section. (This represents the observed divided by the expected frequency of referrals made by the recipient of a job opening.) Base period: First half of April, 1949.

‡ Productivity index (col. 5): The number of placements made (col. 6) divided by the number of job openings available, that is, the number of openings in the section per interviewer. Base period: April, 1949.

§ The number of placements was adjusted for the two interviewers absent for more than five days during April. Since the sectional numbers of placements were not revised, the values in col. 6 add up to more than the two totals shown.

was an effective way to improve an interviewer's placement record only in one of these two groups.

The members of Section B were more co-operative: they discouraged competitive practices by making them ineffective. When they learned about interesting vacancies, they often told one another, but an interviewer who manifested competitive tendencies was excluded from the network of reciprocal information and lost the respect of his co-workers. Any advantage of hoarding jobs was, at least, neutralized by such lack of co-operation, as is indicated by the absence of a relation between competitiveness and productivity in this group. Since competitive practices made an interviewer unpopular and failed to raise his productivity, they were infrequent.

These officials themselves attributed the greater competitiveness in Section A to the ambitiousness of several members: "There is usually one individual who starts it, who becomes a pace-setter. Once it has started, it is too late." The others, so interviewers claimed, have to follow suit. However, the most competitive member of Section A in recounting her reactions when production records were first introduced made it clear that this explanation of competition on the basis of personality characteristics is inadequate:

> When they introduced statistics, I realized how fast I worked. I even wanted to drop lower. I didn't mind working fast as long as it didn't show, but when it showed up like that on the record, I wanted to work less. But you know what happened? Some of the others started to compete with each other and produced more than I did. Then I thought to myself, "Since I can do it, it's silly to let them get ahead of me." I'm only human. So I worked as fast as before.

When statistical records made the superior performance of this interviewer public knowledge, she decided to work less, possibly in response to pressures the others had brought to bear upon her. While complaining about her unfair standards, however, the other members of the section also improved their own performance. Consequently, this interviewer, just like the others, felt constrained by colleagues to compete for an outstanding record. One or two members of Section B, on the other hand, were also accused of competitive tendencies, but their colleagues successfully discouraged their expression in monopolistic practices. It is in this sense that the competitive practices of one group and the co-operative practices of the other were social factors, calling for explanation in sociological rather than psychological terms, as Durkheim has long since emphasized.[3]

Differential conditions affected the development of these two groups. First, the supervisor in Section A relied heavily on performance records in evaluating interviewers: "And here, in the production figures, is the answer to the question: How good are you? Here you see exactly how good the work you did was." Interviewers often mentioned the pressure thus exerted: "[Especially] around rating time, you get this competition. You don't care whether the best person gets the pob, but you try to make the placement yourself." In contrast, the new supervisor in Section B surprised his subordinates by rating them more leniently than they had expected, and not primarily on the basis of production records. Consequently, as one interviewer reported, "we became less anxious about statistics; another experience like that, and we might forget all about placement credit."

Second, a common professional orientation existed only in Section B. While the members of Section A had been assigned, and had received their training, at different times, the majority of those in Section B received their training together after World War II, at a times when intensive counseling had been stressed, since many returning veterans needed occupational advice. One official said of this period:

> When I first came here, in May, 1946, we had a very nice bunch. It was like an all-day consultation; we discussed placements with each other all day long. At that time, the veterans came back, and there was a lot of emphasis on counseling. Nobody asked you how many placements you made, then. The emphasis was on quality, and we consulted with each other all day.

[3] Emile Durkheim, *The Rules of Sociological Method* (Chicago: University of Chicago Press, 1938), pp. 110 and *passim*.

In this situation, the group developed a common professional code, which discouraged speedy placement as constituting defective employment service. In effect, this orientation transformed competitive practices from illegitimate means for desirable ends into illegitimate means for worthless ends. If such practices did occur, they were vigorously opposed on moral grounds as violating the interest of clients. Nevertheless, as will be shown presently, competition could not have been effectively curbed if the supervisor's evaluation practice had engendered acute anxiety over productivity. However, the existence of this code would have made it difficult for the supervisor to judge performance mainly by productivity, since doing so would have stamped him as ignorant of the essentials of good employment service.

No opportunity for the development of a *common* professional code had existed in Section A. Since competitiveness prevailed in this group, the individual whose personal professional standards made him reluctant to compete either became the deviant whose productivity suffered or modified his standards and entered the race with the others.

Third, most members of Section A had been appointed to temporary civil service positions during World War II. They were on probation pending permanent appointments when production records were originally introduced and even afterward remained subject to layoffs due to reductions in staff. Their insecurity led them to strive to impress superiors with outstanding performance. In contrast, all but one of the members of Section B were veterans, whose employment could not be terminated except for cause. As one envious colleague put it, "They felt that nothing could happen to them, because they were veterans, and had super-seniority."

Differences in these three conditions—security of employment, opportunity for the development of a common professional orientation, and the evaluation practice of the supervisor—gave rise to two dissimilar social structures. Productivity was highly valued in Section A and became associated with the individual's standing in the group, while striving for sheer productivity was disparaged in Section B. Thus, whereas the most productive and most competitive member of Section A was considered the best interviewer by her co-workers and was

most popular with them,[4] the most productive member of Section B was least respected and least popular. As a result of these structural differences, co-operative norms prevailed only in Section B.

The interviewers in *both* sections disliked working in a competitive atmosphere. A member of Section A said: "If I see that an interviewer keeps orders on her desk, I take them and put them in the box. . . . Of course, you don't make friends that way." Since the majority in this section, including its most popular members, were highly competitive, to antagonize them was to threaten one's own standing in the group. This deterred interviewers from discouraging competitive practices. Antagonizing a deviant, however, does not endanger one's status. Consequently, since a striver was unpopular in Section B, its members could use sanctions freely to combat competitive practices and enforce co-operative norms.

SOCIAL COHESION AND PRODUCTIVITY. Table 1 shows that the group most concerned with productivity was less productive than the other group. Fifty-nine per cent of the job openings received in Section A were filled, in contrast to 67 per cent in Section B. (The 8 per cent difference is significant on the .01 level.) Another implicit paradox is that competitiveness and productivity were directly related for individuals in Section A but inversely related for the two groups.[5]

Anxious concern with productivity induced interviewers in Section A to concentrate blindly upon it at the expense of other considerations. In their eagerness to make many placements they often ignored their relationships with others as well as official rules. Competitiveness in this group weakened social co-

[4] She was most often mentioned by members of her own section in answer to the questions, respectively, "Who are the best interviewers?" and "Who are your friends in the office?"

[5] For another example of such disparity between individual and corresponding group data see the discussion of promotion opportunities and attitudes toward promotion in Samuel A. Stouffer *et al.*, *The American Soldier* (Princeton: Princeton University Press, 1949), I, 250–54. Kendall and Lazarsfeld discuss the methodological significance of such findings in Robert K. Merton and Paul F. Lazarsfeld (eds.), *Continuities in Social Research* (Glencoe, Ill.: Free Press, 1950), pp. 193–95.

hesion, while co-operativeness in Section B strengthened it. This difference is further shown by the fact that usually none of the members of Section A spent their rest periods together, whereas all but one of those of Section B, a newcomer when this study was being made, did. Social cohesion enhanced operating efficiency by facilitating co-operation and by reducing status anxiety.

Although the members of both groups had occasion to assist one another, greater effort was required to elicit such co-operation in Section A. The social interaction that occurred in the office during the twenty-four busiest hours of one week was recorded and classified as official and private contacts, that is, those directly concerned with a specific job or client, and all others. The frequency of an interviewer's official contacts with colleagues was related to his productivity in Section A (rank correlation = +.98) but not in Section B (rank correlation = +.08). This suggests that only interviewers who kept, as one put it, "hopping around all the time" to retrieve job orders that others kept on their desks were able to make many placements in the competitive section. In the cohesive group, on the other hand, the co-operation needed for making placements occurred as a matter of course, and not only in response to special requests. This effort was not required for high productivity.

To maximize his placements, the interviewer in Section A hoarded jobs and simultaneously tried to prevent others from doing so, thereby antagonizing his co-workers, whose co-operation he needed if he was to do well. The members of this section therefore attempted to conciliate colleagues whom their competitive practices had alienated. Often, shortly after having interfered with her operations, an interviewer paid another a compliment about her work or her apparel. The most competitive interviewer was in the habit of taking time out to joke with her co-workers and was proud of making more placements than anybody else, "nevertheless." Actually, this compensating friendliness, which made her popular despite her competitiveness, helped her to be productive.

In Section A, interviewers had to make special efforts at conciliation in order to make placements, but this was not necessary in Section B. At least, this impression is cor-

roborated by the finding that frequency of private contacts with others was also related to productivity in Section A (rank correlation = +.84) but not in Section B (rank correlation = +.13). The members of the cohesive group, whose operating practices did not put colleagues at a disadvantage, did not have to devote time and energy to solicit and encourage co-operation, since it was not extended reluctantly. Their spontaneous co-operation improved operating efficiency.

Social cohesion also lessened the status anxiety generated by the evaluation system. Such anxiety is most acute in the individual who does not feel integrated in his work group and therefore seeks to derive social recognition from excelling at his task and from approval of superiors. Friendly relations with co-workers made the standing of the individual in the cohesive group independent of his productivity, particularly since fast work was disparaged as a sign of superficial service. The consequent reduction of anxiety in the antiproductivity-oriented group actually raised its productivity.

Fluctuations in productivity illustrate the dysfunction of status anxiety. Section B had not always operated more efficiently than Section A. Its productivity had been lower during the two months preceding the last rating but had abruptly increased then, while that of Section A had declined, as Table 2 shows.

The two groups found themselves in different situations before and after they were rated. The members of Section A were familiar with the rating standards of their supervisor, for she had rated them in previous years. Their anxiety led them to work especially hard immediately before the annual rating. The members of Section B, on the other hand, had never before been rated by their new supervisor. They were also concerned about their record but could not calm their anxiety by concentrating upon certain tasks, because they did not know what the supervisor would stress; the explanation he gave to his subordinates was too vague and adhered too strictly to official procedures to help them to foresee his actual practices. This unfocused anxiety was particularly detrimental to efficient performance. Later, when the interviewers found out that they were not rated primarily on the basis of statistical records, their anxiety largely subsided and their productivity increased. In contrast, the experience of the members of Section A, whose rating was strongly influenced by their production records, intensified their status anxiety, but, when the rating was over, anxiety was no longer channeled into exceptionally hard work, with the result that their productivity declined below that of Section B.

Social cohesion is no guaranty against anxiety in a bureaucracy. Civil service status is too important to officials for them to remain immune to the threat of losing it. But when no such threat is felt, social cohesion reduces anxiety by divesting productivity of its significance as a symbol of status in the work group. Diminished anxiety as well as smoother cooperation then enable those in the cohesive group to perform their tasks more efficiently than the others.

In the absence of social cohesion, competitive striving for an outstanding performance record became a substitute means for relieving status anxiety in Section A. This psychological function of competition is illustrated by the following incident: The interviewers in this section became very irritable, and one of them even became physically ill, when a temporary supervisor, who tried to prevent competitive practices, interfered with their method of allaying anxiety. Status anxiety reduced operating efficiency. Even in the cohesive group, productivity was low when the unknown rating standards of a new supervisor produced

Table 2. Productivity before and after Rating

	SECTION A	SECTION B
December, 1948	0.64 (619)*	0.56 (317)
January, 1949	0.70 (941)	0.56 (472)
February, 1949		
(rating)	0.56 (1,342)	0.60 (477)
March, 1949	0.59 (1,335)	0.71 (448)
April, 1949	0.59 (1,001)	0.67 (433)

* Numbers in parentheses are the numbers of job openings available on which the productivity index—the proportion of these openings that were filled—is based.

acute and diffuse anxiety. Otherwise, however, the cohesive group was more productive, because social cohesion relieved status anxiety by making the individual's standing in the group independent of his productivity. The very competitive striving that undermined the group's cohesiveness also served to lessen the individual's status anxiety in a noncohesive situation. The hypothesis that the cohesiveness of the group and the competitiveness of the individual in the less cohesive group both reduce status anxiety explains the paradox that the *less competitive group* as well as the *more competitive individual* in the competitive group each was particularly productive.

Selections from The Impact of

Budgets on People

CHRIS ARGYRIS

What This Study Tries to Do. The purpose of the study is to examine problems and to raise questions concerning the possible human relations effects budgets have upon supervisors. Because of the nature of the problem this study cannot present final solutions to problems, nor answer questions in any definitive way. It can merely define a wider aspect of the budget problem and suggest possible solutions. Each controller must light up these approaches with his own experience. In short, this study, the first of its kind attempted by the Foundation, is primarily exploratory.

Because of the indefinable limits of the human problems in this area, the research team decided to focus its attention on how the

From *The Impact of Budgets on People,* prepared for the Financial Executives Research Foundation, formerly, Controllers Institute Research Foundation. Copyright 1952 by Controllers Institute Research Foundation. Reprinted with permission of the publisher.

supervisors feel about budgets and how the finance people feel about the same budgets. The group sought answers to questions such as these.

1. How do the finance people see their job?

2. What problems do the finance people see in relation to factory people? What problems don't they perceive?

3. Similarly, how do the factory supervisors see their job?

4. What problems do factory supervisors perceive in relation to the finance people and/or budgets? What problems don't they perceive?

5. What similarities and differences exist between factory people and finance people with regard to values, attitudes, and feelings toward budgets?

It should be pointed out that due to the exploratory nature of the study no recommendations could be made to the managements of the plants studied, which could then be observed in action, checked, and analyzed by the research team. Therefore, it is extremely difficult to present many recommendations based solely upon these findings. There is, however, a growing body of practical suggestions developed in other research work which is relevant to some of the problems unearthed by this report. In our recommendations we have drawn upon these suggestions because they are relevant and, we hope, useful to the controller.

How the Research Task Was Accomplished. The problem of human factors in the use of budgets is an extremely difficult one. Not only is the subject of budgets per se complicated, but, to make matters more difficult, budgets are so closely interrelated with the other parts and functions of organization that it would be an immense task to study carefully and thoroughly the problem as a whole.

The process of preparing manufacturing cost budgets is much the same in all four companies. In all cases the process starts with a meeting of the controller, the assistant controller and a top management group to determine over-all financial goals for the company in the forthcoming year. The controller's staff then translates the financial goals into the detailed cost breakdowns required for departmental budgets. This preliminary budget is sent to all superintendents who are asked to scrutinize the budget carefully and report any alterations they wish made.

Once the superintendents have their budget modifications clearly in mind, a meeting is held with the controller and his staff. Both parties come to the meeting "armed to the teeth" with ammunition to back their demands. After the disagreements are resolved, all parties sign the new budget proposal. The superintendents return to their offices, awaiting the new budget and the expected drive to "put it over."

Some Limitations of the Study. Any study whose approach is purely exploratory must be conducted within the limits of fairly well-defined boundaries. These are some of the more important limitations imposed upon this study by its exploratory nature:

1. None of the plants studied has a supervisory incentive system as a part of its budget system. This seems a serious limitation and points to the need for further research.

2. The report does not include any material concerning the effects budgets have upon the workers in the plant. Casual interviews with workers suggested that they are definitely affected. How much they are affected, and through what channels, is not clear. This problem also deserves further study.

3. Budgets constitute only one of the evaluation processes management uses. As is commonly known, most evaluation processes tend to have "two strikes against them" simply because they tend to set goals for, and make evaluations of, the supervisors. As such, budgets do not escape the usual complaints. Moreover, it appears that many complaints are focused upon the budget because the budget is one of the few evaluation processes that is always in writing, and therefore concrete. Thus, some of the supervisors tend to use it as a "whipping post" in order to release their feelings about many other, and at times totally unrelated, problems.

What Budget People Think Is the Use of Budgets. To the budget people, budgets have an extremely important function in the organization as the "eyes and the ears of the plant." They provide the answers to most questions and the budget people see themselves as the "answer men" of the organization. Consider the following examples:

> First let me say that budgets are the watchdog of this company. What do I mean by that? Two things: First, if we have profit, there's no problem; Second, if we are losing money, what can we do about improvement—any kind of improvement?

> We guard the fields. The budget department has to constantly strive to improve the goods and make the plant better. There is always room to make things better.

There is, therefore, an important emphasis made on budget people constantly finding things that are "sour," looking for weaknesses and, in general, looking for things that are wrong, not right.

Another emphasis is equally important. All the budget people interviewed insisted that the errors found and the weaknesses uncovered should immediately be sent to top management.

> If I see an inconsistency, I'll go to top management and report it. No, I never go

to the supervisor in charge. It is our job to report any inconsistencies to the top management.

Once the information is in top management's hands, it is up to it to take action. In other words, budget results are primarily top management control instruments.

Coupled with the task of finding weaknesses and reporting them to top management is a third emphasis on doing the reporting soon. Budget results can be effective only when they are "hot off the griddle." Whatever pressure budgets may generate to "motivate" a factory man to better his record would be lost if action was not taken immediately.

> It's our philosophy that we've got to get these figures to top management when they're hot. They're no good when the job is cold. As it is now, with our records, top management can get the factory supervisors together and do something right away.

A fourth emphasis is on using the budget as a means for putting pressure on operating supervisors.

> As soon as we examine the budget results and see a fellow is slipping, we immediately call the factory manager and point out, "Look Joe, you're behind on the budget. What do you expect to do about it?" True, he may be batting his brains out already on the problem but our phone call adds a little more pressure—er—well, you know, we let them know we're interested.

Finally, budget people believe that budgets present a goal, a challenge to factory people. They think that without budgets factory people would have nothing "to shoot for"—would lack the help of a great motivating instrument. For example:

> Production budgets set the goals. The budgets, yes, the budgets, set a challenge for those fellows (factory). It's something for them to shoot for. They need something to shoot for. All of us need a goal.

In summary, budget personnel see budgets as performing at least the following important functions:

1. They are a means to make things better. There is always room for improvement. Inconsistencies, errors, weaknesses are constantly being discovered, examined, and reported to top management.

2. Properly used, they are a means of instituting improvements quickly. Budgets are of most value when their results are in the hands of top management as soon as possible.

3. They are a means of putting pressure on factory supervisors.

4. They provide a goal, a motivating force for the factory people.

What Budget People Think Are the Differences between Their Outlook and That of Factory Supervisors. If the budget people see any important differences between the outlook of operating people and themselves, such information should be of value in ascertaining how "basic" are the causes of misunderstanding between the budget and production parts of the organization.

The results indicate that budget people see some very basic differences. For example:

> I would say that factory people have a different outlook on life. They tend to be more liberal toward others.
> The financial people, on the other hand, look at life more coldly. To them, it's all figures. The only thing they look at is what amount of money is involved. It's the total figure that counts.

> The factory supervisors' outlook on things is different. They emphasize today. Yes, they're looking at only the short run. We have to look at things in the long run. We have to see the whole unit. They worry about their individual departments.

> I think you'd almost say there are personality differences between factory and finance. We (finance) tend to approach everything with figures. We have to. We've been retained that way. Factory people approach it without worrying about costs.

> Yes, there are differences. We (finance) have been trained to see things as they are —to study them logically and systematically. We've been trained to look at a problem and say, "Well, this is it, one two, three, bang, that's it."

The differences described above may be clues for understanding the human problems that arise. For example, if the factory supervisors are, in fact, only interested in the short run and if the budget staff does not see the short run as being crucial, then trouble will arise. Similarly, if the budget staff has a basically different outlook on problems from the factory supervisors, this difference will tend to increase disagreements.

What Budget People Think Are Their Problems with Factory Supervisors. The budget people were asked to describe what they felt was the most difficult problem they faced in their relationships with factory supervisors. The majority of the replies fell into a very consistent pattern. The most pressing problem was "selling" budgets to factory supervisors. The budget people believed that the task was almost insurmountable. It was interesting to see that the three most often stated reasons for this problem with factory supervisors were (*a*) lack of education on the part of factory supervisors, (*b*) lack of interest, and (*c*) misunderstanding and/or mistrust of budgets.

What Budget People Think Are Some of the Solutions to These Problems. Most of the solutions suggested by budget people seem to revolve around educating, or training, factory people in the appreciation and use of budgets.

These are some of the suggestions.

1. Supervisors should be taught the use and need for budgets in the company and specifically in their departments.

2. If possible, budgets should be explained so the supervisor would know exactly how and why budgets are constructed the way they are. (Most finance people were quick to caution against overwhelming the factory man with minute details of financial "buzz words." They all pointed out that the explanations should be kept as simple as possible.)

3. Closely connected with the above is the budget staffs' desire that factory people have more acquaintance with, and therefore respect for, the everyday problems of the finance staff in administering budgets.

4. Interestingly enough, most of the top controllers believed that the problems of administering the budget would not be alleviated until finance people, as well as factory people, changed. They felt that the budget people should be given a thorough course in self-understanding and in understanding and getting along with others—in other words, a course in human relations.

These, then, are the human problems involved in the administration of budgets and what can be done about them, as seen by the budget people.

What Factory Supervisors Think Is the Use of Budgets. Just how important are budgets and budget departments to factory supervisors? Each factory supervisor was asked to name the department which affected him the most and then the second most important. Fifty-seven percent considered production control as number one and forty-five percent chose the budget department as number one. Of the fifty-seven percent who picked the production control department as number one, all but one supervisor chose the budget department as the second most important department.

It seems relatively safe, therefore, to say that budgets wield an important influence in the production supervisor's world. Here . . . [is a] typical comment:

> Well, if you want to study a department that has its clutches everywhere, go into the budget department. That's all over this plant.

In general, the supervisors close to the employees hardly ever used budgets. In fact, they suggested that the best way to cause trouble was to mention a budget directly or indirectly to the employees. The supervisors higher up in the line of authority did use them. Of course, their usage varied, but in general the budgets were used. We shall see subsequently that the amount of use by upper-level supervisors was closely related to the way they handled their subordinates.

USE BY FRONT-LINE SUPERVISORS. In all the plants studied the research team obtained a definite impression that budgets were "taboo" with the employees who did the work. The writers could not help but sense an informal, but highly effective group norm of "no one speaks of or uses budgets seriously." This is, of course, merely an impression. No interviews were conducted with the employees to test the impression. Some idea of the validity of this observation may be obtained if one examines parts of the statements made below by the supervisors close to the people. These statements should also give the reader a vivid picture of the feelings and the human problems faced by these supervisors.

> You can't use budgets with the people. Just can't do anything like that. People have to be handled carefully and in our plant, carefully doesn't mean with budgets. Besides, I don't think my people are lazy.

> No, can't do it because some people see budgets as a target against a man. I'll have to admit that we cannot display the budget in front of our people. You have to be careful, you know. The first thing you know you'll have a grievance against you. We don't ask a man to look at a budget. Oh well, what we might do is put it under his nose so he can't help but see it. I should say, if we show the budget to any worker, it's only one out of every six.

> No, no, I couldn't ever use a budget in front of my people. I just wouldn't dare. And, mind you, I don't think my top management would want us to. We wouldn't get any production out if we did.

Budgets, therefore, are far from being "cold pictures" of past production to the people. Rather they are symbols of something which may arouse fear, resentment, hostility, and aggression on the part of the employees toward the company and which may lead to decreased production.

The supervisor is, therefore, forced to refrain from mentioning budgets. He tries to accomplish what top management desires in distributing budget results, by translating these results into informal shop language and thereby calling these results to the attention of the employees. If he is not able to do this, he doesn't mention budgets at all.

The price for mentioning budgets is high. The supervisor who uses them explicitly is faced with a resentful work group which may express this resentment in many different ways, all of which lead to trouble for the supervisor.

It is not difficult, therefore, to see why a supervisor does not dare use budgets as some budget people want him to.

USE BY TOP-FACTORY SUPERVISORS. We have seen that front-line supervisors are not able to use budgets freely with their employees. Top-factory supervisors, on the other hand, seem to use budgets quite frequently and strongly on the supervisors below them.

Clearly, the closer one is to the employees, the less one can use budgets to increase production or arouse interest in production. If such is the case, one begins to wonder about the supervisor who is in the position of receiving all the pressure from above, but cannot pass on the pressure to the people below him. Does all this pressure stay with the supervisor?

What Factory Supervisors Think Are Budget Problems. Although there may be some differences among levels of supervision in the use of budgets, all the supervisors, regardless of their rank, were pretty much agreed concerning the limitations of budgets. Some of the limitations mentioned were:

BUDGET REPORTS ONLY INCLUDE RESULTS, NOT REASONS. Perhaps one of the greatest criticisms of budgets was the fact that they never included the reasons why they were not achieved by a certain supervisor. There was considerable feeling about this problem. Supervisors disliked intensely the fact that their departments would look "sick" on the budget while the reasons for the "sickness" were never published along with the results.

> Budgets never show the reasons why they have not been met. They never take into account all variables that affect production.

The budget might contain the finance man's explanation: e.g., "The reason 'why' this budget has not been met is excess labor costs, or too much waste of time getting the job ready to be produced, etc.," but such reasons were not the real explanations as seen by the supervisors. They wanted the budget to state why they had excess labor costs, or why it took too long to get the job ready.

In other words, the supervisor's why was never included. Only the why of the budget man was included.

The following supervisor sheds additional light on the subject. It is interesting to note that he realizes why the budgets are not broken down further. But it is perhaps more interesting to note that even though he understands why budgets give only the total picture, he still feels quite strongly about them. Such data cannot help but lead one ot wonder if a knowledge about budgets will really alleviate the feelings about them.

As I see it, budgets are for top management. Top management is only interested in the total picture. They just want to see the results. They're just interested in knowing if the goal has been met.

The deviations, the headaches are all ironed out for them at the end of the budget. But, you can bet your boots, they are not ironed out for me. They remain, to remind me of the many things that can go wrong in my department. It's like this: I'm in the forest. I see hundreds of different trees (problems) that go to make it up. Top management is up in the air looking down on the forest. They see a mass of green. Now the budget measures that mass of green, but they don't tell the top management anything about the different trees that make up the green. You might put it this way—my job is to worry about the feelings that go to make up these figures. Finance peoples' job is to worry about the figures without the emotions.

EMPHASIS ON HISTORY. Another closely allied problem is that budgets emphasize past performance. Budgets are historical documents. As such, they are used primarily to project some predictions about the future based on the past.

Factory supervisors, on the other hand, place little emphasis on the past and hardly ever have time to think of the future. Their emphasis is on the present day-to-day situation.

RIGIDITY OF BUDGETS. In addition to the emphasis on the past, supervisors felt there was an equally negative emphasis on rigidity of standards. Once established, budget people seemed to dislike changing standards. Most budget people, the factory supervisors stated, were inflexible.

This rigidity of the finance people, as seen by the factory supervisors, leads to some important feelings on the part of the latter. For example:

I'd say one of the biggest problems is that budgets are set up on past performance. Once they come up with a figure, they hate

to leave it. Two years ago, my budget on errors was 100, now it's 150, but our production has increased a lot more.

Somehow the budget people freeze the figures in their minds and they just don't want to change.

BUDGETS APPLY PRESSURE FOR AN EVER-CHANGING GOAL. One of the more important criticisms the factory people had was the feeling that the people who set the budgets were never satisfied. For example:

If I meet this budget, those guys up there will only raise it.

Or,

You can't let them know that you made the budget without too much trouble. If you do they'll up it as sure as hell.

These were typical remarks made by most of the factory supervisors. (In no case did the top-factory supervisor consider this to be a criticism.) It was quite obvious that the factory supervisors wondered when, if ever, the optimum level would be reached. For example:

They make a budget and then constantly increase it. There's too much of that constant raising and raising that thing. Pretty soon the boys catch on and figure out it's the same old stuff. So they don't respond.

THE IMPLICATION THAT BUDGETS MOTIVATE SUPERVISORS TO DO A BETTER JOB. As we have seen earlier, the finance people perceive budgets as goal-setters for factory supervisors. They feel that the supervisors are "kept on the ball" because of budgets. Some finance people suggest that factory supervisors would be "lost" without budgets. On the other hand, factory supervisors resent quite strongly being thought of as people who would lose their motivation if it were not for budgets.

Some of them agreed that budgets had a function of helping them accomplish their work, but few if any saw budgets as the creator of their motivation. To accept budgets as motivators is to imply that supervisors do not have adequate interest in their jobs. This is seen as an insult to a man's integrity and the factory supervisors resent it strongly. For example:

I don't care much for budgets. I can use them, but I don't need them. My job is to get out the production, and I do the best I know how. What do I need budgets for? Now budgets can't help me in that.

Budget! Well, I know this is the way the other fellows feel about it. They don't want to be bothered with them. We do our job, and we do the best job we can. That's it. No matter what comes out, we know we've done our best.

BUDGETS ARE NOT REALISTIC. Another important criticism made by factory supervisors was that some budgets were purposely kept high so that they were almost impossible to meet. The supervisors definitely and sincerely resent this practice. They resent it primarily for two reasons.

Such a practice places a supervisor in a situation where he can never succeed. One supervisor expressed this when he said:

There's not much sense in setting a budget that's too high. What good is it? If a man doesn't meet it, he's going to say, "to hell with it." It's going to get him to think they're never satisfied. If you ever want to discourage a guy, just give him a budget you know he can't meet.

Such a practice implies that the company does not believe the supervisor's own desire to do a good job is sufficient to meet reasonable budgets. The unrealistic budget is used to spur supervisors on, but it does not work and is resented.

What Factory Supervisors Think Are the Differences between Their Outlook and That of the Budget People. [Earlier] . . . some differences in outlook between financial people and factory people as seen by the financial people were described. What are the differences in outlook as seen by the factory supervisors?

The first four basic differences as seen by the factory supervisors have already been discussed. They were:

1. Finance people are primarily interested in the past and the future. They don't think of the present.

2. Finance people tend to be too rigid once they have set up their figures.

3. Finance people see only the total picture.

They never see the many problems that go to make up the total picture. They worry only about end results.

4. Finance people tend to see life only as a set of figures. They take the emotions out of life and deal only with the cold figures.

Some other differences have not been previously mentioned:

1. Finance people cannot see the other person's point of view. They know almost nothing about the problems a supervisor is faced with daily.

2. Finance people have a language of their own. It is completely different from the language of the shop.

3. The final difference is more in the area of attitudes. It was best expressed by one supervisor who said:

A big problem with budget people, and all finance people for that matter, is that basically they are—well—let's see—yes—sarcastic.

I think that they think they're the whole show. If you're asking for our opinions, we think they have an over-exalted opinion of their position.

What Factory Supervisors Think Are Solutions to Some of These Problems

1. By far the most frequent and most stressed recommendation made by factory supervisors was that the finance people should learn to see the other person's point of view. The supervisors recommended that the finance people be given a "taste" of factory problems. Some typical comments were:

They are not fully acquainted with our everyday production problems. They don't realize our troubles and our difficulties. The best thing to do is to bring them down and see our problems.

I'd tell you what I'd teach them: to know my job. See the problems I have. Bring them down here and see what really goes on.

2. The financial people should undergo some training to learn that budgets are not final. They are merely opinions. One supervisor stated:

Yes, I could recommend a good thing. I wish they could have their thinking about budgets changed. They are too rigid. Budgets are statements of opinions not facts.

That's their big trouble. They think budgets are facts.

3. The financial people should change their belief that the employee is lazy and wants to do as little work as possible. For example:

I'd like to see them change their attitude that employees are out to get them (budget people) and do as little work as they can get away with.

4. Closely related to recommendation (3) above is one that recurred often: finance people should change their belief that the best way to raise production is through pressure.

5. Financial people should be taught that they are not superior to factory supervisors. Some typical comments:

I'd deflate their ego—I'd give them something to take them down a peg.

I'd like to teach them not to think their budgets are too important.

The Problem of Pressure. One of the most common of the factory supervisors' attitudes about budgets was that budgets were used as a pressure device to increase production efficiency. Many cases were cited to support this point. Finance people also admitted that budgets helped "keep people on the ball" by raising their goals and increasing their motivation. The problem of the effects of pressure applied through budgets seems to be the core of the budget problem.

THE CAUSES OF PRESSURE. Employees and front-line supervisors believe that the cause for pressure from the top is due to top management's belief that most employees are basically or inherently lazy. Employees and front-line supervisors also feel that top management believes that employees do not have enough motivation of their own to do the best possible job.

The interviews with top management officials revealed that the employees' beliefs were not totally unfounded, as a few quotations from some of the top management (both line and finance) make clear:

I'll tell you my honest opinion. Five per cent of the people work, ten per cent of the people think they work. And the other eighty-five per cent would rather die than work.

I think there is a need for more pressure. People need to be needled a bit. I think man is inherently lazy and if we could only increase the pressure, I think the budget system would be more effective.

Such feelings, even if they are never overtly expressed toward employees, filter through to the employees in very subtle ways. Budgets represent one of the more subtle ways. Once the employees sense these feelings exist in top management, they may become very resentful.

THE EFFECTS OF PRESSURE. How do people react to pressure? In three of the plants studied factory supervisors felt they were working under pressure and that the budget was the principal instrument of pressure. Management exerts pressure on the work force in many ways, of which budgets is but one. Budgets, being concrete, seem to serve as a medium through which the total effects of management pressure are best expressed. As such they become an excellent point of focus for studying the effect of pressure on people in a working organization.

THE CREATION OF GROUPS. An increase in tension, resentment, suspicion, fear and mistrust may not be the only result of ever stronger management pressures transmitted to supervisors, and in turn, to employees. We know, from psychological research, that people can stand a certain amount of pressure. After this point is passed, it becomes intolerable to an individual. We also know that one method people have to reduce the effect of the pressure (assuming that the employees cannot reduce the pressure itself) is to join groups. These groups then help absorb much of the pressure and the individual is personally relieved.

The process of individuals joining groups to relieve themselves of pressure is not an easy one. It does not occur overnight. The development of a group on such a basis seems to have the following general stages of growth.

First, the individuals "feel" the pressure. They are not certain, but they sense an increase in pressure.

Second, they begin to see definite evidences

of the pressure. They not only feel it, they can point to it.

Since they feel this pressure is on them personally, they begin to experience tension and general uneasiness.

Next, the people usually "feel out" their fellow workers to see if they sense the pressure.

Finding out that others have noted the pressure, the people begin to feel more at ease. It helps to be able to say, "I'm not the only one."

Finally, they realize that they can acquire emotional support from each other by becoming a group. Furthermore, they can "blow their top" about this pressure in front of their group. Gradually therefore, the individuals become a group because in becoming a goup they are able to satisfy these needs:

1. A need to reduce the pressure on each individual.

2. A need to get rid of tension.

3. A need to feel more secure by belonging to a group which can counteract the pressure.

In short, a new, cohesive group has developed to combat management pressure. In a sense, the people have learned that they can be happier if they combine against this management pressure.

Suppose now that top management, aware of the tensions which have been generated and the groups which have been formed, seeks to reduce the pressure. The emphasis on budgets is relaxed. Perhaps even the standards are "loosened." Does this then destroy the group? After all, its primary reason for existence was to combat the pressure. Now, the pressure is gone. The group should eventually disintegrate.

The answer seems to be that the groups continue to exist!

The evidence for this is not as conclusive as it should be. Therefore, the following explanation should be considered primarily in the realm of inference and conjecture rather than scientific fact.

These factors seem to operate to keep the group in existence:

1. There is a "time lag" between the moment management announced the new policy and the time the workers put it into effect.

2. The individuals have made a new and satisfactory adjustment with each other. They have helped to satisfy each other's needs. They

are, as the social scientist would say, "in equilibrium" with each other. Any attempt to destroy this balance will tend to be resisted even if the attempt represents an elimination of a "bad" or unhealthy set of conditions. People have created a stable pattern of life and they will resist a change in this pattern.

3. The individuals fear pressure will come again in the future. Because of this feeling, they will tend to create unreal conditions or to exaggerate existing conditions so that they can rationalize to themselves that pressure still exists and, therefore, the need for the group also exists.

PRESSURE ON FRONT-LINE SUPERVISORS. But what about the foreman? Strong pressures converge upon him. How does he protect himself from these pressures?

He cannot join a group against management, as his work force does. For one reason, he probably has at least partially identified himself with management. For another reason, he may be trying to advance in the hierarchy. Naturally, he would not help his chances for advancement if he joined a group against management.

The evidence of the previous chapter seems to indicate that the line supervisor cannot pass all the pressure he receives to his employees. Time and time again the factory supervisors stated that passing the pressure down would only create conflict and trouble which would lead to a decrease in production.

The question arises, where does the pressure go? How do the supervisors relieve themselves of at least some of the pressure? There is evidence to suggest at least three ways in which pressure is handled by the supervisors:

1. Interdepartmental strife. The foremen release some of the pressure by continuously trying to blame fellow foremen for the troubles that exist. "They are," as one foreman expressed it, "trying to throw the dead cat in each other's backyard."

In three plants observed, much time was spent by certain factory supervisors in trying to lay the blame for errors and problems on some other department.

2. Staff versus factory strife. The foremen released much of the pressure by blaming the budget people, production control people and salesmen for their problems. The data already presented concerning factory supervisors' at-

titudes towards budget people substantiate this point.

3. "Internalizing" pressure. Many supervisors who do not express their feelings about the pressure have in reality "internalized" it and, in a sense, made it a part of themselves. Such damming up of pressure seemed to be expressed in the following ways:

(a) Supervisor A is quiet, relatively non-emotional, seldom expresses his negative feelings to anyone, but at the same time he works excessively. Supervisor A can be found working at his desk long after the others have gone home. As one supervisor expressed it, "That guy works himself to death."

(b) Supervisor B is nervous, always running around "checking up" on all his employees. He usually talks fast, gives one the impression that he is "selling" himself and his job when interviewed. He is forever picking up the phone, barking commands and requesting prompt action.

Both of these types (or a combination of these types) are expressions of much tension and pent up emotions that have been internalized. People working under such conditions finally are forced to "take it easy," or they find themselves with ulcers or a nervous breakdown.

But that is not the end of the problem. Constant tension leads to frustration. A frustrated person no longer operates as effectively as he was accustomed. He finds that he tends to forget things he used to remember. Work that he used to do with pleasure, he now delegates to someone else. He is no longer able to make decisions as fast as he did months ago. Now he finds he has to take a walk or get a cup of coffee—anything to get "away from it all."

SUCCESS FOR BUDGET SUPERVISORS MEANS FAILURE FOR FACTORY SUPERVISORS. Students of human relations agree that most people want to feel successful. We observe people constantly defining social and psychological goals, struggling to meet them, and as they are met, feeling successful.

Finance and factory supervisors are no exception. The typical finance supervisor does his work as best he can. He hopes and expects just praise of this work from his superior. Most of his success comes, therefore, from his superior's evaluation. It is the "boss" who will

eventually say "well done," or commend a promotion. In other words, a finance supervisor measures his success on his job, to a substantial degree, by the reactions of his superior.

The situation is the same for the factory supervisor. He also desires success. Like the finance supervisor, much of his success also derives from the comments and behavior the "boss" exhibits. In short, the factory supervisor is also oriented toward the top for an evaluation of how well he is doing his job.

What is the task of a good and successful finance supervisor? The reader will recall that the finance people perceive their task as being the watchdog of the company. They are always trying to improve the situation in the plant. As one finance supervisor said, "Always, there is room to make it better." And finally, the reader will recall the statement that, "The budget man has made an excellent contribution to this plant. He's found a lot of things that were sour. You might say a good budget man . . . lets top management know if anything is wrong."

In other words, their success derives from finding errors, weaknesses, and faults that exist in the plant. But, when they discover these errors, weaknesses, and faults, they also single out a "guilty party" and implicitly, at least, accuse him of failure. This is true because in finding weaknesses, errors or faults in a certain department, one is at the same time telling the factory supervisors that "things aren't going along as well as they could be." This, naturally, gives many factory supervisors a feeling of failure.

To be sure, such an occurrence will not make every supervisor feel he has failed. Some supervisors do not worry much about their job. Therefore, we find that the supervisor who really feels the failure is the one who is highly interested in doing a good job.

REPORTING SHORTCOMINGS OF THE FOREMAN. The way in which these shortcomings are reported is also important:

Assume that finance man A discovers an error in foreman B's department. How is this error reported? Does the finance man go directly to the factory foreman? In the plants studied the answer, usually, is "no."

The finance man cannot take the "shortest" route between the foreman and himself. For one reason, it may be a violation of policy for a staff man to go directly to a line man. But, more important (from a human point of view), the staff man derives his success when his boss knows he is finding errors. Therefore, his boss would never know how good a job finance man A is doing unless it came to his attention. In short, perhaps because of organizational regulations but basically because much success in industry is derived from above, the finance person usually takes his findings to his own boss, who in turn gives it to his, and so on up the line and across and down into the factory line structure.

Taking the long way around has at least one more positive value for finance people. The middle and top management finance people also derive some success in being able to go to the plant manager and point to some newly discovered weaknesses in the factory. Therefore, not only one man obtains feelings of success, but all interested people up the entire finance structure obtain some feeling of satisfaction.

But, how about the factory people? The answer seems evident. They experience a certain sense of "being caught with their pants down."

Finally, to add insult to injury, the entire incident is made permanent and exhibited to the plant officials by being placed in some budget report which is to be, or has been, circulated through many top channels.

EFFECTS OF FAILURE ON PEOPLE. One might ask: What effects does this kind of failure have upon an individual? If they were insignificant, obviously we would not be concerned. Such is not the case. Feelings of failure can have devastating effects upon an individual, his work and his relationships with others.

Lippitt and Bradford, reporting on some ingenious scientific experiments conducted on the subject of success and failure, state that people who fail tend to:

1. Lose interest in their work.
2. Lower their standards of achievement.
3. Lose confidence in themselves.
4. Give up quickly.
5. Fear any new task and refuse to try new methods or accept new jobs.
6. Expect failure.
7. Escape from failure by daydreaming.
8. Increase their difficulty in working with others.

9. Develop a tendency to blame others, to be over-critical of others' work and to develop troubles with other employees.

On the other hand, people who succeed tend to:

1. Raise their goals.
2. Gain greater interest in the activity in which they are engaged.
3. Gain greater confidence in their ability in the activity.
4. Increase their persistence to future goals.
5. Increase their ability to cooperate and work.
6. Increase their ability to adapt readily to new situations.
7. Increase their emotional control.

In summary, we should point out that finance people aren't inherently "out to get them" as factory people in the plants described them. Rather, they are placed in a social organization where the only way in which they can receive success is to place someone else in failure.

THE WALL BETWEEN FINANCE AND FACTORY PEOPLE. At least two more very interesting conditions are related to this peculiar position which the finance people hold:

First, since the budget people are always looking for weaknesses, errors, and faults, they begin to develop a philosophy of life in which their symbol for success is, not only the error discovered, but the very thought of the discovery of a possible new error. "Weaknesses," "discovery of errors made by others"—which are symbols of failure for others—are symbols of success for the budget people.

The realization and admission by budget people of the peculiar position in which they are placed, leads to the second interesting condition. The budget people tend to become defensive about their work. They don't like placing people in failure, but they have to. Being aware of this difficulty and the negative feelings it may create, they tend to become defensive about queries concerning "their books" or their methods. One has the feeling that, at times, they use their technical "know-how" and language to confuse the factory people. This confusion of the factory people serves, of course, as a defense for the budget man. As one man suggested, "After all, if they don't know anything about budgets, how can they criticize them?" In short, the ignorance of the factory people concerning budgets may become a wall behind which the finance people may work unmolested. It is interesting to note that one of the major causes of insecurity among factory supervisors concerning budgets (i.e., "we can't understand them") is one of the primary factors of security for the budget people.

THE PROBLEM OF DEPARTMENT-CENTER SUPER-VISORS. We have already shown that supervisors are partially evaluated by budget records. The factory supervisor, who desires to be known as being an efficient, effective supervisor, must make certain that his daily, weekly, monthly, and quarterly results compare favorably with the predicted results defined by the budgets. In short, a factory supervisor will feel successful, other things being equal, when he "meets his budget."

The phrase "meets his budget" is crucial.

Such a philosophy overlooks an extremely important point, perhaps described by the statement, "An organization is something different from the sum of the individual parts." The difference of the whole from the sum of the parts lies in the fact that the parts of an organization exist in certain relationships with each other. It is these relationships which create the difference.

WHAT MAKES AN ORGANIZATION. Parts, alone, do not make a whole organization. One cannot conceive of "adding" parts of an organization any more than adding together the hundreds of pieces that make up a watch in order to make the watch run. The crucial problem is to place the parts in correct relationship to each other.

Without laboring the point it seems clear that important relationships between departments are disregarded by an overemphasis on the individual departments. If everyone made certain his own department was functioning correctly, but at the same time, did not pay attention to the functioning of his department in relation to others, then trouble would still arise.

CONTROLLING CONFLICTS AMONG DEPARTMENTS. It might be suggested that the control of the relationships between departments rests with the plant manager, or some higher authority. From his high position, he is best able to control the conflict between departments. The crux of the matter is that this is all the leader

can do, i.e., control conflict. He is unable to eliminate it since the causes for the conflict are not within his reach. Since the top leader controls this conflict, the supervisors increasingly look to the leader to "break up a fight" or settle a dispute. This forces the supervisors to become increasingly dependent upon the leader. Furthermore, the more successful the top leader is, the less the supervisors need to worry about cooperation. They soon learn that the leader will solve any inter-departmental problems.

An example will illustrate the point.

In one of the plants studied a mistake was made on a customer order. The customer sent the material back to the plant. The error was corrected and the material sent back to the customer.

The cost of making the correction was nearly three thousand dollars. The error, especially since it was so large, had to be entered in the budget records. Some department had to be charged with the error. The problem was, who should be charged with the error?

For two months, supervisors of the departments most likely to be blamed waged a continuous campaign to prove their innocence. Each supervisor blamed the others. No one wanted the error on his record. The supervisors actually spent hundreds of man-hours arguing and debating among themselves. Emotions were aroused, people began calling each other names. Finally, two of the supervisors refused to talk to each other. Conflict reigned among the supervisors.

But, the supervisors were not the only persons in conflict. The division manager was also in conflict. He had to make the decision. To charge any supervisor with such an error would certainly invite hostility from that supervisor. This hostility might have further effects in the future. The division manager did not want to risk a weakening of his relationship, especially with a supervisor. But, he had to make a decision.

A meeting was held with the interested supervisors. The problem was discussed until just about everybody and everything that could be blamed, were blamed for the error. The division manager finally "gave in." He decided to place the error under "general factory loss." No department would be affected. The plant, as a whole, would carry the stigma. The division manager expressed his thoughts behind his decision to the research worker as follows:

> Take that big three thousand dollar error. We have to charge it up to someone. One man blames sales, another someone else. Everyone refuses to admit it might be their own fault. They each blame someone else.
>
> Well, I don't know. Perhaps, I thought it might be best to put the whole thing under general factory loss. Or else, they'd be hurt.

Note that the supervisors are willing to have the plant as a whole take the blame. But, they resist any attempts to place the blame on their individual departments.

In summary, budgets and budgeting tend to make the supervisor think of his, and essentially only his, department. Budget records, as administered, foster a narrow viewpoint on the part of the user. The budget records serve as a constant reminder that the important aspect to consider is one's own department and not one's own plant. As a result, supervisors become department centered rather than plant centered.[1]

BUDGETS AS A MEDIUM FOR PERSONALITY EX-PRESSION. The final problem to be discussed became evident only after a series of interviews with different controllers and top factory officials. Then it became obvious that the way people expressed their interest in budgets, and the way in which they described and used them, were directly related to the pattern of leadership they used in their daily industrial life.

For example, if a rather domineering, aggressive, "go-getting" top executive was interviewed, his presentation of the problem would also be made in a domineering, aggressive, "go-getting" manner. Therefore, although it is accurate to state that budgets are composed of "cold, nonhuman symbols" (i.e., figures), it is equally valid to state that once human beings use these "nonhuman figures," they project onto these figures all the emotions and feelings at their command.

Because budgets become a medium of per-

sonality and leadership expression, and since people's personalities and leadership patterns are different, this research study found a number of methods with which top factory executives used budgets. A few of these methods are illustrated by the following comments made by top factory supervisors:

> I go to the office and check that budget every day. I can then see how we're meeting the budget. If it's O.K., I don't say anything. But, if it's no good, then I come back here (smiles) and give the boys a little . . . Well, you know. I needle them a bit. I give them the old . . . hm . . . well . . . you know what . . . the old needle.

> I make it a policy to have close contact, human contact, with all the people in my department.

> If I see we're not hitting the budget, I go out and tell them I have $40,000 on the order.
>
> Well, they don't know what that $40,000 means. They think it's a lot of money so they get to work.

> Human factor, that's important. If you treat a human being like a human being, you can use them better and get more out of them.

> You know, it's a funny thing. If I want my people to read the budget, I don't shove it under their nose. I just lay it on my desk and leave it alone. They'll pick it up without a doubt.

It is hoped that the above descriptions are adequate to convey the point that budgets furnish a means of expression. They serve to permit the user's pattern of leadership to blossom forth.

Summary

This exploratory research has led to the tentative conclusion that budgets and budgeting can be related to at least four important human relations problems:

First, budget pressure tends to unite the employees against management, and tends to place the factory supervisor under tension. This tension may lead to inefficiency, ag-

[1] One method to remedy this problem is to attempt to have the staff person report directly to the factory. For an interesting statement of this case see: Douglas MacGregor, "The Role of the Human Relations Consultant," *Journal for the Study of Social Issues*, Vol. IV, Summer 1948.

gression, and perhaps a complete breakdown on the part of the supervisor.

Second, the finance staff can obtain feelings of success only by finding fault with factory people. These feelings of failure among factory supervisors lead to many human relations problems.

Third, the use of budgets as "needlers" by top management tends to make the factory supervisors see only the problems of their own department. The supervisors are not concerned with the other people's problems. They are not "plant-centered" in outlook.

Finally, supervisors use budgets as a way of expressing their own pattern of leadership. When these patterns result in people getting hurt, the budget, in itself a neutral thing, often gets blamed.

In the preceding pages we have discussed our observations and findings in an extremely complex field—the impact of budgets upon people. Because problems are so complex and our research so obviously exploratory, we undertake the task of suggesting lines of action with considerable humility.

Organizations as Clockworks:

The Simple Steady State

P A R T F O U R

IN THE FIRST three parts, we have been look-ing at the organization and asking, "What is it?" "What does it do?" "Of what does it consist?" We have been developing an anat-omy of organizations. The planned structure provides us with a skeleton to describe form and support for purpose. To this we have added the emergent informal structure. This "fleshed out," underlying structure gives the organization sources of energy, strength, and direction, and it also protects the formal struc-ture and makes it operable. In doing this, the informal structure can hamper and restrict the formal structure.

This however is a static picture. Like a ca-daver on a dissecting table, it gives some idea of what the living thing is like, but only some. The cadaver cannot give us any idea of a smile, the deft return of a ball on a tennis court, or a witty reply in a conversation. Or-ganizations do things. They produce goods, services, satisfactions. They move, they grow, and they sometimes die. These things have not yet touched upon.

When a thing goes into motion, new prop-erties, not existent in the static state, emerge. When a machine begins to move, we develop inertia, friction, and usually sound. When or-ganizations enter a dynamic, moving state, we get interpersonal conflict, underfilled and over-filled positions, shifting of task elements, unan-ticipated interactions, and many other things.

Work Flow

We have said that organizations have out-puts. They also have inputs; raw materials, or-ders, money, human energy, to name a few, which are transformed into the desired outputs as they flow through the organization. There are actually many flows in organizations—raw materials and products, paperwork, orders, in-structions, ideas, knowledge, and money. It is the existence of these flows as they are mani-fested by people filling interconnected roles or positions that first occupy our attention in ex-ploring organizations in motion (Chapple and Sayles). We find that, because of the flows, the actual structure and behavior in organiza-tions are not exactly what the dormant anat-omy suggested. It is both more and less. The work flow connects people separated by geog-raphy, tasks, and outlook in a pervasive de-pendency that confounds simplistic goals and value sets, and leads to unities and conflicts

298

that make organizations both frustrating and vital. The structuring of goals, actions, and interactions anticipated when looking at the anatomy of organizations is present in the ongoing organization. Yet there are other goals, actions, and interactions, not included or seeming to be of only minor importance in the static model, that now assume major importance and fill dominant positions. If we think only in terms of traditional static models, these are a surprise and can appear illegitimate. People in organizations do communicate vertically with superiors and subordinates, as traditional models would suggest, but they also communicate horizontally with others on the same authority level. Often, this is the principal direction of communication. We are interested in both the reason for this, such as work flow and the extent to which machines are used (Simpson), and the consequences for organizational productivity and the satisfactions people derive from the resulting social organization.

The Organization as a System

Directly, more often indirectly, the previous parts of this book have referred to the central importance of the "fit" or integration of the various parts or elements of organizations. We are concerned with the "fit" of the same type of elements like the sequence of tasks to make a product, but also fit between different types of parts like the tasks, the values people performing the tasks have about them, and the worth society places on the products of tasks. This fit or integration of different types of elements, both within and without the organization, is a function of the degree of specialization. Unfortunately, organizations are almost never single purpose or have a single flow or face a single environment and hence seldom have in them people of identical skills and value orientations. Every organization then has several specializations within it. Properly organized each of these specializations can be handled by a subunit of the organization. And there lies the rub. A high degree of specialization may be necessary for the operating team, the laboratory, and the x-ray department to function well; however, their efforts must still be integrated to make the patient well. The more specialized they become, the more difficult becomes the task of integration (Lorsch).

We are, therefore, concerned with the perplexing question of how to increase efficiency by increased specialization while, at the same time, ensuring the necessary overall integration, made increasingly difficult by our increasing specialization. To be successful, organizations must face and solve this problem.

One of the principal factors leading to the differentiation of subunits is that the various flows have different technical requirements. Now only are they different, they are at times incompatible. The question then is: which are the most important, which should suffer the least disadvantage? For many organizations, this is the productive flow that delivers the goods or services efficiently. Such systems are efficiently planned and administered because they are rational systems or, at least, are handled as if they were rational systems by making other parts of the organization buffer and protect this system from disturbances (Thompson). Actually any system, whether it be the technical tasks of doing work in making a product or the task of administering a collective work effort, becomes more formal as we try to make it more efficient and predictable. The more rational administrative effort becomes, the more necessary is the use of rules, procedures, and structures and, also, the more independent from its environment must the organization become (Udy).

We have been exploring organizations in a dynamic state, where they are in motion. They are in motion because of the actions of people in them, actions resulting from the decisions each of them make. It is seldom that these actions can be controlled directly. They, instead, can only be indirectly influenced through the decision-making processes of organization members. The decisions to be made are, in part, dependent upon a person's knowledge of what is to be done, how to do it, and the state of the world. All of these things are influenced by the organization and the position within it that a person occupies. The rationality a person can apply to decision making about organization matters is then constrained or even molded by the structure of the organization he is within. The decision-making capacities of people are remarkable, but limited, and the problems the world brings to us are often far too complex to handle directly or in a whole piece. The ability of organizations to channel, direct, and screen information, to classify and factor problems in a number of ways, and to store past solutions for future use means that organizations can be structured to aid human intellectual problem solving (March and Simon). If people are capable of handling only problems of limited scope in a given period of time, then organizations can, by setting limited objectives, reduce the magnitude of problems that the whole unit will have to handle and, by structuring internal operations, reduce further the magnitude of the problems that individuals within the organization will have to handle. Furthermore, by the complex and pervasive ways in which they influence information movements (e.g. by channeling, editing, and interpreting information), organizations can make decision making easier and more accurate for its members. The same capability can also make decision making more difficult and less accurate. One of our principal concerns, then, is to find the ways in which organizations affect individual and group decision making to ensure that they aid rather than hinder the process.

Adjustments in the System: Filling Positions in the Managerial Hierarchy

When a person joins an organization, say in some managerial capacity, he rapidly finds that the "position" he is given provides him with only the scantiest information about what he is to do. The title may tell him that he is the manager of Product Coordination and a job description may tell him to whom he reports, who reports to him, and may give a list of duties and activities but, probably, little more. How he is to do many of these officially prescribed duties, such as "direct the activities of the following subordinates, . . ." or "coordinate work with the Departments of Sales, Production, Engineering, Finance, and New Market Development," he will find completely unexplained. Furthermore, he will soon find that there are many other duties and activities expected from him that are not contained in any job description. Superiors will expect him to defend company policy, even though he may personally be in disagreement with it. Subordinates will expect him to "go to bat" for them with other officials in the company who control things the subordinates want. Fel-

low managers will expect him to unofficially loan them personnel or materials or to quietly adjust schedules to help them out.

A new manager may well wonder, "How have others handled these problems? How does the manager do his job?" The answers he receives will likely only add to his confusion. Some will tell him that he must think through his plans thoroughly, translate them into detailed clear orders, and follow the progress of subordinates carefully to see that they do what they have been ordered. Others will tell him to bring his subordinates into the planning activities and not to engage in close supervision. Some will say he must follow the orders and instructions of higher management, while others will say that it is impossible to succeed at all unless you get aid from and are willing to give aid to other people in the organization even if this means "bending" rules and official plans and schedules. The problem is that such advice is both correct and incorrect at the same time. Or, to be more precise, it may be correct for some organizations and incorrect for others. There is not generally "correct" behavior for people in organizations. How people behave in one organization may be quite different from the way they behave in another. For that matter the way they behave in one part of an organization may be quite different from the way they act in another part. "Correct" organizational behavior is, in part, determined by the fact that it is manifested by people in an organization and, in part (and this is a large part), by the particular characteristics of that organization or that part of the organization. The technology used, the sizes of the organization, the state of the environment, and other general characteristics of the organization or its subunits are major determinants of requisite behavior. The individual characteristics of the manager and his subordinates, the nature of the social relationship between them, and the skills and abilities of each that go into making the immediate organizational world in which an individual operates have powerful influences on determining which leader behaviors will be functional (Fiedler).

One of the things any person in a position where he has subordinates soon finds out is that the formal authority he has is a gross and clumsy tool. It is often a bit like having a 155 mm howitzer when you want to bring down an enemy sniper from a tree. Hence, most managers find that they must supplement formal authority with their own personal authority, and this takes time and skill to acquire. In attempting to establish influence over subordinates, superiors usually have a number of strategies or devices at their disposal. They can give orders and closely watch subordinates to see that they are carried out. Since such direct supervision is time consuming they may resort to the practice of establishing rules, which can have the effect of standing orders, telling subordinates what to do even when the superior is not present. Such instruments are powerful, but they place high demands on all parties and often have quite unanticipated consequences, which can often frustrate the real objectives of the superior. The reasons for this are that these instruments and their effects are far more complex than appears on the surface (Gouldner; Blau). Interestingly enough, rules, often thought to be coercive in nature, can be used (or more accurately nonactivated) by superiors to develop willing compliance on the part of their subordinates (Blau).

Conflict

However, fitting into an organization involves not only establishing relationships with one's position and subordinates (or superior), it also involves relationships with many others in organizations, with whom one has many other relations of a nonhierarchical nature. Often, the objectives and values of these other parties are so different that these relationships become very difficult. Although all members of the same organization are presumably committed to cooperating, people in different parts of the organization are often in disagreement and in conflict (Dalton; Dutton and Walton).

When such conflicts occur along major work flows, they can disrupt vitally needed coordination. Analysis of the origins of this conflict gives insight as to how it can be avoided or, at least, diminished (Walton; Dutton and Walton).

Organizations in motion, then, have a quite different appearance than they do when at rest. The nice neat appearance of division of work or relationships between positions and duties, authority and rules, reporting relationships and interaction becomes blurred, complex and, at first, confounding. The old neat "fit" among elements is loosened and, in some places, disappears. Strangely enough, a new "fit" begins to appear. People without much formal authority begin to bring about coordination among groups driven apart by the division of work; nonapplication of rules may give superiors authority they cannot acquire by applying them; channeling information so that people do not get "all the facts" helps them make better rather than worse decisions. Organizations in motion, then, present us with a somewhat strange world where many things seem topsy-turvy but where we have gradually been able to see that elements fit together with a different logic than we had previously used. We have hardly uncovered all of the new logic, but we have important parts of this systems model of organizations which we can use to vastly improve our analysis, planning, and predictions of organizations and the behavior of people in them.

Work Flow as the Basis for Organization Design

ELIOT CHAPPLE AND LEONARD SAYLES

Toward a Science of Organization

In the approach to be taken to organizational structure, two elements will appear. The technology or flow of work is the major criterion for designing the structure. This contrasts sharply with a well-established tradition of planning the organization from the top down. Secondly, any tendency to group people and activities together simply because they have or involve similar or purportedly similar functional responsibilities is avoided.

Traditionally, the scientific approach in studying any human group considers the environment and the technology developed to adapt to the environment. Each individual operation involves an implement or machine using some sort of power, a sequence of actions to accomplish the task, and possibly the interaction of several people in some kind of team activity. In this sense, the term "implement" can be applied to any object, a sheet of paper, a loom, an accounting machine, or a bulldozer. The products of business, or of any organization for that matter, result from interrelated techniques, some of which are essential and others secondary.

If an entire technique or series of techniques can be performed by a single individual, such as a silver craftsman who sells his wares himself, no organization results. But, if a division of labor occurs, some interaction between technicians must take place, and organization on the work level results. On the production level, a relatively large number of techniques may be linked together to make up the work

flow through the plant, with a single owner-manager providing the entire management. If there is only a small number of employees and few demands on his time for other activities (for example, if he subcontracts for a larger corporation on a regular basis), the owner may have a foreman in the shop even though the operation does not require one. The ensuing growth of such enterprises usually comes about rather simply with the owner taking a partner who is often a relative. Then, the management begins to specialize, typically with one man selling and the other overseeing production.

Designing the Structure from the Bottom Up. Regardless of the type of business organization—a small retail shop, the trader or merchant acting as intermediary between buyers and sellers, or a bank—a similar elaboration of organization takes place. The division of labor on the work level may involve sales people, clerks recording transactions, or cashiers; as the division of labor proliferates, so does management. The development of specialized managers or of a management division of labor is clearly secondary in the evolution of business to the growth of specialization on the work-flow level. This sequence is of critical importance in designing the organization.

Yet, in many writings about modern business organizations, the prime and determining influence of technological process is lost sight of. In their writings, the designers of the organization, who are perhaps under the spell of a two-dimensional chart, start at the top. Beginning with the directors and the president, they work down, level by level, discussing the functions of the various divisions, considering the relationships of "staff" or "service" departments to the "line," weighing the importance

From Eliot O. Chapple and Leonard R. Sayles, *The Measure of Management*, Macmillan, New York, 1961, pp. 19–45. Reprinted by permission of Macmillan and Company.

of the "span of control," and defining their graphic representations by referring to the nature of executive authority and responsibility. They may casually mention the first-line supervisor, but what he supervises is usually incidental to their recommendations.

The Tradition of Functional Concentration. Most decisions on "proper" organizational structure are based primarily on similarities of activities or functions. Traditionally, organizations are divided into such major functions as sales, production, finance, and personnel. Each may have subsidiary functions such as engineering, training, market research, inventory control, etc., that, in many companies, compete for equal standing with the others. It is usually recognized, of course, that a common location, product, customer, or specialization may vary the design, but within each divisional setup functional considerations predominate.

If a new function or activity is identified or grows in importance, the question always is, "Who will take it over?" For instance, should sales engineering be assigned to the sales division or engineering? It is an important adjunct in making the sale and helping the sales force bring in business. On the other hand, is it wise to divorce the sales engineers from first-hand involvement in engineering activities? What about sales training, another constant source of conflict? The sales division is sure personnel does not understand what it takes to make a salesman, but the personnel division does have a training department with broad responsibility for the entire corporation. Personnel has the specialized skills and specialists to do the training that salesmen are supposed to be incapable of doing well.

The endless arguments about proper placement of organizational activities are usually only temporarily settled. Because only verbal criteria exist, no one can define a function accurately, and no one wins a conclusive victory. In the meantime, the organization may acquire a cover of charts which, like a turtle's shell, conceal what goes on inside the animal.

Organization Based on Actual Work Flow

Clearly, a different approach to the problem of organizational design is needed. The struc-

ture built for members of management can be ignored for the moment to go back to the bottom where the work is done.

This requires looking at the way the technology separates out a series of jobs that must be accomplished if the product is to result. We may manufacture something, buy it for resale, or hire it, as in the case of money, but whatever the business—manufacturing, retailing, banking, or service—we follow certain techniques. There is a beginning, when the process starts, something is done, and the process ends. Put another way, something comes in the door, something is done to it, and it moves on its way out another door to the customer.

In the cases to follow, which are drawn from the authors' field studies, the problems created when the work-flow sequence is not used as a criterion of organizational design, as well as the techniques of analyzing the work process and identifying the work-flow sequences will be examined. By using a comparative point of view, we shall describe a method to isolate some general principles of organization.

Case 1. The Sales-Credit Controversy. In this case, the general sales manager of a manufacturing company was engaged in a major battle with both the credit manager and the treasurer, who was the credit manager's boss. Such conflicts are not rare. Salesmen usually believe the credit department tries to prevent them from making sales, and credit personnel often think the salesmen will sell to anyone, no matter how bad the risk, to get their commissions. This case illustrates the nature of the problem and why management structure and work flow are too often incongruous.

Although interpreted by management as a clash of personalities, the argument between the sales manager and the credit manager stemmed from much more mundane sources. To understand it, it is necessary to look at the actual work flow through their departments and observe the way the work was organizationally split up. The key implement was the salesman's order, which he mailed in to the home office after filling out what the customer required and extending the dollar figures. Figure 2-1a illustrates what happened to the order and how the people who handled it were divided between the various functional divisions.

When the office opened in the morning, the

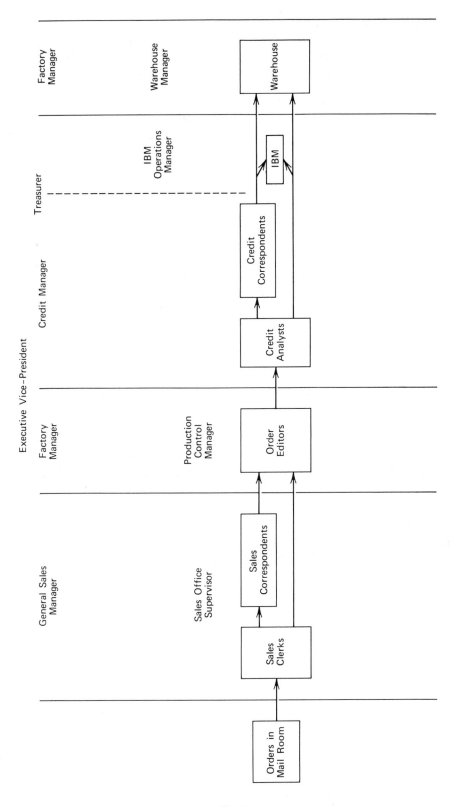

Fig. 2-1a

mail was sorted in the mail room. Orders were separated and taken immediately by a mail boy to the sales office which occupied one section of the large, open general office of the company, a one-floor layout. There, the clerks checked over the orders to see if there were any special problems of handling shipments or questions raised by the salesmen that might require correspondence. Any order presenting a problem was given to a sales correspondent who wrote to the customer or the salesman, if necessary.

When the sales department completed its work, the order was sent to what was called an order-editing department. This was under the jurisdiction of the factory manager because he superintended warehousing. The orders were checked to see that they were correct, the prices up-to-date, the arithmetic accurate, and the goods in stock at the warehouse nearest to the customer. A copy of the order was sent to another warehouse if the closest one did not have stock. If inventory records showed no stock available, the order editor made out a back-order form to be mailed to the customer.

Then one of the editors would take a batch of orders to the credit department, where credit analysts (clerks) checked the credit ratings to be sure each customer's credit was within the limits set by management. They ascertained whether it was permissible to sell on any other terms than C.O.D. and whether the volume of the order was within the limits of his credit rating. If there was a credit problem, i.e., a deviation, the order was given to a credit correspondent who wrote the customer, with a copy for the salesman, telling him his order could not be accepted and stating the terms, if any, on which he could still buy from the company. If the customer was a big-volume account whose credit rating had dropped, the credit manager would make a final decision before the correspondent wrote a letter. It should be mentioned that each salesman had a reference book of the credit ratings for all accounts in his territory and was not supposed to call on any account whose line of credit was below a specified level.

After this processing, the orders were assembled, one copy of each order was sent to the warehouses to be filled and another to be tabulated for accounting purposes. The IBM accounting processing was supervised by the treasurer, and the warehouses were, as mentioned above, under the manager of the factory. Work was organized so that, in theory at least, all of the orders were processed through this office work flow in one day. Thereafter, there was a definite break in timing because accounting did not receive the orders until a batch was completed at the end of each day. The same was true for the warehouses where goods were pulled for shipment and billed.

There was tension between the credit manager and the general sales manager because the credit department, following its procedure faithfully, occasionally canceled an order that a salesman had made, sometimes a large one. Because credit ratings fluctuate, this had happened recently to two large accounts, and the general sales manager was understandably furious. Both customers threatened not to buy from the company again. The situation was more embarrassing because the general sales manager had written each customer a personal letter to thank him for his confidence in their product after the sales correspondent handling the accounts called the orders to his attention.

Reorganization. Now let us look at a series of improvements in the organization. The first and most obvious change in the work flow of handling orders was to reverse the position of the sales and the credit departments. If credit could not be extended, there was no point in checking the accuracy of an order or carrying out the "sales" functions involved. Moreover, this change would prevent recurrences of the kind of embarrassment the general sales manager had undergone. The rearrangement was also more efficient because it eliminated the processing of orders that ultimately would be thrown out. However, it did not deal with more basic issues.[1]

---

[1] The reader may consider the illogical arrangement of having the credit checked after sales correspondents and order editors worked on an order as an obvious mistake that anyone should have recognized. However, because it was not recognized for many years in a relatively alert company, it reflects the strong attraction of organizing by functional specialty. All the sales activities were put together and handled first, with salesmen contacting their own departments. Then, and only then, was it time for the next function to begin, in this case, that of the credit department. Unfortunately, the logic of functional organization is rarely challenged in practice.

As the organization chart (Figure 2-1a) indicates, three separate divisional heads, reporting to the executive vice-president, were involved in the movement of a piece of paper and its carbon from one clerical position to another in the general office. Not only were three separate divisions writing to the customer (sales, credit, and the order editor if he issued a back order) but also there was no assurance that there would be any coordination in what each said. Credit correspondents were accused by sales of being too brusque with customers and they, in turn, accused sales of promising too much.

Many other practical problems of management arose. The policy of the company was to clear the orders in a single day. Tight scheduling was sometimes necessary to get the work completed because volume fluctuates. Absenteeism, inadequate performance, or the assignment of other work to the people in a department would upset the even flow of work. If there was disagreement because one department was holding up another, the only recourse when the immediate supervisors could not agree was to settle the dispute on the level of the executive vice-president. Thus, in heated disagreements between the general sales manager and the credit manager, the executive vice-president had to listen not only to complaints about customer relations, but also to all the petty grievances each had about the performance or management of the other.

The difficulty was created when the work flow was divided into separate pieces on the basis of functional similarities. The solution was to put it back together as a single flow under a single supervisor. He would control the entire flow of an order from the time the paper arrived in the mail room until it left the general office to go to the tabulating department or the warehouse as well as credits, payments, and invoices after the billing was completed. He was responsible for individual performance and could move people around to fit the needs of fluctuating volume. He did not have to argue with other divisions on the management of the process. See Figure 2-1b.

There was still the problem of functional responsibilities. Sales wanted and deserved some voice in the quality of letters sent to customers. Credit, too, had some legitimate concerns, primarily that company policies regarding credit be followed and any cases not under these policies be referred to higher authority. Both departments outlined standards and procedures that could be carried out by the new department. In this way, representatives of sales or credit would only come into the picture when an exceptional situation required higher-level attention. These procedures also included a periodic auditing program so the sales department could satisfy itself that the correspondents' letters to customers were not antagonistic. The credit department checked that this new work unit only made routine credit decisions and all exceptions needing the credit manager's decision actually got to him. As a result, only one correspondent, a credit-sales-order editing specialist, wrote to each customer although several did identical work. In turn, the correspondent was supervised, together with the clericals handling the proceduralized work flow of the order, by one individual. Credit, sales, and factory set the standards of action for which this single supervisor was responsible.

Case 2. Integrating Inspection, Material Handling, and Machine Maintenance. The case just described has many counterparts in manufacturing organizations. Because work flow is more easily associated with traditional production processes, a typical assembly operation has been chosen. Some of the parts are produced directly from raw materials purchased by the company, and others are purchased from subcontractors. Both types of components are combined into subassemblies and final assemblies. Figure 2-2a illustrates the flow of work and the organizational segmentation. The existence of material-handling units between each production unit is typical. They report to the production planning department whose manager reports to the vice-president in charge of manufacturing, rather than to the general superintendent. The inspection units, again reporting through a separate channel of authority to the same vice-president, are less typical. Mechanical maintenance, which also had its own chain of command, was the third specialization organizationally separated from production.

Inspection may appear to be the greatest justification for a separate structure because production people might ignore, or at least slight, the quality problem. On closer examination, however, it could be observed that two

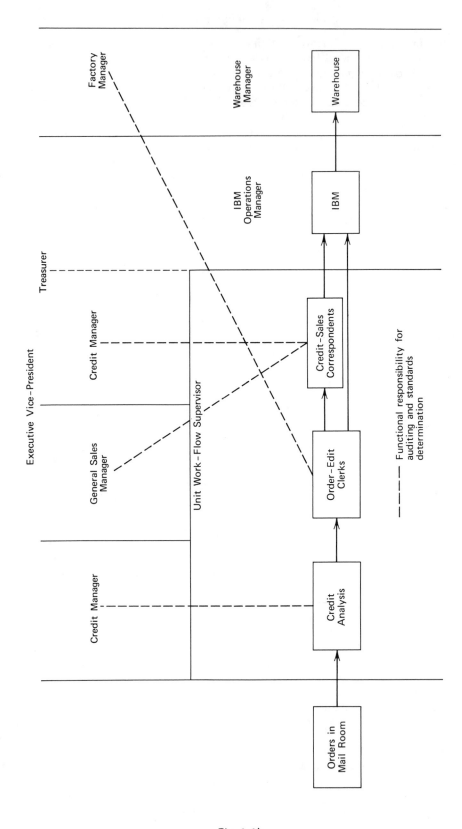

Fig. 2–1b

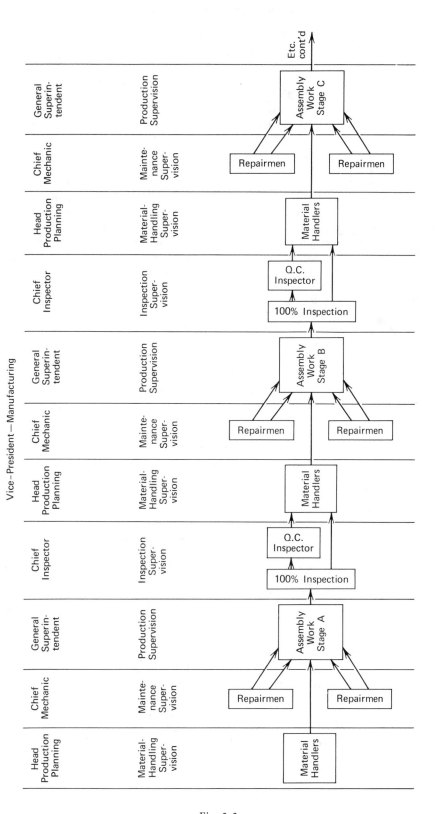

Fig. 2-2a

types of inspection were really being carried on. As a regular part of the finishing operation, a cursory visual check was given to all products by one group of inspectors. This check was paced identically with the production process itself as another step after finishing. There was also a quality-control procedure handled by other inspectors who followed routine sampling methods, quite distinct from the 100 per cent inspection process.

The first group of inspectors was the source of frequent holdups that seriously aggravated the relationship of production and inspection personnel. In retrospect, the obvious basis for the friction over the complete inspection stage can be noted. The source of intramanagement feuds is usually not hard to discover. The 100 per cent inspection stage was clearly an integral part of the finishing work flow. Materials passed through all of the stages, including inspection, at the same rate, or at least were supposed to if production schedules were to be maintained. This meant that the "balancing" problem within this work process was always shuttled back and forth between two separate jurisdictions. Quality-control inspection, on the other hand, involved a different sequence of product movement and had no effect on the flow of work.

The remedial steps were obvious. First, 100 per cent inspection was recognized as a necessary part of the production process and transferred to the general foreman so inspection became merely an audit or visual checking within the production framework. Quality-control inspection, which did not interfere with the flow of work since it was done on a sampling basis, remained where it was. This and other organization changes are illustrated in Figure 2-2b.

Matters were made worse by the material-handling department, which supplied the lines with parts on the basis of a schedule set up by production planning to whom the supervisor of material handling reported. The master schedule for the month's production was broken down by weeks and operations planned around it. However, day-to-day and even hour-to-hour upsets would interfere. A key machine went down. The production rate of a given unit was greater, or slower, than expected. The crucial parts needed to keep production moving were not available, and foremen, general foremen, and superintendents were constantly calling each other, and the material-handling supervisors and the production planning department to straighten things out. The constant arguments could only be settled by the vice-president in charge of manufacturing.

The source of the difficulty was twofold: the scope of production planning, that is, the inherent conflict between a master schedule and the day-to-day variation that every factory experiences, was not adequately analyzed, and, more important, the inevitable lack of coordination between the several units making up a single continuous work-flow system.

In a reorganization, the material-handling units were transferred to production. Units that tied together work groups of two foremen were to report to the general foreman. If departments under the supervision of general foremen were involved, the material-handling reported to the superintendents who bridged the general foremen. Production planning was also re-examined to differentiate between day-to-day and long-range scheduling operations.

The factory manager acquired two planners whose sole responsibility was to control the daily variations and relate them to the long-range schedule, which involved purchasing of parts and raw materials. Thus, control of raw materials, processes, and finished inventories remained unchanged in the organizational structure.

The company was also plagued by a slightly different problem. As the chart in Figure 2-2a indicates, the chief mechanic reports to the vice-president in charge of manufacturing, which is traditional functional specialization. The assumption is that placing all the people concerned with mechanical service together in one department leads to more efficient operation and thereby saves money.

But what happened in this case? The floor mechanics, who repaired the machines, worked under their own foremen. The production foreman used a call light to signal for a mechanic when a machine went down. If the mechanic was already working on a machine in another department, the production foreman had to ask the mechanical foreman to take the mechanic off the job he was doing and send him over to the new machine. The mechanics and their foremen usually objected to this even though the whole line might otherwise be held up. The mechanics complained

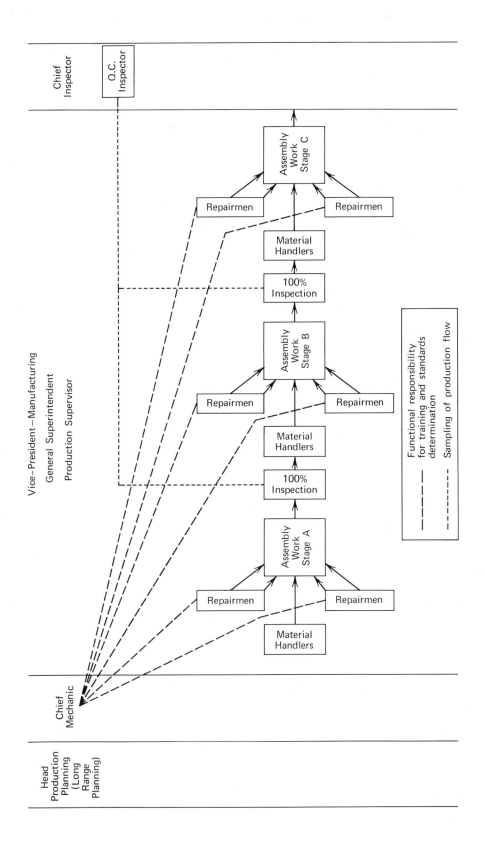

Fig. 2–2b

that most of the breakdowns resulted from bad maintenance by the operators and there would be no trouble if the production foremen would make sure their people kept the machines oiled and adjusted. The production foremen countered by saying the mechanics always fixed the wrong machines, had no understanding of production problems, and usually were just stubborn when they insisted on fixing an unimportant machine, i.e., unimportant to the production foreman at the moment. Moreover, the production foremen were constantly arguing among themselves. If all the mechanics were busy in one department and another department needed one, the first-come, first-served principle was not . . . satisfactory to the man with a rush order to get out.[2]

As in the other cases, the heated arguments were complicated by personalities and also had to be settled on the top-management level. No matter how carefully the vice-president tried to get the foremen to agree on a procedure to determine the importance of any machine breakdown and to emphasize preventive maintenance, the foremen usually ended up in his office.

He finally decided the only way to eliminate the stress was to assign mechanics to the general foremen in production and in some instances superintendents. The mechanical department continued to train the mechanics in its shops, and set up repair performance standards to make sure each mechanic's work met specifications. Most importantly, however, the assignment of mechanics was controlled by production. As a result, the conflicts ended, and the vice-president was able to devote time to more constructive activities than settling intramanagement rows. In terms of cost, the company was better off than before. Although the original centralization of facilities appeared efficient, no additional mechanics were needed for the reorganization, and it reduced delays in the work flow because of mechanical failure, actually saving money for the company.

So far, the examples of work flow have dealt with the processing of paper or materials through a production line. The final case illustrates how work flow also involves people.

[2] Cf. George Strauss, "The Set-Up Man: A Case Study of Organizational Change," *Human Organization*, vol. XIII, no. 2, 1954, pp. 17–25.

Identification of Unit Work Flow

Any organization that has more than one supervisor must decide which employees and, therefore, which processes should be under the jurisdiction or span of control of a given manager. This is the old question of who reports to whom. The preceding text was directed to finding some criterion upon which to base this crucial decision. The case studies were presented to illustrate the significance of technology as the critical determinant of this aspect of organizational structure.

But, this concept of technology needs a more careful explanation than the implications of the cases. It should be clear at the outset that the technology or work method of the organization does not refer primarily to the equipment or to the mechanical, electrical, or chemical processes utilized. Every organization has a method of performing work that involves some sequence of operations. These work flows, so crucial in the cases cited, can be identified wherever there is a sequence of techniques that must be performed in a regular or predetermined order by separate individuals. Thus the technology of the organization is the "who does what with whom, when, where, and how often."

These kinds of work flows are not the same as the work-flow analyses of the industrial engineer, which chart each operation in the production process chronologically. In constructing an organizational structure, the interest is in the person-to-person flow. Thus, one individual may perform what the engineer would identify as several separate operations before the work or paper goes to the next person in the production sequence.[3]

The next step is to separate the elements of the work flow that should be considered as a single supervisory unit, which will be called "unit work flows." The concern here is with the quantitive characteristics of the work flow regardless of whether that which "flows" is a

[3] It is necessary, of course, to know the total time required by each person to complete his activities to determine the duration of that particular stage in the production sequence. This helps establish the rate at which the paper, material, or a person moves through the line. This rate is set by the time required to complete the slowest or longest step in the sequence.

person, paper, or material. These characteristics are necessary to set up criteria to identify the unitary work flows and to understand their implications behaviorally in organization design.

In broad terms, the flow of materials, in a manufacturing company for example, that begins at the receiving dock and finally appears at the shipping door as finished product ready for the customer could be considered a single work flow. However, the time coordinates of the complete process are generally too wide; sometimes a matter of weeks or months are needed to complete the manufacturing cycle. Besides the question of physical contiguity is relevant. Physical location or layout is an important factor in identifying the unit flows that make up an organizational design.

In the example of processing the salesman's order, a controlling factor in the separation of warehousing work flow from the office work flow was location. Although they are physically separate out of necessity, the warehouses could be contiguous. In this case they were located in various parts of the country. Consequently, there was a time lapse between the processing of the orders by the clerical groups and their receipt at the appropriate warehouses.

Yet, even if this time was reduced to a minimum and the location of the warehouse was, so to speak, at the end of the order processing line, the order-filling work flow would still differ quantitatively from the order-processing work flow in its time characteristics. When the day's orders were received in the warehouse, they were sorted according to customer location and given to each order filler in groups having a common shipping route. He then assembled the order from bins or bulk locations and placed it with the order copy (with the amounts checked off) on a conveyer that moved the orders through a checking station, a manifest clerk, a packer, etc. The order-filling work flow did not begin until after the orders for an entire day were processed; the office work flow essentially was done one order at a time. Hence, this procedural difference caused a break in continuous flow similar to the one in geographical location.

If the existing procedural and locational discontinuities can be determined by time criteria, a total work flow can be divided into its unitary parts.[4] Obviously, by changing the technological system, the constituent techniques in a single unit flow can be varied and combined into more inclusive units, through the introduction of a conveyor, for example. Such changes are continually being made in business and require concurrent organizational changes to avoid creating management problems.

Sources of Stress in Organization

A unit work flow becomes segmented and its parts placed under different chains of command largely, although not necessarily entirely, as a result of the emphasis on functional specialization in organizational design. Sales and credit managers were both responsible for the order-processing flow in one company, and chaos resulted. In the second case, material handlers, maintenance employees, and the inspectors all had separate chains of command that conflicted with the management responsible for maintaining production. In the third illustration, the employment and training departments failed to coordinate the induction training procedure with the employment office functions. The true interrelationships among the processes, eventually merged under a single supervisor, had been disguised by artificial functional designations.

However, in one instance the problem was procedural not structural: the sequence within one group had not been thought through in terms of work flow. As a result, orders reached the credit checking clerks after they passed through earlier stages rather than at the beginning of the process which is more efficient.

Let us look more closely at the resulting organizational disturbances. In a situation requiring cooperative endeavors, whether it is a work group, employees and managers, or staff and line officials, each tries to develop a stable pattern of work, of interaction. When these stable patterns are disturbed, individuals experience stress or an uncomfortable feeling of pressure and dissatisfaction. A breakdown in

[4] With the use of statistical techniques, it is possible to determine the homogeneity of the measurements within any unitary flow and to develop accurate criteria to test for discontinuities.

the flow creates opposition as the individuals struggle to restore it. The expected responses from the individuals in the sequence prove inadequate, and new coordination problems arise.

The regularities of actions and interactions disappear when this stress occurs, and erratic variation takes over. The difference is obvious between a smoothly running operation and one with a problem. Under stress, people react emotionally, and, because more than one individual is involved, the reactions usually conflict with each other.

Thus, a vicious circle is established. Something happens in the work situation that causes the relationship of individuals to change or to depart from the normal pattern. This creates a stress, either of opposition or nonresponse, that is further complicated by higher levels of supervision and staff specialists whose unexpected interactions, i.e., outside the usual organization pattern, irritate the disturbed workflow relations. People get upset; they become angry with each other and, depending on their individual characteristics, react temperamentally. These personality conflicts have direct ramifications in the work process because the emotional reactions change the pattern of contact and interaction. Joe is angry with Bill, so he does not check with him before starting a new experimental run. Consequently, a special test that should have been included in the run is left out, and the whole thing has to be done over. To complete the circle, these emotional disturbances damage the work-flow sequence, which causes additional personality stresses.

Robert Guest of the Yale Technology Project described this accurately when he said:

> Foremen are always getting caught in this familiar vicious circle. Material inspection, say has failed to spot some faulty pieces. Something goes wrong at a welding operation. The general foreman is on the foreman's neck to "get it straightened out, or else!" The foreman drops everything to spend time on this one item. He cannot pay attention to the man he was breaking in on a new job. He cannot check on the stock bin which the stock man forgot to replenish. He meant to warn an operator about a safety condition. He knew another man was down in the dumps about a personal problem. By the time he has cleared up the original trouble and satisfied the boss, something else has blown up and the general foreman is roaring down the aisle again.[5]

What produced these stresses and where do these changes come from? They are not directly interactional on the worker level. With rare exceptions, the work flow does not require a direct interactional contact between two contiguous persons as team operations do. That is, the upsets and bickerings are not caused by people who occupy adjacent positions in the flow process and place pressures on one another. In fact, orders could be put on the next desk or on a conveyor without any real contact. Material or parts in an assembly operation usually move from one operator to the next on a conveyor. But, they may also be brought and taken away by service personnel, just as a mail boy may move orders from one group to the next in the office. In these examples, the flow of work does not cause any direct interpersonal problems,[6] except that the action of one person depends on the action of his predecessor, causing him not to act and thus breaking the sequence. As Guest indicates, however, the initiating sources of stress are primarily fluctuations in the rate at which work flows through the supervisory unit. The critical variable is time. Production schedules require tight coordination; holdups must be avoided. If they occur, production suffers and the relationships of the supervisor to his workers and of the workers among themselves change as a consequence.

The objective of any organizational structure is to minimize the incidence of deviations from the established interaction patterns of the work process. The realistic administrator

[5] Robert H. Guest, "Of Time and the Foreman," Personnel, May, 1956, pp. 478–486.
[6] This contrasts with the usual conception of work-flow stress. Among the best known studies in this area is William F. Whyte's work in the restaurant industry. Whyte found stress was caused by the direct pressure emanating from interworker contacts. "Lower-status" runners placed pressure and thus disturbed "higher-status" kitchen personnel, and demanding customers upset the waitress who could not tolerate a high frequency of demands. (William F. Whyte, Human Relations in the Restaurant Industry, McGraw-Hill Book Company, Inc., New York, 1948, pp. 49–59, 104–128.)

knows complete stability is a never-to-be-achieved utopia. Equipment will always break down; employees will always be absent; and changes in procedures will be introduced continuously. Work will not always come through on time, or when it does, the quality may be so poor the normal process time must be increased significantly. Rush orders or a flood of work may press upon his unit. Whatever the type of fluctuation, his interaction patterns have to change. He may have to spend more time with individual workers, supervisors in other departments, engineers, mechanics, maintenance men, or various persons in control positions, such as production planners or factory cost controllers, who occupy a place in the paper-work flow of which the line supervisor also is a part. And, as a result, less time is available to maintain other vital contacts.

Even if his unit flow is not complicated by other supervisors who directly affect him, the supervisor will still have coordination and timing problems in his own unit and in his relations with those who give him work and to whom he transmits it. The possibility of stress is much greater if he does not have control over the key individuals who work directly with his segment of the flow and cannot get a response from them when he needs it, as in the case of the maintenance mechanics, or if he must constantly gear his segment to the next one, as in the examples of the material handling and inspection

This is the major point of the discussion. Although the dynamic organization will always experience changes that cause variations in the work-flow system, most of these can be dealt with effectively by the supervisor affected. But, his job becomes almost impossibly difficult if there is no semblance of stability.[7] If the parts of a unit work flow are distributed among several supervisors, the individual manager cannot hope to maintain any stability in internal relationships because erratic changes

[7] The degree to which the use of functional organization introduces stress and instability is cogently analyzed by James Worthy, Sears Roebuck and Co., in his paper, "Some Aspects of Organization Structure in Relation to Pressures on Company Decision-Making," in *Proceedings of Fifth Annual Meeting of the Industrial Relations Research Association* (ed. L. Reed Tripp), IRRA Publ. 10, 1953, pp. 69–79.

are introduced by individuals whose behavior he cannot control. Because these other supervisors are meeting different organizational needs, they do not and cannot adjust to the requirements of any single manager. Significant irregularities in the rate of flow and significant changes in the interaction of the individuals concerned indicate the existence of a point of organization stress.

In companies where such problems are common, informal working arrangements usually develop over the course of time. Assuming the individual supervisors get along, i.e., the frequency or intensity of stress is not too great or their personalities are not obviously incompatible, they frequently get together to plan the work and discuss their mutual problems. The objective is for each supervisor to create the least upset to the next group in the line. Unfortunately, it is almost impossible because the segmentation of the work flow makes informal arrangements vulnerable to unexpected changes emanating from higher up.

Higher Level Management Problems

Because people, not lines on a chart, are the major concern, the elimination of points of stress within the work flow should be the first consideration of organization design. This means the traditional functional classification must be abandoned and each job analyzed as a part of one or perhaps, as in the case of an executive, many work flows. Merely recognizing that "informal" organization exists and hoping that management will grant it equal importance to the "formal" structure will not solve the problems.

Studies of the informal organization discuss how people actually relate themselves to each other in the process of getting the work done. Thus, the pattern of relationships that evolve in completing the job is what some observers consider the uncontrolled or spontaneous aspect of the organization. The authors believe this aspect must be the objective of the consciously contrived organizational structure. The organization must be designed for people not in the hope that people will somehow fit into it.

Accordingly, the first step is to identify the unit work flows and set their boundaries, placing each one under a single supervisor. As stated previously, these work flows consist not only of the people through whom the material, paper, or person flows, but also all the individuals who help maintain the flow, the mechanics, service people, etc. All the factors required to get the work done should be concentrated under a single person with responsibility centered at the lowest managerial point, not at the highest, as in the examples where top management officials were constantly arbitrating interdepartmental disputes.

Span of Second-level Supervision. So far, a series of unit flows, each with its own supervisor, has been constructed. However, each still depends upon the other. Although the stress points within the unit work flows are eliminated by effective organizational design, areas of interdependence between these units necessarily remain. As noted above, the pace of the work generally shifts between unit work flows, there are different rhythms and sequences, and, as a result, the coordination problems are not as great, but there is still an obvious need to coordinate relationships. In the example, the application of quantitative criteria revealed that orders went to the warehouse or tabulating or material from a fabricating unit to assembly with a definable discontinuity. This indicates the need for at least one further level of supervision, a manager over the unit work-flow managers whose responsibility is to see that they are coordinated into a larger system.

Controls. Combining unit work flows into a work-flow system does not depend upon arbitrary assumptions as to the number of individuals such a manager can supervise. These factors are determined by analysis of the controls the manager has available to maintain the system, not by abstract formulas. Worthy pointed out that in the Sears organization a store manager may have thirty to forty department heads reporting to him.[8] This works not merely because the company does not want a manager spending too much time with any single department head but, more fundamentally, because the department store manager receives daily and weekly reports which

are sufficient to tell him whether significant deviations are occurring in the ratio of stock (inventory) to sales, in markdowns, markups, etc. Consequently, he spends time with subordinates only in cases where managers are in trouble or where the reports suggest difficulties. As the theory of administrative controls is developed, similar control procedures can be adopted for any business operation.

Many companies find it difficult to organize for effective operation because their reporting systems do not adequately pinpoint responsibility. Most administrative controls are by-products of accounting controls. They were developed for financial record keeping, not management control. Consequently, they are issued by the controller as financial documents and, although completely accurate, they are usually so late as to be matters of ancient history and too general because costs are both prorated and arbitrarily assigned. As such, these reports have little use as operating tools.[9] Thus the number of unit work-flow supervisors reporting to the second management level is a function of the state of development of the organization's controls: the measures which assess how things are going in the production process. Primarily, controls signal troubles at the points where two unit work flows come into contact. These juncture points are the potential stress areas that the second level manager oversees. Improvements in management reporting technology, particularly by the computer, will substantially increase the span of control at this management level.

The use of controls is based on the same criterion utilized in defining each of the unit work flows, the time coordinates of the system. The controls should indicate when the individual unit flows are intermeshing with one another. If they show homogeneity, in the statistical sense, in the interrelationships of the component units, the system is operating as

---

[8] William F. Whyte, *Modern Methods in Social Research*, prepared for the Office of Naval Research under Contract Nonr-401(2), pp. 25–28.

[9] There is an increasing concern with what is called "management accounting." However, present practice indicates it has by no means reached its declared goal of defining organizational responsibility within an accounting framework. Too many costs are still allocated and prorated. True managerial accounting cannot be achieved without loosening the bonds placed in the way of organizational change by poor accounting logic.

planned. If the sequential movement of goods, paper, or people between units is stabilized, as reported through appropriate controls, the manager can relax. He must go into action when his controls show stressful situations are developing that require attention and action to avoid complete breakdowns in the system.

Assuming some ingenuity is shown in the development of controls, the number of unit supervisors within the flow is of little significance, because each unit is self-sufficient.

Handling the Staff-Line Relationships

What is to be done with specialists such as the chief mechanic, the chief inspector, the production planning manager, and the credit manager? As pointed out previously, the specialists are responsible for developing standards, the procedures to implement these standards, and auditing results. Although this was mentioned explicitly only in the case of the credit manager, each specialist also plays a part in one or more work flows. The significance of the specialists' development and auditing is that they have been removed from direct work-flow decision. The chief mechanic, for example, does not directly or through the foremen decide on what machine the mechanic is to work. He is responsible for the standards of mechanical repair, the program of preventive maintenance, and the evaluation of the mechanic's performance.

Thus, the unit work-flow supervisor and the chief mechanic have a dual responsibility for performance: the first, for the mechanic's contribution in maintaining the production flow, and the latter for the quality of his work. Both factors must be considered in evaluation and control. Otherwise, it is easy to overemphasize short-term gains in production at the cost of the long-run impact on the mechanical equipment.

Moreover, this shift in responsibility gives the specialist time to develop programs and to carry out his auditing responsibility. Otherwise, he is too busy with the day-to-day operating decisions to determine the source of the problems. Under the pressure of the immediate situation, his only interest would be to put the fire out; he would have little time to see what caused the problem in the first place.

However, the specialists need to be fitted into the organizational system. Because they are concerned with developing programs to expedite the work flow and eliminate stresses both within and between unit work flows that affect the total work-flow system, the specialists inevitably become the specialized assistants of the work-flow system manager. Their responsibility then is to act for him in their respective areas to improve the operation on the unit work-flow level. It is important to note the word "responsibility." In the usual sense of the word, specialists do not have staff responsibility with advisory or consultative relations to the line, nor do they have the responsibility of line supervisors, one step removed. They are actually *of* the staff of the manager and accountable to him for developing, installing, and auditing the results of programs in terms of the major objective of removing stress.

Conclusion: Work Flow and Organization Design

The type of organization design just described, based on the actual work flow within a technological and procedural framework, requires the complete use of time measurements as its basis. Not only is the delimitation of unit work flows dependent on the possession of quantitative criteria, but improvements of the technological process, in its broadest sense, require the examination of how each individual, whether worker, specialist, or supervisor, spends his time. The effective use of the method by any company depends also upon layout and location, the techniques by which paper, materials, or people are handled, and the controls used to signal real or impending deviations.

For example, if the record system is not or cannot be tied to individual responsibility, it is that much more difficult to locate points of stress and, in the absurd but common case, the supervisor may have to spend his time continually "on the floor" looking and listening because he does not routinely receive adequate information about his operation. The exception principle, one of the oldest in management, is useful in organizational planning only if the systems and procedures make its use possible.

The work-flow theory requires the specification of what each person does, when, where, with whom, how long, and how often. Therefore a type of job analysis or job description, to use a somewhat discredited term, is needed to outline the flows for each individual and to specify in quantitative measurements the duration of the action and interaction required to carry them out. These administrative patterns will be discussed in the next chapter, with the executive in mind, but similar, although much simpler, descriptions are necessary for the workers themselves. Any contact, whether it is a mechanic repairing a machine, a service boy bringing parts, or a set-up man making adjustments for a new run, involves some interaction, and the time involved is not simply a matter of the actual physical action.

Variations introduced by personality must also be considered within the organization design that results from the application of work-flow theory to any particular technological system. The supervisor who fails to act when stress is indicated in his control reports, waiting until someone calls it to his attention, hinders the operation of his unit work flow if it is set up on close time tolerances. Similarly, the manager who cannot spend the time with his staff specialists to see that preventive programs are developed and installed always faces stress within his area. In contrast, a staff specialist may find his development and audit responsibilities uncongenial in terms of his personality and, unconsciously, try to build a segregated work unit for himself, isolated from the people with whose performance he is concerned. The results of all of these are damaging to the work-flow system.

Personality and the reactions of the individual to specific types of stress limit both the construction of an organization to a given design and also its operation under the specifications. Fortunately, the same methods used to assess organization design also apply to the evaluation of individual personality and temperament. Through measurements of interaction, it can be determined precisely how an individual adjusts to a given type of organizational position and its potentialities for stress. In this way, it is possible to offset shortcomings either by modifications in the job or by selecting assistants who complement the individual's abilities.

The purpose here has been to suggest criteria upon which to base the design of an organization: the structure must be built from the bottom up and it must be superimposed upon a known technology. In fact, technology, as defined earlier, should be the basis for the distribution and assignment of supervision. Supervisory jobs are largely products of the time coordinates of the production process, regardless of the kind of work the organization does. The significance of this will become more apparent in the next chapter.

Vertical and Horizontal Communication in Formal Organizations[1]

RICHARD L. SIMPSON

Writings on formal organization have stressed communication up and down the line of authority. Instructions move down, information moves up. When two men on the same level communicate, they are supposed to do it indirectly. If Supervisor A must communicate with Supervisor B, the communication goes up one chain from A, then down another to B, with their common superior linking the two chains at the top. According to this view, there is little direct communication between equals, except small talk which is not related directly to work problems.

This process is admittedly cumbersome, but advantages are claimed for it. As Miller and Form explain:

> Although communication between departments on the same level occurs, theoretically it is not supposed to be direct. Reports, desires for services, or criticisms that one department has of another are supposed to be sent up the line until they reach an executive who heads the organizations involved. They are then held, revised, or sent directly down the line to the appropriate officials and departments. The reason for

this circuitous route is to inform higher officials of things occurring below them.[2]

From the literature, one infers that most communications not only should be, but are, vertical rather than horizontal,[3] but this appears to have been assumed, not demonstrated. If we examine the forerunners of modern writings on industry and bureaucracy, it is easy to see how such a belief has arisen. Among the main forerunners are Weber's work on bureaucracy[4] and writings on military organization, public administration, and personnel management.[5] These sources embody much the same viewpoint in that they are concerned with control, accountability, and authority. Bureaucracy, to them, is efficient because it specifies who is responsible to whom, for precisely what activities. From this implicit perspective it is easy to assume that the great advantage of bureaucracy—and the great desideratum in managing one—is the centralization of control so that those on top know exactly what is going on beneath them. This control is

---

From Richard L. Simpson, *Administrative Science Quarterly*, Vol. 4, No. 2, September 1959, pp. 188–196. Reprinted by permission of the *Administrative Science Quarterly*, and the author.

[1] Revision of a paper presented to the American Sociological Society, Seattle, August 28, 1958. The data used here were gathered for a doctoral dissertation. "A Study of Supervisory Reorganization in a Factory Production Department" (University of North Carolina, 1956), under the direction of E. William Noland, to whom the author is indebted as well as to Jack L. Dyer and Ida Harper Simpson for helpful suggestions and criticisms.

[2] Delbert C. Miller and William H. Form, *Industrial Sociology* (New York, 1950), p. 158.

[3] *Ibid.* See also Burleigh B. Gardner and David G. Moore, *Human Relations in Industry* (Chicago, 1950), p. 43; and Wilbert E. Moore, *Industrial Relations and the Social Order* (New York, 1951), p. 94.

[4] See Max Weber, "Bureaucracy," in *From Max Weber: Essays in Sociology*, tr. by H. H. Gerth and C. Wright Mills (New York, 1946).

[5] For examples of traditional thinking about line organization from these fields, see John Robert Beishline, *Military Management for National Defense* (New York, 1950); Luther Gulick, "Notes on the Theory of Organization," in Luther Gulick and L. Urwick, eds., *Papers in the Science of Administration* (New York, 1937); and Walter Dill Scott and Robert C. Clothier, *Personnel Management* (New York, 1926).

319

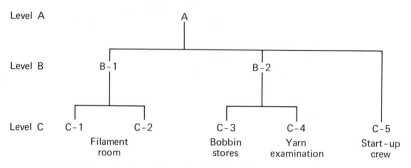

Fig. 1. Organization chart of spinning department supervisors.

best achieved, it might seem, if everyone adheres strictly to the chain of command. It is understandable if writers steeped in this orientation adopt it as their own and assume further that what ought to be, is.

In this paper we shall explore this assumption. The procedure followed will be, first, to test the hypothesis that work-related communications between officials are more often vertical than horizontal; second, to venture an explanation of the results of the test; and, third, to resolve a seeming contradiction in recent research on industrial communications, proposing a new hypothesis concerning mechanization and automation as determinants of supervisory communication patterns.

Research Setting

Interviews were conducted with supervisors in the spinning department of a synthetic textile mill. Spinning was one of three production departments in the mill: chemical, spinning, and textile. The chemical department prepared a liquid which passed through jets, cooled into solid threads, and finally wound onto whirling bobbins in the spinning departments. The spinning department's job was to remove these yarn-filled bobbins from the machines, replace the full bobbins with empty ones, inspect the yarn for defects, and transport the full bobbins to the textile department for final touches.

The supervisors who were studied are listed below, with a description of their responsibilities. Each position is designated by a letter corresponding to its level in the hierarchy. The plant operated continuously, with three shifts working each day, so that some positions

were occupied by more than one man, one for each shift. A chain-of-command chart of spinning supervisors is shown in Figure 1.

Positions and Duties in the Spinning Department

Level A

A. *General foreman*, in charge of the spinning department. Each day he posted brief written instructions covering the work of the entire department. In addition, he was the immediate superior of B-1, B-2, and C-5—the man to whom they felt responsible and to whom they came if they needed authoritative advice. A worked the day shift only, Monday through Friday.

Level B

B-1. *Shift foreman*, in charge of the filament room, where bobbins filled with yarn were removed from the machines and replaced with empty bobbins. Under his direct command were two first-line supervisors in the filament room, C-1 and C-2. Position B-1 was occupied by four men, one for each shift. The shifts rotated on a schedule so that during a 24-hour day period each group of shift workers worked six days in the daytime, then six days in the evening, then six days on the graveyard shift, then were off duty six days.

B-2. *Yarn examination and bobbin stores supervisor*. In salary classification, B-2 was one level below B-1, but in the hierarchy of command he was of the same rank, intermediate between the general foreman and the first-line supervisors. Under his direct supervision were C-3, foreman in charge of bobbin stores, and

C-4, foreman in charge of yarn examination. B-2 worked the daylight hours only, Monday through Friday. At the close of each day he left written instructions for the night shifts.

Level C

C-1 and C-2. *Filament foremen.* These were first-line supervisors, each supervising the work of about 20 women in the filament room. Their immediate superior was B-1. They were shift workers; therefore there were four men holding each position, one on each shift.

C-3. *Bobbin stores foreman.* This first-line supervisor was in charge of the group which maintained a supply of bobbins in good condition and sent bobbins to the filament room as needed. There was one foreman per shift, four in all. The immediate supervisor for C-3 was C-2.

C-4. *Yarn examination foreman.* This first-line foreman supervised the women who examined yarn for quality as it passed from the filament room to the textile department. There was one C-4 per shift. The immediate superior for C-4 was B-2.

C-5. *Start-up crew foreman.* C-5 supervised eight men who shut down and started the filament machines whenever a change was made in the type of yarn being produced. These machine changes were always made in the daytime; therefore C-5 worked the daylight hours only, Monday through Friday, and was responsible directly to A.

Research Procedure

Each supervisor was asked how many *work-related contacts* he had with every other supervisor. The question was: "About how often do you talk with ———— on business? Don't include times when you just say hello or pass the time of day; just the contacts needed to get your work done. . . . What kinds of things do you talk about with him?" Shift workers were told that the question referred only to times when they were on the daylight shift, so as to equalize the times available for contacts between all positions. All interviewing was done in the daytime. If the answer given was indefinite, such as "often" or "hardly ever," the interviewee was asked to estimate a *specific*

number for his average daily or weekly contacts. In this way information was obtained on the frequency and purpose of contacts between every pair of supervisors.

Findings and Interpretation

Table 1 shows the numbers of vertical and horizontal work-related contacts of each supervisor, the proportion of these contacts which were vertical, and the "expected" proportion which would have been vertical if each man had distributed his contacts equally among the other men. Our hypothesis that communication between officials is more often vertical than horizontal cannot be rejected; but neither can it be accepted without qualification.

The contacts of the three men at the higher levels—A, B-1, and B-2—were overwhelmingly vertical; but they could hardly have been otherwise. A, being the only man at his level, could not possibly have any horizontal contacts.[6] B-1 and B-2 could communicate horizontally only with each other, but could communicate downward with several foremen and upward with A. They seldom had to communicate with each other, since the work relations between their sections were coordinated mainly through horizontal contacts between their subordinates, as we shall see later.

On the C foreman level most contacts were horizontal except those of C-3, the bobbin stores foreman. Three of these five foremen—C-1, C-2, and C-5—had markedly fewer vertical and more horizontal contacts than would have occurred on the chance expectation that every man communicates equally with every other man. The contacts of C-4 were mainly horizontal, in about the same proportion as would be expected on the basis of chance. (Our calculation of expected ratio of vertical to total contacts is based on a purely statistical notion of probability and has no necessary relation to the logic of administration. Empiri-

[6] He had horizontal contacts with the chemical and textile department general foremen, but this analysis concerns only within-department contacts. Our impression is that most cross-department contacts at all levels were horizontal. In addition, A had vertical contacts with his superior as did all men at level C with the operatives they supervised.

Table 1. *Estimated Contact Frequencies of Spinning Department Supervisors* *

POSITION	TOTAL CONTACTS PER WEEK	VERTICAL CONTACTS PER WEEK	HORIZONTAL CONTACTS PER WEEK	PROPORTION OF CONTACTS VERTICAL	EXPECTED PROPORTION VERTICAL †
A	12.8	12.8	0	1.000	1.000
B-1	40.0	37.0	3.0	.925	.857
B-2	22.0	19.0	3.0	.864	.857
C-1	30.5	10.0	22.5	.330	.429
C-2	32.6	11.1	21.5	.341	.429
C-3	27.6	15.6	12.0	.565	.429
C-4	20.6	8.6	12.0	.417	.429
C-5	12.5	3.0	9.5	.240	.429
Total	198.6	117.1	81.5	.590	.607

* Estimated contact frequencies for each pair of supervisors were obtained by averaging the estimates made by each man; i.e., by adding the two men's estimates and dividing by two. The estimates of the two men in each reciprocal relationship were in most cases slightly discrepant, but no man in any pair claimed more than twice as many contacts between the two as the other claimed. In the case of "shift" positions occupied by more than one man, the different men's estimates were substantially alike; therefore the figures are felt to be reasonably accurate, though not precise.

† Based on the expectation that every supervisor will communicate an equal amount and divide his communication equally among all other supervisors.

cally, no one would really expect to find all supervisors communicating equally often with all other supervisors.)

The preponderance of horizontal communications reported by four of the five first-line foremen (level C) is understandable if we examine the content of the communications they reported. Very few communications involved the issuing of commands or the reporting of results—the standard types of vertical communications. Most contacts of men at level C involved either (1) joint problem solving or (2) co-ordination of work flow between sections. These were mainly horizontal communications.

Joint problem-solving communication was described by C-1, a filament foreman, in explaining his contacts with C-2, the other filament foreman:

We get together on a lot of problems. If a machine is acting up, or labor is short and we have to make sure all the machines are

properly covered, we talk things over. Things are coming up all the time that we have to work out together.

It is noteworthy that they worked out these problems without consulting or informing their superior.

Co-ordination of work flow between sections often required horizontal contacts. The yarn examination foreman (C-4) might notify a filament foreman (C-1 or C-2) that he was about to run out of yarn for examination. A filament foreman might ask the bobbin stores foreman (C-3) when he could expect to receive a supply of cleaned bobbins. The start-up crew foreman (C-5) and a filament foreman might discuss the next start-up of a filament-spinning machine.

Thus contacts of men at the upper levels were mainly vertical, while contacts of men at the lower levels were mainly horizontal. There remains one exception. C-3, a first-line supervisor, had more vertical than horizontal contacts. Apparently this was because of his position in the work flow. The bobbin stores section of C-3 was often under pressure to furnish bobbins to the filament-spinning section, but C-3 could not control the number of bobbins he received from the textile department for cleaning. Therefore, bobbin stores at times became a bottleneck. When this happened, C-3 sought help from his superior, B-2, who could contact the textile department and try to speed up the flow of bobbins. Problems requiring the attention of B-2 rarely arose in yarn examination, the section supervised by his other subordinate, C-4. The flow of work into yarn examination was set by filament spinning alone and was fairly steady, unlike the flow of work into bobbin stores, which was irregular and required co-ordination with both the textile department and the filament-spinning section. For these reasons B-2 had more downward contacts with one of his subordinates than with the other, and C-3 had more upward contacts than anyone else on his level.

Discussion

Our thesis has been that writers on formal organization have overemphasized vertical communication, in which instructions are given and reports are made, while underemphasizing horizontal communication, in which problems are ironed out and work-flow processes are co-ordinated. In the case we have described, communications of first-line foremen were mainly horizontal because of the mechanized nature of the work. In the spinning department, few instructions were necessary. Each day the general foreman (A) wrote instructions for the entire supervisory force. These instructions actually consisted of information, stating which machines were to produce what kinds of yarn. This brief information told each filament foreman and the start-up crew foreman what to do for the whole day. Beyond that, instructions were seldom needed. The machines set the pace in filament spinning and yarn examination. Only in bobbin stores, where the work depended on co-ordination with another department, were frequent contacts between the foreman and his superior crucial.

This case helps to clear up an apparent contradiction between recent findings by Blau[7] and Faunce.[8] Blau states that in assembly-line work, in contrast to relatively unmechanized work, the machine sets the pace so that the foreman's command function is minimized and he becomes primarily an expediter and joint problem solver. This situation parallels the one observed in the spinning department. Faunce, on the other hand, finds that in highly automated automobile factories there is more direct supervision than in nonautomated (but assembly-line) auto factories. Thus an increase in mechanization results in less supervision according to Blau, but in more supervision according to Faunce.

That the contradiction is more apparent than real becomes evident if we examine the data adduced by Blau, Faunce, and the present writer carefully. Blau and the author find that when there is extensive mechanization, such as that in a traditional auto assembly line or a modern synthetic textile mill, the machine sets the pace so that the need for direct supervision is at a minimum. Faunce is not denying this; he is actually discussing something different. He finds that automation—i.e., mechanization beyond the degree found in the traditional assembly line—increases the frequency and seriousness of machine breakdowns, since the machines are more complex and more interdependent than an old-style assembly-line plants. The machine breakdowns require vertical supervisory communication. Since Blau and Faunce are dealing with different degrees of mechanization, it is not surprising that they find different supervisory patterns in their different industrial settings.

This discussion suggests the following hypothesis: Mechanization reduces the need for close supervision (vertical communication), since instead of the foreman the machines set

[7] Peter M. Blau, Formal Organization: Dimensions of Analysis, *American Journal of Sociology*, 62 (July, 1957), 58–59.
[8] William A. Faunce, Automation in the Automobile Industry, *American Sociological Review*, 23 (1958), 401–407. William H. Form, in discussion from the floor at the convention where an earlier version of this paper was presented, pointed out the relevance of Faunce's study. His comments led us to revise our original conclusions, but he is in no sense to be held responsible for our analysis.

the work pace of his subordinates; but automation (i.e., extreme mechanization) increases the need for vertical communication, to deal with the frequent and serious machine breakdowns. This hypothesis might be stated as a typology: (a) low mechanization, high vertical communication rate; (b) medium mechanization (e.g., the traditional assembly line or the spinning department described above), low vertical communication; (c) high mechanization (i.e., automation), high vertical communication. Comparative research would be needed to test the validity of this typology and discover the precise conditions under which it holds.

Product Innovation and Organization

JAY W. LORSCH

This is an exploratory study of the functioning of two large organizations involved in the complex task of discovering ideas for new products and the improvement of existing ones, and of converting these ideas into products that are feasible and commercially acceptable. From a theoretical standpoint, the study focuses on the problem of obtaining task specialization (*differentiation*) for the units in the organization and of also obtaining an effective unity of effort between these units (*integration*). While the study has as a topical focus the problems connected with discovering new ideas in a research laboratory and converting them into marketable and producible products (the *scientific transfer process*), there is little doubt that any complex organization, whether it be a bank, a retail store, or a manufacturing firm, is confronted with the same issues.

Any organization can be usefully conceived of as a sociotechnical system in which behavior is influenced by a number of interrelated variables, including the individual predispositions of members, social structure, formal organization, and the system's external environment.[1] Organizational systems are involved in constant transactions with their technical and market environment, and the strategy adopted to cope with this environment becomes the organization's primary task.[2] Each system has a number of units that can be conceived of as socio-technical subsystems. Behavior in each of these units is influenced not only by its structure and the predisposition of members, but also by the internal environment of the system of which it is a unit and by the external market and technical environment with which it must cope.

As the system develops strategies to cope with its external environment, these subsystems become differentiated around specific tasks designed to deal with particular sectors of the total external environment. If the system is to be effective in performing its overall task, a means must be provided to integrate the activities of these differentiated subsystems. The relationship between these twin processes of differentiation and integration is the theoretical focus of this study.

Since the publication of *Management and the Worker*,[3] which was the first attempt to study an organization as a social system, there have been a steadily increasing number of studies investigating many aspects of man's relationship to his organizational environment.[4]

From Jay W. Lorsch, *Product Innovation and Organization*, Macmillan, New York, 1965, pp. 1–22. Reprinted by permission of Macmillan Company.

[1] A detailed explanation of this conceptual framework is given in G. Homans, *The Human Group* (New York, Harcourt, Brace & Co., 1950). A modified and more concise statement is presented in P. Lawrence et al., *Organizational Behavior and Administration* (Homewood, Ill., Richard D. Irwin, 1961), pp. 213–222, 534–546.

[2] This topic is dealt with in a paper entitled "Socio-Technical Systems" delivered by E. L. Trist at an open university lecture jointly sponsored by the Departments of Engineering and Psychology at Cambridge University, Nov. 10, 1958. A further development of these ideas is available in A. K. Rice, *The Enterprise and Its Environment* (London, Tavistock Publications, 1963).

[3] F. Roethlisberger and W. Dickson, *Management and the Worker* (Cambridge, Harvard University Press, 1939).

[4] Three such studies are: L. Barnes, *Organizational Systems and Engineering Groups* (Boston, Harvard

These studies have covered such diverse topics as work-group behavior, career development, and man's relation to technology; they have contributed to an increasing knowledge about the psychological and social factors that influence behavior in organizational systems. One area, however, in which there has been limited research is the study of the process of differentiation and integration in large, complex systems.

Problems in obtaining effective working relationships between different departments in an organization are a constant source of concern to administrators, and there have been few studies on this subject. There appears to be a real need, however, to gain additional understanding of the conditions under which effective collaboration between different departments is possible. An increased understanding of the nature of these twin processes and their interrelationship would make not only a theoretical contribution, but also might make it possible to state more precisely how organizations should be designed to enable systems to attain optimal integration while still permitting their parts to be specialized in performing particular parts of the organizational task.

This theoretical focus is closely related to the reasons for selecting the topical focus of scientific transfer. In no other setting do the problems of obtaining effective integration seem more acute than around the development of products. It is a task that requires the close cooperation of research scientists, production engineers, market planners, and sales personnel if it is to be accomplished successfully. Behind these basic functions are financial analysts, purchasing specialists, quality control experts, and so forth, who are required to cooperate in providing various services. All of the personnel who must collaborate in this work are also representatives of highly specialized units, so that there is both a high degree of differentiation and a need for a high degree of integration. Thus organizations involved in the development of new products, as a central part

of their total task, provide an exceptional opportunity to examine the problems associated with differentiation and integration which confront any large, complex organization.

At the outset of this project we recognized that in many respects we were venturing into unchartered waters where prior knowledge was limited and, in some cases, only suggestive. It seemed necessary, therefore, as a first step in any larger research undertaking, to begin with an exploratory study that would examine some hypotheses based on the prior research knowledge, would test these prior findings in a systematic manner, and would seek those emergent findings that could be more systematically studied in later research.

Although there has not been a large amount of prior research into the question of differentiation and integration in large organizational systems, this does not imply that this study is being initiated *de novo*, but rather that we are attempting to confirm and build on several different bodies of research related to the focus of this study. First, there are those few research studies and theoretical articles that have dealt with differentiation and integration in large systems. There is also a growing body of research on the relationship between the task of an organization and its structure. Finally, there are studies that have focused on the values of different occupational groups, as well as several studies examining the phenomena of intergroup relations.

Earlier Research on Integration and Differentiation

Problems of integration and differentiation are not unfamiliar to social scientists. As early as the turn of the century, Herbert Spencer pointed to the tendency for both differentiation and integration to be present in any social system:

> A social organism is like an individual organism in these essential traits; that it grows; that while growing it becomes more complex; that while becoming more complex, its parts acquire increasing mutual interdependence; that its life is immense in length compared with the lives of its component units; . . . that in both cases there is in-

Business School, 1960); H. A. Sheperd, "Patterns of Organization for Applied Research and Development," *Journal of Business* (January, 1956), pp. 52–58; R. Hower and C. Orth, *Managers and Scientists* (Boston, Harvard Business School, 1963).

creasing integration accompanied by increasing heterogeneity.[5]

Spencer also indicated that the dual process of differentiation and integration occurred in social systems of any size, from a society as a whole down to the individual firm.

Elton Mayo, writing a half-century later, made a similar point:

> Every social group, at whatever level of culture, must face and clearly state two perpetual and recurrent problems of administration. It must secure for its individual and group membership:
> 1. The satisfaction of material and economic needs.
> 2. The maintenance of spontaneous cooperation throughout the organization.[6]

Mayo concentrated on the problems of maintaining cooperation, but the first problem is related to the second, in that the satisfaction of material needs has created increased specialization in organizations and this specialization (differentiation) is related to problems of obtaining cooperation (integration). This point is made quite clearly by Chester Barnard:

> Thus, in an important aspect, "organization" and "specialization" are synonyms. The ends of cooperation cannot be accomplished without specialization. The coordination implied is a functional aspect of organization. This function is to correlate the efforts of individuals in such a way with the conditions of the cooperative effort as a whole that purpose may be accomplished.[7]

Barnard goes on to point out that each unit in the organization is a specialization, and that the overall purpose or task of the organization must be broken down into unit tasks. One of the functions of the executive is to integrate the differentiated tasks of these units.

The need for specialization or differentiation occurs as the system attempts to perform the tasks required to cope with its external environment. But this differentiation makes it increasingly necessary to obtain integration of the parts of the system. These references, and others that could be cited, indicate that the issues on which this study focuses are not novel, but the fact remains that only limited research has been conducted on differentiation and integration in organizational systems.

One researcher, A. K. Rice, who has examined this issue in complex organizations, points to the need for each unit or subsystem within the organizational system to be differentiated around a primary task if it is to be viable internally. This means that in complex organizations the differentiated subsystems will be performing discrete tasks, which must be integrated, if the organization is successfully to accomplish its mission. Rice makes this point in the following manner:

> For organization model building the differentiation of operating systems depends upon the discovery of sub-systems with discrete primary tasks. Successive orders of differentiation can continue until primary production systems are reached. Each differentiation requires a corresponding integration to assure that the primary tasks of the parts add up to the whole. . . . In other words, the viability of any grouping of sub-systems for command purposes depends upon the group having a discrete primary task that differentiates it from other groups of the same order of differentiation, and from groups at higher or lower levels of differentiation.[8]

Thus, on the basis of his research, Rice is pointing to the need for both differentiation and integration in large systems. These findings match the positions taken by Spencer, Mayo, Barnard, and others. However, Rice is also pointing to one phenomenon in the process of differentiation and integration which is peculiar to large, complex systems. As the task of the organization is segmented into subtasks, subsystems emerge with certain distinct characteristics that are related to their primary task.

Just what units an organization is divided into may vary somewhat depending upon the

[5] Herbert Spencer, *Autobiography* (New York, 1904), II, p. 56.
[6] Elton Mayo, *The Social Problems of An Industrial Civilization* (Boston, Harvard Business School, 1945), p. 9.
[7] Chester Barnard, *The Functions of The Executive* (Cambridge, Harvard University Press, 1945), pp. 136–137.

[8] Rice, p. 225.

particular requisites of its environment, but it is apparent that there is a general tendency in all large industrial enterprises for activities to be divided into three basic subsystems: Research, Production, and Sales. Wilfred Brown, in his description of the organization at the Glacier Metals Company, notes that these three major subsystems exist in any industrial organization. He describes their activities in the following manner: [9] "They decide what goods or services they seek to provide. [Research] . . . They arrange for the provision of some good or service. [Production] . . . They arrange for the sale of goods or services." [Sales]

In this study, then, the Research, Production, and Sales units are considered the basic subsystems in the organization. They are basic in the sense that, as Brown has pointed out, they are performing the major activities of the firm. The other subsystems that may exist in an enterprise have the function of controlling, servicing, or integrating these three basic functions.

The Dimensions of Differentiation

Up to this point differentiation has been discussed as if it only involved segmenting the organizational task into the tasks of subsidiary units, but previous research studies suggest that we can expect these units to also be differentiated along other dimensions. First, different organizational structures may emerge within each subsystem in relation to their different tasks. These different structures will influence norms and behavior within each unit. Second, other differences in cognitive states and norms may be expected to evolve in relation to the similar professional backgrounds and shared activities of members of one subsystem who are performing a common task. This second type of difference will be referred to as occupational orientation.

Research into the Relationship of Task and Structure. Much of the research on this topic has concentrated on the functionality of different structural patterns for the performance of different tasks and on the tendency for systems or subsystems with similar tasks to have simi-

lar organizational structures. Rather than conceiving of all organizational structures as being identical and imposing the same constraints and opportunities, we now have research data indicating that there are variations among structures within the same system and between different systems and that these different structures tend to be suitable for different tasks.

Hints of a relationship between effective performance of tasks and the structure of the system performing the task can be found in several early experimental studies. For example, Leavitt, building on the earlier work of Bavelas with communication nets in small groups, found that wheel networks in which there was a central coordinating person could more effectively perform a routine task than circle nets where every person communicated only with his two neighbors.[10] Macy, Christie, and Luce conducted an experiment using the same networks and the same-sized groups as Leavitt but with increased complexity of the task.[11] In this experiment they found that the circle net seemed to perform better than the wheel on a complex task.

From these experimental studies we begin to get an indication that a more highly structured pattern such as a wheel network is more effective for performing simple tasks, while a less structured network such as the circle is more effective for complicated tasks. Leavitt, himself, has noted the implications of these findings for real organizational structures:

> One cannot overlook, in this discussion of structure, the implications of the research on communication networks and other recent related work. *Direct* application of this laboratory research to the real world is scarce, though it has had some significant indirect influence on structural planning. In that research, variations in communications nets effect both routine and novel task performance rather significantly. The results suggest that appropriate communications

[9] Wilfred Brown, *Exploration in Management* (London, Heinemann, 1960), pp. 143–145.

[10] H. J. Leavitt, "Some Effects of Certain Communications Patterns on Group Performance" in *Readings in Social Psychology*, ed. Macoby et al. (New York, Holt, Rinehart & Winston, 1958), pp. 546–563.

[11] J. Macy, L. Christie, and K. Luce, "Coding Noise in Task Oriented Groups," *Journal of Abnormal and Social Psychology*, XL (1953), pp. 401–409.

structures might vary considerably within a complex organization depending upon the type of task that any subunit of the organization undertakes.

Thus for programmed repetitive tasks, centralized communication structures seem to operate most efficiently, but with some human costs. For more novel, ill-structured tasks more wide open communications nets with larger numbers of channels and less differentiation among members seem to work more effectively.[12]

Further evidence of this relationship between task and organizational structure can be found in several reports of field research conducted in large organizations. Joan Woodward, in a study of the organizational structure of 203 firms in England, found that among firms involved in unit production, mass production, and those in the process industries, there were differences in such factors as the ratio of managers to other personnel, span of control, and number of levels in the hierarchy. Firms using similar technical methods had similar organizational structures. She also found there was a relationship between successful performance and the organizational structure of companies within each industry. Those firms which were most successful in their industry had organizational characteristics which approximated the median of the organization in their industry.[13]

The significance of Woodward's findings are twofold. First, she found support in field settings for the conclusions of the experimental researchers that there is a relationship between successful task performance and structure. More importantly, she also found a tendency for organizations to adopt a structure consistent with the requirements of their technology.

Burns and Stalker, in a more comprehensive report of research conducted in several English and Scottish firms, also pointed to the relationship between organizational effectiveness and structure in different environments.[14] They examined several firms that had been operating in relatively stable environments and that were attempting to move into the more rapidly changing field of electronics. When these enterprises were operating in a stable market and technical environment, they had developed a quite rigid and highly prescribed organizational structure, which the authors termed "mechanistic." As the companies moved into the changing environment, Burns and Stalker found that a looser and less prescriptive structure was adopted. This they termed "organic." They concluded that the firms that could not succeed in the changing environment failed because of an "inability to adapt the management system to the form appropriate to conditions of more rapid technical and commercial change."[15] The authors also pointed out that neither the organic or mechanistic type exist in a pure form but instead represent a continuum along which firms can be arrayed. Finally, Burns and Stalker make the point that there is a relationship between the different organizational structures and the norms and behavior of members of the system. From this work there is additional evidence of a relationship between task performance and structure in organizational systems. Low structure appears to be appropriate for a changing environment (complex organizational task) and higher structure for a stable environment (routine organizational task). These differences in structure appear to be related to differences in norms and behavior.

One other recent study provides support for the view that there is a relationship between organizational structure and effective task performance. Lawrence and Turner in a study just completed have found data which support their hypothesis that "given certain specified environmental conditions, organizations which operate consistently along either mechanistic or organic lines will perform better in regard to both economic measures and employee satisfaction than inconsistent organizations."[16] They amplify this general hypothesis in two

[12] H. J. Leavitt, "Applied Organizational Change in Industry—Structural Technological and Humanistic Approach," Carnegie Institute of Technology. Mimeo (to appear in Handbook of Organization, March, editor).
[13] Joan Woodward, Management & Technology (London, Her Majesty's Stationery Office, 1958). See especially pp. 16, 24.
[14] T. Burns and G. Stalker, The Management of Innovation (London, Tavistock Publications, 1961). See especially pp. 1–10.
[15] Burns and Stalker, p. 5.
[16] P. Lawrence and A. Turner, Industrial Jobs and the Worker. (Manuscript in preparation.)

more detailed ones that point to the relationship to organizational effectiveness of consistency between organizational structure, leadership style, predispositions of members, and the organization's task. This provides further evidence that organizational structure, as well as these other interrelated factors, may vary with the organizational task.

From both experimental studies and field studies of total organizations, we have found a relationship between structure and different organizational tasks. Yet our central interest at this juncture is in the differences in structure that will occur within one system in relation to the different tasks of the various subsystems. We have already indicated that we expect subsystems to be differentiated in structure and Leavitt was quoted earlier as pointing to these differences. R. H. Hall has recently found evidence that there are, in fact, differences in organizational structure between units and departments and that these differences are related to the different tasks of the units.[17] Units performing a simple routine task tended to have higher structure than those performing more complex tasks.

On the basis of all of these previous findings, we can therefore expect units within any organizational system to be differentiated in structure in relation to their individual tasks. Further, we can expect these structural differences to be related to differences in norms and behavior between the various subsystems. Also we can expect various units to be more or less similar in structure and norms, depending upon the similarity of their tasks. Moreover, we can also expect there will be differences in the degree of structure between systems. These differences in total system structure may also be related to differences in norms and behavior between any two organizations. This is a matter to be considered in more detail subsequently.

Research into the Relationship of Task and Occupational Orientation. The term *occupational orientation* will be used here to denote the cognitive orientations and norms that arise within groups working on the same primary task. We consider the term to include three dimensions: the *orientation toward task, orien-*

tation toward time, and *interpersonal orientation.* Although other researchers have not made this conceptual distinction, there is some research evidence that different norms and mental states do emerge in relation to the differentiated tasks of the various subsystems and the different occupational groups working on these tasks.

Rice, in discussing the discrete tasks of each subsystem, has indicated that there will be differences in "leader-follower patterns" (which is one aspect of what we are terming interpersonal orientation) between the subsystems.[18] In an extensive study of a variety of field situations, Fiedler has found a relationship between certain leadership conditions (task structures, the power position of the leader, and the leader's affective relationship with subordinates), leadership style, and effective task performance. Under both extremely favorable and extremely unfavorable leadership conditions, a managing, controlling leadership style was found to be related to effective task performance. With intermediate leadership conditions, permissive leadership behavior appeared to gain more effective performance.[19]

Fiedler's findings are relevant to our discussion if we recognize that leadership behavior is closely related to the wider interpersonal norms of the subsystem. Although Fiedler is focusing on individual leadership behavior and might find some individual deviation from group norms, we would expect that the leader's behavior would generally be consistent with the norms of the group in which he operates. The introduction of the other conditions in addition to the nature of the task makes us more aware of the complexity of the factors with which we are dealing. However, the important findings for our purposes is that organizational conditions, including different tasks, call for different leadership styles (and presumably different interpersonal orientations).

From both these studies, then, we can anticipate that the different tasks of subsystems will be related to differences in interpersonal orientation. We should also note that although in-

[17] R. H. Hall, "Intraorganizational Structural Variables," *Administrative Science Quarterly* (December 1962), pp. 295–308.

[18] Rice, p. 15.
[19] F. Fiedler, *Technical Report No. 10.* Group Effectiveness Research Laboratory, Department of Psychology, University of Illinois (May 1962). See especially page 14.

terpersonal orientations are influenced by a variety of other factors, including the individual members' predispositions, interpersonal orientation is related to the structure of a particular unit. In a highly structured unit, other things being equal, there would generally be more directive interpersonal norms than in a less highly structured unit. We do not imply that this relationship will be precise or will prevail in all cases, but rather that there will be a tendency in this direction.

Whereas interpersonal orientation concerns norms about dealing with other persons, orientation toward both task and time deal with the members' concerns with particular segments of the organization's environment. The task environment is segmented into a market sector where the companies' products are sold, a scientific sector from which relevant new information is obtained, and a plant sector which determines the technical and economic constraints on processing and production methods. The environment can also be segmented along the dimension of time in that different basic subsystems are concerned with the state of the environment at various stages, ranging from the present to long-term, perhaps five or more years in the future.

No studies have attempted to systematically isolate differences in orientation toward time and task in relation to different subsystem tasks. However, two different types of research have indicated that we can expect to find such differences, as well as differences in other values between the various subsystems. The first type of research deals with values among different occupational groups. Barnes has summarized the major differences between the values of science and those of business:

> Scientists traditionally pursue one set of goals or values. Businessmen seek another. The scientist tends to identify himself with man's search for truth and knowledge. He associates himself with education and learning as they fit the traditions of pure science. One sociologist, R. K. Merton, observes that this value exaltation of pure science protects science from outside influences which would dilute or destroy the value system itself. Science's value system thus performs the function of keeping pure science sacred and independent. H. A. Shepard stresses the need for such a value system as a major

stimulus for basic research. Pareto writes that "the quest for experimental uniformities is an end in itself." Finally, Florence Kluckhohn pictures science's value system as an alternative to, not a part of, America's dominant cultural pattern.

> In contrast to this value system business pursues the values of financial gain and material achievement. These goals explicitly or implicitly serve as the dominant goals for both individuals and corporations. Sales, productivity, and practicality further earmark business and its value system. While this value system encourages both generosity and idealism, both can exist only within the boundaries of reasonable profit and business practicality. In a sense, business has adopted the notion of practicality as its own value, and the American executive tends to respect its connotation of common sense, feet-on-the-ground realism.

> Quite clearly neither of the value systems reflect reality in any exact way. Both represent belief and assumptions. Both are subjective pictures, not objective representations. Each sets up certain "good" goals in life that people "ought to want" if they are to identify themselves with the particular value system. To deny these goals is to choose another value system.[20]

We should note that Barnes is referring to values which underlie the cognitive orientations in which we are interested. The fact that these differences in more fundamental values do exist is an indication that we can expect to find differences in both task and time orientation. It should be remembered that the scientists in the research subsystems we are dealing with have chosen to work in an industrial setting, and it is therefore quite likely that their values will not be entirely those of pure science. However, these researchers will probably be much more oriented to the values of science than will the non-scientists who are members of other subsystems. Finally, Barnes is dealing with business values as if they were homogeneous, and at one level they are. But our interest is in differences in values and cognitive orientations that may exist between different occupational groups within the business culture; e.g., sales executives versus production executives.

[20] Barnes, pp. 20–21.

Anne Roe reports several findings which indicate there are underlying differences between various occupational groups. For example, on the Allport-Vernon Study of Values she reports that persons in sales occupations tended to have significantly higher economic values and significantly lower aesthetic values than the mean of the wider population. Similarly, she found that physical scientists tended to have significantly higher theoretical values and significantly lower aesthetic values than the mean of the population. Extrapolating from this finding, we might expect that members of a sales subsystem would have higher economic values and those in a research subsystem would have higher theoretical values.[21]

She also reports that on the Kuder Preference Record chemical engineers, such as those who might be running a production plant, tended to score high in "dealing with practical problems, rather than imaginary or glamorous ones." Sales occupations tended to be lower than the average population on this dimension of practicality. Chemical engineers tended to be average in "taking the lead in activities"; salesmen tended to be above average on this dimension.[22]

Miner, using the Kuder Preference Record to examine power needs among occupational groups in one organization, found that sales personnel preferred activities dealing with power and authority to a greater extent than the average member of the organization. Manufacturing personnel tended to fall at the mean for the organization; research personnel fell considerably below the mean.[23]

McClelland, in studying the need for achievement of a group of American businessmen, found that of five types of business occupations represented in the study (general management, sales and marketing, finance, engineering, and personnel), only sales and marketing tended to have personnel with a higher need for achievement than the average.[24]

From all of these studies, then, we might expect that members of a sales subsystem would tend to have a higher need for achievement, higher economic values, higher power needs, and to be less practical than those in production or research. Members of the production subsystem would be more likely to be highly practical. Research subsystem members would be more highly theoretical and have lower power needs. This discussion is not intended to be exhaustive but rather suggestive of the differences in underlying values and interests of the various subsystems. We anticipate that these basic differences in values will also be reflected in different orientations toward task and time.

Dearborn and Simon have reported findings which support this expectation. Using a case study as a projective instrument, they found that a group of executives tended to interpret the study situation in terms of their functional specialty. For example, five out of the six sales executives saw the principal problem to be a sales matter, while four out of five production executives perceived that the major need was "to clarify the organization." The researchers summarized their findings as follows:

> We have presented data on the selective perceptions of industrial executives exposed to case material that support the hypothesis that each executive will perceive as most important those aspects of a situation that relate specifically to the activities and goals of his department. Since the situation is one in which the executives were motivated to look at the problem from a company-wide rather than a departmental viewpoint, the data indicate further that the criteria of selection have been internalized.[25]

Studies dealing with intergroup relations present further evidence about differences in mental states and norms between departments. Lawrence and Ronken, in an earlier examination of the scientific transfer process, focused particularly upon the administrative skills required to gain understanding among the several groups involved, so that social conflicts could be resolved to the extent necessary to overcome technological problems arising

[21] Anne Roe, *The Psychology of Occupations* (New York, John Wiley & Sons, 1956), pp. 156–158.

[22] Roe, pp. 158–159.

[23] J. Miner, "Desire for Power as an Organizational Variable," Mimeo, School of Business Administration, University of Oregon.

[24] D. McClelland, *The Achieving Society* (Princeton, D. van Nostrand, 1961), pp. 266–267.

[25] D. Dearborn and H. Simon, "Selective Perception: A Note on the Departmental Identification of Executives," *Sociometry, XXI* (1958), pp. 140–144.

around the new product. They found that one of the factors influencing these social conflicts was differences in assumptions (orientations), particularly around the task.[26] Seiler, in two recent articles concerning interdepartmental relations, reports that there were differences in norms and mental states between departments and that these differences were related to the effectiveness of collaboration.[27]

In summary, prior research about the dimensions of differentiation between subsystems leads us to the following conclusions: first, we can expect that these units will be differentiated in structure in relation to their task; second, they will probably be differentiated in interpersonal orientation, particularly in relation to different tasks and in relation to different subsystem structures. There are underlying value differences between the occupations represented in the various subsystems and they tend to have different cognitive orientations. This fact, plus the findings of two studies of intergroup relations, have led us to conclude that we can expect to find that subsystems will also be differentiated in task and time orientation.

The Relationship Between Differentiation and Integration

Previous Research Findings. It should again be pointed out that few studies have systematically examined the relationship of differentiation to integration. To do so is one of the major objectives of the present study. There are, however, a few studies that have suggested what this relationship may be. Seiler found that the fewer shared norms and values two units had, the more difficult it was for them to collaborate. In our terms, this implies that the greater the differentiation between any two subsystems in structure and occupational orientation, the greater will be the difficulties in integrating their activities.

[26] H. Ronkin and P. Lawrence, *Administering Changes* (Boston, Harvard Business School, 1952), p. 203.
[27] J. Seiler, "Toward a Theory of Organization Congruent with Primary Group Concepts," *Behavioral Science* (July 1963), pp. 190–198; and "Diagnosing Interdepartmental Conflict," *Harvard Business Review* (September–October 1963), pp. 121–132.

One factor that Seiler's work does not consider is the degree of interdependence required between the various subsystems. When the organizational task creates a high need for interdependence, or *requisite integration*, we are predicting that a given amount of differentiation will create even greater problems of integration. We can thus summarize the basic relationship between differentiation and integration by stating that the higher the degree of differentiation in subsystem structure and occupational orientation in relation to requisite integration, the greater will be the problems of integration. We should emphasize that while this differentiation may be costly for obtaining integration, it is necessary for subsystem performance. The problem confronting an organization is to achieve some balance between differentiation and effective integration. The system, if it is to perform effectively, must contain some device to facilitate integration. This point has been made clearly by Eric Miller:

> Role-relationships cluster around the subtasks; such clusters of relationships become potential sub-systems; and areas of less intensive relationships become potential boundaries between sub-systems. Clustering may be functional for sub-task performance, but the associated discontinuities between clusters may be dysfunctional for integrated performance of the total task. It becomes a function of a differentiated managing system to compensate for these discontinuities.[28]

Miller's position that integrating the differentiated subsystems is the function of management, is similar to that taken by Barnard and by Rice. However, there is also some evidence that when there is high requisite integration between subsystems, as in the firms in this study, committees, liaison departments, and similar devices are evolved to accomplish this coordinative function. These devices appear to provide more detailed integration of activities at a lower level in the organization than does reliance on a top management group alone.

Integrative Devices. The existence of these integrative devices is obvious to anyone who has observed the number of committees and

[28] Eric Miller, "Technology, Territory and Time," *Human Relations*, XII, No. 3, p. 245.

similar groups that exist around the new product functions in any organization. Burns and Stalker have pointed to another integrative device, that of liaison specialists "whose job was to move across linguistic and functional frontiers and to act as intermediaries between the people getting on with a job." [29] A further indication of the presence of such devices is provided in the survey conducted by Booz, Allen, and Hamilton.[30] They report a rapid increase in the number of new product departments in companies surveyed. These departments, which often have such labels as Technical Service or Market Planning, have the primary task of integrating the activities of the basic subsystems.

These integrative devices are of two types—structural and processual. Structural devices are major organizational innovations. They involve the differentiation of a separate unit that has as one of its functions the integration of the activities of the basic subsystems. The processual devices may be either temporary project teams or longer-term cross-functional coordinating committees, but in either case they provide the setting in which the process of integration takes place. Although it is possible that these devices may in time become an intrinsic part of the formal system structure, we will consider them as distinct from the structural devices because they always retain their primary function as the locus in which integration activities are carried out. There has been no systematic research into the conditions which influence the performance of the two types of integrative devices. One of our purposes in this study is to examine some of these conditions.

Examining first the conditions that we predict will be necessary for integrative structural devices to be effective, we want to consider the position of the integrative subsystem in relation to the basic subsystems. If an integrative unit is to be effective in linking the basic subsystem, we are predicting that it will have to be intermediate in structure and occupational orientation between the units it is intended to link. Such an integrative unit will have more shared mental states and norms with these units than the basic units have with each other

and thus should be able to obtain a greater unity of effort between them. The integrative unit that is not in this middle position may be more similar to one of the basic units it is linking, but it will necessarily be more differentiated from the other units and this will limit its effectiveness. In the course of this study, then, we will attempt to determine the validity of the following hypothesis:

> If a structural integrative device is effective in integrating basic sub-systems, it will tend to be intermediate between the basic subsystems in structure and occupational orientation.

In exploring the conditions under which processual devices might be effective, we have started with no *a priori* assumptions, other than what factors we are not interested in considering. We are not interested in examining the internal processes of individual groups in order to consider factors such as leadership behavior, the phases of group emotion, or role differentiation. Other researchers have considered, and are still doing research into, the relationship of these variables to group effectiveness. Rather, we are interested in exploring total system structure or norms to see how these may influence the effectiveness of these devices. Out of this exploration we hope to develop some research leads which will enable us later to examine more systematically the factors related to the effectiveness of processual devices.

Hypotheses on the Relationship between Differentiation and Integration. Even assuming the existence of an effective integrative unit, there will be a certain degree of differentiation between it and the basic subsystems. Also there will always be a degree of differentiation between the basic subsystems themselves. In each system we will attempt to test the validity of the following hypothesis:

> Within any organizational system the greater the differentiation between any two subsystems in relation to the requisite integration, the greater will be the difficulties in obtaining effective integration between them.

In comparing this relationship in the two systems, we will consider the influence of the intervening variable of differences in system

[29] Burns and Stalker, p. 9.
[30] Booz, Allen, and Hamilton, *Management of New Products* (New York, 1960), pp. 26–28.

structures and norms. As we have already mentioned, Burns and Stalker have found that systems with low structure tended to operate more effectively in a changing environment than highly structured firms. The authors suggest that in a mechanistic system there is more reliance on higher management for integration, and that in the organic type integration seems to occur at a lower level.[31] This difference and other differences in system structure and norms could influence the relationship between the degree of differentiation among subsystems and the effectiveness of integration of their activities when we compare this relationship in the two organizations. Thus we would only expect the relationship between the degree of differentiation and integration to hold in both systems if other organizational characteristics are similar. In comparing the two systems we are also predicting that system performance (in this study, the rate of product development and innovation) will be related to

[31] Burns and Stalker, p. 11.

the effectiveness of integration. If a system is not obtaining effective integration where the need for it is high, we can expect that there will be dysfunctional consequences in system performance. Our hypothesis about the relationship between differentiation and integration in both systems can therefore be stated as follows:

If other system characteristics are similar, the greater the degree of total differentiation within each system, the greater the problems of integration and the greater the dysfunctional consequences in system performance.

Finally, in terms of this third hypothesis, we will attempt to isolate any differences in overall system characteristics between the two organizations and thus to delineate more precisely some of the factors related to the superior performance of low structured systems in performing scientific transfer in a changing environment.

Rationality in Organizations

Instrumental action is rooted on the one hand in *desired outcomes* and on the other hand in *beliefs about cause/effect relationships*. Given a desire, the state of man's knowledge at any point in time dictates the kinds of variables required and the manner of their manipulation to bring that desire to fruition. To the extent that the activities thus dictated by man's beliefs are judged to produce the desired outcomes, we can speak of technology, or *technical rationality*.

Technical rationality can be evaluated by two criteria: instrumental and economic. The essence of the instrumental question is whether the specified actions do in fact produce the desired outcome, and the instrumentally perfect technology is one which inevitably achieves such results. The economic question in essence is whether the results are obtained with the least necessary expenditure of resources, and for this there is no absolute standard. Two different routes to the same desired outcome may be compared in terms of cost, or both may be compared with some abstract ideal, but in practical terms the evaluation of economy is relative to the state of man's knowledge at the time of evaluation.

We will give further consideration to the assessment of organizational action in a later chapter, but it is necessary to distinguish at this point between the instrumental and economic questions because present literature about organizations gives considerable attention to the economic dimension of technology but hides the importance of the instrumental question, which in fact takes priority. The cost of doing something can be considered only after we know that the something can be considered only after we know that the something can be done.

Complex organizations are built to operate

technologies which are found to be impossible or impractical for individuals to operate. This does not mean, however, that technologies operated by complex organizations are instrumentally perfect. The instrumentally perfect technology would produce the desired outcome inevitably, and this perfection is approached in the case of continuous processing of chemicals or in mass manufacturing—for example, of automobiles. A less perfect technology will produce the desired outcome only part of the time; nevertheless, it may be incorporated into complex organizations, such as the mental hospital, because desire for the possible outcome is intense enough to settle for possible rather than highly probable success. Sometimes the intensity of desire for certain kinds of outcomes, such as world peace, leads to the creation of complex organizations such as the United Nations to operate patently imperfect technologies.

Variations in Technologies

Clearly, technology is an important variable in understanding the actions of complex organizations. In modern societies the variety of desired outcomes for which specific technologies are available seems infinite. A complete but simple typology of technologies which has found order in this variety would be quite helpful. Typologies are available for industrial production (Woodward, 1965) and for mental therapy (Hawkes, 1962) but are not general enough to deal with the range of technologies found in complex organizations. Lacking such a typology, we will simply identify three varieties which are (1) widespread in modern society and (2) sufficiently different to illustrate the propositions we wish to develop.

The Long-linked Technology.[1] A long-linked technology involves serial interdepen-

---

From James D. Thompson, in *Organization in Action*, McGraw-Hill, New York, 1967, pp. 14–24. Reprinted by permission of the publisher.

[1] The notions in this section rest especially on conversations some years ago with Frederick L.

dence in the sense that act Z can be performed only after successful completion of act Y, which in turn rests on act X, and so on. The original symbol of technical rationality, the mass production assembly line, is of this long-linked nature. It approaches instrumental perfection when it produces a single kind of standard product, repetitively and at a constant rate. Production of only one kind of product means that a single technology is required, and this in turn permits the use of clear-cut criteria for the selection of machines and tools, construction of work-flow arrangements, acquisition of raw materials, and selection of human operators. Repetition of the productive process provides experience as a means of eliminating imperfections in the technology; experience can lead to the modification of machines and provide the basis for scheduled preventive maintenance. Repetition means that human motions can also be examined, and through training and practice, energy losses and errors minimized. It is in this setting that the scientific-management movement has perhaps made its greatest contribution.

The constant rate of production means that, once adjusted, the proportions of resources involved can be standardized to the point where each contributes to its capacity; none need be underemployed. This of course makes important contributions to the economic aspect of the technology.

The Mediating Technology. Various organizations have, as a primary function, the linking of clients or customers who are or wish to be interdependent. The commercial bank links depositors and borrowers. The insurance firm links those who would pool common risks. The telephone utility links those who would call and those who would be called. The post office provides a possible linkage of virtually every member of the modern society. The employment agency mediates the supply of labor and the demand for it.

Complexity in the mediating technology comes not from the necessity of having each activity geared to the requirements of the next but rather from the fact that the mediating technology requires operating in *standardized ways*, and *extensively*; e.g., with multiple clients or customers distributed in time and space.

The commercial bank must find and aggregate deposits from diverse depositors; but however diverse the depositors, the transaction must conform to standard terms and to uniform bookkeeping and accounting procedures. It must also find borrowers; but no matter how varied their needs or desires, loans must be made according to standardized criteria and on terms uniformly applied to the category appropriate to the particular borrower. Poor risks who receive favored treatment jeopardize bank solvency. Standardization permits the insurance organization to define categories of risk and hence to sort its customers or potential customers into appropriate aggregate categories; the insured who is not a qualified risk but is so defined upsets the probabilities on which insurance rests. The telephone company became viable only when the telephone became regarded as a necessity, and this did not occur until equipment was standardized to the point where it could be incorporated into one network. Standardization enables the employment agency to aggregate job applicants into categories which can be matched against standardized requests for employees.

Standardization makes possible the operation of the mediating technology over time and through space by assuring each segment of the organization that other segments are operating in compatible ways. It is in such situations that the bureaucratic techniques of categorization and impersonal application of rules have been most beneficial (Weber, 1947; Merton, 1957a).

The Intensive Technology. This third variety we label *intensive* to signify that a variety of techniques is drawn upon in order to achieve a change in some specific object; but the selection, combination, and order of application are determined by feedback from the object itself. When the object is human, this intensive technology is regarded as "therapeutic," but the same technical logic is found also in the construction industry (Stinchcombe, 1959) and in research where the objects of concern are nonhuman.

The intensive technology is most dramatically illustrated by the general hospital. At any moment an emergency admission may require some combination of dietary, x-ray, laboratory, and housekeeping or hotel services, to-

---

Bates. For a different but somewhat parallel analysis of work flows, see Dubin, 1959.

gether with the various medical specialties, pharmaceutical services, occupational therapies, social work services, and spiritual or religious services. Which of these, and when, can be determined only from evidence about the state of the patient.

In the construction industry, the nature of the crafts required and the order in which they can be applied depend on the nature of the object to be constructed and its setting; including, for example, terrain, climate, weather. Organized or team research may draw from a variety of scientific or technical skills, but the particular combination and the order of application depend on the nature of the problem defined.

The development of military combat teams, with a multiplicity of highly skilled capacities to be applied to the requirements of changing circumstances, represents a shift toward the intensive technology in military operations (Janowitz, 1959).

The intensive technology is a custom technology. Its successful employment rests in part on the availability of all the capacities potentially needed, but equally on the appropriate custom combination of selected capacities as required by the individual case or project.

Boundaries of Technical Rationality. Technical rationality, as a system of cause/effect relationships which lead to a desired result, is an abstraction. It is instrumentally perfect when it becomes a closed system of logic. The closed system of logic contains all relevant variables, and only relevant variables. All other influences, or *exogenous variables*, are excluded; and the variables contained in the system vary only to the extent that the experimenter, the manager, or the computer determines they should.

When a technology is put to use, however, there must be not only desired outcomes and knowledge of relevant cause/effect relationships, but also power to control the empirical resources which correspond to the variables in the logical system. A closed system of action corresponding to a closed system of logic would result in instrumental perfection in reality.

The mass production assembly operation and the continuous processing of chemicals are more nearly perfect, in application, than the other two varieties discussed above because they achieve a high degree of control over relevant variables and are relatively free from disturbing influences. Once started, most of the action involved in the long-linked technology is dictated by the internal logic of the technology itself. With the mediating technology, customers or clients intrude to make difficult the standardized activities required by the technology. And with the intensive technology, the specific case defines the component activities and their combination from the larger array of components contained in the abstract technology.

Since technical perfection seems more nearly approachable when the organization has control over all the elements involved,

> *Proposition 2.1:* Under norms of rationality, organizations seek to seal off their core technologies from environmental influences.

Organizational Rationality

When organizations seek to translate the abstractions called technologies into action, they immediately face problems for which the core technologies do not provide solutions.

Mass production manufacturing technologies are quite specific, *assuming* that certain inputs are provided and finished products are somehow removed from the premises before the productive process is clogged; but mass production technologies do not include variables which provide solutions to either the input- or output-disposal problems. The present technology of medicine may be rather specific if certain tests indicate an appendectomy is in order, if the condition of the patient meets certain criteria, and if certain medical staff, equipment, and medications are present. But medical technology contains no cause/effect statements about bringing sufferers to the attention of medical practitioners, or about the provision of the specified equipment, skills, and medications. The technology of education rests on abstract systems of belief about relationships among teachers, teaching materials, and pupils; but learning theories assume the presence of these variables and proceed from that point.

One or more technologies constitute the core of all purposive organizations. But this technical core is always an incomplete representation of what the organization must do to accomplish desired results. Technical rationality is a necessary component but never alone sufficient to provide *organizational rationality*, which involves acquiring the inputs which are taken for granted by the technology, and dispensing outputs which again are outside the scope of the core technology.

At a minimum, then, organizational rationality involves three major component activities: (1) input activities, (2) technological activities, and (3) output activities. Since these are interdependent, organizational rationality requires that they be appropriately geared to one another. The inputs acquired must be within the scope of the technology, and it must be within the capacity of the organization to dispose of the technological production.

Not only are these component activities interdependent, but both input and output activities are interdependent with environmental elements. Organizational rationality, therefore, never conforms to closed-system logic but demands the logic of an open system. Moreover, since the technological activities are embedded in and interdependent with activities which are open to the environment, the closed system can never be completely attained for the technological component. Yet we have offered the proposition that organizations subject to rationality norms seek to seal off their core technologies from environmental influences. How do we reconcile these two contentions?

Proposition 2.2: Under norms of rationality, organizations seek to buffer environmental influences by surrounding their technical cores with input and output components.

To maximize productivity of a manufacturing technology, the technical core must be able to operate as if the market will absorb the single kind of product at a continuous rate, and as if inputs flowed continuously, at a steady rate and with specified quality. Conceivably both sets of conditions could occur; realistically they do not. But organizations reveal a variety of devices for approximating these "as if" assumptions, with input and output components meeting fluctuating environments and converting them into steady conditions for the technological core.

Buffering on the input side is illustrated by the stockpiling of materials and supplies acquired in an irregular market, and their steady insertion into the production process. Preventive maintenance, whereby machines or equipment are repaired on a scheduled basis, thus minimizing surprise, is another example of buffering by the input component. The recruitment of dissimilar personnel and their conversion into reliable performers through training or indoctrination is another; it is most dramatically illustrated by basic training or boot camp in military organizations (Dornbusch, 1955).

Buffering on the output side of long-linked technologies usually takes the form of maintaining warehouse inventories and items in transit or in distributor inventories, which permits the technical core to produce at a constant rate, but distribution to fluctuate with market conditions.

Buffering on the input side is an appropriate and important device available to all types of organizations. Buffering on the output side is especially important for mass-manufacturing organizations, but is less feasible when the product is perishable or when the object is inextricably involved in the technological process, as in the therapeutic case.

Buffering of an unsteady environment obviously brings considerable advantages to the technical core, but it does so with costs to the organization. A classic problem in connection with buffering is how to maintain inventories, input or output, sufficient to meet all needs without incurring obsolescence as needs change. Operations research recently has made important contributions toward this problem of "run out versus obsolescence," both of which are costly.

Thus while a fully buffered technological core would enjoy the conditions for maximum technical rationality, organizational rationality may call for compromises between conditions for maximum technical efficiency and the energy required for buffering operations. In an unsteady environment, then, the organization under rationality norms must seek other devices for protecting its technical core.

Proposition 2.3: Under norms of rationality, organizations seek to smooth out input and output transactions.

Whereas buffering absorbs environmental fluctuations, smoothing or leveling involves attempts to reduce fluctuations in the environment. Utility firms—electric, gas, water, or telephone—may offer inducements to those who use their services during "trough" periods, or charge premiums to those who contribute to "peaking." Retailing organizations faced with seasonal or other fluctuations in demand, may offer inducements in the form of special promotions or sales during slow periods. Transportation organizations such as airlines may offer special reduced fare rates on light days or during slow seasons.

Organizations pointed toward emergencies, such as fire departments, attempt to level the need for their services by activities designed to prevent emergencies, and by emphasis on early detection so that demand is not allowed to grow to the point that would overtax the capacity of the organization. Hospitals accomplish some smoothing through the scheduling of nonemergency admissions.

Although action by the organization may thus reduce fluctuations in demand, complete smoothing of demand is seldom possible. But a core technology interrupted by constant fluctuation and change must settle for a low degree of technical rationality. What other devices do organizations employ to protect core technologies?

> *Proposition 2.4:* Under norms of rationality, organizations seek to anticipate and adapt to environmental changes which cannot be buffered or leveled.

If environmental fluctuations penetrate the organization and require the technical core to alter its activities, then environmental fluctuations are exogenous variables within the logic of technical rationality. To the extent that environmental fluctuations can be anticipated, however, they can be treated as *constraints* on the technical core within which a closed system of logic can be employed.

The manufacturing firm which can correctly forecast demand for a particular time period can thereby plan or schedule operations of its technical core at a steady rate during that period. Any changes in technical operations due to changes in the environment can be made at the end of the period on the basis of forecasts for the next period.

Organizations often learn that some environmental fluctuations are patterned, and in these cases forecasting and adjustment appear almost automatic. The post office knows, for example, that in large commercial centers large volumes of business mail are posted at the end of the business day, when secretaries leave offices. Recently the post office has attempted to buffer that load by promising rapid treatment of mail posted in special locations during morning hours. Its success in buffering is not known at this writing, but meanwhile the post office schedules its technical activities to meet known daily fluctuations. It can also anticipate heavy demand during November and December, thus allowing its input components lead time in acquiring additional resources.

Banks likewise learn that local conditions and customs result in peak loads at predictable times during the day and week, and can schedule their operations to meet these shifts (Argyris, 1954).

In cases such as these, organizations have amassed sufficient experience to know that fluctuations are patterned with a high degree of regularity or probability; but when environmental fluctuations are the result of combinations of more dynamic factors, anticipation may require something more than the simple projection of previous experience. It is in these situations that forecasting emerges as a specialized and elaborate activity, for which some of the emerging management-science or statistical-decision theories seem especially appropriate.

To the extent that environmental fluctuations are unanticipated they interfere with the orderly operation of the core technology and thereby reduce its performance. When such influences are anticipated and considered as constraints for a particular period of time, the technical core can operate as if it enjoyed a closed system.

Buffering, leveling, and adaptation to anticipated fluctuations are widely used devices for reducing the influence of the environment on the technological cores of organizations. Often they are effective, but there are occasions when these devices are not sufficient to ward off environmental penetration.

> *Proposition 2.5:* When buffering, leveling, and forecasting do not protect their technical cores from environmental fluctuations, organizations under norms of rationality resort to rationing.

Rationing is most easily seen in organizations pointed toward emergencies, such as hospitals. Even in nonemergency situations hospitals may ration beds to physicians by establishing priority systems for nonemergency admissions. In emergencies, such as community disasters, hospitals may ration pharmaceutical dosages or nursing services by dilution—by assigning a fixed number of nurses to a larger patient population. Mental hospitals, especially state mental hospitals, may ration technical services by employing primarily organic-treatment procedures—electroshock, drugs, insulin—which can be employed more economically than psychoanalytic or *milieu* therapies (Belknap, 1956). Teachers and caseworkers in social welfare organizations may ration effort by accepting only a portion of those seeking service, or if not empowered to exercise such discretion, may concentrate their energies on the more challenging cases or on those which appear most likely to yield satisfactory outcomes (Blau, 1955).

But rationing is not a device reserved for therapeutic organizations. The post office may assign priority to first-class mail, attending to lesser classes only when the priority task is completed. Manufacturers of suddenly popular items may ration allotments to wholesalers or dealers, and if inputs are scarce, may assign priorities to alternative uses of those resources. Libraries may ration book loans, acquisitions, and search efforts (Meier, 1963).

Rationing is an unhappy solution, for its use signifies that the technology is not operating at its maximum. Yet some system of priorities for the allocation of capacity under adverse conditions is essential if a technology is to be instrumentally effective—if action is to be other than random.

The Logic of Organizational Rationality. Core technologies rest on closed systems of logic, but are invariably embedded in a larger organizational rationality which pins the technology to a time and place, and links it with the larger environment through input and output activities. Organizational rationality thus calls for an open-system logic, for when the organization is opened to environmental influences, some of the factors involved in organizational action become *constraints;* for some meaningful period of time they are not variables but fixed conditions to which the organi-

zation must adapt. Some of the factors become *contingencies,* which may or may not vary, but are not subject to arbitrary control by the organization.

Organizational rationality therefore is some result of (1) constraints which the organization must face, (2) contingencies which the organization must meet, and (3) variables which the organization can control.

Recapitulation

Perfection in technical rationality requires complete knowledge of cause/effect relations plus control over all of the relevant variables, or closure. Therefore, under norms of rationality (Prop. 2.1), organizations seek to seal off their core technologies from environmental influences. Since complete closure is impossible (Prop. 2.2), they seek to buffer environmental influences by surrounding their technical cores with input and output components.

Because buffering does not handle all variations in an unsteady environment, organizations seek to smooth input and output transactions (Prop. 2.3), and to anticipate and adapt to environmental changes which cannot be buffered or smoothed (Prop. 2.4), and finally, when buffering, leveling, and forecasting do not protect their technical cores from environmental fluctuations (Prop. 2.5), organizations resort to rationing.

These are maneuvering devices which provide the organization with some self-control despite interdependence with the environment. But if we are to gain understanding of such maneuvering, we must consider both the direction toward which maneuvering is designed and the nature of the environment in which maneuvering takes place.

REFERENCES

Argyris, Chris. *Organization of a Bank.* New Haven, Conn.: Labor and Management Center, Yale University, 1954.

Belknap, Ivan. *The Human Problems of a State Mental Hospital.* New York: McGraw-Hill Book Company, 1956.

Blau, Peter M. *The Dynamics of Bureaucracy.* Chicago: The University of Chicago Press, 1955.

Dornbusch, Sanford M. "The Military Academy

as an Assimilating Institution." *Social Forces*, 33 (May 1955), pp. 316–321.

Hawkes, Robert W. "Physical Psychiatric Rehabilitation Models Compared." Paper presented to the Ohio Valley Sociological Society, 1962.

Janowitz, Morris. "Changing Patterns of Organizational Authority: The Military Establishment." *Administrative Science Quarterly*, 3 (March 1959), pp. 473–493.

Meier, Richard L. "Communications Overload." *Administrative Science Quarterly*, 7 (March 1963), pp. 521–544.

Merton, Robert K. "Bureaucratic Structure and Personality," in Robert K. Merton (ed.), *Social Theory and Social Structure* (rev. ed.). New York: The Free Press of Glencoe, 1957a.

Stinchcombe, Arthur L. "Bureaucratic and Craft Administration of Production: A Comparative Study." *Administrative Science Quarterly*, 4 (September 1959), pp. 168–187.

Weber, Max. *The Theory of Social and Economic Organization*, A. M. Henderson and Talcott Parsons (trans.), and Talcott Parsons (ed.). New York: The Free Press of Glencoe, 1947.

Woodward, Joan. *Industrial Organization, Theory and Practice*. London: Oxford University Press, 1965.

Administrative Rationality, Social Setting, and Organizational Development

STANLEY H. UDY, JR.

Few if any concepts employed in social science are fraught with so many difficulties as is the concept "rationality." It is used in a bewildering variety of ways, each of which seems to involve its own plethora of philosophical, psychological, and sociological problems. For present purposes we shall let the chips fall where they may and consider social behavior to be *rational* insofar as it is purposefully directed toward explicit empirical objectives and planned in accordance with the best available scientific knowledge.[1] Brushing aside, for the time being, the question of uncertainty—which, though of crucial practical importance, merely complicates the problem in a formal sense—one may say that the most severe difficulties with this concept from a sociological viewpoint seem to appear in situations where it is applied simultaneously to individuals and collectivities in the same context. Historically the classic instance is perhaps the "problem of order" in utilitarian social philosophy; namely, the problem of accounting for the existence of society assuming it to be composed of discrete individuals striving rationally for the same ends in a context of scarce resources. The solution to this problem, of course, as has been widely pointed out, is that neither the individual nor society—particularly the latter—is so rational in its behavior as the utilitarians had supposed. Cultural values distribute ends among categories of persons differentiated in the social structure and, at the same time, mo-

tivate "nonrational" behavior in given circumstances. Social integration is hence possible because there is no reason to suppose that it must occur relative to explicit overall objectives. Not all behavior need be rational; indeed, on the societal level it cannot be.[2]

In the analysis of formal organizations, however, the problem of rationality arises again in a somewhat different form. One may define a *formal organization* as any social group engaged in pursuing explicit announced empirical objectives through manifestly coordinated effort and, at the same time, describe an entity that appears to be culturally universal.[3] A striking feature of such organizations is that the individuals in the system qua members as well as the system as a whole are expected to behave in a rational manner. The classical "problem of order" suggests that this state of affairs is by no means easy to attain; we may reasonably expect some formal organizations to come closer to it and, in this sense, to be "more rational" than others. Such "dual rationality" can be approximated in the case of formal organization only because the members of the organization are at the same time members of a larger society where integrative values can find expression independently of administrative structure.

We may thus presume rationality to be present in a formal organization to the extent that role expectations are based on planning for organizational objectives.[4] In a more so-

From *American Journal of Sociology*, Vol. 68, 1962, pp. 299–308.

[1] Based on Marion J. Levy, Jr., "A Note on Pareto's Logical-Nonlogical Categories," *American Sociological Review*, Vol. XIII (December, 1948), pp. 756–57. The problem of uncertainty of information is, of course, extremely important in other contexts. See, e.g., Herbert A. Simon, *Models of Man* (New York: John Wiley & Sons, 1957), pp. 241–60.

[2] Talcott Parsons, *The Structure of Social Action* (Glencoe, Ill.: Free Press, 1949), pp. 87–94, 697–719.

[3] Stanley H. Udy, Jr., "'Bureaucracy' and 'Rationality' in Weber's Organization Theory," *American Sociological Review*, Vol. XXIV (December, 1959), p. 792 (hereinafter cited as "BR").

[4] Stanley H. Udy, Jr., "Technical and Institutional Factors in Production Organization," *American Journal of Sociology*, Vol. LXVII (November, 1961), p. 248 (hereinafter cited as "TI").

phisticated statement, Cyert and March characterize a rational system as being oriented to produce choices through standardized search procedures in such a way as to "maximize the expected return to the system" in terms of "a well-defined preference ordering over possible future states."[5] Two major determinants of the degree of administrative rationality in an organization thus suggest themselves: The first is the extent to which the structure of the organization defines and motivates planned collective behavior; the second is the degree to which behavior in the social setting is independent of behavior in the organization, from the standpoint of the individual member. This paper will thus first attempt to isolate organizational-structural requisites of rationality and to analyze their interrelations. It will be found that the requisites herein isolated form a Guttman scale in terms of which the organizations studies can be compared as to degree of rationality. Second, we shall explore relationships between the rationality scale and the institutional and social settings of the organizations studies, in an attempt to assess the independence from societal ascription of organizations lying at different points on the scale. Finally, we shall propose some hypotheses about the development of rationality in organization.[6]

[5] R. M. Cyert and J. G. March, *A Behavioral Theory of the Firm* (Englewood Cliffs, N.J.: Prentice-Hall, Inc., 1963).
[6] Rationality is here treated as a *function* of organizational and social structure. In two previous papers we treated rationality as a *structural* category by operationalizing it in terms of presumed structural correlates. In *BR*, Weber's conception of administrative rationality was found to involve limited objectives, a performance emphasis, and segmental participation, as those terms are defined in the present study. In *TI*, degree of rationality was operationalized in terms of the presence or absence of limited objectives and segmental participation, as those terms are herein defined. In view of present considerations these earlier characterizations seem misleading. As indicated below, orientation to limited objectives appears to be the only one of these characteristics that properly forms a part of rationality per se, functionally considered. Performance emphasis, in view of the way it is operationalized, is more properly part of the reward system, and is so considered in *TI*. Segmental participation, along with a new item herein introduced, "specificity of role assignment," may be viewed structurally as

Data and Methods

Data are drawn from 34 formal organizations engaged in the production of material goods in thirty-four nonindustrial societies; information is based on anthropological monographs and the Human Relations Area Files. The method of cross-cultural comparison was used in order to maximize variation in both internal structure and social setting of the organizations studied. It was also decided to limit the analysis to organizations having three or more levels of authority, inasmuch as previous work suggested that only such organizations would be of sufficient complexity to be of interest for present purposes.[7] The 34 organizations studies are part of a sample of 426 organizations in 150 societies assembled for an earlier, more general study of work organization in nonindustrial culture and were drawn in accord with the criteria set forth by George P. Murdock for his "World Ethnographic Sample."[8] Fifty-six of the original 426 cases proved both to have three or more levels of authority and also to offer sufficient data for purposes of the present analysis. Twelve of them, however, had already been employed in an ex post facto extrapolation of a scale containing four of the seven items used in the

an aspect of what one might term "role differentiation and assignment."

These changes, which allow the structural requisites of rationality to cut across the scheme presented in *TI*, suggest some revisions in the model presented there. Briefly, the category "role differentiation and assignment"—with particular reference to its degree of specificity—replaces what is there termed "rationality," and is defined somewhat differently, as indicated above. Assuming more precise ways of measuring it than are presented here, "rationality" could be considered a criterion variable relative to the entire model presented in *TI*. The relationships indicated in *TI* probably remain generally the same despite the change in the one category, although the present results raise some questions about their validity under certain conditions and suggest that some of the operational items are more important than others.
[7] *TI*, pp. 247–54.
[8] George P. Murdock, "World Ethnographic Sample," *American Anthropologist*, Vol. LIX (August, 1957), pp. 664–87.

scale developed in the present study.[9] Since one of our desires was to test the previous result, these 12 cases were dropped, leaving 44 organizations representing 34 societies. Under the not entirely realistic assumption that organizations in different societies represent independent events while those in the same society do not, only one organization per society was finally used, it being drawn at random when the society offered more than one potentially usable case on the basis of a survey of pertinent ethnographic material. Of the resulting 34 organizations representing 34 societies, 11 are African, 12 North American, and the remaining 11 are distributed over the circum-Mediterranean, insular Pacific, east Eurasian, and South American regions.[10] The geographical distribution of the sample is therefore unfortunately somewhat unbalanced. The extent to which this imbalance reflects the actual distribution of complex production organization as opposed to complete data is not known, except that it may be noted that materials on South American societies are quite sparse.

Administrative Rationality and Its Structural Requisites

We shall assume that rationality as herein defined minimally involves orientation to *limited objectives*, defined for present purposes as objectives explicitly restricted only to the production of certain products. This simple criterion of rationality is, of course, far from ideal but represents the closest operational approach possible of our data to "explicit announced objectives" or to "a well-defined preference ordering of future states."[11] We shall thus assert that "highly rational" organizations possess limited objectives in this sense, by definition. The problem now becomes one of exploring the structural requisites of an organizational

orientation to limited objectives. In an earlier study it had been found that all organizations with limited objectives also involved *segmental participation*—that is, explicit definition of the terms of participation by some mutual contractual agreement—but that not all organizations with segmental participation had limited objectives.[12] Since a reasonable common-sense interpretation of this relationship is at hand (unrestricted terms of participation seem likely to invite goal displacement) it was decided to hypothesize that segmental participation precedes limited objectives at the upper end of the rationality scale. Reference was then made to another previous study [13] that found (in a sample different from the present one) the following characteristics to be related to segmental participation on a scale in the following descending order: *Performance emphasis* (expected dependence of the quantity of the reward on the amount and/or quality of work done); *specialization* [14] (the concurrent performance of three of more qualitatively different operations by different members); and *compensatory rewards* (allocation of money or goods in kind by members of higher authority to members of lower authority in return for participation).[15] Reasonable theoretical interpretations seemed possible for these

[12] BR.

[13] BE.

[14] We have elsewhere defined "specialization" as a continuous variable (i.e., the number of different operations performed simultaneously by different members; see my *Organization of Work* [New Haven, Conn.: HRAF Press, 1959], pp. 22–23). In a social context of the type discussed here, however, it seems proper to regard specialization as discontinuous; the number "three" was chosen as the cutoff point because three is the smallest number of roles in one system wherein ego is faced with the problem of defining relationships between two alters in a way independent of ego's relationship with either of them.

[15] See Peter M. Blau and W. Richard Scott, *Formal Organizations* (San Francisco: Howard M. Chandler, 1962), pp. 205–6, 224–25. Blau and Scott regard this characteristic as indicative of "hierarchical dependence." We find that compensatory rewards indeed do represent hierarchical dependence but only one possible form which it may take. Other possible forms would be the use or threat of force, manipulation of approval needs, etc. We would argue that if organization is to be rational it is important that hierarchical dependence be restricted to compensatory rewards.

[9] Stanley H. Udy, Jr., "'Bureaucratic' Elements in Organizations," *American Sociological Review*, Vol. XXIII (August, 1958), pp. 415–18 (hereinafter cited as "BE"). In this earlier study, these characteristics were termed "bureaucratic" elements. It has since seemed appropriate to refer to them as aspects of "role differentiation and assignment" associated with rationality, and to treat "bureaucracy" as another dimension of organization entirely (see BR).

[10] Murdock, *op. cit.*

[11] Cyert and March, *op. cit.*

findings as well. Segmental participation would seem to be difficult without some explicit attention being drawn to performance. Similarly, unless roles are specialized relative to one another such that the particular content of each is stable and discretely identifiable, any emphasis on performance would seem tenuous. Specialization, in turn, is always potentially difficult to institutionalize, since it is always at least partially determined by technical considerations. Functionally, compensatory rewards constitute a mechanism whereby specialization can be "artificially" institutionalized by management through its control over the reward system. Furthermore, there is some reason to believe that compensatory rewards constitute the *only* mechanism that can reliably do this. Empirically, there appear to be only two possible alternatives: manipulation of already-existing social obligations, and the use of force.[16] The first of these alternatives presupposes a fortuitous and highly improbable identity of technical activities and social roles; the second is subject to serious limitations as a continuous mode of control, particularly in organizations that are at all complex. If this line of reasoning is correct, compensatory rewards are requisite to specialization, except under extremely improbable social conditions.

A review of pertinent literature on administration revealed that the items so far mentioned are often assumed to be structural correlates of administrative rationality and suggested two further items on which data were available: *specific job assignment* (continuous assignment by management of particular people to particular roles), and *centralized management* (the existence of a single internal source of ultimate authority).[17] The former was placed on the scale between specialization

and performance emphasis on the grounds that roles had to be specialized to be assigned and that particular people had to be associated with particular roles to be rewarded for performance in a consistent fashion. Centralized management was placed at the beginning of the scale on the grounds that management could not consistently allocate compensatory rewards without being centralized.

The scale suggested by the preceding arguments was tested over our sample with the results shown in Table 1: "X" denotes the presence of a characteristic, "O" its absence. In general, the results are consistent with the hypotheses proposed.

Since much of the theoretical basis of this scale is probabilistic, one would expect some exceptions. Deviant cases were thus examined in detail, and proved to be of two general types. The first involved the absence of expected specialization or performance emphasis —the apparent loci of most of the deviance. The reason why so much deviation centers on these characteristics seems to be that the presence or absence of each of them, in contrast to the other items, is in part a function of purely technical considerations. Certain kinds of tasks, as for example many involving agriculture or construction, are by nature cumulative and do not lend themselves particularly to specialization, although there is no reason why they cannot be otherwise rationally organized. The Tallensi, Tarahumara, and Camayura cases appear probably to be of this variety. They suggest that rationality involves specialization only where the latter is clearly relevant technologically. Similarly, whether or not rationality involves a performance emphasis appears to be technologically relative. Where activities are highly routinized with a minimum of uncertainty involved, performance seems less likely to be emphasized, despite the presence of other rational characteristics. The Nambicuara, Otoro, and Hopi cases may well be of this variety. In sum, it appears that specialization and a performance emphasis tend in effect not to be a part of rational administration unless their presence clearly contributes to technical efficiency in the physical sense.

The other class of exceptions may be purely a function of the research methodology and are thus possibly more apparent than real. A characteristic was coded as "absent" not only when its existence was explicitly denied but

[16] S. H. Udy, Jr., *Organization of Work* (New York, Taplinger Publishing Co.); chap. vii.
[17] See, e.g., Max Weber, *Theory of Social and Economic Organization* (New York: Oxford University Press, 1947), pp. 225–26; *General Economic History* (Glencoe, Ill.: Free Press, 1950), p. 95; H. H. Gerth and C. Wright Mills, *From Max Weber: Essays in Sociology* (New York: Oxford University Press, 1946), pp. 196 ff.; James G. March and Herbert A. Simon, *Organizations* (New York: John Wiley & Sons, 1958), pp. 12–33; and Chris Argyris, *Understanding Organizational Behavior* (Homewood, Ill.: Dorsey Press, 1960), pp. 12–13.

Table 1. Administrative Rationality in 34 Nonindustrial Production Organizations *

ORGANIZATION	LIMITED OBJECTIVES	SEGMENTAL PARTICIPATION	PERFORMANCE EMPHASIS	SPECIFIC JOB ASSIGNMENT	SPECIALIZATION	COMPENSATORY REWARDS	CENTRAL MANAGEMENT
Iroquois	x	x	x	x	x	x	x
Navaho	x	x	x	x	x	x	x
Paiute	x	x	x	x	x	x	x
Sanpoil	x	x	x	x	x	x	x
Sinkaietk	x	x	0	x	x	x	x
Nambicuara	x	x	0	x	x	x	x
Otoro	0	x	0	x	x	x	x
Hopi	0	x	0	x	x	x	x
Tikopia	0	0	x	x	x	x	x
Kabyles	0	0	x	x	x	x	x
Jukun	0	0	x	0	x	x	x
Tallensi	0	0	x	x	0	x	x
Haida	0	0	0	x	x	x	x
Haitians	0	0	0	x	x	x	x
Dahomeans	0	0	0	x	0	x	x
Tarahumara	0	0	0	x	0	x	x
Turkana	0	0	0	x	0	x	x
Camayura	0	0	0	x	0	x	x
Betsileo	0	0	0	0	x	x	x
Trobrianders	0	0	0	0	x	x	x
Pukapukans	0	0	0	0	x	0	x
Malay	0	0	0	0	x	0	x
Bemba	0	0	0	0	0	x	x
Crow	0	0	0	0	0	x	x
Ifaluk	0	0	0	0	0	x	x
Ila	0	0	0	0	0	x	x
Kikuyu	0	0	0	0	0	x	x
Lobi	0	0	0	0	0	x	x
Papago	0	0	0	0	0	x	x
Sotho	0	0	0	0	0	x	x
Winnebago	0	0	0	0	0	x	x
Dogon		0	0	0	0	0	
Tarasco	0	0	0	0	0	0	0
Tibetans	0	0	0	0	0	0	0

* Coefficient of reproducibility = .95.
For references see Udy, *Organization of Work*, pp. 139–58 ff.

also in instances where it was simply not reported, provided the context was such that it seemed reasonable to assume that the ethnographer would have reported it had it been present. This procedure of courts tended to result in "overreporting" absences. On this score the single deviant omissions for the Sinkaietk, Dahomeans, Pukapukans, and possibly the Turkana are dubious; the "absent" characteristics may actually be present. By the same token, the Betsileo case may involve specific job assignments; the description is not entirely clear on this point. General explanations for other exceptions are not apparent.

The results were adjudged to be consistent with the hypothesis, although our interpretation of some of the exceptions suggests the desirability of complicating the model with some

*Table 2. Rationality and Social Involvement ***

SOCIAL INVOLVEMENT †	SCALE TYPE							
	0	1	2	3	4	5	6	7
Compulsory political ascription	2	0	4	3	0	0	0	0
Compulsory kinship ascription	0	1	1	0	0	0	0	0
Compulsory reciprocity	0	0	4	1	0	1	0	0
Self-commitment, kinship or community obligation	0	0	0	0	6	3	0	0
Voluntary self-commitment, self-defined self-interest	0	0	0	0	0	0	2	6

* "Compulsory" social involvement categories collapsed and scale types 0–3, 4–5, and 6–7 combined: $x^2 = 62.79$; $P < .001$; degrees of freedom = 4.
† As indicated by basis of participation.

contextual variables deriving from technology. We suggest that the scale items indicate a cumulative emphasis on specificity of organizational roles and decision rules such that (1) explicit limits for individual rationality are established and motivated, and (2) interrelated procedures relative to collective rationality are established.

The Institutionalization of Rationality

We now wish to explore and explicate the hypothesis that administrative rationality involves relative independence of the organization from its social setting. Central to this hypothesis is the idea of social involvement, developed in a previous paper. *Social involvement* is defined as the institutionalization of participation and motivation in the organization through expectations and obligations existing independently of the organization in the social setting.[18] One would expect socially involved organizations to be less rational on the grounds that they are less independent of the social setting. The presence in the organization of opportunities to express general social values would inhibit the development of highly specific roles and procedures. In addition, one would expect organizations that are not socially involved to be highly rational under an assumption of structural substitution: that is, if functions are not performed in the setting they

would presumably have to be built into the organization.

Rationality was run against a modified version of a social involvement rank order developed in a previous study.[19] The 34 organizations studied were ranked in presumed order of increasing social involvement according to how participation is institutionalized as follows:

1. Participation expected on the basis of voluntary self-commitment and self-defined self-interest.

2. Participation based on voluntary self-commitment defined as a kinship or community obligation.

3. Participation required by compulsory reciprocity.

4. Participation required by compulsory kinship ascription.

5. Participation required by compulsory political ascription, usually sanctioned by bodily punishment.

Results are shown in Table 2. They are consistent with the hypothesis both as to tendency and symmetry, except that the three "compulsory" social involvement categories do not appear to differ from one another in effect.

For further exploratory purposes, the eight *most rational* organizations (those with segmental participation with or without limited objectives) were compared with all other organizations. Another measure of whether or not the organization is institutionalized as in-

[18] *TI*, pp. 248–49.

[19] *Ibid.*

dependent from its setting is the separation of ownership from management. Table 3 compares organizations having *independent proprietorship* ("ownership" separated from "management" in that control over the ultimate disposition of the means of production is not vested in management) with all other organizations with respect to rationality. All the most rational organizations in the sample have independent proprietorships; most of the other ones do not; the relationship is significant at the .05 level.

Table 3. Rationality and Proprietorship *

	MOST RATIONAL ORGANIZATIONS	OTHER
Independent proprietorship	8	7
Other	0	18

$$Q = +1.00$$
$$X^2 = 9.93$$
$$P < .01$$

* One case was omitted owing to lack of data.

We thus conclude that the mechanisms by which rational administration is institutionalized are such as to produce an independence, or segmentation, of the organization from its social setting. As is the case with individual members relative to the organization, so is the case of the organization relative to its social setting; rational administration requires that an "area of discretion" be defined within which manipulative planning is free to occur.

The Social Setting of Rational Organization

The preceding discussion suggests that it is more difficult for rational administration to develop in social settings that emphasize traditional ascriptive relationships. Previous research suggests that this may be especially likely where differences of power and status are ascribed, since such differences seem particularly likely to be part of social involvement patterns.[20] Accordingly, the settings of the most rational organizations were compared with the settings of all other organizations with respect to three presumed indexes of the general presence of ascription in the society concerned: (1) the presence of a hereditary stratification system with at least three classes or castes; (2) the presence of hereditary political succession; (3) the presence of slavery in any form.[21] Combined results appear in Table 4. The hypothesis is rather weakly confirmed; none of the relationships is statistically significant at the .05 level, but all are in the expected direction, and the stratification relationship approaches significance. None of the most rational organizations in the sample existed in a setting with a complex stratification system. Furthermore, Table 5 indicates what at first glance seems to be a surprising finding—rational organization is negatively associated with the existence of a centralized government

[20] *Ibid.*
[21] Data are drawn from Murdock, *op. cit.*

Table 4. Rationality and Ascriptive Elements in Social Setting *

	COMPLEX HEREDITARY STRATIFICATION		HEREDITARY POLITICAL SUCCESSION		SLAVERY	
	PRESENT	ABSENT	PRESENT	ABSENT	PRESENT	ABSENT
Most rational organizations ...	0	7	4	3	2	6
Other organizations ...	10	15	16	7	11	14
	$Q = -1.00$		$Q = -.26$		$Q = -.40$	
	$X^2 = 2.42$		$X^2 = .02$		$X^2 = .29$	
	$P > .10$		$P > .98$		$P > .50$	

* Cases lacking data omitted.

transcending the local community. The relationship, however, is not statistically significant. We report it because, in the type of society dealt with here, strong central government indicates a hierarchical feudal order wherein political power permeates the entire social order, and is hence probably simply another index of ascription. If so, this result is consistent with our hypothesis.[22]

*Table 5. Rationality and General Centralized Government **

	GENERAL CENTRALIZED GOVERNMENT	
	PRESENT	ABSENT
Most rational organizations	1	7
Other organizations	12	13

$$Q = -.73$$
$$X^2 = 2.33$$
$$P > .10$$

* One case omitted owing to lack of data.

Development of Rational Administration

It is very hazardous to attempt to extrapolate hypotheses concerning organizational evolution or development from cross-sectional data of the type on which this study is based. As our earlier theoretical argument indicates, a scale does suggest a structure of requisite elements. It does not, however, indicate prerequisites. One cannot conclude from our scale, for example, that centralized management must precede compensatory rewards in a temporal sequence of development. Similarly, a scale per se implies nothing about causal relationships among the items in it. It simply describes a modal static state of affairs.

One can, however, use such a scale to predict types of problems that different developmental sequences will probably entail. For example, if specialization should be the first rational characteristic to develop in an organi-

[22] It should perhaps be pointed out that political conservatives have been alleging this relationship for some time, though the applicability of the present data to such an argument is probably questionable for the reasons suggested.

zation, the scale implies that such an organization if it is to be stable must immediately develop a centralized management and compensatory rewards. Unless it proves to be the case that rational administrative characteristics are likely to develop simultaneously—and we shall presently see that at least in many cases this is highly unlikely—one may hypothesize that a developmental sequence that follows the scale pattern will probably entail fewer problems and tensions than one which does not.[23]

It is further possible to infer certain constraints and problems that seem likely to arise at specific points in organizational development. First, the institutional system appears to be markedly discontinuous relative to administrative rationality. An increase in rationality beyond specialization evidently involves a radical change in institutional arrangements; ascriptive social involvement is abandoned in favor of self-commitment. Similarly, an increase beyond a performance emphasis involves another such change—the introduction of the norm of self-defined self-interest in commitment, as well as the separation of proprietorship from management. But between points of discontinuity, it appears possible for rationality to fluctuate independently of the institutional system, provided the requisite pattern suggested by the scale is maintained. Thus, for example, given an institutional adjustment to specific job assignments, performance can either be emphasized or not, with no institutional implications one way or the other. By the same token an organization with no rational characteristics at all can develop a centralized management, compensatory rewards, and specialization without encountering institutional difficulties. But if either of these organizations were to proceed further in rational development, its mode of institutionalization would have to change considerably.

The fact that Table 2 is symmetrical suggests that the converse of the preceding argument may also be valid, insofar as obligation to participate is concerned. It appears that if participation is institutionalized as voluntary commitment based on self-defined self-interest, the organization must at least involve segmental participation plus, in principle, the five other

[23] On the other hand it may be impossible to develop administrative rationality without generating problems and tensions.

characteristics lower on the scale. Also, participation based on self-commitment in a context of kinship or community obligations implies an organization at least sufficiently rational to possess specific job assignments, together with specialization, compensatory rewards, and a centralized management. On the other hand, where participation is purely ascriptive or based on compulsory reciprocity, no rational elements need necessarily be present.

One may next ask: In what kinds of social settings is administrative rationality, together with its requisite institutional arrangements, most likely to be found? Owing to gaps in the data, our analysis at this point is necessarily quite fragmentary. In complex hereditary aristocracy, the existence of slavery, hereditary succession to political office, and complex government are viewed as rough indexes of an ascriptive emphasis in the culture concerned. Tables 4 and 5 suggest, as one might suppose, that organizations in settings where ascription is stressed are themselves likely to be highly socially involved, and hence possess nonrational administrative systems. It is particularly noteworthy that complex hereditary stratification is absent from the setting of all the most rational administrative systems. But this relationship is not symmetrical, and the situation with respect to the other social setting variables is not nearly so marked. One infers, therefore, that, to some extent at least, fairly rational organizations can be institutionalized in quite "hostile" settings. Also, it would appear that a propitious setting does not in itself guarantee rational administration. Why might this be so?

We have already seen that certain elements of rationality—notably specialization and performance emphasis—are at least partially functions of technical, as opposed to institutional, influences. If in a more general sense it is the case that administration tends to be no more rational than is technically necessary, one would indeed expect to find instances of relatively nonrational administrative systems in settings where rationality would in principle be possible, merely because in the instances concerned rationality would be technically unnecessary.

A second reason may stem from the type of ascription present in the social setting. Stinchcombe has suggested that where rationality is a general cultural value, ascription may not markedly inhibit rationality in administration, on the grounds that the major effect of ascription is to infuse the organization with general cultural values.[24] It is possible that the Iroquois case in our sample partially illustrates this type of situation. It is known that Iroquois culture placed a high valuation on efficiency and achievement, with socialization measures taken to assure the differential competence of hereditary political officials. And the Iroquois organization in our sample is highly rational, yet exists in a society with a complex government involving hereditary political officials. Complex hereditary stratification is absent, however. Furthermore, participation is based on self-defined self-interest. It may be that a general valuation of rationality simply tends to make possible nonascriptive recruitment in otherwise ascriptive settings. Modern industrial society may largely fit in this category. For even in the presence of a high cultural valuation on efficiency and rationality, ascriptive recruitment can still be disruptive to organizational operations by introducing competing goals and loyalties, however "rationally" they are individually viewed. It would seem that there are limits to the extent to which the effects of ascription on administration can be offset by institutional arrangements.

Conclusions

In a sample of 34 nonindustrial production organizations, seven organizational characteristics associated with administrative rationality were found to scale in a cross-sectional comparative analysis in such a way as to suggest that rationality involves a cumulative emphasis on specificity of organizational roles and decision rules. The rationality scale was further found to be highly negatively associated with the degree to which the organization is socially involved with its setting; administrative rationality appears to require some modicum of organizational independence. Rationality was somewhat less closely negatively associated to settings having traditional ascriptive elements. From these findings it was possible to infer certain differentials in problems of organizational development under varying conditions.

[24] Arthur L. Stinchcombe, "Comment," *American Journal of Sociology*, Vol. LXVII (November, 1961), pp. 255–59.

Cognitive Limits on Rationality

JAMES G. MARCH AND HERBERT A. SIMON

The Concept of Rationality

How does the rationality of "administrative man" compare with that of classical "economic man" or with the rational man of modern statistical decision theory? The rational man of economics and statistical decision theory makes "optimal" choices in a highly specified and clearly defined environment:

1. When we first encounter him in the decision-making situation, he already has laid out before him the whole set of alternatives from which he will choose his action. This set of alternatives is simply "given"; the theory does not tell how it is obtained.

2. To each alternative is attached a set of consequences—the events that will ensue if that particular alternative is chosen. Here the existing theories fall into three categories: (a) *Certainty:* theories that assume the decision maker has complete and accurate knowledge of the consequences that will follow on each alternative. (b) *Risk:* theories that assume accurate knowledge of a probability distribution of the consequences of each alternative. (c) *Uncertainty:* theories that assume that the consequences of each alternative belong to some subset of all possible consequences, but that the decision maker cannot assign definite probabilities to the occurrence of particular consequences.

3. At the outset, the decision maker has a "utility function" or a "preference-ordering" that ranks all sets of consequences from the most preferred to the least preferred.

4. The decision maker selects the alternative leading to the preferred set of consequences. In the case of *certainty*, the choice is unambiguous. In the case of *risk*, rationality is usually defined as the choice of that alternative for

From James G. March and Herbert A. Simon, *Organizations*, Wiley, New York, 1958, pp. 137–171.

which the expected utility is greatest. Expected utility is defined here as the average, weighted by the probabilities of occurrence, of the utilities attached to all possible consequences. In the case of *uncertainty*, the definition of rationality becomes problematic. One proposal that has had wide currency is the rule of "minimax risk": consider the worst set of consequences that may follow from each alternative, then select the alternative whose "worst set of consequences" is preferred to the worst sets attached to other alternatives. There are other proposals (e.g., the rule of "minimax regret"), but we shall not discuss them here.

Some Difficulties in the Classical Theory. There are difficulties with this model of rational man. In the first place, only in the case of certainty does it agree well with commonsense notions of rationality. In the case of uncertainty, especially, there is little agreement, even among exponents of statistical decision theory, as to the "correct" definition, or whether, indeed, the term "correct" has any meaning here (Marschak, 1950).

A second difficulty with existing models of rational man is that it makes three exceedingly important demands upon the choice-making mechanism. It assumes (1) that all the alternatives of choice are "given"; (2) that all the consequences attached to each alternative are known (in one of the three senses corresponding to certainty, risk, and uncertainty respectively); (3) that the rational man has a complete utility-ordering (or cardinal function) for all possible sets of consequences.

One can hardly take exception to these requirements in a normative model—a model that tells people how they *ought* to choose. For if the rational man lacked information, he might have chosen differently "if only he had known." At best, he is "subjectively" rational, not "objectively" rational. But the notion of objective rationality assumes there is some objective reality in which the "real" alternatives, the "real" consequences, and the "real" utilities exist. If this is so, it is not even clear why the cases of choice under risk and under uncertainty are admitted as rational. If it is not so, it is not clear why only limitations upon knowledge of consequences are considered, and why limitations upon knowledge of alternatives and utilities are ignored in the model of rationality.

From a phenomenological viewpoint we can only speak of rationality relative to a frame of reference; and this frame of reference will be determined by the limitations on the rational man's knowledge. We can, of course, introduce the notion of a person observing the choices of a subject, and can speak of the rationality of the subject relative to the frame of reference of the observer. If the subject is a rat and the observer is a man (especially if he is the man who designed the experimental situation), we may regard the man's perception of the situation as objective and the rat's as subjective. (We leave out of account the specific difficulty that the rat presumably knows his own utility function better than the man does.) If, however, both subject and observer are men—and particularly if the situation is a natural one not constructed for experimental purposes by the observer—then it becomes difficult to specify the objective situation. It will be safest, in such situations, to speak of rationality only relative to some specified frame of reference.

The classical organization theory, like classical economic theory, failed to make explicit this subjective and relative character of rationality, and in so doing, failed to examine some of its own crucial premises. The organizational and social environment in which the decision maker finds himself determines what consequences he will anticipate, what ones he will not; what alternatives he will consider, what ones he will ignore. In a theory of organization these variables cannot be treated as unexplained independent factors, but must themselves be determined and predicted by the theory.

Routinized and Problem-solving Responses. The theory of rational choice put forth here incorporates two fundamental characteristics: (1) Choice is always exercised with respect to a limited, approximate, simplified "model" of the real situation. We call the chooser's model his "definition of the situation." (2) The elements of the definition of the situation are not "given"—that is, we do not take these as data of our theory—but are themselves the outcome of psychological and sociological processes, including the chooser's own activities and the activities of others in his environment (Simon, 1947, 1955; March, 1955a; Cyert and March, 1955, 1956; Newell, Shaw, and Simon, 1958).

Activity (individual or organizational) can usually be traced back to an environmental stimulus of some sort, e.g., a customer order or a fire gong. The responses to stimuli are of various kinds. At one extreme, a stimulus evokes a response—sometimes very elaborate—that has been developed and learned at some previous time as an appropriate response for a stimulus of this class. This is the "routinized" end of the continuum, where a stimulus calls forth a performance program almost instantaneously.

At the other extreme, a stimulus evokes a larger or smaller amount of problem-solving activity directed toward finding performance activities with which to complete the response. Such activity is distinguished by the fact that it can be dispensed with once the performance program has been learned. Problem-solving activities can generally be identified by the extent to which they involve *search:* search aimed at discovering alternatives of action or consequences of action. "Discovering" alternatives may involve inventing and elaborating whole performance programs where these are not already available in the problem solver's repertory (Katona, 1951).

When a stimulus is of a kind that has been experienced repeatedly in the past, the response will ordinarily be highly routinized. The stimulus will evoke, with a minimum of problem-solving or other computational activity, a well-structured definition of the situation that will include a repertory of response programs, and programs for selecting an appropriate specific response from the repertory. When a stimulus is relatively novel, it will evoke problem-solving activity aimed initially at constructing a definition of the situation and then at developing one or more appropriate performance programs.

Psychologists (e.g., Wertheimer, Duncker, de Groot, Maier) and observant laymen (e.g., Poincaré, Hadamard) who have studied creative thinking and problem-solving have been unanimous in ascribing a large role in these phenomena to search processes. Search is partly random, but in effective problem-solving it is not blind. The design of the search process is itself often an object of rational decision. Thus, we may distinguish substantive planning—developing new performance programs—from procedural planning—developing programs for the problem-solving process itself. The response to a particular stimulus may involve more than performance—the stimulus may evoke a spate of problem-solving activity —but the problem-solving activity may itself be routinized to a greater or lesser degree. For example, search processes may be systematized by the use of check lists.

Satisfactory versus optimal standards. What kinds of search and other problem-solving activity are needed to discover an adequate range of alternatives and consequences for choice depends on the criterion applied to the choice. In particular, finding the optimal alternative is a radically different problem from finding a satisfactory alternative. An alternative is *optimal* if: (1) there exists a set of criteria that permits all alternatives to be compared, and (2) the alternative in question is preferred, by these criteria, to all other alternatives. An alternative is *satisfactory* if: (1) there exists a set of criteria that describes minimally satisfactory alternatives, and (2) the alternative in question meets or exceeds all these criteria.

Most human decision-making, whether individual or organizational, is concerned with the discovery and selection of satisfactory alternatives; only in exceptional cases is it concerned with the discovery and selection of optimal alternatives. To optimize requires processes several orders of magnitude more complex than those required to satisfice. An example is the difference between searching a haystack to find the *sharpest* needle in it and searching the haystack to find a needle sharp enough to sew with.

In making choices that meet satisfactory standards, the standards themselves are part of the definition of the situation. Hence, we need not regard these as given—any more than the other elements of the definition of the situation —but may include in the theory the processes through which these standards are set and modified. The standard-setting process may itself meet standards of rationality: for example, an "optimizing" rule would be to set the standard at the level where the marginal improvement in alternatives obtainable by raising it would be just balanced by the marginal cost of searching for alternatives meeting the higher standard. Of course, in practice the "marginal improvement" and the "marginal cost" are seldom measured in comparable units, or with much accuracy. Nevertheless, a similar result would be automatically attained if the standards were raised whenever alternatives proved easy to discover, and lowered whenever they were difficult to discover. Under these circumstances, the alternatives chosen would not be far from the optima, if the cost of search were taken into consideration. Since human standards tend to have this characteristic under many conditions, some theorists have sought to maintain the optimizing model by introducing cost-of-search considerations. Although we doubt whether this will be a fruitful alternative to the model we are proposing in very many situations, neither model has been used for predictive purposes often enough to allow a final judgment.

Performance Programs. We have seen that under certain circumstances the search and choice processes are very much abridged. At the limit, an environmental stimulus may evoke immediately from the organization a highly complex and organized set of responses. Such a set of responses we call a *performance program*, or simply a *program*. For example, the sounding of the alarm gong in a fire station initiates such a program. So does the appearance of a relief applicant at a social worker's desk. So does the appearance of an automobile chassis in front of the work station of a worker on the assembly line.

Situations in which a relatively simple stimulus sets off an elaborate program of activity without any apparent interval of search, problem-solving, or choice are not rare. They account for a very large part of the behavior of all persons, and for almost all of the behavior of persons in relatively routine positions. Most behavior, and particularly most behavior in organizations, is governed by performance programs.

The term "program" is not intended to connote complete rigidity. The content of the program may be adaptive to a large number of characteristics of the stimulus that initiates it. Even in the simple case of the fire gong, the response depends on the location of the alarm, as indicated by the number of strokes. The program may also be conditional on data that are independent of the initiating stimuli. It is then more properly called a *performance strategy*. For example, when inventory records show that the quantity on hand of a commodity has decreased to the point where it should be reordered, the decision rule that governs the behavior of the purchasing agent may call upon him to determine the amount to be ordered on the basis of a formula into which he inserts the quantity that has been sold over the past 12 months. In this case, search has been eliminated from the problem, but choice —of a very routinized kind, to be sure—remains.

We will regard a set of activities as routinized, then, to the degree that choice has been simplified by the development of a fixed response to defined stimuli. If search has been eliminated, but a choice remains in the form of a clearly defined and systematic computing routine, we will still say that the activities are routinized. We will regard activities as unroutinized to the extent that they have to be preceded by program-developing activities of a problem-solving kind.

Performance Programs in Organizations

There are several ways to determine what programs a particular organization uses:

1. Observing the behavior of organization members. In relatively routine positions, where the same situations recur repetitively and are handled in terms of fairly definite programs, it is easy to infer the program from behavior. This is a common method for inducting new members of an organization into its procedures.

2. Interviewing members of the organization. Most programs are stored in the minds of the employees who carry them out, or in the minds of their superiors, subordinates, or associates. For many purposes, the simplest and most accurate way to discover what a person does is to ask him.

3. Examining documents that describe standard operating procedures. Programs may be written down, more or less completely and more or less accurately. The relation of a written operating procedure to the actual program that is carried out is complex, for the program may have been written down: (*a*) as an instruction to initiate a new program and communicate it to those who will carry it out; (*b*) as a description of an existing program to instruct new organization members; or (*c*) as an exposition (with or without amendments) of an existing program to legitimize or "formalize" it. There are other possibilities besides these three. In any event, when a document is used as a source of information about a program, the purposes for which it was prepared are relevant to its interpretation.

A person who has been trained in the observation of organizations can extract by these and other techniques a large part of the program that governs routine behavior. This is such a common-sense fact that its importance has been overlooked: Knowledge of the program of an organization permits one to predict in considerable detail the behavior of members of the organization. And the greater the *programming* (6.1) [1] of individual activities in the organization, the greater the *predictability* (6.2) of those activities [6.2:6.1].

To be sure, prediction of behavior from the knowledge of a program has none of the element of "surprise" that we commonly associate with scientific prediction—any more than prediction of the lines that will be uttered by a Hamlet on the stage. It is no less important for its common-sense obviousness.

In general, we would anticipate that programs will be generated by past experience and in expectation of future experience in a given situation. Thus, the greater the *repetitiveness* (6.3) of individual activities, the greater the programming [6.1:6.3.] From this one would predict that programming will be most complete for clerical and factory jobs, particularly when the work is organized largely by process.

The prediction of behavior from a program when tasks are relatively simple and routine is

---

[1] The authors identify variables by such notations as (6.1) and propositions by notations such as [6.2:6.1] (ed.).

illustrated by findings of Guetzkow and Simon (1955) using five-man experimental groups in the Vavelas network. Employing methods-analysis techniques, they were able to predict average trial times of groups to within 10% from a knowledge of the methods the groups were using to perform the task.

If the program determines in some detail the behavior of individuals and groups performing relatively routine tasks, then we can predict behavior to the extent that we can answer the following questions: (1) What motivates members of the organization to accept a program as a determinant of their behavior? What processes, other than motivation, are involved in implementation of programs? This question has already been examined in earlier chapters. (2) What determines the content of a program? To what extent can the program be predicted uniquely from the requirements of the task? How are programs invented and developed, and what are the determinants of this process? (3) What are the consequences of programs, as developed and executed, for the goal and subgoal structure of the organization? (4) What are the predictors of behavior in areas that are not routinized and are unprogrammed? This question will be taken up in the next chapter.

We turn now to the second and third of these questions.

Program Content. The extent to which many human activities, both manual and clerical, can be programmed is shown by the continuing spread of automation to encompass a wider and wider range of tasks. In order to substitute automatic processes for human operatives, it is necessary to describe the task in minute detail, and to provide for the performance of each step in it. The decomposition of tasks into their elementary program steps is most spectacularly illustrated in modern computing machines which may carry out programs involving thousands of such steps. The capabilities of computers have now been extended to many tasks that until recently have been thought to be relatively complex, involving problem-solving activities of a fairly high order. Some examples are several existing computer programs for the automatic design of small electric motors and transformers, a program that enables a computer to discover proofs for certain kinds of mathematical theo-

rems, and a program for translating languages.

Even on routine jobs, *program content* (6.4) varies. We have already mentioned the extreme case: the detailed specification of output, methods, and pace in a man-paced assembly operation. But not all programs are of this type. They may not contain detailed time specifications (e.g., in typical machine-paced operations). In fact, programs usually specify the content of an activity more closely than its timing. They may specify the properties of the product (e.g., in blueprints, tolerances, etc.) rather than the detail of the methods to be used. We need propositions that will explain variations in program content along these dimensions:

(*a*) The extent to which pacing rules are built into the program.

(*b*) The extent to which work activities are detailed in the program.

(*c*) The extent to which product specifications are detailed in the program.

Since performance programs are important aspects of the organizational system, their content will presumably tend to be related to the functions they perform. We can identify two major functions that such programs fulfill, or at least are intended to fulfill. First, they are a part of the control system in the organization. Organizations attempt to control employees by specifying a standard operating procedure and attaching organizational rewards and penalties to it. Second, performance programs are important parts of the coordination system in the organization. They help fulfill the needs for interdepartmental predictability (Blau, 1955).

Insofar as they are to function as controls, the programs must be linked to variables that are observable and measurable. We would expect program content to be a function of the *ease of observing job activities* (6.5), the *ease of observing job output* (6.6), and the *ease of relating activities to output* (6.7) [6.4:6.5, 6.6, 6.7]. Thus, we would predict that programs will contain activity specifications in preference to product specifications to the extent that: (*a*) the activity pattern is easily observed and supervised; (*b*) the quantity and quality of output are not easily observed and supervised; (*c*) the relations between activity pattern and output are highly technical, and are matters of scientific and engineering knowledge, better known to specialists in the organization than to the operatives (Ridley and Simon, 1938).

Conversely, programs will contain specifications of quality and quantity of output to the extent that: (*a*) the activity pattern is difficult to observe and supervise; (*b*) the quantity and quality of output are easily observed and supervised; (*c*) the relations between activity pattern and output are matters of common sense, are matters of skill in the specific occupation for which the operatives are trained, or are highly variable, depending upon circumstances of the individual situation that are better known to the operatives than to supervisors and specialists.

For performance programs to serve as coordinative devices, they must be linked to the coordination needs that are felt by the organization. Consequently, we would hypothesize that program content will be a function of the *need for activity coordination* (6.8) and the *need for output coordination* (6.9) [6.4:6.8, 6.9]. The more minutely other members of the organization need to synchronize or coordinate their activities with the activities of a particular member, the more completely will the program specify the activity pattern and/or the pacing of those activities. But to the extent that the activities of the former depend on the characteristics of the output of the latter, rather than on his activities, the program will specify product characteristics.

These propositions about program content are derived from the assumption that the program will be rationally adapted to the organization's objectives. To the extent that this assumption actually determines program, program content becomes a technological question in exactly the same way as the form of the production function is a technological question. In the experiment with the Bavelas network, mentioned previously, determining the most efficient program for performing the task is an exercise in methods study resting upon knowledge of human physiological constants—the times required to perform certain simple acts. If we assume that over some period of time an organization will actually arrive at an efficient program, we can predict its long-run behavior from our technical analysis.

Suppose, however, that we substitute for the maximizing assumption implicit in this method of prediction the assumption that behavior is rational in the more limited sense described earlier: that programs are sought that will operate "satisfactorily," and that the "best" program is not necessarily sought or found. In this case, predicting the program becomes more difficult. Which of the (presumably numerous) satisfactory potential programs the organization will adopt depends, under these circumstances, upon the procedures it employs to construct new programs and to improve existing ones. These procedures will provide the principal subject matter for the next chapter.

The Structure of Programs. To illustrate further the structure of programs for handling recurrent events, we will describe some formal procedures often used by business concerns for controlling inventory. We will analyze first the common "two-bin" system of inventory control, then a more elaborate system.

In the two-bin system of inventory control, two quantities are established for each item kept in stock: (1) the order quantity (the amount to be purchased on a single order), (2) the buffer stock (the amount that should be on hand when a new order is placed). The program is very simple:

1. When material is drawn from stock, note whether the quantity that remains equals or exceeds the buffer stock. If not:
2. Write a purchase order for the specified order quantity.

Let us call the first step the "program-evoking" step, and the second step the "program-execution" step. The bifurcation is characteristic of programs—a program includes a specification of the circumstances under which the program is to be evoked. In the example just cited, the program specifies certain observations, which are to be made (whether the buffer stock is intact) whenever a certain event occurs (withdrawal of material from stock). A decision to act or not to act (to apply or not to apply the program) is based on the result of the observation.

The program-evoking step may involve only observation auxiliary to some other activity (as in this example), or it may invoke systematic scanning of some part of the environment (e.g., the activity of a quality inspector). Further, a program-execution step by one member of an organization may serve as a program-evoking step for another member. In the example above, the receipt of a purchase order from the inventory clerk is a program-evoking step for the purchasing department.

In our very simple example, the program-execution step requires neither discretion nor problem-solving. In more complicated situations, the program will be a strategy; i.e., action will be contingent on various characteristics of the situation. For example, in a more elaborate inventory control scheme, the purchase quantity may depend on a forecast of sales. Then the program might look like this:

1. When material is drawn from stock, note whether the quantity that remains equals or exceeds the buffer stock. If not:
2. Determine from the sales forecast provided by the sales department the sales expected in the next k months.
3. Insert this quantity in the "order quantity formula," and write a purchase order for the quantity thus determined.

This program, although it is contingent on certain changing facts (the sales forecast), does not allow discretion to the person who executes it—at least in ordinary meanings of the word "discretion." If, however, the organization does not provide the inventory clerk with an official sales forecast, or does not establish a specific order quantity, we would say that the clerk's activity was, to that extent, discretionary. We might discover by observation and interview that the clerk was in fact following a very definite and invariable program, but one stored in his own memory and not recorded in official instructions.

The Nature of Discretion. The amounts and kinds of *discretion* (6.10) available to the organizational participant are a function of his performance program and in particular the extent to which the program specifies activities (means) and the extent to which it specifies product or outcome (ends) [6.10:6.4]. The further the program goes in the latter direction, the more discretion it allows for the person implementing the program to supply the means-end connections. Compare the programs cited earlier with the following alternative program:

1. It is the duty of the inventory clerk to determine when each item should be recorded and in what quantity, and to place orders with the purchasing department. He should perform this function with attention to the costs of holding inventories, the costs of shortages, and the economies associated with bulk orders.

If we interpret the last sentence as enjoining the clerk to minimize the sum of the specified costs, we see that this program specifies a goal, but leaves the means undetermined. To construct, a "rational" program starting from these premises requires the following steps: (1) defining the total cost function in specific terms; (2) estimating the coefficients that appear in the cost function; (3) deriving a formula or "strategy" that specifies the ordering rules as functions of: (*a*) the coefficients that appear in the cost function, (*b*) the sales forecasts (i.e., finding the policy that minimizes step 1), and (4) inserting in the formula the coefficients estimated in step 2, and the sales forecasts.

It is difficult to find a place for discretion within the framework of traditional theories of rational behavior. In the present theory, however, a whole host of phenomena fall under this heading.

First, when a program involves search activities, the actual course of action depends on what is found. We may regard the choice of a course of action after search as discretionary.

Second, when a program describes a strategy, application of the strategy to specific circumstances requires forecasts or other estimates of data. We may regard the application of the strategy to select a course of action as discretionary.

Third, a program may exist in the memory of the individual who is to apply it, having arrived there either as a result of extraorganizational training (e.g., professional training or apprenticeship), or as a product of learning from experience rather than as a result of formal instructions. Under these circumstances we often regard him as behaving in a discretionary fashion.

In all of the cases listed above, the decision process may in fact be highly routinized—the term "discretionary" referring in these instances to the form of the performance program or the source from which it was acquired. These cases need to be distinguished from a fourth meaning of "discretionary": A program may specify only general goals, and leave unspecified the exact activities to be used in reaching them. Moreover, knowledge of the means-ends connections may be sufficiently incomplete and inexact that these cannot be very well specified in advance. Then "discretion" refers to the development and modification of the performance program through problem-solving and learning processes. Although it is difficult to draw a perfectly sharp line between changing a program and changing a datum in applying a strategy, we have already argued that there is an important difference of degree here. With these several meanings of the term "discretionary" in mind, we do not need separate propositions about the amount of discretion, for these will be subsumed under the propositions already noted that specify the form, content, and completeness of programs.

Interrelation of Programs. A program, whether simple or complex, is initiated when it is evoked by some stimulus. The whole pattern of programmed activity in an organization is a complicated mosaic of program executions, each initiated by its appropriate program-evoking step.

Insofar as the stimuli that evoke programs come from outside the organization, the individual pieces of this mosaic are related to each other only in making claims on the same time and resources, and hence in posing an allocation problem. Nevertheless, if the goal of optimizing is taken seriously, this allocation problem will usually complicate the problem-solving process greatly, for it requires the marginal return from activity in response to any particular stimulus to be equated with the marginal return from activities in response to all other stimuli. Hence, all programs must be determined simultaneously.

When the goal is to respond to stimuli in a satisfactory, but not necessarily optimal, fashion, choice is much simpler; for the standards may be set at levels that permit a satisficing response to each stimulus without concern for the others. The organization, under these circumstances, normally has some slack that reduces the interdependence among its several performance programs.

Apart from resource-sharing, there may be other and more integral connections among programs. Program A may be a *higher-level* program, i.e., a problem-solving activity whose goal is to revise other programs, either by con-

structing new ones, reconstructing existing ones, or simply modifying individual premises in existing programs. In this case, the *content* of the lower-level programs that are related to A will depend on A. Or, program A may be a program one of whose execution steps serves as an initiating stimulus for program B.

The inventory example illustrates both possibilities. As to the first, program A may be a forecasting program, or a program for periodic revision of the coefficients in the cost function. As to the second possibility, the order that goes from the inventory clerk to the purchasing department serves to initiate one of the purchasing programs of the latter.

Program and Organization Structure. In organizations there generally is a considerable degree of parallelism between the hierarchical relations among members of the organization and the hierarchical relations among program elements. That is to say, the programs of members of higher levels of the organization have as their main output the modification or initiation of programs for individuals at lower levels.

Any organization possesses a repertory of programs that, collectively, can deal in a goal-oriented way with a range of situations. As new situations arise, the construction of an entirely new program from detailed elements is rarely contemplated. In most cases, adaptation takes place through a recombination of lower-level programs that are already in existence. An important objective of standardization is to widen as far as possible the range of situations that can be handled by combination and recombination of a relatively small number of elementary programs.

Limitation of high-level action to the recombination of programs, rather than the detailed construction of new programs out of small elements, is extremely important from a cognitive standpoint. Our treatment of rational behavior rests on the proposition that the "real" situation is almost always far too complex to be handled in detail. As we move upwards in the supervisory and executive hierarchy, the range of interrelated matters over which an individual has purview becomes larger and larger, more and more complex. The growing complexity of the problem can only be matched against the finite powers of the individual if the problem is dealt with in grosser and more aggregative form. One way in which this is accomplished is by limiting the alternatives of action that are considered to the recombination of a repertory of programs (Simon, 1953b).

We may again illustrate this point with the inventory example. Top management decides upon the total dollar inventories without controlling the distribution of inventories among individual items. Specific inventory control programs are found at lower levels of the organization.

Perception and Identifications

We have seen that humans, whether inside or outside administrative organizations, behave rationally, if at all, only relative to some set of "given" characteristics of the situation. These "givens" include knowledge or assumptions about future events or probability distributions of future events, knowledge of alternatives available for action, knowledge of consequences attached to alternatives—knowledge that may be more or less complete—and rules or principles for ordering consequences or alternatives according to preference.

These four sets of givens define the situation as it appears to the rational actor. In predicting his behavior, we need this specification and not merely a specification of the situation as it "really" is, or, more precisely, as it appears to an outside observer.

The steps that lead, for an actor, to his defining the situation in a particular way involve a complex interweaving of affective and cognitive processes. What a person wants and likes influences what he sees; what he sees influences what he wants and likes.

In the three previous chapters we have examined primarily motivational and affective factors. We have considered the relation between individual goals and organizational goals, the ways in which goals are acquired from reference groups, and the motivational bases for conformity with group goals. Cognition enters into the definition of the situation in connection with goal attainment—determining what means will reach desired ends. But cognition enters into the goal-formation process also, because the goals used as criteria for choice seldom represent "final" or "ultimate" values. Instead, they too reflect the perceived

relations of means to ends and hence are modified by changing beliefs about these relations. Since goals provide the principal bridge between motivations and cognition, we will begin our consideration of cognitive elements in the definition of the situation with the topic of subgoal formation.

Cognitive aspects of subgoal formation. An individual can attend to only a limited number of things at a time. The basic reason why the actor's definition of the situation differs greatly from the objective situation is that the latter is far too complex to be handled in all its detail. Rational behavior involves substituting for the complex reality a model of reality that is sufficiently simple to be handled by problem-solving processes.

In organizations where various aspects of the whole complex problem are being handled by different individuals and different groups of individuals, a fundamental technique for simplifying the problem is to factor it into a number of nearly independent parts, so that each organizational unit handles one of these parts and can omit the others from its definition of the situation. This technique is also prominent in individual and small-group behavior. A large complex task is broken down into a sequence of smaller tasks, the conjunction of which adds up to the accomplishment of the larger. The factorization of a large task into parts can be more elaborate for an organization than for an individual, but the underlying reason is the same: the definition of the situation at any one moment must be sufficiently simple to be encompassed by a human mind.

The principal way to factor a problem is to construct a means-end analysis. The means that are specified in this way become subgoals which may be assigned to individual organizational units. This kind of jurisdictional assignment is often called "organization by purpose" or "departmentalization by purpose."

The motivational aspect of this particular process of subgoal formation is rather simple. Whatever will motivate individuals and groups to accept the tasks assigned them through the legitimate (formal and informal) processes of the organization will provide motivation for subgoals. For the subgoals are implicit or explicit in the definition of the situation as it is incorporated in the task assignment.

When tasks have been allocated to an organizational unit in terms of a subgoal, other subgoals and other aspects of the goals of the larger organization tend to be ignored in the decisions of the subunit. In part, this bias in decision-making can be attributed to shifts in the *focus of attention* (6.11). The definition of the situation that the subunit employs is simplified by omitting some criteria and paying particular attention to others. In particular, we expect the focus of attention to be a function of the *differentiation of subgoals* (6.12) and the *persistence of subgoals* (6.13) [6.11:6.12, 6.13].

The tendency of members of an organizational unit to evaluate action only in terms of subgoals, even when these are in conflict with the goals of the larger organization, is reinforced by at least three cognitive mechanisms. The first of these is located within the individual decision maker, the second within the organizational unit, and the third in the environment of the organizational unit.

In the individual there is reinforcement through selective perception and rationalization. That is, the persistence of subgoals is furthered by the focus of attention it helps to generate [6.13:6.11]. The propensity of individuals to see those things that are consistent with their established frame of reference is well established in individual psychology. Perceptions that are discordant with the frame of reference are filtered out before they reach consciousness, or are reinterpreted or "rationalized" so as to remove the discrepancy. The frame of reference serves just as much to validate perceptions as the perceptions do to validate the frame of reference.

Within the organizational unit there is reinforcement through the *content of in-group communication* (6.14). Such communication affects the *focus of information* (6.15) [6.15-6.14], and thereby increases subgoal persistence [6.13:6.15]. The vast bulk of our knowledge of fact is not gained through direct perception but through the second-hand, third-hand, and *n*th-hand reports of the perceptions of others, transmitted through the channels of social communication. Since these perceptions have already been filtered by one or more communicators, most of whom have frames of reference similar to our own, the reports are generally consonant with the filtered reports of our own perceptions, and serve to reinforce

the latter. In organizations, two principal types of in-groups are of significance in filtering: in-groups with members in a particular organizational unit, and in-groups with members in a common profession. Hence, we may distinguish *organizational* identifications and *professional* identifications. There are others, of course, but empirically these appear to be the most significant.

Finally, there is reinforcement through selective exposure to environmental stimuli. The *division of labor in the organization* (6.16) affects the information that various members receive [6.15:6.16]. This differentiation of information contributes to the differentiation of subgoals [6.12:6.15]. Thus perceptions of the environment are biased even before they experience the filtering action of the frame of reference of the perceiver. Salesmen live in an environment of customers; company treasurers in an environment of bankers; each sees a quite distinct part of the world (Dearborn and Simon, 1958).

There is one important distinction between this source of reinforcement and the two mentioned previously. Reinforcement through selective perception and rationalization and reinforcement through in-group communication serve to explain how a particular definition of the situation, once it becomes established in an individual or group, maintains itself with great stability and tenacity. These mechanisms do not explain, however, what particular definitions of the situation will *become* established in particular environments—they explain behavior persistence and not the origins of behavior. In order to predict what particular subgoals we are likely to find in particular parts of an organization, we must take as our starting point (*a*) the system of subgoal assignment that has resulted from analysis of the organization's goals, and (*b*) the kinds of stimuli to which each organizational unit is exposed in carrying out its assignments. Under the last heading we must include the selective feedback to organizational units of those consequences of action that relate to their particular subgoals.

Through these mechanisms of subgoal formation and subgoal perception, there is selective attention to particular consequences of proposed alternatives, and selective inattention to others. The magnitude of these effects depends in part on variations in the "capacity" of the individual participants in the organization. The smaller the *span of attention* (6.17), the narrower the focus of attention and the more critical the screening mechanisms cited above [6.11:6.17]. One variable of particular importance in determining the span of attention is, of course, the *time pressure* (6.18) involved [6.17:6.18]. In general, we would expect selective perception to be most acute where time is shortest. The relations among these variables are indicated in Figure 6.1.

Other Cognitive Aspects of the Definition of the Situation. All the statements of the last section apply, *mutatis mutandis,* to the other elements of the definition of the situation besides goals and values. That is to say, the definition of the situation represents a simplified, screened, and biassed model of the objective situation, and filtering affects all of the "givens" that enter into the decision process: knowledge or assumptions about future events; knowledge of sets of alternatives available for action; knowledge of consequences attached to alternatives; goals and values (Levin, 1956; Gore, 1956).

Consider just knowledge and assumptions about future and present events—"stipulated facts," "absorption of uncertainty." What the sales of the ABC Company are going to be in 1961 is a question of fact. But this matter of fact may become a matter of organizational stipulation—all action within the organization to which the 1961 sales figure is relevant being based upon an "official" sales forecast. Organizational techniques for dealing with uncertain future and present facts will be discussed in a later section of this chapter.

A related phenomenon is the summarizing of raw information to communicate it further in the organization. The weatherman makes observations of temperature, humidity, barometric pressure, but may communicate only his conclusions in the form of a weather forecast. In organizational communication evidence is replaced with conclusions drawn from that evidence, and these conclusions then become the "facts" on which the rest of the organization acts. One particular form or summarization is classification. When a particular thing has been classified as belonging to a species, all the attributes of the species can be

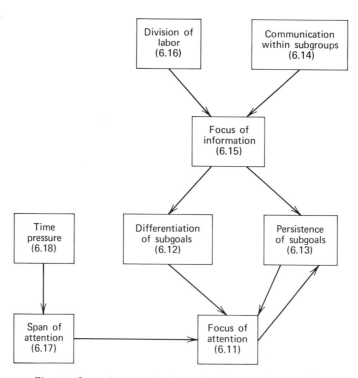

Fig. 6.1. Some factors affecting selective attention to subgoals.

ascribed to the individual instance of it. Priority systems are an example of an important kind of formal classification device.

Similarly, individuals and organizations develop repertoires of programs of action suited to different situations. These are frequently combined with classification systems so that once a situation has been assigned to a particular class the appropriate action program can be applied to it. Such repertoires of performance programs, and the requisite habits and skills for their use, appear to make up the largest part of professional and vocational training.

Knowledge of consequences is intimately related to selective attention to subgoals, and does not require further elaboration here.

The goals that are included in the definition of the situation influence choice only if there are some means, valid or illusory, for determining the connections between alternative actions and goal satisfaction—only if it can somehow be determined whether and to what extent these goals will be realized if particular courses of action are chosen. When a means of testing actions is perceived to relate a particular goal or criterion with possible courses of action, the criterion will be called *operational*. Otherwise the criterion will be called nonoperational. This distinction has already been made in discussing the effects of organizational reward systems.

For some purposes we will need to make the further distinction between cases where means-end relations can be evaluated prior to action, and those where they can be evaluated only after the fact. We will call operational goals in the former case *operational ex ante*, in the latter case *operational ex post*.

The goal of "promoting the general welfare" is frequently a part of the definition of the situation in governmental policy-making. It is a nonoperational goal because it does not provide (either *ex ante* or *ex post*) a measuring rod for comparing alternative policies, but can only be related to specific actions through the intervention of subgoals. These subgoals, whose connection with the broader "general welfare" goal is postulated but not testable, become the operational goals in the actual choice situation. (Speaking strictly, whether a goal is operational or nonoperational is not a yes-no question. There are all degrees of "operationality." It will often be convenient, however, to refer simply to the two ends of the continuum.)

An important circumstance causing the substitution of subgoals for more general goals as criteria of decision is that the former are perceived as operational, the latter as nonoperational. For example, a business firm may understand to some degree how its specific actions affect its share of market, but may understand less surely how its actions affect long-range profits. Then the subgoal of maintaining a particular share of market may become the effective criterion of action—the operational goal.

The distinction between operational and nonoperational goals, combined with the generalization that behavior in organizations is intendedly rational, leads to the consideration of two qualitatively different decision-making processes associated with these two kinds of goals. When a number of persons are participating in a decision-making process, and these individuals have the same operational goals, differences in opinion about the course of action will be resolved by predominately analytic processes, i.e., by the analysis of the expected consequences of courses of action for realization of the shared goals. When either of the postulated conditions is absent from the situation (when goals are not shared, or when the shared goals are not operational and the operational subgoals are not shared), the decision will be reached by predominately bargaining processes. These are, of course, a distinction and prediction made in Chapter 5 and lead to a proposition previously suggested: Rational, analytic processes take precedence over bargaining processes to the extent that the former are feasible. The condition of feasibility is that there be shared operational goals. The proposition, while it has not been much tested, is eminently testable. The goal structure of participants in a decision-making process can be determined by observation of their interaction or by interviewing or opinion-polling techniques. Their understanding of the means-end connections, and of possible methods for testing these connections, can be ascertained in the same way. It is not difficult to code their actual interaction in such a way as to detect the amount of bargaining.

The distinction between operational and non-operational goals has been made the basis for the distinction between unitary and federal organization units (Simon, Smithburg, and Thompson, 1950, pp. 268–72). This distinction will be explored in the next chapter.

The distinction between operational and non-operational goals also serves to explain why a theory of public expenditures has never developed a richness comparable to that of the theory of public revenues. The economic approach to a theory of public expenditures would postulate some kind of "utility" or "welfare" function. A rational expenditure pattern would be one in which the marginal dollar of expenditure in each direction would make an equal marginal contribution to welfare. Although statements of this kind are encountered often enough in the literature of public finance, they are infrequently developed. The reason is that, in the absence of any basis for making the welfare maximization goal operational (because of the absence of an operational common denominator among the subgoals of governmental service), the general statement leads neither to description nor to prescription of behavior (Simon, 1943).

In the literature on organizations, identification with subgoals has generally been attributed to motivation. Hence, in an analysis of conflict among organizational units, the affective aspects of the conflict have been stressed. In the present section, we have seen that cognitive processes are extremely important in producing and reinforcing subgoal identification. Subgoals may replace broader goals as a part of the whole process of replacing a complex reality with a simplified model of reality for purposes of decision and action (Blau, 1955).

What difference does it make whether subgoal identification is motivationally or cognitively produced—whether the attachment to the subgoal has been internalized or is only indirect, through a cognitive link to some other goal? It may make very little or no difference in the short run; indeed, it may be difficult to find evidence from shortrun behavior that would distinguish between these mechanisms. But it may make a great deal of difference in the processes for changing identifications. The greater *the dependence of the identification on cognitive links* to other goals (6.19), the greater the *effectiveness of attention-directing stimuli in changing goal emphasis* (6.20) [6.20:6.19]. By the same token, where identifi-

cation depends on cognitive links, the invention of new techniques for evaluating the means-ends connections between action alternatives and goals will transform bargaining processes into processes of rational analysis. These hypotheses can be tested empirically.

The Division of Work

Insofar as tasks are highly programmed, the division of work is a problem of efficient allocation of activities among individuals and among organizational units—a version of the assignment problem. However, we need to make two distinctions that tend to be overlooked in the classical theory: First, there is a problem of specialization among individual employees, and a problem of specialization among organizational units. There is no reason to suppose that both sets of problems have the same answers or that the same general principles apply to both. Second, the division of work that is most effective for the performance of relatively programmed tasks need not be the same as that which is most effective for the performance of relatively unprogrammed tasks. In the present discussion, we shall be concerned primarily with programmed tasks; the subject of unprogrammed tasks will be reserved for the next chapter.

The economies of individual specialization arise principally from opportunities for using programs repetitively. To develop in a person the capacity to carry out a particular program requires an investment in training. In automatic operations, there is an analogous capital investment in machinery capable of carrying out the program. In the case of a computing machine, a substantial part of this investment actually consists of the cost of programming the machine for the particular operations in question. In all of these cases there are economies to be derived, *ceteris paribus*, from assigning the work so as to minimize this investment cost per unit of program execution.

Programs that are built into machines or acquired by humans usually take the form of generalized means—skills or processing capacities that can be used in executing a wide variety of tasks. Typing skill, for example, is a skill of transforming any manuscript into typewritten form, and typing occurs as a subprogram in a wide range of programs. Similarly, a drill press is a bundle of capacities for drilling holes; the program can be called into play whenever the fabrication of some product requires holes to be drilled.

This rather obvious point underlies the central problem in specializing highly programmed activities. Consider an organization that performs a large number of tasks, each consisting of the fabrication of a product. If we analyze the fabrication process into subprograms, we find that it becomes economical to arrange the work so that there will be specialized means (machines and trained employees) for performing some of these subprograms. But since a number of these specialties will be required for the manufacture of each product, we create in this way considerable interdependence and need for coordination among them. The greater the *specialization by subprograms* (6.21) (process specialization), the greater the *interdependencies among organizational subunits* (6.22) [6.22:6.21].

Interdependence does not by itself cause difficulty if the pattern of interdependence is stable and fixed. For in this case, each subprogram can be designed to take account of all the other subprograms with which it interacts. Difficulties arise only if program execution rests on contingencies that cannot be predicted perfectly in advance. In this case, coordinating activity is required to secure agreement about the estimates that will be used as the basis for action, or to provide information to each subprogram unit about the relevant activities of the others. Hence, we arrive at the proposition that the more repetitive and predictable the situation, the greater the *tolerance for interdependence* (6.23) [6.23:6.3]. Conversely, the greater the elements of variability and contingency, the greater is the burden of coordinating activities that are specialized by process (MacMahon, Millet, and Ogden, 1941).

Thus, we predict that process specialization will be carried furthest in stable environments, and that under rapidly changing circumstances specialization will be sacrificed to secure greater self-containment of separate programs. A second prediction is that organizations, in order to permit a greater degree of process specialization, will devise means for increasing stability and predictability of the environment.

Three important devices come under this heading. All of these devices may be regarded as instances of the more general practice of standardization—of reducing the infinite number of things in the world, potential and actual—to a moderate number of well-defined varieties. The greater the *standardization of the situation* (6.24), the greater the tolerance for subunit interdependencies [6.23:6.24].

The first step in almost all major manufacturing sequences that lead from natural raw materials to finished goods is refining. In steel manufacture, a complex of natural materials—ores, coke, and flux—is reduced to a relatively homogeneous, standard material—pig iron. In the natural textile industries, fibers are transformed into threads of uniform size, strength, and elasticity by carding and spinning processes. In all such cases, the complexity of subsequent manufacturing processes and their contingency on raw materials is reduced by transforming highly variable natural materials into much more homogeneous semimanufactured products. After homogeneity has been attained, subsequent steps in the manufacturing process may again produce great variety in the product—alloy steels in the first example, dyed fabrics in the second. But it is often difficult and expensive to program this subsequent elaboration unless the processing begins with a simple, homogeneous material of known properties.

A second important device for dealing with the interdependencies created by specialization is the use of interchangeable parts. When the fit of two parts is assured by setting minimum and maximum size limits, the interdependency between the units that make them is decreased and the burden of coordination partly removed.

Third, the need for coordinated timing between successive process steps is reduced by holding buffer inventories. If process A precedes process B in the manufacture of some item, then the effect of variations in the rate of process A upon process B can be largely removed by maintaining an inventory of products on which process A has been completed.

Even with such devices, the need for coordination typically remains. The most common device for securing coordination among subprograms where there is a high degree of process specialization is scheduling. A schedule is simply a plan, established in advance, that determines what tasks will be handled and when. It may have greater or less detail, greater or less precision. The *type of coordination* (6.25) used in the organization is a function of the extent to which the situation is standardized [6.25:6.24]. To the extent that contingencies arise, not anticipated in the schedule, coordination requires communication to give notice of deviations from planned or predicted conditions, or to give instructions for changes in activity to adjust to these deviations. We may label coordination based on pre-established schedules *coordination by plan*, and coordination that involves transmission of new information *coordination by feedback*. The more stable and predictable the situation, the greater the reliance on coordination by plan; the more variable and unpredictable the situation, the greater the reliance on coordination by feedback.

Insofar as coordination is programmed and the range of situations sufficiently circumscribed, we would not expect any particularly close relation between the coordinative mechanisms and the formal organizational hierarchy. That is to say, scheduling information and feedback information required for coordination are not usually communicated through hierarchical channels. Hierarchy may be important in establishing and legitimizing programs, but the communication involved in the execution of highly programmed activities does not generally follow the "lines of command" (Bakke, 1950).

In addition, from the standpoint of any particular organization, specialization and the structure of subprograms is as much sociological as it is technological. The organization depends to a great extent upon the training that employees bring to it—training acquired by apprenticeship or in schools. Hence the boundaries of specialization of individual jobs tend to be determined by the structure of trades and professions in the broader social environment.

Communication

On the basis of the foregoing analysis, we may classify the occasions for communication as follows:

1. Communication for nonprogrammed activity. This is a catchall category that will need further analysis later.
2. Communication to initiate and establish programs, including day-to-day adjustment or "coordination" of programs.
3. Communication to provide data for application of strategies (i.e., required for the execution of programs).
4. Communication to evoke programs (i.e., communications that serve as "stimuli").
5. Communication to provide information on the results of activities.

The distinction between the first two categories and the last three is the familiar distinction between communication relating to procedural matters and communication relating to substantive content.

Empirical evidence for the distinction among the last three categories was obtained from a study of the use of accounting data by operating departments in manufacturing concerns. It was found that accounting information was used at various executive levels to answer three different kinds of questions: (*a*) Problem-solving questions: Which course of action is better? This corresponds to our category 3. (*b*) Attention-directing questions: What problems shall I look into? This corresponds to category 4. (*c*) Score-card questions: How well am I (or is he) doing? This corresponds to category 5. Some of the accounting information was also used in connection with less programmed activity (Simon, (Guetzkow, Kozmetsky, and Tyndall, 1954). We will consider this point below.

Communication and Coordination. The capacity of an organization to maintain a complex, highly interdependent pattern of activity is limited in part by its capacity to handle the communication required for coordination. The greater the *efficiency of communication* (6.26) within the organization, the greater the tolerance for interdependence [6.23:6.26]. The problem has both quantitative and qualitative aspects.

As we noted earlier, it is possible under some conditions to reduce the volume of communication required from day to day by substituting coordination by plan for coordination by feedback. By virtue of this substitution, organizations can tolerate very complex interrelations among their component parts in the performance of repetitive activities. The coordination of parts is incorporated in the program when it is established, and the need for continuing communication is correspondingly reduced. Each specific situation, as it arises, is largely covered by the standard operating procedure.

A different method for increasing the organization's tolerance for interdependence is to increase the efficiency of communication by making it possible to communicate large amounts of information with relatively few symbols. An obvious example is the blueprint, which provides a common plan stated in extreme detail. The blueprint employs a carefully defined, highly developed "language" or set of symbolic and verbal conventions. Because of this standardized language, it can convey large quantities of information. The same attention to standardization of language is seen in accounting systems and other reporting systems that employ numerical data.

Accounting definitions and blueprint conventions are examples of a still more general phenomenon: technical languages, whose symbols have definite and common meanings to the members of an organization. Prominent in these technical languages are categories for classifying situations and events.

The role of unambiguous technical terms in permitting coordination by feedback is shown by the Christie-Luce-Macy experiments (Macy, Christie, and Luce, 1953) with "noisy marbles" in the Bavelas network. Participants in the experiment were given some colored marbles, and they were required to discover what color was held by all of them. Control groups were given marbles that had solid colors like "red," "yellow," etc. Experimental groups were given streaked marbles whose colorings did not correspond in any simple way to color designations in common language. Comparison of the performance of the control with the experimental groups showed (a) that the latter were much hindered by the lack of adequate technical vocabulary, and (b) that their performance became comparable to that of the control groups only when they succeeded in inventing such a vocabulary and securing its acceptance throughout the group.

Classification schemes are of particular significance for the program-evoking aspects of communication. When an event occurs that calls for some kind of organization response, the question is asked, in one form or other: "What *kind* of event is this?" The organization has available a repertory of programs, so that once the event has been classified the appropriate program can be executed without further ado. We can make this process more specific with a pair of examples.

The oil gauge on the dashboard of an automobile is an example of the use of classification in program-evoking. For most drivers, the oil pressure is either "all right" or "low." In the first case, no action is taken; in the second case a remedial program is initiated (e.g., taking the automobile to a repair shop). Some auto manufacturers have substituted a red light, which turns on when the oil pressure is not in the proper range, for the traditional gauge. This example also illustrates how substituting standards of satisfactory performance for criteria or optimization simplifies communication.

Similarly, inspection activities often involve dichotomous decisions. In these cases, the choice is not usually between evoking a program or not evoking one (action or inaction), but between different programs. Thus, if the item being inspected meets the standards, one program is evoked (it is passed on for further processing); if it fails to meet standards, another program is evoked (scrapping, or reworking, as the case may be).

One reason that classifying is so economical of communication is that most of the coordination can be preprogrammed; the organization has a repertory of responses to stimuli, and it only needs to know what kind of stimulus it is confronted with in order to execute an elaborate program. On the other hand, if the communication system could handle a more complete description of the program-evoking event, and if the action part of the organization had the capacity to develop programs on the spot to meet present needs, no doubt one could conceive tailor-made programs that would be more accurately adapted to each separate situation than are the preprogrammed responses.

Here again the normative or adaptive problem of organization design is one of balance. If its model of reality is not to be so complex as to paralyze it, the organization must develop radical simplifications of its responses. One such simplification is to have (a) a repertory of standard responses, (b) a classification of program-evoking situations, (c) a set of rules to determine what is the appropriate response for each class of situations. The balance of economies and efficiencies here is exactly the same as it is in all cases of standardization. Note that what we have described in an organizational framework is quite comparable to discrimination learning in individuals. In the individual case, as in the organizational, there is a close relationship between the categories used in the cognitive code and the operational decision rules (Whorf, 1956).

In our culture, language is well developed for describing and communicating about concrete objects. The blueprint has already been mentioned as an important technical device for this purpose. Language is also very effective in communicating about things that can be classified and named, even if they are intangible. Thus, when there are standard repertories of programs, it is easy to refer to them.

On the other hand, it is extremely difficult to communicate about intangible objects and nonstandardized objects. Hence, the heaviest burdens are placed on the communications system by the less structured aspects of the organization's tasks, particularly by activity directed toward the explanation of problems that are not yet well defined. We shall see in the next chapter that this difference in communication difficulty has important implications for the organization of nonprogrammed activities.

Where the available means of communication are primitive—relative to the communication needs—so will be the system of coordination. There will tend to be less self-containment of organizational units and a greater reliance on coordination through communication the greater the efficiency of communication [6.12:6.26]. This relation may sometimes be obscured by the fact that pressure toward coordination (e.g., under conditions of rapid change) may compel attempts at feedback coordination even though available communication is inefficient. It should also be noted that self-containment decreases and interdependencies increase the likelihood of developing an efficient communication code [6.26:6.21].

The Absorption of Uncertainty. The use of classification schemes in communication has further consequences, some of which go back to our earlier discussion of perception and identification. The technical vocabulary and classification schemes in an organization provide a set of concepts that can be used in analyzing and in communicating about its prob-

lems. Anything that is easily described and discussed in terms of these concepts can be communicated readily in the organization; anything that does not fit the system of concepts is communicated only with difficulty. Hence, the world tends to be perceived by the organizations members in terms of the particular concepts that are reflected in the organization's vocabulary. The particular categories and schemes of classification it employs are reified, and become, for members of the organization, attributes of the world rather than mere conventions (Blau, 1955).

The reification of the organization's conceptual scheme is particularly noticeable in *uncertainty absorption* (6.27). Uncertainty absorption takes place when inferences are drawn from a body of evidence and the inferences, instead of the evidence itself, are then communicated. The successive editing steps that transform data obtained from a set of questionnaires into printed statistical tables provide a simple example of uncertainty absorption.

Through the process of uncertainty absorption, the recipient of a communication is severely limited in his ability to judge its correctness. Although there may be various tests of apparent validity, internal consistency, and consistency with other communications, the recipient must, by and large, repose his confidence in the editing process that has taken place, and, if he accepts the communication at all, accept it pretty much as it stands. To the extent that he can interpret it, his interpretation must be based primarily on his confidence in the source and his knowledge of the biases to which the source is subject, rather than on a direct examination of the evidence.

By virtue of specialization, most information enters an organization at highly specific points. Direct perception of production processes is limited largely to employees in a particular operation on the production floor. Direct perception of customer attitudes is limited largely to salesmen. Direct evidence of the performance of personnel is restricted largely to immediate supervisors, colleagues, and subordinates.

In all of these cases, the person who summarizes and assesses his own direct perceptions and transmits them to the rest of the organization becomes an important source of informational premises for organizational action. The "facts" he communicates can be disbelieved, but they can only rarely be checked. Hence, by the very nature and limits of the communication system, a great deal of discretion and influence is exercised by those persons who are in direct contact with some part of the "reality" that is of concern to the organization. Both the amount and the *locus of uncertainty absorption* (6.28) affect the *influence structure of the organization* (6.29) [6.29:6.27,6.28].

Because of this, uncertainty absorption is frequently used, consciously and unconsciously, as a technique for acquiring and exercising power. In a culture where direct contradiction of assertions of fact is not approved, an individual who is willing to make assertions, particularly about matters that do not contradict the direct perceptions of others, can frequently get these assertions accepted as premises of decision.

We can cite a number of more or less "obvious" variables that affect the absorption of uncertainty. The more complex the data that are perceived and the less adequate the organization's language, the closer to the source of the information will the uncertainty absorption take place, and the greater will be the amount of summarizing at each step of transmission. The locus of absorption will tend to be a function of such variables as: (*a*) the needs of the recipient for raw as against summarized information (depending upon the kinds of data used in selecting the appropriate program), (*b*) the need for correction of biases in the transmitter, (*c*) the distribution of technical competence for interpreting and summarizing raw data, and (*d*) the need for comparing data from two or more sources in order to interpret it.

The way in which uncertainty is absorbed has important consequences for coordination among organizational units. In business organizations, expected sales are relevant to decisions in many parts of the organization: purchasing decisions, production decisions, investment decisions, and many others. But if each organizational unit were permitted to make its own forecast of sales, there might be a wide range of such estimates with consequent inconsistencies among the decisions made by different departments—the purchasing department, for example, buying raw materials that the production department does not expect to process. It may be important in cases of this kind to make an *official* forecast and to use this official

forecast as the basis for action throughout the organization.

Where it is important that all parts of an organization act on the same premises, and where different individuals may draw different conclusions from the raw evidence, a formal uncertainty absorption point will be established, and the inferences drawn at that point will have official status in the organization as "legitimate" estimates. The greater the need for coordination in the organization, the greater the *use of legitimized "facts"* (6.30) [6.30:6.8, 6.9].

The Communication Network. Associated with each program is a set of information flows that communicate the stimuli and data required to evoke and execute the program. Generally this communication traverses definite channels, either by formal plan or by the gradual development of informal programs. Information and stimuli move from sources to points of decision; instructions move from points of decision to points of action; information of results moves from points of action to points of decision and control.

Rational organization design would call for the arrangement of these channels so as to minimize the communication burden. But insofar as the points of origin of information and the points of action are determined in advance, the only mobile element is the point of decision. Whatever may be the position in the organization holding the formal authority to legitimize the decision, to a considerable extent the effective discretion is exercised at the points of uncertainty absorption.

In large organizations, specialization of communication functions will be reflected in the division of work itself. Among the specialized communication units we find are (*a*) units specializing in the actual physical transmission of communications: a telephone and teletype unit, messenger group, or the like: (*b*) units specializing in recording and report preparation: bookkeeping and other record-keeping units; (*c*) units specializing in the acquisition of raw information, usually referred to as intelligence units, sometimes as research units; (*d*) units specializing in the provision of technical premises for decision: research units, technical specialists; (*e*) units specializing in the interpretation of policy and organizational goals, a function usually not much separated from the main stem of the hierarchy; and (*f*) units specializing in the retention of information: files, archives units [A-6.25].

In part, communication channels are deliberately and consciously planned in the course of programming. In part, they develop through usage. We will make two hypotheses about such development. First, the greater the communication efficiency of the channel, the greater the *communication channel usage* (6.31) [6.31:6.26]. The possession by two persons, or two organization units, of a common, efficient language facilitates communication. Thus, links between members of a common profession tend to be used in the communication system. Similarly, other determinants of language compatibility—ethnic background, education, age, experience—will affect what channels are used in the organization.

Second, channel usage tends to be self-reinforcing [6.31:6.31]. When a channel is frequently used for one purpose, its use for other unrelated purposes is encouraged. In particular, formal hierarchical channels tend to become general-purpose channels to be used whenever no special-purpose channel or informal channel exists or is known to the communicator. The self-reinforcing character of channel usage is particularly strong if it brings individuals into face-to-face contact. In this case (the Homans hypothesis) informal communication, much of it social in character, develops side-by-side with task-oriented formal communication, and the use of the channel for either kind of communication tends to reinforce its use for the other.

In part, the communication network is planned; in part, it grows up in response to the need for specific kinds of communication; in part, it develops in response to the social functions of communication. At any given stage in its development, its gradual change is much influenced by the pattern that has already become established. Hence, although the structure of the network will be considerably influenced by the structure of the organization's task, it will not be completely determined by the latter.

Once a pattern of communication channels has become established, this pattern will have an important influence on decision-making processes, and particularly upon nonprogrammed activity. We may anticipate some of the analysis of the next chapter by indicating briefly the nature of this influence.

The existing pattern of communication will determine the relative frequency with which particular members of the organization will encounter particular stimuli, or kinds of stimuli, in their search processes [6.11:6.31]. For example, a research and development unit that has frequent communication with sales engineers and infrequent communication with persons engaged in fundamental research will live in a different environment of new product ideas than a research and development unit that has the opposite communication pattern.

The communication pattern will determine how frequently and forcefully particular consequences of action are brought to the attention of the actor. The degree of specialization, for example, between design engineers, on the one hand, and installation and service engineers, on the other, will have an important influence on the amount of awareness of the former as to the effectiveness of their designs.

From our previous propositions concerning time pressure effects, we would predict that the pattern of communication would have a greater influence on nonprogrammed activities carried out with deadlines and under time pressure than upon activities that involve relatively slow and deliberate processes of decision. For, given sufficient time, if particular information is available anywhere in an organization, its relevance to any particular decision is likely to be noticed. Where decisions are made relatively rapidly, however, only the information that is locally available is likely to be brought to bear. We see here another reason why specialization (in this case specialization with respect to possession of information) is tolerated to a greater degree under "steady-state" conditions than when the organization is adapting to a rapidly changing environment.

Organization Structure and the Boundaries of Rationality

It has been the central theme of this chapter that the basic features of organization structure and function derive from the characteristics of human problem-solving processes and rational human choice. Because of the limits of human intellective capacities in comparison with the complexities of the problems that individuals and organizations face, rational behavior calls for simplified models that capture the main features of a problem without capturing all its complexities.

The simplifications have a number of characteristic features: (1) Optimizing is replaced by satisficing—the requirement that satisfactory levels of the criterion variables be attained. (2) Alternatives of action and consequences of action are discovered sequentially through search processes. (3) Repertories of action programs are developed by organizations and individuals, and these serve as the alternatives of choice in recurrent situations. (4) Each specific action program deals with a restricted range of situations and a restricted range of consequences. (5) Each action program is capable of being executed in semi-independence of the others—they are only loosely coupled together.

Action is goal-oriented and adaptive. But because of its approximating and fragmented character, only a few elements of the system are adaptive at any one time; the remainder are, at least in the short run, "givens." So, for example, an individual or organization may attend to improving a particular program, or to selecting an appropriate program from the existing repertory to meet a particular situation. Seldom can both be attended to simultaneously.

The notion that rational behavior deals with a few components at a time was first developed extensively in connection with economic behavior by John R. Commons, who spoke of "limiting factors" that become the foci of attention and adaptation. Commons' theory was further developed by Chester I. Barnard, who preferred the term "strategic factor."

This "one-thing-at-a-time" or "ceteris paribus" approach to adaptive behavior is fundamental to the very existence of something we can call "organization structure." Organization structure consists simply of those aspects of the pattern of behavior in the organization that are relatively stable and that change only slowly. If behavior in organizations is "intendedly rational," we will expect aspects of the behavior to be relatively stable that either (a) represent adaptations to relatively stable elements in the environment, or

(b) are the learning programs that govern the process of adaptation.

An organization is confronted with a problem like that of Archimedes: in order for an organization to behave adaptively, it needs some stable regulations and procedures that it can employ in carrying out its adaptive practices. Thus, at any given time an organization's programs for performing its tasks are part of its structure, but the least stable part. Slightly more stable are the switching rules that determine when it will apply one program, and when another. Still more stable are the procedures it uses for developing, elaborating, instituting, and revising programs.

The matter may be stated differently. If an organization has a repertory of programs, then it is adaptive in the short run insofar as it has procedures for selecting from this repertory a program appropriate to each specific situation that arises. The process used to select an appropriate program is the "fulcrum" on which short-run adaptiveness rests. If, now, the organization has processes for adding to its repertory of programs or for modifying programs in the repertory, these processes become still more basic fulcra for accomplishing longer-run adaptiveness. Short-run adaptiveness corresponds to what we ordinarily call problem-solving, long-run adaptiveness to learning.

There is no reason, of course, why this hierarchy of mechanisms should have only three levels—or any specified number. In fact, the adaptive mechanisms need not be arranged hierarchically. Mechanism A may include mechanism B wthin its domain of action, and vice versa. However, in general there is much asymmetry in the ordering, so that certain elements in the process that do not often become strategic factors (the "boundaries of rationality") form the stable core of the organization structure.

We can now see the relation between Commons' and Barnard's theories of the "limiting" or "strategic" factor and organization structure. Organization will have structure, as we have defined the term here, insofar as there are boundaries of rationality—insofar as there are elements of the situation that must be or are in fact taken as givens, and that do not enter into rational calculations as potential strategic factors. If there were not boundaries to rationality, or if the boundaries varied in a rapid and unpredictable manner, there could be no stable organization structure. Some aspects of structure will be more easily modified than others, and hence we may need to distinguish short-run and long-run structure.

In this chapter, we have been concerned mostly with short-run structure—with programs to respond to sequences of situations requiring adaptive action. The "boundaries of rationality" that have been the source of our propositions have consisted primarily of the properties of human beings as organisms capable of evoking and executing relatively well-defined programs but able to handle programs only of limited complexity.

In the next chapter, we will shift our attention to long-run considerations, and particularly to the processes in organizations that bring programs into existence and that modify them.

REFERENCES

Blau, P. M. *The Dynamics of Bureaucracy.* Chicago, 1955.

Cyert, R. M., and J. G. March. Organizational structure and pricing behavior in an oligopolistic market. *American Economic Review,* 1955, **45**, 129–139.

Cyert, R. M., and J. G. March. Organizational factors in the theory of oligopoly. *Quarterly Journal of Economics,* 1956, **70**, 44–64.

Dearborn, D. C., and H. A. Simon. Selective perception: a note on the departmental identifications of executives. *Sociometry,* 1958, **21**, 140–144.

Gore, W. G., Administrative decision-making in federal field offices. *Public Administration Review,* 1956, **16**, 281–291.

Guetzkow, H., and H. A. Simon. The impact of certain communication nets upon organization and performance in task-oriented groups. *Management Science,* 1955, **1**, 233–250.

Katona, G. *Psychological Analysis of Economic Behavior.* New York, 1951.

Levin, H. S. *Office Work and Automation.* New York, 1956.

MacMahon, A. W., J. D. Millett, and G. Ogden. *The Administration of Federal Work Relief.* Chicago, 1941.

Macy, J., Jr., L. S. Christie, and R. D. Luce. Coding noise in a task-oriented group. *Journal of Abnormal and Social Psychology,* 1953, **48**, 401–409.

March, J. G. An introduction to the theory and measurement of influence. *American Political Science Review,* 1955a, **49**, 431–451.

Marschak, J. Rational behavior, uncertain prospects, and measurable utility. *Econometrica.* 1950, **18**, 111–141.

Newell, A., J. C. Shaw, and H. A. Simon. Elements of a theory of human problem solving. *Psychological Review,* 1958, **65**, 151–166.

Ridley, C. E., and H. A. Simon. *Measuring Municipal Activities.* Chicago, 1938.

Simon, H. A. *Fiscal Aspects of Metropolitan Consolidation.* Berkeley, Calif., 1943.

———. *Administrative Behavior.* New York, 1947.

———. Birth of an organization: the economic cooperation administration. *Public Administration Review,* 1953b, **13**, 227–236.

——— A behavioral model of rational choice. *Quarterly Journal of Economics,* 1955, **69**, 99–118.

———, G. Kozmetsky, and G. Tyndall. *Centralization vs Decentralization in Organizing the Controller's Department.* New York, The Controllership Foundation, 1954.

Simon, H. A., D. W. Smithburg, and V. A. Thompson. *Public Administration.* New York, 1950.

Whorf, B. L. *Language, Thought, and Reality.* New York, 1956.

Strategic Leniency and Authority

PETER M. BLAU

A psychological explanation of the failure to enforce strict discipline among subordinates might attribute it to poor leadership. Some supervisors are overly lenient, it could be held, because inborn or acquired personality traits prevent them from asserting their authority over others and maintaining effective leadership. Note that this explanation assumes as a matter of course that the bureaucratic superior who appears lenient merely indulges his subordinates and is less effective than the disciplinarian in discharging his supervisory responsibilities. Empirical evidence, however, indicates that the very opposite is the case.

A study of twenty-four clerical sections in an insurance company analyzed the relationship between method of supervision and productive efficiency.[1] In closely supervised sections, whose heads gave clerks detailed instructions and frequently checked up on them, productivity was usually lower than in sections where employees were given more freedom to do the work in their own way. Moreover, supervisors who were primarily concerned with maintaining a high level of production, interestingly enough, were less successful in meeting this goal than those supervisors who were more interested in the welfare of their subordinates than in sheer production; in the latter case,

productivity was generally higher. Finally, groups who worked under more authoritarian supervisors were, on the whole, less productive than those supervised in a relatively democratic fashion. Other studies have also found that disciplinarian supervisors are less effective than more liberal ones.[2]

Such findings are often misinterpreted as signifying that democratic ways are superior to authoritarian ones. But this is a rather loose use of the term "democratic," the exact meaning of which is worth preserving. Since "democracy" denotes rule from below (literally, "people's rule") and not from above, one person's supervision of others can, by definition, not be democratic. This is not the place for a discussion of the relation between democracy and bureaucracy; the final chapter is reserved for this purpose. But here it should be noted that tolerant supervisory practices, in contrast to disciplinarian ones, are neither democratic nor an indication that controlling power over subordinates has been surrendered. On the contrary, leniency in supervision is a potent strategy, consciously or unconsciously employed, for establishing authority over subordinates, and this is why the liberal supervisor is particularly effective.

Let us clarify the concept of authority. First, it refers to a relationship between persons and not to an attribute of one individual. Second, authority involves exercise of social control which rests on the *willing* compliance of subordinates with certain directives of the superior. He need not coerce or persuade sub-

---

From *Bureaucracy in Modern Society*. New York: Random House, 1956, pp. 70–79. Copyright 1956 by Random House. Reprinted with permission of the publisher.
[1] Daniel Katz, Nathan MacCoby, and Nancy C. Morse, *Productivity, Supervision and Morale in an Office Situation*. Ann Arbor: Institute for Social Research, University of Michigan, 1950, especially pp. 17, 21, 29.

[2] See for instance, F. J. Roethlisberger and William J. Dickson, *Management and the Worker*. Cambridge: Harvard University Press, 1946, pp. 452–53.

ordinates in order to influence them, because they have accepted as legitimate the principle that some of their actions should be governed by his decisions. Third, authority is an observable pattern of interaction and not an official definition of a social relationship. If a mutinous crew refuses to obey the captain's orders, he does not in fact have authority over his men. Whatever the superior's official rights to command obedience and the subordinates' official duties to obey him, his authority over them extends only to conduct that they voluntarily permit to be governed by his directives. Actual authority, consequently, is not granted by the formal organizational chart, but must be established in the course of social interaction, although the official bureaucratic structure, as we shall see presently, facilitates its establishment.

What are some of the practices of a lenient foreman or supervisor? Above all, he allows subordinates to violate minor rules, to smoke or talk, for example, despite the fact that it is prohibited by management. This permissiveness often increases his power over them by furnishing him with legitimate sanctions that he can use as he sees fit. If an action of his subordinates displease him, the supervisor can punish them by commanding: "Cut out the smoking! Can't you read the sign?" Had he always enforced the rule, this penalty would not have been available to him. Indeed, so crude a use of sanctions is rarely necessary. The mere knowledge that the rule exists and, possibly, that it is enforced elsewhere, instills a sense of obligation to liberal superiors and induces subordinates more readily to comply with their requests.

Whereas the disciplinarian supervisor generally asserts his official prerogatives, the lenient and relaxed one does not. The latter attempts to take the wishes of his subordinates into account in arranging their work schedule, although he has the right to assign their work at his own discretion. Sometimes he goes to special trouble to accommodate a subordinate. Instead of issuing curt commands, he usually explains the reasons for his directives. He calls his subordinates by their first names and encourages their use of his first name (especially in democratically minded American organizations). When one of his subordinates gets into difficulties with management, he is apt to speak up for him and to defend him. These

different actions have two things in common: the superior is not required to do them, and his subordinates greatly welcome his doing them. Such conduct therefore creates social obligations. To repay the supervisor for past favors, and not to risk the cessation of similar favors in the future, subordinates voluntarily comply with many of his requests, including some they are not officially required to obey. By refraining from exercising his power of control whenever it is legitimate to do so, the bureaucratic superior establishes effective authority over subordinates, which enables him to control them much more effectively than otherwise would be possible.

Complementary role expectations arise in the course of interaction between superior and subordinates and become crystallized in the course of interaction among subordinates. As the superior permits subordinates to violate some rules and to make certain decisions themselves, and as they grow accustomed to conform with many of his directives, they learn to expect to exercise discretion in some areas and to follow supervisory directives in others, and he learns to expect this pattern of conduct from them. The members of the work group, by watching one another at work and talking among themselves about the manner in which they perform their duties, develop social consensus about these role expectations and thereby reinforce them. The newcomer to the group, who must be taught "how things are done around here" as distinguished from "what's in the book," provides an opportunity for further affirming this consensus by making it explicit.

The resulting common role expectations are often so fully internalized that employees are hardly aware of being governed by them. The members of one department might find it natural for their supervisor to interrupt their work and tell them to start on a new task. The members of another department in the same organization might consider such a supervisory order as gross interference with their work, since they had become accustomed to using their discretion about the sequence of their tasks, yet readily comply with other directives of the supervision. These role expectations of independence from the supervisor in some areas and unquestioning obedience in others define the limits of his authority over subordinates.

POWER OF SANCTION. The preceding comments apply to informal leadership as well as to bureaucratic authority. The informal leader, like the prudent bureaucratic superior, establishes his authority over his followers by creating social obligations.[3] Once a relationship of authority exists, both bureaucratic superior and informal leader can afford to word their orders as mere suggestions, because even these are readily followed by the rest of the group. Neither of them usually needs sanctions to command obedience, though sanctions are available to both of them in case they wish to use special inducements, since praise or blame of the person in the superordinate position itself exerts a powerful influence.

Nevertheless, there is a fundamental distinction between informal leadership and bureaucratic authority. Informal leadership freely emerges among a group of peers. It is initially the result of personality differences that have become socially magnified. Some members of the group excel in activities that are highly valued by all, whether these are street fighting or solving complex problems; these few will be more respected, and their opinions will carry greater weight. The person in the extreme position, if he also finds ways to obligate the others to him, is expected to be the group's leader.

Bureaucratic authority, on the other hand, prevents the group itself from conferring the position of leadership upon the member of their choice. The voluntary obedience of subordinates must converge upon the individual officially placed in the position of supervisor, irrespective of his personal characteristics. The bureaucratic mechanism that makes this state of affairs a predictable occurrence is the superior's power to impose sanctions, typically in the form of periodic ratings of the performance of his subordinates, which influence their chances of advancement and of keeping their jobs.

The dependency of bureaucratic subordinates upon their immediate superior produced by his rating power engenders frustrations and anxieties for adults. It forces employees to worry about their supervisor's reaction at

every step they take. An effective way to weaken or avoid such feelings is to identify with the bureaucratic system of normative standards and objectives. By making this system a part of their own thinking, employees transform conformity with its principles from submission to the superior's demands into voluntary action. Guided by internalized standards, they are less likely to experience external restraints in performing their duties. Moreover, once the hierarchical division of responsibility has been accepted as a basic principle of the organization, it becomes less threatening to a person's self-esteem to obey the supervisor's directives, since he is known to be duty-bound to issue them, just as it is not degrading to obey the traffic directions of a policeman. Dependence on the superior's rating encourages the adoption of a bureaucratic orientation, for the disadvantages of dependence can thereby be evaded.

It is of crucial importance that this process of identification with bureaucratic standards does not occur in isolation but in a social situation. All members of the work group find themselves in the same position of dependence on their supervisor. (In fact, all members of the bureaucratic organization are, in varying degrees, dependent on their immediate superiors.) Together, they can obtain concessions from the supervisor, because he is anxious to obligate them by granting some of their demands. In exchange, they feel constrained to comply with many of his directives. Typically, a strict definition is given to the limits of this effective authority. Subordinates can often be heard to remark: "That's the supervisor's responsibility. He gets paid for making those decisions." This does not mean that operating employees shirk responsibilities, as indicated by their willingness to shoulder those they define as their own. But the social agreement among the members of the work group that making certain decisions and issuing certain directives is the duty of the supervisor, not merely his privilege, serves to emphasize that following them does not constitute submission to his arbitrary will but conformity with commonly accepted operating principles. In such a situation, which prevails in some organizations though by no means in all, subordinates do not experience the supervisor's exercise of authority over them as domination; neither are they necessarily envious of his responsibilities, since

[3] For a clear illustration of this point in a street corner gang, see William F. Whyte, *Street Corner Society*. Chicago: University of Chicago Press, 1943, pp. 257–262.

they frequently consider their own more challenging than his.

The effective establishment of authority obviates the need for sanctions in daily operations. If a supervisor commands the voluntary obedience of subordinates, he need not induce them to obey him by promising them rewards or threatening them with punishment. In fact, the use of sanctions undermines authority. A supervisor who is in the habit of invoking sanctions to back his orders—"You won't get a good rating unless you do this!"—shows that he does not expect unqualified compliance. As subordinates learn that he does not expect it, they will no longer feel obligated unconditionally to accept his directives. Moreover, employees resent being continually reminded of their dependence on the supervisor by his promises and threats, and such resentment makes them less inclined to carry out his orders.

This is the dilemma of bureaucratic authority: it rests on the power of sanction but is weakened by frequent resort to sanctions in operations. A basic difference, however, should be noted between the periodic rating of the performance of subordinates, which can be called a *diffuse sanction,* and *specific sanctions* recurrently employed to enforce particular commands. Since all employees know that their immediate superior is officially required to evaluate their operations at periodic intervals, this evaluation is neither a sign that he does not expect unqualified compliance with his directives nor a reason for annoyance with him. This diffuse sanction, imposed only annually or every few months, though creating the dependence of subordinates upon their supervisor, does so without constantly endangering their willingness to be guided by his requests, as the habitual use of specific sanctions (including promises of good ratings and threats of poor ones) would.

While the mere fact that the supervisor administers ratings is not resented by his subordinates, low ratings might well antagonize some of them. But bureaucratic mechanisms exist that enable the supervisor to shift the blame for negative sanctions. For example, statistical records of performance, which are kept in many white-collar offices as well as factories, furnish the supervisor with objective evidence with which he can justify low ratings by showing the recipients that the poor quality

of their work left him no other choice. Instead of blaming the supervisor for giving them a poor rating, these employees are forced to blame themselves or to attribute the rating to the "statistics," which are often accused, rightly or wrongly, of failing to measure the qualitative aspects of performance.*

His intermediate position in the hierarchy provides the supervisor with another justification mechanism. He can place the responsibility for giving low ratings or instituting unpopular requirements on his superiors, to whom he is accountable. Oftentimes a supervisor or foreman will tell his subordinates that he does not like certain standards any better than they do but "those brass-hats in the front office" insist on them. In most organizations, one or a few superintendents or assistant managers (or deans) become the scapegoats who are blamed for all negative sanctions and unpopular requirements. Since the attitudes of employees toward these administrators in removed positions is much less relevant for effective operations than their attitudes toward their immediate superior, the displacement of aggression from him to them is in the interest of the organization. Clients or customers can also serve as scapegoats of aggression—the supervisor can blame their demands for instituting procedures that inconvenience employees. And if he joins subordinates in ridiculing clients or customers, a frequent practice in service occupations, the supervisor further reduces antagonism against himself by standing united with the employees against outsiders.

Periodic ratings, then, increase the dependency of the members of a bureaucracy on their superiors but at the same time allow them to escape from disturbing feelings of dependency by internalizing the principles that govern operations. Although the responsibilities the supervisor is required to discharge occasionally arouse the animosity of some subordinates, various mechanisms divert such antagonism from the supervisor to other objects. These two elements of the bureaucratic structure conspire to provide a fertile soil for the establishment of supervisory authority. Together, they permit supervisors to obligate subordinates willingly to follow directives.

Various circumstances, however, can prevent

---

* Of course, quantitative records also facilitate the supervisor's task of evaluating operations.

such favorable conditions in the bureaucratic organization. The disciplinarian supervisor may antagonize subordinates, through recurrent use of sanctions and in other ways, and thereby undermine his effective authority over them as well as their motivation to put effort into their work. The lenient supervisor may be so reluctant to displease subordinates that he refrains from evaluating their performance in accordance with rigorous standards, giving all of them high ratings. This practice invalidates the incentive system, which enhances the interest of employees in accomplishing specified results in their operations. The manipulative supervisor may employ devious techniques to conceal from subordinates his attempts to impose his arbitrary will upon them, for example, by frequent and unwarranted utilization of scapegoats. While manipulative techniques have a fair chance of being successful in temporary pair relationships, as between customer and salesman, their chances of success in relatively permanent relationships within a group are very slim. For sooner or later, some member is apt to see through them, and he is not likely to keep this a secret. Once they are discovered, manipulative techniques have a boomerang effect. Employees who realize that their superior tries to manipulate them are prone to suspect all of his statements and generally to resist his efforts to influence their performance.

These and other disruptive tendencies can be observed in hierarchical organizations, but methods of supervision that encourage operating efficiency are also evident. In the absence of a much larger body of information about bureaucracies than we now possess, it is impossible to know which of these opposite conditions is more frequent. Nevertheless, the fact that authority is sometimes effectively exercised without domineering subordinates or lowering their morale, rare as this may be, demonstrates that such a state of affairs is actually possible and not merely a utopian ideal type.

About the Functions of Bureaucratic Rules

ALVIN W. GOULDNER

Wherever bureaucratic patterns are found to be relatively entrenched, it must be assumed that their "career" has resulted in a net balance of gains greater than that of the losses, though it would be foolhardy to assume that there had been *no* losses at all. Above all, this means that the *consequences* which are brought about by bureaucratic methods of administration must be examined if their *survival* is to be understood. Here the problem is not one of motives or opportunities, or intentions and powers; it is rather a question of the practical results which sustain bureaucratic patterns once initiated. In fine, the questions are: What gains were secured by bureaucratic procedures; what problems were actually mitigated; what tensions were eased by their use?

The Problem of "Close Supervision"

The problem may be opened by reviewing a point touched upon before: If a supervisor viewed a worker as unmotivated, as unwilling to "do a job," how did the supervisor respond; how did he attempt to solve this problem? He usually attempted to handle this by directing the worker more closely, by watching him carefully, and explicitly outlining his work obligations. As one foreman said: "If I catch a man goofing off, I tell him in an a,b,c, way exactly what he has to do, and I watch him like a hawk 'til he's done it." This was precisely what Peele did when he first entered the plant as manager and found that the workers were resisting him.[1]

From *Patterns of Industrial Bureaucracy*. Glencoe: Free Press, 1954, pp. 157–180. Reprinted with permission of the publisher.
[1] Students of industrial behavior will at once note

At first glance this might appear to be a stable solution; it might seem as if "close supervision" would allow the supervisor to bring the problem under control. Actually, however, there were commanding reasons why supervisors could not rest content to supervise their workers closely and to remind them endlessly of what had to be done. One motive was fairly obvious: The supervisor could not watch all of his men all of the time. As a surface fore-

that we have been led back to the lair of a hoary problem whose origins, however indeterminate, have a certifiable antiquity. John Stuart Mill, for example, had long since observed the connections between "close supervision" and the managerial estimate of workers' motivation to work: "The moral qualities of the laborers are fully as important to the efficiency and worth of their labor as the intellectual . . . it is well worthy of meditation, how much of the aggregate of their labor depends upon their trustworthiness. All the labor now expended in watching that they fulfill their engagement, or in verifying that they have fulfilled it, is so much withdrawn from the real business of production to be devoted to a subsidiary function rendered needful not by the necessity of things but by the dishonesty of men. Nor are the greatest precautions more than very imperfectly efficacious, where, as is now almost invariably the case with hired laborers, *the slightest relaxation of vigilance is an opportunity eagerly seized for eluding performance of their contract.*" (Our emphasis—A. W. G.) Longmans, Green and Co., Ltd., London, 1926 edition, pp. 110–111. More recently, the problem of "close supervision" has been given careful attention at the University of Michigan. One of the most theoretically sophisticated accounts of this work is to be found in Daniel Katz and Robert Kahn, "Human Organization and Worker Motivation," in *Industrial Productivity*, edited by L. Reed Tripp, Industrial Relations Research Association, Madison, Wisconsin, 1951, pp. 146–171.

man remarked, "As soon as I turn my back on some of these guys, they slip me the knife."

There is, though, one basis on which the supervisor could feel confident that workers would do their jobs even when he was *not* around; that is, if the supervisors believed that workers themselves wanted to do what was expected of them. As John Stuart Mill remarked in this connection, "Nor are the greatest *outward* precautions comparable in efficacy to the monitor *within*." [2] Indeed, it may be suspected that this was *one* of the factors alerting management to the problem of the worker's motivation; for a motivated worker made the job of supervision earlier.

There is, however, another consideration that made "close supervision" a dangerous solution to the problem of the unmotivated worker. Specifically, workers viewed close supervision as a kind of "strictness" and punishment. In consequence, the more a supervisor watched his subordinates, the more hostile they became to him. Workers shared standardized conceptions of what a "good" or legitimate foreman should be like, and almost universally, these insisted that the good foreman was one who "doesn't look over your shoulder." From the workers' standpoint a "driving" foreman was "bad," and they would retaliate by withholding work effort. As a hopper worker asserted:

> If the foreman doesn't work well with us, we don't give him as good work as we can . . . I just don't care, I let things slide.

In other words, close supervision enmeshed management in a vicious cycle: the supervisor perceived the worker as unmotivated; he then carefully watched and directed him; this aroused the worker's ire and accentuated his apathy, and now the supervisor was back where he began. Close supervision did not solve his problem. In fact, it might make the worker's performance, in the super's absence, even less reliable than it had been.

Must it be supposed, however, that "close supervision" *invariably* corrodes the relationship between the worker and his superior? Does it do so under any and all conditions? What is there *about* close supervision which

disturbs relations between workers and supers? To consider the last question first: Notice that close supervision entails an intensification of *face-to-face* direction of the worker. In such a context, it becomes very *evident* exactly "who is boss." This, in turn, suggests one of the distinctive conditions which underpin the strains induced by close supervision; for ours is a culture in which great stress is placed upon the *equality* of persons, and in such a cultural context *visible* differences in power and privilege readily become sources of tension, particularly so if status differences do not correspond with traditionally prized attributes such as skill, experience, or seniority.

Close supervision violated norms of equality internalized by workers, and they responded by complaining that the supervisor was "just trying to *show* who is boss." Workers' devotion to this norm was indicated also by their preference for supervisors who did not act as if they were "better than anyone else"; they insisted that supervisors, or for that matter other workers, should not behave like "big shots." In other words, they were hostile to those who put forth claims of personal superiority.[3]

Again, workers expressed the feeling that close supervision violated their culturally prescribed expectations of equality by saying that such a supervisor was "trying to make a *slave* out of us."

Supervisors, as well as workers, were frequently oriented to the same egalitarian norms. For example, the production manager for the entire Company expressed these sentiments in the following way:

> "Here's the real secret to successful human relations: The real key lies in treating your employees like human beings. *I'm no better than any one of the plant workers.* Oh,

[2] Mill, *ibid.* [sic], p. 111. This statement was deleted from the third (1852) edition. (Our emphasis—A. W. G.)

[3] That this is a culturally induced sentiment, as significant in a military as in an industrial setting, may be inferred from the warning addressed to U. S. Army officers during the last war: ". . . do not make the mistake of thinking of yourself as a superior individual . . . ," officers were cautioned in "Military Courtesy and Discipline," W. D. Man. FM 21-50, June 15, 1942, quoted in S. A. Stouffer, E. A. Suchman, Leland C. DeVinney, Shirley A. Star, and Robin M. Williams, Jr., *The American Soldier*, Vol. 1, Princeton University Press, Princeton, N. J., 1949, p. 387.

maybe I can afford a little better car, or a home in Penmore.[4] I can send my kids for a music lesson while they can't. *But these things don't make me any better than them.*"

To the extent that a supervisor was oriented to norms of equality, the continual exercise of direct face-to-face supervision might be expected to create tensions for him. As one board plant foreman confided: "Sometimes I wonder who the hell am I to tell these guys what to do."

THE EXPLICATIONAL FUNCTIONS OF BUREAU-CRATIC RULES. In this context, some of the functions performed by bureaucratic rules can perhaps be more readily discerned. First, it can be noted that the rules comprise a functional equivalent for direct, personally given orders. Like direct orders, rules specify the obligations of the worker, enjoining him to do particular things in definite ways. Usually, however, rules are given, or are believed to be given, more deliberation than orders, and thus the statement of obligations they explicate can be taken to be definitive. Since the rules are also more carefully expressed, the obligations they impose may be less ambiguous than a hastily worded personal command.[5] Looked at in this light, rules are a form of *communication* to those who are seen as desirous of evading responsibilities, of avoiding commitments, and of withholding proper and full performance of obligations. Comprising in one facet an explicit body of obligations, the rules serve to draw a worker's *attention* to managerial expectations and to dissolve the residues of diffuseness which may allow the

worker to "hedge." Thus, on the one hand, the rules explicate the worker's task while on the other, they shape and specify his relationships to his superior. Stated in the language of the political scientist, the rules serve to narrow the subordinate's "area of discretion." The subordinates now have fewer options concerning what they *may* or *may not* do, and the area of "privilege" is crowded out by the growing area of "obligation."

It might be asked, why were work obligations comparatively diffuse in the mine, but much more explicit on the surface? An illustration previously used was the situation in which a group of workers were standing around, waiting for the mine head to assign them. He stepped out of his office and said, "One of you, clean out the rock crusher."

How was a *specific* individual chosen for this "dirty" job? This was the question asked a worker who had been through the situation. "It's simple," he replied. "We all just turn around and *look* at the newest guy in the group and he goes and does it." In other words, there existed an *informal* norm among miners to the effect that *new* workers got the dirty jobs; it was a norm to which the men were so sensitive that a mere "look" could bring the expected results. The informal group among miners spontaneously and with solidarity acted to enforce its norms. The informal group and its norms, then, constituted a functional equivalent for bureaucratic rules to the degree, at least, that it served to allocate concrete work responsibilities and to specify individual duties. It would appear, therefore, that the explication of obligations provided by bureaucratic rules is particularly necessary where there is no other instrumentality, specifically an effective informal group, which does this.[6]

---

[4] A middle class suburb in the area.

[5] Mill also saw the function of rules as a definitive statement of explicit obligations. He insisted that the successful conduct of a business required two things, "fidelity and zeal." Fidelity, easier to obtain than zeal, could be partly ensured when "work admits of being reduced to a *definite set of rules;* the violation of which conscience cannot easily blind itself, and on which responsibility may be enforced by the loss of employment." Nevertheless, he conceded, many things needed for business success cannot be reduced to "distinct and positive obligations." Finally, in this connection, he adds "the universal neglect by domestic servants of their employer's interest, wherever these are not protected by some fixed rule, is a matter of common remark . . ." *Ibid.*, p. 139.

[6] This situation is in seeming contrast to one described by William Foote Whyte in his perceptive, *Human Relations in the Restaurant Industry*, McGraw-Hill Book Co., New York, 1948. Whyte recounts an incident in which a supervisor gave an order to two women, without specifying which one was to carry it out. Whyte remarks, "For effective action, orders and directions must be definite and clear as to what must be done, *how* and *when* it is to be done, and *who is to do it*." (*Ibid.*, p. 261.) Our own formulations are not necessarily in contradiction to Whyte's practical strictures. From our viewpoint, however, Whyte's conclusions should be limited to situations in which informal co-

THE SCREENING FUNCTIONS OF RULES. A second, less obvious, function of bureaucratic rules can be observed if we notice that, in part, they provide a substitute for the personal repetition of orders by a supervisor. Once an obligation was incorporated into a rule, the worker could not excuse himself by claiming that the supervisor had failed to tell him to do a specific thing. To take one example: The worker who operated a machine without using the safety guard could not "pass the buck" by saying that the supervisor neglected to mention this when he gave him a task. Since there existed a standing rule that "safety guards should always be used," the supervisor need not warn the worker of this every time he instructed him to use a machine.

Once standing rules have been installed, there are fewer things that a supervisor has to direct a worker to do; thus the frequency and duration of worker-foreman interaction in their *official* capacities is somewhat lessened. Morever, even if the super does intervene in his capacity as a superior, he need not appear to be doing so on his own account; he is not so apt to be seen as "throwing his weight around." He can say, as one foreman said about the no-absenteeism rule: "I can't help laying them off if they're absent. *It's not my idea.* I've got to go along with the rules *like everyone else.* What *I* want has nothing to do with it." In other words, the rules provide the foreman with an impersonal crutch for his authority, screening the superiority of his power which might otherwise violate the norm of equality. Instead, equality presumably prevails because, "like everyone else," he, too, is bound by the rules which the plant manager has sanctioned.

Differences in power which are not justifiable in terms of the group's norms, or which violate them, seem to establish a situation requiring the utilization of impersonal control techniques. Impersonal and general rules serve in part to obscure the existence of power disparities which are not legitimate in terms of the group's norms.[7] The screening function of the rules would seem, therefore, to work in two directions at once. First, it impersonally bolsters a supervisor's claim to authority without compelling him to employ an embarrassing and debatable legitimation in terms of his personal superiority. Conversely, it permits *workers* to accept managerial claims to deference without committing them to a merely personal submission to the supervisor that would betray their self-image as "any man's equal."

THE "REMOTE CONTROL" FUNCTION OF RULES. It would be a mistake, however, to continue assuming that management instituted rules only when it perceived workers as unmotivated. For top management was often as much concerned with the low motivation of those in the lower echelons of its own ranks, i.e., middle management, as it was with workers'.

[7] William F. Whyte has made an observation in his restaurant studies which, if reconceptualized, in effect constitutes an interesting example of this pattern. Whyte points out that tension arises between the waitresses and the pantry help who fill their orders, under several conditions: when the waitresses are *younger* than the pantry people—even though both groups are women; or when those in the pantry are *men*. It would seem that these tensions emerge because *traditional* criteria of authority in our society are being violated. That is, younger people are initiating action for older people, while our cultural prescriptions prefer that power be vested in older folk. Again, women are initiating action for men, while the culture prescribes that men should wield the power. In an acute analysis, Whyte makes the following interpretation of the "insignificant-looking spindle" on which the waitresses place their orders, and from which the pantry people take them. "Wherever the people on the receiving end of the orders are related to the order givers as males vs. females, or older vs. younger, then it is important for the pantry help to have some *impersonal* barrier to block the pressure from themselves." (*Ibid.*, p. 75.) In other words, instead of having the waitresses orally inform the pantry help of what they want, the waitresses can now write it out and place their order on the spindle. The pantry personnel can pick the order off the spindle without coming into direct interaction with the waitresses and without seeming to take orders from those culturally prescribed as inferiors. The spindle thus masks the existence of a relationship which violates internalized cultural prescriptions.

hesion among workers has deteriorated so that they are unable to apply pressure to get the work done themselves, or if they are *unwilling* to do so. Our earlier point, about the tensions generated by close supervision, leads us to suspect that Whyte's prescriptions of detailed orders signify the presence of a motivational problem which may only be further exacerbated by the remedy he proposes.

This was quite evident in Peele's feeling that foreman and supervisors were "shirking." It was also a pattern that was more generally evident. Thus, for example, if all supervisors could be "counted on" to enforce safety regulations there would have been no need for the main office to employ a "safety engineer" to check upon safety conditions in the local plants.[8]

The problem of handling the "enemy within" was sometimes more difficult than that of coping with those in the "out-group." For at least on the factory level, in-group and out-group could stand face to face and might sniff watchfully at each other, and could place their confidence for a while in "close supervision." But what could the safety engineer, for example, do to control some twenty-five plants? How could he control the supervision of safety work throughout the entire Company by means of "close supervision" alone? (Notice that the safety engineer's problem was only an extreme case of a common problem; it was not qualitatively different from that experienced by many of the plant's middle managers).

In some way the safety engineer had to utilize a "spot check" system. That is, he made occasional visits to a plant, spending a little while there, and then moved on to another factory. If, however, each plant was to operate on a unique basis, each having its own distinctive techniques for handling safety, it would be difficult for the safety engineer to make his *own* judgment about plant conditions. He would be forced to place greater reliance on local management, which was precisely what he wanted to avoid. Insofar as he had established certain general rules applying to all plants, he could go to each one and "see for himself." He could "tell at a glance" whether the rules concerning machine guards or debris on the floor were being followed. In part, then, the existence of general rules was a necessary adjunct to a "spot check" system; they facilitated "control from a distance" by those in the higher and more remote reaches of the organization.[9]

There was another aspect of the rules which was also helpful to control from a distance. This was their *public* character. Because the rules were publicly known, an "enemy" could be used to control an "ally." For example, when the safety engineer inspected a plant he was not averse to speaking to workers whom he himself characterized as "troublemakers." The safety engineer told of a plant tour which he had made while in the company of a "troublemaker." This worker showed the engineer that there was a pile of debris in front of the blacksmith's bench, and took him to another spot and showed him how a machine had had its guard removed. He could only do this because the rules were public knowledge, and like everyone else, the "troublemaker" knew what they were. On the basis of these observations the safety engineer could then apply pressure to the supervisors. In sum, the *public* character of the rules enabled deviance to be detected by the *out-group*. This enlargened the information channels open to the heads of the in-group, in turn enabling them to keep their own junior officers in line.

These considerations lead us to expect that bureaucratic rules flourish, other things being equal, when the senior officers of a group are impressed with the recalcitrance of those to whom they have delegated a measure of com-

---

[8] Safety rules are discussed more fully in Chapter X [of *Patterns of Industrial Bureaucracy*].

[9] Some further implications of this, in the context of labor relations problems, may be seen from the comments of Frederick H. Harbison and Robert

Dubin about the General Motors Company: "A rigid grievance procedure has made it easier for the corporation to control the decisions and actions of management's rank and file. Thousands of plant managers, department superintendents and foremen have been dealing with union representatives on a day-to-day basis. Many of them have been inexperienced in labor relations, and some were bound to make mistakes. *The existence of a system of rules has made it easier to top company officials to locate quickly those spots where local management has been 'off base.'*" (Our emphasis—A. W. G.) *Patterns of Union-Management Relations*, Science Research Associates, Chicago, 1947, pp. 83–84. The remote control function of bureaucratic measures has also been noted by Franz Neumann and Julian Franklin. For example, Franklin writes: "Rigid hierarchy and a precisely articulated framework of offices and functions make it possible for discretionary policy to be set at *one point* outside the bureaucracy and then to be administered automatically at all levels of the hierarchy." "The Democratic Approach to Bureaucracy," *Readings in Culture, Personality and Society*, Columbia College, N. Y., n. d., p. 3.

mand. In other words, bureaucratic patterns are particularly useful to the degree that distrust and suspicion concerning role performance has become diffuse and directed to members of the "in-group," as well as to those on the outside; and when, as the Old Testament puts it, "A man's enemies are the men of his own house."

THE PUNISHMENT LEGITIMATING FUNCTIONS OF RULES. Faced with subordinates who were only reluctantly performing their roles, or at least, who were seen in this way, management was experiencing a status-threatening and hence aggression-provoking situation. The supervisor wanted to eliminate these threats when they arose and to prevent their recurrence. These were the supervisor's needs which emerged from his relations with workers when the latter began to behave apathetically ("goldbricking") or disobediently ("talking back"). On another level, the personality plane, the supervisor was beginning to "burn up" and was getting set to "blow his top." He was, in brief, accumulating a cargo of aggression with which he had to do something.

Why didn't the supervisor express his aggression and "tell the worker off"? Why didn't he *punish* the worker, thereby killing two birds with one stone; namely, unburdening himself of hostile feelings and compelling the worker to conform to his expectations? After all, punishment, or the infliction of "pain, failure, or ego-degradation" [10] upon the worker might help to bolster the supervisor's threatened status and salve his wounded ego.

There was one important drawback. Among surface workers in particular, and for the Company as a whole, supervisors were expressly forbidden, formally, to express aggression. As seen when contrasting miners with the more bureaucratized surface workers, the overt expression of aggression was taboo among the latter. Moreover the Company "labor relations manual" asserted that "A *friendly* attitude toward . . . all employees will provide the basis for sound Company-employee relations in each plant." The manual also insisted that one of the characteristics of every good employee was an "ability to *control emotion*."

[10] Norman F. Maier, *Frustration*, McGraw-Hill Book Co., 1949, p. 194.

In the face of these proscriptions, it was difficult to express aggression openly.

In our society, moreover, it is not permissible to inflict a punishment under any and all conditions. There seems to be a deep-grooved inscription in our culture which asserts that punishment is permissible only on the condition that the offender could know *in advance* that certain of his behaviors are forbidden.[11] This is one of the sentiments which underlies the rejection of *ex post facto* laws in our legal structure. If it has become a formally announced legal principle that "ignorance of the law is no excuse," this has, in part, been necessary because traditional folkways informally insist that ignorance of the law constitutes an extenuating circumstance.

Within the plant, orientation to this traditional norm was expressed in several ways. First, the frequent claim that so-and-so was a good foreman because he gave his workers a "second chance," a factor in the "indulgency pattern," implied that such a foreman did *not* take the first opportunity that presented itself to inflict a punishment. Instead he used this first deviaion as an occasion to *warn* the worker that future infractions would meet with punishment.

That punishments which were not preceded by warnings were only doubtfully legitimate, in the eyes of plant personnel, can be inferred from the introduction of the formal warning notice. One of the functions of the *worker's signature* on the warning notice was to forestall a claim that he had not been warned and could not, therefore, be punished. Day, the old personnel manager, complained precisely of this point after he had been demoted, saying, "Why didn't Peele tell me about it long before now, instead of just replacing me?"

Bureaucratic rules, then, serve to legitimate the utilization of punishments. They do so be-

[11] Here, again, there is evidence suggesting that we are dealing with a culturally induced sentiment rather than one peculiar to this factory or to industrial phenomena alone. On the basis of their wartime studies of the U. S. Armed Forces, the authors of *The American Soldier* suggest that punishment is more likely to be effective if "the men are given specific *advance* warning about the consequences of an occurrence of the offense, since *most men consider fair warning as a condition for fair punishment*." *Ibid.*, p. 425. (Our emphasis—A. W. G.)

cause the rules constitute statements in advance of expectations. As such, they comprise explicit or implicit *warnings* concerning the kind of behavior which will provoke punishment.

In actuality, the establishment of a rule explicating an obligation is frequently accompanied by a specific statement of the punishment, i.e., another rule specifying the punishment which will result if the first rule is violated. Two things, rather than one, have thus been clarified: (1) what is expected of the man and (2) what will happen to him if he does *not* fulfill these expectations. For example, the no-absenteeism rule did not merely state that the worker must not be absent without cause; it also specifically provided that he was to be layed off a like number of days for those which he took.

In brief, when rules explicate obligations, they are producing consequences recognized and intended by most participants in the situation. When rules explicate a punishment, however, they are legitimating the use of punishments, a consequence sometimes not at the center of the group's intention or awareness. The relationship between the explicational and the punishment functions of rules is like the relation between the locomotive and the trains which it pulls. Attention can all too readily be diverted to the noisy, smoking locomotive in the vanguard, while the attached trains carrying the pay load are easily neglected.

An example of the punishment function of the rules occurred in the dehydrating section of the mill: There were a number of large vats, used to heat and dehydrate the gypsum into powder, which occasionally needed to be cleaned out. A rule specified that the man who went down into one of these vats must wear a harness with a rope leading up to the top; there was also supposed to be someone at the top holding onto the rope and watching the man inside. These precautions stemmed from the fear that a man at the bottom of a vat could be killed by fumes or smothered by a cave-in of the "cake" covering the inside of the vat.

One day a main office executive passed through the plant on an inspection tour and noticed a rope leading down into a vat. He looked over the side and saw a worker cleaning it out, but there was no one around at the top watching the man and guarding the rope. Immediately the executive looked for the man's foreman, who was not to be seen. After a search, however, he discovered the foreman doing exactly the same thing, cleaning out a vat without having someone watch him. The executive then "raised hell" with the foreman and took it to higher plant authorities.

In short, the first thing the executive did when he discovered the infraction of vat-cleaning rules, was to look for someone to punish and blame. Instead of calling the man up from the vat, he left him down there. Instead of doing something to forestall an accident, the manifest function of this rule, he exploited the situation as an opportunity to inflict a punishment.

The rules thus channel aggression, providing permissible avenues for its expression and legitimating the utilization of punishments. To the extent that possible objects of punishment and aggression are members of the "in-group," as suggested in our discussion of the "remote control" function of rules, it becomes all the more necessary to legitimate meticulously the use of these control measures. For, by and large, aggression and punishments directed toward in-group members are not preferred patterns of behavior in our culture and require especially unambiguous justification. Bureaucratic rules are thereby particularly functional in a context in which reliance upon the in-group has been shaken. . . .

THE APATHY-PRESERVING FUNCTION OF BUREAU-CRATIC RULES. Nor is this the last of paradoxes. For though bureaucratic rules were fostered by situations involving worker apathy, or its semblance, the rules actually contributed to the preservation of work apathy. Just as the rules facilitated punishment, so, too, did they define the behavior which could permit punishment to be *escaped*. . . . The rules served as a specification of a *minimum* level of acceptable performance. It was therefore possible for the worker to *remain* apathetic, for he now knew just how *little* he could do and still remain secure.

For example, after Peele had ruled that workers could not "punch in early" and accumulate a little overtime in that way, one mill worker said acidly.

Well, if that's the way he wants it, that's the way he wants it. But I'll be damned if I put in any overtime when things get rough and they'd like us to.

Said another worker:

O.K. I'll punch in just so, and I'll punch out on the nose. But you know you can lead a horse to water and you can lead him away, but it's awful hard to tell just how much water he drinks while he's at it.

This, of course, is the stuff of which "bureaucratic sabotage" is made. "Bureaucratic sabotage" is deliberate apathy fused with resentment, in which, by the very act of conforming to the letter of the rule, its intention is "conscientiously" violated. The worker's feeling and attitudes toward his work were thus essentially left untouched by the bureaucratic rules. The worker could, as it were, take any attitude toward his work that he wished, so long as he conformed to the rules. The rules did little to modify *attitudes* toward work, but were significant primarily as guidelines for *behavior*. In the last analysis, it would seem that proliferation of bureaucratic rules signify that management has, in effect if not intention, surrendered in the battle for the worker's motivation. In his study of *Social Organization*, Charles Horton Cooley came to much the same conclusion:

Underlying all formalism, indeed, is the fact that it is psychically cheap; it substitutes the outer for the inner as more tangible, more capable of being held before the mind *without fresh expense of thought and feeling*.[12]

And again:

. . . the merely formal institution does not enlist and discipline the soul of the individual, but takes him by the outside, his soul being left to torpor or to irreverent and riotous activity.[13]

Thus bureaucratic rules may be functional for subordinates, as well as for superiors; they permit "activity" without "participation"; they enable an employee to work without being emotionally committed to it.

[12] C. H. Cooley, *Social Organization*, Chas. Scribner's Sons, 1919, p. 349. (Our emphasis—A. W. G.)
[13] *Ibid.*, p. 343.

This function of bureaucratic rules is of peculiar importance since it suggests one of the inherent sources of bureaucratic rules' instability; for the rules do not seem to *resolve* the very problem, worker apathy, from which they most directly spring. Insofar as formal rules merely "wall in," rather than resolve, worker apathy, it may be expected that other mechanisms more competent to muster motivations will challenge and compete with them.[14]

BUREAUCRATIC RULES AND CLOSE SUPERVISION. What does this mean in terms of the problem of "close supervision"? It implies that bureaucratic rules do not eliminate the need for "close supervision" but, instead, primarily function to reduce the tensions created by it. Insofar as close supervision springs from management's perception of workers as failing to perform their role-obligations and as being unmotivated, the institution of rules in no way suffices to resolve this problem. The rules do not recharge the worker's motivation, but merely enable him to know what management's exectations are and to give them minimal conformance. Thus the tensions originally spurring supervisors to use "close supervision" remain untouched.

It is, instead, the secondary problems created by close supervision that are somewhat mitigated by bureaucratic rules: With the rules,

[14] It may well be that this is one of the organic contradictions of bureaucratic organization that make it susceptible to infiltration and displacement by "charismatic" elements, which involves loyalty to leadership based on belief in the leader's unusual *personal* qualities. Weber vaguely explained the vulnerability of bureaucracy as a breakdown of its efficiency in the face of new problems and accumulating tensions. He did little to analyze the specific nature of these tensions and tended to focus on their origins in the environment, neglecting their inner-organizational sources. We are suggesting, in effect, that bureaucratic authority is supplanted by charismatic when it is no longer possible to bypass the question of motivation. Charismatic leadership, it has been widely noted, has an ability to arouse new enthusiasms and to ignite irrational sources of motivation inaccessible to the bureaucrat. Indeed, some observers have insisted that this is one of the distinctive characteristics of modern totalitarianism. Thus George Orwell, in his *1984*, brings this novel to its climax when his hero is being tortured not merely to confess, nor to conform—but to *believe*.

the supervisor is now enabled to show that he is not using close supervision on his own behalf, but is merely transmitting demands that apply equally to all (the screening function); the supervisor is now more able to use a "spot-check" system to control workers with whom he cannot have frequent interaction (the remote control function); he now has a clear-cut basis for deciding, and demonstrating to his superiors if need be, that workers are delinquent in their role-performances (the explicational function); he now has firm grounds for punishing a worker if he finds him withholding obligation-performance (the punishment-legitimating function); or he can relax the rules, thereby rewarding workers, if they do perform their role obligations as he wants them to (the leeway function). In general, then, the rules reduce certain role tensions.

To repeat: These various functions of the rules largely serve to mitigate tensions *derivative* of "close supervision," rather than to remove all the major tensions which *create* it. Indeed, the rules now make close supervision feasible. The rules thus actually perpetuate one of the very things, i.e., close supervision, that bring them into being. The dynamics of the situation are of this sort:

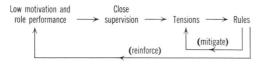

One may well wonder how bureaucratic rules could be perpetuated and sustained, if they actually removed the tensions leading to close supervision, rather than mitigating the tensions stemming from it. For if this happened low motivation would be raised to a satisfactory level; there would then be less need for close supervision; hence fewer tensions would be generated by it, and, in consequence, there would be less need for these tensions to be reduced by bureaucratic rules. To put it more sharply, bureaucratic rules seem to be sustained not only because they mitigate some tensions, but, also, because they *preserve* and allow other *tensions* to persist. If bureaucratic rules are a "defense mechanism," they not only defend the organization from certain tensions (those coming from close supervision),

but they also *defend other tensions* as well (those conducing to close supervision).[15]

It should not be supposed, however, that all the consequences of bureaucratic rules are equally reinforcing to low motivation and thereby to close supervision. Obviously, the apathy-preserving function of the rules does this most directly. It may be taken as "given," however, that punishments are more likely to impair motivation, and thus encourage close supervision, than rewards,[16] other things being equal. It therefore seems warranted to conclude that the punishment function is more apt to reinforce low motivation, and with it close supervision, than is the leeway function.

[15] This seems to have some bearing on certain more *general* problems involved in the functional analysis of organizations, which can be elucidated by comparing our approach with that employed by Philip Selznick. (See Selznick, "Foundations of the Theory of Organization," *American Sociological Review*, Feb., 1948, pp. 25–35). Selznick emphasizes the utility of concepts describing organization defensive mechanisms. He suggests that organizations develop recurrent defensive mechanisms, in a manner analogous to the human personality. These mechanisms, he holds, reduce tensions to the organization from threats which impinge upon it from its environment. Selznick illustrates this with the concept of "cooptation": Thus when the leadership body of a group loses the consent of a segment of the group over which it claims authority, a tension is established. One of the defensive mechanisms which may then become operative to reduce this tension, according to Selznick, is the "cooptation" of a prominent member of the dissenting segment onto the leadership body. This "formal" cooptation may extract increased consent from the sub-group, thereby reducing the tension experienced by those claiming authority. For example, an imperial colonial administrative body may coopt a tribal chief to the imperial administrative organ. Now, in what sense has the tension been reduced? One thing seems clear at least: The conditions which originally motivated the tribesmen to withdraw consent may in no way have been altered by the cooptation. Actually, the cooptation may safeguard the tensions which the tribesmen are experiencing and which led them to withhold consent. By inhibiting verbalization of their grievances, by directing attention and energies away from them, the cooptation of the tribal leader may allow these tensions to remain concealed and to continue to fester. In other words, defense mechanisms may actually defend the circumstances which produce the tension itself.
[16] Cf., N. R. F. Maier, *ibid.*

Hence we should expect that the more a specific administrative pattern is organized around the punishment functions of rules, the more it will impair motivation and reinforce the need for close supervision.

The discussion of management's perception of both workers and middle management, and the analysis of close supervision, suggest that the extreme elaboration of bureaucratic rules is prompted by an abiding distrust of people and of their intentions. Quite commonly, such rules serve those whose ambitions do not generate the ready and full consent of others; they diminish reliance upon and withhold commitments to persons who are viewed as recalcitrant and untrustworthy. In the extreme case, they seem to comprise an effort to *do without people altogether*. This could not be stated with greater frankness than in the words of Alfred Krupp, the munitions manufacturer:

> What I shall attempt to bring about is that *nothing shall be dependent upon the life or existence* of any particular person; that nothing of any importance shall happen or be caused to happen without the foreknowledge and approval of the management; that

the past and the determinate future of the establishment can be learned in the files of the management *without asking a question of any mortal*.[17]

If the several assessments made in various parts of this chapter are assembled into a complete diagnosis, it appears that bureaucratic rules proliferate when a social organization is riven by the following tensions: (1) Managerial distrust and suspicion become pervasive and are directed, not only toward workers, but also toward members of the managerial in-group as well. (2) Disturbances in the informal system which result in the withholding of consent from the formally constituted authorities; the informal group is either unwilling or unable to allocate work responsibilities and gives no support to management's production expectations. (3) Finally, the appearance of status distinctions of dubious legitimacy, in an egalitarian culture context, which strain the formal authority relationships.

[17] Quoted in Frederick J. Nussbaum, *A History of the Economic Institutions of Modern Europe*, F. S. Crofts and Co., New York, 1933, p. 379. (Our emphasis—A. W. G.)

Engineer the Job to Fit the Manager

FRED E. FIEDLER

What kind of leadership style does business need? Should company executives be decisive, directive, willing to give orders, and eager to assume responsibility? Should they be human relations-oriented, nondirective, willing to share leadership with the men in their group? Or should we perhaps start paying attention to the more important problem of defining under what conditions each of these leadership styles works best and what to do about it?

The success or failure of an organization depends on the quality of its management. How to get the best possible management is a question of vital importance; but it is perhaps even more important to ask how we can make better use of the management talent which *we already have*.

To get good business executives we have relied primarily on recruitment, selection, and training. It is time for businessmen to ask whether this is the only way or the best way for getting the best possible management. Fitting the man to the leadership job by selection and training has not been spectacularly successful. It is surely easier to change almost anything in the job situation than a man's personality and his leadership style. Why not try, then, to fit the leadership job to the man?

Executive jobs are surprisingly pliable, and the executive manpower pool is becoming increasingly small. The luxury of picking a "natural leader" from among a number of equally promising or equally qualified specialists is rapidly fading into the past. Business must learn how to utilize the available executive talent as effectively as it now utilizes physical plant and machine tools. Your financial expert, your top research scientist, or your production genius may be practically irreplaceable. Their jobs call for positions of leadership and responsibility. Replacements for these men can be neither recruited nor trained overnight,

and they may not be willing to play second fiddle in their departments. If their leadership style does not fit the job, *we must learn how to engineer the job to fit their leadership style.*

In this article I shall describe some studies that illuminate this task of job engineering and adaptation. It will be seen that there are situations where the authoritarian, highly directive leader works best, and other situations where the egalitarian, more permissive, human relations-oriented leader works best; but almost always there are possibilities for changing the situation around somewhat to match the needs of the particular managers who happen to be available. The executive who appreciates these differences and possibilities has knowledge that can be valuable to him in running his organization.

To understand the problems that a new approach would involve, let us look first at some of the basic issues in organizational and group leadership.

Styles of Leadership

Leadership is a personal relationship in which one person directs, coordinates, and supervises others in the performance of a common task. This is especially so in "interacting groups," where men must work together cooperatively in achieving organizational goals.

In oversimplified terms, it can be said that the leader manages the group in either of two ways. He can:

Tell people what to do and how to do it.
Or share his leadership responsibilities with his group members and involve them in the planning and execution of the task.

There are, of course, all shades of leadership styles in between these two polar positions, but the basic issue is this: the work of motivating and coordinating group members has to be done either by brandishing the proverbial stick or by dangling the equally proverbial carrot.

From *Harvard Business Review*, September–October 1965, pp. 115–122. Reprinted by permission of the publisher.

The former is the more orthodox job-centered, autocratic style. The latter is the more nondirective, group-centered procedure.

Research evidence exists to support both approaches to leadership. Which, then, should be judged more appropriate? On the face of it, the first style of leadership is best under some conditions, while the second works better under others. Accepting this proposition immediately opens two avenues of approach. Management can:

Determine the specific situation in which the directive or the nondirective leadership style works best, and then select or train men so that their leadership style fits the particular job.

Or determine the type of leadership style which is most natural for the man in the executive position, and then change the job to fit the man.

The first alternative has been discussed many times before; the second has not. We have never seriously considered whether it would be easier to fit the executive's job to the man.

Needed Style?

How might this be done? Some answers have been suggested by a research program on leadership effectiveness that I have directed under Office of Naval Research auspices since 1951.[1] This program has dealt with a wide variety of different groups, including basketball teams, surveying parties, various military combat crews, and men in open-hearth steel shops, as well as members of management and boards of directors. When possible, performance was measured in terms of objective criteria—for instance, percentage of games won by high school basketball teams; tap-to-tap time of open-hearth shops (roughly equivalent to the tonnage of steel output per unit of time); and company net income over a three-year period. Our measure of leadership style was based on a simple scale indicating the degree to which a man described, favorably or unfavorably, his least-preferred co-worker

(LPC). This co-worker did not need to be someone he actually worked with at the time, but could be someone the respondent had known in the past. Whenever possible, the score was obtained before the leader was assigned to his group.

The study indicates that a person who describes his least preferred co-worker in a relatively favorable manner tends to be permissive, human relations-oriented, and considerate of the feelings of his men. But a person who describes his least-preferred co-worker in an unfavorable manner—who has what we have come to call a low LPC rating—tends to be managing, task-controlling, and less concerned with the human relations aspects of the job. It also appears that the directive, managing, and controlling leaders tend to perform best in basketball and surveying teams, in open-hearth shops, and (provided the leader is accepted by his group) in military combat crews and company managements. On the other hand, the nondirective, permissive, and human relations-oriented leaders tend to perform best in decision- and policy-making teams and in groups that have a creative task—provided that the group likes the leader or the leader feels that the group is pleasant and free of tension.

Critical Dimensions. But in order to tell which style fits which situation, we need to categorize groups. Our research has shown that "it all depends" on the situation. After reviewing the results of all our work and the findings of other investigators, we have been able to isolate three major dimensions that seem to determine, to a large part, the kind of leadership style called for by different situations.

It is obviously a mistake to think that groups and teams are all alike and that each requires the same kind of leadership. We need some way of categorizing the group-task situation, or the job environment within which the leader has to operate. If leadership is indeed a process of influencing other people to work together effectively in a common task, then it surely matters how easy or difficult it is for the leader to exert his influence in a particular situation.

LEADER-MEMBER RELATIONS. The factor that would seem most important in determining a man's leadership influence is the degree to which his group members trust and like him,

[1] Conducted under Office of Naval Research contracts 170–106, N6-ori-07135 and NR 177–472, Nonr-1834 (36).

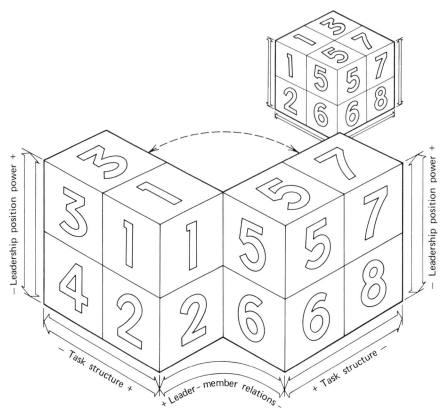

Exhibit I. A model for classifying group-task situations.

and are willing to follow his guidance. The trusted and well-liked leader obviously does not require special rank or power in order to get things done. We can measure the leader-member relationship by the so-called socio-metric nomination techniques that ask group members to name in their group the most influential person, or the man they would most like to have as a leader. It can also be measured by a group-atmosphere scale indicating the degree to which the leader feels accepted and comfortable in the group.

THE TASK STRUCTURE. The second important factor is the "task structure." By this term I mean the degree to which the task (a) is spelled out step by step for the group and, if so, the extent to which it can be done "by the numbers" or according to a detailed set of standard operating instructions, or (b) must be left nebulous and undefined. Vague and ambiguous or unstructured tasks make it difficult to exert leadership influence, because nei-

ther the leader nor his members know exactly what has to be done or how it is to be accomplished.

Why single out this aspect of the task rather than the innumerable other possible ways of describing it? Task groups are almost invariably components of a larger organization that assigns the task and has, therefore, a big stake in seeing it performed properly. However, the organization can control the quality of a group's performance only if the task is clearly spelled out and programmed or structured. When the task can be programmed or performed "by the numbers," the organization is able to back up the authority of the leader to the fullest; the man who fails to perform each step can be disciplined or fired. But in the case of ill-defined, vague, or unstructured tasks, the organization and the leader have very little control and direct power. By close supervision one can ensure, let us say, that a man will correctly operate a machine, but one cannot ensure that he will be creative.

It is therefore easier to be a leader in a structured task situation in which the work is spelled out than in an unstructured one which presents the leader and his group with a nebulous, poorly defined problem.

POSITION POWER. Thirdly, there is the power of the leadership position, as distinct from any personal power the leader might have. Can he hire or fire and promote or demote? Is his appointment for life, or will it terminate at the pleasure of his group? It is obviously easier to be a leader when the position power is strong than when it is weak.

Model for Analysis. When we now classify groups on the basis of these three dimensions, we get a classification system that can be represented as a cube; see Exhibit I. As each group is high or low in each of the three dimensions, it will fall into one of the eight cells.

From examination of the cube, it seems clear that exerting leadership influence will be easier in a group in which the members like a powerful leader with a clearly defined job and where the job to be done is clearly laid out (Cell 1); it will be difficult in a group where a leader is disliked, has little power, and has a highly ambiguous job (Cell 8).

In other words, it is easier to be the well-esteemed foreman of a construction crew working from a blueprint than it is to be the disliked chairman of a volunteer committee preparing a new policy.

I consider the leader-member relations the most important dimension, and the position-power dimension the least important, of the three. It is, for instance quite possible for a man of low rank to lead a group of higher-ranking men in a structured task—as is done when enlisted men or junior officers conduct some standardized parts of the training programs for medical officers who enter the Army. But it is not so easy for a disrespected manager to lead a creative, policy-formulating

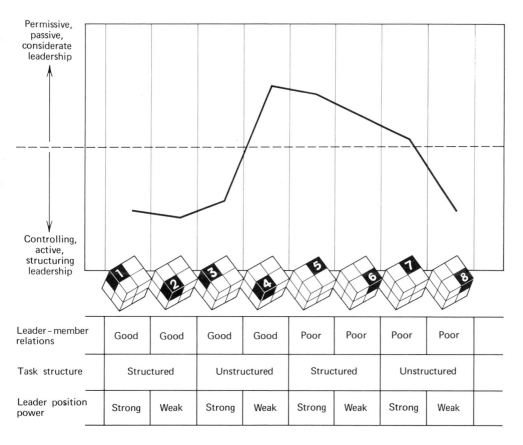

Exhibit II. How the style of effective leadership varies with the situation.

session well, even if he is the senior executive present.

Varying Requirements. By first sorting the eight cells according to leader-member relations, then task structure, and finally leader position power, we can now arrange them in order according to the favorableness of the environment for the leader. This sorting leads to an eight-step scale, as in Exhibit II. This exhibit portrays the results of a series of studies of groups performing well but (a) in different situations and conditions, and (b) with leaders using different leadership styles. In explanation:

The *horizontal* axis shows the range of situations that the groups worked in, as described by the classification scheme used in Exhibit I.

The *vertical* axis indicates the leadership style which was best in a certain situation, as shown by the correlation coefficient between the leader's LPC and his group's performance.

A positive correlation (falling above the midline) shows that the permissive, nondirective, and human relations-oriented leaders performed best; a negative correlation (below the midline) shows that the task-controlling, managing leader performed best. For instance, leaders of effective groups in situation categories 1 and 2 had LPC-group performance correlations of −.40 to −.80, with the average between −.50 and −.60; whereas leaders of effective groups in situation categories 4 and 5 had LPC-group performance correlations of .20 to .80, with the average between .40 and .50.

Exhibit II shows that both the directive, managing, task-oriented leaders and the nondirective, human relations-oriented leaders are successful under some conditions. Which leadership style is the best depends on the favorableness of the particular situation for the leader. In very favorable or in very unfavorable situations for getting a task accomplished by group effort, the autocratic, task-controlling, managing leadership works best. In situations intermediate in difficulty, the nondirective, permissive leader is more successful.

This corresponds well with our everyday experience. For instance:

Where the situation is very favorable, the group expects and wants the leader to give di-

rections. We neither expect nor want the trusted airline pilot to turn to his crew and ask, "What do you think we ought to check before takeoff?"

If the disliked chairman of a volunteer committee asks his group what to do, he may be told that everybody ought to go home.

The well-liked chairman of a planning group or research team must be nondirective and permissive in order to get full participation from his members. The directive, managing leader will tend to be more critical and to cut discussion short; hence he will not get the full benefit of the potential contributions by his group members.

The varying requirements of leadership styles are readily apparent in organizations experiencing dramatic changes in operating procedures. For example:

The manager or supervisor of a routinely operating organization is expected to provide direction and supervision that the subordinates should follow. However, in a crisis the routine is no longer adequate, and the task becomes ambiguous and unstructured. The typical manager tends to respond in such instances by calling his principal assistants together for a conference. In other words, the effective leader changes his behavior from a directive to a permissive, nondirective style until the operation again reverts to routine conditions.

In the case of a research planning group, the human relations-oriented and permissive leader provides a climate in which everybody is free to speak up, to suggest, and to criticize. Osborn's brainstorming method [2] in fact institutionalizes these procedures. However, after the research plan has been completed, the situation becomes highly structured. The director now prescribes the task in detail, and he specifies the means of accomplishing it. Woe betide the assistant who decides to be creative by changing the research instructions!

Practical Tests. Remember that the ideas I have been describing emanate from studies of real-life situations; accordingly, as might be expected, they can be validated by organizational experience. Take, for instance, the dimension of leader-member relations described

[2] See Alex F. Osborn, *Applied Imagination* (New York, Charles Scribner's Sons, 1953).

earlier. We have made three studies of situations in which the leader's position power was strong and the task relatively structured with clear-cut goals and standard operating procedures. In such groups as these the situation will be very favorable for the leader if he is accepted; it will be progressively unfavorable in proportion to how much a leader is disliked. What leadership styles succeed in these varying conditions? The studies confirm what our theory would lead us to expect:

The first set of data come from a study of B-29 bombers crews in which the criterion was the accuracy of radar bombing. Six degrees of leader-member relations were identified, ranging from those in which the aircraft commander was the first choice of crew members and highly endorsed his radar observer and navigator (the key men in radar bombing), to those in which he was chosen by his crew but did not endorse his key men, and finally to crews in which the commander was rejected by his crew and rejected his key crew members. What leadership styles were effective? The results are plotted in Exhibit III.

A study of anti-aircraft crews compares the 10 most chosen crew commanders, the 10 most rejected ones, and 10 of intermediate popularity. The criterion is the identification and "acquistion" of unidentified aircraft by the crew. The results shown in Exhibit III are similar to those for bomber crew commanders.

Exhibit III also summarizes data for 32 small-farm supply companies. There were member companies of the same distribution system, each with its own board of directors and its own management. The performance of these highly comparable companies was measured in terms of percentage of company net income over a three-year period. The first quarter of the line (going from left to right) depicts endorsement of the general manager by his board of directors and his staff of assistant managers; the second quarter, endorsement by his board but not his staff; the third quarter, endorsement by his staff but not his board; the fourth quarter, endorsement by neither.

As can be seen from the results of all three studies, the highly accepted and strongly rejected leaders perform best if they are controlling and managing, while the leaders in the intermediate acceptance range, who are neither rejected nor accepted, perform best if they are permissive and nondirective.

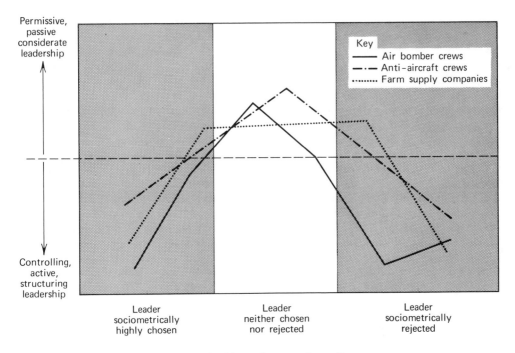

Exhibit III. How effective leadership styles vary depending on group acceptance.

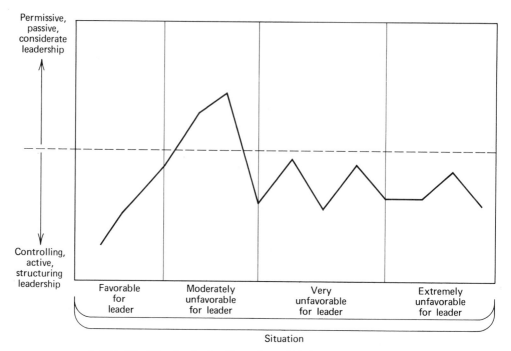

Permissive,
passive,
considerate
leadership

Controlling,
active,
structuring
leadership

| Favorable for leader | Moderately unfavorable for leader | Very unfavorable for leader | Extremely unfavorable for leader |

Situation

Exhibit IV. Effective leadership styles at Belgian Naval Training Center.

Now let us look at some research on organizations in another country:

Recently in Belgium a study was made of groups of mixed language and cultural composition. Such teams, which are becoming increasingly frequent as international business and governmental activities multiply, obviously present a difficult situation for the leader. He must not only deal with men who do not fully comprehend one another's language and meanings, but also cope with the typical antipathies, suspicions, and antagonisms dividing individuals of different cultures and nationalities.

At a Belgian naval training center we tested 96 three-man groups, half of which were homogeneous in composition (all Flemish or all Walloon) and half heterogeneous (the leader differing from his men). Half of each of these had powerful leader positions (petty officers), and half had recruit leaders. Each group performed three tasks: one unstructured task (writing a recruiting letter); and two parallel structured tasks (finding the shortest route for ships through 10 ports, and doing the same for 12 ports). After each task, leaders and group members described their reactions—including group-atmosphere ratings and the indication of leader-member relations.

The various task situations were then arranged in order, according to their favorableness for the leader. The most favorable situation was a homogeneous group, led by a well-liked and accepted petty officer, which worked on the structured task of routing a ship. The situation would be especially favorable toward the end of the experiment, after the leader had had time to get to know his members. The least favorable situation was that of an unpopular recruit leader of a heterogeneous group where the relatively unstructured task of writing a letter came up as soon as the group was formed.

There were six groups that fell into each of these situations or cells. A correlation was then computed for each set of six groups to determine which type of leadership style led to best team performance. The results, indicated in Exhibit IV, support the conclusions earlier described.

Of particular interest is the fact that the difficult heterogeneous groups generally required controlling, task-oriented leadership for good performance. This fits the descriptions of successful leader behavior obtained from executives who have worked in international business organizations.

Conclusion

Provided our findings continue to be supported in the future, what do these results and the theory mean for executive selection and training? What implications do they have for the management of large organizations?

Selection & Training. Business and industry are now trying to attract an increasingly large share of exceptionally intelligent and technically well-trained men. Many of these are specialists whose talents are in critically short supply. Can industry really afford to select only those men who have a certain style of leadership in addition to their technical qualifications? The answer is likely to be negative, at least in the near future.

This being the case, can we then train the men selected in one leadership style or the other? This approach is always offered as a solution, and it does have merit. But we must recognize that training people is at best difficult, costly, and time-consuming. It is certainly easier to place people in a situation compatible with their natural leadership style than to force them to adapt to the demands of the job.

As another alternative, should executives learn to recognize or diagnose group-task situations so that they can place their subordinates, managers, and department heads in the jobs best suited to their leadership styles? Even this procedure has serious disadvantages. The organization may not always happen to have the place that fits the bright young man. The experienced executive may not want to be moved, or it may not be possible to transfer him.

Should the organization try to "engineer" the job to fit the man? This alternative is potentially the most feasible for management. As has been shown already, the type of leadership called for depends on the favorableness of the situation. The favorableness, in turn, is a product of several factors. These include leader-member relations, the homogeneity of the group, and the position power and degree to which the task is structured, as well as other,

more obvious factors such as the leader's knowledge of his group, his familiarity with the task, and so forth.

It is clear that management can change the characteristic favorableness of the leadership situation; it can do so in most cases more easily than it can transfer the subordinate leader from one job to another or train him in a different style of interacting with his members.

Possibilities of Change. Although this type of organizational engineering has not been done systematically up to now we can choose from several good possibilities for getting the job done:

1. *We can change the leader's position power.* We can either give him subordinates of equal or nearly equal rank or we can give him men who are two or three ranks below him. We can either give him sole authority for the job or require that he consult with this group, or even obtain unanimous consent for all decisions. We can either punctiliously observe the channels of the organization to increase the leader's prestige or communicate directly with the men of his group as well as with him in person.

2. *We can change the task structure.* The tasks given to one leader may have to be clarified in detail, and he may have to be given precise operating instructions; another leader may have to be given more general problems that are only vaguely elucidated.

3. *We can change the leader-member relations.* The Belgian study, referred to earlier, demonstrates that changing the group composition changes the leader's relations with his men. We can increase or decrease the group's heterogeneity by introducing men with similar attitudes, beliefs, and backgrounds, or by bringing in men different in training, culture, and language.

The foregoing are, of course, only examples of what could be done. The important point is that we now have a model and a set of principles that permit predictions of leadership effectiveness in interacting groups and allow us to take a look at the factors affecting team performance. This approach goes beyond the traditional notions of selection and training. It focuses on the more fruitful possibility of organizational engineering as a means of using leadership potentials in the management ranks.

Conflicts between Staff and Line Managerial Officers

MELVILLE DALTON

In its concentration on union-management relations, industrial sociology has tended to neglect the study of processes inside the ranks of industrial management. Obviously the doors to this research area are more closely guarded than the entry to industrial processes through the avenue of production workers, but an industrial sociology worthy of the name must sooner or later 'extend its inquiries to include the activities of all industrial personnel.

The present paper is the result of an attempt to study processes among industrial managers. It is specifically a report on the functioning interaction between the two major vertical groupings of industrial management: (1) the *staff* organization, the functions of which are research and advisory; and (2) the *line* organization, which has exclusive authority over production processes.

Industrial staff organizations are relatively new. Their appearance is a response to many complex interrelated forces, such as economic competition, scientific advance, industrial expansion, growth of the labor movement, and so on. During the last four or five decades these rapid changes and resulting unstable conditions have caused top industrial officials more

From *American Sociological Review*, Vol. 15, June 1950, pp. 342–351. Reprinted with permission of the author and the publisher, American Sociological Association.

and more to call in "specialists" to aid them toward the goal of greater production and efficiency. These specialists are of many kinds including chemists, statisticians, public and industrial relations officers, personnel officers, accountants, and a great variety of engineers, such as mechanical, draughting, electrical, chemical, fuel, lubricating, and industrial engineers. In industry these individuals are usually known as "staff people." Their functions, again, for the most part are to increase and apply their specialized knowledge in problem areas, and to advise those officers who make up the "line" organization and have authority [1] over production processes.

This theoretically satisfying industrial structure of specialized experts advising busy administrators has in a number of significant cases failed to function as expected. The assumptions that (a) the staff specialists would be reasonably content to function without a measure of formal authority [2] over production, and that (b) their suggestions regarding improvement of processes and techniques for control over personnel and production would be welcomed by line officers and be applied, require closer examination. In practice there is often much conflict between industrial staff and line organizations and in varying degrees the members of these organizations oppose each other.[3]

The aim of this paper is, therefore, to present

and analyze data dealing with staff-line tensions.

Data were drawn from three industrial plants [4] in which the writer had been either a participating member of one or both of the groups or was intimate with reliable informants among the officers who were.

Approached sociologically, relations among members of management in the plants could be viewed as a general conflict system caused and perpetuated chiefly by (1) power struggles in the organization stemming in the main from competition among departments to maintain low operating costs; (2) drives by numerous members to increase their status in the hierarchy; (3) conflict between union and management; and (4) the staff-line friction which is the subject of this paper.[5] This milieu of tensions was not only unaccounted for by the blue-print organizations of the plants, but was often contradictory to, and even destructive of, the organizations' formal aims. All members of management, especially in the middle and lower ranks,[6] were caught up in this conflict system. Even though they might wish to escape, the obligation of at least appearing to

---

[1] *Inside* their particular staff organization, staff officers also may have authority over their subordinates, but not over production personnel.

[2] To the extent that staff officers influence line policy they do, of course, have a certain *informal* authority.

[3] Some social scientists have noted the possibility of staff-line friction, and industrial executives themselves have expressed strong feelings on the matter. See Burleigh B. Gardner, *Human Relations in Industry* (Chicago: Richard D. Irwin, Inc., 1945) and H. E. Dimock, *The Executive in Action* (New York: Harper & Brothers, 1945). Dimock believes that we are too "staff-minded" and that we should become more "executive-minded" (p. 241). A high line officer in a large corporation denounced staff organizations to the writer on the ground of their "costing more than they're worth," and that "They stir up too much trouble and are too theoretical." He felt that their function (excepting that of accountants, chemists, and "a few mechanical engineers") could be better carried out by replacing them with "highly-select front-line foremen [the

lowest placed line officers] who are really the backbone of management, and pay them ten or twelve thousand dollars a year."

[4] These plants were in related industries and ranged in size from 4,500 to 20,000 employees, with the managerial groups numbering from 200 to nearly 1,000. Details concerning the plants and their location are confidential. Methodological details concerning an intensive study embracing staff-line relations and several other areas of behavior in one of the plants are given in the writer's unpublished doctoral thesis, "A Study of Informal Organization Among the Managers of an Industrial Plant," (Department of Sociology, University of Chicago, 1949).

[5] Because these conflict areas were interrelated and continually shifting and reorganizing, discussion of any one of them separately—as in the case of staff-line relations—will, of course, be unrealistic to some extent.

[6] From bottom to top, the line hierarchy consisted of the following strata of officers: (1) first-line foremen, who were directly in charge of production workmen; (2) general foremen; (3) departmental superintendents; (4) divisional superintendents; (5) assistant plant manager; (6) plant manager. In the preceding strata there were often "assistants," such as "assistant general foreman," "assistant superintendent," etc., in which case the

carry out formal functions compelled individuals to take sides in order to protect themselves against the aggressions of others. And the intensity of the conflict was aggravated by the fact that it was formally unacceptable and had to be hidden.

For analytical convenience, staff-line friction may be examined apart from the reciprocal effects of the general conflict system. Regarded in this way, the data indicated that three conditions were basic to staff-line struggles: (1) the conspicuous ambition and "individualistic" behavior among staff officers; (2) the complication arising from staff efforts to justify its existence and get acceptance of its contributions; and, related to point two, (3) the fact that incumbency of the higher staff offices was dependent on line approval. The significance of these conditions will be discussed in order.

MOBILE BEHAVIOR OF STAFF PERSONNEL. As a group, staff personnel in the three plants were markedly ambitious, restless, and individualistic. There was much concern to win rapid promotion, to make the "right impressions," and to receive individual recognition. Data showed that the desire among staff members for personal distinctions often over-rode their sentiments of group consciousness and caused intra-staff tensions.[7]

The relatively high turnover of staff personnel [8] quite possibly reflected the dissatisfactions and frustrations of members over inability to achieve the distinction and status they hoped for. Several factors appeared to be of importance in this restlessness of staff personnel. Among these were age and social differences between line and staff officers, structural differences in the hierarchy of the two groups, and the staff group's lack of authority over production.

With respect to age, the staff officers were significantly younger than line officers.[9] This would account to some extent for their restlessness. Being presumably less well-established in life in terms of material accumulations, occupational status, and security, while having greater expectations (see below), and more

---

ment in which he hoped to introduce it, but was rebuffed by the superintendent who privately acknowledged the merit of the scheme but resented the staff officer's "trying to lord it over" him. The staff organization condemned the behavior of its member and felt that he should have allowed the plan to appear as a contribution of the staff group rather than as one of its members. The officer himself declared that "By G— it's my idea and I want credit. There's not a damn one of you guys [the staff group] that wouldn't make the same squawk if you were in my place!"

[8] During the period between 1944 and 1950 turnover of staff personnel in these plants was between two and four times as great as that of line personnel. This grouping included all the non-managerial members of staff and line and all the hourly-paid (non-salaried) members of management (about 60 assistant first-line foremen). Turnover was determined by dividing the average number of employees for a given year (in line or staff) into the accessions or separations, whichever was the smaller.

[9] Complete age data were available in one of the larger plants. Here the 36 staff heads, staff specialists, and assistants had a mean age of 42.9 years. This value would have been less than 40 years, except for the inclusion of several older former line officers, but even a mean of 42.9 years was significantly less (C.R. 2.8) than that of the 35 line superintendents in the plant who had a mean age of 48.7 years. The age difference was even more significant when the staff heads were compared with the 61 general foremen who had a mean age of 50.0 years. And between the 93 salaried first-line foremen (mean age of 48.5 years) and the 270 salaried nonsupervisory staff personnel (mean age of 31.0 years) the difference was still greater.

---

total strata of the line hierarchy could be almost double that indicated here.

In the staff organizations the order from bottom to top was: (1) supervisor (equivalent to the first-line foreman); (2) general supervisor (equivalent to the general foreman); (3) staff head—sometimes "superintendent" (equivalent to departmental superintendent in the line organization). Occasionally there were strata of assistant supervisors and assistant staff heads.

The term "upper line" will refer to all strata above the departmental superintendent. "Middle line" will include the departmental superintendent and assistants. "Lower line" will refer to general and first-line foremen and their assistants.

"Lower," "middle," and "upper" staff will refer respectively to the supervisor, general supervisor and staff head.

"Top management" will refer to the upper line and the few staff heads with whom upper line officers were especially intimate on matters of policy.

[7] In a typical case in one of the plants, a young staff officer developed a plan for increasing the life of certain equipment in the plant. He carried the plan directly to the superintendent of the depart-

energy, as well as more life ahead in which to make new starts elsewhere if necessary, the staff groups were understandably more dynamic and driving.[10]

Age-conflict [11] was also significant in staff-line antagonisms. The incident just noted of the young staff officers seeking to get direct acceptance by the line of his contribution failed in part—judging from the strong sentiments later expressed by the line superintendent—because of an age antipathy. The older line officers disliked receiving what they regarded as instruction from men so much younger than themselves, and staff personnel clearly were conscious of this attitude among line officers.[12] In staff-line meetings staff officers frequently had their ideas slighted or even treated with amusement by line incumbents. Whether such treatment was warranted or not, the effects were disillusioning to the younger, less experienced staff officers. Often selected by the organization because of their outstanding academic records, they had en-

tered industry with the belief that they had much to contribute, and that their efforts would win early recognition and rapid advancement. Certainly they had no thought that their contributions would be in any degree unwelcome. This naiveté [13] was apparently due to lack of earlier first-hand experience in industry (or acquaintance with those who had such experience), and to omission of realistic instruction in the social sciences from their academic training. The unsophisticated staff officer's initial contacts with the shifting, covert, expedient arrangements between members of staff and line usually gave him a severe shock. He had entered industry prepared to engage in logical, well-formulated relations with members of the managerial hierarchy, and to carry out precise, methodical functions for which his training had equipped him. Now he learned that (1) his freedom to function was snared in a web of informal commitments; (2) his academic specialty (on which he leaned for support in his new position) was often not relevant [14] for carrying out his formal assignments; and that (3) the important thing to do was to learn who the informally powerful line officers were and what ideas they would welcome which at the same time would be acceptable to his superiors.

Usually the staff officer's reaction to these conditions is to look elsewhere for a job or make an accommodation in the direction of

[10] One might also hypothesize that the drive of staff officers was reflected in the fact that the staff heads and specialists gained their positions (those held when the data were collected) in less time than did members of the line groups. E.g., the 36 staff officers discussed above had spent a median of 10 years attaining their positions, as against a median of 11 years for the first-line foremen, 17 years for the general foremen, and 19 years for the superintendents. But one must consider that some of the staff groups were relatively new (13–15 years old) and had grown rapidly, which probably accelerated their rate of promotions as compared with that of the older line organization.

[11] E. A. Ross in *Principles of Sociology* (New York: D. Appleton-Century Co., 1938) pp. 238–48, has some pertinent comments on age conflict.

[12] Explaining the relatively few cases in which his staff had succeeded in "selling ideas" to the line, an assistant staff head remarked: "We're always in hot water with these old guys on the line. You can't tell them a damn thing. They're bull-headed as hell! Most of the time we offer a suggestion it's either laughed at or not considered at all. The same idea in the mouth of some old codger on the line'd get a round of applause. They treat us like kids."

Line officers in these plants often referred to staff personnel (especially members of the auditing, production planning, industrial engineering, and industrial relations staffs) as "college punks," "slide-rules," "crackpots," "pretty boys," and "chair-warmers."

[13] John Mills, a research engineer retired from the telephone industry, has noted the worldly naiveté of research engineers in that field in his *The Engineer in Society* (New York: D. Van Nostrand Co., 1946).

[14] Among the staff heads and assistants referred to earlier, only 50 per cent of those with college training (32 of the 36 officers) were occupied with duties related to their specialized training. E.g., the head of the industrial relations staff had a B.S. degree in aeronautical engineering; his assistant had a similar degree in chemical engineering. Considering that staff officers are assumed to be specialists trained to aid and advise management in a particular function, the condition presented here raises a question as to what the criteria of selection were. (As will be shown in a separate paper, the answer appeared to be that personal—as well as impersonal—criteria were used.) Among the college-trained of 190 line officers in the same plant, the gap between training and function was still greater, with 61 per cent in positions not related to the specialized part of their college work.

protecting himself and finding a niche where he can make his existence in the plant tolerable and safe. If he chooses the latter course, he is likely to be less concerned with creative effort for his employer than with attempts to develop reliable social relations that will aid his personal advancement. The staff officer's recourse to this behavior and his use of other status-increasing devices will be discussed below in another connection.

The formal structure, or hierarchy of statuses, of the two larger plants from which data were drawn, offered a frustration to the ambitious staff officer. That is, in these plants the strata, or levels of authority, in the staff organizations ranged from three to five as against from five to ten in the line organization. Consequently there were fewer possible positions for exercise of authority into which staff personnel could move. This condition may have been an irritant to expansion among the staff groups. Unable to move vertically to the degree possible in the line organization, the ambitious staff officer could enlarge his area of authority in a given position only by lateral expansion—by increasing his personnel. Whether or not aspiring staff incumbents revolted against the relatively low hierarchy through which they could move, the fact remains that (1) they appeared eager to increase the number of personnel under their authority,[15] (2)

the personnel of staff groups *did* increase disproportionately to those of the line,[16] and (3) there was a trend of personnel movement from staff to line,[17] rather than the reverse, presumably (reflecting the drive and ambition of staff members) because there were more positions of authority, as well as more authority to be exercised, more prestige, and usually more income in the line.

Behavior in the plants indicated that line and staff personnel belonged to different social status groups and that line and staff antipathies were at least in part related to these social distinctions. For example, with respect to the item of formal education, the staff group stood on a higher level than members of the line. In

---

[15] This was suggested by unnecessary references among some staff officers to "the number of men under me," and by their somewhat fanciful excuses for increase of personnel. These excuses included statements of needing more personnel to (1) carry on research, (2) control new processes, (3) keep records and reports up-to-date. These statements often did not square with (1) the excessive concern among staff people about their "privileges" (such as arriving on the job late, leaving early, leaving the plant for long periods during working hours, having a radio in the office during the World Series, etc.); (2) the great amount of time (relative to that of line officers) spent by lower staff personnel in social activities on the job, and (3) the constantly recurring (but not always provoked) claims among staff personnel of their functional importance for production. The duties of middle and lower staff personnel allowed them sufficient time to argue a great deal over their respective functions (as well as many irrelevant topics) and to challenge the relative merit of one another's contributions or "ideas." In some of the staffs these discussions could go on intermittently

for hours and develop into highly theoretical jousts and wit battles. Where staff people regarded such behavior as a privilege of their status, line officers considered it as a threat to themselves. This lax control (in terms of line discipline) was in part a tacit reward from staff heads to their subordinates. The reward was expected because staff superiors (especially in the industrial relations, industrial engineering, and planning staffs) often overlooked and/or perverted the work of subordinates (which was resented) in response to pressures from the line. This behavior will be noted later.

[16] In one of the larger plants, where exact data were available, the total staff personnel had by 1945 exceeded that of the line. At that time the staff included 400 members as against 317 line personnel composed of managerial officers and their clerical workers, but not production workers. By 1948 the staff had increased to 517 as compared with 387 for the line (during this period *total* plant personnel declined over 400). The staff had grown from 20.8 per cent larger than the line in 1945 to 33.6 per cent larger in 1948, and had itself increased by 29.3 per cent during the three years as against a growth in the line of 22.1 per cent. Assuming the conditions essential for use of probability theory, the increase in staff personnel could have resulted from chance about 1.5 times in a hundred. Possibly post-war and other factors of social change were also at work but, if so, their force was not readily assessable.

[17] This movement from staff to line can disorganize the formal managerial structure, especially when (1) the transferring staff personnel have had little or no supervisory experience in the staff but have an academic background which causes them to regard human beings as mechanisms that will respond as expected; (2) older, experienced line officers have hoped—for years in some cases—to occupy the newly vacated (or created) positions.

the plant from which the age data were taken, the 36 staff officers had a mean of 14.6 years of schooling as compared with 13.1 years for 35 line superintendents, 11.2 years for 60 general foremen, and 10.5 years for 93 first-line foremen. The difference between the mean education of the staff group and that of the highest line group (14.6–13.1) was statistically significant at better than the one per cent level. The 270 non-supervisory staff personnel had a mean of 13.1 years—the same as that of the line superintendents. Consciousness of this difference probably contributed to a feeling of superiority among staff members, while the sentiment of line officers toward staff personnel was reflected in the name-calling noted earlier.

Staff members were also much concerned about their dress, a daily shave, and a weekly hair-cut. On the other hand line officers, especially below the level of departmental superintendent, were relatively indifferent to such matters. Usually they were in such intimate contact with production processes that dirt and grime prevented the concern with meticulous dress shown by staff members. The latter also used better English in speaking and in writing reports, and were more suave and poised in social intercourse. These factors, and the recreational preferences of staff officers for night clubs and "hot parties," assisted in raising a barrier between them and most line officers.

The social antipathies of the two groups and the status concern of staff officers were indicated by the behavior of each toward the established practice of dining together in the cafeterias reserved for management in the two larger plants. Theoretically, all managerial officers upward from the level of general foremen in the line, and general supervisors in the staff, were eligible to eat in these cafeterias. However, in practice the mere taking of one of these offices did not automatically assure the incumbent the privilege of eating in the cafeteria. One had first to be invited to "join the association." Staff officers were very eager to "get in" and did considerable fantasying on the impressions, with respect to dress and behavior, that were believed essential for an invitation. One such staff officer, a cost supervisor, dropped the following remarks:

There seems to be a committee that passes on you. I've had my application in for three years, but no soap. Harry [his superior] had

his in for over three years before he made it. You have to have something, because if a man who's in moves up to another position the man who replaces him doesn't get it because of the position—and he might not get it at all. I think I'm about due.

Many line officers who were officially members of the association avoided the cafeteria, however, and had to be *ordered* by the assistant plant manager to attend. One of these officers made the following statement, which expressed more pointedly the many similar spontaneous utterances of resentment and dislike made by other line officers:

There's a lot of good discussion in the cafeteria. I'd like to get in on more of it but I don't like to go there—sometimes I have to go. Most of the white collar people [staff officers] that eat there are stuck-up. I've been introduced three times to Svendsen [engineer], yet when I meet him he pretends to not even know me. When he meets me on the street he always manages to be looking someplace else. G—d— such people as that! They don't go in the cafeteria to eat and relax while they talk over their problems. They go in there to look around and see how somebody is dressed or to talk over the hot party they had last night. Well, that kind of damn stuff don't go with me. I haven't any time to put on airs and make out I'm something that I'm not.

COMPLICATIONS OF STAFF NEED TO PROVE ITS WORTH. To the thinking of many line officers, the staff functioned as an agent on trial rather than as a managerial division that might be of equal importance with the line organization in achieving production goals. Staff members were very conscious of this sentiment toward them and of their need to prove themselves. They strained to develop new techniques and to get them accepted by the line. But in doing this they frequently became impatient, and gave already suspicious line officers the impression of reaching for authority over production.

Since the line officer regards his authority over production as something sacred, and resents the implication that after many years in the line he needs the guidance of a newcomer who lacks such experience, an obstacle to staff-line cooperation develops the moment this sore spot is touched. On the other hand, the staff officer's ideology of his function leads him to precipitate a power struggle with the line organization. By and large he considers himself as an agent of top management. He feels bound to contribute something significant in the form of research or ideas helpful to management. By virtue of his greater education and intimacy with the latest theories of production, he regards himself as a managerial consultant and an expert, and feels that he must be, or appear to be, almost infallible once he has committed himself to top management on some point. With this orientation, he is usually disposed to approach middle and lower line with an attitude of condescension that often reveals itself in the heat of discussion. Consequently, many staff officers involve themselves in trouble and report their failures as due to "ignorance" and "bull-headedness" among these line officers.

On this point, relations between staff and line in all three of the plants were further irritated by a rift inside the line organization. First-line foremen were inclined to feel that top management had brought in the production planning, industrial relations, and industrial engineering staffs as clubs with which to control the lower line. Hence they frequently regarded the projects of staff personnel as manipulative devices, and reacted by cooperating with production workers and/or general foremen (whichever course was the more expedient) in order to defeat insistent and uncompromising members of the staff. Also, on occasion (see below), the lower line could cooperate evasively with lower staff personnel who were in trouble with staff superiors.

EFFECT OF LINE AUTHORITY OVER STAFF PROMOTION. The fact that entry to the higher staff offices in the three plants was dependent on approval of top line officers had a profound effect on the behavior of staff personnel. Every member of the staff knew that if he aspired to higher office he must make a record for himself, a good part of which would be a reputation among upper line officers of ability to "understand" their informal problems without being told. This knowledge worked in varying degrees to pervert the theory of staff-line relations. Ideally the two organizations cooperate to improve existing methods of output, to introduce new methods, to plan the work, and

to solve problems of production and the scheduling of orders that might arise. But when the line offers resistance to the findings and recommendations of the staff, the latter is reduced to evasive practices of getting some degree of acceptance of its programs, and at the same time of convincing top management that "good relations" exist with officers down the line. This necessity becomes even more acute when the staff officer aspires (for some of the reasons given above) to move over to the line organization, for then he must convince powerful line officers that he is worthy. In building a convincing record, however, he may compromise with line demands and bring charges from his staff colleagues that he is "selling out," so that after moving into the line organization he will then have to live with enemies he made in the staff. In any case, the need among staff incumbents of pleasing line officers in order to perfect their careers called for accommodation in three major areas: [18] (1) the observance of staff rules, (2) the introduction of new techniques, and (3) the use of appropriations for staff research and experiment.

With respect to point one, staff personnel, particularly in the middle and lower levels, carried on expedient relations with the line that daily evaded formal rules. Even those officers most devoted to rules found that, in order not to arouse enmity in the line on a scale sufficient to be communicated *up* the line, compromising devices were frequently helpful and sometimes almost unavoidable both for organizational and career aims. The usual practice was to tolerate minor breaking of staff rules by line personnel, or even to cooperate with the line in evading rules,[19]

[18] The relative importance of one or more of these areas would vary with the function of a given staff.
[19] In a processing department in one of the plants the chemical solution in a series of vats was supposed to have a specific strength and temperature, and a fixed rate of inflow and outflow. Chemists (members of the chemical staff) twice daily checked these properties of the solution and submitted reports showing that all points met the laboratory ideal. Actually, the solution was usually nearly triple the standard strength, the temperature was about 10 degrees Centigrade higher than standard, and the rate of flow was in excess of double the standard. There are, of course, varying discrepancies between laboratory theory and plant practice, but

and in exchange lay a claim on the line for cooperation on critical issues. In some cases line aid was enlisted to conceal lower staff blunders from the upper staff and the upper line.[20]

Concerning point two, while the staff organizations gave much time to developing new techniques, they were simultaneously thinking about how their plans would be received by the line. They knew from experience that middle and lower line officers could always give a "black eye" to staff contributions by deliberate mal-practices. Repeatedly top management had approved, and incorporated, staff proposals that had been verbally accepted down the line. Often the latter officers had privately opposed the changes, but had feared that saying so would incur the resentment of powerful superiors who could informally hurt them. Later they would seek to discredit the change by deliberate mal-practice and hope to bring a return to the former arrangement. For this reason there was a tendency for staff members to withhold improved production schemes or other plans when they knew that

___

the condition described here resulted from production pressures that forced line foremen into behavior upsetting the conditions expected by chemical theory. The chemists were sympathetic with the hard-pressed foremen, who compensated by (1) notifying the chemists (rather than their superior, the chief chemist) if anything "went wrong" for which the laboratory was responsible and thus sparing them criticism; and by (2) cooperating with the chemists to reduce the number of analyses which the chemists would ordinarily have to make.
[20] Failure of middle and lower staff personnel to "cooperate" with line officers might cause the latter to "stand pat" in observance of line rules at a time when the pressures of a dynamic situation would make the former eager to welcome line cooperation in rule-breaking. For example, a staff officer was confronted with the combined effect of (1) a delay in production on the line that was due to an indefensible staff error; (2) pressure on the line superintendent—with whom he was working—to hurry a special order; and (3) the presence in his force of new inexperienced staff personnel who were (a) irritating to line officers, and (b) by their inexperience constituted an invitation to line aggression. Without aid from the line superintendent (which could have been withheld by observance of formal rules) in covering up the staff error and in controlling line personnel, the staff officer might have put himself in permanent disfavor with all his superiors.

an attempt to introduce them might fail or even bring personal disrepute.

Line officers fear staff innovations for a number of reasons. In view of their longer experience, presumably intimate knowledge of the work, and their greater remuneration, they fear[21] being "shown up" before their line superiors for not having thought of the processual refinements themselves. They fear that changes in methods may bring personnel changes which will threaten the break-up of cliques and existing informal arrangements and quite possibly reduce their area of authority. Finally, changes in techniques may expose forbidden practices and departmental inefficiency. In some cases these fears have stimulated line officers to compromise staff men to the point where the latter will agree to postpone the initiation of new practices for specific periods.

In one such case an assistant staff head agreed with a line superintendent to delay the application of a bonus plan for nearly three months so that the superintendent could live up to the expedient agreement he had made earlier with his grievance committeeman to avoid a "wildcat" strike by a group of production workmen.[22] The lower engineers who had devised the plan were suspicious of the formal reasons given to them for withholding it, so the assistant staff head prevented them (by means of "busy work") from attending staff-line meetings lest they inadvertently reveal to top management that the plan was ready.

The third area of staff-line accommodations growing out of authority relations revolved around staff use of funds granted it by top management. Middle and lower line charged that staff research and experimentation was little more than "money wasted on blunders," and that various departments of the line could have "accomplished much more with less money." According to staff officers, those of

___

[21] Though there was little evidence that top management expected line officers to refine production techniques, the fear of such an expectation existed nevertheless. As noted earlier, however, some of the top executives *were* thinking that development of a "higher type" of first-line foreman might enable most of the staff groups to be eliminated.
[22] This case indicates the over-lapping of conflict areas referred to earlier. A later paper will deal with the area of informal union-management relations.

their plans that failed usually did so because line personnel "sabotaged" them and refused to "cooperate." Specific costs of "crack-pot experimentation" in certain staff groups were pointed to by line officers. Whatever the truth of the charges and counter-charges, evidence indicated (confidants in both groups supported this) that pressures from the line organization (below the top level) forced some of the staff groups to "kick over" parts of the funds appropriated for staff use [23] by top management. These compromises were of course hidden from top management, but the relations described were carried on to such an extent that by means of them—and line pressures for manipulation of accounts in the presumably impersonal auditing departments—certain line officers were able to show impressively low operating costs and thus win favor [24] with top management that would relieve pressures and be useful in personal advancement. In their turn the staff officers involved would receive more "cooperation" from the line and/or recommendation for transfer to the line. The data indicated that in a few such cases men from accounting and auditing staffs were given general foremanships (without previous line experience) as a reward for their understanding behavior.

SUMMARY. Research in three industrial plants showed conflict between the managerial staff and line groups that hindered the attainment of organizational goals. Privately expressed attitudes among some of the higher line executives revealed their hope that greater control of staff groups could be achieved, or that the groups might be eliminated and their functions taken over in great part by carefully selected and highly remunerated lower-line officers. On their side, staff members wanted more recognition and a greater voice in control of the plants.

All of the various functioning groups of the plants were caught up in a general conflict system; but apart from the effects of involvement

in this complex, the struggles between line and staff organizations were attributable mainly to (1) functional differences between the two groups; (2) differentials in the ages, formal education, potential occupational ceilings, and status group affiliations of members of the two groups (the staff officers being younger, having more education but lower occupational potential, and forming a prestige-oriented group with distinctive dress and recreational tastes); (3) need of the staff groups to justify their existence; (4) fear in the line that staff bodies by their expansion, and well-financed research activities, would undermine line authority; and (5) the fact that aspirants to higher staff offices could gain promotion only through approval of influential line executives.

If further research should prove that staff-line behavior of the character presented here is widespread in industry, and if top management should realize how such behavior affects its cost and production goals—and be concerned to improve the condition—then remedial measures could be considered. For example, a corrective approach might move in the direction of (1) creating a separate body [25] whose sole function would be the coordination of staff and line efforts; (2) increasing the gradations of awards and promotions in staff organizations (without increase of staff personnel); (3) granting of more nearly equal pay to staff officers, but with increased responsibility (without authority over line processes or personnel) for the practical working of their projects; (4) requiring that staff personnel have a minimum supervisory experience and have shared repeatedly in successful collaborative staff-line projects before transferring to the line; (5) steps by top management to remove the fear of veiled personal reprisal felt by officers in most levels of both staff and line hierarchies (This fear—rising from a dis-

[23] In two of the plants a somewhat similar relation, rising from different causes, existed *inside* the line organization with the *operating* branch of the line successfully applying pressures for a share in funds assigned to the *maintenance* division of the line.
[24] The reader must appreciate the fact that constant demands are made by top management to maintain low operating costs.

[25] This body, or "Board of Coordination," would be empowered to enforce its decisions. Membership would consist of staff and line men who had had wide experience in the plant over a period of years. The Board would (a) serve as an arbiter between staff and line; (b) review, screen, and approve individual recommendations submitted; and (c) evaluate contributions after a trial period. Such a body would incidentally be another high status goal for seasoned, capable, and ambitious officers who too often are trapped by the converging walls of the pyramidal hierarchy.

belief in the possibility of bureaucratic impersonality—is probably the greatest obstacle to communication inside the ranks of management); (6) more emphasis in colleges and universities on realistic instruction in the social sciences for students preparing for industrial careers.

Interdepartmental Conflict and Cooperation: Two Contrasting Studies

JOHN M. DUTTON *and* RICHARD E. WALTON

This report compares and contrasts emergent behavioral patterns in two district organizations. It focuses on how personnel of functionally interdependent departments enter into the process of joint decision-making and otherwise relate to each other. The study is based on data gathered through field observations and interviews. The analytical approach is to describe behavior in tactical terms, characterizing the participants in these two lateral relationships as behaving instrumentally and adaptively, albeit not always effectively.

Although the organizational literature on lateral relationships is meager when compared with the studies on leadership and authority, both M. Dalton and G. Strauss have published insightful accounts of tactical patterns in lateral relationships in several firms they have studied.[1] Dalton's studies have focused upon relations between production and maintenance and between "line and staff." Strauss analyzes the tactical patterns of purchasing agents in their relations with other departments. This article adds another account of conflict in the lateral relations between another pair of departments—sales and production. In the organizations reported upon here, sales and production represented the two most important functions and both were "line" departments. Moreover, their interdependence was intense, frequent, and central to the core activities of both departments.

The two case studies of conflict and collaboration presented here are especially fruitful objects of analysis because they are placed in the same general technological, economic, and

From *Human Organization*, Vol. 25, No. 3, Fall 1965, pp. 207–220. Reprinted by permission of the publisher.
The authors wish to acknowledge the support for the study provided by Purdue Research Foundation, and the contributions of H. G. Fitch as research assistant.

market context and within the same overall organizational structure. The two company districts had the same basic task. Within each district, production and sales tasks included independent and interdependent aspects. Yet the two emergent relationships differed dramatically. In the Elgin district, production and sales each adopted a narrow, exclusive goal structure and engaged in reciprocal organizational strategies and tactics of conflict. In sharp contrast, each of the two parties at Bowie adopted goals that embraced the other's operating objectives and pursued strategies of collaboration.

The discussion first analyzes the technological and economic interdependencies of the production and sales departments. Subsequently the relationship syndrome is described point by point in each district. The discussion then turns to the stabilizing processes in each relationship; the factors which may account for the different patterns in the two districts; and the consequences of these patterns for the participants and for the larger organization.

Areas of Interdependence Between Production and Sales

Peerless was a large manufacturer which owned and operated more than a dozen widely dispersed plants.[2] The company produced a wide line of metal windows, doors, and sashes for sale to industrial customers and to the building industry. Products ranged from simple metal frames to complex all-weather doors and sashes and included both standard industry items and products made to customer order specifications. Individual order quantities varied from a few dozen to several thousand items. Items were produced only upon receipt of firm customer orders.

Each company plant was a relatively self-sufficient unit, dependent on its own resources for obtaining and producing customer orders in a profitable manner within its geographical area. Each district consisted of a production plant and a sales area. Responsibility for company field operations was divided at the home office between a general sales manager and a general production manager. Several regional production managers and several regional sales managers provided a link between the home office and the subordinate managers in the various districts. Especially important for the study was the fact that no position of overall general management responsibility was established for any of the districts or regions. Thus, coordination between sales and production was largely an *ad hoc* arrangement in each district.

Important areas of interdependence which called for some degree of joint decision-making between production and sales at Peerless metal fabricating plants included acceptance of new orders, scheduling, and quality control.

Order Acceptance. Obtaining orders was a responsibility of the district sales personnel. New orders required designing and cost estimating, and often involved hard negotiating with customers on price and terms of delivery. Decisions which affected both production and sales were frequently made in day-to-day order procurement activities. Salesmen would have liked, essentially, to sell any and all orders they could. The buyer's market they faced inclined them to let customers exercise great influence over product design. However, some orders were less profitable for production than others. Given the plant's staff and equipment, some were technically only marginally feasible. Others were feasible but not economical. The potential participants in decisions regarding new designs and order acceptance included: 1) the sales manager, salesman, service manager, and product designer; and 2) the production manager, plant superintendent, production control manager, and shipping manager.

Top management's expectations were that designs and order acceptance would be decided on the basis of a full search for alternatives and a balanced examination of the implications for both departments. Beyond this, sales could seek orders to balance production facilities. Similarly, production, by experimenting with new, initially costly orders, could assist in building profitable sales volume in the company's competitive market.

Scheduling Decisions. Production was a rapid and complex operation. Each day many different standard and specialty orders passed through several fast-moving stages of fabrication and assembly work to the shipping department for direct delivery to customers.

Both sales and production had a strong interest in scheduling. Responsibility for scheduling orders for production was assigned to the production manager. The sequence of orders produced was important to sales, however, because lead time was short between order receipt and the delivery date required. Consequently, sales officials were concerned that the sequence of orders through the plant reflect their customer priorities.

Production's stake in scheduling decisions was equally important. A large number of scheduling sequences was technically possible for a set of current orders, but widely varying costs were attached to these sequences.

Coordination between sales and production was also required in the handling of customer requests for revision of delivery dates and order quantities, and in resolving the problems arising from plant congestion and equipment breakdowns. Changes in the production schedule which resulted from these problems placed special potential strain on the sales-production relationship.

The formal organizational plan called upon sales and production personnel to balance customer priority on the one hand and production cost and inconvenience on the other hand. Ideally they would share accurate information relevant to these considerations, collaboratively weight the factors, and reach a decision through consensus.

Quality Control. Opportunities for quality errors were numerous because of the nature of company operations. Sales was responsible for securing complete and correct order specifications. Production was responsible for producing orders free from defects and in the quantity stipulated. Each party possessed information of value to the other. Production possessed information on defective and marginal orders which it could reveal or conceal. Sales was in a position to ascertain whether a customer could accept an order of marginal quality; also sales was frequently the first to be informed by the customer of an error or defect and could conceal or reveal this knowledge. Sales officials felt the threat of losing customers by failing to maintain quality in a competitive market. Production appreciated the need to maintain minimum standards in the area of product quality but was subject to production performance criteria, including raw material waste control and machine and labor utilization, which sometimes competed with quality considerations. Moreover, once a quality error or loss occurred, the expense was charged against either sales or production. Thus, both had an incentive to avoid unnecessary bad marks on their respective records, and each had reason to be less concerned about those defects charged against the other department. Notwithstanding these divisive incentives, both parties were ultimately dependent—for sales and production volume—upon an acceptable level of quality.

Analysis of the organizational setting thus revealed a potential toward both collaboration and conflict at the district level. Sales was more sensitive than production to volume, and production more concerned than sales with cost factors. In addition, the fact that plant production and district sales did not report to a common superior allowed each to choose to concentrate on its separate functions to the exclusion of the other's interests.

The Elgin Plant—A Conflict Relationship

The Elgin plant was the largest and one of the oldest plants in the company, with many employees of long-time service. Plant layout and equipment were typical and posed no particular problems, save in shipping, where space was cramped.

Bargaining and Other Dynamics of the Conflict Relationship. Maintenance of a bargaining approach to joint decision-making imposed particular requirements on the social system, as well as on the process of information handling and exchange in joint decisions. Each party required a conflict-oriented frame of reference consistent with a bargaining approach to joint decisions. Bargaining also imposed a need for particular, supporting patterns of atti-

tudes and interaction. These Elgin behavior patterns can be analyzed in terms of strategy and tactics employed to implement a bargaining relationship.

Goals and Orientation to Decision-Making. Officials in each of the two departments adopted narrowly defined objectives for their own department. That each department perceived the other as adopting divisive rather than unifying objectives can be seen in the comments of Elgin sales versus production officials.

Sales officials: Sales is customer oriented. Production is interested only in cost. . . . Production only sees plant waste in costly orders and low output. . . . Sales' job is service—delivery when the customer wants it. . . . Sales' main job is to build volume in customer orders.

Production officials: Our goal is to run orders efficiently. Many opportunities arise to reduce costs . . . but the salesmen don't know enough about production to recognize these things. . . . New items often give us problems. . . . Many times the salesmen try to sell ideas that cannot be produced economically or even at all!

These statements go beyond superficial confirmation of the departmental division of labor intended by top management. The two parties were aware of the existence of larger, overall district goals. But they chose not to adopt district goals as superordinate and not to coordinate their departments in the maximum interest of these goals.

Information-Handling. Lack of understanding of each other's department problems characterized the approach to joint decision-making at Elgin. The parties also failed to communicate, or delayed communicating, relevant information to each other. These conditions at Elgin were legitimized by the viewpoint of each party which saw problems of the other as "their problem, not ours."

Scheduling decisions, for example, were subject to mutual influence but were arrived at through demand-counterdemand, exaggeration, pressure maneuvers, and so on. Padding of needs for prompt and urgent handling of customer orders by sales officials was at the heart of the bargaining process. Production personnel, however, privately discounted sales requests as "obviously padded." On the other hand, production would exaggerate the difficulty it anticipated with a given request, whereas sales would assume that production constraints were more fanciful than real.

Quality control decisions exhibited the same bargaining pattern, including deliberate distortion and concealment. Sales engaged in overstatement of quality needs and production discounted sales quality requests.

The withholding of information stemmed in part from fear of raising future performance expectations and from fear of home office sanctions. If production (or sales) was too accommodating in scheduling decisions, they might create high expectations and, therefore, future problems for themselves. Similarly, full disclosure of quality defects might bring home office sanctions.

Because each department usually possessed more flexibility than it was willing to admit, it limited the number and type of contacts with the other, thus reducing the risk of revealing the true facts to the other.

Freedom of Movement. At Elgin each party sought to gain maximum freedom for itself and to limit the other's freedom. On the one hand, each party attempted to fix future performance obligations and to establish jurisdictional limits *for* the other. On the other hand, each party engaged in tactical violations of limits imposed *by* the other.

Elgin sales was particularly active in circumventing formal procedures. Sales found production lacking in understanding, consideration, and competence and therefore attempted to take direct, unilateral action on their problems even when this violated procedures and usurped jurisdictional authority from production. This type of behavior is succinctly summarized in a sales official's comments:

> When production refuses, we have to act to satisfy customers. For instance, production often claims not to have material to produce an order. So we get on the phone to locate and purchase material. Production then, of course, claims that we are not within our rights. But we can't solve our problems by turning customers away.

To counteract this behavior, and to satisfy its generally felt need for caution and certainty in the conflict bargaining process, production further emphasized jurisdictional limits, restricted interaction, and formalized decision-rules to govern interdepartmental relations. The resulting oscillation between emphasis on rigid rules on the one hand, and unilateral action on the other, heightened the dilemma for each party of either choosing dependence on a reluctant peer or risking independent action. These tendencies are shown in the following comments by members of both units.

> Problems are resolved on a jurisdictional basis: "You take care of your part and we'll take care of ours." Each group decides who's responsible for what part of the problem and then goes its separate way; each party tries to hold out for the least possible action on his part.

> The relationship between sales and production doesn't permit very much innovation on new orders. Production tends to resist, saying "Do it the old way," and finding lots of reasons not to try new ideas. However, sales needs new designs and depends on production for help. But if sales goes ahead with a new design alone, production feels their rights are infringed on.

The difficulties in joint decisions on scheduling resulted in a supreme attempt to formalize relationships between the parties on the handling of this problem. The parties at Elgin negotiated a written agreement which stipulated procedures for scheduling customer orders. The new scheduling agreement established the minimum production lead time on customer orders, and the plant capacity, and set forth a detailed plan of organization and procedures for scheduling customer orders. Under the plan two new expediters, plus the production control manager and service manager, were to constitute the sole contacts between sales, the production office, and the plant production floor.

This remarkably formal and explicit signed agreement was an expression of the two-unit relationship at Elgin. Its twofold significance was that it was produced by the bargaining relationship and that it was widely heralded at the plant as a forward step. Apparently the agreement controlled the tension and conflict between the departments. It strengthened tendencies already present to limit interaction between sales and production. Since members of the units found these exchanges both punitive and unrewarding, the plan provided welcome relief. The agreement delegated the scheduling problem to a small group and, as a consequence, numerous persons were able to withdraw from an uncomfortable relationship.

Sales was inclined to initiate more contacts than production. While the agreement tended to restrict interaction in scheduling, sales remained active in other areas, such as quality control. Here sales employed the tactic of circumventing formal procedures by exploiting special relationships with a person in production. Contrary to policy, this official permitted sales people into the plant to check on customer complaints.

Both parties frequently used pressure tactics to achieve their ends. The two types commonly employed were hierarchical relationships and "commitment tactics." At Elgin both sales and production turned to their regional and home office superiors as a means of resolving differences. For example, both managers frequently refused to accept responsibility for a given quality error. As a result disagreements were carried all the way up to the home office general sales and general production managers for a decision.

Another type of behavior, referred to in bargaining theory as "commitment tactics," was tactical to the conflict approach. One manager would attempt to influence a joint decision by structuring the situation so as to be seen by the other as irrevocably or maximally committed to his preferred position. For example, a sales official would often call the production planning manager to get a promise on delivery while holding the customer on another telephone line in order to "put the pressure on" production.

Production also used commitment tactics, sometimes by presenting sales with a *fait accompli*. This was not uncommon when an order cancellation or delay by the customer would be inconvenient to production. A sales official commented:

> Production will try to get a customer to take an order when the latter wants to cancel. Production has sometimes waited until the order was in production or has asked us to tell the customer the order was already in process.

Production will also ship ahead of time when they have an order completed before the planned delivery date. They will do this even when they *know* the customer does not want the order early and has no place to store it.

Blaming was also tactically used both as a form of punishment and as a means of avoiding responsibility for failures in performance. The conflict about who was to blame for errors, losses, and delays was especially intense. The sales manager commented:

> Recently a customer received an order with oversize frames in it. He was willing to sort out the bad items himself if we could give him credit. But the production manager wouldn't do it. He wouldn't take the loss in production.
>
> We finally had to take the credit as sales expense. However, we delayed so long that the customer lost patience and we got the whole order back to rehandle ourselves.

At Elgin this pattern was often carried to the point of attributing every problem or negative result to the other fellow. Moreover, not only was the other party perceived as responsible for what was bad, but he was also seen as erroneously accepting credit for what was good! For example, production personnel charged that sales people took a lot of credit for work on new designs done in production.

Attitudes. The attitudes of the parties supported the bargaining approach to joint decision-making. Each department used the terms "we" and "they" to distinguish between the two groups and to compare "good" and "bad" motives. Each found occasion to report unfavorable attributes of the other, such as the lack of integrity of a plant foreman who expected personal gifts for helping a salesman. Also, each saw the other as lacking in understanding and competence. Vindictiveness was revealed in anecdotes in which one party expressed satisfaction at making the other "squirm."

The atmosphere at Elgin went beyond the use of stereotypes and obstructive behavior. Attitudes approached resignation and despair, and a lack of hope that any accommodation could be reached that would permit interdepartmental problem-solving. Efforts which had been made to improve relationships had failed. The service manager reported:

> The production planner and I tried business lunches together. But we quit after a while. We weren't getting anywhere. We also tried customer service meetings. These didn't work either. People's feelings got involved. There were personality conflicts. Production felt they weren't getting a hearing. They started to make these meetings gripe sessions against sales.

There was little or no interaction that was not related to work, and when members of sales and production did meet, the atmosphere was cautious and hostile. It was apparent at these meetings that the parties were holding back information. It was also apparent that each party brought up topics and made statements that were designed to make the other party feel uncomfortable. For instance, one party would point out errors and oversights by the other or would verbally reprimand the other for withholding information.

The Bowie Plant—A Collaborative Relationship

The Bowie plant had been acquired by the company within the past ten years. It had been purchased complete with equipment from its former owners, and many of the plant personnel had remained after the purchase. Bowie was somewhat smaller than the average plant but was fully equipped and could produce the company's complete product line.

Problem-Solving and Other Dynamics of the Collaborative Relationship. At Bowie members of the two groups interacted frequently to resolve problems that arose in the course of their work. They enjoyed these contacts, as the following scene indicates:

> The production manager burst into the sales managers office and handed him a sample of a new part. "Try that," he said.
> "It certainly seems stronger," the sales manager replied. He tried to twist the sample in his hand and also tried to bend it under his foot. "It certainly is!" he exclaimed.
> "We'll run a trial on this in the plant and see how it works out," said the production manager, and then left.
> The sales manager explained the incident, saying, "We were having trouble with this part. Frank, the production manager, got an idea from a toy he got for his kids and came to see me about it. He gave the idea to Tom, the designer, who worked it over to make it easier to produce. We think it is a very good idea."

In this incident a production man and a sales person cooperated with each other to develop an idea for an improved product. They saw the problem as a joint task for both sales and production and provided social support for each other in their attempts to solve the problem.

At Bowie problem-solving was the approach to joint decision-making used in all areas of interdependence, including new designs, scheduling, and quality control. Maintenance of this approach required a collaborative orientation from each party and a supporting pattern of interaction.

Goals and Orientation to Decision-Making. Members of the Bowie organization tended to define objectives for themselves which embraced both production and marketing functions. The sales manager's comment was especially direct in this respect.

> You build a plant to make a certain product mix. Then you have to try to go out and sell this mix.
> In planning sales we try to develop a program to obtain business to keep all machines in the plant operating. There's a big capital investment out there and you can get terrible imbalances among departments if you don't exercise control.
> You also, however, have to sell what's there in the market. You can't tool up to produce what isn't there. The ideal is a balance between the market and the production setup.

The production manager had a similar view. For example, he indicated sufficient concern about missed deliveries that his remarks could have been confused with those emanating from sales.

Information-Handling. In contrast with Elgin, both Bowie departments evidenced an understanding of the other's problems. For instance, the scheduling task at Bowie, as at Elgin, contained conflict potential: Customers tended to give short lead time and initiated requests for revised delivery dates; production officials had reasons peculiar to their task for preferring one schedule over another; breakdowns in bottleneck equipment occurred, etc. Distortion or rationing in the handling of information, however, did not develop. For example, the "padding" of sales requests which marked the scheduling process at Elgin occurred at Bowie only in a minor way, if at all. The salesmen at Bowie were more inclined than at Elgin to probe for the customer's real needs so that unnecessary demands were not passed on to production. The following salesman's comments are indicative of this understanding and consideration:

> The customers are educated not to expect delivery within a certain period of time. There are exceptions, but why foul up production scheduling to accommodate customers who don't anticipate their own needs?
> You do have to take the customer's needs into account. You can't be late. We have established an understanding with production. If our minimum delivery rule doesn't satisfy customers, then we contact production through the service manager.

Each party tried to anticipate problems, not only for itself but also for the other. Recall that at Elgin production was reluctant to inform sales of errors or slightly defective product runs. At Bowie, production people were encouraged to go to the service manager and tell him about an error. Sales would then phone to see if the customer was willing to accept the product anyway. The customer frequently cooperated if he was approached this way. The production manager commented on other areas in which he was benefited by sales:

> We have few problems in avoiding uneconomical or unprofitable orders. The sales manager is good about this. He gives me a look-see on possible problem orders insofar as cost is concerned. We look at these together and compare revenue and cost considerations.
> I also go to sales to *ask* for certain types

of business. We may need finishing work of a particular type, for instance.

This degree of understanding at Bowie had not always existed. In the past salesmen had obtained every order they could. Certain steps were being taken to further increase salesmen's understanding of production problems, including giving young salesmen firsthand experience in production.

Constraints at Bowie limited the degree to which the parties could be helpful to one another in jointly solving problems. One constraint was a lack of relevant cost information. The sales manager cited specific orders for small lots and complex items which were of doubtful profitability, but in the absence of cost information he could not be certain. This situation was viewed as a mutual problem rather than an intergroup issue, however.

Freedom of Movement. At Bowie the parties generally tried to increase freedom of movement. Cooperation and procedures were adequate enough so that there was little or no incentive to circumvent the rules or formal procedures. Where deviations did exist, they did not present an issue. A member of the production organization said:

> Sales people are not supposed to come out on the floor but sometimes they do. I don't think there's anything wrong with it as long as the salesmen don't stop and talk to the machine operators. And they don't do this as far as I know.

There was flexibility in decision-making rules. No arrangement existed at Bowie comparable to the Elgin scheduling agreement. No minimum delivery rule was established. It was generally understood that quick delivery promises were risky, but the service manager was delegated authority by both parties to "play-it-by-ear."

In more general terms, there was a complete absence of attempts by either party to fix future performance for the other party or to force commitments from the other that would limit its future freedom. This freedom was accompanied by a relatively open interaction pattern. The sales and production managers met daily several times, as did their office subordinates, the service manager and production control manager. There were few restrictions on the movements of any member of the plant organization.

Although Bowie's interaction system was more open than Elgin's, there were certain restrictions in selected decision areas at Bowie. These limits were, however, pursuant to the collaboration pattern rather than exceptions to it. Limited interaction was especially notable in day-to-day scheduling decisions, as shown by a sales official's comment:

> People are generally free to come and go in the plant and office. However, we don't want salesmen to try to persuade the foremen to get their orders. By the same token we don't want foremen to ask salesmen for changes in orders. We do have lines of communication on scheduling matters through the service manager.
>
> We confine our scheduling contacts with production to the service manager. As soon as you have a number of people doing it, you lose control.

These comments indicated conditions where limited interaction could be beneficial to the collaborative relationship. Successful collaboration on scheduling required both cooperative criteria and adequate decision-rules. Scheduling was an extremely complex cognitive task. Limited interaction was beneficial to the scheduling system for the following reasons: First, it enabled the service manager to reject untimely distractions for the production scheduler when the latter was involved in the intricate task of constructing a schedule. Second, it kept the information on scheduling channeled through the position where cooperative criteria were applied. Influence exerted in a non-controlled pattern was often sub-optimal in effect; for instance, when a salesman operated with incomplete data and inadequate rules in seeking to persuade a foreman to give preference to a particular order.

Closely related to open interaction patterns and freedom of movement was flexibility at Bowie in the establishment of positions and the performance of tasks. The leading instance of flexibility was a quality control plan. This plan, which had been devised at the Bowie plant and was unique within the company, employed a quality control man who rotated continuously through all departments in the plant watching for errors. Although the system contained the normal instances of laxness, and although this person, in performing his difficult task, encountered instances of friction from individuals, he was generally supported by both departments.

Another instance of organizational innovation was the establishment of the office of general manager serving both sales and production personnel. Home office approval had been secured for this move but the plant had taken the initiative on this change. The appointed official, the service manager, had extensive experience in production control as well as sales service and, in this smaller plant with its collaborative patterns, was well-qualified for an over-all coordinating position.

Bowie presented a further contrast to Elgin in searching for solutions in lieu of using pressure tactics. Whereas at Elgin the sales official held the customer on the phone while making requests of production, in order to increase his own commitment to this request, at Bowie the sales official did not need this leverage to find out what production could or could not do. Therefore, he was free to try to influence the customer—or at least to test the customer's real needs.

> Because production tells us in advance that we will not make our schedule on a particular order, we can call the customer and ask for an extra few days. You find that 90 percent of the time if you call him first, you can get extra time. It's when he has to call you that you get in trouble. The customer is apt to wait until about 4 p.m. on the promised delivery date and then call and say, "Where are you?" If he learns then that no delivery is to be made, he loses confidence. If you call him, he will go to bat for you. If you don't, you embarrass him; he may not need the order but his attitude will be that he does!

There were hierarchical appeals within the plant. But it appeared that the issues which were bucked up raised appropriate questions for plant officials. They were not cases where power was needed to accomplish the obvious, as was the tendency at Elgin. Similarly, extra-plant relations were largely used to implement the *jointly* developed policies of the sales and production managers. By working closely with the home office, the sales and production managers had jointly secured transfer orders from other districts to level production through low periods and had obtained home office approval for the production of certain items for inventory, also a unique arrangement within the company.

Regional and home office sales and production officials were not used as courts of appeal. Superiors set budget goals and cost controls and established payoffs for performance but they were not feared or seen as arbitrators. The sales manager stated:

> I have little contact with the regional manager and the home office. We don't depend on them. There is very little contact, on my part at least, and I feel there is little contact by the production manager.

The production manager's views on the use of the regional manager were similar to those of sales. He was a younger manager in training; nevertheless, he acknowledged the importance of working with sales, perhaps at some cost to his training relationship. He said:

> I don't use the regional manager as a court of appeal. The regional manager is training me. But it has never reached the point where I can't work out any problems with the sales manager. We feel we can reach an equitable solution together.

The tendency at Bowie was to attempt to diagnose problems regarding defective joint decision-rules rather than to find a "scapegoat" or to place blame on the other party. This pattern contrasted sharply with that at Elgin. Although much less energy was dissipated over the question of who was to blame, this was not because there was no penalty associated with accepting responsibility. There was as much penalty at Bowie as at Elgin.

The sales manager opposed pinpointing responsibility for errors because of the defensive atmosphere created by this procedure.

> We have a company quality control program. Its aim is to pinpoint losses. This aim can work against you because your people then try to avoid getting pinned for the error. However, we're not so interested in who created the problem as in what practices created the problem and how to correct these practices.

Not all officials wholly agreed with this position. The production manager was more inclined to support formal home office procedure —but for internal control purposes, not as an interdepartmental weapon. The quality control manager was still more favorably disposed to this procedure as an additional support for him in his task of maintaining quality. He also provided the researchers with information which, while it didn't change the general impression reported above, did confirm that the departments at Bowie were not always successful in avoiding the question of "blame."

Attitudes. The attitudes of both sales and production at Bowie have already been seen to support the problem-solving approach used in joint decision-making. Statements of members of the Bowie plant-district organization indicated that production and sales got along well. Personal relationships developed from work relationships. Members shared an interest in one another's affairs and saw each other off the job. Instances were revealed where members went out of their way to help another person.

The fact that liaison members at Bowie showed less strain than at Elgin was perhaps an indication of the differences in attitudes at the two plants. The Bowie service manager was well aware of the differences and potential conflict between sales and production in his district. However, he found his situation quite tolerable. And the quality control manager, who would be caught in the interdepartmental cross-pressure if anyone was, expressed the desire for *more* informal contacts.

Thus, the attitudes supported the blurring of departmental lines; encouraged trust and support between the two parties, and avoidance of punishing contacts; and furthered attempts to integrate the two units.

Strategy and Tactics: A Comparative Summary

The patterns of behavior at Bowie were in sharp contrast with those at Elgin. Elgin employed a bargaining, and Bowie a problem-solving, approach to joint decisions. The patterns of goal orientation, information-handling, interaction and attitudinal structure strategical to these contrasting approaches are summarized in Table 1.

Table 1. Summary of Two Contrasting Approaches to Interdepartmental Relations

	ELGIN: A BARGAINING APPROACH	BOWIE: A PROBLEM-SOLVING APPROACH
1. Goals and orientation to decision-making	1. With regard to respective goals and orientation to decision-making, each department emphasized the requirements of its own particular task, rather than the combined task of the plant sales district as a whole.	1. Each department stressed common goals whenever possible and otherwise sought to balance goals. Each party perceived the potentials for interdepartmental conflict in the separate task structures but nevertheless stressed the existence of superordinate district goals and the benefits of full collaboration for each party. Each saw the relationship as cooperative.
2. Information-handling	2. With respect to the strategic question of information exchange, each department (a) minimized the other's problems or tended to ignore such considerations as it did recognize; and (b) attempted to minimize or distort certain kinds of information communicated.	2. Each department (a) sought to understand the other's problems and to give consideration to problems of immediate concern to the other; and (b) endeavored to provide the other with full, timely, and accurate information relevant to joint decisions.
3. Freedom of movement	3. Several tactics were employed which related to the strategic question of freedom of movement. Each department sought to gain maximum freedom for itself and to limit the degrees of freedom for the other by the use of the following tactics: (a) attempting to circumvent formal procedures when advantageous; (b) emphasizing jurisdictional rules; (c) attempting to fix the other's future performance obligations; (d) attempting to restrict interaction patterns; (e) employing pressure tactics—hierarchical appeals and commitment tactics—whenever possible; (f) blaming the other for past failures in performance. Relations were laden with threats, hostility, and the desire for retaliation. Interdepartmental interactions were experienced as punishing by both sides. Contacts were limited to a few formal channels circumscribed by a rigid	3. Each department explored ways it could increase its freedom of movement toward its goals with the following behavior: (a) accepting informal procedures which facilitated the task; (b) blurring the division between production and sales in tasks and positions; (c) refraining from attempts to fix the other's future performance; (d) structuring relatively open interaction patterns; (e) searching for solutions rather than employing pressure tactics; (f) attempting to diagnose defects in rules for decision-making rather than worrying about placing blame. Relations were characterized by mutual support. Department officials were independent of higher authority. Home office was asked to support initiatives of joint proposals from the plant.

	ELGIN: A BARGAINING APPROACH	BOWIE: A PROBLEM-SOLVING APPROACH
	rule structure. Department officials depended on higher authority. Home-office managers were called upon to resolve opposing views, to suggest solutions, and to support one party against the other.	
4. Attitudes	4. Each department developed attitudes in support of the above bargaining strategy and tactics.	4. Each department adopted positive inclusive and trusting attitudes regarding the other.

The above comparative summary sharpens our understanding of the patterns of behavior which were strategical and tactical to the interdepartmental conflict at Elgin. How general are these particular patterns of interdepartmental conflict?

It is interesting to note certain contrasts and similarities in our observations and those of Strauss.[3] Whereas striving for status and authority seemed to be a major aspect of the strategic conflict engaged in by Strauss's purchasing agents, status was neither an objective nor a preoccupation underlying the conflict behavior of the sales and production managers in the present study. These managers were merely intent upon doing well in their assigned task (narrowly defined). Several possible reasons for these differences can be offered: First, the sales and production managers were relatively high status; second, unlike the purchasing agents, who could attract the notice of higher management only by enlarging their responsibilities, assuming new initiative, etc., the sales and production managers were measured by higher management in terms of their routine performance; third, the sales and production managers, within their functional areas, had opportunities for upward mobility not available to the purchasing agents.

Despite these strategic differences, certain important similarities are noted in the implementing tactics used to pursue conflict in the two settings; namely, increase in formality, fixing of obligations, appeal to superiors, and selective circumvention of procedures.

There are fewer similarities between the conflict behavior patterns reported here and those described by Dalton.[4] The present study involved two dominant actors in a bipolar district organization, whereas Dalton's participants were in a multi-person and multi-group field; hence, the importance of bargaining strategies (information control, decision-rule framework, etc.) in this study and the importance of coalition strategies (alliances, favors, cliques, etc.) in Dalton's work. Nevertheless, many tactics such as blaming, hierarchical appeals, and formalization were often common to both bargaining and coalition strategies.

Stability in Lateral Relationships

How were these contrasting patterns maintained at Elgin and Bowie respectively? Apart from what ever forces might explain the emergence of either relationship, each pattern achieved added stability because it was self-reinforcing, reciprocal, and regenerative.

Self-Reinforcing Processes. There were important self-reinforcing processes within the orientation and behavioral patterns of a given party to a relationship. Perception of divisive goals by production (or sales) led to a bargaining orientation at Elgin. Bargaining called for the use of tactics such as concealment, distortion, threat. Implementing these tactics, in turn, required circumscribed interaction patterns and negative attitudes toward the other party. However, once adopted, each of these tactical patterns had a feedback effect reinforcing the others and the basic orientation to goals. That is, for example, unfriendly and suspicious attitudes reinforced the tendency to circumscribe interactions, to distort information, and to attend to divisive goals.

Precisely the same type of feedback and reinforcement tendencies existed within superordinate goal orientation, the problem-solving approach, full information exchange, open interaction patterns, and positive attitudes at Bowie.

The effect of these feedback and reinforcement processes within either approach to a relationship (once these components had achieved the apparent internal consistency found in these two cases) was to create some momentum and stability for the relationship itself. Because many elements of the total behavioral pattern would have to change together in order to achieve stability at some other point on the conflict-collaboration continuum, forces toward change greater than those which established the relationship in the first place would have to be brought to bear.

Reciprocal Patterns. In a given plant the pattern was reciprocal for the two parties. At Elgin, where one department adopted a narrow goal structure, the other did likewise. Where one party rationed or distorted information, the other did also. Where one attempted to limit the activities of the other, both did. Where one expressed antagonistic feelings, the other, too, reciprocated. Perhaps the pattern could not have been otherwise for long, because for one party to have been free and candid in providing information and in accommodating the other's needs without assurances of reciprocal treatment would have been even more self-defeating than to pursue a defensive bargaining relationship.

The elements of the pattern at Bowie—which were the opposite of those just described—were also reciprocated. Although there were temptations to "cheat" on these patterns (for the temporary benefit that might accrue), both sides appreciated the fact that they enjoyed the larger benefits of collaboration precisely because there was reciprocity. This reciprocal nature of the emergent pattern was facilitated by the degree of symmetry which existed in the underlying structure of their interdependence: Each party had substantial initiative and ability to make the effective decision in one or more of, the areas of decision-making vital to both departments. Es-

pecially important for the maintenance of a collaborative pattern is an allowance for both parties to be equally and similarly rewarded by the benefits of collaboration.

Regenerative Relations. Relations were also regenerative at each plant. The experience of older hands was communicated to new members. Only in exceptional cases did individuals resist the conditioning effect of the prevailing plant culture. Within each department existing patterns of behavior were encouraged and alternative patterns discouraged. Except for a single plant official at Elgin who cooperated with sales, the other sporadic attempts to achieve an element of collaboration between sales and production invariably collapsed in failure. The converse, and of equal significance, was Bowie's tendency to resist bargaining. Occasional attempts by Bowie individuals at concealment, threat, and division were greeted with stern and prompt disapproval. Sanctions at each plant thus supported the present behavior patterns and rejected the major alternative.

Antecedents to Lateral Relationships

What factors explain the emergence of the divergent patterns in these two districts of the same company? Conflict relationships are sometimes explained in terms of contextual factors, such as payoff structure or difficulty of the task, and sometimes attributed to the personal characteristics of the principals in the relationship.

It has already been noted that the formal organizational plan in Peerless contained forces toward both conflict and collaboration at the district level. But at Elgin the parties acted on the conflict potential and ignored the collaboration potential. At Bowie the reverse was true. Why? Although to date we have not collected systematic data to test the many explanatory hypotheses we believe plausible, this intensive investigation is suggestive of the effect of certain factors.

Contextual Factors. Although the same types of contextual forces may have been acting on the principals in both districts, the magnitude of these forces may have been different —and even subtle differences in the two districts may explain the contrasting responses.

For example, although the districts operated under a common formal plan (including performance criteria and reward structure), the plan could be interpreted differently by the several regional managers who supervised the Elgin and Bowie districts. That is, one or both of the regional production and sales managers responsible for supervising the Elgin district managers may have placed relatively more emphasis on performance of the separate sales (or production) department.

Similar differences were possible in the nature of the task. Although each pair of sales and production departments performed basically similar functions for the total system, slight differences here might have made great differences in the stress and strain on the production and sales interaction. Two circumstances of this nature can be cited which may have influenced the relationship.

First, compared to Elgin, Bowie seemed to enjoy a relatively large degree of home office support, particularly in terms of achieving a balanced plant load. Extensive arrangements had been made via the home office for providing orders for Bowie production during the slow season by transferring orders from other plants. It was not wholly clear whether this arrangement was possible because of the plant's reputation at the home office or because of the collaborative relationship at Bowie. It was clear, however, that the resulting arrangement was perceived as highly advantageous by Bowie production and that Bowie production gave credit for the plan both to Bowie sales and to the home office.

Secondly, compared to Bowie, Elgin was an older plant and was handicapped by lack of space, especially in shipping. Significantly, perhaps, this plant experienced problems of congestion and errors in delivery not mentioned at Bowie. In addition, Elgin operated a special department which produced a unique product for the whole firm. This utilized space, time, materials and labor at Elgin in such a way as to restrict the amount of the plant's resources available to Elgin sales. This technological limitation on production's ability to respond to the needs or demands of sales could have been a factor promoting conflict.

Personal Characteristics. There was an important comparability in the Elgin and Bowie situations in terms of the work background of the sales managers. At both districts the sales managers possessed production as well as sales experience. In neither case, however, did the production managers have experience in sales.

Direct familiarity with another department's operations—the problems, the possibilities, and the performance criteria involved—increases one's ability to initiate a collaborative pattern beneficial to both departments. For example, the first party is able to differentiate among those demands he would make on the other in terms of how much inconvenience would be involved for the latter. Similarly, he may be able to identify the relatively important task demands of the other and respond selectively to them. Also, the first party may possess emotional empathy for the other, which affects the timing and manner of presenting his requests or demands on the other.

Thus, in terms of background and experience, the sales managers in both districts were in a position to take the initiative in developing a collaborative pattern. Structurally—in terms of the work flow—sales was also advantageously situated to play an initiative role. With few exceptions, production produced only to customer order, and action by sales preceded action by production much of the time. Another precondition—and our final similarity—was that the Elgin sales manager, like the one at Bowie, had shown some personal interest in working toward a collaborative pattern.

But the differences between the personal characteristics of the principals in the two districts may help explain why a collaborative pattern developed in one but not the other. There were differences in the personal styles of the two sales managers; differences in the cognitive and interpersonal skills of the two production managers; and differences in the degree of status congruity within the two relationships.

First, we can present a brief summary statement about Bowie for use as a benchmark for examining the same factors at Elgin. At Bowie the sales manager was markedly senior to the newly promoted Bowie production manager "in training." The young Bowie production manager was eager to learn, both trusted and took direction from his sales counterpart, appeared to be relatively skilled in interpersonal relations, and was willing to experiment. The

Bowie sales manager was also skilled in interpersonal relations and used a permissive, albeit somewhat paternal, approach in dealings with his younger production counterpart.

The Elgin sales manager had been promoted to his position fairly recently. Although his background included several years of work in production, his primary orientation was toward sales. He found resourceful use for his production knowledge in the pursuit of sales goals; believed that production as well as sales should seek innovative new products; and was convinced that greater customer service was required to cope with prevailing competitive market conditions. His leadership style was forceful and he aggressively sought ways to achieve sales goals. He was similarly action-oriented in his dealings with production.

The background and personality of the Elgin production manager were quite different from those of the sales manager. He was a veteran of long service (all in production work) with the company. During his early years of company experience, the industry's products were in great demand and industry capacity was short. He spoke with nostalgia of these earlier times:

> I remember when customers took anything. During the war we doled out orders to customers. They felt you were doing them a favor to promise delivery in two months. I can remember how we allocated so many items to each customer.

The Elgin manager apparently found the current demands upon production increasingly difficult to cope with. In the past two years he had steadily gained weight, become increasingly defensive, and sought to substitute outside activities for painful plant relationships. Another member of the plant organization spoke about the production manager, saying:

> The production manager has changed. He was relaxed when he first came here. Since he came, however, he has become more and more suspicious. People have become more and more afraid of him. He dresses down his production control manager terribly. He is stubborn and just won't cooperate.

A possible explanation for his worsening problem was his limited range of cognitive skills. Clues to these factors were contained in his comments on past events and in his methods of handling the relationship with sales. His perception of the district management problem was limited to a rigid view of plant costs as a function of customer order input.

In addition to inherent cognitive difficulties, the plant manager experienced interpersonal problems. The behavior he exhibited in this particular relationship may reflect a more general personal style for resolving problems in lateral relations where goal conflict exists. He seemed to have two approaches, either open conflict with the adversary or collusion with members of the other side. He related anecdotes regarding his style in dealing with the union that were of a collusive pattern.

The Elgin production manager may also have experienced much that was socially incongruent in the current situation. An older man, and accustomed to being in a position where production was dominant, he was increasingly required to act in response to the demands of a young man whose goals and demands for an involved and tension-filled relationship ran counter to his own experience and desires. The corrosive effect of this situation on his physical and mental well-being may have been an apparent result.

Thus, at Bowie, a young and open production manager was being guided by a nondirective, senior sales manager with an overall production-sales district outlook; whereas at Elgin, an older conservative, reticent production manager was being "pushed" by a younger ambitious sales manager with a dominantly sales point of view.

Conflict in Lateral Relationships

Consequences for Organizational Performance. Negative consequences of conflict for performance were widespread and pronounced in all areas of interdependence in the lateral relationship. Conflict was accompanied by relatively fewer new designs, more frequent acceptance of unprofitable orders, loss of profitable orders, greater plant congestion, poorer customer delivery service, dismissal of crews for lack of work, refusal of overtime when customer orders were unfinished, shipment of orders of marginal and substandard quality to customers, and return of defective orders by customers. Some of these consequences were attributable rather directly to a competitive orientation to decision-making. Other consequences, such as the acceptance of new, unprofitable orders resulting from a lack of information exchange on prospective new designs, stemmed from behavior tactical to the maintenance of competitive goal orientation. Still other consequences were the result of behavior that was retaliatory. Attempts by sales, for example, to blame production for quality defects led production to refuse to accept customer inspection for defects. Loss of orders and extra charges for return freight were the result.

This apparently wholesale indictment of the conflict pattern must be qualified. Conflict is sometimes exhilarating and motivating, sometimes debilitating and discouraging.[5] Conflict had the latter effect in the conflict plant studied here, in part because of the severity of the pattern, and in part because of the particular configuration of interdependencies in the two tasks involved. It is possible that a more moderate conflict pattern would have had high motivational effects; and that a different type of task interdependence would have greatly reduced the negative effects of the conflict tactics described here, or indeed have involved different, more innocuous tactics.

Consequences for Individuals. Conflict had apparent psychological and professional consequences for the principals and their leading subordinates. Participants in the conflict relationship showed greater anxiety and frustration. Such reaction may well be a function of individual tolerance for conflict and deserves further study.

Professional consequences also appeared to stem from the relationship. Participants in the conflict relationship were criticized by their superiors both at the plant and at the home office, and during interviews a number reported contemplating leaving the company. By contrast, at the integrative plant a number of persons commented on their prospects for being moved to more responsible company positions in the future.

Organizational "Hotspots" with Interdependent Tasks. Some positions were especially sensitive to conflict. The plant scheduling task seemed a position where severe, day-to-day crosscurrents were encountered. While both plants limited interaction in this area, their solutions were sharply different. At Bowie, the sales and production managers were kept in close contact with the problem. The service manager played a central role and employed cooperative criteria in scheduling. Moreover, his problems were widely recognized and he was insulated from damaging forays by the avoidance of unilateral action on scheduling. At Elgin, on the other hand, the parties had negotiated a highly formal solution which kept the principals as remote from the scheduling activity as possible. The two new expediter positions which were created served to "referee" scheduling problems for the parties. A competitive game continued, for high stakes, despite the existence of the scheduling agreement. Neither the principals nor the schedulers or expediters were protected from the bargaining practices of the parties. At Elgin considerable turnover and shifting characterized these scheduling positions.

Three tentative conclusions could be drawn from these comparisons: 1) Some task positions in organizations can be structurally sensitive to stress. 2) It is possible to protect members of the organization from the consequences of such inherently stressful tasks. 3) Lateral relationships dominated by conflict and competition do not provide such safeguards.

Summary

The comparative summary of the behavioral syndromes at Elgin and Bowie given in Table 1 shows sharply contrasting interdepartmental relations at the two plants. Both of these contrasting syndromes were deemed to be stable and resistant to change. The stability of each relationship was insured by reinforcement, where on element of a strategy was held in place by all the other elements; by reciprocation, where each party confirmed the appropriateness of the strategy of the other; by regeneration, where tradition and social pressure ensured that new members would maintain the prevailing pattern.

Analysis of these contrasting cases indicated that such contextual factors as more task facilitation from the home office for Bowie and less adequate equipment at Elgin might have contributed to the different degrees of conflict in the emergent relationships. Also contributing —in the same direction—were a more aggressive personal style of influence on the part of the Elgin sales manager; less adequate cognitive and interpersonal skills on the part of the Elgin production manager; and more status incongruity in the relationship between sales manager and production manager at Elgin.

Finally, the analysis indicated that the conflict relationship at Elgin had numerous and important negative effects on overall performance. However, it is apparent that sound judgments as to the effect of a generally competitive or conflictful relationship can be made only on the basis of an analysis of the specific elements of the relationship patterns and an analysis of the task, especially with regard to the interdependence of sub-tasks. It is also apparent that a conflict relationship can have significant negative effects for individual personal and professional well-being.

NOTES AND REFERENCES

1. M. Dalton, *Men Who Manage*, Wiley, New York, 1959. G. Strauss, "Tactics of Lateral Relationship: The Purchasing Agent," *Administrative Science Quarterly*, VII (September, 1962), 161–186; "Work-Flow Frictions, Interfunctional Rivalry, and Professionalism: A Case Study of Purchasing Agents," *Human Organization*, XXIII (Summer, 1964), 137–149.

Other notable treatments of lateral relations are: E. R. Chapple and L. Sayles, *The Measure of Management*, Macmillan, New York, 1961; H. A. Landsberger, "The Horizontal Dimension in a Bureaucracy," *Administrative Science Quarterly*, VI (December, 1961), 298–332; and J. A. Seiler, "Diagnosing Interdepartmental Conflict," *Harvard Business Review*, XLI (September–October, 1963), 121–132.

R. E. Walton, "Theory of Conflict in Lateral Organizational Relationships," *Proceedings of the International Conference on Operational Research and Social Sciences*, Cambridge, England, September, 1964 presents a theory of lateral relationships which the authors are testing in a comparative field study of six or more plants. In the six-plant study relatively fewer variables are subjected to statistical treatment. In the present study we subject two more comprehensive cases to intensive clinical analysis.

2. Company data are disguised for protection of the firm and of individual employees. The essential elements of the lateral relationships discussed have been preserved while names, places, and setting have been altered.

3. G. Strauss, *op. cit.* (1962).

4. M. Dalton, *op. cit.*

5. See J. A. Seiler, *op. cit.*

Determinants of and

Constraints on Structure

PART FIVE

IN THIS LAST SECTION, we shall not consider many if any new elements of organization but, instead, we shall concern ourselves with the variation these elements can have and some of the ways in which they are combined. We have noted that some elements such as individual attitudes or sentiments are natural or spontaneous, while others such as job content or assignment are more formal and can be chosen, hence, they can be specified through decision making.

One of our first concerns was to make clear that between some of the controllable elements and the desired results that they were thought to produce, there are natural or spontaneous elements. Hence a supervisor may decide that he will watch an employee very closely (increase direct supervision) to make sure that an important job gets done in the desired fashion (desired result or goal). The close supervision may so change the employee's attitude (natural element) that he deliberately holds back or makes mistakes because of his anger and resentment. Here we are examining a fairly direct casual chain, and our concern is to be sure that important links are not missed.

Later we examined the systems characteristics of organizations and noted that there were a great many elements and that most of them were in some way or another interconnected. Hence the superior in the hypothetical situation above decided to increase the amount of direct supervision because he perceived that the employee had displayed an apathetic attitude toward his work lately and had decided to "take no chances." Furthermore, the employee had been apathetic about his work because of his disgust with a new company policy that restricted each employee to the immediate department in which he worked, thereby keeping this employee from visiting friends in another department during break and lunch periods. The company, in turn, had established this rule because of pressure from its principal customer, the U. S. Air Force, which had insisted that such measures were necessary because of the secret nature of the equipment the company was making. Here we find decisions made about one formal element meshing in a most complex way with other formal elements and, also, with many natural or spontaneous elements.

Toward the end of the proceeding section, we introduced another type of model, the conditional model. The systems model urges us to remember the numerous interconnections be-

424

tween elements. The conditional models take us the next step and tell us what values these elements must have to produce certain interconnections. A systems model might suggest to us that we should consider whether the behavior of a teenage daughter has so distracted her father's attention that when he goes to look for a gas leak in the basement, he absent-mindedly lights a match and causes an explosion. The conditional model tells us that *if* the concentration of escaped gases in the air is above a certain level and below another level, there will be an explosion when a match is ignited. Going back to our hypothetical supervisor, were he to call the employee in for a counseling session in connection with a regular performance review program, the utility of the interview would be conditional upon his attitude toward his supervisor and, hence, dependent upon whether the interview occurred before or after the increase in direct supervision. Such a model helps us make more precise statements about the way elements in organization fit together and what is or will occur. As yet we are just beginning to use such models and to gather data to test them. This work, although at the moment of modest quantity, does tell us some of the limits or constraints on combinational possibilities of organization elements, and we shall consider a few of the more important of these now.

The Effects of Scale

One thing that theorists have long speculated upon is the influence that the size of the organization will have on its structure and performance. As the overall organization got larger, it is argued, all components of the organization would not just become proportionately larger or more numerous. There would, instead, be a nonproportional change with size. This leads to a perplexing question, namely, what form or forms would the nonproportional relationship take? For example, if we were to compare one organization with another twice its size, would we find twice as many personnel involved in carrying out the managerial function or half as many? Would the changes among the elements be linear or curvilinear? Some of the attempts to find answers to this have yielded conflicting results, on the surface at least. One study would show

that as organizations get larger, the number of persons engaged in administrative work becomes proportionally larger. Another study, however, would show them becoming proportionally smaller. The explanation for this inconsistency seems to rest upon the effects of some other organization elements involved. If increased size also means that these other factors come into play or become more important, they can make the organization more complex and thereby make the administrative slice proportionately larger (Anderson and Warkov). Without these additional factors, increased size may make, through specialization, the administrative task more efficient and, thus, able to be carried out by proportionately fewer people. The crucial factor influencing this aspect of structure, then, seems to be organizational complexity, with size being but one of several important factors to be considered.

General characteristics of organizations seem to change also with size. It is usually held that as organizations become larger they become bureaucratic. This can include a number of things, among them that there are more rules, jobs become more specialized and more structured, and there is more direct and closer supervision exercised by superiors. Even among these elements, variations are the nonproportional, since some research that the use of rules increases more rapidly than surveillance (Rushing).

Development of Organization Roles

The degree to which a person's activities are directed in an organization and the selection of the means, rules or surveillance, through which this is effected seems to be influenced by a number of other organization and extraorganization elements. The complexity of the technology and the skills possessed by subordinates vary inversely with the use of rules and surveillance (Bell 1966), while the predictability of demands upon subordinates varies directly with their use (Bell 1965). These results are to be anticipated from the concept of an organization being a rational system, discussed by Thompson in Part Four.

All of these elements, directly or indirectly, culminate in defining the position or role that some member of the organization is going to fill. Throughout, we have been suggesting what the effect will be for this person. It is time to examine again and in some detail what a few of these effects will be.

Implicit in what has been said above is that while the position of the individual in the organization may be prescribed in great or little detail and may include goals, programs, or both, there will be a logical consistency in these statements. In reality, this is seldom if ever the case. The occupant of an organizational position may find some subgoals specified in great detail without much specification on acceptable, or even workable, procedures. In other areas, he may find considerable detail on method, but with only vague suggestions of what they are to accomplish. There will also be still other vast areas about which practically nothing is said and for which he is to supply his own details. The opposite situation may face other people who will find not only many goals and procedures spelled out for them but also that some of them are inconsistent with others, such as the situation when the production manager is urged to keep costs down, which means long production runs, and is also urged to promptly service customer demands for delivery and design changes, which would mean short and frequent production runs. The impact of these underdefined and overdefined situations is important, interesting and, at times, surprising (Frank).

There are numerous reasons for this surprise, one of the most important being that we know very little about how formal specifications of goals, duties, and the impact of technology, rules, etc., get transformed into roles. If we had a better understanding of this process we would not only be able to better understand roles that emerge but also to differentiate those elements that actually contribute to a role from those that, by chance, appear simultaneously with them. One of the more interesting studies into how roles evolve appears in this section (Guetzkow).

In addition to the above factors, which influence the degree of autonomy an organizational member receives, there is that of deliberate policy or design. Some organizations are deliberately intended to be centralized, to pro-

vide considerable direction from above, while others are intended to be decentralized, giving organization members considerably more autonomy. Many of the formal considerations for choosing a decentralized style were presented earlier by Drucker. There are, however, other factors that have to be taken into account when choosing one style over another. In general, a centralized organization is a more efficient organization (Morse and Reimer) when efficiency is a matter of getting out standard products under predictable conditions and efficiency is measured in output per man or some similar measure. A more decentralized organization of the same size doing similar work would be less efficient; however, the attitudes of organization members will be more positive toward their work and the organization (Morse and Reimer). Centralized organizations are efficient, however, in part because of the high degree of specialization that has to be coordinated from above through managerial effort. We have noted that as organizations get larger, this task of coordination also becomes more complex and so do the parts of the organization concerned with carrying out this work. Ultimately, it seems that the organization reaches a size in which the complexity of the administrative activities and the increasingly negative attitudes of a large number of organization members in positions where their activities are increasingly more specified creates conditions whereby a fundamental shift in the style of the organization becomes desirable and, perhaps, even essential. The decentralized organization, with its effect of thrusting decision making further down into the organization, simplifies the administrative setup, increases autonomy, makes the organization more flexible, and stimulates member feeling of integration into the organization and motivation to work. Typically, although not necessarily, centralized organizations have their primary departments set up on a fundamental basis. Significant decentralization, however, requires that the primary units be less interdependent and that they be of a product or geographical nature. Needless to say, some organizations can meet this requirement very easily, while others would find it almost impossible.

Organizational Size and Functional Complexity:
A Study of Administration in Hospitals

THEODORE R. ANDERSON AND SEYMOUR WARKOV

One of the important problems in any organization is the coordination of the various activities which occur within it. This coordination function is normally performed by the administrative component of the organization. The relative size of this component is an important dependent variable in much organization theory. In particular, the coordination of activities is alleged to become relatively more difficult (requiring a more than proportionately greater expenditure of time or energy or both) with an increased number of personnel and with a greater variety of role activities or tasks.

For example, Durkheim asserted that growing density of population in a society results in increasingly complex forms of organization.[1] Similarly, both Spencer and Simmel propose that an increase of size necessitates more complex forms of communication.[2] It is commonly claimed that, in addition to its effect on organizational complexity, growth also brings about a disproportionate increase in the size of the administrative component.[3] Finally, more and more complex tasks may require that the coordination of an organization's differentiated components be accomplished by an increasingly larger administration.[4]

Despite the apparently widespread interest in the concomitants of organizational size and complexity, few systematic researches have been undertaken to test the basic hypotheses. There are not many comparative studies of several large-scale organizations, presumably because of the expense of gathering data on such organizations. The tendency in research has been, instead, to focus attention upon one or at most a very few organizations. These studies present illustrative material and, at times, suggestive conclusions, but they do not represent tests of the hypotheses or conclusions.

Terrien and Mills provide one of the two systematic empirical studies in this general area. They make the Parkinsonian proposal that "the relationship between the size of the administrative component and the total size of its containing organization is such that the

From *American Sociological Review*, Vol. 26, Feb. 1961, pp. 23–28. Reprinted with permission of the authors and the publisher, American Sociological Association.

[1] Emile Durkheim, *On the Social Division of Labor in Society,* translated by George Simpson, New York: Macmillan, 1933, Part 2.

[2] Herbert Spencer, *Principles of Sociology*, New York: Appleton, 1898, Vol. I, pp. 525–528; Georg Simmel, "The Number of Members as Determining the Sociological Form of the Group," translated by A. W. Small, *American Journal of Sociology*, 8 (1902–1903), pp. 1–46.

[3] For a general discussion of this and other points relating to organizational size, and a review of the literature, see Theodore Caplow, "Organizational Size," *Administrative Science Quarterly*, I (March, 1957), pp. 484–505.

[4] See, e.g., Max Weber, *The Theory of Social and Economic Organization*, translated by A. M. Henderson and T. Parsons, New York: Oxford University Press, 1947, pp. 324–337.

larger the size of the containing organization, the greater will be the proportion given over to its administrative component."[5] Data on school districts of California support this hypothesis in that the administrative component contained a higher mean percentage of the total staff in large than in small school districts. Bendix, in the other systematic study, presents evidence pointing in the opposite direction. Using data drawn from German industrial experience between 1907 and 1933, he shows that the percentage of administrative salary workers (of all employees) declines with increasing size of establishment for concerns with at least six employees. On the other hand, the per cent of salaried technicians increases with growing size.[6] This paper presents further data bearing upon these contrasting hypotheses and upon the hypothesis relating organizational complexity to the relative size of the administrative component.

DATA AND METHOD. Relevant data were secured for Veterans Administration hospitals in the United States for the year 1956. These data were derived from reports on the number of hospital personnel in various structural categories which are published monthly by the Central Office of the Veterans Administration.[7] Only hospitals discharging at least 40 tuberculous patients were included in the sample.[8] In 1956, there were 51 such hospitals; two were eliminated for technical reasons.[9]

[5] F. C. Terrien and D. C. Mills, "The Effect of Changing Size Upon the Internal Structure of an Organization," *American Sociological Review*, 20 (February, 1955), p. 11.

[6] Reinhard Bendix, *Work and Authority in Industry*, New York: Wiley, 1956, p. 222, Table 7.

[7] *Supplement, VA Statistical Summary*, Washington, D.C.: Central Office, Veterans Administration, January to December, 1956.

[8] These were originally assembled for the purpose of studying medically unsanctioned withdrawal from hospitals on the part of tuberculosis patients. See Seymour Warkov, *Irregular Discharge from Veterans Administration Tuberculosis Hospitals: A Problem of Organizational Effectiveness*, Ph.D. thesis, Yale University, 1959. The analysis reported in this paper, however, is not based upon this study.

[9] One hospital was eliminated because in fact it comprised two separate hospitals; the second because its administrative personnel were combined with those of another hospital in the statistical summary.

Thus 49 Veterans Administration hospitals, each with a substantial number of tuberculous patients, make up the final sample.

The dependent variable, the relative size of the administrative component, was measured by the per cent of all employees classified in the category, "General Hospital Administration." This component includes the Manager's Office, the Registrar's Office, and the Fiscal, Personnel, and Supply units.[10] The first independent variable, organizational size, was measured by the Annual Average Daily Patient Load (hereafter called ADPL) and was estimated for 1956 from the three months of February, May, and October. An alternative measure of organizational size is the total hospital labor force—that is, the denominator of the dependent variable. For the two groups of hospitals studied here (see below) these two measures of size are essentially equivalent. The correlations between these measures within each group of hospitals being .966 and .977, only one measure of size, namely, ADPL, was utilized in the main analysis.

The second independent variable, organizational complexity, was inferred from structural characteristics of the hospitals in the sample, which were divided into two distinct groups. Nineteen were classified as Tuberculosis Hospitals by the Veterans Administration. The percentages of the ADPL in these hospitals with pulmonary tuberculosis ranged from a low of 44 to a high of 100, with a median of 91.5 per cent. The other 30 hospitals were classified as General Medicine and Surgery Hospitals (hereafter called GM&S). A wide range of diseases are regularly treated in these hospitals, including internal diseases and psychiatric illness as well as tuberculosis. The percentages of the ADPL with pulmonary tuberculosis in this second group ranged from a low of three to a high of 41, with a median of 16.5 per cent. It is assumed in this paper that the TB hospitals are less complex organizationally than are the GM&S hospitals in that fewer types of diseases are treated on a regular basis.

The concept of organizational complexity poses serious methodological and measurement

[10] The Annual estimate for this component is based on the table reporting full-time equivalent hospital personnel employed in VA hospitals, *Supplement, VA Statistical Summary*, June, 1956.

problems. Udy's recent attempt to clarify the concept and to measure the degree of complexity suggests that it comprises three elements: the number of tasks performed, the maximum number of specialized operations ever performed at the same time, and the existence or non-existence of combined effort.[11] Using these criteria, it is reasonable to consider the GM&S hospitals as more complex because, not only are all tasks performed in the TB hospitals also carried out in the GM&S hospitals, but many other services that are regularly rendered in the GM&S hospitals are not provided in the TB hospitals. Of course, these two groups of hospitals also differ in many ways other than in complexity. For this reason, conclusions about complexity should be interpreted with caution.

It is important to note that the design used here permits the influence of size to be studied independently of the influence of complexity. All of the TB hospitals have about the same complexity. Furthermore, all of the GM&S hospitals have at least approximately the same degree of complexity, although some variation probably exists among them. Thus, within each category, complexity is sufficiently constant so that any relationship between size and proportion of personnel in administration is not substantially influenced by complexity. Other hospitals were excluded from the analysis because their inclusion would tend to confound the effects of complexity and size. The size of the sample used here is sufficient to demonstrate statistically the impact of the data upon the hypotheses; it is believed that the avoidance of a confounding effect is more important for the purpose at hand than an increase in sample size.

RESULTS. The emperical results may be presented as replies to a series of questions. First, is there a relationship between type of hospital and organizational size? The data indicate that the GM&S hospitals are significantly and substantially larger than are the TB hospitals. In 1956, the mean ADPL (or size) of the GM&S hospitals was 770 and only 335 for the TB hospitals.

Second, do GM&S and TB hospitals differ

[11] Stanley H. Udy, Jr., "The Structure of Authority in Non-Industrial Production Organizations," *American Journal of Sociology*, 64 (May, 1959), pp. 582–584.

with respect to the proportion of personnel in administration? The fact that about 12.5 per cent of the employees were in administration in both types of hospitals is clearly inconsistent with previous research findings and speculations. According to existing theory, larger, more complex hospitals have a higher proportion of staff in administration. The interpretation of this contrary finding is deferred for the moment.

Third, is there a relationship between hospital size and percentage of personnel in administration? Since the GM&S hospitals were so much larger than the TB hospitals it seemed unreasonable to treat them as a single homogeneous group. Hence, this question was asked of each hospital type.

The TB hospitals were divided into three categories, with roughly one-third of them in each. The mean per cent of employees in administration within each category is shown by the following figures:

SIZE:	UNDER 250	250– 400	ABOVE 400
No. of hospitals	5	8	6
Mean per cent	15.6	12.0	10.7

It is clear that the larger the hospital the *smaller* the per cent of all personnel in administration. An analysis of variance of these data indicates significance beyond the .01 level. Further, Eta^2 is .577, indicating that 58 per cent of the variance in percentage of employees in administration can be accounted for by variations in size. Thus size is a powerful explanatory variable, although in a direction opposite to that expected.

That this result is not a peculiarity of TB hospitals is indicated by the results for the GM&S hospitals. Here, different size categories were used so as to place, as in the former case, approximately one-third of the hospitals in each, with the following results:

SIZE:	UNDER 600	600– 900	ABOVE 900
No. of hospitals	12	9	9
Mean per cent	14.0	12.0	11.0

Again, the larger the hospital the *smaller* the per cent of all personnel in administration.

These results are also significant beyond the .01 level, and Eta^2 is .556, almost identical to the figure for the TB hospitals. This divergent finding, then, has some degree of generality, applying at least to two quite different types of Federal hospitals.[12]

Fourth, is the relationship between size of hospital and proportion of personnel in administration linear? The fact that within each type of hospital Eta^2 proved to be significantly greater than r^2 provides a negative answer. A scatter diagram of these data (not presented here) suggests that the slope of the regression line becomes more horizontal as size increases. It is possible that the slope might actually become positive with sufficiently large hospitals, but this is only a speculation, in view of the limitations of the present data.

Finally, if size is controlled or held constant, do the hospital types differ in per cent of employees in administration? This is in fact the case, but the hospital types differ so much in size that all of the observations cannot be brought to bear upon the question (especially because the size regressions are not linear). In particular, only one size category (between 300 and 600) included an appreciable number of each type of hospital. Furthermore, within this reasonably narrow range, the GM&S and TB hospitals had roughly the same size distribution. In this range, the 11 TB hospitals averaged only 11.1 per cent of personnel in administration; the corresponding figure is 14 per cent for the 12 GM&S hospitals. This difference is significant at the .01 level. Thus, the earlier finding of no overall difference in the average per cent of employees in administration appears to be entirely a function of the size differential between the two types of hospital. In general, if GM&S hospitals may be considered to be more complex than TB hospital, then these data tend to confirm the hypothesis that organizational complexity and the relative size of the administrative component are positively related, as expected. However, the data refute, at least for these organizations, the hypothesis that organizational size and relative size of the administrative component are positively related; indeed they suggest perhaps the counter hypothesis.

DISCUSSION. On the surface, at least, the findings reported in this paper are in direct contradiction to those reported by Terrien and Mills. Moreover, these results are substantially at variance with what is apparently the common conception (among sociologists and others) of the relationship between organizational size and the relative size of the administrative component. There appear to be, in general, two ways to resolve these discrepancies. First, either or both sets of data may be inadequate in some way to test the hypothesis under discussion. Second, these two sets of data may not, in fact, be directly comparable. In the latter case, it should be possible to develop theoretical statements consistent with both sets of findings.

Both sets of data are derived from relatively straightforward enumeration procedures conducted by state and federal agencies. For fiscal and other reasons the accuracy of these data is important within the agencies concerned. There is no reason to suspect that either set of basic data is in substantial error, certainly not to the degree necessary to eliminate the conclusion in contradiction to the earlier study.

Another possible explanation of this finding is that the administrative component was incorrectly identified or categorized in at least one of the two studies. There is no doubt that some administrative activities are performed by personnel who are not so classified. However, there is no reason to believe that the proportion of such personnel is substantially greater (or lesser) in large than in small organizations, which have a specialized, designated administrative component. Accordingly, it is reasonable to conclude that both the findings of Terrien and Mills and of the present investigation accurately reflect organizational processes which are (therefore) not directly comparable. If so, an explanation is called for which renders these findings mutually consistent.

The following propositions are offered as one possible resolution of the apparent discrepancy between the two sets of findings. The propositions are based upon the fact that some of the school districts studied by Terrien and Mills include more than one school and

---

[12] It is important to emphasize the fact that an inverse relationship is not an artifact of the measure of size used here. Identical results were obtained using the labor force measure of size.

upon the assumption that the larger school districts incorporate more schools than do the smaller districts. In contrast, each of the organizations in the present study has a single location. Thus:

1. The relative size of the administrative component *decreases* as the number of persons performing identical tasks in the same place increases.[13]

2. The relative size of the administrative component *increases* as the number of places at which work is performed increases.

3. The relative size of the administrative component *increases* as the number of tasks performed at the same place increases (or as roles become increasingly specialized and differentiated).

If these propositions are correct, then Terrien and Mills' findings may be interpreted as confirming the second proposition and *not* as nullifying the first proposition. Our findings, on the other hand, support the first and third propositions but do not bear upon the second one. Given this interpretation, the relative size of the administrative component in a single school should decline as school size increases, provided that the organizational complexity of the schools is held constant. In practice, it might prove difficult to devise an effective measure of organizational complexity within schools. These propositions are presented tentatively, of course, pending further investigation of these and other types of organizations.

At least one alternative means of rectifying the two sets of findings is available. The school districts and hospitals may differ in the extent to which they are subject to centralized authority. Where the central authority is powerful, special constraints may inhibit the emergence of the relationship between size and administration that would otherwise occur. In particular, some special bureaucratic constraint may operate within government hospitals which inhibits the "free" growth of the administrative component.

It is also important to recognize that these propositions, even if confirmed empirically, are not necessarily sufficient to explain all structural and temporal variations in the relative size of the administrative component. Specifically, the inclusion of a proposition concerning the routinization of roles would undoubtedly improve the general explanation of variations in the relative size of the administrative component. Routinization is not discussed in this paper because the apparent contradiction between the two sets of findings could be resolved without taking it into account.

On the other hand, these propositions appear to explain adequately the apparent overall increase in the relative importance of administrative activities within organizations during the past several decades (as evidenced by the rapid rise in the per cent employed in clerical occupations, for instance). It is often suggested that this increase in administration is a function of the sheer growth in organizational size. If our propositions are correct, however, the explanatory variable is organizational complexity rather than organizational size. Clearly, more systematic studies are required before any such conclusions can be considered to be substantially confirmed.

[13] This proposition appears to be consistent with commonplace observations. For example, as any teacher knows, administering a test in the same room to four times more students than usual does not require four times as many proctors. An alternative possibility is that the inverse relationship holds up to a point, and then becomes positive, thus producing an overall U-shape. Our data suggest that the curve flattens out eventually, but do not suggest the existence of an upturn.

Organizational Size, Rules, and Surveillance[1]

WILLIAM A. RUSHING

Although the assumption that organizational size has far-ranging effects on other organizational characteristics is widely accepted, there are few generalizations concerning the effect of size that find consistent factual support. Several studies have examined the relationship between organizational size and the proportion of organizational personnel who are administrative personnel, but the results are strikingly inconsistent (Blau and Scott, 1962, pp. 222–227); the relationship between size and managerial succession has come under recent empirical scrutiny, but here, too, findings are inconsistent (Gordon and Becker, 1964); the effect of organizational size on work performance has also been examined, but findings in this area are unclear (Thomas, 1959). Still, most students of organizations will nevertheless agree that size is an important determinant of organizational behavior and structure. Robert Dubin (1958) has gone so far as to assert, for example, that size is probably the most important variable in fostering the growth of bureaucracy in an organization.

In this paper concern is with the effect of organizational size on two characteristics of bureaucratic organization—surveillance and formal rules (including record keeping to evaluate participant performance). These variables are sometimes referred to as supervision and administration based on the files, respectively; both are, or course, aspects of organizational control structures. Since problems of organizational control undoubtedly increase with increases in organizational size, both variables should be affected by organization size. It is the hypothesis of this paper, however, that size has a differential effect on the two variables. In brief, the hypothesis asserts that with an increase in organizational size, organizational dependence on administration based on the files increases at a faster rate than organizational dependence on surveillance. The hypothesis is a special case of Boulding's principle of nonproportional structural growth, which states that different components of organizational structure are differentially affected when organizations increase in size (Boulding, 1953).

Size has also been an important independent variable in small-group experimental research (Thomas and Fink, 1963), and the effects of surveillance (Day and Hamblin, 1964) and rules (norms) (Hare, 1962) have also been studied. But the effects of group size on the latter two variables have not been studied a great deal; in particular, the *differential* effect of size on them has not been explored. This is a serious gap in small-group research in as much as both surveillance and rules are vital components of group processes in most groups. A further concern of this paper, therefore, is the development and clarification of hypothesized relationships, between these three variables that could be tested experimentally.

Organization Size, Rules, and the Costs of Surveillance

As noted, rules and surveillance are both aspects of organizational control. Participant performance may be controlled through surveillance procedures—e.g., by supervising work closely, inspecting the quality and quantity of work, etc. This, of course, requires personal observation and face-to-face contact between supervisor and supervisee. Conduct may also be controlled through more impersonal mechanisms—e.g., through the routinization of performance in formal rules and by keeping written records of work performance, sup-

[1] A version of this paper was read at the annual meetings of the Pacific Sociological Association, Salt Lake City, April 22–24, 1965. I want to thank Robert B. Hagedorn, Reece McGee, Richard H. Ogles, and Walter L. Slocum for their comments on an earlier draft.

432

ported, of course, by rewards and punishments. Performance may be specified in such detail that participants are rarely in doubt as to their work duties; and records of work performance allow the inspection of participant performance, thus making continual direct observations of the work process less necessary.

Thus, while surveillance and administration based on the files perform similar functions, they nevertheless differ. Surveillance necessitates the presence of a supervisor to make direct observations of work performance, whereas rules and record keeping do not—at least to the same extent. This difference has an important consequence. Effective control through rules and record keeping is more efficient than equally effective control by surveillance. For if control is achieved by the former method, the time, effort, and expense involved in the latter may be considerably reduced.[2] (This does not say, of course, that increases in formal rules and procedures will themselves have no costly consequences. When records and rules replace direct contact, several unanticipated dysfunctional consequences are likely, such as, for examples, decreases in morale and "corrective feedback" from subordinates. These undesirable consequences may nevertheless be the price that organizations must pay for increased formal organization, which large size may require.)

In other words, rules and record keeping may achieve the same results that surveillance

does; but they do so at fewer costs. The use of surveillance requires that values be forgone that would not otherwise be forgone if more impersonal mechanisms of control were employed; the values of time, effort, and expense of supervisory personnel, for examples. (The definition of cost as "value forgone" is adopted from Homans, 1961, p. 59.) Formal rules and record keeping may reduce these costs since they eliminate the need for supervisory personnel and may allow the allocation of more time to nonsurveillance activities. Furthermore, surveillance costs may include more than time, effort, and monetary expense; case studies by Blau, Gouldner, and Rushing reveal that surveillance may involve interpersonal frictions—awkwardness, uncomfortableness, embarrassment, insults, and resentments—that are by-products of face-to-face contact between superordinates and subordinates (Blau, 1955, p. 40; Gouldner, 1954a, pp. 160–62; and Rushing, 1964). Impersonal rules and record keeping may reduce such costs, since the frequency of superiors' face-to-face directives to and evaluations of subordinates are reduced.

Because of surveillance costs and because modern organizations are rationally oriented to the pursuit of specified goals at a minimum of costs, it is assumed in this paper that organizational attempts to maintain control through surveillance procedures tend to decrease relative to more impersonal mechanisms of control. A deduction from this assumption is, of course, the proposition that organizational use of formal rules and record keeping will increase with an increase in the costs of surveillance. It is assumed furthermore that such costs *increase* with organizational size.

In small organizations control through surveillance may be relatively easily achieved through informal face-to-face relationships; surveillance is often the by-product of superordinates and subordinates working side-by-side in organizational activities. Since surveillance requires little special effort and additional time, costs are minimal; for example, superordinates do not have to forgo the performance of their own activities to assure the adequate work performance of subordinates. When an organization grows, however, there are more subordinates to supervise, so that it becomes increasingly efficient to rely more on rules for exerting control. The historical growth of hospitals provides an example.

[2] Peter M. Blau (1955, p. 35) notes, for example, that the use of performance records in one organization "not only provided superiors with information which enabled them to rectify poor performance but often *obviated the need* for doing so." (Emphasis supplied.) Elsewhere Blau and Scott (1962, p. 179) state that "The superior no longer needed to check frequently on the work of subordinates, and his task of critically evaluating their performance became *easier and less onerous.*" (Emphasis supplied.) Blau (1956) notes in more general terms that "evaluation on the basis of standards that specify results to be accomplished constrains employees to discipline themselves and renders close supervision . . . superfluous." This is not to say that the use of formal rules and record keeping are the only cost-reducing replacements for surveillance. The routinization of work performance through machine technology could be another. Our present concern, however, excludes other mechanisms by which behavior may be controlled and routinized.

When hospitals were small and jobs relatively simple, control was assured through the direct supervision of directors of nursing and the hospital administrator. With increased size, however, this practice became too costly:

> When hospitals grew in size and complexity . . . the administrator who tried to retain full supervision of details . . . began to find his day so crowded with trivial matters that he had no time left for problems of general policy. Either he had to neglect some areas while he concentrated on others, or he faced the necessity of making basic changes in the pattern of organization. (Burling, Lentz, and Wilson, 1956, p. 319.)

One such change was to resort to more formal procedures and record keeping.

> One way an administrator could maintain order in a mushrooming organization was to tighten paper controls. For example, where one department head had been ordering his own supplies and another asked the administrator for them by word of mouth, now both were asked to submit formal requisition sheets at stated times of the week. (Burling, Lentz, and Wilson, p. 319.)

In short, procedures involving written rules and records were introduced for "discovering mistakes and assigning responsibility in the absence of close immediate supervision" (Burling, Lentz, and Wilson, p. 320) which large size made impossible. Greater reliance was placed on administration based on the files.

There are several factors which accompany size that probably contribute to surveillance costs. The fact that the number of potential social relationships which must be controlled grows at a much faster rate than absolute size itself [the actual rate for two-person relationships alone is $N(N-1)/2$] may cause surveillance processes to become increasingly costly as organizational size increases. Also, increases in size will almost inevitably increase the physical distance between participants and superiors who are responsible for participant work performance. The costs of surveillance obviously must increase when the distance between supervisors and supervisees increases. Gouldner has spoken of rules under such circumstance as serving a "remote control" function: they facilitate " 'control from a distance' "

by those in the higher and more remote reaches of the organization," eliminating the necessity for continuous personal inspection (1954a, p. 107). And the advantage of using performance records rather than direct surveillance to assure general conformity to organizational work standards in large organizations where superiors and subordinates are physically separated has been noted by Blau, who states: "[The] function of strengthening uniform administrative control is especially important for a large organization, where the top administrator is expected to exercise control over thousands of operating officials dispersed over a wide area and many hierarchical levels removed from his position" (Blau, 1955, p. 35).

Furthermore, as Blau's quote implies, social distance may be involved. As organizations increase in size, the number of hierarchical levels increases; consequently, the supervisor and supervisees may be several hierarchical levels apart. But since interpersonal friction is likely to increase with an increase in social distance (Homans, pp. 299–307), face-to-face contact required by surveillance is likely to increase organizational tensions. Rules may serve as lubricants to eliminate such costs.

As bureaucracies expand, the diversity of values and points of view carried by members of the organization will usually increase, leading to an increase in organizational conflict. But since surveillance relationships between conflicting parties are particularly disruptive, conflict is apt to be followed by more impersonal agents of control. More than one writer has noted the role of social conflict in generating formal rules and expectations (for examples see Kerr, 1954; Gouldner, 1954b; Dubin, 1957; and Mack and Snyder, 1957).

Finally, with an increase in size there is less direct personal contact between organizational participants, leading to communication failures. Codified standard operating procedures, originating from positions high in the hierarchy, contain uniform information and "messages" on which consistent decisions may be made. In fact, Dunlop, in his analysis of formal rules in industrial organizations, seems to tie the process, whereby large organizations replace informal surveillance with formal codified rules, to problems of communication created by large organizations (Dunlop, 1958).

In sum, the argument being advanced is that

both surveillance and administration based on the files may control participant conduct, but that the former is more costly than the latter. Since bureaucratic organizations are oriented to achieving maximum efficiency, there is a tendency for them to reduce their reliance on the former relative to their reliance on the latter. And since the costs of surveillance are likely to increase with increases in organizational size, as organizations increase in size they should become increasingly dependent on codified rules, relative to surveillance procedures. This does not say, of course, that there is a negative correlation between organizational size and extent of organizational surveillance. It only asserts that organizational dependence on surveillance, *relative to dependence on codified rules and record keeping*, and organizational size are negatively correlated.

Measures

To test this hypothesis, measures of organizational size and extent of organizational dependence on surveillance and administration based on the files are required. In the ideal case, these measures would be based upon the study of individual organizations. Since data of this nature are not available, measures are derived from the 1960 United States population figures reported in *Occupation by Industry* and the 1958 edition of the *United States Census of Manufactures* and the *Statistical Abstract*. The first is based on household enumeration and gives the number of individuals per occupation by industry, while the other two are based on establishment reports and gives the number of establishments per industry. Measures are computed for two different groups of industries.

The first group includes twenty general industrial categories from the construction, mining, and manufacturing industries, as listed in the census (see Table 1). The second group consists of subcategories of the general manufacturing categories; for example, "rubber products" and "miscellaneous plastic products" are subcategories of the general category, "rubber and miscellaneous plastic products."[2] In

all, *Occupation by Industry* lists sixty-one subcategories. However, several are residual and heterogeneous in nature (e.g., "not specified food industries"), and were eliminated from the analysis.[3] A further problem is that, unlike the general categories, subcategory titles in *Occupation by Industry* and *Census of Manufactures* are not always the same. Fortunately, industries in both sources are classified according to the Standard Industrial Classification code (SIC). However, since the SIC used in the two sources is not comparable in every case,[4] only those industries were included in which the difference in total personnel reported in the two sources did not deviate by more than thirty percent (i.e., when the ratio of the two figures was between .70 and 1.30). This gave a total sample of forty-one. (For reasons to be noted below (footnote 5), analysis is actually based on only forty.)

For the measure of organizational size, the mean number of employees per establishment is derived for each industry. Industries are ranked on mean organizational size, and Spearman rank correlation coefficients between mean size and a surveillance-formal rules index are computed for each group. The surveillance-formal rules index is a measure of the extent to which organizations in the various industries depend upon surveillance relative to formal rules. It is computed as follows.

The mean number of foremen and inspectors per industry is the measure of surveillance personnel. The total number of persons engaged in surveillance functions would, of course, be a better measure. But since foremen and inspectors are the only occupational categories listed in the census data for which surveillance is the sole function, only they are included in the measure.

For the measure of formal rules, we take our clue from Max Weber. Weber argued that bureaucratic management is based on rules; he further stated that it is administration based on the files, i.e., management based on written documents (Weber, 1946). In other words,

---

[2] Three categories ("electrical machinery," "furniture and fixtures," and "tobacco") are included

in both groups. These categories appear alone with no subcategories.

[3] The plastics category is included, even though it is a "miscellaneous" category, because it is the only plastics category listed. Its elimination has no effect on the results.

[4] *Occupation by Industry*, p. IX.

formal rules are written documents and are found in the files. If this is true, a growth of the files must occur when the number of formal rules increases. And since an increase in the files will require that additional file clerks be employed, the number of file clerks should be an index of the number and extensity of formal rules in an organization. Measures of formal rules, then, are derived from the number of file clerks in the various industries.

The mean number of file clerks in organizations from each industry is combined with the mean number of foremen and inspectors, and a surveillance-formal rules index is obtained. The index is computed by dividing the mean number of foremen and inspectors by the mean number of file clerks for each industry. Since the index expresses the ratio of foremen and inspectors to file clerks, a high ration indicates high reliance on surveillance relative to reliance on formal rules, while low dependence on surveillance relative to formal rules is indicated when the ratio is low.[5] The rank order of industries on this index is determined and Spearman rank-order correlations computed. If the hypothesis is true, the correlations between the two rank orders should be negative.

Findings

Analysis of the twenty general industrial categories reveals, as predicted, a negative correlation between organizational size and the surveillance-formal rules index. The ratio of foremen and inspectors to file clerks decreases as mean organizational size increases, as Table 1 indicates. The Spearman rank correlation of $-.40$ is significant at the .05 level of significance. Analysis based on the forty subcategories gives a rank correlation of $-.29$, also significant at the .05 level. Hence, data support the hypothesis.

[5] The pottery industry was eliminated from the analysis because it has no file clerks. (Only in rare instances does the census report figures for occupations by industry when the number of incumbents is less than twenty; apparently the pottery industry has fewer than twenty file clerks.) To have computed a measure for this industry would have given an unrealistically high index value.

Discussion

Results are thus consistent with Boulding's principle of nonproportional structural growth and its corollary of compensatory change (1953); they also support Thibaut and Kelley's analysis of the relationship between rules and surveillance (1959). Although the former is a structural hypothesis that includes no concepts relevant to psychological properties or the behavior of individuals, while the latter consists precisely of such concepts, the predictions of one are consistent with the predictions of the other. Some may be inclined, therefore, to view these two interpretations as competing interpretations of the data at hand. The two interpretations are not necessarily mutually exclusive alternatives, however, for both may be correct. Taken together, they provide a coherent explanation of the results.

Thibaut and Kelley's framework is actually a framework for the analysis of interpersonal power and influence processes. Nevertheless, it has direct relevance to the problem of organizational control and the hypothesis of this paper. It states that individuals attempt to realize good "outcomes"—i.e., they attempt to maximize rewards and minimize costs, and that they achieve good outcomes by influencing the acts of others. Consequently, the value received from the influence's act will vary depending upon its costs to the influence agent, assuming rewards are constant. Costs of exerting influence would include such things as time, energy, and interpersonal strain. Although it is possible to influence behavior through surveillance or by imposing binding rules, the latter entail fewer costs.

> [Rules] serve as substitutes for the exercise of personal influence and produce more economically and efficiently certain consequences otherwise dependent upon personal [face-to-face] processes. . . . [Rules] are social inventions that accomplish more effectively what otherwise would require [face-to-face] influence. (Thibaut and Kelley, 1959, pp. 130, 134.)

If we replace the individual-individual dyad of the Thibaut-Kelley framework with the organization-participant relationship, an analysis closely paralleling the above is possible. The

Table 1. *Rank Correlation between Mean Organizational Size and Ratio of Mean File Clerks to Mean Foremen and Inspectors for Twenty General Manufacturing Categories*

INDUSTRY	TOTALS				FIRM MEAN				RANK		d	d²
	FIRMS [a]	EMPLOYEES [b]	FOREMEN AND INSPECTORS [b]	FILE CLERKS [b]	SIZE	FOREMEN AND INSPECTORS	FILE CLERKS	RATIO OF MEAN FOREMEN AND INSPECTORS TO MEAN FILE CLERKS	MEAN SIZE	RATIO OF MEAN FOREMEN AND INSPECTORS TO MEAN FILE CLERKS		
Transportation equipment	6,607	1,818,604	83,368	3,983	275.3	12.62	.6028	20.94	1	16	−15	225
Primary metal industries	6,446	1,227,382	76,527	886	190.4	11.87	.1374	86.39	2	4	−2	4
Electrical machinery	8,091	1,480,209	66,715	3,951	182.9	8.245	.4883	16.88	3	19	−16	256
Petroleum and coal pdts.	1,608	281,353	14,801	725	175.0	9.204	.4508	20.42	4	18	−14	196
Tobacco	504	86,209	4,508	121	171.0	8.944	.2400	37.27	5	12	−7	49
Textile mills	7,675	963,050	40,838	875	125.5	5.32	.1140	46.67	6	9	−3	9
Paper and allied pdts.	5,271	583,743	27,758	658	110.7	4.232	.1248	41.92	7	10	−3	9
Rubber and misc. plastic pdts.	4,462	389,602	22,050	527	87.3	4.941	.1181	41.83	8	11	−3	9
Leather and leather pdts.	4,534	349,851	14,530	182	77.16	3.205	.0401	79.93	9	5	4	16
Chemical and allied pdts.	11,309	857,786	45,379	1,700	75.84	4.012	.1503	26.69	10	14	−4	16
Machinery, exc. electrical	29,839	1,579,825	66,480	3,220	52.95	2.228	.1079	20.67	11	17	−6	36
Fabricated metal industries	24,782	1,292,248	60,989	2,351	52.14	2.461	.0948	25.95	12	15	−3	9
Food and kindred products	41,619	1,822,373	74,058	1,338	43.79	1.779	.0321	55.42	13	6	7	49
Stone, clay, and glass pdts.	15,022	602,614	28,228	561	40.12	1.879	.0373	50.86	14	8	6	36
Apparel and other fab. textile pdts.	29,297	1,159,707	33,953	1,180	39.58	1.156	.0403	28.76	15	13	2	4
Furniture and fixtures	10,160	375,495	16,837	317	36.96	1.655	.0312	53.04	16	7	9	81
Printing, publishing and allied industries	35,368	1,147,918	24,146	5,153	32.38	.6827	.1457	4.68	17	20	−3	9
Lumber and wood pdts., exc. furniture	37,789	682,323	37,569	121	18.06	.9942	.0032	310.69	18	1	17	289
Mining and quarrying	43,000 [c]	653,979	38,039	344	15.2	.8846	.0080	110.58	19	2	17	289
Construction	466,000 [c]	3,062,038	110,153	1,106	6.57	.236	.0024	98.33	20	3	17	289

$\Sigma d^2 = 1,880$
$r_s = -.41$
$p = <.05$ (one-tail test)

[a] From *United States Census of Manufacturers: 1958*, Vol. 1, Table 3, pp. 6–23.
[b] From *Occupation by Industry*, United States Census of Population, 960, Table 2, pp. 12–66.
[c] From *Statistical Abstract*, 1963, p. 488.

central problem, insofar as the present paper is concerned, is the organization influencing, that is, exerting control over, its participants. This can be done with either rules (i.e., administration based on the files) or surveillance, but, as noted above, the former method may be less costly. In the organizational context this means that rules may control the work process with communications which originate at a distance from the work level—i.e., farther up the hierarchy, so that constant face-to-face supervision and inspection either by persons higher in the hierarchy or by persons hired specifically for this purpose, become less necessary. Without the communication of such rules, however, control of participant behavior must depend more on personal surveillance at the work level, thus raising organizational costs. But since industrial organizations are oriented to reducing costs where they can, they will tend to reduce their dependence on surveillance and rely more on rules whenever the costs of the former increase. And as was previously noted, surveillance costs will usually increase with organizational size. Consequently, a relationship between organizational size and the relative organizational dependence upon rules and surveillance would be expected.

This analysis is, of course, consistent with Boulding's hypothesis of nonproportional structural growth, which asserts that all organizational variables do not change at the same rate as structure grows, and the corollary of compensatory change, which asserts that compensation accompanies this unequal growth —that is, the rapid growth of some variables compensates for the slower growth of other variables (1953). In terms of the variables of the present study, the growth of rules compensates for the relatively slower growth in surveillance personnel. The compensation has reference, of course, to organizational control. Thus, Boulding's hypothesis, *as it would apply to rules and surveillance*, is a special case of Thibaut and Kelley's analysis of rules and surveillance, which in turn is a special case of their more general theory of rewards, costs, and outcomes. (The Thibaut and Kelley deductions can also be made from the work of George C. Homans, who employs a similar framework in *Social Behavior: Its Elementary Forms*.) Data, then, are supportive of both a structural and a psychological theory [in the sense in which structural and psychological are

used by Homans (1964)], the former being a special instance of the latter.

Actually, however, a more direct test of the hypothesis would require data of a different nature. The hypothesis, particularly as it relates to Boulding's formulations, refers to organizational growth over time—as *an* organization gets bigger, it depends more on impersonal rules and records relative to personal surveillance. But since the data refer to comparisons among organizations at *one* point in time, support for the hypothesis is necessarily indirect.

More direct tests of the hypothesis could be pursued in two primary directions. First, an organizational survey could be conducted in which all relevant variables (such as type of industry, product produced, covertness of participant performance, etc.) are held constant, with size alone being allowed to vary. If the proposed hypothesis is valid, measures of surveillance and rules should be affected along the lines suggested above. Second, since the hypothesis has direct implications for the social-psychological level of analysis where small group interaction processes become focal, a series of small-group experiments testing the effects of varied size on group control strategies seem to be in order. The size-control strategies hypothesis, after all, applies to relatively small task groups outside as well as inside complex organizations. Such research may actually reveal certain aspects of the group process more precisely than studies of complex organizations were able to show; it might, for example, reveal the precise point in group size that groups begin relying more on rules and norms, relative to their use of surveillance mechanisms, to control the conduct of their members.

Finally, the hypothesis, and the above supporting data, may throw additional light on analyses of organizations in individual industries. In this respect a few remarks concerning Arthur Stinchcombe's analysis of the construction industry (1959) are in order, since the findings of the present paper may suggest different conclusions than those drawn by him. Stinchcombe contrasts "bureaucratic control" —administration based on the files—with control based on professional self-discipline. Roughly the same distinction has been made by Parsons, Gouldner, and others. Various writers have recognized that Weber's formulations fail to include the phenomenon of professional self-discipline, or professional authority, and is, therefore, inadequate for describing important organizational processes in universities, hospitals, law firms, and other organizations which contain high-level professional personnel. Stenchcombe extends this argument to the construction industry.

He uses the proportion of clerks in the administrative component of organizations as an index for administration based on the files, and finds that construction is lower on the index than certain other industries. He concludes, therefore, that control in the construction industry is maintained, more so than in other industries, through the self-discipline of craft workers. Data in the present study suggest that another mechanism of control may also exist. Table 1 shows that the mean size of construction firms is smaller than any other industry, and that the ratio of foremen and inspectors to file clerks for construction ranks toward the top. This suggests that administration based on the files may be supplemented in the construction industry by surveillance as well as by professional self-discipline. In any case, surveillance processes appear to be more important in the construction industry than they are in other industries.

This conclusion is consistent with the observations of Sherman Maisel, who, on the basis of his study of the construction (housebuilding) industry, concludes that work performance in this industry "is under strict supervision and 'pushing' by the foremen." This appears to be a consequence of size, for he continues: "There is little formality in . . . the organization . . . of these firms. The relatively small size of the management group encourages personal contact. *Few, if any, special organizational techniques are used*" (Maisel, 1953, pp. 100, 127). Richard R. Myers, in a study of construction firms in Detroit, also notes the importance of the foreman's function, since building workers are organized "in primary labor groups around foremen . . . who direct the work of their crews on the job" [6] (Myers, 1962, pp. 132, 126).

These observations suggest, therefore, that in the construction industry surveillance, rather than self-discipline, may compensate for "special organizational techniques," such as administration based on the files. This conclusion seems to be all the more warranted in light of the fact that the mean number of foremen and inspectors may actually be a more conservative estimate of the actual number of foremen and inspectors in the construction industry than it is for other industries. This is so because the figure does not include "working foremen"; since construction work, according to Maisel, is usually organized in "small work crews under foremen who perform supervision as an *added* duty" (1953, p. 115), there may be a higher proportion of working foremen in the construction industry than in other industries. Evidence suggests, therefore, that surveillance processes are important components indeed of the social control processes in the construction industry.

Conclusions

Data from this small study support the hypothesis that organizational growth is nonpro-

---

[6] However, Myers, contrary to Maisel, notes certain limitations of the foremen's surveillance role. It is limited because: (1) the foreman is subject to union control; (2) foremen and journeymen frequently exchange positions (a foreman may, on a subsequent job, become a craft worker, subject to the control of an individual who was formerly under his control); and (3) the weak power position of building firms. If Myers' analysis is correct, it would indicate that what autonomy the building craftsman has is due, not to his self-discipline, but to power. His additional finding, however, that the construction foreman is likely to hire his friends if they are available, suggests another dimension of social control in work organizations. When one's power to control subordinates is restricted, one may attempt to maintain control by hiring persons *personally* known to be persons who have "good judgment" and "initiative" (Myers, 1962, p. 135).

It is not possible to know how general Myers' findings concerning the limitations of the foreman's supervisory function actually are. The somewhat different conclusions of Maisel may be due to the fact that the two studies took place at different times in different geographical settings. For example, the high postwar demand for construction labor which outran the available supply in Detroit (Myers, 1962, p. 127) very likely limited the scope of the building firms' control (and the control of its representatives—i.e., foremen) over its employees in Myers' study.

portional insofar as surveillance procedures and administration based on the files are concerned, thus supporting Boulding's hypothesis of nonproportional structural growth. Findings suggest that with organizational growth, formal rules increase at a faster rate than surveillance procedures. If the assumption that surveillance costs increase with organizational size is granted, data support Thibaut and Kelley's hypothesis concerning the cost-reducing function of rules.

It is possible, of course, that variation in the surveillance-rules index may be due to factors other than size. There is reason to believe, for example, that surveillance may vary depending upon the value placed on participant autonomy, level of productivity, dispersion of personnel, covertness of performance, as well as other variables. Although there is no reason to believe that these variables are systematically associated with size, in this sample of diverse industries, it is possible that they are. In this event, the observed correlation may be spurious, in that size has no independent effect on the surveillance-rules index but is nevertheless correlated with it because size is associated with other factors that do have an independent effect on the index. Furthermore, since there is considerable variation in size among the firms of any one industry, indices based on means are not the best measures possible, even if they are the best available. For more conclusive evidence on the validity of the hypothesis, observational studies of the rule-making process in a sample of organizations are required.

REFERENCES

Blau, P. M. *Dynamics of bureaucracy.* Chicago: The University of Chicago Press, 1955.

Blau, P. M. *Bureaucracy in modern society.* New York: Random House, 1956. P. 82

Blau, P. M., and Scott, W. R. *Formal organizations.* San Francisco: Chandler, 1962.

Boulding, K. E. Towards a general theory of growth. *Canadian Journal of Economics and Political Science*, 1953, **19**, 335.

Burling, T., Lentz, Edith M., and Wilson, R. N. *The give and take in hospitals.* New York: Putnam, 1956.

Day, R. C., and Hamblin, R. L. Some effects of close and punitive styles of supervision. *American Journal of Sociology*, 1964, **69**, 599–510.

Dubin, R. Industrial conflict and social welfare. *Conflict Resolution*, 1957, **1**, 219.

Dubin, R. *The world of work.* Englewood Cliffs: Prentice-Hall, 1958, P. 368.

Dunlop, J. T. *Industrial relations systems.* New York: Holt, 1958. P. 44.

Gordon, G., and Becker, S. Organizational size and managerial succession: A reexamination. *American Journal of Sociology*, 1961, **65**, 261–69.

Gouldner, A. W. *Patterns of industrial bureaucracy.* Glencoe: The Free Press, 1954a.

Gouldner, A. W. *Wildcat strike.* Yellow Springs, Ohio: The Antioch Press, 1954b.

Haas, E., Hall, R. H., and Johnson, N. J. The size of the supportive component in organizations: A multi-organizational analysis. *Social Forces*, 1963, **42**, 9–17.

Hare, A. P. *Handbook of small group research.* New York: The Free Press of Glencoe, 1962. Pp. 21–63.

Homans, G. C. *Social behavior: Its elementary forms.* New York: Harcourt, Brace and World, 1961.

Homans, G. C. Contemporary theory in sociology. In Robert E. L. Faris (ed.), *Handbook of modern sociology.* New York: Rand McNally, 1964. Pp. 961–963, 967, 973.

Kerr, C. Industrial conflict and its mediation. *American Journal of Sociology*, 1954, **60**, 232, 235, 236.

Mack, R. W., and Snyder, R. C. The analysis of conflict—toward an overview and synthesis. *Conflict Resolution*, 1957, **1**, 219.

Maisel, S. J. *Housebuilding in transition.* Berkeley: University of California Press, 1953.

Myers, R. R. "Interpersonal Relations in the Building Industry." In Sigmund Nosow and William H. Form, *Man, work, and society.* New York: Basic Books, 1962, Pp. 126–37.

Rushing, W. A. *The psychiatric professions: Power, conflict, and adaptation in a psychiatric hospital staff.* Chapel Hill: The University of North Carolina Press, 1964, Pp. 81–82, 91–92.

Stinchcombe, A. L. Bureaucratic and craft administration of production: A comparative study. *Administrative Science Quarterly*, 1959, **4**, 168–87.

Thibaut, J. W., and Kelley, H. L. *The social psychology of groups.* New York: Wiley, 1959.

Thomas, E. J. Role conceptions and organizational size. *American Sociological Review*, 1959, **24**, 30–37.

Thomas, E. J., and Fink, C. F. Effects of group size. *Psychological Bulletin*, 1963, **60**, 371–384.

The Influence of Technological Components
of Work Upon Management Control[*]

GERALD D. BELL

When considering close versus distant supervisory activities managers often have couched their thoughts in terms of (a) how many subordinates might most efficiently be controlled, (b) whether a personal, or more distant superior-subordinate relationship might be most effective, and (c) how the degree of competence of the subordinates affected supervisory duties.

In attempting to determine the merits of close versus distant supervision, relatively less thought has been given to the degree of predictability of work situations that confront subordinates on their jobs.[1] This factor would seem to be highly significant for determining optimal levels of closeness of supervision. For the degree to which subordinates are faced by non-predictable, unique events would seem to set limits upon the effectiveness of close supervision. Correspondingly, it would seem that the degree of closeness of supervision present in any department or organization would influence the degree of rule-usage existing in that unit.

This paper explores the relationships between: (a) predictability of subordinates' work demands and closeness of supervision, and (b) closeness of supervision and rule-usage. Predictability is thought to be a techological component of the work situation, while the latter two variables are considered to be dimensions of management control.

Predictability and Closeness of Supervision

The predictability concept refers to *situations* that occur while a worker is performing his job. It does not refer to how routinely an employee carries out his tasks. The degree of predictability can be defined by the extent to which a worker could, if he were asked, sit down the night before he goes to work and make a list of the precise events that would confront him on the following work day. Those individuals who could consistently and accurately estimate the events that would develop in relation to their work would be considered to have predictable jobs. On the other hand, those who could not estimate the actual events that would confront them on their work would be considered to have unpredictable jobs.[2]

From *Journal of The Academy of Management*, Vol. 8, No. 2, 1965, pp. 127–132.
[*] The author is greatly indebted to Stanley H. Udy, Jr., Elton F. Jackson, and Chris Argyris, who throughout the formulation of the investigation provided keen analytical critiques of the notions presented in this paper. Enthusiastic support was received from Anthony J. DeLuca, Administrator of the Griffin Community Hospital. Part of the research is based on the author's dissertation, "Formality Versus Flexibility in Complex Organizations: A Comparative Investigation Within a Hospital." Unpublished Ph.D. dissertation, Yale University, 1964.
[1] James G. March and Herbert A. Simon, *Organizations* (New York: John Wiley and Sons, Inc., 1958).

[2] Readers interested broadly in this kind of theorizing and investigation might want to pursue the work of Elliott Jacques and others at Glacier Metal Works; the author's manuscript, "Predictability of Work Demands and Professionalization as Determinants of Worker's Discretion"; and, an article by Elmer Burak scheduled to appear in this journal.

We have hypothesized that *the more unpredictable the work demands* of a subordinate's job, *the more distant the supervision* will be. This is because the more subordinates face unexpected events in their work, the less likely it is that the supervisor will be able to or find it desirable to direct closely the subordinates' activities, unless he devotes himself to only one or two subordinates. And in the latter case there comes a point when the supervisor might as well be doing the job himself rather than studying each unique event, making decisions, and then instructing his subordinates on how to perform the tasks. It would seem to be more efficient, in situations where the work demands are highly unpredictable, to recruit competent subordinates and to train them to handle unexpected events effectively by exerting their own discretion.

We are suggesting that unpredictable work demands will encourage supervisors to loosen their control over subordinates, and that highly predictable work situations make it more feasible for management to increase its control over subordinates' activities. We have hypothesized then that *the more predictable the work demands, the closer the supervision.*

Before testing this hypothesis, let us briefly discuss the relationship between closeness of supervision and rule-usage, and then analyze the findings for both of these associations.

Closeness of Supervision and Rule-Usage

We have hypothesized that, as closeness of supervision increases, the utilization of rules will also increase. For predictable tasks, supervisors are assumed to be encouraged closely to control the workers' activities. And, since administrators desire closely to supervise subordinates' activities, we have hypothesized that they will also be likely to establish more rules and regulations for workers to follow in performing their tasks than they would if there were an absence of close supervision and an absence of predictability. In this sense, of course, rule-usage is a means by which administrators regulate activities. We have hypothesized then, that *the closer the supervision, the more rules will be utilized.*

Relevant Literature

An illustration of the suggested relationships is evident in Blau's study of an unemployment agency which supplied personnel to clothing manufacturers. The activities performed in this agency were very unpredictable. They were characterized ". . . by alternating seasons of feverish activity and widespread layoffs, by erratic variations in demand due to changes in fashions . . ." which required speed in operations.[3] At the same time, the supervisors, who at first closely controlled the subordinates, tended to lessen the closeness of their supervision in order to meet the demands of the non-predictable tasks. Furthermore, since the supervisors tended not to supervise closely they also tended to disregard the pervasive set of rules which had been established at first to control the workers' activities.[4]

In a similar analysis, Stinchcombe indicates that administrators, confronted with critical problems of instability, as in the case of the construction industry, will find it uneconomical closely to supervise clerks who process communications. In turn, since there will be less closeness of supervision, there will be little opportunity for and value in teaching clerks rules for channeling communications.[5] Consequently, there will be many unpredictable activities to be performed; thus, a lack of closeness of supervision, and few rules. Similar processes to these can be distinguished in investigations by Walker,[6] Simpson,[7] Faunce,[8] and others.

[3] Peter M. Blau, *The Dynamics of Bureaucracy* (Chicago: University of Chicago Press, 1955), p. 24.

[4] *Ibid.,* p. 25.

[5] Arthur L. Stinchcombe, "Bureaucratic and Craft Administration of Production: A Comparative Study," *Administrative Science Quarterly* (September, 1959), p. 177.

[6] Charles R. Walker, *Toward the Automatic Factory* (New Haven; Yale University Press, 1957).

[7] Richard L. Simpson, "Vertical and Horizontal Communication in Formal Organizations," *Administrative Science Quarterly* (September, 1959), pp. 188–196.

[8] William A. Faunce, "Automation in the Automobile Industry: Some Consequences for In-plans Social Structure," *American Sociological Review,* 23 (1958), pp. 401–407.

Research Design

To test the notions presented above, interviews were conducted in The Griffin Community Hospital located in Derby, a small city near New Haven, Connecticut. The sample selected for study within the hospital was composed of the 204 full-time, day-shift employees. These day-shift workers are distributed throughout 30 departments in the hospital.

The data were collected mainly by two methods. First, informal observations and interviews were conducted from January through June, 1963. Secondly, a questionnaire was used which was pre-tested at Grace New Haven Hospital, revised, and pre-tested again at the same institution. They were then distributed in the Griffin Hospital in mid-May and the final follow-ups were completed in the second week of June, 1963. An 84 percent return was obtained. The dimensions studied here are on an ordinal scale of measurement, and thus, Kendall's Tau rank order correlation was used for most of the analysis. A relatively high proportion of respondents were (a) Catholics (62%), (b) nurses (30%), (c) over 40 years of age (61%), (d) married (57%), and (e) had completed high school (54%).

Predictability of Tasks and Closeness of Supervision

Predictability was measured by asking respondents two questions.

First, they were asked, "If you wrote a list of the exact activities you would be confronted by on an average work day, what per cent of these activities do you think would be interrupted by unexpected events?" There were five possible responses to this question ranging from 0 to 20% of my daily activities are usually interrupted by unexpected events, to 80 to 100% of my activities are interrupted.

The second indicator of predictability was established by asking the respondents, in a later section of the questionnaire, the following question: "Every job is confronted by certain routine and repetitive activities. What per cent of the activities or work demands connected with your job would you consider to be of a routine nature?" These questions were given equal weight in determining each individual's predictability score; the respondents' answers to the above questions were summed; and, then individuals were ranked from high to low in nine categories of predictability according to their scores on the above two questions.

The statistical association between the responses to these two questions was both positive and significant beyond the .001 level of significance ($r_e = .52$), thus lends some credence to the assumption that these two indicators represent the same concept (predictability).

An index of closeness of supervision was established by asking the respondents two questions.

First, they were asked, "How often does your supervisor keep a close check on what you are doing and closely observe your work?" There were five possible responses to this question ranging from very often to very seldom.

The second indicator of closeness of supervision was determined by asking respondents, "To what extent does your immediate supervisor influence what you do in a typical work week?" Again there were five possible responses to this item ranging from 0 to 20% of my activities to 80 to 100% of my activities. The respondent's scores on these two questions were added and the workers were ranked into nine categories of closeness of supervision.

The analysis showed that the two indices were moderately associated. (The Kendall's Tau rank order correlation between the two questions was $r_e = .54$, p<.001.) [9] Thus, the

---

[9] Since the measure of closeness of supervision utilized here involves the workers' perceptions of how closely they are supervised it is possible that their estimates could be biased by many personality and social-background factors. Holding the extent of the "real closeness of supervision" constant, for example, a high authoritarian worker might believe he is not closely supervised while a non-authoritarian individual might feel that he is very closely controlled. With this limitation in mind we attempted to control for, at least partially, possible selective perception biases by asking the supervisors how closely they controlled their subordinates' work performance. Then supervisor's scores on closeness of supervision in each of the departments were correlated with the average closeness of supervision score as deter-

relationship was consistent with our assumption that we were measuring the same underlying variable (closeness of supervision).

Assuming that our indices of predictability and closeness of supervision were generally valid, we next related these two variables. A rank order correlation was computed for the association between predictability and closeness of supervision. The correlation indicated that the hypothesis was supported well beyond the .001 level of significance. ($r_c = .78$, $p < .001$)

For those jobs in which the work tasks were highly predictable the supervisors tended to exert relatively close control over the subordinates. For jobs in which the activities were unpredictable, there was a lack of close supervision. Controls were made for professionalization, discretion, and rule-usage, and the basic association between predictability and closeness of supervision remained unaltered.

It is possible, of course, that managements' control might affect the degree of predictability of an employee's job. However, this relationship or causal direction would seem to be weaker than that predicted above. For example, regardless of how closely a supervisor might control his sales force, the salesman will presumably be confronted by many unexpected events due to the uniqueness of individual customers whom he meets, even though management might assign the salesman fairly homogeneous clients. Similarly, researchers would probably face many unexpected situations regardless of the fact that they might have an all encompassing set of rules which instruct them to act or react in certain ways in all situations. Unexpected events might well

---

mined by the subordinates' estimates. The supervisors' estimates, of course, were subject to the same type of perception biases; however, the likelihood of both the subordinate and the supervisor in the same department having biased estimates is probably small.

The relationship between these two factors was both positive and significant at the .01 level, and thus lends some support to our measure of closeness of supervision. (Kendall's Tau $r_c = .63$, $p. < .01$). This support is only partial, however, since we had to consider departments as the unit of analysis and thus we did not have the supervisors' corroborating estimate of closeness of control for each subordinate. This later estimate would appear to be a more valid index upon which future research might be based.

continue to occur regardless of the manner in which the employees handled these unexpected situations.

Closeness of Supervision and Rule-Usage

The extent to which rules and regulations control an individual's task performance was measured by one question. Respondents were asked, "To what extent do hospital rules, regulations, and customs determine or influence what you do during an average work week?" There were five possible answers to this question. They ranged from 0 to 20% of my activities to 80 to 100% of my activities. Although there was only one question used to establish the rule-usage variable, it appeared to be a fairly accurate indicator of the general concept of rule-usage. Typical of the comments that respondents made with regard to this question was the following:

> I don't have to worry about what to do on my job because they've [people in hospitals] been doing this work for years . . . so I just came to work and they showed me how to do the job like it had always been done.

This worker's job was clearly specified and delimited because customary rules were established. In turn, the worker was required to exercise little discretion in carrying out his duties because he merely followed the rules.

The rank order correlation between closeness of supervision and rule-usage supported the proposition. The higher the closeness of supervision, the more that rule-usage was present ($r_c = .42$, $p < .003$). The association between these two variables, however, is rather weak; thus, closeness of supervision appears to explain only a relatively small part of the presence or absence of rules in connection with any given job. Controls were made for predictability, professionalization, and discretion, and did not alter the relationship between closeness of supervision and rule-usage.

A partial explanation for finding a somewhat moderate relationship between closeness of supervision and rule-usage could be that management control which takes the form of direct "personal supervision" will reduce the utility of rules. Another partial explanation could be that closeness of supervision might have been confounded by some of the respondents with style of supervision. That is to say, some managers might closely regulate their subordinates' activities, but in such a friendly manner that the subordinates might not perceive the fact that their behavior is being closely checked. On the other hand, some supervisors might relate to their subordinates in a very authoritarian, impersonal manner and subordinates might perceive this style of supervision as being "close control" supervision, regardless of the actual extent to which the supervisors regulate or restrict their behavior. These questions at least indicate the poten-

tial value of future research concerned with the measurement of these separate variables.

Conclusions

We explored the relationships between the degree of predictability of the work demands of subordinates' jobs and closeness of supervision. The analysis indicated that the more unpredictable the work environment the less there will be close supervision. Further, as closeness of supervision increases, the extent of rule-usage also increases. These relationships point to the important pressures that technological components of the work situation place upon management control.

Predictability of Work Demands and Professionalization as Determinants of Workers' Discretion *

GERALD D. BELL

Assume that you have been asked by the president of a large firm to advise him on the most desirable levels of decentralization in order to control the activities of different departments within his organization. Upon what factors would you be likely to base your decision?

A recent investigation indicates that to establish appropriate levels of decentralization, one's decisions should be, at least partially, based on: the types of productive tasks workers perform in general; and, the degree of predictability of work demands, in particular.[1]

This paper provides a partial explanation of several non-administrative cause for differences in the degrees of discretion workers exert in performing their tasks. Specifically we attempt to trace the influence of two factors upon discretion. One is the *predictability of work demands;* the other is the *professionalization of jobs.* Before attempting to analyze these relationships, let us take a brief view of the research design and the components of discretion.

From *Journal of The Academy of Management,* Vol. 9, No. 1, March 1966, pp. 20–28.

* The author is greatly indebted to Stanley H. Udy, Jr., Elton F. Jackson, and Chris Argyris, who throughout the formulation of the investigation provided keen analytical critiques of the notions presented in this paper. Enthusiastic support was received from Anthony J. DeLuca, Administrator of The Griffin Community Hospital. The many months of discussion held with the administrator are greatly appreciated. Part of the research is based on the author's dissertation, "Formality Versus Flexibility in Complex Organizations: A Comparative Investigation Within a Hospital," unpublished Ph.D. dissertation, New Haven, Connecticut: Yale University, Department of Sociology, 1964.

[1] See the author's forthcoming article, "Formality Versus Flexibility in Complex Organizations: The Discretionary Model."

Research Design

The investigation was conducted in the Griffin Community Hospital in Derby, a small city near New Haven, Connecticut. The sample was composed of the 204 full-time, dayshift employees within the hospital. These dayshift workers were distributed throughout 30 departments in the hospital.

Data Collection. The data were collected mainly by two methods. First, informal observations and interviews were conducted from January through June, 1963. Second, a questionnaire was used which was pre-tested at Grace New Haven Hospital, revised, and pre-tested again at the same institution. It was then distributed in the Griffin Hospital in mid-May and the final follow-ups were completed in the second week of June, 1963. An 84 percent return was obtained. The dimensions studied were on an ordinal scale of measurement, and thus, Kendall's Tau rank order correlation was used for the analysis.

A relatively high proportion of respondents were: (a) Catholics (62%); (b) nurses (30%); (c) over 40 years of age (61%); (d) married (57%); and, (e) had completed high school (54%).

Components of Discretion. For each task that a worker performs he is confronted by the opportunity to exert a certain degree of discretion or judgment in order to carry out his tasks. Jaques offers as examples of discretionary content the following:

being left to decide what experiments to do and how to do them in order to carry forward a piece of research; having to choose the best feeds and speeds for an improvised job on a machine; having to decide whether

446

the finish on a piece of work would satisfy some particular customer; having to choose from among several possible methods of manufacture in providing an estimate of cost; having to plan and organize one's work in order to get it done within a prescribed time.[2]

We have considered the discretion a worker exercises to be directed in differing degree, toward three main aspects of task performance. These are: (1) which tasks to perform; (2) how to perform them; and, (3) in which sequence to complete them.

For the first dimension, some tasks are clearly established and the employee makes few decisions in selecting the activities he performs. For other jobs, the tasks are not clearly delineated for the worker, and thus, he has the potential for exerting much discretion in determining which activities he performs. In the second case, jobs vary according to how much discretion the worker exerts in choosing how to perform his tasks. And in the third, jobs vary according to the quantity of discretion exercised by the worker in determining the time or sequence in which the tasks are to be performed.

Measurement of Discretion. Since the amount of discretion exercised by an employee is assumed to be directed toward the above three dimensions, we attempted to measure discretion by asking questions designed to determine the actual number of decisions made with regard to each of these areas. For these questions, each respondent was interviewed in person in order to increase the validity and reliability of the responses.

The respondents were first asked to list the main tasks performed during a typical work week, and then to indicate for which of these tasks they used their own judgment concerning whether or not to perform them, how, and when to perform them. The scores were summed and the respondents were ranked according to the total percent of decisions they made.

Intercorrelations between these three indicators of discretion are all highly significant (all were above $r_e = .71$, p<.001) and this finding

is consistent with our assumption that we are tapping the same general variable, which we have labeled discretion. This measure, however, is still far from perfect. It is possible, for example, that the high intercorrelations between the three indicators of discretion are due to the fact that respondents confounded these dimensions. Similarly, it is possible that personality, background dispositions, or other factors might have influenced individual's responses.[3]

In an attempt to provide some additional validating evidence of our discretion measure, the respondents were asked in a later section of the questionnaire, "To what extent do you control your job and the general pace of work?" The respondents' scores on discretion were positively and significantly related to their answers on the above question; ($r_e = .58$, p<.001) and thus, although this association does not eliminate the possibility of perception biases, it does lend some support to the validity of the discretion measure.

To provide evidence with which other researchers might compare the measures of discretion developed here with their experience and knowledge concerning jobs in various types of enterprises, we have computed the average discretion score for each major type of occupation in the hospital and have presented it in Chart 1.

A further aid in evaluating the discretion measure can be provided by referring to the descriptions for the above categories in the *Dictionary of Occupational Titles.* Brief descriptions for the major jobs in the hospital lend further credence to our measure of discretion (see Chart 2). The jobs rated high on the discretion measure are described as comprising tasks that require much judgment, and decision-making effort. On the other hand, jobs rated low on discretion have been characterized as involving very little choice-behavior on the worker's part.

---

[2] Elliott Jaques, *The Measurement of Responsibility* (Cambridge: Harvard University Press, 1956), p. 34.

[3] We attempted to eliminate individual perception biases by asking them to list the specific tasks they performed and to discuss the extent of discretion they exerted in performing each aspect of their tasks. By utilizing the above process it appeared that fairly accurate discretion scores could be determined for each respondent. Jaques reports similar findings in his efforts to measure discretion, *op. cit.*

Causes of Discretion

Predictability refers to the extent to which a worker is confronted by unexpected events while performing his tasks. Predictability then is concerned with the uniqueness of work situations presented to an employee while he carries out his job.

Chart 1. Occupations and Their Average Discretion Scores

OCCUPATION	AVERAGE DISCRETION SCORE (FOR THE THREE DISCRETION QUESTIONS)
1. Housekeeping, laundry, etc.	1.3
2. Dietary helpers	1.4
3. Cooks	2.0
4. Nurses' Aides	2.2
5. X-ray technicians	2.3
6. Orderlies	3.0
7. Laboratory technicians	3.0
8. Pharmacists	3.0
9. Secretaries	3.1
10. Plumber, carpenter, (semi-skilled workers)	3.2
11. Dietary supervisors	3.7
12. Nurses (staff)	4.5
13. Assistant department head (nursing)	4.9
14. Assistant department head (others)	5.0
15. Department head (nursing)	5.2
16. Department head (others) *	5.4
17. Doctors	5.6
18. Administrators	5.7

* Three of these 18 department heads were M.D.'s. The total scores of the respondents in each occupational category were summed and then divided by the number of employees in each category.

Predictability and Discretion. A subtle point that might cause some confusion is the fact that predictability as we are defining it does not refer to the degree to which a person can predict what *he will do* on his job, or how uniformly he performs his tasks; rather, it refers to the extent to which unexpected events confront an employee regardless of how he handles these unexpected events. An employee might have a job, such as a sales job, and regardless of how little discretion he exercised in selling his products, or how routinely he performed his duties, certain unexpected events would presumably continue to arise because of the unique characteristics of his customers, their needs, wants, and so forth. Similarly, even if a scientist were told what to do each day, this would not stop some unexpected results such as explosions, fires, and new discoveries from occurring. The predictability concept, then, refers to the uniqueness of the situations presented to a worker, rather than to the routines with which he carries out his tasks.[4]

Predictability is thought to affect discretion directly because when work demands are unpredictable they tend to present the employee with novel problems toward which he has the opportunity to utilize his judgment in completing the tasks.

This assumes, of course, that the worker is motivated to carry out his tasks efficiently, and that other factors such as supervisory control are at a minimum. If a surgeon, for example, is operating on a patient and opens the patient's stomach and finds an unexpected object inside he will have the opportunity, and it is assumed he will be encouraged to alter his activities or to utilize his discretion to meet the exigencies of the situation. In the same manner, let us assume that a stock broker meets a new customer and begins his "sales pitch" by presenting an image of an intellectual. He then begins to perceive that he is presenting the wrong image because the customer sympathizes with

[4] It should also be noted here that it would seem to be theoretically possible for a worker to utilize his discretion to eliminate some of the unpredictable features of his work situation. This possibility would seem, however, to be limited to some degree by the fact that a worker could control the technological characteristics of his tasks to only a certain extent. For instance, a salesman could sell a more homogeneous clientele, but these customers would still present many unique personality differences. Similarly, a researcher might attempt to specialize his research; however, he would still be confronted by many of the unusual difficulties encountered in research.

Chart 2. Occupations and Their Descriptions

1. *Housekeeping:* Keeps premises clean, orderly condition, sweeps floors and disposes of waste or litter. Scrubs floors. Polishes metal fixtures and fittings. Frequently works in evenings, after daytime employees have left the premises.

2. *Dietary Helpers:* Portions food *in accordance* with diets in a hospital *under* the *direction* of a Dietitian; weights out proper amounts of *specified* foods, and may perform some cooking *as directed*. Places food on dishes and on trays to be delivered to patients. May wash and scour equipment used, such as mixers, fruit juice reamers, carts, pantry shelves, and refrigerator compartments.

3. *Cook:* Prepares and cooks meals, *follows daily instructions* given by employer: peels, washes, trims, and otherwise prepares vegetables and meats for cooking.

4. *Nurses aide:* Assists professional nursing staff in hospitals by performing *routine* or *less skilled tasks* in the care of patients: bathes and dresses patients. Answers call bells, makes beds. Serves food and nourishment. Assists patients in walking. Gives alcohol rubs and performs other services. Cleans rooms and equipment.

5. *X-ray technicians:* Assists medical practitioners by operating X-ray equipment: prepares patient for X-ray treatment, fixing lead plates to patient to protect portions not to be exposed to the X-ray. Manipulates switches to time length and regulates intensity of exposure. Develops film photographically and dries them. May specialize in X-rays of certain parts of body.

6. *Pharmacist:* Compounds and dispenses medicines and preparations as directed by prescriptions prepared by licensed physicians and dentists. Performs routine assays and tests to determine identity, purity, and strength of drugs. Preserves drugs, medicines, biologicals, or chemicals. Maintains stock of drugs, chemicals, and other pharmaceutical supplies.

7. *Dietitian:* Applies the principles of nutrition to the feeding of individuals and groups: *Plans* menus and special diets with proper nutritional value. *Determines* dietetic value of foods and food products. Purchases food, equipment and supplies. *Supervises* chefs and other food service employees. Maintains sanitary conditions. Prepares educational nutrition materials.

8. *Nurse:* Performs various nursing duties requiring education, experience, and skill in the art of caring for ill and injured persons: administers medicines, ointments, and drugs as instructed by a physician. Observes symptoms, and takes and records the temperature, pulse, and respiration of patients, and charts these according to standard practice.

9. *Department head nurse: Directs* the activities of a nursing staff in a hospital; *establishes* policies to be executed by subordinates. Sets a standard and scope of service to be rendered. *Directs* personnel policy policy establishing factors, such as qualifications for employment and scales of wages.

10. *Physician:* A classification title for persons of recognized experience, educational, and legal qualifications, who are engaged in such phases of medicine as *diagnosing, prescribing* medicines for, and otherwise treating diseases and disorders for the human body, and performing surgery and operations.

11. *Administrators:* Advises governing board or independently *determines* policies and *defines* scope of services rendered. *Formulates* procedures for prosecution of program so that requirements of clients will most effectively be met. *Coordinates* work of agency with that of other community organizations to avoid duplication of community services. *Oversees* research activities directed at gathering facts pertinent to planning and execution of program. *Determines* hiring qualifications and establishes performance standards for paid and volunteer workers. *Coordinates* work of subordinates. May *direct* solicitation of funds and public-relations program. May *establish* budget and *direct* fiscal management of organization.

anti-intellectuals. The broker will presumably consider a change in his behavior. That is, he will use his discretion to formulate a new image in order to carry out his task more adequately.

Relevant Research. Although he does not directly refer to predictability, Gouldner's descriptions of miners' work activities implicitly points to the connection between predictability and discretion. The miners exerted their own judgment and skills in performing their many non-uniform tasks and in executing a variety of types of jobs. They were more "generalists" than specialists in comparison to the surface workers, and their tasks tended to be quite unpredictable.[5]

Correspondingly, in Janowitz's analysis of the changing structure of the military, although he also does not explicitly refer to the predictability concept, the close causal sequence flowing from predictability to discretion can be inferred from his work. In his terms:

> Close-order formations based on relatively low fire-power could be dominated and controlled by direct and rigid discipline. But continuously since the development of the rifle bullet more than a century ago, the social organization of combat units has been altering so as to throw the solitary soldier of his own and his primary group's social and psychological resources.[6]
>
> [That is, the non-predictability of combat has encouraged the utilization of discretion on the part of the soldiers.]

More and more frequently the decision to fire or not to fire, or in Janowitz's terms, the need for improvisation, has been distributed to many infantrymen; and consequently, the broadest decentralization of initiative at the point of contact with the enemy has taken place.[7]

In a similar view, Thompson and Tuden assert that when there is complete understanding and knowledge, or in our terms complete predictability, of the causation, means, and goals of the solution to a problem, decision-making is merely a technical or mechanical matter. "In its extreme form this situation requires no choice since the problem solution appears as common sense."[8]

And finally, the causal nexus between predictability and discretion is exemplified in Stinchcombe's research. In the relatively predictable mass production industry decisions were most often made outside the work milieu and communicated through well-established communication channels down to the workers. On the contrary, in construction work the majority of decisions were made at the level of the work crew since the work was so non-predictable.[9]

Predictability was measured by asking respondents two questions. First, they were asked, "If you were to write a list of the exact activities you would be confronted by on an average work day, what percent of these activities do you think would be interrupted by unexpected events?" There were five possible responses to this question ranging from 0% to 20% of my daily activities are usually interrupted by unexpected events to 80% to 100% of my activities are interrupted.

The second indicator of predictability was established by asking the respondents, in a later section of the questionnaire: "Every job is confronted by certain routine and repetitive demands. What percent of the activities or work demands connected with your job would you consider to be of a routine nature?" These questions were given equal weight in determining each individual's predictability score and the respondents answers to the above questions were summed. Individuals were then ranked from high to low in nine categories of predictability according to their scores on the above two questions.

The statistical association between the responses to these questions, is both positive and

---

[5] Alvin W. Gouldner, *Patterns of Industrial Bureaucracy* (Glencoe, Illinois: The Free Press, 1954), p. 109.

[6] Morris Janowitz, "Changing Patterns of Organizational Authority: The Military Establishment," *Administrative Science Quarterly* (March, 1959), p. 481.

[7] *Ibid.*

[8] James D. Thompson and Arthur Tuden, "Strategies, Structure, and Processes of Organizational Decision," in James D. Thompson, *et al., Comparative Studies in Administration* (Pittsburgh: University of Pittsburgh Press, 1959), p. 198.

[9] Arthur Stinchcombe, "Bureaucratic and Craft Administration of Production: A Comparative Study," *Administrative Science Quarterly*, IV (September, 1959), p. 180.

significant well beyond the .001 level of significance ($r_e = .52$), and thus lends credence to the assumption that these two indicators are representing the same concept which we have labeled predictability.

Assuming that our indices of discretion and predictability are generally valid, we next relate predictability to discretion. This association tends to support our hypothesis. (Kendall's Tau rank order correlation is $r_e = -.51$, p<.001). The individuals who estimate that they have the most predictable and routine work demands tend to estimate that they exercise the least discretion. On the contrary, when a worker is faced with many novel and unique situations on his job, he seems to carry out his tasks by utilizing much of his own initiative and judgment. Furthermore, the significant relationship between predictability and discretion was not altered when controls were made for rule-usage, professional training and closeness of supervision.

Professionalization and Discretion. The second variable which is considered to influence discretion is the degree to which particular jobs are professionalized. Professional training is thought to bring with it a certain degree of discretion because professionalized workers are trained to exercise and to expect to be given discretion with regard to the problems they face in their work. In Stinchcombe's terms, craft administration differs from mass production administration ". . . by substituting professional training of manual workers for detailed, centralized planning of work." [10]

In a similar light, Thompson and Bates rehearse the notion that the university must be highly decentralized since "knowledge" is given recognition as the basis for authority more so than title or seniority. In turn, knowledge is a highly specialized item. Discretion over academic activities is controlled less by university executives than by professional members of the faculty. Marcson also indicates that the nature of professionals' tasks acts as a force toward decentralization of authority for these workers.

We have hypothesized here that *the higher the degree of professional training, the more discretion employees will exercise in performing their tasks.*

[10] *Ibid.,* p. 175.

The measurement of professional training consisted of two factors. First, respondents were asked to indicate the amount of professional training they had attained. There were six possible answers to this question ranging from no professional training to six or more years. Second, the respondents were asked, "To what extent do the standards of your profession influence what you do on your job during an average work week?" Five possible answers were provided for this question ranging from 0 to 20% of my activities to 80% to 100% of my activities.

These two questions were given equal weight in determining the respondents' final professionalization score. The worker's two scores on the above questions were combined and the respondents were then ranked into 9 categories from high to low, of professional training. The rank order correlation between these two questions indicates that they are positively and significantly related. (Kendall's Tau rank order correlation is $r_e = .64$, p<.001).

By then relating professionalization to discretion the data indicate that our hypothesis is moderately supported ($r_e = .50$, p<.001). The higher the professionalization of jobs, the more discretion is initiated by the worker in completing his tasks.[11] This relationship was maintained furthermore when controlling for predictability, rule-usage, position within the organization, and closeness of supervision.[12] These findings indicate that the training and skills that individuals acquire in their professional socialization tend to be transferred into the organizational setting and to be conducive to the exertion of discretion by the professional workers.

Conclusions

We have attempted to explore two nonmanagerial determinants of the amounts of discretion workers exert in their daily produc-

[11] James D. Thompson and F. L. Bates, "Technology, Organization and Administration," *Administrative Science Quarterly* (December, 1957), p. 333.
[12] Simon Marcson, *The Scientist in American Industry* (Princeton, New Jersey: Princeton University Press, 1960), p. 44.

tive activities. The data indicate, first of all, that the more unpredictable the work demands which confront an employee, the more the likelihood that he will exert a high degree of discretion. Second, the data point to the fact that the more professional training an employee has, the more discretion he tends to exert in carrying out his duties.

These findings offer tentative suggestions to administrators concerning the most efficient levels of decentralization of authority for given work activities and thus units within the organization. Departments in which the productive activities are unpredictable, and which employ mostly professional workers would seem to resist rigid control and central regulation. Efficiency would probably be enhanced if management allowed unpredictable, professional units to be fairly flexible and discretionary in their forms of organization.[13] Correspondingly, in this latter instance, the supervisory-subordinate relationship would probably operate more smoothly than if administrators attempted closely to regulate their subordinates activities.

[13] This topic is explored in the author's forthcoming article, "The Influences of Technological Components of Work Upon Management Control."

Administrative Role Definition and Social Change

ANDREW GUNDER FRANK

My intent is to suggest how the degree to which organizational roles are defined is important for the extent and speed of social change. I shall propose three ideal types of administrative organization which are distinguished by the degree of definition of their administrative roles and sets of roles. The three types are: 1) *under-defined*, in which role expectations of administrative behavior are not well spelled out; 2) *well-defined*, in which administrative roles are explicitly and coherently defined; and 3) *over-defined*, in which role expectations cannot be satisfied by role incumbents. Thus, I disregard the now popular distinction between formal and informal organization and approach the study of social behavior which is inconsistent with well-defined (Type II) roles by introducing two additional ideal types of organization instead. The question I am posing is

How do these three types of organization differ in their implications for vitality and change?

The sources and indices of vitality and change on which I shall focus are change in the definition of administrative roles, initiative, adaptation to environmental change, and transformation of one organizational type into another due to change of the whole set of roles and their interrelations.

To introduce the discussion of the three ideal types of organization and their implications for change, it will be useful to consider a study of administrative organization which relies on the ideal type of well-defined roles: *The Hoover Commission Report on Organization of the Executive Branch of the Government.* Some findings and recommendations of the Hoover Report may be summarized:

From *Human Organization*, Vol. 22, No. 4, Winter, 1963–1964, pp. 238–242. Reprinted by permission of the publisher.

First finding. The executive branch is not organized into a workable number of major departments and agencies which the President can effectively direct, but is cut up into a large number of agencies which divide responsibility. *Second finding.* The line of command and supervision from the President down through his department heads to every employee, and the line of responsibility from each employee of the executive branch up to the President has been weakened, or actually broken, in many places and in many ways. *Fifth finding.* Many of the statutes and regulations that control the practices and procedures of the government are unduly detailed and rigid.

Any systematic effort to improve the organization and administration of the government, therefore, must: 1. Create a more orderly grouping of the functions of government into major departments and agencies under the President. 2. Establish a clear line of control from the President to these department and agency heads and from them to their subordinates with correlative responsibilities from these officials to the President, cutting through the barriers which have in many cases made bureaus and agencies partially independent of the Chief Executive. 5. Enforce the accountability of administrators by a much broader pattern of controls so that the statutes and regulations which govern administrative practices will encourage, rather than destroy, initiative and enterprise.

Only by taking these steps can the operations of the executive branch be managed effectively, responsibly, and economically.

(Hoover, n.d.: Chapter 1)

The criteria of "effectiveness, responsibility and economy" which underlay the Commission's diagnosis and prescriptions are not spelled out explicity. But we may infer that

453

they are a piece with such traditionally accepted canons of good administration as comprehensive overview of policy-making, unified policy, clear and explicit definition of objectives, precision in relating decisions to antecedent objectives (Smithies, 1955), consistency, stability, and due process in decision-making (Pennock, 1952), "authority commensurate with responsibility," etc.

My purpose in this paper is to question the propriety of such canons to, and the effectiveness of, the attendant prescriptions for "the vitality of democracy itself" and to advance an alternative approach to this "field of inquiry which concerns every citizen." Dahl (1956), Lindblom (1959), and Gilbert (1958), among others, have already argued that administrative theory and practice such as that exemplified by the Hoover Commission do not necessarily contribute to responsible (read, responsive?) democracy. Although I subscribe to these young Turk approaches, I shall make no more than passing direct references to issues of power, responsibility, and responsiveness in the political-administrative process. Instead, I wish to focus my attention on organizational and administrative *vitality* and *change*. To do so, I shall regard the administrative organization recommended by the Hoover Report as an example of only one type of organization, which I label "well-defined"; and I shall compare its effects on vitality and change with those of two other ideal types of administrative organization.

I. Under-Defined Administrative Roles

The first ideal type of administrative organization I want to advance is characterized by under-defined administrative roles. In this type of organization, the expectations of particular roles may be under-defined, or defined expectations may not be matched by sanctions. In either event, a further aspect of this ideal type of organization is that the relations among roles is under-defined, so as to leave *lacunae* in the role set. My conception of this type of organization is largely distilled from my participation, this past year, in giving birth to Monteith College, a new general education college at Wayne State University. Those, who for lack of personal familiarity with a similar new

institution cannot visualize this type of organization, may wish to call the normless anomie of Durkheim to mind as a model.

In examining the implications of under-defined roles for change, it appears important to classify the responses of role incumbents as a) active or b) passive. As the following discussion will suggest, if member behavior is active, change will be relatively large, and if member behavior is passive, change will be relatively small. In distinction to Type III (over-defined role organizations) and this distinction is crucial to the whole argument of this paper, under Type I organization the degree of activeness and passiveness of individual behavior is not organizationally, but ideosyncratically, determined by individuals themselves, or it is culturally determined in a way which I do not understand.

A. Under-defined roles permit individuals actively to take the determination of their own and others' destinies into their own hands if they so wish. Active response to under-defined roles may result in many different *ad hoc* responses to situations in which guiding norms either do not exist or are not enforceable by existing sanctions. Active individuals may take substantial initiative in defining roles for themselves or others and, by doing so, for incumbents who will succeed them in these roles in the future. Active individuals may adapt their role definitions and/or their *ad hoc* responses to changing circumstances in their own or the administrative environment. Thus, they—and with them the entire political process—may be responsive to pressures from various interest groups.

B. In distinction to Type III organization, under-defined roles do not impose organizationally generated pressure on members to engage in any of these activities. They can, if they wish, be relatively passive only to the few existing norms or leave it to others, similarly situated, if any, to define their roles for them.

As time passes, individual response to under-defined roles would thus seem to change the whole set of role definitions and the more so the more active is individual behavior. In this way, the very administrative process which, in response to under-defined roles, results in changing the definitions of roles, and relations among them, also serves to transform Type I organization into an organization of Type II or Type III. The more contemporary role definition is influenced by strong leadership from a single person, the more likely is it that the original Type I organization will be replaced by the well-defined roles of Type II. The more leadership in current role definition is distributed among several people, the more likely are the under-defined roles of Type I to be replaced by the over-defined roles of Type III.

II. Well-Defined Administrative Roles

In the second ideal type of administration organization in which particular roles are well-defined, the means available to incumbents are quite adequate to the performance of their roles, while the relations among the roles are defined so as to yield a coherent and internally consistent set of roles. To some readers this ideal type may be reminiscent of social structure as visualized by Radcliffe-Brown and the anomie-avoiding social structure of Durkheim and Merton, in which institutionally given means are just adequate to the achievement of culturally defined roles. If we add hierarchy to the ideal type of well-defined roles, we get an idealization of the administrative organization advanced in the Hoover Report, or, more generally, an analog of the ideal type of Weberian bureaucracy. Although I hold with Lindblom (1959), and others that strict examples of this type of well-defined role organization can hardly be found in any existing organizations, and although it has, nonetheless, received the lion's share of attention elsewhere, it will be instructive to review some of its implications for administrative vitality and change. All of us who have ever been clients of an organization, bureaucratic or otherwise, which resembles the ideal type of well-defined roles have noticed, and I venture to say suffered and denounced, the conformity and ritualism in role performance to which Type II organization gives rise. Systematic analysis of the sources of the behavior may be found in Parsons' (1955) analysis of *The Social System* and Merton's (1947) discussion of "Social Structure and Anomie," and "Bureaucratic Structure and Personality." These studies help to confirm the contention that well-defined roles prohibit individual initiative and make ritual perfor-

mance easy, if not mandatory. They thus impede individual initiative in *ad hoc* behavior and innovation in his own and others' roles. At the same time, well-defined role organization lacks provision for individual and institutional adaptation to changes in the administrative environment; and deviation from role expectations endangers the very coherence of well-defined, well-articulated role organization.

Charges of unresponsiveness to the interests of outsiders and to policy changes initiated by newly appointed, and quickly disappointed, officials inside bureaucracies are, of course, commonplace and consistent with the above analysis. But interpretation of this unresponsiveness in the context of our three ideal types suggests that laying the blame at the door of bureaucracy itself, as is also commonplace, may be putting the blame in the wrong place. Comparing this resistance to change, this lack of vitality, with the administrative process under the other two types of organization suggests that the source of this inflexibility lies not so much in bureaucracy as it does in well-defined roles. For, as our examination of these other ideal types suggests, organization, bureaucratic or otherwise, with under- or over-defined roles does not suffer from such inflexibility. I infer that, if the Hoover Commission wishes to

> encourage, rather than destroy, initiative and enterprise [quoted on page 2]

by establishing

> a clear line of control . . . with correlative responsibility,

that is substituting well-defined roles for under- or over-defined ones, then the Commission is barking up the wrong tree.

We may see further that the same organizational obstacles which impede internally generated (innovation) and externally generated (adaptation) change results in failure of the whole role set to be transformed. Thus Type II organization does not provide for its own metamorphosis into Type I or Type III organization. An important practical result is that, failing to ride with the punches, Type II organization effectively resists pressure from the outside until that pressure either subsides or builds up enough to topple the institution by revolution rather than evolution.

III. Over-Defined Administrative Roles

Over-definition of roles may be the result a) of excessive role expectations which establish a single performance target beyond the role incumbent's means to achieve or the result b) of conflicting role expectations which prohibit complete role performance by the incumbent because the standards or norms of the roles are themselves in conflict. Again, the articulation of the whole set of roles is also over-defined in that the expectations for the various roles are not mutually compatible. It should be stressed that, to make a role overdefined, more of its expectations must be sanction*able*—though not sanction*ed*—than can ever be fulfilled by its incumbent. These sanctions need not, however, be external; they can quite well be sanctions of conscience.

A. Over-defined roles with merely excessive —but not conflicting—expectations are reminiscent of the anomie-producing social structure, discussed by Merton (1957), in which the culturally defined goals of people are beyond their institutionally prescribed means. Analyzing individual response to such anomie, Merton recognized four kinds of deviant behavior, all of which—in our terms—may be regarded as involving changing role definitions, or adaptation. Pursuing quite different interests in his path-breaking recent book, Albert Hirschman (1959) builds his whole *Strategy of Economic Development* around the gap between goals and means of over-defined roles with excessive expectations. His argument is that the imbalance implicit in what I am calling over-defined role organization will generate the initiative and enterprise desired by the Hoover Commission and so sorely needed by countries anxious to enjoy rapid economic change. That is, Hirschman argues that biting off more than you can chew is the best way to learn quickly to chew more. Holland Hunter (1959) makes the same argument in a still unpublished paper on Soviet economic planning and proceeds to examine how excessive the bite—in other words, how over-defined the roles—may be before you begin to choke.

Thus, the pressure which the excessive expectations of over-defined roles exert on their incumbents provides people with incentive themselves to initiate *ad hoc* behavior and changes in role definition which render the administrative process innovative and adaptive. Such behavior may involve simulating role performance, or creation of alternative means of role performance, or gradually changing the expectation for one's own role (such as letting a part of it atrophy through nonperformance), or changing another's role, etc. But, whatever the response to excessive expectations, the cumulation of such administrative behavior may transform the set of roles toward one that is well-defined (Type II) or more likely toward one that is over-defined, but by conflicting role expectations (Type III, B).

B. Conflicting expectations render a role, or indeed a set of roles, over-defined because, due to their very internal inconsistency, they cannot possibly be satisfied. The type of administrative process organized by such conflicting role expectations was suggested to me by my study of Soviet economic planning and has been analyzed by me and others under the term "conflicting standards organization." Under this type of organization, the very conflict among role expectations renders simultaneous sanctioning of all expectations impossible and makes differences in the selection of expectations to be sanctioned over time and among different incumbents quite likely. But such differential sanctioning changes the role definitions themselves. Similarly, unlike well-defined roles which cannot be easily changed lest the role set become not well-defined, or over-defined but non-conflicting roles (Type III, A) which cannot be changed too much lest they conflict, already conflicting role definitions can be and are changed with abandon without undermining this type of organization. Moreover, the pressures of conflicting expectations —and they probably are considerable—induce individual role incumbents to innovate and adapt energetically and almost continually. Contrary to the organizational possibilities of both under-defined and well-defined roles, there is nothing in the demands of conflicting role organization which prevents building a strongly sanctionable demand for individual initiative into the role definition. Thus, in stark contrast to the internal and external unresponsiveness of administration under well-defined roles, administration under conflicting role expectations can contain built-in provisions for internally generated innovations and externally stimulated adaptation.

Comparison and Policy Implications of the Three Ideal Types

The main conclusion we may derive from the foregoing analysis is that, paradoxically, administrative behavior in response to the under-defined roles of Type I and the over-defined roles of Type III resemble each other more than either resembles the behavior arising out of the well-defined roles of Type II, because both under- and over-definition of roles impose a much wider range of discretion on individual decision-makers than do well-defined roles. It is the relative lack of discretion permitted by well-defined roles which organizationally inhibits changes in role definition, initiative, and adaptation under our first ideal type of organization. It is the contrastingly wide range of discretion permitted by under-defined and demanded by over-defined roles which results in the change-producing, role-defining, innovation, and adaptive behavior of role incumbents under Types I and III organization. Whatever other beneficial effects the Hoover Commission medicine might have, improving the vitality of the patient—the therewith of democracy in the United States—would not seem to be one of them.

The under-defined roles of Type I and the over-defined roles of Type III differ from each other, in turn, in that over-definition of roles results in built-in pressures for innovative and adaptive administrative behavior on the part of role incumbents, while under-defined roles need merely permit the same. In this connection, I am moved to disagree with Blau's (1955) contention that initiative only occurs with job security. Blau seems to have based this conclusion on his study of a federal law enforcement agency which witnesses substantial definition of their roles by incumbents. This feature suggests that this agency, partially at least, exemplified our under-defined role organization. And given the permissiveness without pressure which characterizes underdefined roles, job security might *be* a requirement for individual initiative; I do not know. But over-defined role organization certainly does not need to provide such job security to witness individual initiative. On the contrary, with over-defined roles, initiative is one result of the quest for job security.

In view of these organizationally fostered differences in individual behavior and consequently in the vitality and changeability of the administrative process, it may be worthwhile to speculate on the possibility that these organizational types also differ in their suitability for various administrative tasks. We have seen that the permissiveness of under-defined roles can result in widespread individual search for new role definitions. Thus, the under-defined role organization of Type I may be particularly suitable for a research institution or a group which is trying to develop new *raisons d'être* in a changing world. I believe this conclusion is consistent with the finding at Rand on the organization of research and development in military technology (Klein, 1960).

The same permissiveness of under-defined roles which can result in widespread search militates against change under forced draft. Such change, as we have seen, can, however, be produced by pressures of over-defined roles. Yet over-defined roles still permit individuals a substantial range of discretion. Thus, an institution which, like underdeveloped countries, is trying to lift itself by its bootstraps, might well benefit from over-defined roles. If there is only a single desired direction of change, and it is known, reliance on excessive role expectations may be suitable. If, as is more usually the case, the objectives are several and/or themselves largely unknown, organization with conflicting role expectations may well be in order (compare Lindblom, 1959 a, b). Administrative processes which do not occur in, and are not intended to result in, a substantially changing world can still profit from organization through relatively well-defined roles.

Different degrees of role definition may also be associated with various administrative roles within an organization. Thus, under-defined roles may be associated with the heads of organizations who, to use Selnick's (1957) term, must offer "Leadership in Administration." Junior executives and their middle management brethren elsewhere may often find themselves in over-defined roles. The more under-defined the leadership roles, the more is middle management likely to experience conflicting role expectations as time passes. The low man on the totem pole may still find himself in a well-defined role. Were we to combine these inferences of degree of definition of individual roles with the above inferences on organizational types, we might arrive at some strategies for organizational decision-making not unlike those of Thompson and Tuden (1959) who relate preferences about possible outcomes of organizational decisions with beliefs about ends of decision-makers with their agreement on means.

We have seen that individual behavior under the permissiveness of under-defined roles (I) seems to involve changes in role definition which transform under-defined role organization (I) into one of well-defined (II) or over-defined (III) roles. Over-defined roles might in time become well-defined. But is surely unlikely, in contrasts, that well-defined roles (II) would become either under-defined (I) or over-defined (III), or that over-defined role organization (III) would easily be transformed into under-defined role organization (I). Should this suggestion be well taken, the implications are quite far-reaching: An institution with well-defined roles which, like my university (Wayne), wishes to initiate the under-defined roles which seem to permit and foster research, may find it more difficult to transform the first set of roles into the second than to abolish or disregard the well-defined ones and start with under-defined ones from scratch. With possibly something like this in mind, Wayne did not try to reform its existing Liberal Arts College, but created a second one, Monteith College, instead.

In brief, the well-defined roles of Type II organization permit only very limited flexibility and require sufficient external pressure for change to result in revolutionary change of an institution which relies on it. The under- and over-defined roles of Type I and Type III organization, on the other hand, provide for internally generated initiative and externally induced adaptation.

REFERENCES

Peter Blau, *The Dynamics of Bureaucracy*, Chicago, 1955.

Robert Dahl, *A Preface to Democratic Theory*, Chicago, 1954.

Andrew Gunder Frank, "Organization of Economic Activity in the Soviet Union," *Wetwirtschaftliches Archiv*, LXXV, No. 1 (March, 1957), 104–156.

Andrew Gunder Frank, "Goal Ambiguity and Conflicting Standards: An Approach to the Study of Organization," *Human Organization*, XVII, No. 4 (Winter, 1958–59), 8–13.

A. G. Frank and Ronald Cohen, "Organization and Change Under Conflicting Standards: Russia and Africa," unpublished.

Charles Gilbert, "The Framework of Administrative Responsibility," *The Journal of Politics*, XXI, 373–407.

Albert Hirschman, *The Strategy of Economic Development*, New Haven, 1958.

Herbert Hoover, *et al. The Hoover Commission Report*, McGraw-Hill, New York, n.d.

Holland Hunter, "On Planning to Catch Up," mimeographed.

Burton Klein, "The Decision Making Problem in Development," Rand Corporation Monograph, P-1916, February 19, 1960.

Charles Lindblom, "The Science of 'Muddling Through'," *Public Administration Review*, XIX, No. 2 (Spring, 1959), 79–88.

Charles Lindblom, "Decision Making in Taxation and Expenditure, National Bureau Conference in Public Finances, mimeographed.

Robert Merton, "Social Structure and Anomie," in *Social Theory and Social Structure*, The Free Press, Glencoe, Ill., 1957.

Robert Merton, "Bureaucratic Structure and Personality," *ibid.*

Talcott Parsons, *The Social System*, The Free Press, Glencoe, Ill., 1955.

J. Roland Pennock, "Responsiveness, Responsibility, and Majority Rule," *The American Political Science Review*, XLVI (Sept., 1952), 790–807.

John Phelan, "Authority and Flexibility in the Spanish Bureaucracy," *Administrative Science Quarterly* (June, 1960).

Arthur Smithies, *The Budgetary Process in the United States*, New York, 1955, as quoted and paraphrased in Lindblom, 1959.

James Thompson and Arthur Tuden, "Strategies, Structures and Processes of Organizational Decision," in J. D. Thompson *et al.* (eds.), *Comparative Studies in Administration*, Pittsburgh, 1959.

Differentiation of Roles in Task-Oriented Groups

HAROLD GUETZKOW

An important feature in the development of groups is the differentiation of roles into an organizational structure.[1] In newly forming groups such differentiation often accompanies the occupancy of the developing positions by particular persons. In this work on the development of experimental organizations in a laboratory, factors related to these two processes have been isolated.

The first part of this inquiry demonstrates the distinction between role differentiation and development of organizational structure. The second part analyzes group processes and personal characteristics associated with role differentiation.

Description of Experiment

The experiments reported in this paper used the communication situation initially suggested by Bavelas (2). The two laboratory "runs" analyzed in this report involved 76 groups of five men each operating in the experimental

From Harold Guetzkow, "Differentiation of Roles in Task-Oriented Groups," in Dorwin Cartwright and Alvin Zander, eds., *Group Dynamics Research and Theory*, Row, Peterson & Co., Evanston, Ill., 1960, pp. 683–704. Reprinted by permission of the publisher.
[1] See Guetzkow and Simon (6), and Guetzkow and Dill (5); full details of the experimental procedures are described in a microfilm (1). The research was supported by a grant from the research funds of the Graduate School of Industrial Administration, Carnegie Institute of Technology. Hearty thanks are due to Messrs. K. Hellfach, A. D. Martin, and F. Metzger and to Mrs. Martha Pryor, Miss Anne E. Bowes, Mrs. Marion Bement, and to Mrs. Janet Stein for aid in conducting the investigation and help in analyzing its results. The manuscript was prepared during 1956–57, at the Center for Advanced Study in the Behavior Sciences. My collaborators, Professors W. R. Dill and H. A. Simon, helped in the development of ideas included in this paper in their usual stimulating way.

problem-solving situation designed by Leavitt (8), but modified to permit study of the group's handling of its operating task separately from its organization problem.

The task was identical to that used by Leavitt: the five subjects each had five pieces of a standard set of six pieces of information; their task on a given trial was to determine which piece was common and then to identify this common piece for the experimenter.

None of the participants had been exposed to this laboratory situation before. Each group worked for about two hours during which time the operating task was repeated twenty times. The time needed for each completion of the repeated task varied from over two minutes to less than one minute. The five subjects were seated around a circular table, screened from each others' view by five radial partitions. Intertrial periods of not more than two minutes each provided opportunity for work on the group's organizational problems. After the preliminary instruction period, there was no oral communication among the participants. During the task trials, the subjects passed messages through slots in their partitions to each other on precoded cards. During the intertrials, messages were written by the subjects on blank cards and then exchanged among themselves. Each subject was given a letter, which was used by him in identifying his message and the slots which opened into each cubicle. When the missing information had been obtained by each, the experimenter was so informed and the task trial was ended by the automatic sounding of a bell. By a signaling arrangement, the subjects were allowed to terminate the intertrial period at any time they wished before the end of the two minutes allowed them.

Three hundred and eighty male freshmen engineering students at Carnegie Institute of Technology served as subjects for the experiments. The groups were equated with respect to the average and the spread of intellectual ability among their five members through the use of ACE Psychological Examination scores. Each group was composed of one man from each of the Carnegie quintiles.

The task problem had been reduced to a routine through the pre-experimental instructions and practice period. The urgent problem before each group was how to organize itself, given its communication net. Three types of nets were used in a quartet of variations (see Fig. 1). Twenty of the groups operated without restriction, *all-channels* being open for communication ("All-Channel" groups). Twenty-one groups were placed in a *circle* net in which the members could communicate only with those immediately to their left and right ("Circle" groups). Twenty groups were placed in the circle net during the task trials, but these communication restrictions were removed during the intertrial period ("Circle-all-channel" or "Circle-AC" groups). Fifteen of the groups operated with severe restrictions in a *wheel* arrangement in which the four spokes could communicate only with the hub ("Wheel" groups). The apparatus could be easily rearranged for the different groups by mechanically closing or opening the communication slots. The subjects were not told by the experimenter of the pattern used in arranging their net either before or during their work period in the laboratory.

Organization as Task Specialization

There were large differences among the 76 groups in the four nets as to whether and how they organized themselves for the performance of their operating tasks (5, 178–179). In the groups which differentiated, it was possible for the experimenter to distinguish three roles on the basis of the interactions portrayed in their task messages.

1. Some participants performed the specialized functions of receiving information, forming the solution, and then sending answers; these organized activities may be thought of as constituting a "keyman" role.

2. Other participants would merely send their own missing information to others and then later receive the answer to the problem; this package of actions is designated as the "endman" role.

3. Some individuals usually passed on the missing information of others as well as their own, and then, if they received the answer, relayed the answer to one or more neighbors; this grouping of activities is designated as the "relayer" role.

When two or three roles are performed simultaneously in an interlocked fashion within a group, one obtains hierarchical structures (5). In the Wheel and All-Channel groups, one typically obtained a two-level hierarchical organization, with four endmen sending their information to the keymen, who in turn formed the solution and communicated the answer to the endmen. In the third of the Circle and Circle-AC groups which organized, the hierarchical structure had three levels, with two relayers serving as intermediaries between two endmen and the keyman.

In the so-called "unorganized" Circle and Circle-AC groups, the subjects eventually all received information about the four missing symbols and then each formed his own solution to the problem. In such situations there was no need to exchange answers. Sometimes the information exchanges became stable, developing quite systematic "each-to-all" pat-

   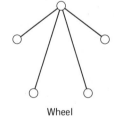   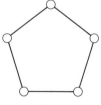

All-channel   Wheel   Circle

Fig. 1. Open channels used in the three nets.

terns. But because each participant performed identical functions (often in an identical way), there sometimes was no role specialization in these "unorganized" groups.

As has been argued elsewhere (4, 380–81), it seems fruitful to distinguish "organizations" from face-to-face, "small" groups, by virtue not of their size but of the relatively large amount of indirect, mediated interaction which occurs among the members of the former. When these mediated interactions are more or less stably structured in somewhat elaborate arrangements in "organized" groups, it is convenient to distinguish them from the "unorganized" groups in which the interactions, although mediated, are unstable and less involved. As is usually the case in working with a set of multi-dimensional characteristics, these bipolar typologies are not discrete.

man who sometimes also behaved as endman or relayer, was classified only as "keyman," as long as the keyman role had been occupied for a minimum of four consecutive trials. If an individual qualified both as relayer and endman, he was "classified according to the role he held for the longer period of time" (quotation from coding instructions).

A second person, using the code written by the first coder, agreed in assigning the same role (including "no role") to 85% of the subjects represented in Table 1. There was variation in the accuracy with which different types of groups could be categorized. The agreement among the coders was 100% for the Wheel groups, 95% for the organized Circle and Circle-AC groups, and 85% for persons in the All-Channel groups. Persons in the unorganized Circle and Circle-AC groups were

Table 1. Distribution of Roles (Number of Persons in Role)

ROLE	ALL-CHANNEL		CIRCLE AND CIRCLE-AC, ORGANIZED *		CIRCLE AND CIRCLE-AC, UN-ORGANIZED *		WHEEL	
Keymen	23 †	23%	15 †	21%	30 †	23%	15	20%
Relayers	17	17%	28	40%	39	30%	0	0
Endmen	46	46%	27	38%	35	27%	60	80%
Persons without roles	14	14%	0	0%	26	20%	0	0%
Totals	100		70		130		75	

* One Circle-AC group was omitted from this and subsequent tabulations because of its marginality to both the organized and the unorganized categories. The Circle group which developed a "chain" in sending information while using a three-level hierarchy arrangement for returning the answers (6, 246) was classified as "organized" in the study, although it was omitted in an earlier analysis (5, Tables 3 and 4).

† The classification of more than one person per group as a keyman results when two persons within a single group played that role at different times.

A quantitative description of the extent and type of role specialization which occurred in the various groups is presented in Table 1. The coder assigned individuals to roles by following the definitions given above. To be classified as occupying a role, it was necessary for an individual to have performed the specified behaviors for four or more consecutive trials. Sometimes an individual occupied two or three roles during the course of the twenty trials. To avoid multiple classifications, a key-

more difficult to classify, as is indicated in an agreement of 71% by the two coders. The accuracy of classification of persons in the three different roles varied too: 85% for keymen, 63% for relayers, and 78% for endmen.

Examine the results presented in Table 1. In the All-Channel groups, the inability of three of the twenty groups to organize is reflected in 14% of the subjects having differentiated no roles for any four consecutive trials. In these All-Channel groups, six of the seventeen organized groups used a three-level hierarchy in returning answers from keymen to endmen, as evidenced in the relayers reported in Table 1. The organization of two-level hierarchies in all of the Wheel groups after the fourth or fifth trial is reflected in the assumption of keymen roles by 20% of the members and occupancy of endmen roles by the remaining 80%

Compare the role specialization in the 14 organized groups with that which occurred in the 26 unorganized groups in the Circle and the Circle-AC nets. Although only 20% of the members of the latter groups failed to develop operationally identifiable roles, all of these groups were unorganized. Had the 26 persons without roles been members of common groups, one still could account for only five or six of the 26 groups which failed to organize. Nor can one account for the failure to organize because of an insufficiency of keymen— there being slightly more in the unorganized than in the organized Circle and Circle-AC groups (23% to 21%). There is a deficit of relayers and endmen. But if the persons who did differentiate relayer and endman roles were collected into common groups (along with sufficient keymen). 18 to 19 of the 26 "unorganized" groups might have been organized. Examination of the actual distribution of the roles in the 26 unorganized groups in the Circle and Circle-AC nets reveals there is a full complement of one keyman, two relayers, and two endmen in 14 of the groups. The difficulty, then, is not in the failure of the members to develop individually appropriate role behaviors.

The failure lay in the groups' inabilities to interlock their roles appropriately at the proper times. Further analysis (5, 202) revealed that this inability was largely caused by the failure of the groups to communicate during the intertrial periods about their organizational problem. Thus, the development of unorganized groups is due fundamentally to the failure to interlock roles into an organization, not to a dearth of differentiated roles.

Factors Associated with Role Differentiation

The finding that roles emerge before groups become organized indicates that conditions associated with the differentiation of roles may be different from those associated with the macro-organization of the group. Let us first explore factors which are associated with role differentiation. In the discussion we will compare them with our hypotheses about macro-organizational development, as analyzed elsewhere (5). In displaying the co-relations which exist among the variables in this paper, we will conform to the common practice of stating many of our hypotheses in the form of causal interrelationships. It is understood that the data supporting the hypotheses do not demonstrate the existence of causality.

Factors associated with role differentiation may be viewed as of two kinds—those *external* environmental factors which induce role formation because of the task components, and those *internal* processes involved in the establishment of particular persons in particular roles.

Role Formation as Induced by Requirements of External Environment

Task Characteristics. Role formation would seem to be intimately associated with the functions demanded by the tasks. Our operational description of the three roles in terms of the components of the task is: information exchange, solution formation, and answer exchange. But the task characteristics did not determine just how the components should be assembled into differentiated roles—nor whether these roles need be continuously played by one set of individuals or interchanged among them. In Table 2, we have hypothesized the various combinations in which the task components might have been assembled in functional roles. All but one were found to have occurred. By its vary nature, the task did not allow persons to specialize only in solution formation, for to form solutions on receipt of information from one's colleagues was imperative. The selection of particular combinations, with the one exception, therefore was not due to the task characteristics themselves.

Communication Restrictions. The communication restriction was an important factor in inducing particular forms of role differentiation. The use of a circle net by the Circle and

Circle-AC groups necessitated the use of three- rather than two-level hierarchies. But these restrictions did not necessitate the use of hierarchy roles, as was demonstrated in the evolution of a set of interlocked but identical roles in a "round-robin." In this form of organization, each participant received missing information, added his own symbol to the compilation, and then routed it around the "robin" so that each could form his own solution. The all-channel net was not nearly so restrictive—and other ways of interlocking roles were developed (5, 178). Even the most restrictive variation used—the wheel net—did not prescribe completely the nature of the role differentiation as one of the subjects in the "spokes" of

layers vs. keymen, $t = 2.13$, $p<.05$; relayers vs. endmen, $t = 2.33$, $p<.05$). Countrariwise, there were no such contrasts in the times at which the three roles were differentiated in the communication restricted Circle and Circle-AC groups. The average of the first trials at which differentiation occurs for the keymen, relayers, and endmen in these two types of organized groups were 6.9 ($\sigma = 2.7$), 6.2 $\sigma - 3.2$, and 6.5 ($\sigma - 4.2$), respectively, with none of the differences significant.

Thus, two pieces of evidence indicate that the development of roles is prescribed to an extent by differences in communication restriction. The type of role which may be developed is prescribed in part by the communi-

Table 2. Functional Roles as A Priori Combination of Task Components

TASK COMPONENTS	ROLE DESCRIPTIONS
Information Sending (IS) alone	Endmen.
Solution Forming (SF) alone	No role exists.
Answer Sending (AS) alone	Relayers in structures in which 2-level hierarchies are used for information exchange and 3-level ones for answer exchange.
IS and SF combinations	All persons in "round-robins" used for information exchange, and in many "each-to-all" groups.
IS and AS combinations	Relayers in groups using 3-level hierarchies for both information and answer exchanges.
IS and SF and AS combinations	Persons in "each-to-all" and "round-robin" groups, in which exchanges include both information and answers.

the wheel (who in our experiments actually all played endman roles) could have been "keyman" with the evolution of a "lieutenant keyman" at the hub.

The time of role differentiation also seems to have been prescribed in part by the communication restrictions. In the All-Channel groups, the average of the numbers of the trials on which the keymen first differentiated their roles was 5.2 ($\sigma = 4.2$). The endmen differentiated their roles soon thereafter, averaging 5.7 trials ($\sigma = 3.4$). The relayers lagged, averaging 8.1 ($\sigma = 3.9$) as the trial of their differentiations. The differences between relayers and both keymen and endmen are significant (re-

cation restrictions; the time at which the roles emerge also is determined in part by the same communication restriction.

Group Goal. The differentiation of roles in these experimental groups would seem to have its central origin in the efficiency goals posited by the experimenter in the instruction, "Your team is competing with the other five-man groups to see which group is fastest at getting the answer. The shorter the time, the better your team score." Two preconceptions may have been evoked in our subjects: a crude notion of the inverse relation of the volume of messages to efficiency of performance, and a cultural bias favoring hierarchical arrangements. Groups adopting an each-to-all solution averaged .84 minutes per task trial during their three fastest trials; groups adopting a hierarchical organization averaged .47 minutes. The division of labor increased for efficient group performance. This division of labor was expressed in the differentiation of relatively stable roles. Role stability may have been enhanced by the goal, for with but twenty trials in all there may have been reluctance to experiment with change.

That such role specialization need not be attached stably to particular persons is evidenced in one pilot variation (3) in which the goal instruction was changed to induce interindividual instead of intergroup competition. In four pilot groups run within an all-channel net, the members were informed their success would be evaluated individually in terms of the rapidity with which each reported the solution to the experimenter rather than in terms of their group's overall performance. Three of the groups bogged down, developing no organization. The members of the fourth group developed a quasi-stable coalition among themselves, the terms of which were to organize a two-level hierarchy in which the keyman role was passed trial-by-trial from person to person —so that each member could report the solution first on one out of every five trials.

Summary. Three facets of the task environment, as imposed by the experimenter, seem to be orderable in terms of their impact on the role formation in the experimental situations as follows: task characteristics (weakest), communication restrictions, and group goal (strongest).

Internal Processes Involved in the Differentiation of Roles

Had the experimenter so chosen, it probably would have been comparatively easy—given the authority relationships obtaining between experimenters and subjects (6, 235)—to have designated that three functional roles should be employed and then to have assigned particular subjects to these roles. Had that been done, both role formation and occupant assignment would have been an initial condition in the experiment constituting part of the external environment. Although research work is needed on the impact of different modes for the designation of positions and their occupancy, there experiments focused on organizational development without formal designation devices.

The mechanisms involved in the establishment of certain persons in particular positions may be divided into those rooted in the action characteristics of the group, and those rooted in the personal characteristics of the members. These experiments yield more information about the former than the latter, as no detailed personality assessments were made of the participants.

Mechanisms Related to Group Interaction

In the wheel net, selection of particular people for keyman and endman roles was a function of communication restrictions. In the other three nets, however, the five persons were placed in functionally equivalent communication points at the beginning of the first trial. What happens as the group develops to establish particular persons in particular roles?

Establishment by Chance. During the first few trials there was much random activity; the subjects seemingly sent information to each other without rhyme or reason. These initial chance-like events, then, might be thought of as selecting a person who, once having served as solution-former, continues thereafter in the key position. On the basis of this "chance" hypothesis, the persons forming the solution on the first trial eventually would occupy keyman roles as the organization differentiated.

In those 18 All-Channel, 18 Circle, and 18 Circle-AC groups in which one or more keymen become differentiated, it is possible to check the extent to which the solution-formers on the first trial become keymen in the semi- or fully stabilized organizational structures. The hypothesis is tested in Table 3. There is no significant difference between the proportion of persons who become keymen from among those who formed solutions on the first trial and the proportion who become keymen from among those who fail to form solutions. "Being lucky" in becoming a solution-former "by chance" on the initial trial does not help one become keymen in subsequent trials. These results contradict the hypothesis and indicate that some other mechanisms must be involved in selecting out the keymen.

Establishment by Withholding Information. The "common symbol" problem made it possible for an individual to insure himself of the key role by withholding his information from the others, provided the latter did not try to use the same device. This procedure was used by only one subject. In fact, there was only a gradual decline in the number of information messages the keymen sent, even after they had become the solution-formers and answer-senders. This means we must look elsewhere for an explanation of how certain persons became the keymen.

to understanding the nature of their communication net and to inquiries about and evaluations of proposed organizational plans. The average numbers of such units in their messages over the 19 intertrials for persons within the three roles are presented in Table 4. These findings indicate that keymen and relayers, in general, tend to send more messages concerning their perception of the structure than do endmen, although the differences are significant only in the All-Channel groups.

The coding used on the intertrial messages indicates the amount of effort the subjects devoted to perceiving their situation. This measure has ambiguity in its meaning—more effort may be stimulated by the inadequacy of perceptions, and contrariwise, more effort may yield superior levels of perception. At the end

Table 3. Selection of Keymen by Chance on First Trial

	ALL-CHANNEL	CIRCLE	CIRCLE-AC
Total number of persons who formed solutions:	42	46	45
number who became keymen	10	15	11
% keymen	24%	33%	24%
Total number who failed to form solutions:	43	44	45
number who became keymen	12	10	10
% keymen	38%	23%	22%
Total number of group members:	85	90	90
number who became keymen	22	25	21
% keymen	26%	28%	23%

Role Differentiation on the Basis of Situational Perceptions. Was role development associated with differences in the adequacy of the subjects' perception of the organizational situation? Our procedures yielded two sets of data from which estimates of such perceptions were obtained. During the intertrial periods participants exchanged messages in efforts to perceive the structure of the communication net and their emerging organization. At the end of the experiment, the participants were asked to eplain how their groups were organized and to diagram the communication net.

The All-Channel, Circle, and Circle-AC groups devoted an average of 16, 29 and 21 per cent of their intertrial messages, respectively,

of the experiment, open-ended questionnaires were given the participants about the functioning of the group, about each participant's own role within the group, and about the group's communication net. On the basis of this information, it was possible to decide whether each participant described his own role and that of his colleagues correctly or incorrectly, or omitted mention of some persons. The accuracy of organizational perceptions of the subjects was conceived as a ratio of the number of correct observations minus the incorrect observations to the total number of roles operationally identified by the experimenters (Table 2). The average of these ratios for persons occupying various roles is presented in

Table 5. In interpreting these figures, it must be remembered that an omitted response on the part of the subject does not necessarily imply lack of knowledge—it may indicate communication failure in the open-ended questionnaire, as no individual probing was undertaken by the experimenters. The results are somewhat disparate with those obtained from the intertrial message measure (Table 4). This is not unexpected, since the correlation between the two estimates is but .13 (significant at the 5% level), based on 258 of the subjects.

The superiority of the keymen and relayers compared with the endmen found in Table 4 holds for the organized Circle and Circle-AC groups in Table 5, but fails to be the case in the All-Channel groups. This discrepancy between Tables 4 and 5 may reflect the difference in time at which the two measures sampled perceptual aedquacy. Did the complete absence of communication restrictions allow endmen in the All-Channel groups finally to gain knowledge of the organization situation equal to that of their keymen and relaying colleagues, even though they did not *send* messages about these matters during the course of their organizational development?

A second discrepancy between Tables 4 and

Table 4. Intertrial Messages about Situation by Roles * (Number of Units Sent in 19 Intertrials)

ROLE	ALL-CHANNEL		CIRCLE AND CIRCLE-AC, ORGANIZED		CIRCLE AND CIRCLE-AC, UNORGANIZED	
	MEAN	STANDARD DEVIATION	MEAN	STANDARD DEVIATION	MEAN	STANDARD DEVIATION
Keymen	5.1	4.6	8.1	6.3	5.0	4.3
Relayers	6.8	6.4	6.4	5.5	6.5	5.4
Endmen	3.3	3.5	5.8	4.7	5.2	5.1

Significant tests: In the All-Channel groups a t-test of Relayers *vs.* Endmen was significant ($t = 2.7$, $p < .01$), as was the t-test of (Keymen plus Relayers) *vs.* Endmen ($t = 2.6$, $p < .02$).
* Number of persons occupying each role is given in Table 1.

Table 5. Accuracy of Organizational Perception by Roles * (Correct minus Incorrect Role Identifications over Total Roles Present)

ROLE	ALL-CHANNEL		CIRCLE AND CIRCLE-AC, ORGANIZED		CIRCLE AND CIRCLE-AC, UNORGANIZED	
	MEAN	STANDARD DEVIATION	MEAN	STANDARD DEVIATION	MEAN	STANDARD DEVIATION
Keymen	.52	.35	.68	.46	.16	.42
Relayers	.50	.37	.58	.45	.18	.35
Endmen	.50	.39	.37	.47	.02	.29

Significance tests: t-tests of (Keymen plus Relayers) *vs.* Endmen were significant both in the Circle and Circle-AC, Organized groups ($t = 2.1$, $p < .05$), and in the Circle and Circle-AC, Unorganized groups ($t = 2.0$, $p < .05$).
* Number of persons occupying each role is given in Table 1.

Table 6. Intertrial Messages Concerned with Specific Organizational Proposals by Roles * (Number of Units Sent in 19 Intertrials)

ROLE	ALL-CHANNEL		CIRCLE AND CIRCLE-AC, ORGANIZED		CIRCLE AND CIRCLE-AC, UNORGANIZED	
	MEAN	STANDARD DEVIATION	MEAN	STANDARD DEVIATION	MEAN	STANDARD DEVIATION
Keymen	7.1	2.1	4.0	3.2	0.6	1.4
Relayers	2.9	3.4	1.7	2.4	0.5	0.9
Endmen	2.8	4.2	1.2	1.8	0.4	0.7

Significance tests:

	All-Channel	Circle and Circle-Ac, Organized
Keymen vs. Relayers	$t = 4.7, p < .001$	$t = 2.6, p < .02$
Keymen vs. (Relayers + Endmen)	$t = 3.2, p < .01$	$t = 3.6, p < .001$

* Number of persons occupying each role is given in Table 1.

Table 7. Intertrial Messages Concerned with Promulgation of Specific Proposals by Roles * (Number of Units Sent in 19 Intertrials)

ROLE	ALL-CHANNEL		CIRCLE AND CIRCLE-AC, ORGANIZED		CIRCLE AND CIRCLE-AC, UNORGANIZED	
	MEAN	STANDARD DEVIATION	MEAN	STANDARD DEVIATION	MEAN	STANDARD DEVIATION
Keymen	1.2	1.6	1.1	2.0	0.4	0.7
Relayers	1.8	2.3	1.2	1.8	0.3	0.6
Endmen	2.7	3.0	1.4	2.1	0.5	1.3

Significance tests: In the All-Channel groups a t-test of Keymen vs. Endmen was significant ($t = 2.2, p < .05$).
* Number of persons occupying each role is given in Table 1.

5 is that in the unorganized Circle-AC groups there was no significant difference between the keymen-relayers and the endmen in intertrial messages (Table 4), while there was in the accuracy measure obtained at the end of the experiment (Table 5). This finding confirms the time-honored proposition that effort does not always bring achievement. The new findings, thus, do not entirely contradict our earlier hypothesis that relative adequacy of perceiving the organizational situation is associated with occupancy of keyman and relayer roles.

Role differentiation on the Basis of Organizational Planning. Although there was no designation of roles by the experimenter, did the participants overtly plan roles for themselves and for others in the course of their intertrial communications? Members of the All-Channel, Circle, and Circle-AC groups respectively devoted 30%, 12%, and 14% of their intertrial messages to organizational planning activities. These planning message units were of three kinds—specific messages, either (a) proposals of oneself or another individual as keyman, or (*b*) promulgations of specific suggestions, and (*c*) more general, somewhat abstract proposals, such as "Why don't we all send our messages clockwise?" The average numbers of these three types of planning messages sent during the course of the 19 intertrials by persons within each role are presented respectively in Tables 6, 7, and 8.

In the specific messages incorporating organizational proposals (Table 6), the differences between the keymen and the other roles are dramatic. About half of these messages are particular plans, proposing oneself as keyman, and most of these proposals were disseminated by the endmen and the relayers (Table 7).

ganized groups. However, in Tables 5 through 8, there are impressive differences between the two types of groups, ranging from a ratio of 1 to 2 to a ratio of 1 to 6. Thus, the accuracy and planning measures are related not only to role formation, but as importantly to the interlocking of roles into group structures.

Summary. The role of keyman clearly is not determined by chance factors operating in the initial trial. Nor did the persons who became keymen bludgeon their way into occupancy of the role by withholding their own piece of information from the other members of their group. It seems that keymen and relayers es-

Table 8. Intertrial Messages Concerned with General Organizational Matters by Roles * *(Number of Units Sent in 19 Intertrials)*

ROLE	ALL-CHANNEL		CIRCLE AND CIRCLE-AC, ORGANIZED		CIRCLE AND CIRCLE-AC, UNORGANIZED	
	MEAN	STANDARD DEVIATION	MEAN	STANDARD DEVIATION	MEAN	STANDARD DEVIATION
Keymen	2.8	3.8	1.7	2.2	1.0	2.2
Relayers	2.1	2.2	1.3	1.4	0.5	1.2
Endmen	0.7	2.1	1.1	2.2	1.1	2.2

Significance tests: In the All-Channel group *t*-tests of the Endmen *vs.* Keymen ($t = 3.0$, $p < .01$) and *vs.* the Relayers ($t = 2.2$, $p < .05$) are both significant.

* Number of persons occupying each role is given in Table 1.

The more general planning messages (Table 8) indicate an ordering of the roles somewhat similar to those found in the intertrial messages concerned with perceiving the organizational situation (Table 4). As in the perceptual messages, the keymen were more given to generalized planning than the endmen.

So far, no use has been made of comparisons between the All-Channel and organized Circle and Circle-AC groups versus the unorganized Circle and Circle-AC groups, exhibited in Tables 4 through 8. These data, along with the role differences already discussed enable us to distinguish between factors which induce role formation versus those which relate to both role formation and the interlocking of roles into a social structure. The volume of intertrial messages displayed in Table 4 is approximately the same for both organized and unor-

tablish themselves by having more adequate perceptions of their organizational situations than do endmen—and that keymen, in turn, gain their special position of leadership in these experimental situations by self-designation of the key role to themselves, the designation being relayed by the other members of the group to each other.

Mechanisms Related to Personal Characteristics

Role Differentiation by Means of Intellectual Ability. Intellectual ability is often related to role occupancy, as documented in Stogdills' survey of the leadership literature (11). An American Council on Education Psychological Examination score was obtained on each subject.[2] The ACE is a general aptitude test of intellectual ability, both quantitative and verbal. These data allow us to check whether role occupancy is associated with intelligence in these experimental situations, as well as to determine indirectly whether intelligence played a part, *per se*, in the interlocking of the roles into organizational structures. In composing the groups, the experimenters matched subjects so that each group had one person coming from each of five ACE levels. Thus, no group could fail to organize because of low intellectual ability.

tional, four-year college norms.[3] In the Circle and Circle-AC groups which organized, the keymen and relayers are associated in intellectual level, being superior to the endmen at the 10% level ($t = 1.7$), not as sharply as the keymen are superior to the relayers and endmen in the All-Channel groups. Thus, role differentiation is associated with intellectual ability.

Can these contrasting results, in which relayers and endmen are similar in the All-Channel groups while keymen and relayers are associated in the organized Circle and Circle-AC groups, be related to our earlier findings

Table 9. Intellectual Ability by Roles * *(Raw Scores for Total ACE Test)*

ROLE	ALL-CHANNEL		CIRCLE AND CIRCLE-AC, ORGANIZED		CIRCLE AND CIRCLE-AC, UNORGANIZED	
	MEAN	STANDARD DEVIATION	MEAN	STANDARD DEVIATION	MEAN	STANDARD DEVIATION
Keymen	138.5	18.8	129.9	22.9	131.9	21.2
Relayers	122.1	16.9	132.5	20.3	125.1	18.8
Endmen	125.3	20.3	123.2	18.8	125.1	23.3

Significance tests: t-tests of Keymen *vs.* (Relayers plus Endmen) are significant both in the All-Channel groups ($t = 3.0, p < .01$) and in the Circle and Circle-AC, Unorganized groups ($t = 5.3, p < .001$).
* Number of persons occupying each role is given in Table 1.

Did the varying intellectual ability of the subjects induce differences in role occupancy among the five persons all of whom initially had equipotential locations within the social situation? The average raw ACE scores for persons in the three roles are presented in Table 9. In the All- Channel groups, there is a significant difference ($t = 2.0, p<.05$) between the ACE scores of the keymen and both the relayers and the endmen. These differences are not calculational artifacts; the raw scores place the "average" keyman (average $= 138.5$) at the 89th percentile, with the relayers and endmen (average $= 124.4$) at the 74th percentile on na-

with regard to accuracy of organizational perceptions and amount of planning activity? Both keymen and relayers in the Circle and Circle-AC groups who finally were successful in organizing themselves were shown to have been more adequate in their perceptions of the organization, as they differentiated their roles. Gaining such superior perception of the organizational structure was not difficult in the All-Channel groups, as there were no communication restrictions. Superior intelligence was not necessary in the All-Channel groups for perceptual accuracy.

Further, consider the strong association between ACE scores and success in designating one's self as keyman in the All-Channel

[2] Through the courtesy of Drs. Roland Moore and Robert Morgan of Carnegie Tech's Bureau of Measurement and Guidance, scores were provided for approximately 90% of our subjects; the remaining 10% were tested by the experimenters in a special session before they were assembled with the others into the groups.

[3] Percentiles based on Table 5, data for men in 94 four-year colleges, *Norms Bulletin American Council in Education Psychological Examination for College Freshmen*, 1949 Edition; Educational Testing Service, Princeton, N.J.

groups. This state of affairs is reflected also, in a diluted way, in the superior ability of the keymen in the unorganized Circle and Circle-AC groups. Thus, it would seem that superior intellectual ability is a prerequisite to the establishment of oneself in both keyman and relayer roles in the more restricted Circle and Circle-AC groups.

These interpretations would be less tenuous had the data revealed a clear relationship between intelligence and accuracy in perception of organizational structure and planning the specific role establishment. Then one might argue that intelligence expresses itself in superior organizing activity. But the product-moment correlations between ACE scores and the accuracy measure (r = .03) and the volume of specific planning (r = .06) are nearly zero. This would seem, then, to mean that although intelligence may be a necessary prerequisite for role differentiation, its presence does not insure the effective occupancy of roles and their intermeshing into a social system. This latter interpretation is further supported by the fact that although all groups were equated in intelligence, 66% of the Circle and Circle-AC groups failed to organize by interlocking their roles.

Role Differentiation Because of Personal Ascendance. If intellectual ability is a limiting rather than an enhancing factor, what personal characteristics might be responsible for inducing the heightened activity in organizational development? The important part self-designation played in role establishment for the keymen suggests that social ascendance might be a fruitful variable to explore. The Guilford-Zimmerman "A" scale was administered to participants in the second "run" before they developed their groups. When a table analogous to the one made for ACE scores is constructed for these self-rated questionnaires (Table 10), the keymen are seen to be clearly more ascendant than the relayers and endmen.

Note the relation between ACE scores for the organized Circle and Circle-AC groups and the importance of ascendance. It would seem that although superior intelligence is needed for both keymen and relayers, higher amounts of personal ascendance distinguish the keymen from the relayers. Personal ascen-

dance predicts the occurrence of self-nomination as keyman.

The fact that identical findings were obtained for both organized and unorganized Circle and Circle-AC groups indicates that ascendance was *not* associated with the interlocking of roles into organizational structures. This contrasts with the parts played by perceptual accuracy, planning, and intellectual ability—all three of which were integrally involved in the development of structure as well as in the distribution of occupants in differentiated roles.

Table 10. Personal Ascendance of Subjects by Roles * *(Raw Sums on G-Z A Scale)* †

ROLE	CIRCLE AND CIRCLE-AC, ORGANIZED		CIRCLE AND CIRCLE-AC, UNORGANIZED	
	MEAN	STANDARD DEVIATION	MEAN	STANDARD DEVIATION
Keymen	5.9 (n = 11)	2.1	6.0 (n = 13)	2.0
Relayers	4.2 (n = 20)	2.0	4.8 (n = 24)	1.5
Endmen	4.6 (n = 19)	1.2	4.9 (n = 23)	1.4

Significance tests: t-tests of Keymen *vs.* (Relayers plus Endmen) are significant both in the Organized (t = 2.4, p < .05) and in the Unorganized (t = 2.2, p < .05) Circle and Circle-AC groups.
* Number of persons occupying each role is given in parentheses under each mean.
† Ascendance scores are not available for either the All-Channel or Wheel groups, as the bulk of the All-Channel groups and all the Wheel groups were completed during the first experimental run; see footnote 3 in (5) for further details.

Summary. Only two variables were available for the analysis of the relation of personal characteristics to the development of roles. Intellectual ability seems to be a necessary, but not sufficient, factor. Ascendance, on the other hand, seems necessary for the distribution of persons among the differentiated roles but does not determine whether groups with differentiated roles will develop interlocked structures of their roles.

Discussion

Planning of the Organization vs. Interlocking Roles. In the previous macro-analysis of these data it was concluded (5, 186–187): "although some explicit understanding of the net and of the evolution of the organization is necessary, understanding *per se* is not sufficient to induce the development of continuing, differentiated organizations." An analogous state of affairs seems to prevail with respect to the existence of roles: although differentiation of roles is imperative for articulation, such differentiation is not sufficient in itself to induce an interlocking of the roles. Murray puts it vividly (9, 451), "It is not so much that a man is obliged (expected) to do certain things, but that he is obliged (in order to integrate his actions with others) to do them at a fixed time."

In the earlier report considerable support was adduced for the conclusion that communication restriction operates by reducing the planning (5, 194–195). The results of the present role analysis indicate that in this experimental situation planning is deficient, not in securing behavioral differentiation of the functional roles, but in its failure to plan the interlocking of the performed roles.

In the previous paper it was hypothesized (5, Table 4) that the sending of specific proposals for organizing the groups was a necessary condition for induction of organization. This analysis indicates that those specific proposals were related integrally to achievement of an interlocking of already differentiated roles. Thus, it is now less difficult to understand why only the specific planning messages rather than the more general ones were found in the macro-analysis to be crucial (5, Table 4). Participants cannot articulate roles by exchanging notes about general organizational plans. To interlock particular roles, it seems, one must get specific.

The discrepancy noted in Tables 4 and 5 dramatically supports an interpretation that the participants must have highly specific knowledge of each other's roles in planning.

The unorganized Circle and Circle-AC groups at the end of the experiment (Table 5) only minimally understood the roles which were being played—even though they devoted almost as many of their intertrial messages to such activity (Table 4). Those individuals who had a more accurate (averaging approximately 53%) knowledge of the roles were able to interlock their roles much more adequately than those without such detailed knowledge (averaging approximately 12%).

Examination of the accuracy averages presented in Table 5 suggests that the knowledge needed for interlocking the roles is relatively widespread throughout the group, as would necessarily be the case if the hypothesis that roles are systems of reciprocated interactions is valid. The equal need for knowledge about the other individuals' roles is vividly exhibited in the startling equality of role perceptions among all participants, regardless of their performed role, in the All-Channel groups. The modification that certain minimal amounts of such knowledge can make is indicated in the gradient of knowledge exhibited among persons in different functional roles. In Table 5, for the Circle and Circle-AC groups which organized, the endmen seem to be able to articulate themselves into the organization, even though they possess but half (37%) of the knowledge possessed by the keyman (68%). Note, however, that the 37% is twice that possessed by the persons (i.e., relayers) with the greatest amount of knowledge (18%) in the unorganized Circle and Circle-AC groups.

The ease with which various roles are perceived may be calculated from the accuracy scores used originally for Table 5 by re-averaging the accuracies with which particular roles are perceived *by* all the members of the group. These new calculations are presented in Table 11. The keymen are more easily visible in the All-Channel and in the organized Circle and Circle-AC groups than are the relayers or endmen.

The figures used to generate Table 11 also yield the accuracy with which one perceives one's own role as contrasted with the accuracy with which one perceives the roles being played by the others. The average overall accuracy with which each participant described his own role was 45%. This compares with an accuracy of 29% for these same partic-

Table 11. Accuracy with Which Particular Roles Are Perceived* *(Correct Minus Incorrect Role Identifications over Total Roles Present)*

PERCEIVED ROLE	ALL-CHANNEL		CIRCLE AND CIRCLE-AC, ORGANIZED		CIRCLE AND CIRCLE-AC, UNORGANIZED	
	MEAN	STANDARD DEVIATION	MEAN	STANDARD DEVIATION	MEAN	STANDARD DEVIATION
Keymen	.71	.31	.68	.28	.04	.29
Relayers	.48	.50	.43	.30	.07	.30
Endmen	.35	.44	.45	.31	.03	.39

Significance tests:

	All-Channel	Circle and Circle-Ac, Organized
Keymen *vs.* Relayers	$t = 2.7, p < .05$	$t = 3.0, p < .02$
Keymen *vs.* (Relayers + Endmen)	$t = 6.2, p < .001$	$t = 2.8, p < .02$

* The number of perceptions made of each role is the number of persons in each role, as given above (Table 1), multiplied by five (as each person in the group had opportunity to observe each role, including the instance when the role was his own).

ipants in perceiving the roles of others, a statistically significant difference ($t = 3.9$, $p<.001$). Thus, not only do roles have varying visibility, but in this experimental situation persons see their own roles with more accuracy than they perceive the roles of others.

That self-perceptions are the result of interactions has been posited by Cooley, James, and Mead (10, 316–318). By noting the different accuracies of participants in the three communication situations, we have empirical evidence to support this long held proposition. In the All-Channel groups, the participants had no communication restrictions imposed by the net within which they operated; in this situation the group members perceived their own roles with an accuracy of 59%. In the organized Circle and Circle-AC groups, despite the net imposed restriction, the members had worked out relatively stable communication patterns at the end of the experiment; their accuracy of self-perception was 51%. In the unorganized Circle and Circle-AC groups, however, where adequate communications were never developed, the accuracy of self-perceptions was but 29%. The difference between the organized and unorganized Circle and Circle-AC groups is statistically significant ($t = 2.0$, $p<.05$).

These findings about role self-perception are analogous to those obtained for group opinion by Travers (12), who presents evidence that group members estimate group opinion more accurately with more interaction.

Position consensus vs. Organization Integration. This experiment generated evidence on the relation of perception to behavior in a way impossible when one is restricted to an interview or questionnaire. For example, members of the Survey Research Center at The University of Michigan have studied whether "the degree of integration existing within an organization at any time stems in part from the degree of consensus or sharing of expectations about the behavior of people who occupy various positions" (7, 20). But, using a verbal survey methodology, they necessarily limited their definition of "integration" to personal judgments by role-occupiers of such variables as felt conflict, feelings of "easy relations," and satisfaction with participation. In this study it was possible to relate consensus to two objective measures of "integration," namely organizational complexity and organizational efficiency.

The test of the relation of consensus to organizational complexity is contained in Table 5. We may use our accuracy measure (Table 5) as an index of the extent to which role expectations were shared, for at least to the extent the participants agreed with the experimenter, to that extent they share their expectations about the roles. If we measure organizational complexity by the extent to which the Circle and Circle-AC groups were organized, we find that the "integrated" groups (i.e., the "organized" groups) have some four times as much consensus ("accuracy") as did the less "integrated" groups (i.e., the "unorganized" groups).

By correlating the efficiency with which each of 68 groups performed its task (average time on three fastest trials) with the overall accuracy of the members of the groups in perceiving their roles, it is established ($r = -.73$) that consensus relates to integration, when one measures integration through an objective performance index, too.

It is assuring to find that both methodologies lead to the same conclusion, namely, that greater consensus about position is associated with greater degrees of organization integration, defined subjectively or objectively.

As this discussion intimates, the term "integration" is ambiguous. The three subjective meanings ("felt conflict," "easy relations," and "participation satisfaction") and the two objective meanings ("organizational complexity" and "performance efficiency") suggest that much further work will be needed to delineate useful definitions of integration, so that the scope of the proposition relating consensus to integration may be specified more adequately.

Conclusions

This experimental study of the differentiation of roles in task-oriented groups allowed the separation of processes involved in role formation from those involved in interlocking roles into organizational structures. In both phases, the establishment of role systems was related to external and internal factors operating on the group. Within the internal processes, it was possible to distinguish further those factors which operated to allow role formation as well as those which induced interlocking roles into organizational structures.

The study tapped only a few of the totality

of the mechanisms involved. The findings may, however, be summarized as hypotheses about the processes which were uncovered:

1. In task-oriented groups which begin their existence with no *a priori* roles, the development of performed roles does not necessarily provide the group with the ability to interlock these roles into organizational structures.

2. The possibility of an interlocked role system is increased:

   a. when the activities comprising the tasks can be assembled into functional positions,

   b. when the perception of the role differentiation processes by the members is more explicit,

   c. when there is planning of a more specific nature,

   d. and when greater intellectual ability is available in the group.

3. The establishment of individuals in leadership-followership roles is related to the same intra-group factors as those related to the establishment of the organizational structure (2b, 2c, and 2d), with the addition that persons characterized by personal ascendance tend to occupy leadership roles.

REFERENCES

1. ADI Auxiliary Publication Project, Photo-duplication Service, Library of Congress, Washington 25, D.C., Document No. 4590.

2. Bavelas, A. Communication patterns in task-oriented groups *Journal of Acoustical Society of America*, 1950, **22**, 725–730.

3. Dill, W. R., & McKee, R. L. An experiment to compare the effects of competitive and of cooperative motivations on group behavior. May, 1953. (Typewritten manuscript.)

4. Guetzkow, H., & Bowes, Anne E. The development of organizations in a laboratory. *Management Science*, 1957, 3, 380–402.

5. Guetzkow, H., & Dill, W. R. Factors in the organizational development of task-oriented groups. *Sociometry*, 1957, **20**, 175–204.

6. Guetzkow, H., & Simon, H. A. The impact of certain communication nets upon organization and performance in task-oriented groups. *Management Science*, 1955, **1**, 233–250.

7. Jacobson, E., Charters, W. W., Jr., & Lieberman, S. The use of the role concept in the study of complex organizations. *Journal of Social Issues*, 1951, **7**, 18–27.

8. Leavitt, H. J. Some effects of certain com-

munication patterns on group performance. *Journal of Abnormal and Social Psychology,* 1951, **46**, 38–50.

9. Murray, H. Toward a classification of inter-actions. In T. Parson & E. A. Shils (Eds.), *Toward a general theory of action.* Cambridge: Harvard Univ. Press, 1951, pp. 434–464.

10. Newcomb, T. M. *Social psychology.* New York: Dryden, 1950.

11. Stogdill, R. M. Personal factors associated with leadership: Survey of the literature. *Journal of Psychology,* 1948, **25**, 35–71.

12. Travers, R. A study in judging the opinions of groups. *Archives of psychology.* New York, 1941, No. 266.

The Experimental Change of a Major Organizational Variable[1]

NANCY C. MORSE

AND

EVERETT REIMER

This experiment is one in a series of studies of social behavior in large-scale organizations undertaken by the Human Relations Program of the Survey Research Center. Its primary aim is to investigate the relationship between the allocation of decision-making processes in a large hierarchial organization and (a) the individual satisfactions of the members of the organization, (b) the productivity of the organization.

Reprinted by permission of the American Psychological Association and the authors. From *Journal of Abnormal and Social Psychology*, **52** (1956), pp. 120–129.

[1] This is a short description of an experiment done while the authors were on the staff of the Human Relations Program of the Survey Research Center, University of Michigan. Financial support for field work and analysis of the data came from the Rockefeller Foundation, the Office of Naval Research Contract No. N6 onr-232 Task Order II, and the company in which the research was done. In addition to the authors the field staff of the experiment included: Arnold Tannenbaum, Frances Fieder, Gilbert David, Arlene Kohn Gilbert, Barbara Snell Dohrenwend, Ann Seidman, Jean Kraus Davison, and Winifred Libbon. The analysis staff included: Nancy Morse, Arnold Tannenbaum, Arlene Kohn Gilbert, and Ruth Griggs. The experiment will be described fully in a book now in preparation. Floyd H. Allport provided extensive assistance on the theoretical problems of the study. The experiment was under the general direction of Daniel Katz, director of the Human Relations Program during the field phase of the experiment, and Robert Kahn, director of the Human Relations Program during the analysis phase. The authors wish to express their appreciation to the staff members on the experiment and to the people in the company who cooperated in the experiment. They also want to thank particularly Daniel Katz, Robert Kahn, Arnold Tannenbaum, Carol Kaye, and Jane Williams for their helpful comments and criticisms of this article.

The results of several previous studies suggested that the individual's role in decision-making might affect his satisfaction and productivity. The effectiveness of decision-making in small groups shown by Lewin, Lippitt and others (4, 5) and the successful application of small-group decision-making to method changes in an industrial setting by Coch and French (1) both indicated the possibilities for enlarging the role of the rank and file in the ongoing decision-making of an organization. The practical experience of Sears, Roebuck and Co. with a "flat," administratively decentralized structure, described by Worthy (8), pointed in the same direction, as did the survey findings by Katz, Maccoby, and Morse (2) that supervisors delegating greater authority had more productive work groups. The logical next step seemed to be the controlled testing of hypotheses concerning the relationship between role in organizational decision-making and two aspects of organizational effectiveness: satisfaction and productivity. Two broad hypotheses were formulated:

Hypothesis I. An increased role in the decision-making processes for rank-and-file groups increases their satisfaction (while a decreased role in decision-making reduces satisfaction).

Hypothesis II. An increased role in decision-making for rank-and-file groups increases their productivity (while a decreased role in decision-making decreases productivity).

Both these hypotheses deal with the effects on the rank and file of different hierarchical allocations of the decision-making processes of the organization. The rationale for the satisfaction hypothesis (I) predicts different and more need-satisfying decisions when the rank and file has decision-making power than when the upper echelons of the hierarchy have that

475

power. Furthermore, the process of decision-making itself is expected to be satisfying to the majority of people brought up in American traditions. Underlying the productivity hypothesis (II) was the consideration that local unit policy-making would increase motivation to produce and thus productivity. Motivation should rise when productivity becomes a path for greater need satisfaction. The productivity hypothesis predicts a higher degree of need satisfaction (as does Hypothesis I) *and* an increase in the degree of dependence of satisfactions upon productivity under conditions of greater rank-and-file decision-making. It is expected that when rank-and-file members work out and put into effect their own rules and regulations, their maintenance in the organization (and thus their satisfactions) will depend much more directly upon their performance.

Procedure

The experiment was conducted in one department of a nonunionized industrial organization which had four parallel divisions engaged in relatively routine clerical work. The design involved increasing rank-and-file decision-making in two of the divisions and increasing upper-level decision-making in the other two divisions. The time span was one and one-half years: a before measurement, one-half year of training of supervisors to create the experimental conditions, one year under the experimental conditions, and then remeasurement. The two pairs of two divisions each were comparable on relevant variables such as initial allocation of the decision-making processes, satisfaction and productivity, as well as on such background factors as type of work, type of personnel, and type of supervisory structure.

The rank-and-file employees were women, mostly young and unmarried, with high-school education. The usual clerk's plans were for marriage and a family rather than a career. The population used in the analysis except where noted is a subgroup of the clerks, the "matched" population. These clerks were present throughout the one and one-half year period, and their before and after questionnaires were individually matched. While they comprise somewhat less than half of the clerks present in these divisions at any one time, they

are comparable to the total group, except on such expected variables as length of time in the division, in the work section, and on the job.

One aspect of the work situation should be mentioned, as it bears on the adequacy of the setting for a test of the productivity hypothesis. The amount of work done by the divisions was completely dependent upon the flow of work to them, i.e., the total number of units to be done was not within the control of the divisions. With volume fixed, productivity depends upon the number of clerks needed to do the work, and increased productivity can be achieved only by out-placement of clerks or by foregoing replacement of clerks who leave for other reasons.

The Development of the Experimental Conditions. Creating the experimental programs included three steps: (*a*) planning by research staff and company officials; (*b*) introducing the programs to the division supervisory personnel and training of the supervisors for their new roles; and (*c*) introduction to the clerks and operation under the experimental conditions.

The experiment was carried out within the larger framework of company operations. The introduction, training, and operations were in the hands of company personnel. The experimental changes were not made through personnel shifts; the changes were in what people did in their jobs with respect to the decision-making processes of the organization.

Two main change processes were used in both the Autonomy program, designed to increase rank-and-file decision-making, and in the Hierarchically-controlled program, designed to increase the upper management role in the decision-making processes. First, there were formal structural changes to create a new organizational environment for the divisions in each program. In both programs the hierarchical legitimization of new roles preceded the taking of the new roles.[2] In the Autonomy program authority was delegated by upper

[2] Weber and others have used the word "legitimization" to refer to the acceptance by subordinates of the authority of superiors. We are using the word in quite a different sense. By hierarchical legitimization we mean the formal delegation of authority by superiors to subordinates. This delegation *legitimizes* the subordinates' utilization of this authority.

management to lower levels in the hierarchy with the understanding that they would re-delegate it to the clerical work groups. In the Hierarchically-controlled program, authority was given to the higher line officials to increase their role in the running of the divisions and to the staff officials to increase their power to institute changes within the two divisions in that program. Second, there were training programs for the supervisors of the divisions to ensure that the formal changes would result in actual changes in relations between people. (For a longer description of the change programs see Reimer [6].)

Measurement. The results of the changes were gauged through before and after measurements and through continuing measurements during the experimental period. The major emphasis was on the attitudes and perceptions of the clerks as reflected in extensive questionnaires. In addition, the training programs and the operations phase of the experiment were observed. Before and after interviews were conducted with the supervisory personnel of the division. Data from company records such as productivity rates, turnover figures, etc., were also included.

The data reported here will be confined to material most pertinent to the testing of the two hypotheses. For other related aspects of the experiment, see Tannenbaum's study of the relationship of personality characteristics and adjustment to the two programs (7), Kaye's study of organizational goal achievement under the Autonomy program (3), as well as forthcoming publications.

Results [3]

Success of Experimental Manipulation. The first question was to discover whether or not the change programs were successful in creating the conditions under which the hypotheses could be tested. Two types of data are pertinent. The first is descriptive data concerning

[3] For the statistical tests used in this section, we have assumed that the individuals were randomly chosen, while the selection of individuals by divisions undoubtedly results in some clustering effect. The levels of significance should, therefore, be considered as general guides rather than in any absolute sense.

the actual operations of the two programs. The second is perceptual data from the clerical employees themselves indicating the degree to which they saw changes in their role in organizational decisions.

The operations of the divisions in fact changed in the direction expected. In the Autonomy program the clerical work groups came to make group decisions about many of the things which affected them and which were important to them. The range of the decisions was very great, including work methods and processes, and personnel matters, such as recess periods, the handling of tardiness, etc. Probably the most important area in which the clerks were not able to make decisions was the area of salary. Some of the work groups were more active in the decision-making process than others, but all made a very great variety of decisions in areas important to them. In the Hierarchically-controlled program the changes decreased the degree to which the employees could control and regulate their own activities. One of the main ways in which this greater limitation was manifested was through the individual work standards that staff officials developed for the various jobs. Also the greater role of upper line and staff officials in the operation of the divisions meant that the indirect influence which the clerks could have on decisions when they were made by division managers and section supervisors was reduced.

The clerks were operating under different conditions in the two programs as the result of the experimental changes, but did they perceive these changes? The method of measuring the perception of changes in decision-making was by asking clerks about their part and about the part of people above their rank in decisions with respect to a wide variety of areas of company operations, or company systems. The following questions were asked about each major area of company operations or system: "To what degree do company officers or any employees of a higher rank than yours decide how the ———— System is set up and decide the policies, rules, procedures or methods of the ———— System?" (followed by a line with the landmark statements: not at all, to a slight degree, to some degree, to a fairly high degree and to a very high degree) and, "To what degree do you and the girls in your section decide how the ———— System is set up and decide the policies, rules, procedures or methods of the ——— System?" (followed by line with the same landmark statements as the first question).

The extreme degree of perceived hierarchical control of the decision-making processes would be shown by the clerks answering that employees of a higher rank than theirs made the decisions, "to a very high degree" and the clerks made them "not at all." Table 1 shows the number of systems where there are half or more of the clerks endorsing these two statements for the before situation and for the two experimental situations. (The Autonomy program is designated in Table 1 and thereafter as Program I and the Hierarchically-controlled program as Program II.) Questions were asked for 27 company systems in the before measurement and 24 systems in the after measurement.

to the rank and file as perceived by the clerks was measured by assigning scores from 1 to 9 for the landmark positions on the scales for the two questions and then dividing the score for upper-level decision-making by the score for rank-and-file decision-making. The theoretical range for the resulting index is from 9.0 to 0, with numbers less than 1 indicating greater local control than upper-level control. Table 2 includes the average index scores for the systems from the before and after measurements calculated by division.

Table 2 indicates the change in the divisions in the Autonomy program toward greater perceived rank-and-file role in decision making, but also shows that the upper levels are seen as still having the major role in the after situation. (The downward shift in perceived decision-making control in the Autonomy pro-

Table 1. *Number of Company Systems in Which Clerks Perceive Very High Upper Level Control of Decision-Making Allocation*

	NUMBER OF SYSTEMS IN WHICH HALF OR MORE CLERKS GAVE SPECIFIED RESPONSE		
	BEFORE	AFTER	
	ALL	PROGRAM I	PROGRAM II
RESPONSE	DIVS.	DIVS.	DIVS.
Upper levels decided policies to a very high degree	20	7	24
Clerks did not decide policies at all	25	9	23
Total number of systems measured	27	24	24

Table 1 shows that the clerks perceived the decision-making processes for most of the company operations measured as located at hierarchial levels above their own, prior to the introduction of the experimental changes. The experimental changes in the Autonomy program divisions resulted in their seeing decision-making activities as much less exclusively confined to levels above theirs. The changes in the Hierarchically-controlled program were less striking but they resulted in the clerks judging that all of the systems about which they were asked in the after situation had their policies molded to a very high degree by people above their level.

The relative role of the hierarchy compared

gram is significant above the 1 per cent level by the Student's t test for paired data. A statistically significant, but slight, change toward greater upper-level control took place in the Hierarchically-controlled program.)

Both Tables 1 and 2 show that the clerks in the Autonomy program perceive as predicted a significant shift away from upper-level control when their before-after answers are compared, and that the clerks in the Hierarchically-controlled program see some increase in upper-level control over policy-making, even though it was already perceived as highly controlled from above before the experiment.

These measures of successful experimental manipulation suggest that the conditions in the

Table 2. Effect of Change Programs on Perception of Decision-Making Allocation

EXPERIMENTAL GROUPS	INDEX OF PERCEIVED DECISION-MAKING ALLOCATION				
	BEFORE MEAN	AFTER MEAN	DIFF.	SE DIFF.	N
Program I					
Div. A	5.69	4.39	− 1.30 *	.24	61
Div. B	6.49	4.08	− 2.41 *	.26	57
Average	6.08	4.24	− 1.84 *	.18	118
Program II					
Div. C	6.15	6.87	+ .72 *	.22	44
Div. D	6.78	7.13	+ .35	.26	44
Average	6.41	7.00	+ .59 *	.17	88

Note. Higher values correspond to perception of predominance of upper levels of organization in decision-making.
* Significant at the 1% level.

two programs are sufficiently different to permit tests of the experimental hypotheses.

Hypothesis I

This hypothesis states that an increase in the decision-making role of individuals results in increased satisfactions, while a decrease in opportunity for decision-making is followed by decreased satisfaction. The general hypothesis was tested for a variety of specific areas of satisfaction. The attitudinal areas to be reported include: (a) self-actualization and growth, (b) satisfaction with supervisors, (c) liking for working for the company, (d) job satisfaction, (e) liking for program. Student's one-tailed t test for paired data was used for tests of significance. Results reaching the 5 per cent level or above are considered significant.

Self-Actualization. One of the hypotheses of the study was that greater opportunity for regulating and controlling their own activities within the company structure would increase the degree to which individuals could express their various and diverse needs and could move in the direction of fully exploiting their potentialities. An increase in upper-management control on the other hand was predicted to decrease the opportunities for employee self-actualization and growth.

Five questions were used to measure this area: 1, Is your job a real challenge to what you think you can do? 2, How much chance does your job give you to learn things you're interested in? 3, Are the things you're learning in your job helping to train you for a better job in the company? 4, How much chance do you have to try out your ideas on the job? 5, How much does your job give you a chance to do the things you're best at? These five items, which were answered by checking one position on a five-point scale, were intercorrelated and then combined to form an index.[4] Table 3 shows the means for the four divisions and two groups on the self-actualization and growth index.

While both groups of clerks indicated that their jobs throughout the course of the experiment did not give them a very high degree of self-actualization, the experimental programs produced significant changes. In the Autonomy program, self-actualization increased significantly from before to after, and a corresponding decrease was shown in the Hierarchically-controlled program. At the end of the experimental period, the Autonomy program is significantly higher on this variable than the Hierarchically-controlled program.

[4] The items were intercorrelated by the tetrachoric method. When these correlations were converted to z scores the average intercorrelation was .62, corrected for length of test, a reliability index of .89 was obtained.

Table 3. *Effect of Change Programs on Feelings of Self-Actualization on Job*

EXPERIMENTAL GROUPS	INDEX OF PERCEIVED SELF-ACTUALIZATION				
	BEFORE MEAN	AFTER MEAN	DIFF.	SE DIFF.	N
Program I					
Div. A	2.67	2.74	+.07	.09	52
Div. B	2.18	2.39	+.21 *	.11	47
Average	2.43	2.57	+.14 *	.07	99
Program II					
Div. C	2.43	2.24	−.19	.14	43
Div. D	2.30	2.23	−.07	.10	38
Average	2.37	2.24	−.13 *	.07	81

Note. Scale runs from 1, low degree of self-actualization to 5, a high degree.
* Significant at the 5% level, one-tailed t test for paired data.

Satisfaction with Supervision. A variety of indices were developed in order to test the hypothesis that the Autonomy program would improve satisfactions with supervisors and that the Hierarchically-controlled program would reduce such satisfactions. Two general types of attitudes were separately measured: (*a*) satisfaction with relations with supervisors and (*b*) satisfaction with supervisors as a representative. These two types of attitudes were studied before and after the experimental period with respect to three levels of supervision: the first-line supervisor, the assistant manager of the division, and the manager of the division. The following three questions were asked for each of these levels in order to tap the clerks' degree of satisfaction with relations with supervisors:

1. How good is your supervisor (assistant manager, manager) at handling people?
2. Can you count on having good relations with your supervisor (assistant manager, manager) under all circumstances?
3. In general, how well do you like your supervisor (assistant manager, manager) as a person to work with?

These three questions were combined to form indices of satisfaction with relations with supervisors, assistant manager, and manager. (The items were intercorrelated for the satisfaction with relations with supervisor index.

Through converting to z scores, the average inter-correlation of items is found to be .78. Correcting for length of test, i.e., using three items to form the index rather than one, the reliability index is .91 with an N of 360.)

Table 4 shows that in general there was a shift toward greater satisfaction with supervisors in the Autonomy program and toward less satisfaction with supervisors in the Hierarchically-controlled program. The divisions, however, show certain characteristic differences in satisfaction at the outset and shift in the expected direction to different degrees.

Both divisions in the Hierarchically-controlled program show a decrease in satisfaction with the first-line supervisor, although the changes are not statistically significant. The after differences between the Autonomy and the Hierarchically-controlled programs are, however, significant.

Satisfaction with relations with both the assistant manager and the manager increased significantly in the Autonomy program and decreased significantly in the Hierarchically-controlled program. Each of the divisions within the groups likewise shifted in the hypothesized directions for the two managerial indices. In the Autonomy program the assistant manager index shifted in the right direction for both divisions, but the changes were not statistically significant when each division was tested separately.

Table 4. *Effect of Change Programs on Satisfaction with Relations with Three Levels of Supervision*

EXPERIMENTAL GROUPS	INDEX OF SATISFACTION				
	MEAN BEFORE	MEAN AFTER	DIFF.	SE DIFF.	N
RELATIONS WITH SUPERVISOR					
Program I					
Div. A	4.18	4.15	−.03	.09	62
Div. B	3.19	3.50	+.31 *	.14	54
Average	3.71	3.80	+.09	.08	116
Program II					
Div. C	3.80	3.67	−.13	.11	46
Div. D	3.43	3.29	−.14	.16	45
Average	3.64	3.48	−.16	.10	91
RELATIONS WITH ASSISTANT MANAGER					
Program I					
Div. A	3.49	3.61	+.12	.12	59
Div. B	3.97	4.11	+.14	.11	53
Average	3.71	3.86	+.15 *	.08	112
Program II					
Div. C	3.80	3.34	−.46 **	.12	43
Div. D	3.57	3.22	−.35 **	.11	43
Average	3.64	3.28	−.36 **	.08	86
RELATIONS WITH MANAGER					
Program I					
Div. A	3.84	4.11	+.27 **	.08	62
Div. B	4.04	4.20	+.16 *	.09	52
Average	3.93	4.15	+.22 **	.06	114
Program II					
Div. C	3.23	2.59	−.64 **	.15	43
Div. D	3.87	3.37	−.50 **	.13	40
Average	3.50	3.01	−.49 **	.10	83

Note. Degree of Satisfaction with Relations with Supervision: five point scale ranging from 1, low degree of satisfaction to 5, high degree of satisfaction.
* Significant at the 5% level one-tailed *t* test for paired data.
** Significant at the 1% level.

Thus while the employees were generally quite satisfied with their relations with their different supervisors, the experimental programs did have the expected effects of increasing the satisfactions of those in the Autonomy program and decreasing the satisfaction of those in the Hierarchically-controlled program. The effects of the programs appear to be most evident in attitudes toward the managerial level and least marked in attitudes toward the first-line supervisors, probably because the managers occupy the key or pivotal positions in the structure (see Kaye, [3]).

The second type of attitude toward supervisors measured was satisfaction with the supervisors as representatives of the employees.

Table 5. The Effect of Change Programs on Satisfaction with Three Levels of Supervision as Representatives of Employees

EXPERIMENTAL GROUPS	INDEX OF SATISFACTION				
	MEAN BEFORE	MEAN AFTER	DIFF.	SE DIFF.	N
SUPERVISOR AS REPRESENTATIVE OF EMPLOYEES					
Program I					
Div. A	3.98	4.06	+.08	.12	59
Div. B	2.91	3.43	+.52 **	.14	49
Average	3.48	3.74	+.26 **	.09	108
Program II					
Div. C	3.73	3.67	−.06	.13	45
Div. D	3.52	3.16	−.36 *	.18	41
Average	3.59	3.43	−.16	.11	86
ASSISTANT MANAGER AS REPRESENTATIVE OF EMPLOYEES					
Program I					
Div. A	3.32	3.75	+.43 **	.14	51
Div. B	3.54	3.76	+.22 *	.13	53
Average	3.43	3.75	+.32 **	.09	104
Program II					
Div. C	3.07	2.81	−.26 *	.12	41
Div. D	3.23	2.92	−.31 *	.13	42
Average	3.15	2.86	−.29 **	.10	83
MANAGER AS REPRESENTATIVE OF EMPLOYEES					
Program I					
Div. A	3.82	4.37	+.55 **	.11	57
Div. B	3.76	3.96	+.20 *	.10	53
Average	3.79	4.17	+.38 **	.07	110
Program II					
Div. C	2.70	2.19	−.51 **	.13	41
Div. D	3.14	2.92	−.22	.16	30
Average	2.92	2.52	−.40 **	.10	71

Note. Five-point scale ranging from 1, low degree of satisfaction to 5, high degree of satisfaction.
* Significant at the 5% level one-tailed t test for paired data.
** Significant at the 1% level.

Three questions were asked employees as a measure of this type of satisfaction:

1. How much does your supervisor (assistant manager, manager) go out of her (his) way to help get things for the girls in the section?
2. How effective is she (he) in helping you and the other girls get what you want in your jobs?

3. How much does your supervisor (assistant manager, manager) try to help people in your section get ahead in the company?

These three items were intercorrelated for the attitudes toward the supervisor as a representative index and the average intercorrelation was .83 with a corrected reliability of .94 (N of 340).

The findings for the three levels of supervision on the satisfaction with supervisors as representatives index are shown in Table 5.

The employees' attitudes toward their supervisors as effective representatives of their interests show significant changes in the predicted directions in the two programs. Those in the Autonomy program became more satisfied than they had been previously, while those in the Hierarchically-controlled program became less satisfied. On satisfaction with the first-line supervisor as a representative both Division B in the Autonomy program and Division D in the Hierarchically-controlled program shifted significantly in the hypothesized directions, although the other two divisions

do you like working for ——— (the name of the company)?"

The answers for this question presented in Table 6 indicate an increase in favorableness toward the company under the Autonomy program and a decrease under the Hierarchically-controlled program.

All of the changes are significant in the predicted direction, except for the before-after difference in Division B which is only at the 10 per cent level of significance.

Job Satisfaction. Three questions were used as an index of job satisfaction:

1. Does your job ever get monotonous?

Table 6. The Effect of Change Programs on Satisfaction with the Company

EXPERIMENTAL GROUPS	INDEX OF SATISFACTION WITH COMPANY				
	BEFORE MEAN	AFTER MEAN	DIFF.	SE DIFF.	N
Program I					
Div. A	4.16	4.32	+.16 *	.09	62
Div. B	3.83	4.02	+.19	.13	53
Average	4.01	4.18	+.17 *	.08	115
Program II					
Div. C	4.04	3.80	−.24 *	.14	46
Div. D	4.26	3.95	−.31 **	.12	43
Average	4.15	3.88	−.27 **	.09	89

Note. Five-point scale, ranging from 1, low degree of satisfaction to 5, high degree of satisfaction.
* Significant at the 5% level one-tailed t test for paired data.
** Significant at the 1% level.

did not shift significantly. The two program groups were not matched on degree of satisfaction with manager and assistant manager as a representative at the beginning of the experiment, as there was significantly more satisfaction in the Autonomy program divisions than there was in Program II. However, the changes for both groups of divisions were statistically significant and in the predicted direction. For attitude toward manager all of the division differences are in the predicted direction and all except Division D are statistically significant.

Satisfaction with the Company. One general question was used to measure company satisfaction: "Taking things as a whole, how

2. How important do you feel your job is compared with other jobs at (the company)?
3. In general, how well do you like the sort of work you're doing in your job?

These three questions showed an average intercorrelation of .47 with a corrected reliability of .73 (N of 369). The results on this index are reported in Table 7.

While the trend for the changes in job satisfaction are in the direction predicted, the differences are not sufficiently great to be statistically significant except for Division C. The lack of change in job satisfaction in the Autonomy program may be due to the fact that job content remained about the same. It is also possible that the increases in complexity and variety of their total work were offset by a rise in their level of aspiration, so that they expected more interesting and varied work.

Satisfaction with the Program. In the after measurement additional questions were asked concerning attitudes toward the programs. Most of these questions were open-ended and required the employee to write her response in her own words. Although less than half of the clerks taking the after measurement filled them out, the results on questions relevant to the satisfaction hypothesis deserve brief mention. The clerks in the Autonomy program typically: wanted their program to last indefinitely, did not like the other program, felt that

appear to be verified. Increasing local decision-making increased satisfaction, while decreasing the role of rank-and-file members of the organization in the decision-making decreased it.

Hypothesis II

This hypothesis predicts a direct relationship between degree of rank-and-file decision-making and productivity. Thus, in order for the hypothesis to be verified, productivity should increase significantly in the Autonomy program, and should decrease significantly in the Hierarchically-controlled program.

Table 7. The Effect of Change Programs on Job Satisfaction

EXPERIMENTAL GROUPS	INDEX OF JOB SATISFACTION				
	BEFORE MEAN	AFTER MEAN	DIFF.	SE DIFF.	N
Program I					
Div. A	3.29	3.29	0	.08	58
Div. B	3.03	3.09	+.06	.09	55
Average	3.16	3.19	+.03	.06	113
Program II					
Div. C	3.14	2.94	−.20 *	.10	42
Div. D	3.12	3.07	−.05	.12	46
Average	3.13	3.00	−.13 *	.07	88

Note. A five-point scale ranging from 1, low degree of satisfaction to 5, a high degree of satisfaction.
* Significant at the 5% level one-tailed *t* test for paired data.

the clerks were one of the groups gaining the most from the program and described both positive and negative changes in interpersonal relations among the girls. The clerks in the Hierarchically-controlled program, on the other hand, most frequently: wanted their program to end immediately, liked the other program and felt that the company gained the most from their program. Not one single person in the Hierarchically-controlled program mentioned an improvement in interpersonal relations as a result of this program. All of the noted changes were for the worse, with increases in friction and tension being most frequently mentioned.

Taking all of these results on the attitudinal questions together, the first hypothesis would

We have previously described the problems of assuming a direct relationship between motivation to produce and productivity in a situation in which volume is not controllable by employees and level of productivity depends upon the number of people doing a fixed amount of work. The Autonomy program was handicapped by both the fact that increasing productivity required reducing the size of their own work group and the fact that upper management staff and line costs were not included in the measure of costs per volume of work.

The measure of productivity, then, is a measure of clerical costs. These clerical costs are expressed in percentage figures, calculated by dividing the actual clerical costs by a constant standard of cost expected for that volume. Since this way of estimating productivity makes the higher figures indicate lower productivity, we have reversed the signs for purposes of presentation. The results for this measure are shown in Table 8.

The clerical costs have gone down in each division and thus productivity has increased. All these increases in productivity are statistically significant (by t tests). In addition, the productivity increase in the Hierarchically-controlled program is significantly greater than that in the Autonomy program. These increases in productivity do not seem to be accounted for by a general rise in productivity

than would at first appear evident. In this company turnover, however, is not high and much of the turnover that does occur is due to personal reasons (marriage, pregnancy, etc.) rather than on-the-job reasons. Out of the 54 employees who left the company from the four divisions during the time of the experiment, only nine resigned for other jobs or because of dissatisfaction. Out of these nine, however, all but one were in the Hierarchically-controlled program. In the exit interviews conducted by the company personnel department 23 of the girls leaving made unfavorable comments about pressure, work standards, etc. Nineteen of these girls were

Table 8. Comparison of the Four Divisions on Clerical Productivity for Year Control Period and Year Experimental Period

	INDEX OF PRODUCTIVITY				
EXPERIMENTAL GROUPS	MEAN CONTROL PERIOD	MEAN EXPERIMENTAL PERIOD	DIFF. %	SE DIFF.	N
Program I					
Div. A	46.3%	55.2%	+ 8.9 *	1.3%	12
Div. B	51.0	62.0	+11.0 *	1.3	12
Average	48.6	58.6	+10.0 *	1.2	24
Program II					
Div. C	50.2	63.2	+13.0 *	1.2	12
Div. D	46.8	62.0	+15.2 *	1.1	12
Average	48.5	62.6	+14.1 *	.9	24

Note. Higher values correspond to greater productivity.

* Significance at the 1% level.

throughout the company, since the divisions outside the experimental groups which were most comparable to them showed no significant gain in productivity during this period. The rise in productivity appears to be the result of the experimental treatments. The two divisions initially low in productivity showed the greatest differential change. Division D increased its productivity the most of the four while Division A increased the least.

A second measure of the organizational costs of the two programs is the degree of turnover which could be attributed to on-the-job factors. A method of control and regulation which reduces clerical costs, but which produces the hidden costs of training new employees is of greater cost to the organization

from the Hierarchically-controlled program.

These results indicate that the productivity hypothesis is clearly not verified in terms of direct clerical costs, since the Hierarchically-controlled program decreased these costs more than the Autonomy program, contrary to the prediction. The indirect costs for the Hierarchically-controlled program are probably somewhat greater. But even when this is considered the evidence does not support the hypothesis.

Discussion

The results on productivity might suggest a "Hawthorne effect" if it were not for the satisfaction findings. The increase in satisfaction under the Autonomy program and the decrease under the Hierarchically-controlled program make an explanation of productivity changes in terms of a common attention effect unlikely.[5]

The Hierarchically-controlled program reduced staff costs by ordering reductions in the number of employees assigned to the tasks. Increases in productivity for Divisions C and D were brought about as simply as that. This temporary increase in one measure of productivity is not surprising and is traditional history in industry. In the Autonomy program, decrease in costs was more complex but can be simply stated as follows. The Autonomy program increased the motivation of the employees to produce and thus they did not feel the need for replacing the staff members who left the section. In addition, they were willing to make an effort to try to outplace some of their members in other jobs which they might like. The reductions in staff in the two programs came about in different ways. Those occurring by order in the Hierarchically-controlled program surpassed in number those occurring by group decision in the Autonomy program, but it is not clear how long the superiority of the Hierarchically-controlled program would have lasted.

The results of the experiment need to be placed in a larger theoretical framework in order to contribute to the understanding of the functioning of large-scale organizations. We shall first consider briefly the role and function of the social control processes, as it is these processes which were changed by the experimental manipulations.

The high degree of rationality which is characteristic of the institutional behavior of man is achieved through a complex system for controlling and regulating human behavior. Hierarchy is a requirement because human beings must be fitted to a rational model. There are essentially two functions which the usual hierarchy serves: a *binding-in* function and a *binding-between* function. By *binding-in*

[5] It is unlikely that even in the Hawthorne experiment the results were due to attention. There were a number of changes in addition to an increase in attention, including relaxation of rules, better supervisors, no change in piece rates despite raises in productivity—to name a few.

we mean insuring that there will be individuals present to fill the necessary roles. The role behavior required by the organization must be a path to individual goals. Money is the most important means used for binding-in, but all ways to motivate a person to enter and remain in the system are means of binding-in. By *binding-between* we mean the insurance of the rationality of action, that is, the setting up and continuation of institutional processes which will accomplish the ends for which the organization is designed. The role behavior of individuals must be integrated into a pattern to produce interrelated action directed toward the goals of the organization. The development of assignments, work charts, job specifications, etc., are but a few examples of the many means used by organizations for binding-between.

Any means for controlling and regulating human behavior in a large organizational setting, then, needs to serve these two functions. The experiment shows that the allocation of decision-making processes to the upper hierarchy results in a greater emphasis on the binding-between function, while the function of binding-in is handled by an external reward system. Such a direct stress on the binding-between function was shown in the Hierarchically-controlled program and resulted in the increase in productivity (an indication of binding-between) and a decrease in employee satisfaction (an indication of degree of binding-in) and some increase in turnover (another indication of binding-in).

The greater allocation of the decision-making processes to the rank-and-file employees in the Autonomy program resulted in an emphasis on both the binding-between and the binding-in functions. Thus there was both an increase in productivity and an increase in satisfaction. While the program is addressed primarily to the binding-in function, in such a context the binding-between function is also served.

The problems of the Hierarchically-controlled system are maintaining the employee effectively "bound-in" to the organization and continuing favorable relations between the supervisory personnel who have involvement in the organization and the rank and file who must do the work. Indications of these problems are dissatisfaction, distortions in communications up the hierarchy, the tendency to "goof off" and cut corners in the work, and the greater turnover.

The Autonomy program is an integrated means of handling both the binding-between and the binding-in functions, but it requires in the long run that the organization be willing to grant employee decision-making in the key areas of binding-in such as pay and promotions. The granting of "safe" areas of decision-making and the withholding of "hot" ones is not likely to work for long. It is necessary for the rank and file to be sufficiently bound in to the organization for them to want to make decisions which are rational for the system. But the rationality of their decisions will also depend upon the orientation of the key supervisors whose values they will interiorize. (Thus the clerks in Division B were more organizationally oriented than those in Division A—see Kaye [3].)

Summary

A field experiment in an industrial setting was conducted in order to test hypotheses concerning the relationship between the means by which organizational decisions are made and (a) individual satisfaction, and (b) productivity.

Using four parallel divisions of the clerical operations of an organization, two programs of changes were introduced. One program, the Autonomy program involving two of the divisions, was designed to increase the role of the rank-and-file employees in the decision-making processes of the organization. The other two divisions received a program designed to increase the role of upper management in the decision-making processes (the Hierarchically-controlled program). The phases of the experiment included: (a) before measurement, (b) training programs for supervisory personnel lasting approximately 6 months, (c) an operations period of a year for the two experimental programs, and (d) after measurement. In addition, certain measurements were taken during the training and operational phases of the experiment. Findings are reported on the question of the experimental "take" and on the general hypotheses on individual satisfactions and productivity. Briefly, it was found that:

1. The experimental programs produced changes in decision-making allocations in the direction required for the testing of the hypotheses.

2. The individual satisfactions of the members of the work groups increased significantly in the Autonomous program and decreased significantly in the Hierarchically-controlled program.

3. Using one measure of productivity, both decision-making systems increased productivity, with the Hierarchically-controlled program resulting in a greater increase.

The relationship of the findings to the so-called "Hawthorne effect" is examined and the experimental programs and their results are considered in the light of a theoretical description of the role of the control and regulation processes of large organizations.

REFERENCES

1. Coch, L., & French, J. R. P., Jr. "Overcoming Resistance to Change." *Hum. Relat.*, 1948, 1, 512–532.
2. Katz, D., Maccoby, N., & Morse, Nancy. *Productivity, Supervision and Morale in an Office Situation.* Ann Arbor: Survey Res. Center, Univer. of Michigan, 1950.
3. Kaye, Carol. *The Effect on Organizational Goal Achievement of a Change in the Structure of Roles.* Ann Arbor: Survey Res. Center, 1954 (mimeographed).
4. Lewin, K. "Group Decisions and Social Change." In G. E. Swanson, T. M. Newcomb, & E. L. Hartley (Eds.). *Readings in Social Psychology* (2nd Ed.). New York: Holt, 1952, 459–473.
5. Lippitt, R., & White, R. K. "An Experimental Study of Leadership and Group Life." In G. E. Swanson, T. M. Newcomb, & E. L. Hartley (Eds.). *Readings in Social Psychology* (2nd Ed.). New York: Holt, 1952, 340–354.
6. Reimer, E. *Creating Experimental Social Change in an Organization.* Ann Arbor: Survey Res. Center, 1954 (mimeographed).
7. Tannenbaum, A. *The Relationship Between Personality Variables and Adjustment to Contrasting Types of Social Structure.* Ann Arbor: Survey Res. Center, 1954 (mimeographed).
8. Worthy, J. C. "Factors Influencing Employee Morale." *Harvard Bus. Rev.*, 1950, 28, 61–73.

Author Index

Allen, L. A., 16
Allport, T. W., 243
Amannheim, K., 240
Archibald, K., 129
Arensberg, C. N., 174, 217
Argyris, C., 22, 104, 216, 217, 340
Autonetics Division of North American Aviation, Inc., 155

Babchuck, N., 218
Back, K., 19
Bakke, E. W., 22, 58, 245
Bales, R. F., 122
Bamforth, K., 218
Banfield, E. L., 115, 125
Barnard, C. I., 57, 58, 120, 150, 183, 198, 236, 327, 371
Barnes, L., 325, 331
Barton, A. H., 123
Bates, F. L., 119
Bavelas, A., 120, 357
Beard, C. A., 107
Becker, H., 245
Becker, S., 432
Beer, S., 24
Beishline, J. R., 319
Belknap, I., 341
Bendix, R., 117, 121, 428
Bentz, V. J., 227
Berger, M., 116
Bierstedt, R. K., 116, 120
Bion, W. R., 274
Blau, P. M., 118, 323, 345, 356, 433, 442, 457
Boulding, K., 24, 122, 432, 436, 438
Brach, E. F. L., 16
Breton, R. 126
Brown, A., 101
Brown, W., 328
Buck, A. E., 107
Burak, E., 441
Burke, K., 242
Burns, T., 3, 329

Cadwallader, M. L., 23
Cannon, W. P., 175
Caplow, T., 427
Cartwright, D., 121

Chappel, E. D., 174, 184, 217
Christie, L., 328, 367
Clothier, R. C., 319
Coch, L., 20, 475
Coleman, J. R., 122
Collins, O., 217
Commons, J. R., 371
Comte, 26
Cooley, C. H., 385, 472
Coon, C. S., 184
Copeland, L., 205
Cottrell, W. F., 19
Cyert, R., 344

Dahl, R. A., 121, 454
Dahrendorf, R., 121
Dale, E., 100
Dalton, M., 18, 218, 407, 417
Davis, J., 224
Davis, K., 18
Davis, K., 156, 247
Davis, R. C., 17
Day, R. C., 432
Dean, L. R., 126
Dearborn, D., 332, 361
Deutsch, K. W., 23, 122
Dewey, J., 214
Dickson, W. J., 18, 178, 197, 200, 229, 244, 298, 325, 373
Dornbusch, S., 339
Doutt, J. T., 20
Drucker, P. F., 182
Dubin, R., 382, 432
Duffy, D. J., 115
Dunlop, J. T., 434
Durkheim, E., 4, 427, 455

Easton, D., 26, 121
Eddington, A., 26
Emerson, H., 6
Etizioni, A., 119

Faris, E., 247
Faunce, W., 323, 442
Fayol, H., 6, 86, 120
Festinger, L., 19
Fieldler, F., 330

Fink, C. F., 432
Form, W. H., 319
Fowler, I., 219
Freedman, R., 224
French, J. R. P., 20, 475
Friedrich, C. J., 117
Fromm, E., 232

Gaddis, P. O., 153
Gardner, B. B., 18, 319, 398
General Motors Corporation, 133
Gilbert, C., 454
Goffman, E., 223
Golembiewski, R. T., 99
Goode, W., 218, 219
Gordon, G., 432
Gore, 362
Gouldner, A. W., 6, 226, 378, 434, 450
Graicunas, V. A., 17, 48
Gross, E., 218
Gulick, L., 319
Guetzkow, H., 366, 459
Gusfield, J. R., 223
Guttman, L., 124

Haire, M., 21, 22, 99
Hall, R. H., 330
Hamblin, R. L., 432
Hamlin, F., 154
Harbison, F. H., 282
Hare, A. P., 432
Hartmann, H., 119
Hawley, A. H., 58, 224
Hawthorne studies, 7, 158
Hempel, C. G., 116
Henderson, L. J., 21
Henderson, W., 198
Hiller, E. T., 243
Hirschman, A., 456
Hogan, W., 102
Homans, G., 5, 22, 160, 222, 325, 370, 434, 438
Hoover Commission, 453
Horsfall, A. B., 217
Hoslett, S. D., 20
Hughes, E. C., 243, 245
Hunter, H., 456

Jacobson, E., 126
Jacques, E., 119, 216, 414, 417
James, W., 472
Janowitz, M., 119, 239, 450
Juran, J. M., 18

Kafka, F., 59
Kahn, R., 378
Kaplan, A., 15
Katona, G., 353
Katz, D., 373, 378, 475
Kaye, C., 487

Kelley, H. L., 436
Kerr, C., 434
Keynes, M., 26
Klein, B., 457
Kluckhohn, F., 331
Koffka, K., 246
Koontz, H., 16
Kornhauser, A., 124
Kozmetsky, 366
Kroeber, A. L., 217

Landecker, W. S., 224
Laski, H. J., 241
Lasswell, H. D., 121, 241
Lawrence, P., 216, 322, 329, 333
Lazarsfeld, P. F., 279
Leavitt, H., 118, 328, 459
Lentz, E. M., 434
Levin, H. S., 362
Levy, M. J., 58, 223, 343
Lewin, K., 475
Lindblom, C., 454, 455, 457
Lippet, R., 61, 475
Lipset, S. M., 217
Lombard, G. F., 216
Lowell, A. L., 244
Luce, K., 328, 367

MacCoby, N., 373, 475
MacGregor, D., 294
Mack, R. W., 434
MacMahon, 365
Macy, J., 328, 367
Maier, N. F., 383
Mailer, N., 125
Maisel, S. J., 439
Mandeville, M. J., 115
Mannheim, C., 241
March, J. G., 21, 118, 131, 344, 353, 441
Marschak, J., 24
Martindale, D., 224
Marx, K., 127
Mayo, E., 18, 179, 200, 216
McClelland, D., 332
Mead, G. H., 472
Meier, R., 341
Merton, R. K., 118, 123, 223, 226, 230, 237, 238, 243, 279, 331, 455
Mill, J. S., 378
Miller, D. C., 319
Miller, E., 333
Miller, W. B., 119
Millett, J. D., 365
Mills, C. W., 224
Mills, D. C., 428
Miner, H. M., 224
Miner, J., 332
Mishler, E. G., 124
Monachesi, E. D., 224

Montgomery, Bernard Law, 101
Mooney, J. D., 27
Moore, D., 18, 319
Moore, W. E., 319
Morse, N., 124, 373, 475
Murdock, G., 344
Myers, R., 439

Nadel, S. F., 223
New Jersey Bell Telephone Company, 150
Newcomb, T., 58, 235
Newell, A., 353
Newman, W. H., 17
Nettler, G., 124
Neuman, F. L., 122

O'Donnell, C., 16
Ogden, 365

Pareto, 21
Parsons, T., 58, 121, 122, 124, 125, 224, 233, 241, 343, 455
Pennock, J. R., 454
Perth, H., 224
Pfiffner, J. M., 102
Presthus, R. V., 15
Pruger, F. V., 230
Purcell, T. V., 126

Rabany, C., 241
Radcliffe-Brown, H., 455
Reiley, 27
Reissman, L., 227
Remarque, M., 125
Rice, A. K., 218, 325, 327, 330
Riesman, D., 233
Roe, A., 332
Roethlisberger, F. J., 18, 178, 197, 200, 229, 244, 373
Rohrer, J., 215
Ronken, H., 216, 333
Ross, E. A., 400
Roy, D., 217, 218

Saltonstall, R., 20
Schachter, S., 19
Scott, W. D., 319
Scott, W. G., 7
Scott, W. R., 432, 433
Seashore, S., 220
von Seeckt, H., 100
Seiler, J., 333
Selznick, P., 58
Serdenburg, R., 15
Sheppard, H. L., 124
Sherif, M., 215

Shills, E. A., 122, 124, 233, 239
Simmel, G., 120, 427
Simon, H. A., 21, 58, 102, 104, 115, 116, 117, 118, 216, 332, 343, 353, 360, 361, 364, 441, 459
Simpson, R. L., 442
Small, A. W., 427
Smith, A., 26
Smithburg, D. V., 102, 116, 117, 216, 364
Smithies, A., 454
Snyder, R. C., 434
Spencer, H., 327, 427
Stahl, O. G., 99
Stalker, G. M., 3, 329
Stewart, F., 102
Stinchcombe, A., 351, 438, 442, 450
Stouffer, S. A., 279, 379
Strauss, G., 217, 219, 407
Sykes, G. M., 125

Tannenbaum, A., 477
Taylor, F. W., 6, 16
Terrien, S. C., 428
Thibaut, J. W., 436
Thomas, E. J., 432
Thompson, A. T., 205
Thompson, J. D., 119, 450, 458
Thompson, V. A., 102, 116, 117, 119, 216, 364
Tripp, L. R., 278, 378
Trist, E., 218
Tuden, A., 450, 458
Tyndall, G., 366

Udy, S. H., 343, 345, 429
Urwick, L. F., 100, 118

Vleck, A., 152

Walker, C. R., 442
Waller, W., 198
Watson, J., 61
Weber, M., 58, 116, 117, 127, 241, 243, 319, 346, 427, 435, 476
Weinbert, S. J., 205
White, L. D., 101
Whorf, B. L., 368
Whyte, W. F., 126, 205, 214, 215, 218, 219, 314, 316, 380
Willerman, B., 126
Willoughby, W. F., 107
Wilson, L., 229
Wilson, R. N., 434
Woodward, J., 329
Worthy, J., 315, 475

Zetterberg, 121

Subject Index

Absenteeism, 274
Acceptance, 122
Accountability, 94, 319
Action program, 371
Activities, 29, 160, 179
Activity, defined, 173
  and interaction, 181, 188
  and sentiment, 188
  source of, 353
Adaptation, 60
  long-run, 371
  to role demands, 61
  short-run, 371
Adjustment to new experience, 54
Administrative component of organizations, 430, 431
  control, 434
  function, 89
  organization, 454
  rationality and organizational development, 343
  rationality structural requisites of, 345
  role definition, 453
  roles, over-defined, 456
    under-defined, 454
    well-defined, 455
  vitality, 454
  work, number of persons engaged in, 425
Alienation, 121, 124
Alternatives of action, 371
Anomie, 456
Assumptions, 72
Attitudes, 415
Attraction, 179
Auditing, responsibility of specialists, 317
Authority, 29, 69, 94, 105, 115, 319, 375
  basis for, 115, 119
  charismatic, 117, 118
  of competence, 119
  formal, 116, 119, 301
  functional, 116
  legal-rational, 120
  legitimate, 6, 113, 159
  of line over staff, 403
  personal, 301
  of position, 118
  relations, 115
  as a right, 106
  source of, 3
  and strategic lenientcy, 373
  types of, 69
  traditional and charismatic, 120
Autonomy of subordinate managers, 140-143
  degree of, 70

Balance as a linking process, 23
Behavior, deviant of, 235
Bargaining, 409
  emergent patterns, 158, 407
  intended, 164
  learning desire, 231
  predictability of, 15
  prescribed acceptable forms, 15
  reasons for conforming, 232
  of staff personnel, 399
  unanticipated, 164
  unpredictable, 13
Behavioral school, 6
Belief, purpose, 111
Bible, 5
Board of directors, 3, 88
Boundaries of rationality, 371
Bricklaying, 95
Budgets, perceptions of, 283-287
Buffering, 339
Bureaucracy, 319
  characteristics of, 29
  competition and, 276
  cooperation and, 276
  dehumanization of, 35
  increase of, 247
  permanancy of, 37
  and personality, 240, 254-256
Bureaucratic control, 438
Bureaucratic methods of administration, 378
Bureaucratic offices, 241
Bureaucratic rules, apathy preserving function of, 384
  and close supervision, 385
  explicational of, 380
  functions of, 378
  punishment for aginimating function of, 383
  remote control function of, 381
  screening function of, 281

Central and divisional management, functions of, 136
Centralized and decentralized organization, 70
Central management, 346
Certainty, 352
Change, 454
Classical doctrine of organizations, 16
  school of organization, 3, 6
Classification of organizations, analytical base for, 121
Clients, 129
Close supervision, 378
  and mechanization, 323
  and predictability of work, 441, 443
  and rule usage, 442
Codes of behavior, 52
Cohesiveness and productivity, 279
Collaborative relationship, 412
Collectivity, 60
Commitment, 124
Communication, 23, 44, 162, 361
  and coordination, 366
  in decision making, 366
  efficiency of, 366
  grapevine in, 20
  horizontal, 319
  joint problem solving, 323
  limits to, 47
  net, 460
  network in decision making, 369
  pattern of, 370
  restrictions, 462
  vertical, 319
Compensation, impact on prestige, 220
Compensatory rewards, 345
Competition, and structural conditions, 277
Competitive actions, 251
Compliance, 121
  coercive, 127
  normative, 127
  relationship, 121
  utilitarian, 127
Component selection, 154
Concentration of the means of administration, 35
Conflict, 301
  among departments, 293
  between line and staff, 397
Conflicting expectations, 456
Conflict relationship, dynamics of, 409
Conformity, 229
Congruent relationships, 126
Control, 316, 319
  centralization of,
Control and adaptation, 14
Cooperation, 407
  employee good will, 51
  enforced, 97
  of engineers and scientists, 326
Coordination, 60, 105, 323, 357, 365

and balance, 82
and communication, 366
by cross functional committees, 334
effect of division of work on, 108
by feedback, 366
by plan, 366
between sales and production, 408
spontaneous, 69
type of, 366
Corporal punishment, 127
Cosmopolitans, 164, 223
Costs, unanticipated, 65
Cultural emphasis in developing organizational members, 60
Custom, 169
Customers, 129
  basis for departmentation, 79
Cybernetics, 24

Data relationships, 180
Decentralization, aims of, 135-36
Decision, scope of the, 70
Decision making, 352
  allocation of, 486
  processes, 299
  and productivity, 475
  routinized and problem solving, 353
  and satisfaction, 475
Dedication, 20
Delegation, 146
  basic, 76
  reasons for not, 147
Demoralization, 61
Departmentalization, interrelation of systems of, 107
Departmentation, 76
Department management function, 92
Dependency, 15
Differentiation, 325
  dimensions of, 328
  of subunits, 299
Direction, operational, 155
Discipline, 113
Discretion, of organization members, 358
Division of work, 16, 18, 65, 73, 361, 364
  criteria for, 83
  effects of work patterns, 263-272
  horizontal, 65
  methods for, 76
  and responsibility, 97
  sources of economy from, 73-74
  task, 68
  vertical, 66
Doctrine, 111
Duty, 117
Dynamic organization, 315
Dysfunctional consequences of structures, 164

Effectiveness of cooperation, 44
Elites, 122

Emergent structure, 13
Empirical models, 6
  theory, 99
Employee, 129
Endogenous variables, 11
Environment, benign, 72
  and organization structure, 329
  physical, 52
  state of, 300
Environmental fluctuations, organization response
    to, 339-341
Equilibrium, 23
Esprit de corps, 69
Ethical sanctification, 116, 118
Executive authority, 303
Executive function, inculcation of belief, 43
  manpower pool, 388
  officer, 76
Executive organization, 49
Exogenous factors, 11
External balance, problems of, 51
  systems, 160, 176

Federalism, 135
Flow of work, 322-324
Flows, 14, 298
  matrix of, 14
  see also Work flows
Formal organization concepts, 72
Freedom of movement, 410, 413
Frustration and alienation, 5
Functional activities, 58, 59
  organization, 76, 304
  process, 17, 18
Functions of organizations, 51

Goal-based theories, 99
Goal of corporate policy, 139
Goals, 64
  displacement of, 243
  manifest and operational, 198
  of organization, 24
  and orientation to decision-making, 412
Group, behavior, elaboration of, 185
  behavior in large organizations, 215
  command, 215
  decision, 220
  defense, 272
  friendship, 215, 216
  goal, 463
  impact on output standards, 219
  informal, 220
  interaction, 464
  interest, 215
  internal dynamics, 222
  reference, 118
  small, 159
  task, 217
Group-oriented attachments, 122

Hawthorne effect, 485
Hierarchical control, 486
Hierarchical levels, and organization size, 434
Hierarchy, 30, 241
Homeostatic properties of systems, 23
Horizontal relationships, 122
Human organization, 52
Human relationships, instability of, 15

Idea-oriented attachments, 122
Individualism, as a reaction to structure of work,
    272
Individual within an organization, 13
Informal leadership positions, 20, 159
Informal organization, 159, 197, 272
Informal organization, characteristics of, 161, 197
  functions of, 198
  neo-classical view of, 19
  as a product of the formal, 160
  survival of, 20
  see also Organization, informal
Informal structure, 13
Informal superior position, 159
Information-handling, 409, 412
Inmates, 129
Innovation, 23
Inspection, 307
Institutional authority and sanctions, 233
Institutionalizing organizational tasks, 3
Instrumental action, 336
Integration, 299, 325
  requisites, 333
Integrative devices, 333
Interaction, 160
  and activity, 188
  defined, 173
  horizontal, 321-23
  lateral, 205
  pyramid of, 182
  and sentiment, 186
  vertical, 205, 321-323
Interdepartmental conflict, 407
  disputes, 316
Interdependence, tolerance for, 365
Interdependency, 4
Interdependent tasks, 421
Internal equilibrium, 51
  relations, 315
  systems, 160, 161, 185
Interpersonal relationships and size of group, 48
Intervening factors, 8
Involvement, 121
  alienative, 124
  calculative, 125
  moral, 125
  in the organization, 125, 128
  remuneration with calculative, 126

Job activities, 356
Job enlargement, 258

496   Subject Index

Job output, 356
Job rotation, 257
Jurisdictional competency, 30

Lateral relationships, antecedents to, 418
   conflict in, 420
   stability in, 417
Leader behaviors, 300
   directive, 389
   member relations, 389
   nondirective, 389
Leadership, 127
Leadership style, 388
   and task performance, 330
Learning, 371
Learning experiences, 164
Least-preferred coworker, 389
Legitimacy, 116
Line, 99
Line, conflicts with staff, 397
Line organization, 134
Locals, 164, 223
Location as basis of departmentation, 79

Management, 97
   control, 441
   division of labor, 303
   general, 89
   of initiative and incentive, 97
   middle, 457
Management problems, higher level, 315
Managerial incentive, 140
Mass production, 250
   and attitudes, 251
   effect on supervisory position, 260
   effect of wage structure, 260
Matrix or project form of organization, 71
Means-end analysis, 360
Measure of organization performance, 144-145
Mechanical pacing, 251
Member, 129
Motivation, from budgets, 287
Motivations of the individuals, 58
Mutuality of interest, 111

Neutralization, 123
Normative model, 6, 352
Norms, 161, 162, 432

Objective, definition of, 112
Objectives, 64
   limited, 345
Offices, 58, 59
One-line authority, 103
Opinions, forming, 162
Optimizing as an objective, 371
Organization, 7
   charts, 66
   complexity, 425

definition of, 40
design, 303
efficiency, 45
efficient, 426
elements, 161
formal, 16, 22
goal, 58-59
goals of, 46
as an impersonal system, 46
informal, 22
integration, 472
neo-classical, 17
objectives of, 105
performance, effect of lateral relationships on,
   420
product innovation and, 325
purpose of, 42
size of, 86
size, limits to, 48-49
   functional complexity, 427
   policy, 14
   rules and surveillance, 432
   and surveillance cost, 438
stress, 315
structure, 17, 312, 328-330
survival of, 40-41, 84
of systems, 22
traditional view, 15
Organizational identifications, 361
   rationality, 338
   segmentation, 304
   style, 70, 72
Organizations, two orientations in study of, 58
Output standards, 219

Participants, lower, 122
   lower versus higher, 130
Perception, 360
   effects of change programs on, 479
Performance, two ways of looking at, 3
Placement of organizational activities, 304
Plans, 64
Policies, jointly developed, 414
Political obligation, 117
Position, 116
Positive commitment, 121
Positive sentiments, 160
Power, 100, 121
   basis of, 122
   coercive, 122
   economic, 123
   institutional, 116
   neutralization of, 123
   normative, 122
   position, 38, 122, 391
   remunerative, 122
   social, 122
   structure, 123

Predictability, 355
  of work and workers' discretion, 446
Pressure, from budgets, 287
  effects of, 289
  multiplicity of, 160
  problems from 298
Prestige scale, 53
Pride in work, 244
Primary groups, 55
Problem solving, 371
Procedural discontinuities, 313
Procedures, 317
Processes, 60
Product form of organization, 76
Production schedules, 68
Productivity, measure of, 484
Productivity of bureaucracy, 281
Professional codes, 279
  identifications, 361
  self-discipline, 438
Professionalization and workers' discretion, 446
Professionals, codes of behavior, 245
Program, 59
  content, 356-7
  direction, 155
  evoking, 357
  execution, 357
  functions, 100
  interrelation of, 359
  management, 151
  and organization structure, 101
  performance, 354, 355
  structure of, 357
Programming, 355
Project or matrix form of organization, 71
Property space, three-dimensional, 123
Proximity of people, 15

Quality control, 408
Quota restriction, 200

Rank, 122
Rational administration, development of, 350
Rational behavior, 343, 360
Rationality, concept of, 352
  cognitive limits on, 352
  in organizations, 336
Rational organization, social setting of, 349
Rational program, 358
Reciprocal influences, 160
Reciprocal patterns, 418
Regenerative relations, 418
Relay assembly test room, 55
Repetition and interest in work, 255
Repetitiveness, 355
Reporting relationships, 109-10
Representatives, 122
Responsibility, 94, 304

  allocation of, 60
  avoidance of, 148-9
Risk, in rational decision making, 352
Role, 60
Role, differentiation, 459, 464
  on the basis of situational perceptions, 465
  because of personal ascendance, 470
  by means of intellectual ability, 468
  differentiations on the basis of organizational planning, 467
  manifest and latent, 223
Role expectations, complimentary, 374
  performances, 128
  theory, 223
Roles, sets of, 453
Routinized, 356
Rules, 432, 434, 436
  and categorization, 241
  for motion, 97

Salary based upon status, 33
Sanctions, 115, 118, 376
Satisfaction, effect of change programs on, 481, 484
  with the company, 483
  from work, 158
Satisfactions, 51
Satisficing as an objective, 371
Scalar process, 17, 18
Scapegoating, 274
Scheduling decisions, 408
Scientific transfer problem, 325
Search, 353
Segmental participation, 345
Selection, of office holders by merit, 32
  and training, 97, 388
Self-actualization, effect of change programs on feelings of, 480
Self-reinforcing processes, 417
Sentiment, 160, 178
  and activity, 188
  defined, 174
  and interaction, 186
Situation, standardation of, 365
Size, effect of, 425
Size of organizations, 300
Slack in organizations, 61
Social control, 19, 229
Social change, 453
Social distance, 53
  and interpersonal friction is likely, 434
Social order, 164
Social organization, 55
Social ranking, 163
Socio-reality, 52
Sociotechnical system, 325
Social relations, need for, 217
  unstable, 9
Social separation, 292

Social system, total, 176
Social systems, 167
Span of attention, 362
Span of control, 316
Span of control, 16, 17, 19
Specialization, 4, 327, 345
  degree of, 299
  by subprograms, 365
  task, 460
Specific job assignment, 346
Stability, 315
Staff, 99
  alter ego concept of, 101
  colleague style, 100
  conflicts with line, 397
  control function of, 102
  ideal styles, 100
  neutral and inferior instrument concept of, 101
  service function of, 102
Staff-line relationships, 317
Staff specialists, 54
Standard operating procedures, 434
Standards, satisfactory vs. optimal, 354
Status, 20, 189
  differentials, 62
  hierarchies, 163, 164, 189
  men and women, 192
  negro and white, 192
  occupational hierarchy, 191
  organizational differences, 191
  placing people and, 192
  problems coming from, 193
  and seniority, 191
  structures, number of, 164
  symbols, 193
  and wages, 190
Steady-state and specialization, 370
Strategic leniency and authority, 373
Stress, potential areas of, 316
Structure, 18, 58, 59
  process and product, 11
  mechanistic, 329
  organic, 329
  relationship of task and, 328
  task, 390
Structure and norms, 330
Subgoal, differentiation of, 361
  formation, 360
  persistance of, 361
Subordinate, dependency of, 375
Supervision as representative of employees, 482

Surveillance, 432
Surveillance costs and organizational size, 438
Sustaining functions, 100
System of human interrelations, 52
Systems, classification of, 25

Task, and interpersonal orientation, 330-331
  and structure, 328-330
Task oriented groups, 459
Task structure and leadership style, 330
Technical advantages of bureaucratic organizations, 34
Technical base, 161
Technical organization, 52
Technical rationality, 336
  boundries of, 338
Technological components of work, 441
Technological framework, 317
Technology, 300, 312, 336
  as flow of work, 303
  variations in, 336
Tenure of office, 33
Threatening condition, 72
Time measurements, 317
Time pressure, 362
Top management, levels of, 87
Trained incapacity, 242
Training, 101
Trusteeship function, 88
Turnover, 9
  and employee attitudes, 51

Unanticipated consequences, 158, 201
Uncertainty, 343, 352
  absorption of, 368

Values, 163
  as a product, 163
  shared, 163
Vertical relationships, 122, 125
Vocabulary, shared, 162

Wages and status, 190
Win-lose situations, 291
Workers reaction to mechanical pace, 254
Work flow, 303, 312
  theory, 317
  unit, 312, 315
Work flows, see Flows
Work restrictions, 159
Work standard, 162